Hearth to Heart
Beta Sigma Phi

Hearth to Heart
Beta Sigma Phi

EDITORIAL STAFF

Managing Editor	Mary Cummings
Executive Editor	Debbie Seigenthaler
Project Managers	Georgia Brazil, Shirley Edmondson Maribel S. Wood
Editors	Mary Jane Blount, Linda Jones Mary Wilson
Associate Editors	Lucinda Anderson, Carolyn King Elizabeth Miller, Judy Van Dyke
Typographers	Sara Anglin, Jessie Anglin Walter Muncaster
Award Selection Judges	Bill Ross, Debbie Seigenthaler Charlene Sproles
Art Director	Steve Newman
Illustrator	Barbara Ball
Test Kitchen	Charlene Sproles
Essayist	Lory Montgomery

Cover Photograph: Hershey Foods Corporation; Page 1: Favorite® Recipes Press; Page 2: Oregon Washington California Pear Bureau

© Favorite Recipes® Press, A Division of Heritage House, Inc. MCMLXLV
  P.O. Box 305141, Nashville, Tennessee 37230

ISBN: 0-87197-438-X
Library of Congress Number: 95-70536

All rights reserved. No part of this book may be reproduced in any form or by any means without prior written permission of the Publisher excepting brief quotes in connection with reviews written specifically for inclusion in a magazine or newspaper.

Manufactured in the United States of America
First Printing 1995

Recipes for photographs are on pages 213.

Contents

Introduction 6

Mouthwatering Menus 7

The Treasure Box 25
    (Crafts)

Just for Starters 35
    (Appetizers and Beverages)

It's a Toss-Up 53
    (Soups and Salads)

The Main Event 73
    (Meats)

Delectable Dishes 85
    (Poultry and Seafood)

From the Garden 103
    (Vegetables and Side Dishes)

Just Loafing Around 115
    (Breads)

Rise and Shine 127
    (Breakfast and Brunch)

Rave Reviews 143
    (Cakes and Pies)

Sweet Treats 171
    (Candy, Cookies and Desserts)

Spouses' Specials 197

Metric Equivalents 214

Merit Winners 216

Index 218

Order Information 225

Beta Sigma Phi

Linda Rostenberg

Dear Beta Sigma Phi Sisters:

Every year, the staffs of Favorite Recipes® Press and Beta Sigma Phi International rack their brains to come up with a new cookbook concept that's a little bit different from all the others—something that will excite the cooks in our crowd! Well, we hit the Big Casino with this year's concept—thousands and thousands of recipes came piling in, resulting in not just one, but two fabulous cookbooks to enjoy this year.

Hearth to Heart: Hearty, Healthy Recipes for the Family on the Go and **Just Desserts** are just what you (and friends, and family) need. In the **Hearth to Heart** cookbook, you'll find favorite kitchen and family-tested recipes that can be prepared without much fuss. (You'll also see that we're helping you eat a little smarter and healthier, too. The healthier recipes are easily recognizable by the ♥ symbol beside their title.) As a special treat, we've got a section of recipes submitted by Beta Sigma Phi husbands and men friends, too.

For those who appreciate some frankly fattening goodies, you'll find wonderful sweet breads, punches, cakes, cookies, pies, tortes and more in **Just Desserts**. (Every Beta Sigma Phi seems to be equipped with a certified sweet tooth.)

And the fun doesn't stop there! We certainly hope you were a winner in our annual cooking contest. As usual, we've awarded prizes in various food categories; these "best-of-the-best" recipes are specially marked by a diamond symbol ✤ in the cookbooks.

Pages and pages of pure eating pleasure-that's what these new Beta Sigma Phi cookbooks are all about! This year and every year, we say thanks to you for making our cookbooks possible. By sharing your family's favorites, you help us create a Beta Sigma Phi heirloom of sorts. Think about that the next time you and your sorority sisters get together to nosh, to nibble . . . to think great thoughts and make dreams come true.

Yours in Beta Sigma Phi,

Linda Rostenberg
Beta Sigma Phi International
Executive Committee

Mouth-Watering Menus

Whether you work in the home, at an office, (or both), the days just never seem to be long enough. Sometimes it's hard to find time to eat, let alone cook a family meal. And entertaining . . . with your busy schedule? Well, if you think entertaining is out of the question with your hectic lifestyle, this book is for you. Every menu on these pages has been developed to help even the busiest folks create delicious meals with ease. Beta Sigma Phi sisters all over the country have shared their secrets and tips for successful gatherings. From a casual after-work buffet to an elegant dinner party, you'll find ideas to make every occasion unforgettable. Welcoming friends and family into your home should be a joyous occasion. All it takes is a little planning, some taste-tempting recipes, and a little imagination. With Hearth to Heart by your side, you'll discover that entertaining can be what it should be—relaxing and fun for you as well as your guests.

All-Occasion Dinner

Beef Rouladen with Bow Tie Noodles
Spinach Salad
Creole-Style Green Beans
Texas Sheet Cake
Champagne Potlatch Punch

See index for similar recipes.

We make this menu for special occasions, like my sixty-eighth birthday party where my four children each made a portion.

Margaret A. Hook, Laureate Delta
Phoenix, Arizona

BEEF ROULADEN WITH BOW TIE NOODLES

8 breakfast steaks or 2 packages rouladen	6 or 7 slices bacon
Accent to taste	4 or 5 pickles, sliced lengthwise
Pepper to taste	All-purpose flour
Dijon or German mustard to taste	2 packages bow tie noodles
2 medium onions	

Place steaks on flat surface. Sprinkle with Accent and pepper. Spread mustard on each steak. Slice onions in half; slice again. Place 1 onion slice on end of each steak. Slice bacon into pieces width of steaks. Place bacon slice on onion slice. Place pickle slice on onion and bacon. Roll up, beginning with end with onion slice. Secure with toothpicks. Cook in skillet over medium heat for 40 minutes to 1 hour or until browned. Remove from skillet. Place in saucepan. Add 2 to 2 1/2 cups water or enough to cover. Simmer for 1 hour. Remove rouladen. Make gravy using flour to thicken and adding water if needed. Return rouladen to saucepan. Keep warm. Prepare noodles according to package directions. Serve with rouladen and gravy. Yield: 8 servings.

TEXAS SHEET CAKE

1 1/2 cups margarine	1 cup sour cream
1 cup water	1/2 cup margarine
1/4 cup baking cocoa	1/4 cup baking cocoa
2 cups all-purpose flour, sifted	6 tablespoons milk
2 cups sugar	1 (16-ounce) package confectioners' sugar
1/2 teaspoon salt	1 teaspoon vanilla extract
1 teaspoon baking soda	1 1/2 cups chopped nuts
2 eggs	

Preheat oven to 375 degrees. Combine 1 1/2 cups margarine, water and 1/4 cup cocoa in saucepan. Bring to a boil. Remove from heat. Combine flour, sugar, salt and baking soda in bowl. Add eggs and sour cream; mix well. Pour into greased 10-by-15-inch baking pan. Bake for 22 minutes. Combine 1/2 cup margarine, 1/4 cup cocoa and milk in saucepan. Cook until heated through. Remove from heat. Add confectioners' sugar, vanilla and nuts; mix well. Spread over warm cake. Let cool. Cut into squares or rectangles to serve.
Yield: 30 to 40 servings.

Basic-Is-Best Dinner

Lasagna — Parmesan Salad
Spumoni Ice Cream
Red Wine

See index for similar recipes.

This was a surprise birthday dinner for my son's 25th birthday with 12 dear friends. Everyone loved it. I also served this same meal when my husband's boss, Vic, who is Italian came to visit for his annual review. Vic had seconds and my husband had the best review and salary increase ever! Sometimes "basic is best!"

Lynda L. Utterback, Preceptor Alpha Rho
Overland Park, Kansas

LASAGNA

9 lasagna noodles	1 jar sliced mushrooms
1 1/2 pounds ground beef	2 cups grated mozzarella cheese
1/2 onion, chopped	3 cups grated Cheddar cheese
1 tablespoon Tones Italian seasoning	Parmesan cheese to taste
1 quart spaghetti sauce	

Preheat oven to 350 degrees. Cook noodles according to package directions. Rinse; pat dry. Brown ground beef in skillet, stirring until crumbly. Drain off fat. Add onion, Italian seasoning and spaghetti sauce; mix well. Simmer for 5 to 10 minutes. Place 3 noodles in 9-by-13-inch baking dish. Add layer of meat sauce, mushrooms and cheeses. Top with 3 more noodles; repeat layers, ending with meat sauce. Top with generous amount of cheese. Cover with cooking foil. Bake for 15 minutes. Remove foil; bake for 15 minutes longer or until top is browned. Yield: 6 servings.

♥ PARMESAN SALAD

1 clove of garlic, minced
1/2 teaspoon salt
1/4 teaspoon pepper
Dash of dry mustard
2 tablespoons grated Parmesan cheese
1 tablespoon lemon juice
1/4 cup vegetable oil
1 head lettuce, torn into bite-sized pieces
Grated Parmesan cheese to taste

Combine garlic, salt, pepper and mustard in salad bowl; mix well with fork. Stir in Parmesan cheese, lemon juice and vegetable oil. Heap lettuce on top dressing. Do not mix. Refrigerate until ready to serve. Sprinkle lightly with additional Parmesan cheese. Toss carefully until lettuce is coated with dressing. Yield: 8 servings.

✤ Candlelight Gourmet Dinner

Gingered Shrimp Roughy
Almond-Orange Salad
Asparagus-Rice Pilaf
Tropical Pineapple Dreams

See index for similar recipes.

To raise money at a local auction, a Bed and Breakfast Inn and I donated a honeymoon package that included a candlelight gourmet dinner. I prepared and served this menu. It was such a hit that we received numerous requests for a repeat. I also served this at a sorority dinner and received rave reviews. It is so easy and elegant.

Lois C. Black, Beta Rho
Leesville, South Carolina

♥ GINGERED SHRIMP ROUGHY

1/3 cup lite mayonnaise
1/3 cup lite sour cream
1/2 teaspoon dried minced onion
1/4 teaspoon ground ginger
1/4 teaspoon dillweed
Dash of salt
1/4 cup peeled boiled small shrimp
1 pound orange roughy
1 tablespoon margarine
1/4 cup toasted sliced almonds
Lemon wedges
Fresh dill sprigs

Mix mayonnaise, sour cream, onion, ginger, dillweed, salt and shrimp in microwave-safe dish. Chill for 1 hour. Brown roughy in margarine in skillet for 5 to 7 minutes or until flakes. Keep warm in serving dish. Microwave shrimp mixture for 3 minutes, stirring after each minute. Spoon over roughy. Sprinkle with almonds. Garnish with lemon wedges and dill. Yield: 4 servings.

♥ ALMOND-ORANGE SALAD

1 head leaf lettuce
1 small bunch spinach
1 (11-ounce) can mandarin oranges, drained
1/4 cup toasted sliced almonds
4 slices turkey bacon, crisp-fried, crumbled
Poppy Seed Dressing

Rinse lettuce and spinach; drain. Tear into bite-sized pieces. Layer lettuce, spinach, oranges, almonds and bacon in order listed. Serve with Poppy Seed Dressing. Yield: 4 servings.

POPPY SEED DRESSING

3/4 cup lite olive oil
1/3 cup honey
1/4 cup red wine vinegar
2 tablespoons dried minced onion
1 tablespoon Dijon mustard
1/2 teaspoon salt
3 tablespoons poppy seeds

Combine all ingredients in blender container. Process for 30 seconds. Yield: 1 to 1 1/2 cups.

♥ ASPARAGUS-RICE PILAF

1 (16-ounce) can asparagus tips
1 1/2 cups instant rice
1 small onion, chopped
1/4 cup chopped carrot
1 tablespoon minced garlic
1 tablespoon olive oil
Salt and pepper to taste

Drain asparagus reserving liquid. Prepare rice according to package directions, replacing equal amount of water with reserved asparagus liquid. Keep warm. Sauté onion, carrot and garlic in olive oil in skillet until tender. Place asparagus in microwave-safe dish. Microwave until warm. Mix rice, onion mixture, salt and pepper in serving bowl. Top with asparagus. Yield: 4 servings.

♥ TROPICAL PINEAPPLE DREAMS

1 fresh pineapple
8 ounces lite cream cheese, softened
1/4 cup sugar
1 1/2 cups lite whipped topping
1 small package toasted coconut pudding mix
1 kiwifruit, peeled, sliced
1/4 cup toasted sliced almonds

Slice pineapple lengthwise into 4 pieces, leaving top attached to each piece. Scoop out pineapple, making a boat. Discard core. Cut pineapple into bite-sized pieces. Blend cream cheese and sugar in mixer bowl until fluffy. Add 1 cup whipped topping. Prepare pudding mix according to package directions using low-fat milk. Place 1/4 cream cheese mixture in each boat. Top with pineapple, then pudding, dividing equally. Place dollop of whipped topping in center. Garnish with kiwifruit slices and toasted almonds. Yield: 4 servings.

10 / Menus

Celebration Dinner

Roast Beef Au Jus
Deviled Egg Salad
Tomato-Rice Salad
Yorkshire Pudding
Roasted Potatoes
Brussels Sprouts
Sherry Trifle
Coffee — Tea

See index for similar recipes.

About 2½ years ago my youngest daughter arrived home from California after 10 years. She tired of the hectic living in a big city and missed her family. Eight of us celebrated her return and enjoyed this dinner.

Beatrice G. Busko, Laureate Gamma
Great Falls, Montana

ROAST BEEF AU JUS

1 (6-pound) boned rolled beef rib roast
½ cup all-purpose flour
4 cups water
½ teaspoon salt
⅛ teaspoon pepper
Horseradish

Preheat oven to 450 degrees. Place roast in roasting pan. Roast for 15 minutes. Reduce oven temperature to 350 degrees. Continue roasting for 15 to 20 minutes per pound or to desired doneness. Remove roast to serving platter. Keep warm. Stir flour into juices in roasting pan. Brown over medium heat. Add water, stirring until gravy boils and thickens. Gravy will be thin. Add salt and pepper. Serve roast sliced with gravy and horseradish. Yield: 8 servings.

DEVILED EGG SALAD

8 lettuce leaves
8 hard-cooked eggs
½ cup mayonnaise
1⅛ teaspoons lemon juice
1⅛ teaspoons sugar
1¾ tablespoons milk
Paprika to taste
Parsley sprigs

Arrange lettuce on 8 individual salad plates. Cut eggs lengthwise into halves. Place 2 egg halves, cut-side down, on each lettuce leaf. Mix mayonnaise, lemon juice, sugar and milk in bowl. Spoon over eggs. Sprinkle with paprika. Garnish with parsley. Yield: 8 servings.

♥ TOMATO-RICE SALAD

2 cups salted water
1 cup long-grain rice
5 or 6 tomatoes
1 cup sliced fresh mushrooms
4 green onions, sliced
2 tablespoons chopped parsley
¼ cup vegetable oil
1 teaspoon prepared mustard
1 teaspoon salt
¼ cup lemon juice
¼ teaspoon garlic powder
½ teaspoon basil
2 teaspoons sugar
¼ teaspoon pepper

Bring salted water to a boil in saucepan. Stir in rice. Cover; reduce heat to simmer. Cook until tender and water is absorbed. Rinse with cold water; drain. Dip tomatoes in boiling water for 1 minute. Remove skins and chop. Combine tomatoes, mushrooms, onions and parsley in large bowl. Add rice; mix well. Mix remaining ingredients in bowl. Pour half the dressing over salad; toss. Add more dressing if too dry. Yield: 8 servings.

YORKSHIRE PUDDING

1 cup all-purpose flour
½ teaspoon salt
2 eggs
1 cup milk
Vegetable oil

Combine flour, salt, eggs and milk in mixer bowl. Beat for 5 minutes or until smooth. Let stand for 1 hour. Preheat oven to 425 degrees. Place ¼ teaspoon oil in each muffin cup. Heat in oven until hot. Fill cups ½ full of batter. Bake on center shelf of oven for 20 minutes or until brown. Serve with gravy as the English do. Yield: 8 servings.

SHERRY TRIFLE

1 sponge or pound cake
⅓ cup raspberry jam
⅓ cup Sherry
2 packages custard pudding mix
1 cup whipping cream
1 teaspoon vanilla extract
1 tablespoon sugar
Almonds, slivered or halved
Maraschino cherries

Cut cake into 10 slices the size of deck of cards. Spread 5 slices with jam. Top with remaining slices. Cut each "sandwich" into cubes. Place cubes in glass bowl. Sprinkle with Sherry. Let stand to absorb. Prepare custard according to package directions. Pour about 3 cups warm custard over cake. Cover with foil to prevent crust from forming. Chill. Combine cream, vanilla and sugar in mixer bowl; beat until stiff. Spread over chilled custard. Garnish with almonds and cherries, placing 8 cherries around edge and 3 in center. Yield: 8 servings.

Louise Crump, Preceptor Epsilon Gamma, Warren, Ohio, makes Baby Carrots by combining 2 pounds scraped baby carrots and ½ teaspoon sugar in saucepan. Add water to cover. Bring to a boil. Simmer, covered, for 10 minutes or until just tender. Place on warm serving platter. Garnish with cilantro.

Family Favorite Dinner

Hearty Beef Stew
Fruit Salad
Sweet Mixed Pickles
Rolls
Ice Cream with Hot Fudge Sauce

See index for similar recipes.

This recipe for stew was given to me by my mom. It was a favorite of my dad's whose parents were homesteaders in Rouleau, Saskatchewan, so my grandma made it in large quantities to feed the whole family as well as the farmhands. Over the years it has had many fine tunings so that each generation can reinvent it. I've passed it on to my own daughter.

Donna Oldridge, Laureate Psi
Ottawa, Ontario, Canada

HEARTY BEEF STEW

2 pounds boneless lean beef chuck, cut into 1-inch cubes
2 or 3 onions, cut into quarters, sliced
3 to 4 cups water
1 tablespoon salt
1 large turnip, cut into 1-inch chunks
5 or 6 carrots, cut into 2-inch pieces
6 or more potatoes, cut into 1-inch chunks
2 stalks celery, cut into 2-inch pieces
1 teaspoon pepper
1 tablespoon sugar
1 envelope dried onion soup mix
3 to 5 drops of Tabasco sauce

Brown beef and onions in large saucepan. Add water and salt. Simmer until beef is almost tender. Remove beef from liquid; set aside. Cook turnip in liquid until about 2/3 done. Remove turnip; set aside. Repeat procedure for carrots, potatoes and celery, cooking each separately. Add pepper, sugar, onion soup mix and Tabasco sauce to remaining liquid. Add enough flour to thicken, stirring until smooth. Add more water if necessary. Return beef and vegetables to sauce. Simmer until beef and vegetables are tender. Yield: 8 servings.

Debbie Eastcott, Chi, Shoal Lake, Manitoba, Canada, makes Monty's Beans by mixing 1 (19-ounce) can pork and beans, 1 (19-ounce) can apple pie filling, 1/2 cup dark brown sugar and 1/2 to 1 teaspoon dry mustard in casserole. Bake in preheated 350-degree oven for 45 minutes. Yield: 6 servings.

Mouthwatering Menus / 11

♥ HOT FUDGE SAUCE

3 tablespoons butter
6 tablespoons baking cocoa
1/3 cup boiling water
3/4 cup Sugartwin
2 tablespoons white corn syrup
Dash of salt
1 teaspoon vanilla extract or Brandy

Melt butter in 1 1/2-quart microwave-safe saucepan. Stir in cocoa. Add boiling water gradually. Add Sugartwin, syrup and salt; mix well. Microwave on High for 3 to 4 minutes, stirring 1 or 2 times. Add vanilla. Serve over ice cream or use for fresh fruit dip. Yield: 1 cup.

Foyers Group Dinner

Pork Tenders Supreme
Dill Rice
Parsnips and Peas
Pineapple Fluff Salad
Hot Rolls
Peach Pie
Coffee — Tea

See index for similar recipes.

The Foyers Group in our church is made up of three couples. The first time they came to our home, I served this menu. I enjoyed cooking and what fun to see friends enjoying it. There wasn't must left!

Irene E. Brubaker, Beta Master
Lincoln, Nebraska

PORK TENDERS SUPREME

1/4 teaspoon garlic salt
All-purpose flour
4 large pork tenders
1/2 (10-ounce) can cream of mushroom soup

Preheat oven to 350 degrees. Mix garlic salt with enough flour to coat pork tenders in bowl. Coat pork tenders well with flour mixture. Place in oven cooking bag. Add mushroom soup. Bake for 45 minutes. Test for doneness. Bake for 15 minutes longer if needed. Yield: 4 servings.

DILL RICE

3 cups cooked rice
1 teaspoon dillweed
2 tablespoons butter

Combine rice, dillweed and butter in bowl; mix well. Yield: 4 to 6 servings.

Grandma's Moving Dinner

*Filipino Roast
Potatoes Maître d'Hôtel
Asparagus with Mushroom Sauce
Baked Beets
Dressed Lettuce
Marshmallow Custard*

See index for similar recipes.

When I was a little girl I visited my grandparents while my parents were moving to another army base. My grandma had this menu the evening before my mom, who had come for me, and I left for our new home.

Gini Gabower, Laureate Gamma
Wausau, Wisconsin

FILIPINO ROAST

1 1/2 pounds ground round steak
1/2 pound ground fresh pork
1 small onion, finely chopped
1 green pepper, finely chopped
1 cup soft bread crumbs
1 teaspoon salt
1/4 teaspoon pepper
1 egg, slightly beaten
3 thin slices bacon
2 cups canned tomatoes

Preheat oven to 400 degrees. Combine steak, pork, onion, green pepper, bread crumbs, salt, pepper and egg in bowl; mix well. Shape into roll. Place in roasting pan. Place bacon over top. Pour tomatoes over and around roast. Bake for 1 hour and 15 minutes. Remove from oven. Lift bacon slices. Bake for 15 minutes longer or until bacon is crisp and golden. Remove roast to hot platter. Serve with gravy made from pan juices. Yield: 6 servings.

BAKED BEETS

6 medium beets, rinsed
2 tablespoons butter or margarine, melted

Preheat oven to 350 degrees. Wipe beets dry. Bake until soft. Peel and slice. Serve hot with melted butter over top. Yield: 6 servings.

MARSHMALLOW CUSTARD

2 eggs
2 tablespoons sugar
2 cups half and half
1/2 teaspoon vanilla extract
6 large marshmallows

Preheat oven to 325 degrees. Beat eggs slightly in bowl. Add sugar, half and half and vanilla; mix well. Place 1 marshmallow in bottom of 6 custard cups. Pour custard mixture over marshmallows, dividing equally. Place custard cups in pan of hot water. Bake for 40 minutes or until silver knife inserted in custard comes out clean. Let cool in refrigerator. Serve in cups. Yield: 6 servings.

Home-For-The-Weekend Special Dinner

*Low-Fat Chicken Enchiladas
Mexican Rice
Black Beans
Queso Especial*

This is my family's favorite meal. We eat it at least once each time our oldest two come home for the weekend.

Gayle Myers, Alpha Psi Zeta
Lampasas, Texas

♥ LOW-FAT CHICKEN ENCHILADAS

4 chicken breasts
1 onion, chopped
1 clove of garlic
1 jalapeño pepper, seeded, chopped
1 tablespoon olive oil
1 small can chopped green chilies
12 corn tortillas
Vegetable oil
2 cups fat-free sour cream
1 to 2 cups chicken broth
1 cup grated Colby Jack cheese

Preheat oven to 375 degrees. Boil chicken breasts in water to cover in saucepan until tender. Remove chicken, reserving broth. Bone chicken; cut into bite-sized pieces. Sauté onion, garlic and jalapeño pepper in olive oil in skillet until tender. Add green chilies and chicken; mix well. Heat tortillas in vegetable oil in skillet; drain. Spoon chicken mixture on warm tortillas. Roll up to enclose filling. Place in 9-by-13-inch glass baking dish. Place sour cream in bowl. Add chicken broth to make desired consistency. Pour over enchiladas. Sprinkle with cheese. Bake for 15 to 20 minutes or until cheese is melted. Yield: 4 to 6 servings.

MEXICAN RICE

1 cup chopped onions
2 cloves of garlic, minced
1 jalapeño pepper, seeded, chopped
2 tablespoons olive oil
1 cup Comet rice
1 tablespoon plus 1 teaspoon chicken and tomato bouillon
2 1/4 cups water
1/2 cup frozen peas and carrots
1/2 cup frozen corn

Sauté onions, garlic and jalapeño pepper in olive oil in skillet until tender. Stir in rice. Sauté until rice begins to turn golden. Dissolve bouillon in 1 cup water. Stir into rice; add remaining water. Reduce heat to low; cover. Cook for 15 to 20 minutes or until rice is tender, stirring frequently. Defrost vegetables in microwave. Add to rice. Cover. Remove from heat. Let stand for 5 minutes. Serve. Yield: 4 to 6 servings.

BLACK BEANS

1 (16-ounce) package black beans
2 cups chicken broth
1 large onion, chopped
2 cloves of garlic, minced
2 stalks celery, chopped
3 jalapeño peppers, seeded, chopped
1/2 cup coarsely chopped cilantro
2 cups water

Rinse beans; drain. Place in large saucepan. Add chicken broth and remaining ingredients. Bring to a boil. Boil for 15 minutes, stirring frequently. Reduce heat. Simmer for 1 1/2 hours or until beans are tender. Add water as needed. Yield: 6 to 8 servings.

QUESO ESPECIAL

2 large ripe avocados
1 tablespoon lemon juice
1/4 teaspoon coarsely ground garlic powder
2 medium tomatoes, chopped
1 medium purple onion, chopped
1/2 clove of garlic, finely minced
1 jalapeño pepper, seeded, chopped
3/4 cup coarsely chopped cilantro
1 pound Velveeta cheese

Peel and seed avocados. Mash avocados with lemon juice and garlic powder in bowl. Combine tomatoes, onion, garlic, jalapeño pepper and cilantro in large bowl. Place Velveeta cheese in microwave-safe dish. Microwave until melted. Spoon avocado mixture into small serving bowls. Pour cheese over avocado mixture. Top with tomato mixture. Yield: 2 to 4 servings.

Sharlene Guggemos, Preceptor Mu Tau, Georgetown, Texas, makes Converted Pickles by placing 1 quart sliced dill pickles, well drained, in glass jar or crock. Add 2 teaspoons celery seeds, 2 teaspoons mustard seeds and 2 cups sugar. Cover. Stir several times a day for 3 days. Place back in jar. Store in refrigerator. These pickles are very good and different!

Mouthwatering Menus / 13

Lakeside Breakfast

Potato Kugel
Baked Lakeside Eggs
Angel Buns — Jams and Jellies
Orange Juice

After a week at "The Mountain Top" Elderhostel, Jan and I spent a few days in the mountains overlooking Lake Sequoyah in Highlands, North Carolina. Lakeside lodging combines a scenic, peaceful atmosphere with a delicious breakfast.

Jane R. Crouch, Preceptor Eta Psi
Palatka, Florida

POTATO KUGEL

6 baking potatoes, peeled, grated
Vegetable oil
2 tablespoons mayonnaise
3 eggs, slightly beaten
1/2 cup milk
Salt and pepper to taste
Sour cream or applesauce

Preheat oven to 350 degrees. Sauté 1 grated potato in vegetable oil in skillet until golden. Add to grated potatoes in bowl. Add mayonnaise, eggs, milk, salt and pepper; mix well. Pour into greased baking dish. Bake for 1 1/2 hours. Serve with sour cream. Yield: 6 servings.

BAKED LAKESIDE EGGS

Scallions, finely chopped
4 eggs
4 teaspoons half and half
Grated Cheddar cheese

Preheat oven to 450 degrees. Coat 4 baking cups with nonstick vegetable cooking spray. Place small amount of scallions in each cup. Top with 1 egg. Add 1 teaspoon half and half. Sprinkle cheese on top. Bake for 10 minutes or to desired doneness. Yield: 4 servings.

♥ ANGEL BUNS

1 envelope quick-active dry yeast
1 tablespoon sugar
1/4 cup warm water
2 cups low-fat baking mix
1/4 cup milk

Dissolve yeast and sugar in warm water in bowl. Mix in baking mix and milk until dough forms. Shape into smooth ball on surface dusted with baking mix. Knead for 10 minutes. Roll out to 1/2-inch thickness. Cut with 2-inch biscuit cutter dipped in baking mix. Place on ungreased cookie sheet. Let rise in warm place for 30 minutes. Preheat oven to 425 degrees. Bake for 6 to 8 minutes or until golden brown. Yield: 9 to 11 buns.

Moving Day Special Dinner

Nutty Chicken Dijon with White Rice
Summer Salad Bowl
Broccoli Spears
Crescent Rolls
Lime Meringue Cake
White Wine — Coffee

See index for similar recipes.

The moving van had pulled away from the curb. Cardboard boxes had been unpacked. I was hanging pictures on great room walls when the call came. My husband was bringing a co-worker home for dinner. I put away my hammer. After a quick trip to the grocery, I began preparing my special Lime Meringue Cake. At 5 o'clock that evening the aroma of Nutty Chicken Dijon simmering in an electric skillet filled the kitchen. On the counter was a leafy green Summer Salad Bowl. Luscious Broccoli Spears were cooking in the humming microwave. I calmly draped a peach colored cloth over an antique oak table top. "This is the first time that we have entertained in our new dining room," I told our guest.

Martha S. Phares, Delta Omicron
Irmo, South Carolina

NUTTY CHICKEN DIJON WITH WHITE RICE

1 medium red or green bell pepper, cut into strips	2 tablespoons dry white wine
5 teaspoons peanut oil	1/4 teaspoon cornstarch
1 pound boneless skinless chicken breasts, cut into thin strips	3 tablespoons chopped dry roasted unsalted peanuts
1/4 cup Dijon mustard	2 cups hot cooked rice

Sauté bell pepper in 2 teaspoons peanut oil in electric skillet over high heat until tender-crisp. Remove from skillet. Sauté chicken in remaining oil in same skillet until tender. Remove chicken from skillet. Blend mustard, wine and cornstarch in bowl. Add to skillet. Cook at Medium-High, stirring constantly, until mixture thickens. Return chicken and pepper to skillet. Cook for 3 to 4 minutes or until heated through. Stir in peanuts. Serve over hot rice. Yield: 4 to 6 servings.

SUMMER SALAD BOWL

Several lettuce leaves	1 cup sliced radishes
4 cups torn lettuce	1 carrot, shredded
2 cups sliced raw cauliflower	Grated cheese to taste
1 cup bias-cut celery	Italian dressing

Line salad bowl with lettuce leaves. Arrange torn lettuce, cauliflower, celery, radishes and carrot in bowl. Sprinkle with cheese. Serve with Italian dressing. Yield: 4 to 6 servings.

♥ LIME MERINGUE CAKE

1/4 cup frozen egg substitute, thawed	1/2 cup skim milk
1/2 cup sugar	1/4 teaspoon lemon extract
2 tablespoons reduced-calorie margarine, melted	Nonstick vegetable cooking spray
1 1/2 cups sifted cake flour	4 egg whites
2 teaspoons baking powder	1/2 teaspoon cream of tartar
1/2 teaspoon grated lime rind	1/2 cup sugar
1/4 teaspoon salt	Lime Custard
	Lime slices
	Lime rind curls

Preheat oven to 350 degrees. Beat egg substitute in mixer bowl at high speed until foamy. Add 1/2 cup sugar and melted margarine gradually, beating well. Combine flour, baking powder, rind and salt in bowl. Add to sugar mixture alternately with milk, mixing well after each addition. Add lemon extract. Coat 9-inch cake pan with cooking spray. Pour batter into pan. Bake for 25 minutes. Let cool completely. Beat egg whites and cream of tartar in mixer bowl at high speed until soft peaks form. Add 1/2 cup sugar gradually, beating until stiff peaks form. Place cooled cake on ovenproof serving plate. Spoon Lime Custard onto cake. Spread meringue over cake and custard. Bake for 12 minutes. Garnish with lime slices and rind curls. Yield: 12 servings.

LIME CUSTARD

1 cup water	2 tablespoons grated lime rind
1/2 cup frozen egg whites, thawed	1/4 cup lime juice
1/2 cup sugar	1 tablespoon reduced-calorie margarine
3 tablespoons cornstarch	

Combine water and egg whites in bowl. Combine sugar with cornstarch in saucepan. Add egg mixture, lime rind and lime juice, stirring constantly. Cook, stirring constantly, over medium heat until mixture boils. Boil for 1 minute or until slightly thickened. Remove from heat. Stir in margarine. Cover. Chill. Yield: 1 1/4 cups.

Old-Fashioned Wartime Picnic

*Scotch Eggs
Bread and Butter
Apples and/or Oranges
Orange Juice*

These Scotch eggs take me back to my childhood in Dundee, Scotland, during the war years when food was scarce. My mother and aunts made a special effort to save enough food ration coupons to make one day a year a special memory. When one or two of the men were home on leave from the war, about 15 to 20 of us would go on a "Family Picnic" to Fife, Scotland. We took the ferryboat "Fifie" across the River Tay which was two miles wide. It was very exciting. After docking, our first stop was the Ice Cream Shop where everyone was given a small cone that cost one penny. On the three-mile walk to Windmill Park, we stopped at a hole in the wall which spouted fresh spring water to fill our containers which we later mixed with concentrated orange juice supplied by the government. When we reached the park, the adults spread the tablecloth and set out the Scotch eggs, bread spread with butter (a rare treat), one apple or orange each (if available) and a glass of orange juice. We played baseball and soccer until time to go. Upon reaching the dock, we rushed to the Ice Cream Shop which was now the "Chip Shop." We were given a small bag of chips, the adults had fish and chips and each kid was given 1 or 2 bites of fish. After a quiet ferry trip home, each family agreed a good time was had by all and my mother was thanked for making the Scotch eggs. Looking back, life seemed much simpler then. Ah! Well. "Those were the days."

Moira Welsh
Winnipeg, Manitoba, Canada

SCOTCH EGGS

*1 tablespoon all-purpose flour
1/2 to 3/4 cup quick-cooking oats
2 slices soft bread, crumbled
1 egg
Salt and pepper to taste
1/4 cup chopped onion (optional)
Seasonings to taste
1 pound bulk sausage
6 small hard-cooked eggs
All-purpose flour*

Preheat oven to 350 degrees. Combine 1 tablespoon flour, oats, bread, egg, salt, pepper, onion and seasonings in bowl. Add sausage; mix well. Divide mixture into 6 equal portions. Roll eggs in flour. Mold 1 portion around each egg. Roll in flour. Fry in skillet until browned. Place in baking pan. Bake for 20 minutes. Drain off fat. Serve hot or cold. Yield: 6 servings.

A Favorite Dinner

*Avocado Sandwiches
Potato or Corn Chips
Low-Fat Sausage Soup
Sun Tea*

See index for similar recipes.

The Low-Fat Sausage Soup is a great way to use broth leftover from boiling meats or potatoes and leftover vegetables. I remember my mother and grandmother freezing broth from boiled (Newfoundland) dinners, potatoes, vegetables, etc. for those days when the pantry was close to bare. I love to cook this way. It is now called recycling.

Linda Jones, Omega Omicron
Riverview, Florida

♥ LOW-FAT SAUSAGE SOUP

*1 to 1 1/4 pounds Italian sausage
3 quarts vegetable, chicken or potato broth
1 (15-ounce) can tomatoes, crushed
4 carrots, sliced diagonally into 1/4-inch slices
2 onions, chopped
2 stalks celery, cut diagonally into 1/4-inch slices
1 green or red bell pepper, sliced
1 cup whole or sliced mushrooms
Cubed potatoes
2 tablespoons dried parsley
2 cloves of garlic, minced
1 teaspoon ground pepper
Pinch of dillweed
Cooked pasta or rice
Parmesan cheese*

Cut sausage diagonally into 1-inch thick pieces. Brown on both sides in skillet; drain off fat. Place broth in saucepan. Bring to a boil. Add tomatoes, carrots, onion, celery, green pepper, mushrooms and potatoes. Bring to a boil. Add parsley, garlic, pepper and dillweed. Turn heat down. Simmer for 20 minutes. Add sausage. Simmer for 15 minutes longer. Add pasta. Heat. Top each serving with Parmesan cheese. Yield: 6 to 8 servings.

16 / Menus

Outdoor Grilling Party

Kabobs
Fat-Free Potato Salad
Fresh Fruit Dessert

My husband made a major career change and upon graduation invited his school comrades and spouses to a backyard cookout. The day was sunny and gorgeous and the backyard was in full bloom. The tables, made with plywood sheets and sawhorses, were decorated with colorful antique cloths, cloth napkins, multi-colored insect repellant candles and potted flowers. Being conscious of environment and nutrition, we used no disposable dishware. The flowers and most of the food served came from our organic garden. Guests made their own kabobs which encouraged discussion and left little room for lulls in conversation or activity. It was an excellent event, creative menu, and everyone had a ball!

Kerry Adams, Alpha Gamma
Omaha, Nebraska

KABOBS

4 cups bite-sized pieces chicken
4 cups cubed flank or tenderloin steak
2 cups cubed orange roughy
2 cups fresh mushrooms
2 cups chopped green peppers
3 cups cherry tomatoes
2 cups chopped eggplant
2 cups onion wedges
2 cups fresh pineapple chunks

Preheat grill. Place ingredients in individual bowls in shallow pans of ice to chill until cooking time. Garnish ice with edible flowers such as marigolds, nasturtiums, violets and roses. Thread ingredients on skewers. Grill over hot coals to desired doneness. Yield: variable.

♥ FAT-FREE POTATO SALAD

5 cups cubed cooked new potatoes
2 pound radishes, sliced
1 pound green onions, sliced
4 or 6 dill pickles, chopped
1/4 cup fresh dill sprigs
2 cups fat-free mayonnaise
1/4 cup stone-ground mustard
Dill sprigs

Place potatoes, radishes, onions, pickles and 1/4 cup dill in salad bowl. Add mayonnaise; toss gently. Add mustard. Chill. Garnish with dill sprigs. Yield: 16 servings.

FRESH FRUIT DESSERT

Fat-free whipped topping
Fresh apple wedges
Fresh peach wedges
Fresh whole strawberries
1 angel food cake, cubed
Low-fat fruit yogurt

Place whipped topping in serving bowl in center of serving plate. Arrange fruit on serving plate with cake cubes. Place yogurt in serving bowl for dipping. Yield: 16 servings.

Surprise Birthday Party

Sliced Ham and Turkey
Macaroni-Shrimp Salad
Fruit Salad
Frog-Eye Salad
Potato Salad
Lettuce Salad
Veggie Tray
Rolls
Birthday Cake
Coffee — Punch

See index for similar recipes.

This was a surprise "70th" birthday party for my mother. It was buffet for 100 people in a retirement complex. The salads were served in punch bowls, and the table looked elegant. We were asked to do it again — every Sunday!

Aliene Gribas, Laureate Iota
Havre, Montana

MACARONI-SHRIMP SALAD

1 (5-pound) package macaroni
18 hard-cooked eggs, chopped
2 medium onions, chopped
10 celery stalks, chopped
3 (4-ounce) cans shrimp pieces
2 1/2 to 3 cups mayonnaise-type salad dressing
1 cup dill relish
1/2 cup mustard
1 cup milk

Cook macaroni according to package directions; drain. Combine macaroni, eggs, onions, celery and shrimp in large bowl; mix well. Combine remaining ingredients in bowl; mix well. Pour over macaroni mixture; mix well. Refrigerate until serving time. Yield: 75 to 100 servings.

FROG-EYE SALAD

1 cup sugar
2 tablespoons all-purpose flour
2 1/2 teaspoons salt
1 3/4 cups pineapple juice
2 eggs, beaten
1 tablespoon lemon juice
1 package acini-de-pepe
3 quarts water
1 tablespoon vegetable oil

Combine sugar, flour, salt, pineapple juice and eggs in saucepan. Cook over moderate heat until thick, stirring constantly. Add lemon juice. Let cool. Cook pasta in water and oil according to package directions. Drain; let cool. Combine sauce and pasta in large bowl; mix well. Place in airtight container. Refrigerate overnight. Yield: 8 servings.

POTATO SALAD

3 cups mayonnaise-type salad dressing
1 cup sweet pickle relish
1 1/2 cups prepared mustard
1 cup milk
5 pounds cooked potatoes, cubed
2 medium onions, chopped
18 hard-cooked eggs, chopped
10 celery stalks, chopped

Combine salad dressing, relish, mustard and milk in bowl; mix well. Add additional milk for desired consistency. Combine remaining ingredients in large bowl; mix well. Pour dressing over potato mixture; mix well. Refrigerate overnight. Yield: 75 to 100 servings.

Vegetarian Company Dinner

Vegetarian Lasagna
Garlic French Bread
Apple-Almond Salad
Carrot Cake

See index for similar recipes.

I use this menu frequently for company. I am vegetarian and many of our friends tease me about eating "rabbit food." Vegetarian food can be very good. I served this dinner prior to our chapter meeting when I gave a program on vegetarianism. None of the members knew the topic of my program. When asked if they noticed anything unusual about our dinner, not one of the girls figured out that there was no meat.

Leslie Peacock, Xi Upsilon Rho
Oxnard, California

Mouthwatering Menus / 17

VEGETARIAN LASAGNA

2 carrots, diagonally sliced
1/3 cup chopped onion
2 cloves of garlic, minced
2 tablespoons olive oil
1 (15-ounce) jar meatless spaghetti sauce
1/4 cup water
1 1/2 teaspoons crushed dried oregano
3/4 teaspoon salt
3/4 teaspoon crushed dried basil
1 1/2 cups fresh sliced mushrooms
1 small zucchini, sliced
2 eggs, beaten
1 1/2 cups cream-style cottage cheese, drained
1/4 cup grated Parmesan cheese
1 (10-ounce) package chopped spinach, thawed, drained
Nonstick vegetable cooking spray
6 ounces lasagna noodles, cooked, rinsed, drained
2 1/2 cups shredded mozzarella cheese

Preheat oven to 375 degrees. Cook carrots, onion and garlic in hot olive oil in medium skillet until onion is tender but not brown. Stir in spaghetti sauce, water, oregano, salt and basil. Simmer, covered, for 15 minutes or until carrots are tender. Stir mushrooms and zucchini into skillet. Cook, uncovered, for 5 minutes or until zucchini is tender. Combine eggs, cottage cheese and Parmesan cheese in bowl; mix well. Stir in spinach; mix well. Spray 9-by-13-inch baking pan with cooking spray. Arrange single layer of lasagna in bottom of pan. Top with 1/3 spinach mixture, then 1/3 spaghetti sauce. Sprinkle with 1/2 cup grated mozzarella cheese. Repeat layers. Bake, covered, until heated through. Top with remaining mozzarella cheese. Return to oven for 3 minutes or until cheese is melted. Let stand for 10 minutes before serving. Yield: 8 servings.

APPLE-ALMOND SALAD

1/4 cup vegetable oil
2 tablespoon sugar
2 tablespoons malt vinegar
1/4 teaspoon salt
1/8 teaspoon almond extract
6 cups torn mixed greens
3 medium apples, cut into wedges
1 cup thinly sliced celery
2 tablespoons sliced green onions
1/3 cup slivered almonds

Combine oil, sugar, vinegar, salt and almond extract in jar with tight-fitting lid. Shake to mix well. Refrigerate for several hours. Combine remaining ingredients in bowl. Pour salad dressing over salad; toss gently to coat. Serve immediately. Yield: 8 servings.

Barbara Ann Wilson, Laureate Beta Tau, Waterford, Ontario, Canada, makes Pickled Beets by cooking fresh medium-sized beets in saucepan until tender. Let cool. Peel off skins. Pack in sterilized jars. Combine 2 cups sugar and 1 cup white vinegar in saucepan. Cook, stirring, until well dissolved. Pour over beets; seal. Do not use until after 6 months. Sorority sisters love them. The recipe has been in her family for 3 generations.

❖ The-Way-To-A-Man's-Heart Dinner

Pasticcio
Greek Salad
Garlic Bread
Boutari-Red (Greek Wine)

See index for similar recipes.

I was visiting my future husband in Kitimat and was going to meet his grown sons for the first time. I wanted to cook something special. As we gathered around the dining table, I had Greek music playing, the lights dimmed and the candles lit. They loved the meal and the atmosphere and accepted me immediately. They both cook it for their girl friends now. The way to a man's heart is definitely through his stomach!

Marlene Collier, Preceptor Gamma Epsilon
Kitimat, British Columbia, Canada

PASTICCIO

3 cups cooked macaroni, drained
2 eggs, lightly beaten
1/3 cup grated Parmesan cheese
1 1/2 pounds ground beef
2 cups sliced mushrooms
1 cup chopped onion
1 (14-ounce) can tomato sauce
1 teaspoon garlic powder
1 teaspoon dried oregano
1 teaspoon basil leaves
1/2 teaspoon salt
1/4 teaspoon pepper
1/8 teaspoon ground cinnamon
1/3 cup butter or margarine
1/3 cup all-purpose flour
1/4 teaspoon ground nutmeg
3 cups milk
2 eggs, slightly beaten
1/3 cup grated Parmesan cheese

Preheat oven to 350 degrees. Combine macaroni, eggs and cheese in bowl. Spread over bottom of greased 9-by-13-inch baking dish. Cook ground beef, mushrooms and onion in large skillet until tender and browned, stirring until crumbly; drain off fat. Stir in tomato sauce, garlic powder, oregano, basil, 1/4 teaspoon salt, pepper and cinnamon. Simmer, uncovered, while preparing topping. Melt butter in large saucepan. Stir in flour, 1/4 teaspoon salt and nutmeg; mix well. Add milk. Cook, stirring, until thick and bubbly. Stir into eggs gradually; return to saucepan. Cook over low heat for 1 minute. Spread meat filling over macaroni. Spread topping over all. Sprinkle with Parmesan cheese. Bake for 35 to 40 minutes or until flavors blend. Yield: 8 to 10 servings.

GREEK SALAD

3 tomatoes, chopped
1 English cucumber, chopped
1 medium red onion, thinly sliced
1 large green pepper, thinly sliced
1 cup Greek olives or black olives
1/2 cup feta cheese, crumbled
1/4 cup red wine vinegar
3/4 cup olive oil
1 teaspoon basil
1/2 teaspoon oregano
1/2 teaspoon salt
Dash of ground pepper

Combine tomatoes, cucumber, onion, green pepper, olives and feta cheese in salad bowl. Combine remaining ingredients in small bowl; mix well. Add dressing to salad. Toss to coat. Serve immediately. Yield: 6 servings.

Romantic Social

Cupid's Casserole
Fantasy Fondue
Passion Fruits with Prosciutto
Sweetheart Salad
Italian Love Cake
Passionate Punch
Hugs and Kisses Cornucopia

See index for similar recipes.

This sorority social event was centered around romance. The table setting had a white lace tablecloth and white lace place mats with a red tablecloth showing through. A chocolate-coated cornucopia filled with hugs and kisses candy was a favor for everyone's place setting. For the fun part, we had a Hot Lips Contest. Everyone was given a heart-shaped piece of paper and a sample tube of lipstick and asked to write their name on the back. After putting the lipstick on, they kissed the heart-shaped paper. All the kisses were placed on a large poster board. The social committee decided who had the hottest lips. Everyone had a great time. At the end of the evening, we sipped on a cup of tea and had a "Hearth to Heart" talk!

Debbie Meegan, Pennsylvania Preceptor Beta Phi
Lemont Furnace, Pennsylvania

CUPID'S CASSEROLE

1 (16-ounce) package frozen mixed vegetables (broccoli, cauliflower and carrots)
1/2 cup chopped onion
1/2 cup sliced celery
1/2 teaspoon crushed dried thyme leaves
2 tablespoons margarine or butter
1 (10-ounce) can cream of broccoli soup
1 (10-ounce) can cream of chicken soup
1 cup milk
3 cups chopped cooked chicken
1/4 teaspoon pepper
2 cups baking mix
1/2 cup water

Preheat oven to 375 degrees. Cook vegetables according to package directions; drain. Cook onion, celery and thyme in hot margarine in 2-quart saucepan over medium heat until onion is tender, stirring occasionally. Add soups and milk; stir until smooth. Combine chicken, cooked vegetables and pepper in casserole. Add soup mixture, stirring gently to mix. Mix baking mix and water in bowl until soft dough forms; beat vigorously 20 strokes. Smooth dough gently into a ball on floured cloth-covered board. Knead 5 times. Roll dough to 1/2-inch thickness. Cut dough with floured heart-shaped cookie cutter. Place heart-shaped biscuits on top chicken mixture. Bake for 30 minutes or until golden brown. Yield: 8 servings.

FANTASY FONDUE

1 clove of garlic, halved
1 cup dry white wine
2 cups grated Swiss cheese
1 cup grated Gruyère cheese
1/4 teaspoon dry mustard
2 teaspoons cornstarch
1 tablespoon Cognac or Kirsch
1 small loaf French bread, cut into 1-inch cubes

Rub cut surface of garlic over side and bottom of fondue pot. Discard garlic. Pour wine into fondue pot. Place over low heat until bubbles rise to surface. Combine Swiss cheese, Gruyère cheese, mustard and cornstarch in medium bowl. Stir cheese mixture slowly into hot wine until mixture is blended and smooth. Stir in Cognac gradually. Keep warm over very low heat. Swirl French bread cubes through warm mixture using fondue forks. Yield: 2 1/2 cups.

♥ PASSIONATE PUNCH

1 (12-ounce) can frozen orange juice, thawed
1 (12-ounce) can frozen lemonade, thawed
1 (12-ounce) can frozen pineapple juice, thawed
1 1/2 cups sugar
2 quarts ginger ale
Ice fruit ring

Dilute juices according to can directions. Combine juices and sugar in large container; chill. Pour into large chilled punch bowl. Add ginger ale just before serving. Float ice fruit ring in punch. Yield: 32 cups.

Labor Day Supper

Steak Teriyaki
Red Potatoes with Lemon
Fancy Sliced Tomatoes
Corn on the Cob
Hard Rolls — Garlic Toast
Peach or Apple Kuchen with Ice Cream

See index for similar recipes.

After a busy summer, Labor Day was the day to wind down and the day of a new beginning — a new school year. For several years, I had made a traditional supper. The children anxiously looked forward to this meal. And every year, I had to prepare more steak as their appetites grew larger. This was also a chance to use the sweet corn, tomatoes and new potatoes from our garden plus the fruit in season.

Judy Mosley, Xi Upsilon
Dresbach, Minnesota

STEAK TERIYAKI

1 1/2 pounds sirloin steak
1/3 cup soy sauce
2 cloves of garlic, minced
1 tablespoon dark brown sugar
2 tablespoons vegetable oil
1/2 teaspoon monosodium glutamate
3/4 teaspoon ground ginger
8 ounces fresh mushrooms, sliced

Cut steak into bite-sized pieces. Combine next 6 ingredients in bowl; mix well. Add steak. Marinate for 3 to 4 hours, turning occasionally. Preheat grill. Grill over hot coals to desired doneness, basting often with marinade. Sauté sliced mushrooms in 2 to 3 tablespoons marinade. Serve with steak. Yield: 6 servings.

FANCY SLICED TOMATOES

Unpeeled tomatoes, sliced
Sweet onions, sliced
Salt and pepper to taste
Dried basil
Sugar
Vinegar
Olive oil

Place layer of tomatoes in 8- to 10-inch shallow serving bowl. Top with layer of onions. Sprinkle with salt, pepper, basil, 1/2 teaspoon sugar, 1 teaspoon vinegar and 1 teaspoon olive oil. Repeat layers, depending on number of servings. Refrigerate for several hours before serving to blend flavors. Yield: variable.

Old-Fashioned Thanksgiving Dinner

Baked Turkey
Turkey Dressing
Mashed Potatoes — Yams
Green Bean Casserole
Chicken with Fried Rice
Green Salad — Cranberries
Deviled Eggs — Relish Dish
Rolls
Pumpkin Pie — Chocolate Pie
Lemon Meringue Pie — Chess Pie
Beverages

See index for similar recipes.

Thanksgiving at our house has always been a big family gathering. I do the turkey, but take the giblets to my mother for her special dressing. We all have our favorite dishes. Everyone loves the deviled eggs. And of course, a favorite pie. We always begin by going around the table sharing something for which we are thankful and then clasping hands.

Roberta Griffith, Xi Upsilon Rho
Oxnard, California

TURKEY DRESSING

Giblets from turkey
1 onion, chopped
2 stalks celery
1 tablespoon butter
2 (6-ounce) packages stuffing mix
3 eggs
Milk
4 green onions, chopped
3 hard-cooked eggs, chopped
1/2 pan cooked corn bread
3 slices bread, crumbled
1 teaspoon sage or poultry seasoning
1/4 cup chopped nuts (optional)
Salt and pepper to taste

Preheat oven to 350 degrees. Cook giblets in water to cover for 2 hours. Reserve broth. Sauté onions and celery in butter in skillet. Add to stuffing mix in large bowl; mix well. Add eggs; mix well. Add milk to broth to make 2 cups. Add broth-milk mixture to stuffing mixture. Stir until moistened. Add remaining ingredients; mix well. Place in 9-by-13-inch baking pan. Bake for 45 minutes. Pierce with fork when done. Spoon more broth over top to prevent dryness. Yield: 8 to 12 servings.

Snow-Day Lite Supper

Spicy Tomato Soup
Vegetable Salad
Cheese Straws
Chocolate-Filled Caramel Buns

See index for similar recipes.

When we have a blizzard-type snow storm and lose our electrical service, we all pitch in and carry an armful of firewood into the house, build a roaring fire and prepare this supper. We spend the evening telling stories and sharing each other's company. This has been a tradition in our family for 31 years.

Joycee Davis, Preceptor Zeta
Lowell, Arkansas

VEGETABLE SALAD

1 cup vegetable oil
1/2 cup vinegar
2 tablespoons lemon juice
6 tablespoons parsley flakes
2 teaspoons salt
2 teaspoons sugar
1 teaspoon chopped sweet basil
1/2 teaspoon cayenne
Flowerets of 1 bunch broccoli
Flowerets of 1 head cauliflower
1 bunch green onions, chopped
1 large green pepper, chopped
1 large cucumber, sliced
1 large tomato, chopped

Mix oil, vinegar, lemon juice, parsley flakes, salt, sugar, basil and cayenne in bowl. Combine vegetables in bowl. Pour dressing over vegetables; mix to coat. Let stand for 2 hours before serving. Yield: 8 servings.

CHOCOLATE-FILLED CARAMEL BUNS

2/3 cup ready-to-spread caramel-pecan frosting supreme
20 pecan halves
2 (10-ounce) cans refrigerator flaky biscuits
20 milk chocolate candy kisses

Preheat oven to 370 degrees. Grease 9-inch square baking pan. Spread frosting over bottom of pan. Press pecans into frosting. Separate dough into 20 biscuits. Wrap 1 biscuit around each candy kiss to completely enclose kiss. Pinch edges to seal. Arrange over frosting and pecans. Bake for 28 to 32 minutes or until golden brown. Let stand for 3 minutes. Invert onto serving plate. Yield: 20 servings.

Soup Get-Together

Super Soups
Stacked Breadsticks
Rainbow Sherbet

See index for similar recipes.

This menu is great for big family get-togethers. It allows each member who brings an ingredient for the soup(s) to be creative. Some ingredients are necessary, but others may be added by personal choice. The best part is that it is all done ahead of time. Serve the soup bases in heated Crock•Pots. Other ingredients should come ready to be added to the soup and at room temperature so they will heat through. My chapter served the soup on opening day several years ago. A sign-up list took care of the ingredients and any special creations added by sorority sisters!

Mary Swetich, Xi Tau
Ely, Nevada

SUPER SOUPS

Chicken Soup Base
Beef Soup Base
Miniature Meatballs
4 ounces full cooked ham strips, cut into thin strips
1 to 2 cups cubed cooked chicken
1 cup cooked peas
2 carrots, cooked, finely shredded
2 potatoes, cooked, cubed
2 cups fine strips fresh spinach
1 pound sliced mushrooms

Prepare soup bases and meatballs ahead of time; chill. Prepare other ingredients to add to soup. Guests select their choice of soup base and add any or all other ingredients. Bring each soup base to a boil in Crock•Pot at serving time, stirring occasionally. Yield: 15 to 20 cups.

CHICKEN SOUP BASE

1/2 cup chopped onion
1/2 cup shredded carrot
1/2 cup chopped celery
3 cups chicken broth
1/4 cup margarine
1/3 cup all-purpose flour
1/8 teaspoon nutmeg
4 cups milk

Cook vegetables in broth in large covered saucepan for 20 minutes or until done. Pour into blender container. Process until smooth. Melt margarine in saucepan. Stir in flour and nutmeg. Stir in puréed vegetables and milk. Cook until thickened. Let cool in refrigerator. Bring base to a boil at serving time or keep hot in Crock•Pot. Add additional milk if too thick. Yield: 8 cups.

BEEF SOUP BASE

8 cups beef broth
1 small onion, sliced
1 cup celery leaves
5 sprigs fresh parsley
2 bay leaves
2 cloves of garlic
1 teaspoon dried basil
Chopped green onions (optional)

Combine first 7 ingredients in 4-quart saucepan. Bring to a boil. Simmer for 20 minutes; strain. Refrigerate or keep warm in Crock•Pot. Bring to a boil prior to serving. Add onions just before serving. Yield: 8 cups.

MINIATURE MEATBALLS

1 egg, beaten
1/4 cup milk
1 tablespoon mustard
1/2 teaspoon salt
1 cup soft bread crumbs
1 pound lean ground beef or turkey

Combine all ingredients in bowl; mix well. Shape into tiny meatballs. Brown in skillet for 10 to 15 minutes; drain off fat. May bake in baking pan in preheated 325-degree oven for 10 to 15 minutes if desired. Yield: 8 servings.

STACKED BREADSTICKS

1 1/2 cups all-purpose flour
1 package yeast
3/4 cup milk
2 tablespoons margarine
1 tablespoon sugar
1/2 teaspoon salt
2 tablespoons melted margarine
2 to 3 tablespoons sesame or poppy seeds
1 egg yolk, beaten
1 tablespoon water

Preheat oven to 375 degrees. Combine 3/4 cup flour and yeast in mixer bowl. Heat milk, 2 tablespoons margarine, sugar and salt in saucepan just until warm and margarine is melted, stirring constantly. Add to flour mixture, stirring constantly. Beat at Low speed of mixer for 30 seconds, scraping side of bowl constantly. Beat for 3 minutes at High speed. Stir in as much of remaining flour as possible with wooden spoon. Turn out onto lightly floured surface. Knead in enough remaining flour for 6 to 8 minutes to make moderately stiff, smooth and elastic dough. Shape dough into ball. Place in lightly greased bowl. Turn once; cover. Let rise in warm place for 45 minutes to 1 hour or until doubled in bulk. Punch dough down. Turn out onto lightly floured surface. Let rest for 5 minutes. Divide into 3 portions; divide each portion into 6 pieces. Let rest for 5 minutes. Roll each piece into 8-inch long rope. Place 7 ropes parallel on greased baking sheet, about 1/4 inch apart. Brush with margarine. Sprinkle with sesame seeds. Place 6 ropes on top. Brush with margarine. Top with sesame seeds. Place 5 ropes on top. Brush with margarine. Top with sesame seeds. Cover. Let rise for 40 minutes. Combine egg yolk with water in bowl. Brush over top. Sprinkle with sesame seeds. Bake for 20 minutes. Let cool. To serve, let each diner pull off a stick. Yield: 18 breadsticks.

Potluck Dinner for a Special Friend

Microwave Stuffed Meat Loaf
Refrigerator Potatoes
Scalloped Corn
Fruit Salad
Garlic Bread
Cherry Cheesecake

See index for similar recipes.

I am a registered nurse in an outpatient surgical center in our community hospital. We treated an elderly female patient three times a week for 10 years. A year after being admitted to a nursing home, her health began to fail. The nurses in our unit had this potluck dinner for her 3 days before Christmas. We cherish the memories of our special friend and the potluck dinner.

Jean Mortensen, Beta Sigma Phi
Arlington, Nebraska

MICROWAVE STUFFED MEAT LOAF

1 slice white bread
1 1/2 pounds ground beef
2 to 3 stalks celery
1/2 large onion
1 egg
2 tablespoons water
Salt and pepper to taste
1 (4-ounce) package dried beef
1 (4-ounce) can mushrooms, drained
1 (4-ounce) package grated mozzarella cheese
1 (16-ounce) can spaghetti sauce

Place bread in blender container. Process to fine crumbs. Add to ground beef in bowl; mix well. Place celery, onion, egg, water, salt and pepper in blender container. Purée. Add to meat mixture; mix well. Press meat onto waxed paper to form 8-by-12-inch rectangle. Top with dried beef, mushrooms and cheese. Roll up as for jelly roll using waxed paper as a guide. Place in microwave-safe baking dish. Pour 1/2 spaghetti sauce over meat roll. Tent with waxed paper. Microwave at full power for 8 to 8 1/2 minutes. Rotate 1/2 turn. Microwave for 8 to 8 1/2 minutes longer. Let stand for 10 minutes before serving. Heat remaining spaghetti sauce in saucepan. Serve with meat loaf. Yield: 6 to 8 servings.

Christmas Brunch

Ham with Ham Glaze
Eggs Mornay
Warm Bananas in Brandy Sauce
Danish Ebelskive
Orange Juice — Tomato Juice
Punch

See index for similar recipes.

About 20 years ago when my three boys were gone from home, we decided to exchange Christmas gifts at Mom's on Christmas — brunch included. Since then it's become a tradition with family, neighbors and friends. Everyone wants to be invited for Mom's fabulous brunch.

Donna J. Myers, Preceptor Beta Nu
La Habra, California

EGGS MORNAY

12 hard-cooked eggs, cubed
1/4 cup butter
1/4 cup all-purpose flour
1/2 teaspoon salt
1/4 teaspoon pepper
1/4 teaspoon nutmeg
2 cups chicken stock
1 cup light cream
1/4 teaspoon cayenne
2 cups cubed Cheddar cheese
2 cups buttered bread cubes

Preheat oven to 350 degrees. Place eggs in bottom of buttered 9-by-12-inch glass baking dish. Combine next 9 ingredients in bowl; mix well. Pour over eggs. Top with buttered bread cubes. Bake for 20 to 25 minutes or until bubbly. Yield: 12 servings.

WARM BANANAS IN BRANDY SAUCE

4 bananas
1 (8-ounce) can pineapple chunks
1/2 cup margarine
1/2 cup packed dark brown sugar
1/2 cup pecans
1/4 cup pineapple or apricot preserves or marmalade
1/2 teaspoon ground cinnamon
1/4 cup Brandy

Cut bananas into 1 to 2-inch pieces. Drain pineapple, reserving 2 tablespoons juice. Combine reserved juice, margarine, brown sugar, pecans, preserves and cinnamon in bowl; mix well to dissolve brown sugar. Place bananas in 2-quart flat microwave-safe baking dish. Pour sauce over bananas. Add Brandy. Microwave for 3 to 5 minutes. Yield: 8 to 10 servings.

Mouthwatering Menus / 23

Christmas Dinner

Chicken Breasts Melvina
Potatoes Sylvia
Turnip Puff Diane

See index for similar recipes.

I have shared this dinner with many of our family and friends. Christmas dinner for our chapter this year was the most special. There were 10 of us ladies. We were able to sit together at a new 3-by-10-foot table my husband had built this year. The table looked so pretty with the decorations and place mats I had made. It was nice to be able to make this dinner the day before and to enjoy it with the rest of the ladies.

June C. Davies, Zi Zeta Rho
Caledon, Ontario, Canada

CHICKEN BREASTS MELVINA

1/3 cup all-purpose flour
1 teaspoon salt
1/4 teaspoon pepper
8 whole boneless skinless chicken breasts, split
1/2 clove of garlic, minced
1 cup chopped onion
1 pound fresh mushrooms
6 tablespoons butter
1 cup dry vermouth
1 cup chicken stock
1 (10-ounce) can cream of mushroom soup
White grapes (optional)

Preheat oven to 350 degrees. Mix flour, salt and pepper in bowl. Coat chicken. Sauté garlic, onion and mushrooms in butter in skillet for 3 to 4 minutes. Remove from skillet. Cook chicken in skillet, turning after 5 minutes. Cook for 3 minutes longer. Add onion mixture. Simmer for 5 minutes. Add vermouth, stock and soup. Simmer for 5 minutes longer. Transfer to buttered 9-by-13-inch baking dish. Bake for 45 minutes. Garnish with grapes. Yield: 8 servings.

TURNIP PUFF DIANE

2 cups mashed cooked turnip
Butter
Salt
Ground ginger
1 cup soft bread crumbs
1 tablespoon sugar
1/4 teaspoon ground mace
1 egg
1/2 cup milk

Preheat oven to 350 degrees. Season turnip with butter, salt and ginger in bowl; mix well. Add bread crumbs, sugar, mace, 1/8 teaspoon ginger and 1/4 teaspoon salt. Mix egg and milk in bowl. Stir into turnip mixture. Pour into greased 1-quart casserole. Dot with 1 tablespoon butter. Bake for 45 minutes. Yield: 8 servings.

An Oriental Dinner

Chasu
Won Tons
Mah-Fry Chicken
Egg Foo-Yung
Fried Rice
Hot Tea

See index for similar recipes.

On January 1, 1987, my husband and I were invited to a New Year's family dinner with oriental friends. It was by tradition a big celebration. The mother made the above plus more. It is the best oriental dinner I have ever had.

Julie Chandler, Upsilon
Weiser, Idaho

CHASU

1 (4-pound) pork loin roast
1/2 cup soy sauce
2 tablespoons sugar
1/2 teaspoon molasses
1/4 cup catsup
1 clove of garlic, chopped
Hot mustard

Cut roast into 1 1/2-by-1 1/2-by-5-inch strips. Combine soy sauce, sugar, molasses, catsup and garlic in bowl; mix well. Add pork strips. Marinate for 2 hours. Preheat oven to 350 degrees. Bake pork strips for 1 hour, basting frequently. Let stand for a few minutes before slicing. Serve with hot mustard. Yield: 8 servings.

WON TONS

2 green onions, chopped
1 pound cooked pork, finely chopped
1/2 cup mushrooms, finely chopped
1/2 cup water chestnuts, finely chopped
1 tablespoon soy sauce
Salt to taste
Dash of monosodium glutamate
Won ton shells
Vegetable oil for frying

Combine green onions, pork, mushrooms, water chestnuts, soy sauce, salt and monosodium glutamate in saucepan. Cook over moderate heat until mixture is dry. Let cool. Place 1 teaspoon pork mixture on 1 corner of each won ton shell. Fold over 2 or 3 times. Pinch 2 opposite free corners of shell together, leaving fourth corner free. Deep-fry in hot oil until golden. Drain. Yield: 8 servings.

✤ Elegant New Year's Day Dinner

Roasted Marinated Pork Loin
Tiered Cheese Terrine
Cream of Asparagus Soup
Onion-Cream Cheese Whipped Potatoes
Marinade Gravy
Baked Sauerkraut
Toasted Almond Biscuits
Homemade Strawberry Preserves
Crème Brûlée

See index for similar recipes.

We enjoyed this dinner in our new home this year with 15 friends and family members. We celebrated a traditional pork and sauerkraut beginning complete with fine china, fresh linens, brass chargers and candles. We anticipate that 1995 will continue to be as wonderful as the beginning. Fellowship and fine food truly warm the heart.

Carol Webb, Xi Alpha Rho
Danville, Kentucky

CREAM OF ASPARAGUS SOUP

2 large leeks
2 tablespoons butter
4 cups ready-to-serve chicken broth
2 potatoes, peeled, chopped
1/2 teaspoon salt
1/4 teaspoon pepper
1 pound asparagus
1/2 cup whipping cream

Trim roots and leaves from leeks, leaving only white and about 2 inches of green sections. Split lengthwise; slice crosswise about 1/4 inch thick. Sauté leeks in butter in saucepan until softened. Stir in chicken broth, potatoes, salt and pepper. Bring to a boil over high heat. Trim 1 1/2 inches from asparagus tips; reserve for garnish. Trim off woody stem ends; discard. Chop remaining asparagus into 1-inch pieces. Add to boiling soup. Reduce heat. Simmer, uncovered, for 10 minutes or until vegetables are tender. Transfer soup to blender container. Purée until smooth. Return soup to saucepan. Stir in cream. Heat through. Garnish each serving with steamed asparagus tips. Yield: 6 servings.

ONION-CREAM CHEESE WHIPPED POTATOES

10 medium potatoes, peeled, quartered
1/4 cup chopped onion
8 ounces cream cheese, softened
1/4 cup butter or margarine
1/2 teaspoon salt
1/4 teaspoon pepper
Milk

Boil potatoes and onion in water to cover in large covered saucepan over medium-high heat until tender; drain. Place in large mixer bowl; beat until smooth. Add cream cheese, butter, salt and pepper. Beat until well blended. Add milk for desired consistency. Serve with Marinade Gravy. Yield: 6 to 8 servings.

MARINADE GRAVY

2 1/2 cups water
4 chicken bouillon cubes
Marinade reserved from roast
1/4 cup cornstarch
3/4 cup water
Pepper to taste

Bring 2 1/2 cups water and bouillon to a boil in medium saucepan. Add reserved marinade. Shake cornstarch, water and pepper in gravy shaker until smooth and well blended. Pour cornstarch mixture into bouillon mixture. Stir over medium heat until thickened. Serve over whipped potatoes. Yield: 4 cups.

BAKED SAUERKRAUT

1 (16-ounce) can sauerkraut
1/4 teaspoon gourmet ground pepper

Preheat oven to 350 degrees. Place sauerkraut and pepper in medium casserole. Bake, covered, for 30 minutes. Yield: 4 servings.

CRÈME BRÛLÉE

8 egg yolks
6 tablespoons sugar
4 cups heavy whipping cream
2/3 cup packed dark brown sugar
2 cups fresh raspberries or strawberries

Beat egg yolks in blender container at high speed until lemon colored. Beat in sugar gradually. Heat cream in saucepan over medium heat. Stir 1/2 the hot cream mixture into egg mixture. Stir hot cream-egg mixture into saucepan. Cook over low heat until thickened. Do not boil. Pour into individual ovenproof serving dishes. Refrigerate for 6 hours. Preheat oven to 550 degrees. Remove dishes from refrigerator. Place immediately into jelly roll pan or broiler pan of cold water. Sprinkle with brown sugar. Broil until brown sugar begins to melt. Remove from oven. Garnish with fresh raspberries. Yield: 8 servings.

The Treasure Box

When you think about gifts you have received in the past, isn't it usually those handmade treasures that mean the most. How often have you marveled at a beautiful centerpiece or darling Christmas ornament and thought to yourself, "I wish I could do that." Well, now you can. Our simple, easy-to-follow directions are created for all levels of skill—from the experienced to those who are "craft impaired." Many can be completed in just a short time. You'll find lots of rainy day projects that are perfect for keeping your youngsters occupied and away from the television for a few hours! Plus, you'll have the fun of sharing some good old fashion family time together. It's never too late to get started on items for your next bazaar or fund raisers . . . and don't forget Christmas gifts and decorations. Think of the pleasure you'll have when you say, "I made it myself."

26 / Crafts

Starfish Santa and Snowman

This jolly Santa and snowman with out-stretched arms began as starfish swimming the seas. A quick makeover with paint and scraps turns the little starfish into ornaments to treasure.

MATERIALS FOR STARFISH SANTA

Medium flat paintbrush
Acrylic paints: Red, Black, White, Face Color, Gold
Starfish
Hot glue gun
7 inches jute

DIRECTIONS

☐ Paint all but outer tips of both front and back of starfish red.
☐ Paint black boots and white fur cuffs on front and back of leg tips.
☐ Paint appropriately colored hands and white cuffs on front and back of arm tips.
☐ Paint white top to cap on front and back of remaining tip.
☐ Paint white brim of cap and white beard on front.
☐ Paint face and black dot eyes and black belt with gold buckle.
☐ Glue looped jute to back of Santa ornament for hanger.

MATERIALS FOR STARFISH SNOWMAN

Medium flat paintbrush
Acrylic paints: White, Black, Orange
Starfish
Hot glue gun
Purchased black hat, 1/2-inch to 3/4-inch diameter
7 inches jute
Scraps of plaid fabric

DIRECTIONS

☐ Paint both sides of starfish white.
☐ Paint black dot eyes and buttons and orange carrot nose.
☐ Glue hat to top of head.
☐ Glue looped jute to back of snowman ornament for hanger.
☐ Cut a 1/4 by 7-inch piece from plaid fabric.
☐ Wrap around snowman's neck for scarf, and glue in place.

The Treasure Box / 27

DIRECTIONS

☐ Clean and dry holder.

☐ Tear masking tape into irregular pieces, and apply them randomly over entire holder.

☐ Overlap tape pieces, and add as many layers as need to cover the design and color of the original holder.

☐ Use rag to apply a heavy coat of shoe polish to holder. Wipe off excess and let dry.

Gifts from the Hearth

Fresh bread baked in unique shapes and gaily wrapped is always a welcome gift. And, if time is especially short, let your favorite bakery, do the cooking for you. Add a decorative bow and you're set.

Leather-Look Bill Holder

Here's a gift little ones can make for Dad that's both inexpensive and easy. You just recycle old napkins or stationery holders picked up at yard sales and flea markets into attractive bill holders.

MATERIALS

Plastic, metal, or wooden napkin holder or stationery holder
Wide masking tape
Cloth rag
Brown shoe polish

Fun Frames

Everyone loves pictures. Make these colorful craft foam frames for your favorite little tyke's room. Choose just the right photo to display, and watch little eyes go round with delight and fascination. This button frame is a wonderful way to display favorites from your button collection.

MATERIALS FOR FOAM FRAMES

Craft foam:
  yellow and blue for Stars and Moon design
  red, green, and blue for Christmas Tree design
Hole punch
Crafter's cement
2 (3½-by-5-inch) clear acrylic frames
Super glue
See Pattern

Tree
Cut 1 from green craft foam.

Small Star
Cut 1 from blue craft foam.

DIRECTIONS

☐ Transfer patterns to craft foam, and cut out. Punch holes in red foam to make tree ornaments.
☐ Use crafter's cement to glue designs to frame, referring to illustration for placement. Use super glue to glue ornaments to tree.

Clever Candlesticks

These simple candle cups allow you to convert all sorts of things into candlesticks. They're communion cups (available at church supply stores) that have been painted and then glued onto the heads of 1½-inch nails. You can stick them in fruit (just make sure the fruit doesn't tend to roll!), use them in foam inserted in floral arrangements, or display them in logs. You might want to paint your candle cups red and green for the holidays and add ¼-inch wide picot ribbon bows. For a twist, try using white or metallic paints.

The Treasure Box / 29

MATERIALS FOR BUTTON FRAME

Crafter's cement
Assorted buttons
1 (5-by-7-inch) clear acrylic frame

DIRECTIONS

☐ Place photo in frame to be sure button design complements photo.

☐ Glue buttons randomly around edge of frame, overlapping as desired. (Note: Cement allows buttons to be moved slightly before it sets.)

Moon
Cut 1 from yellow craft foam.

Star
Cut 2 from blue craft foam.

Surprise Gift Bags

It seems as though there are always lots of little presents to pull together at Christmas—the list keeps growing to include teachers, babysitters, children's friends, neighbors, and co-workers. Unfortunately, time and money can run short. Here are three versions of a simple cloth gift bag that will fit many needs. The small bag is filled with potpourri and rolled over a twig, becoming a charming sachet. The medium bag is bursting with peppermint candies and rolled over a candy cane. And the large bag contains a dry soup mix. It's rolled over a wooden spoon. If your recipe isn't too precious to divulge, you can also attach a recipe card.

MATERIALS

Pinking shears
Fabric scraps:
(Note: Cut to size with pinking shears.)
3½-by-12-inch strip for small bag
4-by-15-inch strip for medium bag
5-by-18-inch strip for large bag
Twig, candy cane, wooden spoon
Cord, ribbon, or yarn:
12 inches for small bag
18 inches for medium and large bags

DIRECTIONS

☐ Fold strip in half with right sides facing and short ends together. Stitch side seams with a ¼-inch seam allowance. Turn.

☐ Fill bag as desired, ¼ to ⅓ full. Roll top of bag over twig, candy cane or spoon. Tie ribbon around bag, and knot ends to secure.

Gingerbread Man Spiced Mug Mats

Rest a hot mug on this cheerful little fellow and you'll release the delicious aroma of cloves. That's because these mats have whole cloves tucked between layers of batting. They're a wonderful gift for that person you tell all your secrets to over a cup of coffee or tea.

MATERIALS FOR GINGERBREAD MAN SPICED MUG MATS

1 (6-inch) square of linen-weave cotton fabric
Paintbrushes: medium flat, small round
Acrylic paints: Brown, Brick Red, Green, White
2 (5-inch) squares of thin quilt batting
1 (6-inch) square of red Christmas print fabric
Whole cloves
See Patterns or Illustration

The Treasure Box / 31

DIRECTIONS

☐ Transfer pattern to linen-weave fabric.

☐ Paint gingerbread man with thin coat of brown paint. Paint red berries and green holly leaves. Paint white details and red heart on gingerbread man. Use a clean brush for each color, and allow paint to dry between coats.

☐ Position batting pieces in center of wrong side of both fabric squares.

☐ Place backing piece right side down, and sprinkle cloves over batting. Wrap fabric edges to inside over batting, and pin on fabric side.

☐ Wrap fabric over batting on front piece, and pin to backing piece. Topstitch front and back pieces together 1/4 inch from edges.

Southwestern Placesetting

Corral your guests with a western theme: bandanas, badges, and boots make a great table setting and good favors.

Fast and Festive Centerpieces

Christmas topiaries stand guard over the center of a festive dining table. Simply glue candies or cookies to styrofoam cones.

Dressed Up Napkin Rings

These sparkling napkin rings are an easy accent to make for the dinner table. Simple wooden napkin rings can be unearthed at garage sales and flea markets. Use a bit of paint and ribbon, and you have five or so golden rings adding the perfect festive note.

MATERIALS FOR NAPKIN RINGS

Wooden napkin rings
Fine sandpaper
Paper towels
Gold acrylic paint
1/2-inch wide gold wire-edge ribbon
Hot glue gun
Nailheads, buttons, or other baubles

DIRECTIONS FOR NAPKIN RINGS

☐ Rough surface of rings with sandpaper. Wipe clean of dust with damp paper towel and let dry.

☐ Wipe gold paint lightly over surface with paper towel, adding coats as needed to get desired effect.

☐ Cut one 8-inch long piece of ribbon for each ring. Form small bows from each ribbon piece, and glue onto rings.

☐ Glue nailheads with prongs bent in, buttons, or other baubles over center of bows.

Glitter Stars

Spangle your tree with simple little stars made from glitter stems. These 12-inch long stems may be purchased at most craft stores and are simply wire that is covered with sparkling red tinsel. To make small stars, just bend the wire about every 2 1/4 inches, and twist the ends around each other. To make larger stars, attach 2 stems together, bend about every 4 1/2 inches, and twist the ends.

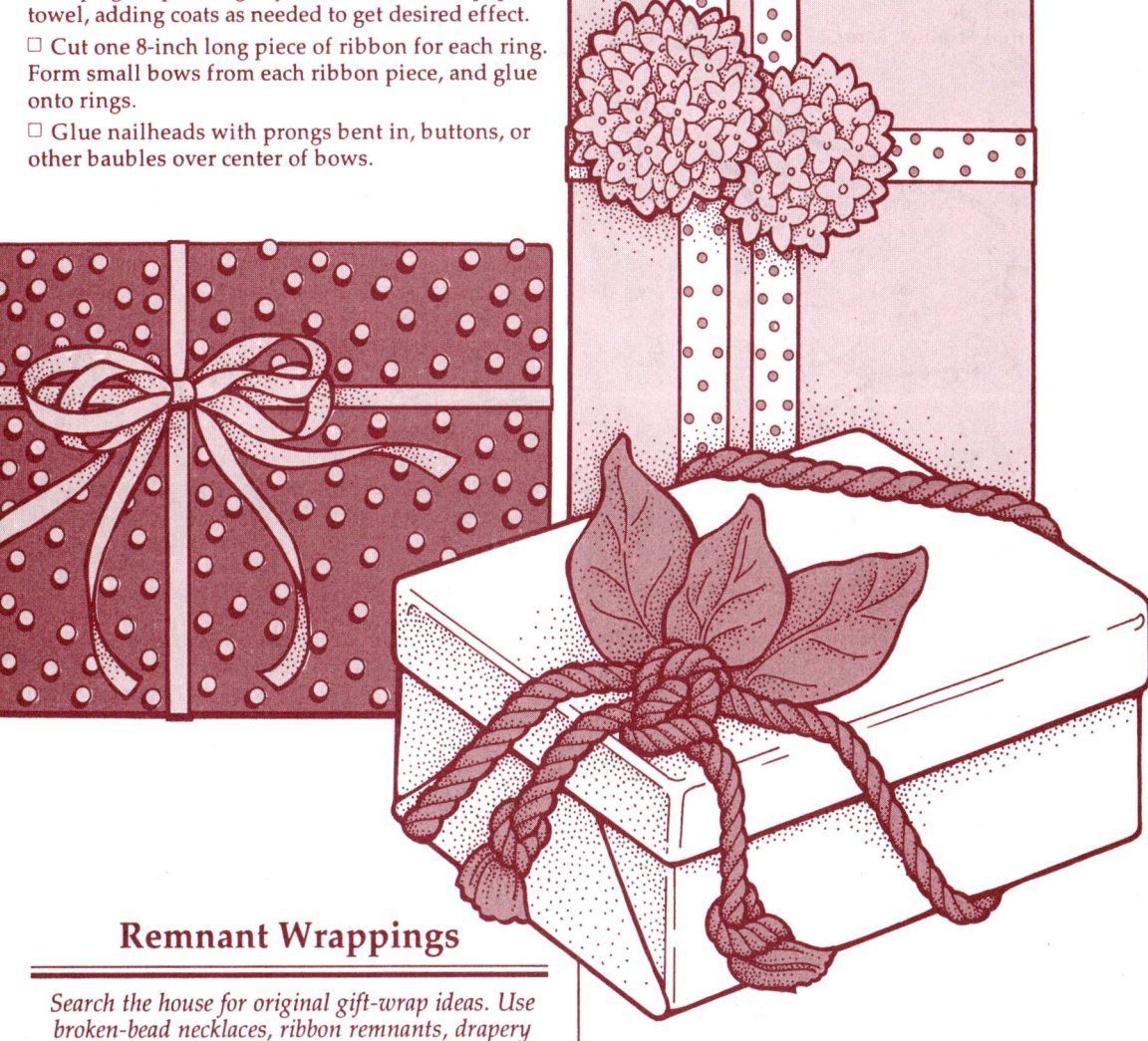

Remnant Wrappings

Search the house for original gift-wrap ideas. Use broken-bead necklaces, ribbon remnants, drapery cord or gold-sprayed dried flowers and leaves.

34 / Crafts

Sequined Sweatshirt

If you're looking for some glitter for holiday parties, here's a shirt with coordinated accessories that you can throw together even at the last minute. Scribbled paint forms the shirt's tree, and masses of sequins form the flash.

MATERIALS FOR SHIRT

Dressmaker's chalk
Solid color sweatshirt
Tulip™ Pearl Fabric Paint: Gold, Ruby Red, Jade
Multi-colored sequins: 5mm, 8mm, and 12mm
See Patterns

DIRECTIONS FOR SHIRT

☐ Use dressmaker's chalk to sketch tree pattern on front of shirt.

☐ Scribble-paint tree and trunk with gold, red and jade paint colors.

☐ Scatter sequins over still-wet paint on tree but not trunk, and press gently into paint. Let dry.

☐ Turn inside out, and hand wash in cold water. Lay flat to dry.

Just for Starters

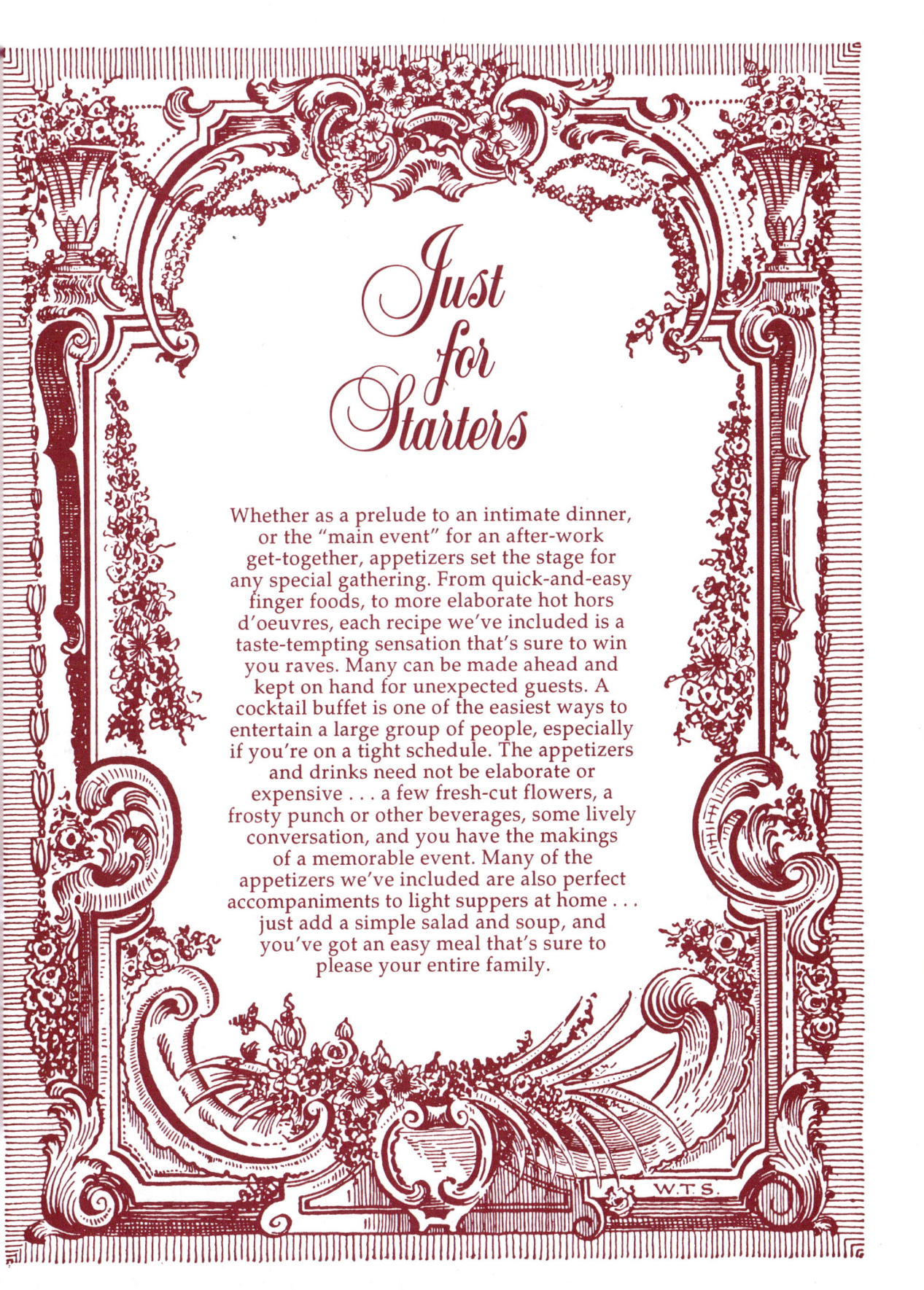

Whether as a prelude to an intimate dinner, or the "main event" for an after-work get-together, appetizers set the stage for any special gathering. From quick-and-easy finger foods, to more elaborate hot hors d'oeuvres, each recipe we've included is a taste-tempting sensation that's sure to win you raves. Many can be made ahead and kept on hand for unexpected guests. A cocktail buffet is one of the easiest ways to entertain a large group of people, especially if you're on a tight schedule. The appetizers and drinks need not be elaborate or expensive . . . a few fresh-cut flowers, a frosty punch or other beverages, some lively conversation, and you have the makings of a memorable event. Many of the appetizers we've included are also perfect accompaniments to light suppers at home . . . just add a simple salad and soup, and you've got an easy meal that's sure to please your entire family.

36 / Appetizers

BEEF AND CHEESE BALL

16 ounces cream cheese, softened
1 cup small-curd cottage cheese
2 teaspoons grated onion
2 teaspoons Worcestershire sauce
3 to 4 dashes of Louisiana hot sauce
3 packages dried beef, cut into small pieces

Combine cream cheese, cottage cheese, onion, Worcestershire sauce and hot sauce in medium bowl, mixing by hand. Add half the beef to mixture. Shape into ball. Roll in remaining beef. Cover with plastic wrap. Chill for 5 to 6 hours or overnight. Serve with favorite crackers. Yield: 16 to 20 servings.

Margaret Sanders, Xi Epsilon Nu
Cape Girardeau, Missouri

CHEESE BALL

16 ounces cream cheese, softened
2 tablespoons butter or margarine
1/2 jar Old English sharp cheese
1/2 package blue cheese
2 tablespoons chopped onion
1 tablespoon Worcestershire sauce
2 tablespoons Milnot cream
1 tablespoon salad dressing (optional)
1/2 cup chopped pecans
Parsley flakes

Combine first 8 ingredients in bowl; mix until cheeses are blended. Shape into ball. Combine pecans and parsley flakes in small bowl. Roll cheese ball in pecan mixture. Chill until firm. Serve with crackers of choice. May add more cream for creamier consistency. Yield: 16 to 20 servings.

LaNita Llewellyn, Laureate Psi
Logansport, Indiana

♥ "A DIET" CHEESE BALL

At only 10 grams of fat per serving, no one can believe this is a diet appetizer! One dieting friend ate all of it!

6 ounces shredded Cheddar cheese
1/2 cup low-calorie cream cheese, softened
1 tablespoon finely chopped green bell pepper
1 tablespoon finely chopped onion
1 tablespoon finely chopped red bell pepper
1 teaspoon Worcestershire sauce
1/2 teaspoon lemon juice
1/2 teaspoon paprika
2 ounces chopped walnuts or fresh parsley

Combine first 8 ingredients in bowl; mix well. Shape into ball. Roll in walnuts. Chill until firm. Serve with melba toast and fresh fruit. Yield: 4 servings.

Lysle Barmby, Xi Omicron
Bragg Creek, Alberta, Canada

♥ CARROT-CHEESE BALLS

2 cups shredded or chopped carrots
8 ounces lite cream cheese, softened
1 cup shredded low-calorie Cheddar cheese
1 clove of garlic, minced
1/4 cup Grape Nuts or Nutrigrain Nuggets
1 tablespoon chopped fresh parsley

Press carrots between paper towels to remove excess moisture. Combine Cheddar cheese and cream cheese in medium bowl; mix well. Add carrots and garlic; mix well. Chill, covered, for 1 hour. Combine cereal and parsley in bowl; mix well. Shape cheese mixture into ball; roll in cereal mixture. Wrap in waxed paper. Chill for 1 hour or until firm. Yield: 16 to 20 servings.

Barbara Bain, Preceptor Beta Psi
Beaumont, Texas

YULETIDE HAM-CHEESE BALL

16 ounces cream cheese, softened
8 ounces sharp cheese, shredded
2 teaspoons grated onion
2 teaspoons Worcestershire sauce
1 teaspoon lemon juice
1/2 teaspoon paprika
1 teaspoon mustard
1/2 teaspoon salt
1 (2-ounce) can deviled ham
2 tablespoons chopped parsley flakes
2 tablespoons chopped pimentos
1 cup chopped pecans

Combine first 11 ingredients in large bowl; mix well. Chill until almost firm. Shape into ball. Roll in pecans. Wrap in foil. Chill overnight. Sprinkle with additional paprika and parsley. Yield: 16 servings.

Marge Baker, Laureate Beta Upsilon
Warrensburg, Missouri

FRUIT COCKTAIL BALL

This was such a success at our "in-house" office brunch, it became part of our office cookbook!

8 ounces cream cheese, softened
1 (3-ounce) package French vanilla instant pudding mix
2 tablespoons orange juice
1 (16-ounce) can fruit cocktail, drained
1/2 cup sliced almonds
1 box butter crackers

Combine cream cheese, pudding mix and orange juice in bowl. Add fruit cocktail; mix well. Shape into ball. Cover with sliced almonds. Chill for 2 hours or until firm. Serve with crackers. Yield: 12 servings.

Sue Schmalfuss, Beta Gamma
Annapolis, Maryland

TUNA BALL

This is inexpensive, delicious and easy to prepare.

3 hard-cooked eggs, chopped	1 teaspoon chopped parsley
8 ounces cream cheese, softened	1 teaspoon Worcestershire sauce
2 tablespoons minced onion	1/4 teaspoon salt
	1 (7-ounce) can tuna

Combine all ingredients in bowl; mix well. Chill, covered, for 2 hours. Shape into ball. Chill until firm. Serve with crackers. Yield: 6 to 8 servings.

Linda Tucker, Tau Beta
Newtown, Missouri

BAGEL DIP

2 cups sour cream	2 teaspoons Accent
1 1/2 cups mayonnaise or mayonnaise-type salad dressing	1 medium onion, finely chopped
2 tablespoons parsley flakes	2 (2-ounce) package corned beef, chopped
2 teaspoons dillweed	1 package frozen bagels

Combine first 7 ingredients in bowl; mix well. Chill overnight. Cut partially thawed bagels into bite-sized pieces; thaw completely. Serve with dip. Yield: 16 to 20 servings.

Sonia Koehler, Theta Omicron
Sioux Center, Iowa

BEER-CHEESE FONDUE DIP

1 unsliced round loaf light rye bread	3/4 cup warm beer
2 (5-ounce) jars Old English cheese	3 tablespoons margarine or butter, melted
1 (8-ounce) jar Cheez Whiz	1 teaspoon Worcestershire sauce
1/2 (8-ounce) jar jalapeño hot salsa Cheez Whiz	Dash of Tabasco sauce
	1/4 cup finely chopped onion
1 (5-ounce) package crumbled blue cheese	1 clove of garlic, minced

Remove top and center of bread, leaving 1/2-inch thick sides to form bread bowl; reserve top and center. Cut reserved bread into bite-sized pieces. Place in plastic bag until ready to serve. Combine next 8 ingredients in food processor container. Process until well blended. Add onion and garlic; blend well. Pour cheese mixture into bread bowl. Chill for 1 hour before serving. Serve bread bowl on platter surrounded by bread pieces. Cheese mixture may be stored in bowl overnight and placed in bread bowl 1 hour before serving. Yield: 16 to 20 servings.

Donna J. Kelley, Xi Eta Eta
Smithton, Pennsylvania

CHEESE DIP WITH PITA CHIPS

1 package Gouda cheese	1/2 cup grated Cheddar cheese
8 ounces cream cheese	Pita bread
1 (10-ounce) package frozen spinach, drained	1/2 cup butter or margarine
1 (4-ounce) can mild green chilies	Lemon pepper to taste
1/4 cup milk	Cumin to taste

Preheat oven to 400 degrees. Process first 6 ingredients in food processor until well blended. Place mixture in 4-inch square baking pan. Bake for 20 minutes or until bubbly. Cut pita bread into triangles and open. Brush with butter. Sprinkle with lemon pepper and cumin. Place in baking pan. Broil until crisp. Serve with dip. Yield: 4 servings.

Diana Meixler, Gamma Rho
Pinetop, Arizona

♥ MEXICAN BEAN DIP WITH PITA CHIPS

4 (6-inch) pita breads	1/3 cup packed fresh coriander leaves
1 (16-ounce) can white beans, drained, rinsed	1/2 teaspoon salt
1 (4-ounce) can chopped green chilies	1/4 cup chopped onion
2 cloves of garlic, chopped	3 ripe tomatoes, seeded, chopped

Preheat oven to 250 degrees. Cut each pita into 12 triangles. Arrange in single layer on ungreased baking sheet. Bake for 15 to 20 minutes or until firm and dry, like chips. Let cool. Process beans, chilies, garlic, coriander and 1/2 teaspoon salt in food processor until puréed. Place in serving bowl. Stir in onion and tomatoes. Serve with cooled chips. Yield: 12 servings.

Beverly Burnap, Xi Gamma Iota
Thendora, New York

♥ MEXICAN FIESTA DIP

16 ounces reduced-calorie cream cheese, softened	1 medium green pepper, minced
	1 medium onion, minced
1 (8-ounce) jar picante sauce	1 cup grated reduced-calorie cheese
1 head lettuce, shredded	1 package fat-free baked tortilla chips
3 large tomatoes, chopped	

Combine cream cheese and picante sauce in bowl. Spread evenly in bottom of 9-by-13-inch dish. Top with lettuce, tomatoes, green pepper, onion and cheese. Chill for 2 to 4 hours. Serve with tortilla chips. Yield: 6 to 10 servings.

Kacy Scoggin, Xi Beta Theta
Hastings, Nebraska

♥ PICO DE GALLO

1 (8-ounce) jar picante chunky sauce
2 or 3 large avocados, cubed
2 or 3 green onions, chopped
1 large tomato, cubed
1 tablespoon canola oil
1 tablespoon lemon juice
Dash of lite salt
Tortilla chips

Pour picante sauce into bowl. Add next 6 ingredients, stirring lightly. Chill. Serve with tortilla chips. Yield: 6 to 8 servings.

Kathy Harris, Pi Chi
Harlingen, Texas

OUT-OF-THIS-WORLD DIP

8 ounces cream cheese, softened
Peanut butter
Sliced green onions
Chutney
Bacon bits
Toasted angel flake coconut
Crackers

Layer cream cheese in serving dish to make 1/2-inch layer. Add 1-inch layer of peanut butter. Layer next 4 ingredients in order listed. Serve with crackers. Yield: 8 to 12 servings.

Carol Rabel, Nu Gamma
Spencer, Iowa

SPINACH AND ARTICHOKE DIP

1 (10-ounce) package frozen chopped spinach, thawed
12 ounces Monterey Jack cheese, shredded
12 ounces mozzarella cheese, shredded
1/2 cup grated Parmesan cheese
1/2 cup sour cream
1/2 cup mayonnaise
1 (14-ounce) jar marinated artichoke hearts, drained, chopped
4 to 5 slices provolone cheese
Salsa
Tortilla chips

Preheat oven to broil. Drain spinach. Combine spinach and next 6 ingredients in microwave-safe dish; mix well. Microwave on High until bubbly. Top with provolone cheese. Broil until cheese is melted and lightly browned. Serve with salsa and tortilla chips. Yield: 16 to 20 servings.

Pamela Lang, Iota Xi Theta Pi
Grinnell, Iowa

♥ SKINNY DIP

1 (15-ounce) can garbanzo beans, drained
1/2 cup plain yogurt
1/4 cup nonfat buttermilk salad dressing
2 tablespoons fine dry seasoned bread crumbs
2 teaspoons lemon juice
1/4 teaspoon crushed red pepper
2 tablespoons chopped pitted ripe olives
Fresh vegetables or crackers

Process first 6 ingredients in food processor until smooth. Stir in olives. Chill, covered, for 1 hour. Serve with vegetables or crackers. Yield: 8 servings.

Sharon Duncan, Preceptor Nu
Fort Smith, Arkansas

SENSATIONAL CRAB DIP

2 cups mayonnaise
1 cup cottage cheese
3/4 cup finely minced onion
1 teaspoon garlic salt
1/2 teaspoon salt (optional)
1/2 teaspoon freshly ground black pepper
1/2 to 3/4 teaspoon caraway seed
1/2 teaspoon celery salt
1 teaspoon dry mustard
1 to 2 teaspoons Worcestershire sauce
1 to 2 teaspoons chili sauce
1/4 teaspoon Tabasco sauce
2 (6-ounce) cans crab meat, chilled
Crackers or fresh vegetables

Combine first 12 ingredients in large bowl. Chill, covered, overnight. Drain crab meat. Add to chilled mixture; mix well. Serve with crackers or vegetables. Yield: 16 to 20 servings.

Bobbie Weatherill, Laureate Beta Omega
Port Orchard, Washington

NORTHSHORE SHRIMP DIP

8 ounces cream cheese
Juice of 1 lemon
1 1/2 pounds boiled shrimp, cut into small pieces
Chopped green onions to taste
2 tablespoons milk
Mayonnaise
1/2 tablespoon Worcestershire sauce
Salt to taste
Pepper to taste
Potato chips or crackers

Soften cream cheese with lemon juice in bowl. Add shrimp and green onions. Add milk and enough mayonnaise to make of desired consistency for dipping. Add Worcestershire sauce, salt and pepper; mix well. Chill overnight. Serve with potato chips or crackers. Yield: 8 to 12 servings.

Karen K. Loyd, Eta Rho
Mandeville, Louisiana

ALL AMERICAN REUBEN SPREAD

2 cups sour cream
1 cup mayonnaise
2 cups shredded Swiss cheese
1 (8-ounce) can sauerkraut, drained
8 ounces deli corned beef, cut up
1/4 cup chopped onion
Dark bread

Combine first 6 ingredients in large bowl; mix well. Chill, covered, for 2 hours or longer. Serve with dark bread. Yield: 6 to 7 cups.

Joan Mendro, Laureate Zeta
Williston, North Dakota

LAYERED CHEESE SPREAD

- 32 ounces cream cheese, softened
- 1/2 teaspoon pepper
- 2 tablespoons chopped green onions
- 1/3 cup grated Parmesan cheese
- 1 (9-ounce) package frozen chopped spinach, well drained
- 1/4 cup chopped onion
- 1 cup shredded Cheddar cheese
- 2 (2-ounce) jars chopped pimentos, well drained (optional)
- Crackers

Line 5-by-9-inch loaf pan with plastic wrap. Beat half the cream cheese until creamy. Stir in pepper and green onions. Spread in bottom of lined pan. Combine Parmesan cheese, spinach and onion in separate bowl; mix well. Spread over cream cheese layer. Combine remaining cream cheese and Cheddar cheese in same bowl until well blended. Stir in pimentos. Spread over spinach layer. Cover with plastic wrap. Press evenly and firmly on top of loaf to seal layers. Chill for several hours or overnight. Lift cheese loaf from pan with plastic wrap. Remove top plastic wrap. Invert loaf onto serving plate. Remove remaining plastic wrap. Garnish as desired with shredded cheese or parsley sprigs. Serve with crackers. Yield: 5 cups.

Maureen Johnson, Pi
Killarney, Manitoba, Canada

♥ PIMENTO SPREAD WITH HERBED CROSTINI

This recipe has almost no calories but a lot of flavor and crunch. I like it hot so I double the jalapeños.

- 2 sundried tomato halves
- 1/4 small jalapeño pepper
- 1 clove of garlic
- 1/4 cup drained pimento
- 1/4 teaspoon red wine vinegar
- 1/4 teaspoon dried basil
- 1/8 teaspoon ground pepper
- 2 cloves of garlic, minced
- 3 tablespoons olive oil
- 1 baguette or French stick
- 2 tablespoons minced fresh parsley

Preheat oven to broil. Cover tomatoes with boiling water in bowl. Let stand for 2 minutes; drain. Process jalapeño pepper and 1 clove of garlic in food processor until minced. Add tomatoes and next 4 ingredients. Process until smooth. Place in small serving bowl. Combine 2 cloves of garlic with olive oil in small bowl. Let stand until oil takes on garlic flavor. Slice baguette; brush slices with garlic and olive oil mixture. Sprinkle parsley on slices. Broil until toasty. Spread with pimento mixture. Serve immediately. Yield: 2 to 4 servings.

Liane Wobito, Eta Lambda
Stouffville, Ontario, Canada

PIMENTO CHEESE

- 10 ounces shredded Swiss cheese
- 10 ounces shredded Cheddar cheese
- 1 quart mayonnaise
- 1 tablespoon onion flakes
- 1 large jar chopped pimentos

Combine all ingredients in large bowl; mix well. Chill, covered, overnight. Yield: 6 to 7 cups.

Donna Laney, Xi Alpha Tau
Monroe, North Carolina

♥ CRETON (PORK SPREAD)

This is a French-Canadian recipe and was always served during our Christmas Eve celebratioin.

- 1 1/2 pounds ground lean pork
- 1 large onion, chopped
- 1 can mushrooms (optional)
- 1 teaspoon salt
- 1/8 teaspoon pepper
- 1 teaspoon ground cloves
- 1 teaspoon ground cinnamon
- 4 cloves of garlic, coarsely chopped
- Crackers or French bread

Place pork, onion and mushrooms in saucepan. Add enough water to cover. Add next 5 ingredients; mix well. Bring to a boil; reduce heat. Simmer for 1 to 1 1/2 hours, stirring occasionally. Let cool; drain. Process mixture in food processor until onion and garlic are finely chopped. Spoon into 3 medium containers. Chill until serving time. Freezes well. Serve with crackers or French bread. Yield: 16 to 20 servings.

Sally Radigan
Scarborough, Ontario, Canada

FOIE GRAS

- 1/4 cup currants
- 2 tablespoons porto
- 1 Granny Smith apple
- 1 small onion, finely chopped
- 1 clove of garlic, minced
- 12 ounces chicken livers, trimmed, cubed
- 1/4 teaspoon thyme
- 1/3 cup butter or margarine, melted
- 1 teaspoon salt
- Freshly ground pepper to taste
- Freshly ground nutmeg to taste

Combine currants and porto in small glass dish. Microwave on High for 1 minute. Peel, core and chop apple. Combine apple, onion and garlic in 2-quart microwave-safe casserole. Microwave, covered, on High for 5 to 6 minutes or until tender. Add livers and thyme. Microwave, covered, on Medium for 7 minutes or until livers lose their color, stirring once. Purée mixture in food processor. Add butter; process until smooth. Add salt, pepper and nutmeg. Fold in currants. Spoon into serving dish. Chill, covered, for 4 hours or until firm. Yield: 1 1/2 to 2 cups.

Joan E. Couture, Preceptor Beta
Pincourt, Quebec, Canada

GOOD LIVER PASTE

8 ounces cream cheese, softened
1 (8-ounce) smoked liver sausage, chopped
1 tablespoon finely chopped onion
2 teaspoons lemon juice
1 teaspoon Worcestershire sauce
Salt to taste
Pepper to taste
Chopped parsley

Combine cream cheese, sausage, onion and lemon juice in bowl. Add remaining ingredients; mix well. Chill until firm. Yield: 1 1/2 to 2 cups.

Sue Foster, Preceptor Beta
Grand Rapids, Michigan

SURIMI SALAD (CRAB SALAD)

1 pound imitation crab, shredded
4 ounces shredded mozzarella cheese
4 ounces shredded Cheddar cheese
2 tablespoons Parmesan cheese
2 tablespoons chopped onion
1 cup mayonnaise
2 tablespoons lemon juice
Salt and pepper to taste
Crackers

Press crab with paper towels to remove excess moisture. Combine crab, mozzarella cheese, Cheddar cheese, Parmesan cheese, onion, mayonnaise, lemon juice, salt and pepper in bowl; mix well. Place in airtight container. Chill until serving time. Serve with crackers. Store in airtight container. Yield: 20 servings.

Shannon Hollingsworth, Xi Nu
Cody, Wyoming

BRUSCHETTA

1 clove of garlic, minced
3 to 4 ounces smoked salmon, chopped
4 ounces mozzarella cheese, shredded
1 tomato, chopped
3 ounces toasted pine nuts
2 to 3 tablespoons extra virgin olive oil
Fresh basil
Small toast pieces

Combine garlic, salmon and cheese in bowl. Add tomato, pine nuts, olive oil and basil; mix well. Serve with toast. Yield: 6 to 8 servings.

Tien Parsons, Gamma Xi
Fulton, Missouri

SALMON PÂTÉ

4 ounces cream cheese, softened
2 teaspoons grated onion
1 teaspoon lemon juice
1/2 to 1 teaspoon horseradish
1/2 teaspoon liquid smoke
1/8 teaspoon salt
1 (7-ounce) can pink salmon, drained
Red food coloring (optional)
Parsley
Paprika
Crackers

Combine cream cheese with onion and lemon juice in bowl. Add horseradish, liquid smoke and salt; mix well. Remove bones and dark skin from salmon. Add salmon to cheese mixture; mix well. May add small amount of red food coloring if desired. Shape into ball. Chill. Garnish with parsley and paprika. Serve with crackers. Yield: 4 to 6 servings.

Tammy Kilpatrick, Gamma Omega
Lazo, British Columbia, Canada

SAVORY HERBED BAKED BRIE

1 (2-pound) 8-inch wheel Brie
1 sheet frozen puff pastry
1/4 cup chopped parsley
1 clove of garlic, minced
1 teaspoon rosemary
1 teaspoon thyme
1 teaspoon marjoram
8 thin slices hard salami, chopped
1 egg, slightly beaten
Crackers
Fruit

Place Brie in freezer for 30 minutes. Let pastry stand at room temperature for 20 minutes. Preheat oven to 350 degrees. Place parsley, garlic and herbs in small bowl; mix well. Slice Brie into 2 layers. Spread herb mixture on bottom layer. Sprinkle with salami. Replace top layer. Unfold puff pastry sheet. Roll into 12-by-18-inch rectangle on floured surface. Place Brie in center of pastry. Fold up pastry to enclose Brie; cut off excess pastry. Brush edges with egg; press to seal. Place seam-side down on lightly greased baking sheet. Brush with remaining egg. Cut 4 steam vents in top. Bake for 30 minutes. Let stand for 15 minutes. Serve with crackers and fruit. Yield: 15 to 20 servings.

Amy Gubbrud, Lambda
Belle Fourche, South Dakota

CREAM CHEESE TARTE

1/2 purple onion, chopped
8 ounces puff pastry, chilled
1/2 cup cream cheese, softened
1/4 cup sour cream
1 tablespoon all-purpose flour
Dash of salt
Freshly ground black pepper
6 ounces crisp-fried bacon, crumbled

Preheat oven to 425 degrees. Sauté onion lightly in small saucepan; drain and let cool. Roll puff pastry to 1/4-inch thickness on lightly floured surface. Combine cream cheese, sour cream, flour, salt and pepper in bowl; mix until very smooth. Spread mixture on pastry, leaving 1/2-inch margin all around. Sprinkle evenly with cooled onion and bacon. Gather edges together forming a central "knot." Place in pie pan. Bake for 12 to 15 minutes or until golden brown. Yield: 6 servings.

Joy Dacquisto, Xi Gamma
Winnipeg, Manitoba, Canada

BLEU CHEESE PEPPER STRIPS

8 ounces bleu cheese, softened
1/3 cup minced radishes
1/4 cup snipped chives
3 tablespoons minced parsley
2 tablespoons butter, softened
Pepper to taste
1 red bell pepper
1 green bell pepper

Combine bleu cheese, radishes, chives, parsley, butter and pepper in bowl; mix well. Set aside. Cut peppers into quarters; remove insides. Fill each pepper strip with blue cheese mixture. Halve each quarter lengthwise. Arrange on platter, alternating colors. Chill for 30 minutes. Yield: 16 strips.

Chris Sebba, Zeta Rho
Redlands, California

CHEESY BREAD APPETIZERS

2 1/2 cups all-purpose flour
1 cup butter or margarine
1 cup sour cream
3 cups shredded Cheddar cheese
Seasoned salt to taste
Paprika to taste

Combine flour, butter and sour cream in bowl; mix well. Divide dough into 4 equal portions. Wrap in foil. Chill until firm. Preheat oven to 350 degrees. Roll dough, 1/4 at a time, into 12-by-16-inch rectangle. Sprinkle with seasoned salt and 3/4 cup cheese. Roll up jelly roll fashion, starting with 12-inch side. Seal edges and ends. Place seam side down on ungreased cookie sheet. Bake for 30 minutes or until golden brown. Cut rolls halfway through at 1-inch intervals with sharp knife. Sprinkle with paprika. Serve warm or let cool. Yield: 24 servings.

Lorraine Barker, Preceptor Gamma Eta
Lawrenceburg, Indiana

FRIED CHEESE SQUARES

1/4 cup all-purpose flour
2 eggs
1 tablespoon water
1/2 teaspoon seasoned salt
24 bite-sized pieces Gouda, mozzarella, Brie, Gruyère or Cheddar cheese
1 cup fine dry bread crumbs
Oil for deep frying

Place flour in shallow dish. Combine eggs, water and salt in small bowl. Beat with fork until blended. Coat cheese pieces with flour and bread crumbs. Dip into egg mixture. Repeat to insure thick coating. Deep fry a few pieces at a time in hot oil; brown on both sides. Remove with slotted spoon; drain. Yield: 24 squares.

Lana Hart, Laureate Beta Eta
Delta, British Columbia, Canada

HOT CHEESE SQUARES

1 pound butter or margarine, softened
4 jars Old English cheese
1 tablespoon Tabasco sauce
1 tablespoon onion powder
2 teaspoons dillseed
2 teaspoons Worcestershire sauce
2 teaspoons Beau Monde
Dash of cayenne pepper
3 loaves Pepperidge Farm bread, thinly sliced

Combine butter and cheese in large bowl. Add next 6 ingredients; mix well. Trim crust from bread. Spread butter mixture on bread slices. Place 3 slices layered together. Ice sides with butter mixture. Cut into 4 squares. Freeze on 10-by-15-inch cookie sheet. Store in plastic bag. Preheat oven to 350 degrees. Place frozen squares on greased 10-by-15-inch cookie sheet. Bake for 15 to 20 minutes or until lightly browned on top. Yield: 20 servings.

Frances J. Stuart, Laureate Delta Delta
Fort Worth, Texas

GOUGÈRES (GOO-SHARE)

With a subtle taste and bouquet of melted cheese, these charming French pastries remind me of the miniature popovers like my grandmother made. They can be refrigerated for days and served as a party hors d'oeuvre or as an accompaniment to a first course. Needless to say, they are best when accompanied by a glass of sturdy red wine and the camaraderie of Beta Sigma Phi sisters!

1 cup water
5 tablespoons butter or margarine
1 teaspoon salt
1/4 teaspoon freshly ground pepper
1/4 teaspoon freshly ground nutmeg
1 cup all-purpose flour
1 cup grated Swiss or Gruyère cheese
5 large eggs, at room temperature
1/2 tablespoon water

Preheat oven to 425 degrees. Combine 1 cup water, butter, salt, pepper and nutmeg in saucepan; bring to a boil. Heat until butter is melted; remove from heat. Add flour. Beat with wooden spoon until mixture leaves side of pan. Add cheese; beat until blended. Beat in 4 eggs, 1 at a time, until thoroughly blended. Beat until mixture is smooth, shiny and firm. Drop by small spoonfuls onto greased cookie sheet. Beat remaining egg with 1/2 tablespoon water in small bowl. Brush tops of uncooked puffs with egg wash. Bake in upper third of oven for 20 minutes or until golden brown and doubled in size. Serve hot or cold. Yield: 36 gougères.

Geraldine McEwan, Preceptor Alpha Omicron
Black Mountain, North Carolina

Appetizers

CHARRITOS

Tortilla chips
Refried beans
Longhorn and Monterey Jack cheeses, grated
Chorrizo
Salsa Mexicana
3 to 4 tablespoons sour cream

Preheat oven to 300 degrees. Spread chips on large pizza pan. Drizzle with refried beans. Reserve enough cheeses for topping. Sprinkle remaining cheeses over chips. Bake for 5 minutes or until cheeses are melted. Fry chorrizo in skillet until browned; drain excess fat. Arrange chorrizo over chips. Sprinkle with Salsa Mexicana. Top with sour cream in center. Sprinkle remaining cheeses over top. Yield: 12 to 16 servings.

Ariene Walker, Laureate Alpha Beta
La Mirada, California

MEXICAN CHEESECAKE

16 ounces cream cheese, softened
1 1/2 envelopes taco seasoning
3 eggs
2 cups shredded Cheddar cheese
1 small can chopped green chilies
1 cup sour cream
Taco chips

Preheat oven to 350 degrees. Combine cream cheese and taco seasoning in bowl; mix well. Add eggs, 1 at a time, mixing well after each addition. Fold in cheese and green chilies. Place in greased 10-inch springform pan. Bake for 40 minutes. Let cool for 10 minutes. Top with sour cream. Bake for 5 minutes longer. Refrigerate for 2 hours. Serve with taco chips. Yield: 16 servings.

Cheryl Kiger, Laureate Gamma Epsilon
Holland, Ohio

PIZZA CHEESE BREAD

24 French bread rolls
Butter or margarine
12 ounces Cheddar cheese, grated
1 large onion, chopped
1 cup mayonnaise
3 drops of Tabasco sauce
1 tablespoon barbecue seasoning salt
1 teaspoon celery salt
1 tablespoon paprika
2 tablespoons dried parsley flakes
1 teaspoon pepper
1/2 teaspoon salt
2 tablespoons Worcestershire sauce

Preheat oven to 350 degrees. Split rolls. Spread with butter. Place on 2 large cookie sheets. Combine remaining ingredients in bowl; mix well. Spread mixture on buttered rolls. Bake for 15 minutes or until cheese is melted and bubbly. Yield: 12 servings.

Cindy McIntire, Theta Alpha
Gridley, California

HERBED CHEESE BITES

1/3 cup fine dry bread crumbs
8 ounces cream cheese, softened
3/4 cup cream-style cottage cheese
1/2 cup grated Swiss cheese
1 tablespoon all-purpose flour
1/4 teaspoon crushed basil leaves
1/8 teaspoon garlic powder
2 eggs
Sour cream

Preheat oven to 375 degrees. Grease twenty-four 1 3/4-inch miniature muffin cups with vegetable cooking spray. Sprinkle bread crumbs on bottom and side of each cup. Shake to remove excess crumbs. Combine cheeses, flour, basil, garlic powder and eggs in small mixer bowl. Beat at low speed until just combined; do not overbeat. Place 1 tablespoon cheese mixture in each cup. Bake for 15 minutes. Let cool in cups for 10 minutes. Remove; let cool thoroughly. Serve topped with sour cream. Yield: 24 cheese bites.

Ella M. Turner, Xi Zeta Omicron
Carrying Place, Ontario, Canada

❧ RASPBERRY-GLAZED CHEESE PIE

2 cups grated Cheddar cheese
2 cups grated provolone cheese
1/4 cup mayonnaise-type salad dressing
8 green onions, chopped
1 cup chopped pecans
18 cooked slices bacon, chopped
1 1/2 cups raspberry preserves
Chopped green onions
Crackers

Combine first 6 ingredients and 1 cup preserves in large bowl; mix well. Line 9-inch pie plate with plastic wrap, leaving enough wrap around edge to cover top of pie. Place mixture in pie plate. Chill, covered, for several hours. Lift pie by wrap, turning upside down onto serving platter. Remove wrap. Spread remaining preserves over pie. Garnish with additional chopped green onions. Serve with crackers. Yield: 12 servings.

Colette Iberg, Xi Mu Rho
Pocahontas, Illinois

FINGER CHICKEN PIE

1 cup margarine, softened
1 cup cream cheese, softened
2 cups all-purpose flour
2 1/2 cans chicken spread

Combine margarine and cream cheese in bowl; mix well. Add flour; mix well. Chill overnight. Preheat oven to 400 degrees. Roll out dough on lightly floured surface until thin. Cut into circles with can. Spread 1/2 teaspoon chicken spread in center of each circle. Fold and crimp edges with fork. Place on ungreased cookie sheet. Bake for 12 minutes, turning after 6 minutes. Yield: 12 servings.

Peggy Ritchie, Beta Zeta Phi
Wichita Falls, Texas

CHICKEN CUPS

2 cups chopped cooked chicken
1 cup ranch-style salad dressing
1 1/2 cups shredded Monterey Jack cheese
1 1/2 cups shredded Cheddar cheese
1 small can sliced black olives
1/2 cup chopped red bell pepper
1 package won ton wrappers

Preheat oven to 350 degrees. Combine chicken, salad dressing, cheeses, olives and red bell pepper in bowl; mix well. Place wrappers in greased muffin cups. Bake for 5 minutes. Fill each wrapper with chicken mixture. Bake for 5 minutes longer. Serve warm. Yield: 24 servings.

Nancy Burkhardt, Xi Gamma Gamma
Richmond, Indiana

♥ GINGER CHICKEN-BACON BITES

12 ounces boneless skinless chicken breasts
1/4 cup orange marmalade
1/2 teaspoon ground ginger
2 teaspoons soy sauce
1/8 teaspoon garlic powder
12 slices bacon
1 (8-ounce) can whole water chestnuts

Cut chicken into 24 bite-sized pieces. Combine marmalade, ginger, soy sauce and garlic powder in large bowl. Add chicken. Let marinate, covered, for 30 minutes. Arrange bacon slices on unheated rack of broiler pan. Broil 4 to 5 inches from heat for 1 to 2 minutes or until partially crisp; drain. Cut bacon and water chestnuts in half crosswise. Drain chicken pieces. Wrap each bacon piece around 1 chicken piece and 1 water chestnut half. Place on broiler pan. Broil for 3 to 5 minutes. Yield: 24 servings.

Carla Soper, Xi Epsilon Delta
Topeka, Kansas

HOT BUFFALO WINGS

5 pounds chicken wings
1 cup margarine
2 to 2 1/2 ounces Louisiana hot sauce
3/4 to 1 teaspoon basil
2 1/2 tablespoons lemon juice
2 envelopes dry lite Italian dressing mix

Cook chicken wings. Combine margarine, hot sauce, basil, lemon juice and dressing mix in large saucepan. Simmer until hot and thoroughly mixed. Add chicken wings; toss for 2 minutes. Place on paper plates to absorb grease. Do not use paper towels. Serve warm. Place in Crock•Pot on Low to keep warm during parties. Yield: 16 to 20 servings.

Linda Reece, Xi Alpha Omega
Story, Wyoming

♥ LEMONADE CHICKEN WINGS

3 pounds chicken wings
1 (12-ounce) can lemonade concentrate
1/2 cup soy sauce
3 cloves of garlic

Remove tips from wings. Cut each wing into 2 pieces. Place in plastic bag. Combine lemonade concentrate, soy sauce and garlic in bowl. Pour over wings; seal bag. Marinate for 4 hours or overnight, turning occasionally. Place wings on lightly greased preheated grill 5 inches from heat. Grill for 15 to 20 minutes, turning to cook evenly. Baste with marinade the last 5 minutes of grilling. Yield: 10 servings.

Mae Belle Herczeg, Lambda Master
Vancouver, British Columbia, Canada

MARINATED CHICKEN WINGS

1 cup soy sauce
1/4 cup unsweetened pineapple juice
1/4 cup vegetable oil
1 teaspoon brown ginger
1 cup water
1 cup sugar
1 teaspoon garlic powder
10 to 25 chicken wings

Combine first 7 ingredients in large bowl; mix well. Add wings. Let marinate for 8 hours or overnight, turning occasionally. Preheat oven to 350 degrees. Bake for 1 hour, turning after 30 minutes. Serve immediately or keep hot. Yield: 10 to 25 servings.

Shirley Dorcy, Xi Beta Delta
Maple Grove, Minnesota

MEAT PUFFS

1 cup water
1/2 cup butter or margarine
1 cup all-purpose flour
4 eggs
16 ounces cream cheese, softened
2 (4-ounce) cans chicken spread
1 teaspoon dillweed

Preheat oven to 400 degrees. Combine water and butter in saucepan; bring to a rolling boil. Stir in flour. Stir vigorously over low heat until mixture forms ball. Remove from heat. Beat in eggs all at once. Continue beating until smooth. Drop dough by scant 1/4 cupfuls onto cookie sheet. Bake for 35 to 40 minutes or until puffed and golden brown. Let cool. Combine cream cheese, chicken spread and dillweed in bowl; mix well. Cut tops off puffs. Fill with chicken mixture. Chill until serving time. Yield: 18 puffs.

Nancey Trimble, Preceptor Nu
Milton-Freewater, Oregon

Lucina M. Daily, Epsilon Psi, El Paso, Texas, makes Curried Chicken Balls by mixing 4 ground cooked chicken breasts, 1/2 teaspoon curry powder, 1/4 teaspoon salt and enough liquid salad dressing to make into 1-inch balls. Shape into balls. Roll in chopped walnuts. Chill. Serve with toothpicks.

HAM FINGERS

8 ounces cream cheese, softened
1 teaspoon dill
1/2 teaspoon garlic powder
1/2 teaspoon onion powder
8 to 12 ham slices
1 red bell pepper, thinly sliced
1 yellow bell pepper, thinly sliced

Combine cream cheese, dill, garlic powder and onion powder in bowl; mix well. Spread on ham slices. Place 1 slice each red and yellow pepper on each slice. Roll up slices. Yield: 8 to 12 servings.

Rosemary Bolon, Xi Gamma Psi
St. Marys, Georgia

HONEY HAM TORTILLA ROLLS WITH HONEY DIP

1 (4-ounce) can honey ham spread
3 ounces cream cheese, softened
1 teaspoon honey
1/4 cup crushed pineapple, drained
1 tablespoon chopped green onions
4 (8-inch) flour tortillas
6 tablespoons mayonnaise
1/4 cup mustard
2 tablespoons honey

Beat ham spread and cream cheese together in mixer bowl until smooth. Stir in 1 teaspoon honey, pineapple and green onions. Spread 1/4 cup mixture on each flour tortilla to within 1/2 inch of edge. Roll up each tortilla starting from 1 edge. Wrap in plastic wrap. Chill for 2 to 8 hours. Mix mayonnaise, mustard and 2 tablespoons honey in small bowl. Cut each tortilla into 1/2-inch slices. Arrange on platter with dip. Yield: 12 servings.

Margaret Doherty, Xi Alpha Alpha Omicron
Ennis, Texas

PASTRY SWIRLS

1 (2-pastry) package frozen puff pastry, thawed
3/4 cup honey mustard
1 1/2 cups Parmesan cheese
8 ham slices
1 egg, beaten
2 teaspoons water

Preheat oven to 375 degrees. Roll out 1 pastry on lightly floured surface to 12 inches in diameter. Spread half the mustard on top pastry. Sprinkle half the Parmesan cheese over mustard. Place 4 ham slices on top, pressing down lightly. Roll each end of pastry to middle. Repeat with remaining ingredients. Chill for 20 minutes. Slice each pastry into 24 pieces. Place on baking sheets lined with waxed paper. Flatten lightly with hand. Combine egg and water in bowl. Brush over top of pastries. Bake for 25 minutes or until golden brown. Yield: 48 swirls.

Penny Legge
Dartmouth, Nova Scotia, Canada

ROLLED HAM-CRAB TORTILLAS

16 ounces cream cheese, softened
1 small onion, chopped
1 medium green bell pepper, chopped
1 cup shredded Cheddar cheese
1/2 teaspoon garlic salt
2 (2-ounce) packages sliced pressed cooked ham or chipped beef
1 (5-ounce) package chopped imitation crab meat
1 (10-count) package large flour tortillas

Mix first 5 ingredients in bowl. Reserve half the cheese mixture. Spread remaining mixture on 5 tortillas to within 1/2 inch of edge. Arrange 4 ham slices over mixture. Roll up tortillas tightly, starting with 1 side. Wrap each tortilla in plastic wrap. Chill for 3 hours to overnight. Add crab meat to remaining cheese mixture. Spread on remaining tortillas. Roll and wrap as directed. Remove wrap; cut each tortilla into 3/4-inch slices. Yield: 64 tortillas.

Laurie Stein, Lambda Eta
Manning, Iowa

HILO HOT DOGS

1 cup apricot preserves
1/2 cup tomato sauce
1/3 cup vinegar
1/4 cup Sherry
2 tablespoons soy sauce
2 tablespoons honey
1 tablespoon vegetable oil
1 teaspoon salt
1/4 teaspoon ground ginger
16 to 20 hot dogs

Combine first 9 ingredients in saucepan; mix well. Heat until warm. Pour into chafing dish to keep warm. Cut hot dogs into 1-inch pieces. Microwave or steam until warm. Add to sauce. Use forks or toothpicks to dip. Yield: 8 to 10 servings.

Donna J. DeLancey, Laureate Alpha Epsilon
Vail, Arizona

MEATBALLS TO GO

4 pounds ground beef
1 cup Parmesan cheese
1 cup dried bread crumbs
2 cups fresh bread crumbs
1 green bell pepper, chopped
4 eggs
Garlic salt to taste
Salt and pepper to taste
1 teaspoon oregano
1 can whole cranberry sauce
1 can chili sauce

Preheat oven to 350 degrees. Combine first 6 ingredients in large bowl. Add garlic salt, salt, pepper and oregano; mix well. Shape into 200 meatballs. Place on baking sheet. Bake for 45 minutes; drain. Place 20 meatballs in each freezer ziplock bag. Store in freezer until ready to use. To serve, combine cranberry sauce and chili sauce in saucepan; mix well. Add 1 bag meatballs. Heat and serve. Repeat with remaining meatballs as needed. Yield: 200 meatballs.

Paulette R. Crowley, Xi Gamma
Lewiston, Maine

♥ TERIYAKI MINIATURES WITH SWEET SOUR SAUCE

When I was a Major in the Air Force, I took this as a potluck dish to my squadron's Christmas party the night my husband proposed. It brings back wonderful memories and is still one of our all-time favorites.

2 tablespoons soy sauce
2 tablespoons water
2 teaspoons sugar
1/4 cup minced onion
1/2 teaspoon garlic powder
1/4 teaspoon ginger
1 pound lean ground beef
1 cup soft bread crumbs
1/4 cup packed dark brown sugar
1/4 cup vinegar
2 tablespoons soy sauce
1 cup water
2 bouillon cubes
1/2 onion, cut into strips
1/2 green pepper, cut into chunks
2 stalks celery, cut up
3 tablespoons cornstarch
1 can pineapple tidbits, drained
1/2 cup maraschino cherries with juice (optional)

Combine first 6 ingredients in bowl; mix well. Let stand for 10 minutes. Add ground beef and bread crumbs; mix well. Shape into 3/4-inch meatballs. Cook in nonstick saucepan until browned. Combine next 8 ingredients in saucepan; mix well. Bring to a boil; boil for 20 minutes. Combine cornstarch with small amount of cold water. Add cornstarch mixture and pineapple to boiled mixture. Cook, stirring constantly, until thickened. Add cherries and juice; mix well. Serve over meatballs. Yield: 24 servings.

Michele Beard, Mu
Tonopah, Nevada

♥ JALAPEÑO PASTRAMI CAKE

16 ounces low-calorie cream cheese, softened
3/4 cup lite mayonnaise
12 ounces pastrami, finely chopped
1 (4-ounce) can chopped peppers
1 (4-ounce) can chopped black olives
2 cloves of garlic, minced
1 small onion, chopped
1 (10-count) package medium flour tortillas

Combine cream cheese and mayonnaise in bowl; mix well. Reserve 1 cup mixture for topping. Add next 5 ingredients to cream cheese mixture in bowl; mix well. Spread mixture on each tortilla. Stack in glass dish. Spread reserved cream cheese mixture over top. Refrigerate, covered, overnight. Cut into small slices with sharp knife to serve. Yield: 12 servings.

Imogene Morrison, Preceptor Nu Kappa
Vallejo, California

Rose Mary Delaquila, Nu Lambda, Fort Myers, Florida, makes C.C.C. Dip by arranging 1 can crab meat, drained and rinsed, on 8 ounces softened cream cheese. Top with 1/2 jar cocktail sauce. Serve on round platter with crackers.

ARMADILLO EGGS

1 (8-ounce) can whole jalapeño peppers
1 (6-ounce) package grated Monterey Jack cheese
1 1/2 cups baking mix
1 (16-ounce) package bulk breakfast sausage
2 eggs, beaten
1 package oven-fry mix for pork

Preheat oven to 350 degrees. Cut peppers in half; remove seeds. Combine cheese, baking mix and sausage in bowl; mix well. Place mixture around pepper halves to form egg shapes. Dip into eggs; roll in oven-fry mix. Place on cookie sheet. Bake for 25 minutes. Yield: 18 servings.

Nancy Barton, Laureate Zeta Xi
Austin, Texas

PINWHEELS

I made over 500 pinwheels for our council tea and brought home no leftovers!

8 ounces cream cheese, softened
2 teaspoons milk
1/8 teaspoon garlic powder
1 (4-ounce) can diced green chilies, drained
1 tablespoon minced onion
Dash of salt
8 (8- to 10-inch) flour tortillas
4 ounces thinly sliced deli-style roast beef
4 ounces thinly sliced deli-style turkey
3 tablespoons chopped cilantro leaves (optional)
1 (2-ounce) can sliced pitted ripe olives, drained

Combine cream cheese, milk and garlic powder in bowl; mix well. Stir in chilies, onion and salt. Moisten both sides of each tortilla lightly with water. Spread 2 rounded tablespoons cream cheese mixture on each tortilla. Layer roast beef on half the tortillas. Layer turkey on remaining tortillas. Sprinkle cilantro and olives over tortillas. Roll up; wrap each in plastic wrap. Chill for 1 hour or up to 8 hours. Trim 1/2 inch from each end of rolls; discard. Cut each roll into 6 slices. Yield: 48 pinwheels.

Becky Reisen, Pi Omicron
Dunedin, Florida

SAUSAGE BALLS

1 package stove-top chicken stuffing
2 eggs
1 pound bulk pork sausage
1/2 cup warm water

Preheat oven to 350 degrees. Place stuffing with seasoning package in bowl. Add eggs, sausage and water; mix well. Shape into balls. Place on cookie sheet. Bake for 12 to 15 minutes on each side. Let cool. Store in ziplock bag. Yield: 16 servings.

Phyllis Johnson, Preceptor Iota Chapter
Tampa, Florida

COLD DEVILED SHRIMP

2 pounds shrimp
1 quart water
1 lemon, thinly sliced
1 red onion, thinly sliced
1/2 cup black olives
2 tablespoons chopped pimento, drained
1/2 cup lemon juice
1 tablespoon wine vinegar
1/4 cup vegetable oil
1 clove of garlic, pressed
1/2 bay leaf, broken
1 tablespoon dry mustard
1/4 teaspoon cayenne pepper
1 teaspoon salt
Freshly ground pepper to taste

Peel and devein raw shrimp. Place 1 quart water and shrimp in saucepan. Bring to a boil. Boil for 3 minutes. Drain at once. Place shrimp in large bowl. Pit and drain olives. Add olives, lemon slices, onion slices and pimento to shrimp; mix well. Combine remaining ingredients in separate bowl; mix well. Add to shrimp mixture; mix well. Place in glass jar with lid. Refrigerate until serving time or up to 1 week, stirring occasionally. Yield: 8 to 12 servings.

Mary Jane Smith, Xi Epsilon Psi
Port Lavaca, Texas

SHRIMP NACHOS

1 (15-ounce) can refried beans
16 ounces nacho chips
8 ounces hot cooked shrimp
8 ounces shredded mozzarella or Monterey Jack cheese
1 tomato, chopped
Chives

Heat beans according to can directions. Preheat oven to broil. Spread chips in pizza pan. Spoon beans over chips. Place shrimp over beans. Sprinkle cheese over shrimp. Broil for 5 to 7 minutes or until cheese is melted. Garnish with tomato and chives. Serve immediately. Yield: 8 servings.

Brenda Herndon, Xi Beta Rho
Nokesville, Virginia

♥ VIETNAMESE SPRING ROLLS

3 cups cooked rice
2 teaspoons ground ginger
4 large cabbage leaves, cut into 12 pieces
1 large carrot, peeled, thinly sliced
12 rice paper wrappers
12 cooked jumbo shrimp
Peanut sauce

Combine rice and ginger in medium bowl. Steam vegetables in saucepan until tender-crisp. Immerse 1 wrapper at a time into pan of steaming water for 30 seconds or until softened and transparent. Place 1/4 cup rice mixture, 1 cabbage piece, carrot slice and shrimp in center of each wrapper. Roll up, folding sides to inside as for burrito. Arrange on serving platter with peanut sauce in center. Chill for 30 minutes. Yield: 12 to 15 rolls.

Julie Hibbert, Kappa
Lethbridge, Alberta, Canada

♥ GOLDEN SHRIMP SHELLS

24 cooked large shrimp, rinsed, drained
2 teaspoons garlic powder
1/4 teaspoon hot pepper sauce
1 tablespoon olive or vegetable oil
1 (8-ounce) can crescent rolls
2 tablespoons grated Parmesan cheese
Cocktail sauce

Preheat oven to 375 degrees. Stir-fry shrimp with garlic powder and pepper sauce in oil in medium skillet for 1 minute. Remove from heat. Remove rolls from can; do not unroll. Cut each roll into 12 slices. Place, cut-side down, 1 inch apart on greased cookie sheet. Press half of each dough slice to flatten. Place 1 shrimp on flattened half of each slice. Fold remaining half of dough slice over shrimp; do not seal. Openings may occur between dough layers. Sprinkle each with Parmesan cheese. Bake for 11 to 13 minutes or until golden brown. Serve warm with cocktail sauce. Yield: 24 shells.

Shelley Bay, Xi Gamma Lambda
Shattuck, Oklahoma

ARTICHOKE APPETIZERS

Although I was reluctant to try these the first time, they are delicious and super easy to make.

1/2 cup mayonnaise
1/2 cup Parmesan cheese
1 loaf cocktail-size pumpernickel bread
1 (14-ounce) can artichoke hearts, drained

Preheat broiler. Combine mayonnaise and Parmesan cheese in small bowl; mix well. Place 1 spoonful mixture on each bread slice. Cut each artichoke heart into quarters. Place 1 piece on each bread slice. Arrange on baking sheet. Broil for 2 to 3 minutes or until lightly browned. Yield: 24 appetizers.

Marcia Nestler, Preceptor Delta Delta
Eldridge, Iowa

♥ PICKLED CARROT STICKS

These are great to crunch on while grilling burgers.

1 1/2 cups cider vinegar
1 1/2 cups water
1 cup sugar
2 tablespoons dillseed
3 or 4 cloves of garlic
2 pounds carrots, cut into sticks

Combine vinegar, water and sugar in large saucepan. Bring to a boil, stirring until sugar is dissolved. Add remaining ingredients. Cook, covered, for 6 to 8 minutes. Remove from heat; let cool. Chill for 8 hours. Strain and serve. Yield: 14 to 16 servings.

Julia M. Gibson, Preceptor Gamma Delta
Centreville, Virginia

CUCUMBER PARTY SANDWICHES

1 (1-ounce) envelope dry original ranch party dip mix
8 ounces cream cheese, softened
2 loaves small square party rye bread
2 or 3 cucumbers, sliced
Dillweed to taste

Combine dip mix and cream cheese in bowl; mix well. Chill for 1 hour. Spread mixture on each bread square. Top with cucumber slice. Sprinkle with dillweed. Chill, covered, until serving time. Yield: 24 sandwiches.

Dianne Shively, Alpha Nu
Cincinnati, Ohio

DATE-NUT LETTUCE SANDWICHES

8 ounces cream cheese, softened
2 tablespoons chopped dates
2 tablespoons chopped toasted walnuts
1 tablespoon sour cream
1/4 teaspoon grated orange peel
8 slices whole wheat bread
1 cup finely shredded lettuce

Combine first 5 ingredients in small bowl; mix well. Spread mixture evenly on 1 side of 4 bread slices. Sprinkle lettuce evenly over mixture. Top with remaining bread slices. Cut each sandwich into fourths. Yield: 16 sandwiches.

Ann Doucet, Laureate Zeta Gamma
Deer Park, Texas

❖ GARDEN GREEK APPETIZER

8 ounces cream cheese, softened
8 ounces feta cheese, crumbled
1/4 cup plain yogurt
1 clove of garlic, minced
1/4 teaspoon black pepper
2 tomatoes, seeded, chopped
1 medium seedless cucumber, chopped
3 green onions, finely chopped
3 black olives, finely chopped
Mini pitas or assorted crackers and breads

Process first 5 ingredients in food processor until smooth. Spread cheese mixture in 10-inch pie plate. Chill until firm. Top with tomatoes, cucumber, green onions and black olives. Serve with mini pitas. Yield: 10 to 12 servings.

Robin Campbell, Lambda Omega
Bolton, Ontario, Canada

Jeannie Kiser, Laureate Alpha Alpha, St. Albans, West Virginia, makes Mock Cream Cheese by mixing 1/4 cup softened margarine and 1 cup unsalted dry cottage cheese in blender. Add skim milk, 1 teaspoon at a time, to make desired consistency. Store, tightly covered, in refrigerator.

STUFFED JALAPEÑO PEPPERS

1 (12-ounce) can whole jalapeño peppers
8 ounces shredded Monterey Jack cheese
1 1/2 cups baking mix
1 pound bulk pork sausage
1 package Shake 'n' Bake
2 eggs, slightly beaten

Preheat oven to 350 degrees. Cut each pepper in half; remove seeds. Stuff with cheese. Place pepper halves back together to make a whole. Combine baking mix and sausage in medium bowl. Shape into small patties. Wrap patties around peppers, enclosing peppers. Roll each in Shake 'n' Bake. Place on cookie sheet. Bake for 30 minutes. Yield: 10 to 12 servings.

Sunny Jaquez, Alpha Epsilon Epsilon
Seminole, Texas

♥ MARINATED PEPPERS

3 pounds mixed peppers (bell peppers, green chilies, banana peppers and jalapeño peppers)
1/2 cup olive oil
3 tablespoons lemon juice
1/2 teaspoon salt
3 cloves of garlic, peeled

Preheat oven broiler to 500 degrees. Arrange peppers on foil-covered 9-by-13-inch baking sheet. Broil, turning frequently, until peppers are wrinkled and charred on all sides. Place peppers in sealed paper bag for 1 hour. Peel and remove stems, seeds and pith, rinsing under cold water. Drain well; pat dry. Slice into 1-inch wide strips. Combine remaining ingredients in large bowl; mix well. Add pepper strips. Stir gently to combine. Chill, covered, for 24 hours. Yield: 12 servings.

Kristy Tomson, Nu Epsilon
Medicine Lodge, Kansas

MEXICAN SNACK SQUARES

2 (8-ounce) cans refrigerator crescent rolls
1 (16-ounce) can refried beans
1 cup sour cream
2 tablespoons taco seasoning mix
1 cup chopped tomatoes
6 ounces shredded Cheddar cheese
1/2 cup sliced green onions
1/2 cup chopped green pepper
1/2 cup sliced black olives

Preheat oven to 375 degrees. Unroll rolls. Place crosswise in 10-by-15-inch baking pan. Press firmly to seal perforations. Bake for 14 to 19 minutes or until lightly browned. Let cool completely. Spread beans over crust. Combine sour cream and taco mix in small bowl; mix well. Spread over beans. Sprinkle remaining ingredients over top. Chill, covered, for 1 hour. Cut into squares. Yield: 48 squares.

Beverly Scott, Laureate Beta Chi
Elma, Washington

48 / Appetizers

TORTILLA ROLL-UPS

2 (10-ounce) packages frozen chopped spinach, thawed
1 cup sour cream
1 cup mayonnaise
1 envelope ranch salad dressing mix
6 green onions, chopped
1/2 can water chestnuts, chopped
1 (10-count) package flour tortillas, at room temperature

Drain spinach; squeeze dry. Combine sour cream, mayonnaise and dressing mix in large bowl. Add spinach, green onions and water chestnuts; mix well. Spread mixture evenly on each tortilla; roll up. Wrap each tortilla in plastic wrap. Place, seam side down, on cookie sheet. Chill for several hours or overnight. Slice tortillas into 1-inch thick slices to serve. Yield: 80 roll-ups.

Lillian Richards, Xi Epsilon Beta
Woodstock, Virginia

FREEZER MUSHROOM ROLLS

2/3 cup butter or margarine
2 teaspoons lemon juice
4 (10-ounce) cans mushrooms, drained, finely chopped
4 green onions, chopped
2 tablespoons butter or margarine
6 tablespoons all-purpose flour
2 cups half and half
Salt and pepper to taste
2 loaves sandwich bread, crusts removed

Melt 2/3 cup butter in saucepan. Add lemon juice. Add mushrooms; cook over medium heat for 5 minutes. Add green onions. Remove from heat. Melt 2 tablespoons butter in large saucepan. Stir in flour. Blend in half and half gradually. Add salt and pepper. Add mushroom mixture. Cook, stirring constantly, over medium heat for 8 minutes or until very thick. Refrigerate, covered, until cool. Roll out 48 bread slices until very thin. Spread 1 heaping tablespoon chilled mixture on each bread slice. Roll up jelly roll fashion. Store rolls in airtight container in freezer for up to 3 months. To serve, defrost rolls. Preheat oven to 400 degrees. Place rolls in baking pan. Bake, seam side down, for 8 minutes or until golden brown. Bake frozen rolls in preheated 350-degree oven for 15 to 20 minutes or until golden brown. Cut rolls in half; serve warm. Yield: 96 rolls.

Doreen Greason, Xi Gamma Mu
Aurora, Ontario, Canada

Paula Kella, Clive, Iowa, makes Pickled Mushrooms by mixing 1/2 cup red wine vinegar, 1/3 cup vegetable oil, 1 thinly sliced small onion, 1 teaspoon mustard, 2 teaspoons dried parsley flakes and 1 tablespoon dark brown sugar in saucepan. Bring to a boil. Add 12 ounces mushroom crowns. Simmer for 5 minutes. Chill, covered, for 8 hours.

CHEESY MUSHROOM PUFFS

3 ounces cream cheese, softened
1 (2-ounce) can mushrooms, drained, chopped
2 tablespoons chopped pimento
2 drops of Tabasco sauce
1 tablespoon chopped onion
1 (8-ounce) can refrigerator crescent rolls
1/3 cup finely chopped walnuts

Preheat oven to 375 degrees. Blend first 5 ingredients in mixer bowl. Separate rolls into 4 sections. Press perforations to seal. Spread 1 tablespoon cream cheese mixture on each section. Roll up, starting with larger side; seal. Roll in walnuts. Place, seam side down, on ungreased cookie sheet. Bake for 15 to 20 minutes or until lightly browned. Cut into bite-sized pieces. Yield: 8 servings.

Ann Marie Phillips, Delta Gamma
Jamestown, New York

HONGOS (MUSHROOMS)

2 eggs, separated
1 cup all-purpose flour
1 tablespoon cornstarch
1/8 teaspoon salt
1/2 cup lukewarm water
1 cup grated cheese
1 pound fresh mushrooms, rinsed
Vegetable oil for deep frying

Beat egg whites in mixer bowl. Mix flour, cornstarch, salt, water and egg yolks in large mixer bowl. Fold in egg whites. Place cheese around mushroom stems or remove stems and stuff mushroom buttons. Heat 1-inch deep oil in frypan. Dip mushrooms in batter. Deep-fry until browned on all sides. May add water as batter thickens. Yield: 12 servings.

Cathy Chavez, Epsilon Omicron
Cimarron, New Mexico

MUSHROOM TOASTIES

1 pound fresh mushrooms, chopped
1/4 cup butter or margarine
3 tablespoons Sherry
1/2 cup 2% milk or cream
2 tablespoons cornstarch
Salt and pepper to taste
Dash of cayenne pepper
1 container 68% vegetable oil spread
1 loaf thinly sliced bread

Preheat oven to 450 degrees. Sauté mushrooms in butter in saucepan, simmering until almost dry. Add Sherry, milk, cornstarch and seasonings; cook until thickened. Spread both sides of bread with vegetable oil spread. Place mushroom filling on half the bread slices. Top with remaining slices. Cut into triangles. Place on cookie sheet. Bake for 6 to 10 minutes or until browned. Yield: 8 to 12 servings.

Jean Castle, Preceptor Alpha Upsilon
Jamestown, New York

STUFFED MUSHROOMS

1/2 onion, minced
2 cans minced clams, drained
6 tablespoons butter or margarine
1 teaspoon Italian seasoning
1/4 teaspoon Creole seasoning
1/2 cup cracker crumbs
1 pound fresh mushrooms
Paprika to taste

Preheat oven to 350 degrees. Sauté onion and clams in butter in saucepan. Add seasonings and crumbs; mix well. Rinse mushroom caps; place in baking pan. Stuff with clam mixture until heaping. Garnish with paprika. Bake for 15 minutes. Yield: 32 mushrooms.

Betty E. Stisser, Zi Beta Upsilon
Angel Fire, New Mexico

STUFFED MUSHROOM CAPS

2 pounds fresh medium mushrooms
1/2 cup margarine
Garlic salt to taste
1 small onion, chopped
8 ounces cream cheese, softened

Preheat oven to broil. Rinse mushrooms; remove stems. Cook mushroom caps lightly in margarine and garlic salt in skillet. Remove from skillet; set aside. Chop half the mushrooms stems. Sauté chopped stems and onion in skillet for 5 minutes; do not overcook. Combine stems and onion with cream cheese in bowl. Stuff mushrooms caps with mixture. Sprinkle garlic salt in greased 9-by-13-inch glass baking dish. Place stuffed mushrooms in dish. Broil until browned. Yield: 24 mushrooms.

Joy Brooks, Preceptor Beta Omega
Emporia, Kansas

MINI JARLSBERG-ONION QUICHES

1 cup finely chopped sweet Spanish onions
1 tablespoon butter or margarine
3 (8-ounce) cans refrigerator buttermilk biscuits
3/4 cup grated Jarlsberg cheese
3/4 cup milk
2 eggs
1 tablespoon Dijon-style mustard
2 tablespoons minced parsley

Preheat oven to 375 degrees. Sauté onions in butter in skillet for 5 minutes or until softened; set aside. Cut each biscuit in half crosswise. Press each half in bottom and up side of buttered 1-inch muffin cup. Spoon 1 teaspoon onion into each cup. Top with 1 teaspoon cheese. Combine remaining ingredients in bowl; beat well. Spoon into muffin cups, dividing equally. Bake for 10 to 12 minutes or until set. Yield: 36 quiches.

Joanie Clark, Xi Beta Epsilon
Pottsville, Pennsylvania

BAKED POTATO SKINS

4 baked potatoes
1/2 cup grated Cheddar cheese
1/2 cup grated Gruyère cheese
Salt and pepper to taste
4 cooked slices bacon, chopped
Paprika to taste
Sour cream (optional)

Preheat broiler. Slice potatoes in half lengthwise. Scoop out 3/4 of pulp; set aside for other use. Place skins on cookie sheet. Broil 4 inches from heat for 8 minutes. Sprinkle with cheeses. Season with salt and pepper. Add bacon and paprika. Broil for 4 to 5 minutes. Serve with sour cream. Yield: 4 servings.

Norma Losoney, Xi Kappa Omega
Pickerington, Ohio

ZUCCHINI PUFFS

1/2 cup shredded zucchini
1/4 cup mayonnaise
1 1/2 tablespoons finely chopped onion
1 cup grated Swiss cheese
4 to 6 slices French bread
Parmesan cheese

Preheat broiler. Press zucchini between paper towels. Mix zucchini and next 3 ingredients in bowl. Spread on bread slices. Cut into serving pieces. Sprinkle with Parmesan cheese. Broil for 3 to 5 minutes or until puffy and golden brown. Yield: 4 to 6 servings.

Barbara Firor, Laureate Delta Nu
Anaheim Hills, California

VEGETABLE KABOBS

1 head cauliflower
1 large stalk broccoli
10 ounces cherry tomatoes, rinsed
8 ounces whole mushrooms, rinsed
2 yellow crookneck squash, cut into 1/2-inch pieces
7 ounces black and green olives
2 cups Italian dressing

Rinse cauliflower and broccoli; divide into flowerets. Thread vegetables on skewers. Garnish with olives on ends. Place on waxed paper. Brush with Italian dressing. Let drain and serve. Yield: 24 servings.

Bennie Hanebrink, Preceptor Alpha Tau
Grain Valley, Missouri

THREE ALARM FIRE

1 (12-ounce) jar pineapple preserves
1 (10-ounce) jar apple jelly
1/2 (8-ounce) jar prepared horseradish
1 tablespoon dry mustard
8 ounces cream cheese
Wheat or bran crackers

Mix first 4 ingredients in bowl. Pour over cream cheese. Serve with crackers. Yield: 12 to 18 servings.

Mary McCormack, Xi Beta Epsilon
Marshall, Minnesota

♥ DR. PEPPER JELLY

This is a wonderful spread for buttery crackers or toast.

3 1/2 cups sugar
2 1/4 cups Dr. Pepper
1/4 cup lemon juice
Few drops of red food coloring (optional)
4 ounces liquid pectin

Combine sugar, Dr. Pepper and lemon juice in large saucepan. Add food coloring; mix well. Bring to a boil over high heat, stirring constantly. Stir in pectin at once. Bring to a full rolling boil. Boil for 1 minute, stirring constantly. Remove from heat. Skim off foam with metal spoon. Pour quickly into hot sterilized jars; seal. Let cool. Store in cool dry place. Allow several days to set. Yield: 5 (6-ounce) glasses.

Anita Brown, Preceptor Xi Zeta
Abilene, Texas

♥ HONEY-FRUIT SNACK

Nonstick vegetable cooking spray
1/3 cup honey
1/4 cup packed dark brown sugar
2/3 cup slivered almonds
5 cups whole grain Total cereal
1 (6-ounce) package mixed dried fruit bits

Preheat oven to 350 degrees. Spray 10-by-15-inch baking pan with nonstick cooking spray. Combine honey and brown sugar in 3-quart saucepan. Bring to a boil over medium heat, stirring constantly; remove from heat. Stir in almonds and cereal until completely coated. Spread in prepared pan. Bake for 8 minutes, stirring frequently. Stir in fruit bits. Bake for 5 minutes longer. Let cool for 5 minutes. Loosen mixture with metal spatula. Let stand for 1 hour or until firm. Store in airtight container. Yield: 7 cups.

Trudy Ruch, Xi Eta
Omaha, Nebraska

♥ MICROWAVE BITS AND BITES

1/4 cup butter or margarine
1/2 teaspoon ginger
1/2 teaspoon celery seeds
1/2 teaspoon onion powder
1/2 teaspoon Tabasco sauce
1 teaspoon garlic powder
4 teaspoons Worcestershire sauce
1/2 teaspoon soya sauce
1 cup peanuts
1 cup pretzels
1 cup chow mein noodles
2 cups Cheerios
2 cups Shreddies

Melt butter in microwave-safe casserole. Add ginger, celery seed, onion powder, Tabasco sauce, garlic powder, Worcestershire sauce and soya sauce. Stir in remaining ingredients; mix well. Microwave on High for 3 minutes; stir. Microwave for 2 minutes longer. Store in sealed container. Yield: 7 cups.

Sue Hood, Eta Zeta
Simcoe, Ontario, Canada

♣ CRANBERRY SALSA

1 pound fresh cranberries
1 unpeeled orange
1 large unpeeled apple, cored
2 fresh jalapeño peppers
2 cups sugar
1 teaspoon lime juice
8 ounces cream cheese
Crackers

Wash fruit. Remove stems and seeds from jalapeño peppers. Place fruit, jalapeño peppers, sugar and lime juice in food processor. Chop with knife blade. Let stand for 48 hours. Serve over cream cheese with crackers. Yield: 8 to 12 servings.

Carol James, Xi Alpha Mu
Midland, Texas

♥ CABBAGE SALSA

2 to 4 fresh jalapeño peppers
1/2 head cabbage, chopped
1/4 to 1/2 cup chopped fresh cilantro
3 or 4 green onions, chopped
1/2 fresh lemon chopped
1 tablespoon garlic powder
1 tablespoon salt
1 tablespoon pepper
Vinegar to taste
1 large tomato, chopped
1 large avocado, chopped
Tortilla chips

Rinse jalapeño peppers; cut in half. Remove seeds and membranes; set aside. Chop peppers. Combine peppers, cabbage, cilantro and green onions in large bowl. Add lemon, garlic powder, salt, pepper and vinegar; mix well. Add tomato and avocado. Add reserved pepper seeds and membranes for hot, hot, hot salsa! Serve with tortilla chips. Yield: 8 to 10 servings.

Vicki Olivas, Beta Sigma
Pasco, Washington

♥ SALSA CRUDA

3 (16-ounce) cans stewed tomatoes, drained
1 (8-ounce) can green chilies, chopped
1 large onion, chopped
1 to 3 jalapeño peppers, chopped
1 teaspoon crushed garlic
1 (8-ounce) can tomato sauce (optional)
1 teaspoon cumin
1 teaspoon cilantro
1/2 teaspoon oregano
1/4 teaspoon salt
1/4 teaspoon pepper
2 tablespoons lime or lemon juice

Chop tomatoes in food processor. Place tomatoes, chilies, onion and jalapeño peppers in large bowl. Add garlic, tomato sauce, cumin, cilantro, oregano, salt, pepper and lime juice; mix well. Refrigerate, covered, overnight. Add more tomatoes if too hot. Yield: 12 to 24 servings.

Krysta Gribble, Gamma Upsilon
Ephrata, Washington

BRAZILIAN FLOAT

2 ounces unsweetened chocolate
2 cups milk
1/3 cup sugar
2 cups freshly brewed double-strength coffee
1 pint coffee ice cream
Chocolate curls

Combine chocolate, milk and sugar in saucepan. Heat slowly until chocolate is melted. Stir in coffee. Beat vigorously with rotary beater until foamy; chill. Pour into 4 tall glasses. Place scoop of ice cream on top. Garnish with chocolate curls. Yield: 4 servings.

Elizabeth Libby, Preceptor Sigma
Penticton, British Columbia, Canada

♥ GRAPE JUICE FLOAT

3 cups grape juice
1/2 cup lemon juice
1 cup apple cider
1/4 cup sugar
1 cup ginger ale
1 pint orange sherbet

Combine grape juice, lemon juice and cider in large bowl. Add sugar. Add ginger ale just before serving. Fill 4 glasses 3/4 full. Top with scoop of sherbet. Serve immediately. Yield: 4 servings.

Marie Emilie Quick, Alpha Gamma Theta
Owensville, Missouri

♥ RHUBARB JUICE

10 to 12 stalks rhubarb
5 cups water
Sugar to taste

Cut up rhubarb. Freeze for 24 hours. Place in 2 thicknesses of cheesecloth in colander. Let drain into large bowl. Add water and sugar. Yield: 6 servings.

Patsy A. Weatherdon, Preceptor Kappa
Salisbury, New Brunswick, Canada

♥ STRAWBERRY SHRUB SODA

3 cups fresh whole strawberries, finely chopped
3 tablespoons raspberry vinegar
1 tablespoon plus 1/2 teaspoon sugar
2 cups seltzer, chilled
3/4 cup strawberry sorbet

Combine strawberries, vinegar and sugar in medium bowl. Stir to mix well. Place mixture in six 8-ounce glasses, dividing equally. Add 1/3 cup seltzer to each glass. Top each with 2 tablespoons sorbet. Serve immediately. Yield: 6 servings.

Sharon Andrews, Preceptor Theta Iota
Tampa, Florida

Duffy Hoagland, Epsilon Omicron, Claremore, Oklahoma, makes Root Beer by mixing 2 1/2 gallons water, 5 pounds sugar and 2 ounces root beer concentrate in 5-gallon container. Add carefully 5 pounds dry ice; stir occasionally until dry ice is dissolved. Add 2 1/2 gallons water; stir.

Just For Starters / 51

STRAWBERRY-WATERMELON SLUSH

1 pint fresh strawberries
2 cups seeded cubed watermelon
1/3 cup sugar
1/3 cup vodka (optional)
1/4 cup lemon juice from concentrate
2 cups ice cubes

Clean and hull strawberries. Combine strawberries and next 4 ingredients in blender container; blend well. Add ice gradually, blending until smooth. Serve immediately. Yield: 4 servings.

Kellie Linden, Xi Theta Pi
Grinnell, Iowa

CALIFORNIA LEMONADE

2 lemons, thinly sliced
1 lime, thinly sliced
1/3 cup sugar
1 (750-milliliter) bottle white wine
5 cups ice cubes

Combine lemon and lime slices with sugar in 2 1/2-quart pitcher. Press slices with wooden spoon to extract some juice and dissolve sugar. Stir in wine and ice cubes. Use a Chardonnay for drier mix or a late-harvest Riesling for sweeter flavor. Yield: 12 servings.

Tamela Smothers, Theta Chi
Chesapeake, Virginia

CHAMPAGNE PUNCH

This is a great punch to serve at a bridal shower.

1 (6-ounce) can frozen pink lemonade concentrate, thawed
1 1/2 cups water
1/2 cup Curaçao
1/4 cup honey
1 (750-milliliter) bottle champagne, chilled

Combine concentrate, 1 1/2 cups water, Curaçao and honey in punch bowl; mix well. Add champagne; mix well. Serve in chilled glasses. Yield: 10 servings.

Poly Wagner, Xi Chi
Louisville, Kentucky

REFRESHING MARGARITAS

2 shots gold Tequila
1/2 (6-ounce) can frozen limeade
6 ounces beer
Crushed ice
Salt to taste

Place Tequila, limeade and beer in blender container. Add ice to fill; blend. Serve with salt on rim of glasses. Yield: 4 servings.

Stasi Seay, Xi Gamma Pi
Paso Robles, California

Cindy Krizek, Alpha, Abilene, Kansas, makes French Iced Coffee by dissolving 2 cups sugar in 3 cups strong hot coffee in rectangle plastic container. Add 2 cups cream, 1 quart milk and 2 teaspoons vanilla extract; mix well. Cover and freeze. Remove from freezer 2 to 2 1/2 hours before serving. Mix well. Serve slushy. Great for brunch and showers.

52 / Beverages

♥ ICED TEA

2 quarts iced tea
1 (6-ounce) can frozen lemonade
1 cup pineapple juice
1 cup sugar
Fresh mint leaves

Combine tea, lemonade, pineapple juice and sugar in large container; mix well. Place mint leaves in glasses. Add tea. Yield: 6 to 8 servings.

Connie Riley, Xi Eta Eta
Acme, Pennsylvania

♥ CRAN TEA

The original recipe came from The Wedgewood Inn, Jackson, California.

Presweetened instant lemon tea mix
Cran-Tea Base
Club soda
Lemon slices

Prepare tea according to package directions. Mix equal amounts of tea and Cran-Tea Base in container. Serve over ice or serve hot. Add shot of club soda and lemon slice to each serving. Yield: variable.

CRAN-TEA BASE

2 quarts cranberry juice
1 cinnamon stick
1 teaspoon whole cloves
1 teaspoon allspice
1 cup pineapple juice

Combine all ingredients in large saucepan. Mull over low heat for 40 to 50 minutes; let cool. Remove spices. Add pineapple juice. Yield: 2 quarts.

Maureen Eastman, Xi Upsilon Omicron
Angels Camp, California

KILLER COFFEE

This takes the place of cappachino and is best served after a meal.

1 cup hot brewed coffee
1 tablespoon Kahlua
1 tablespoon Brandy
1 tablespoon Baileys
1 tablespoon Grand Marnier

Pour coffee into serving cup. Add remaining ingredients; mix well. Yield: 1 serving.

Leslie Hansen, Xi Epsilon Xi
New Hampton, Iowa

MOOSE MILK

We always serve Moose Milk at our chapter Christmas party. We think it brings us good luck!

1 cup vodka
1 cup cold coffee
$1/2$ cup Crème de Cacao
2 cups vanilla ice cream
Crushed ice

Combine first 4 ingredients in blender container; blend. Add enough ice to thicken. Yield: 4 servings.

Sue Walk, Xi Lambda
Cheyenne, Wyoming

GLÖGG

10 cloves
1 cinnamon stick
5 cardamom seeds
$1/2$ (1-fifth) bottle Ruby Port
2 quarts Burgundy
1 pound raisins
2 cups sugar
1 (1-fifth) bottle Brandy

Place cloves, cinnamon and cardamom in cloth sack; tie securely. Combine Port, Burgundy, raisins, sugar and spice sack in large saucepan. Heat slowly until raisins get puffy. Turn off heat; pour in Brandy. Strain and bottle. Raisins are delicious in oatmeal cookies. Yield: 16 to 20 servings.

Helen L. Graham, Xi Xi
Corona, California

HOT WINE DRINK

2 quarts apple cider
$1 1/2$ quarts cranberry juice
$1/4$ cup packed dark brown sugar
4 cinnamon sticks
1 teaspoon whole cloves
1 (1-fifth) bottle Rosé

Combine first 5 ingredients in large saucepan. Heat slowly until very hot. Add wine just before serving; reheat. May be kept hot in coffee urn. The longer the time heated, the more potent the spice. May also be served cold. Yield: 16 to 20 servings.

Donna Mack, Xi Delta Gamma
Manassas, Virginia

DANDELION TONIC

My Dad paid me 5 cents a quart to pick the blossoms. I never saw the finished product. As I grew older, I realized he took it to the Saturday night barn dances for the men folk. Sometimes Mother had to drive the Model T home. I never knew why!

2 quarts fresh dandelion blossoms
4 quarts boiling water
3 pounds sugar
Juice of 4 lemons
Juice of 2 oranges
1 yeast cake
1 egg white, beaten

Check blossoms for insects. Place in 5-gallon crock. Pour water over blossoms. Let stand for $1 1/2$ days. Strain; discard blossoms. Add sugar and juices; stir well. Let stand for 24 hours. Mash yeast in small amount of liquid mixture. Add to crock; stir well. Let stand. Stir in egg white when scum rises. Let stand for 3 days. Strain and bottle. Yield: 4 quarts.

Nadine E. Thomas, Xi Epsilon
Hoquian, Washington

Lynn Hamilton, Preceptor Zeta Phi, St. Peters, Missouri, makes Apple Dip by mixing 8 ounces softened cream cheese, 1 cup peanuts, crushed, $3/4$ cup dark brown sugar and $1/2$ teaspoon vanilla extract in bowl. Serve with apple slices.

It's a Toss-Up

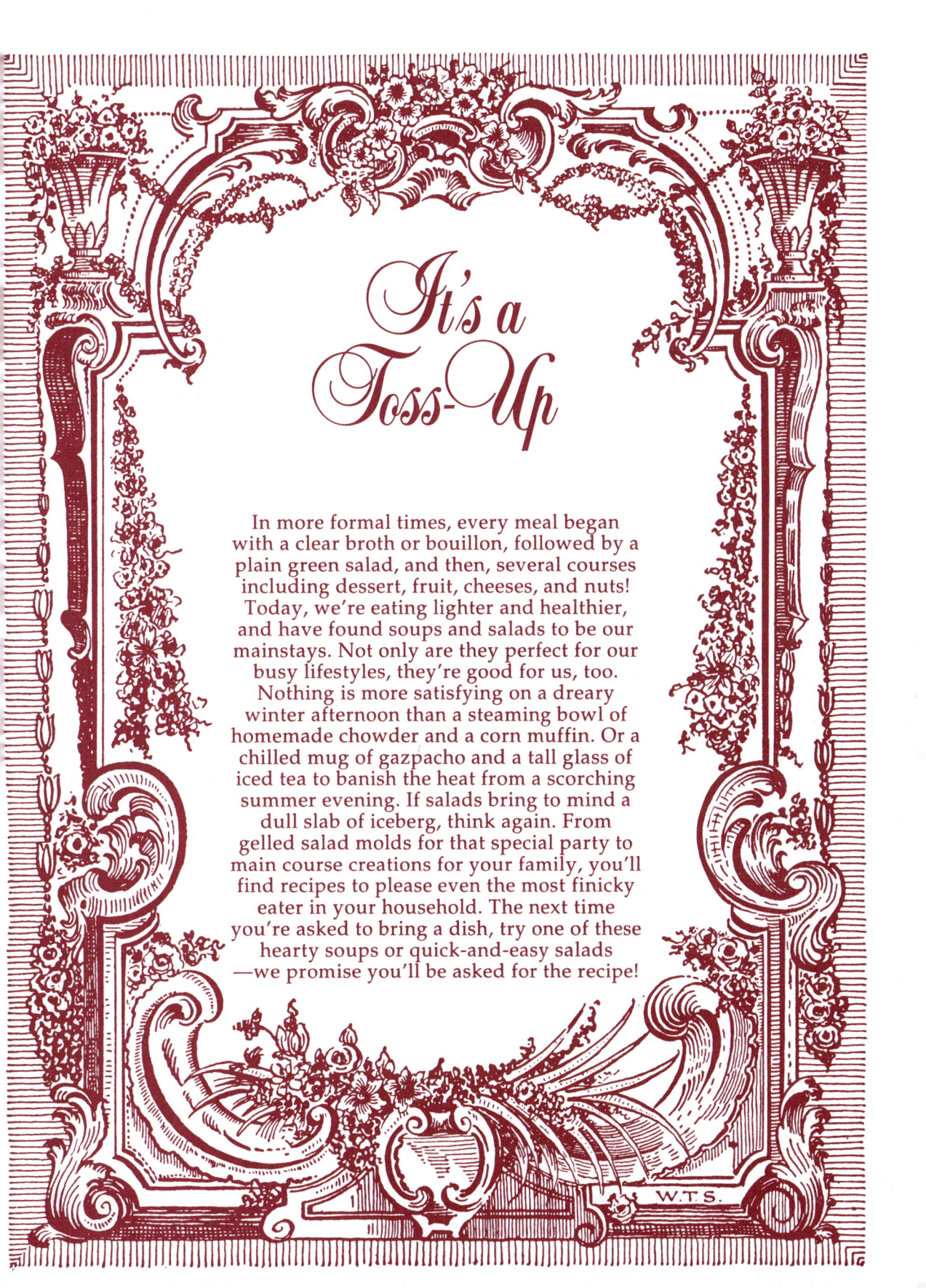

In more formal times, every meal began with a clear broth or bouillon, followed by a plain green salad, and then, several courses including dessert, fruit, cheeses, and nuts! Today, we're eating lighter and healthier, and have found soups and salads to be our mainstays. Not only are they perfect for our busy lifestyles, they're good for us, too. Nothing is more satisfying on a dreary winter afternoon than a steaming bowl of homemade chowder and a corn muffin. Or a chilled mug of gazpacho and a tall glass of iced tea to banish the heat from a scorching summer evening. If salads bring to mind a dull slab of iceberg, think again. From gelled salad molds for that special party to main course creations for your family, you'll find recipes to please even the most finicky eater in your household. The next time you're asked to bring a dish, try one of these hearty soups or quick-and-easy salads —we promise you'll be asked for the recipe!

54 / Soups

CANADIAN SOUP

6 large potatoes, chopped
2 large onions, chopped
3/4 cup carrots
3/4 cup celery
3 cups water
16 ounces chicken broth
18 ounces Velveeta cheese
1 cup light cream or milk
Salt and pepper to taste
1/4 cup chopped parsley
6 ounces Canadian bacon or ham, chopped
1/4 cup cornstarch
1/2 cup water

Combine potatoes, onions, carrots, celery and water in large kettle. Bring to a boil. Simmer, covered, for 20 minutes. Add next 6 ingredients; mix well. Cook over low heat, stirring frequently, for 15 minutes. Combine cornstarch and 1/2 cup cold water in bowl. Add to soup gradually, stirring constantly. Cook for 10 minutes or until thickened. Yield: 10 servings.

Becky Wachs, Theta Sigma
Hays, Kansas

♥ BARLEY PEASANT SOUP

1 pound beef stew meat, cut into 1/2-inch cubes
1 tablespoon olive oil
2 cups chopped onions
1 cup sliced celery
2 cloves of garlic, minced
5 cups water
5 cups beef broth
2 cups sliced carrots
1 1/2 cups pearl barley
1 can garbanzo beans, rinsed, drained
1 can kidney beans, rinsed, drained
4 cups sliced zucchini
3 cups diced plum tomatoes
2 cups chopped cabbage
1/4 cup snipped fresh parsley
1 1/2 teaspoons Italian seasoning
1 teaspoon dried thyme
Salt and pepper to taste
Grated Parmesan cheese

Brown meat in oil in large kettle. Add onions, celery and garlic. Cook until meat is no longer pink. Add water and broth; bring to a boil. Add carrots and barley. Reduce heat. Simmer, covered, for 45 minutes to 1 hour. Add beans, zucchini, tomatoes, cabbage, parsley and seasonings. Simmer for 15 to 20 minutes. Top individual servings with Parmesan cheese. Yield: 16 to 20 servings.

Pam Robbins, Zeta Eta
Haysville, Kansas

♥ BLACK BEAN SOUP

1 pound chili-ground beef chuck
2 tablespoons vegetable oil
1/2 cup sliced green onions
1 1/2 cups water
1 (19-ounce) can black beans soup
2 (15-ounce) cans black beans
1 cup medium-hot chunky salsa
1 (10-ounce) can Ro-Tel tomatoes and green chilies
1/4 cup sour cream
Rice
Corn bread

Brown beef in oil in large kettle. Add onions. Cook for 5 minutes; drain off fat. Add water and remaining ingredients. Cook, uncovered, for 15 minutes. Serve over rice and with corn bread. Yield: 8 to 12 servings.

Bettie Hill, Preceptor Lambda Tau
Dallas, Texas

♥ BLACK FOREST POTATO SOUP

This recipe came from the "Milwaukee Journal" and was chosen as the best soup from Wisconsin.

1 pound boneless beef chuck roast
Salt and pepper to taste
1 to 2 tablespoons vegetable oil
2 quarts beef stock or beef bouillon
1 pound potatoes, peeled, chopped
1/2 pound green beans, cut diagonally into 1-inch pieces
2 large or 3 small leeks, sliced
2 carrots, sliced
2 tomatoes, skinned, chopped
1 cup sliced celery
Salt and pepper to taste
Minced chives to taste
Minced parsley to taste
Toasted rye bread

Season roast with salt and pepper. Sear roast in oil in large kettle; drain off fat. Add beef stock; bring to a boil. Simmer, covered, for 1 hour. Skim off fat as it rises to top. Add vegetables. Simmer for 30 minutes longer or until vegetables and beef are tender. Remove beef. Cut into bite-sized pieces; return to kettle. Season to taste. Heat to serving temperature. Garnish with chives and parsley. Serve with toasted rye bread and a salad. Yield: 6 to 8 servings.

Bernice F. Swoboda, Xi Alpha Epsilon
Two Rivers, Wisconsin

SAUERKRAUT-BEEF SOUP

This recipe was given to me by a friend. It is a German recipe that has been handed down through her family.

1 (3- to 4-pound) beef roast
8 medium potatoes, cubed
1 (32-ounce) can sauerkraut, drained
1 1/2 cups barley
50 to 60 ounces beef broth
3 eggs
All-purpose flour

Place roast in large kettle. Add small amount of water. Simmer, covered, until tender. Cut roast into bite-sized pieces; return to kettle. Add potatoes, sauerkraut, barley and beef broth. Cook slowly over medium heat for 1 1/2 hours. Add additional broth for desired consistency. Beat eggs and enough flour to make consistency of dough. Bring soup to a boil. Drop dumplings into soup by 1/2 teaspoonfuls. Cook for 25 minutes longer. May reheat, adding additional broth or water. Freezes well. Yield: 12 to 16 servings.

Teresa Downham, Upsilon
Laurel Springs, New Jersey

HAMBURGER SOUP

2 pounds ground beef
1 onion, chopped
1 (19-ounce) can tomatoes
3 (10-ounce) cans beef consommé
2 (10-ounce) cans tomato soup
1 large can vegetable cocktail
2 cups frozen peas
2 cups frozen corn
2 cups chopped potatoes
1/2 cup rice
Salt and pepper to taste
2 cups water

Sauté ground beef and onion in saucepan, stirring until crumbly; drain. Add tomatoes; mash. Add consommé, soup and vegetable cocktail. Add vegetables, rice, salt and pepper. Stir in water. Simmer for 3 hours. Yield: 20 servings.

Pamela Wells, Zeta
Grand Falls-Windsor, Newfoundland, Canada

♥ MEATBALL-VEGETABLE SOUP

1 pound extra-lean ground beef
1 egg
1 teaspoon salt
1/4 teaspoon pepper
1 quart beef broth
8 green onions with tops, cut into 1/2-inch pieces
3/4 cup thinly sliced celery
3/4 cup thinly sliced carrots
1 (48-ounce) can tomato juice
1/2 cup rice
1 bay leaf
1 teaspoon dried basil leaves
2 tablespoons soy sauce
Minced parsley

Combine ground beef, egg, salt and pepper in bowl. Shape into 1-inch balls. Bring broth to a boil in large saucepan. Drop meatballs into broth. Add onions, celery, carrots, tomato juice, rice, bay leaf and basil. Simmer, covered, for 30 minutes, stirring occasionally. Remove bay leaf. Stir in soy sauce. Garnish with parsley. Yield: 8 servings.

Janice Carter, Xi Gamma Epsilon
Mohave Valley, Arizona

HEALTHY VEGETABLE AND HAM SOUP

1 quart tomato juice
1 (10-ounce) can beef broth
1 broth can water
2 (2-inch thick) smoked ham shanks
1 can peeled tomatoes with onion and green pepper
1 cup chopped white onion
2 stalks celery, sliced
2 carrots, sliced
1 clove of garlic, crushed
1 leek, thinly sliced
2 cups finely shredded cabbage
1/2 cup peas
1/2 cup small shell macaroni
1 can small white beans, drained
1 can kidney beans, drained
Salt and pepper to taste
Grated Parmesan cheese

Place tomato juice, beef broth, 1 broth can water and ham shanks in large kettle. Bring to a boil; reduce to simmer. Simmer for 1 1/2 hours. Remove shanks from kettle. Chop meat; return to stock. Add next 7 ingredients. Simmer for 45 minutes or until vegetables are just tender. Add next 5 ingredients. Simmer for 10 to 12 minutes or until macaroni is done. Top with Parmesan cheese. Yield: 8 servings.

Cynthia L. Duncan, Delta Sigma
Louisville, Colorado

♥ CHICKEN-SUCCOTASH STEW

2 slices bacon, cut into 1-inch pieces
4 boneless skinless chicken breasts
3 tablespoons all-purpose flour
3/4 teaspoon salt
1 onion, chopped
2 cloves of garlic, minced
2 medium red potatoes, thinly sliced
2 (14- to 16-ounce) cans stewed tomatoes
1 (12-ounce) can whole-kernel corn, drained
1 (10-ounce) package frozen fordhook lima beans
1 chicken-flavored bouillon cube
1 tablespoon basil
3 cups hot water

Cook bacon in 8-quart kettle over medium-high heat until browned. Remove from kettle; drain. Reserve 1 tablespoon bacon drippings in kettle. Cut chicken into bite-sized pieces. Combine flour and salt in bowl. Coat chicken with flour mixture. Sauté chicken with onion and garlic in reserved bacon drippings until chicken is browned. Add remaining ingredients. Bring to a boil over high heat. Reduce heat to medium. Cook, covered, for 10 minutes or until chicken and vegetables are tender. Sprinkle with bacon. Yield: 8 to 12 servings.

Maxine L. Young, Lambda Master
Tacoma, Washington

TACO SOUP

1 1/2 pounds ground turkey or beef
1 medium onion, chopped
1 green bell pepper, chopped
Garlic powder to taste
1 can stewed tomatoes
1 (8-ounce) can tomato sauce
1 can kidney beans, undrained
1 can pinto beans, undrained
1 can hominy, drained
1 envelope taco seasoning
1 envelope dry ranch dressing mix

Brown turkey with onion and green pepper in large saucepan, stirring until crumbly. Add garlic powder; drain. Combine turkey mixture and remaining ingredients in kettle; mix well. Bring to a boil. Simmer for 30 minutes. Yield: 8 servings.

Susan MacLeod, Xi Omega Nu
Rosenberg, Texas

♥ TURKEY SOUP

This dish is great for a low-sodium low-fat diet, especially if low-sodium low-fat ingredients are used.

1 1/2 pounds ground turkey
1 large onion, chopped
4 carrots, sliced
4 stalks celery, sliced
1 (28-ounce) can tomatoes
1 quart water
1/4 cup uncooked rice or barley
2 medium potatoes, chopped
1 small bay leaf
1/2 teaspoon thyme
1/2 teaspoon basil
4 teaspoons Chili Powder
4 drops of Tabasco sauce
1/3 teaspoon dillweed
1/3 teaspoon pepper
1 (15-ounce) can kidney beans
1 (15-ounce) can green beans, drained, rinsed
1 (15-ounce) can whole-kernel corn

Brown turkey and onion in large kettle, stirring until crumbly. Add carrots, celery, tomatoes and water. Bring to a boil. Stir in rice. Simmer for 30 minutes. Add potatoes, bay leaf, thyme, basil, Chili Powder, Tabasco sauce, dillweed and pepper. Cook for 30 minutes. Add beans and corn. Cook for 5 minutes. Add additional water or unsalted tomato juice if mixture becomes too thick. Yield: 6 to 8 servings.

CHILI POWDER

3 tablespoons paprika
2 teaspoons finely crushed oregano
1 teaspoon ground cumin
1 teaspoon turmeric
1 teaspoon garlic powder
1/4 teaspoon red pepper

Combine paprika, oregano, cumin, turmeric, garlic powder and red pepper in bowl; mix well.
Yield: 4 to 5 tablespoons.

Jean G. Holroyd, Laureate Kappa
Vancouver, Washington

♥ THREE-BEAN CHILI

1 pound 97% fat-free ground turkey
1 large onion, chopped
1 (15-ounce) can red kidney beans
2 (15-ounce) cans pinto beans
1 (15-ounce) can great northern beans
1 envelope chili mix
2 (15-ounce) cans diced tomatoes
1/2 cup grated low-fat sharp Cheddar cheese
1/2 cup fat-free sour cream

Brown turkey and onion in heavy 5-quart kettle, stirring until crumbly. Add beans, chili mix and tomatoes. Bring to a boil over medium heat; reduce heat. Simmer for 45 minutes. Garnish with cheese and dollop of sour cream.
Yield: 8 to 10 servings.

Lois C. Black, Delta Phi
Batesburg-Leesville, South Carolina

♥ CRAB SOUP

2 quarts water
2 cups thinly sliced carrots
1/2 cup coarsely chopped celery
1/4 cup butter or margarine
1 1/2 tablespoons Old Bay seasoning
1 tablespoon Worcestershire sauce
3 cups chopped potatoes
1 (16-ounce) can crushed tomatoes
1 1/2 pounds fresh Maryland crab meat

Place water in large stockpot. Bring to a boil. Add next 5 ingredients; return to a boil. Reduce heat. Simmer for 30 minutes. Add potatoes. Cook for 20 to 30 minutes, stirring occasionally. Add tomatoes. Simmer for 10 minutes. Add crab meat just before serving.
Yield: 12 servings.

Mary Dilworth, Mu Eta
Centerville, Ohio

CREAM OF CRAB-BROCCOLI SOUP

8 ounces frozen Alaska King crab, thawed
1 (10-ounce) package frozen chopped broccoli
1/2 cup chopped onion
3 tablespoons butter or margarine
2 tablespoons all-purpose flour
2 cups milk
2 cups half and half
2 chicken bouillon cubes
1/2 teaspoon salt
1/8 teaspoon pepper
1/8 teaspoon cayenne pepper
1/4 teaspoon thyme

Drain and slice crab. Cook broccoli in saucepan according to package directions. Sauté onion in butter in 3-quart saucepan; blend in flour. Add milk and half and half. Cook, stirring constantly, until thickened and smooth. Dissolve bouillon cubes in hot soup. Add seasonings, crab and broccoli; heat through.
Yield: 6 servings.

Tahnell Vogt, Laureate Pi
Highland Village, Texas

♥ FISH STEW

3/4 cup chopped onions
1/2 cup chopped parsley
1/4 cup olive oil
3 large ripe tomatoes, chopped
3 cups chicken broth or clam juice
1 cup water
1 large potato, chopped
2 large bay leaves
Salt and pepper to taste
1 1/2 pounds salmon, cut into chunks
1 1/2 pounds white fish, cut into chunks

Sauté onions and parsley in olive oil in saucepan. Add tomatoes and broth. Bring to a boil. Add water, potato, bay leaves, salt and pepper. Cook, covered, for 10 minutes. Remove bay leaves. Add salmon and white fish. Cook gently for 10 to 12 minutes. Pour into tureen or serve in soup bowls. Yield: 4 servings.

Doris V. Ray, Eta Master
Portland, Oregon

BAY CHOWDER

3 medium potatoes, chopped
3 medium carrots, chopped
1 celery stalk, chopped
1 medium onion, chopped
2 cups chicken stock or broth
1/2 teaspoon salt
1/4 teaspoon pepper
1/2 bay leaf
1/2 teaspoon thyme
8 ounces fresh mushrooms, sliced
1 1/2 tablespoons butter or margarine
1 pound fresh scallops
1/2 cup dry white wine
1 cup heavy cream
1 egg yolk, slightly beaten
1 tablespoon chopped parsley

Combine potatoes, carrots, celery, onion, stock, salt, pepper, bay leaf and thyme in large saucepan; cover. Bring to a boil; reduce heat. Simmer for 15 minutes or until vegetables are tender. Remove bay leaf. Purée vegetables in food processor until smooth. Sauté mushrooms in butter in large saucepan for 5 minutes. Add scallops and wine. Cook for 1 minute. Combine cream and egg yolk in bowl. Stir into scallop mixture until smooth. Add vegetable mixture; heat thoroughly. Garnish with parsley. Yield: 8 servings.

Anne B. Aho, Xi Delta Nu
Mount Vernon, Ohio

LARGE GOURMET CHOWDER

6 medium potatoes, cut up
2 cans lobster, thawed
1 (10-ounce) can baby clams
1/2 cup butter or margarine
5 medium onions, chopped
1 to 2 pounds scallops
3 or 4 haddock filets, chopped
1 package imitation crab meat
1 package frozen shrimp, thawed
1 quart whipping cream
1 litre half-and-half blend
1/2 cup chopped parsley
1/2 teaspoon salt
1/2 teaspoon pepper
1/2 teaspoon garlic salt
1/2 teaspoon rosemary
1/2 teaspoon thyme
1/4 teaspoon basil

Cook potatoes in saucepan in water to cover. Drain, reserving water. Drain lobster and clams, reserving juices. Melt butter in large heavy saucepan. Cook onions in butter until transparent. Add lobster juice, clam juice and potato water. Bring to a boil. Reduce heat to low. Add potatoes, lobster, clams, scallops, haddock, crab and shrimp. Cook for 5 minutes. Add remaining ingredients. Bring to a simmer; do not boil. Yield: 15 servings.

Gail Abraham, Beta
Halifax, Nova Scotia, Canada

♥ ITALIAN CLAM CHOWDER

2 (6-ounce) cans minced clams
3/4 cup sliced celery
1 small onion, chopped
1/2 cup chopped green bell pepper
2 tablespoons olive oil
2 cans low-salt chicken broth
1 cup sliced carrots
2 (14-ounce) cans stewed Italian tomatoes
1/2 teaspoon sweet basil
1/2 teaspoon pepper
1 cup small shell-shaped pasta

Drain clams, reserving liquid. Sauté celery, onion and green pepper in olive oil in large saucepan until tender. Add broth, carrots, tomatoes, basil and pepper. Stir in reserved clam liquid. Bring to a boil; reduce heat. Simmer, covered, for 20 minutes. Add pasta. Simmer, uncovered, for 8 to 10 minutes. Add clams; heat through. Yield: 6 to 8 servings.

Jeannie Pessano, Preceptor Alpha
Ocean City, New Jersey

♥ THEY-WON'T-BELIEVE-IT FRUIT SOUP

2 cups strawberries
1 1/3 cups non-fat dry milk
1 teaspoon vanilla extract
6 teaspoons sugar or equivalent sweetener
1/2 cup cold water
1/4 cup cold orange juice
4 mint sprigs

Combine strawberries, dry milk, vanilla, sugar and water in blender container. Blend until smooth. Pour into bowl; chill. Add orange juice at serving time. Beat with wire whisk until smooth. Pour into soup bowls. Garnish with mint sprigs. Yield: 4 servings.

Kathy Hahne, Epsilon
Edmond, Oklahoma

♣ ♥ TOMATO AND BLACK BEAN SOUP

2 tablespoons plus 2 cups defatted beef stock
1 medium onion, chopped
1/4 teaspoon minced garlic
3 (15-ounce) cans black beans
3 large ripe tomatoes, chopped
1 (28-ounce) can tomatoes, drained, chopped
1 teaspoon salt
1/2 teaspoon pepper
4 cups seashell pasta, cooked al dente

Combine 2 tablespoons beef stock, onion and garlic in nonstick skillet coated with nonstick vegetable cooking spray. Cook for 4 minutes or until onion is tender. Add 1 can undrained black beans and ripe tomatoes. Simmer for 5 minutes. Pour into stockpot. Add canned tomatoes; simmer for 5 minutes. Drain remaining beans, mashing half with fork. Add to stockpot. Add 2 cups beef stock, salt and pepper. Simmer for 4 to 5 minutes. Add pasta; heat through. Yield: 14 servings.

Jennifer Taylor, Preceptor Beta Phi
Vancouver, Washington

CUBAN BLACK BEAN SOUP

2 pounds dry black beans
2 green bell peppers, chopped
4 onions, chopped
1/2 cup olive oil
1 (8-ounce) can tomato sauce
2 bay leaves
1 tablespoon garlic powder
1 tablespoon pepper
1 teaspoon cumin seed
1 tablespoon ground oregano
1/2 teaspoon salt
3 tablespoons vinegar
1/4 cup white wine
1 (4-ounce) jar chopped pimentos
2 tablespoons sugar
5 to 6 cups cooked white or yellow rice
Sour cream

Cover beans with water in large saucepan; let soak overnight. Cook in same water over medium heat for 4 to 5 hours or until soft. Add water as needed; stir. Sauté green peppers and onions in olive oil in large skillet. Add tomato sauce; stir. Add bay leaves, garlic powder, pepper, cumin seed and oregano. Add tomato mixture, salt, vinegar, wine and pimentos to beans. Cook for 1 hour. Remove bay leaves. Add sugar. Cook for 30 minutes. Serve over rice with dollop of sour cream. Freezes well. Yield: 10 servings.

Nancy Hodge, Xi Delta Delta
Mooresville, North Carolina

BEAN AND RICE SOUP

This is an old recipe handed down from generation to generation in Vermont.

1 1/2 cups navy beans
8 ounces salt pork, chopped
1 cup macaroni
1 cup instant rice

Soak beans in water to cover in bowl overnight. Place in saucepan. Cover with water. Cook for 2 hours or until soft. Add salt pork. Cook until tender. Add macaroni. Cook until soft. Add rice; cook until tender.
Yield: 10 to 12 servings.

Joyce C. Sammet, Laureate Alpha Tau
Lake Mary, Florida

♥ MY FAVORITE LENTIL SOUP

2 tablespoons olive oil
1 large onion, chopped
3 large carrots, coarsely grated
1/2 teaspoon crushed thyme leaves
1/2 teaspoon crushed marjoram leaves
1 (28-ounce) can tomatoes with juice, chopped
7 cups beef, chicken or vegetable broth
1 1/2 cups dried lentils, rinsed
1/2 teaspoon salt
1/4 to 1/2 teaspoon pepper
1/3 cup chopped fresh parsley
4 ounces Cheddar cheese, grated

Heat oil in large saucepan. Sauté onion, carrots, thyme and marjoram, stirring constantly, for 5 minutes. Add tomatoes, broth and lentils. Bring to a boil; reduce heat. Simmer, covered, for 1 hour or until lentils are tender. Add salt, pepper and parsley. Simmer for a few minutes longer. Sprinkle each serving with cheese.
Yield: 8 servings.

Martha Hollett, Alpha Iota
Plymouth, Indiana

♥ LENTIL AND VEGETABLE SOUP

This is a low-cost, low-fat and low-calorie soup for cold weather to give you "get-up and go."

1 tablespoon olive oil
2 1/2 cups chopped red, green and yellow bell peppers
2 cups chopped onions
1 teaspoon minced garlic
3 1/2 cups chicken broth
2 cups water
1 pound dried lentils, sorted, rinsed
2 cups sliced carrots
2 large potatoes, cut into 1-inch chunks
1 pound fresh or 1 (10-ounce) package frozen spinach
8 ounces reduced-fat kielbasa sausage
Salt to taste
Italian bread

Heat oil in 8-quart stockpot over medium heat. Add peppers, onions and garlic. Cook for 6 to 8 minutes or until vegetables are tender. Add broth, water, lentils, carrots and potatoes. Bring to a boil. Simmer, covered, for 50 minutes or until lentils are tender, stirring occasionally. Stir in spinach and sausage. Add salt. Simmer for 8 to 10 minutes longer. Serve with Italian bread.
Yield: 8 servings.

Kathryn DeFillipo, Preceptor Chi
Plainfield, New Jersey

BROCCOLI-CHEESE SOUP

3 cups water
1 (10-ounce) package frozen chopped broccoli
3 chicken bouillon cubes
1/4 cup chopped onion
1/2 cup butter or margarine
4 1/2 tablespoons all-purpose flour
2 1/2 cups milk
8 ounces cream cheese, softened
Salt and pepper to taste

Combine water, broccoli, bouillon and onion in large saucepan. Bring to a boil. Melt butter in large saucepan. Stir in flour. Add milk gradually, stirring until thickened. Add cream cheese, stirring until cream cheese is melted. Add broccoli mixture. Heat through, stirring constantly. Add salt and pepper. Yield: 6 servings.

Kay Meyers, Alpha Omega
Sioux Falls, South Dakota

Wanda B. Burkett, Delta Phi, Batesburg, South Carolina, makes Corn Chowder by combining 1 can cream of potato soup, 1 can cream of onion soup, 1 (15-ounce) can cream-style golden sweet corn and 2 soup cans water in saucepan. Simmer for 30 minutes over medium heat, stirring often.

BROCCOLI SOUP

3/4 cup chopped onion
2 tablespoons margarine
6 cups water
6 chicken bouillon cubes
1 (8-ounce) package fine
  egg noodles
2 (10-ounce) packages
  chopped broccoli
1/2 teaspoon garlic
  powder
6 cups milk
1 pound American
  cheese, grated

Sauté onion in margarine in large saucepan until transparent. Add water and bouillon. Bring to a boil. Add noodles. Cook for 3 minutes. Stir in broccoli and garlic powder. Cook for 4 minutes. Add milk and cheese. Cook until cheese is melted. Yield: 8 servings.

Shelby Bauer
Ida, Kansas

CHEESY BROCCOLI AND CAULIFLOWER SOUP

6 cups water
6 chicken bouillon cubes
1 1/2 cups frozen mixed
  vegetables
2 1/2 cups cubed potatoes
1 (10-ounce) package
  chopped cauliflower
1 (10-ounce) package
  frozen chopped
  broccoli
2 (10-ounce) cans cream
  of chicken soup
1 pound Velveeta
  cheese

Place water, bouillon cubes, frozen mixed vegetables and potatoes in large saucepan. Bring to a boil; boil for 15 minutes. Add cauliflower and broccoli. Bring to a boil; boil for 10 minutes. Add soup and cheese. Simmer over very low heat until heated through.
Yield: 24 servings.

Cathy Maddox, Xi Beta Beta
Lincoln, Nebraska

ROASTED CARROT AND BRIE SOUP

2 1/2 tablespoons butter
  or margarine
3 cups coarsely chopped
  carrots
1/2 cup coarsely chopped
  Spanish onion
6 cups chicken stock
Salt and pepper to taste
3 ounces Brie cheese,
  cut into small pieces
3/4 cup whipping cream

Preheat oven to 450 degrees. Place butter in 9-inch baking pan. Bake until melted. Add carrots and onion. Roast for 20 minutes or until lightly browned. Transfer mixture to heavy saucepan. Add chicken stock. Season with salt and pepper. Simmer for 30 minutes or until carrots are soft. Pour 1/3 of soup into blender container. Add 1/3 of cheese to container. Blend until smooth. Place in large saucepan. Repeat with remaining soup and cheese. Add whipping cream. Season to taste.
Yield: 6 to 8 servings.

Karin Parakin, Zeta Gamma
Port Hardy, British Columbia, Canada

♥ CABBAGE-TOMATO SOUP

1 (46-ounce) can V-8
  juice
1 small head cabbage,
  chopped
2 beef bouillon cubes
2 cups frozen green
  beans
4 bay leaves
4 ounces sliced onion
6 ribs celery, chopped
3 tablespoons parsley
  flakes
4 medium carrots,
  chopped
Salt and pepper
  to taste

Combine all ingredients in kettle. Heat until almost boiling; reduce heat. Simmer, covered, for 1 hour or until vegetables are tender. Remove bay leaves. Serve hot.
Yield: 6 to 8 servings.

Joan M. Zuments, Preceptor Lambda
Arvada, Colorado

GREEN CHILI-CHEESE SOUP

1 (14-ounce) can lite
  chicken broth
1 (10-ounce) can Cheddar
  cheese soup
1 (10-ounce) can cream
  of mushroom soup
1 (10-ounce) can cream
  of celery soup
1 pound lite Velveeta
  cheese, cubed
2 (8-ounce) cans chopped
  green chilies
2 1/2 cups skim milk
Chopped tomatoes
Tortilla chips

Combine chicken broth and soups in large saucepan; mix well. Heat over medium heat until mixed and bubbly. Reduce heat to low. Add cheese, green chilies and milk, stirring occasionally, until cheese is melted. Top individual servings with tomatoes and tortilla chips.
Yield: 8 servings.

Elaine Wilson, Xi Beta Alpha
Artesia, New Mexico

♥ CREAMY FIVE-ONION SOUP

1/4 cup butter or
  margarine
1 yellow onion,
  chopped
1 red onion, chopped
2 leeks, chopped
1 bunch green onions,
  chopped
3 ounces shallots,
  chopped
1 tablespoon basil
1/2 cup all-purpose flour
2 (10-ounce) cans beef
  broth
1 cup white wine
1 tablespoon pepper
2 cups heavy cream
3 to 4 ounces shredded
  Gruyère cheese

Melt butter in stockpot. Add onions and basil. Sauté until tender; do not brown. Add flour to make a roux. Cook for 5 minutes, stirring constantly. Remove from heat. Add beef broth, stirring until smooth. Add wine and pepper. Cook over medium heat for 20 minutes, stirring occasionally. Add cream. Cook for 15 minutes longer. Stir in cheese. Serve hot. Yield: 8 servings.

Lynne Owens, Xi Alpha Theta
Gardnerville, Nevada

FRENCH ONION SOUP

4 large onions, sliced	Garlic Melba toast
6 beef bouillon cubes	3 ounces shredded
6 cups water	Parmesan cheese
2 cups white Zinfandel wine	

Separate onion rings. Place in Crock•Pot. Add bouillon cubes, water and wine. Cook on High for 3 to 4 hours or until onions are tender. May simmer on Low all day. Preheat oven to broil. Ladle soup into mugs. Top with toast and cheese. Broil for 2 to 3 minutes or until cheese is melted and bubbly. Yield: 6 to 8 servings.

Sharon Van Winkle, Xi Alpha Omega
Story, Wyoming

♥ MINESTRONE

1/3 cup olive oil	1 (16-ounce) can tomatoes
1/4 cup butter or margarine	5 ounces fresh spinach, coarsely shredded
1 large onion, chopped	2 medium zucchini, chopped
2 large carrots, chopped	6 beef-flavored bouillon cubes
2 stalks celery, chopped	1 teaspoon salt
2 medium potatoes, chopped	2 (16- to 20-ounce) cans kidney beans
8 ounces fresh green beans, cut into 1-inch pieces	1/2 cup grated Parmesan cheese
6 cups water	
1/2 small head cabbage, shredded	

Heat olive oil and butter in 8-quart kettle over medium heat. Add onion, carrots, celery, potatoes and green beans. Cook for 20 minutes or until vegetables are lightly browned, stirring occasionally. Add water, cabbage, tomatoes with liquid, spinach, zucchini, bouillon cubes and salt. Bring to a boil over high heat, stirring to break up tomatoes. Reduce heat to low. Simmer, covered, for 40 minutes or until vegetables are tender, stirring occasionally. Do not overcook. Stir in beans. Cook for 15 minutes longer or until soup is slightly thickened. Ladle soup into bowls. Sprinkle cheese on top. Yield: 8 to 16 servings.

Connie Parsons, Preceptor Alpha Gamma
Glenrock, Wyoming

PARSNIP SOUP

1 1/2 tablespoons butter or margarine	3/4 teaspoon sage
6 or 7 parsnips, peeled, chopped	3 cloves
1 tart apple, peeled, chopped	2/3 cup milk
6 cups chicken stock	Salt and pepper to taste
	Parsley
	Croutons

Melt butter in large saucepan. Add parsnips and apple. Cook, covered, for 10 minutes. Add chicken stock, sage and cloves. Bring to a boil. Simmer, covered, for 30 minutes. Remove cloves. Let cool slightly. Purée mixture in blender or food processor. Return to saucepan. Add milk. Heat gently; do not boil. Season with salt and pepper. Garnish with parsley and croutons.
Yield: 8 servings.

Elsbeth Gibson, Laureate Alpha
Fredericton, New Brunswick, Canada

BLACK-EYED PEA SOUP

6 slices bacon	4 (15-ounce) cans black-eyed peas
1 large onion, chopped	2 (14-ounce) cans beef broth
1 clove of garlic, minced	
1 teaspoon salt	1 (10-ounce) can chopped tomatoes and green chilies
1/2 teaspoon pepper	
1 (4-ounce) can chopped mild green chilies	

Cook bacon in large stockpot over medium heat until crisp. Remove bacon; drain and crumble. Add next 5 ingredients to pan drippings. Sauté until onion is transparent. Add bacon and remaining ingredients. Increase heat to medium-high. Bring to a boil. Remove from heat. Yield: 12 to 14 servings.

Debbie Seab, Xi Alpha Sigma
Moss Point, Mississippi

♥ PEA POD-POTATO SOUP

1/4 cup chopped green onions	1 (8-ounce) can sliced water chestnuts
2 tablespoons butter or margarine	1/2 teaspoon salt
	1/8 teaspoon pepper
2 medium potatoes, peeled, chopped	1/4 teaspoon ginger
	1/8 teaspoon dry mustard
5 cups chicken broth	Sliced green onions
1/2 cup plain yogurt	
8 ounces Chinese pea pods, stemmed, cut up	

Sauté chopped green onions in butter in 2-quart saucepan until soft. Add potatoes and broth. Simmer for 20 minutes. Purée, 1/2 at a time, in blender. Return to saucepan. Stir 2 tablespoons puréed potato mixture into yogurt. Add yogurt to puréed potato mixture. Stir in pea pods, water chestnuts and seasonings. Bring to a boil over medium heat. Serve in individual bowls. Garnish with green onions. Yield: 8 servings.

Sharon Culen, Xi Alpha Iota
Rochester, Minnesota

Penne Mathews, Preceptor Beta Phi, College Station, Texas, makes Avocado Soup by combining 3 finely mashed avocados, 3 tablespoons lemon juice, 3 tablespoons piquante sauce, 3 cups chicken broth and dash of salt in bowl; mix well. Chill.

CHEESE-POTATO SOUP

8 cups water
5 potatoes, chopped
5 potatoes, shredded
1 bunch celery
1 pound carrots, shredded
1 large onion, shredded
4 (10-ounce) cans cream of celery soup
1 pound Velveeta cheese, cubed
2 cups chopped or wafered ham

Place water, potatoes, celery, carrots and onion in large saucepan. Cook over medium heat until potatoes are tender. Add soup, cheese and ham. Cook over low heat until cheese is melted. Yield: 24 servings.

Wanda Fouts, Theta Sigma
Hays, Kansas

I'M-IN-A-HURRY HEARTY POTATO SOUP

1 (24-ounce) package frozen potatoes
1 cup chopped onions
1 cup chopped celery
1 (16-ounce) package frozen crinkle-cut carrots
1/4 cup margarine
4 chicken bouillon cubes
6 cups water
1/2 cup all-purpose flour
1 (14-ounce) can evaporated milk
1 pound Velveeta cheese, cubed

Combine potatoes, onions, celery, carrots, margarine, bouillon cubes and water in large saucepan. Bring to a boil. Cook over low heat for 15 minutes. Combine flour with enough water in small bowl to make paste. Add evaporated milk, cheese and flour mixture to saucepan, mixing well. Simmer gently for 10 minutes. Do not boil. Yield: 8 servings.

Carmel-Beth Kemerling, Mu Lambda
Tarkio, Missouri

♥ CHEESY CHUNKY TOMATO SOUP

1/4 cup chopped celery
1/4 cup chopped green bell pepper
1/4 cup chopped green onions
1/4 cup margarine
1/4 cup Parmesan cheese
2 (10-ounce) cans tomato soup
2 soup cans water
2 cans stewed tomatoes
1 tablespoon basil
1 teaspoon chopped garlic
1/4 cup shredded Cheddar cheese
Tabasco sauce to taste

Sauté celery, green pepper and onions in margarine in saucepan. Add Parmesan cheese. Sauté until combined. Add soup, water and tomatoes; mix well. Add basil and garlic. Bring to a boil. Simmer for 10 minutes. Add Cheddar cheese and Tabasco sauce. Simmer for 5 minutes longer. Yield: 12 to 16 servings.

Bette Deniston, Preceptor Alpha Epsilon
Carbondale, Illinois

♥ TOMATO SOUP

1 onion, finely chopped
2 tablespoons olive oil
1 clove of garlic, crushed
4 pounds tomatoes or 3 (28-ounce) cans tomatoes
2 tablespoons sugar
2 bay leaves
1/2 teaspoon thyme
1/2 teaspoon mint
1/2 teaspoon basil
Pinch of cayenne pepper
1/2 teaspoon salt
Pepper to taste

Sauté onion in oil in large saucepan until softened. Add remaining ingredients. Cook, uncovered, over low heat for 20 minutes or until tomatoes have softened and liquid has reduced. Remove bay leaves. Purée soup in blender. Return to saucepan. Cook until creamy. Serve hot. Yield: 8 servings.

Patricia McCauley, Xi Alpha Kappa
Addison, Ontario, Canada

WATERCRESS SOUP

1 1/2 pounds zucchini
1 tablespoon unsalted butter or margarine
3 leeks without tops, chopped
4 cups chicken stock or canned broth
1 bunch watercress, tough stems removed
1/3 cup heavy cream (optional)
Salt to taste
Freshly ground pepper to taste

Trim ends off zucchini. Peel and chop. Melt butter in large heavy saucepan over low heat. Add leeks. Cook for 5 minutes or until soft but not brown. Add zucchini. Increase heat to medium high. Sauté for 2 minutes; do not brown. Add stock. Bring to a boil. Reduce heat to moderate. Simmer for 5 minutes or until zucchini is just tender. Add watercress. Simmer for 1 minute. Purée soup in blender until smooth. Add cream. Add salt and pepper. Yield: 4 to 6 servings.

Kris Dungan, Gamma Gamma
Duluth, Minnesota

ZUCCHINI SOUP

1 pound Italian hot sausage
2 cups 1/2-inch celery pieces
2 pounds zucchini, cut into 1/2-inch pieces
2 (28-ounce) cans tomatoes
1 teaspoon sugar
1 cup chopped onions
2 teaspoons salt
1 teaspoon Italian seasoning
1 teaspoon oregano
1/2 teaspoon basil
1/4 teaspoon garlic powder
2 green bell peppers, cut into 1/2-inch pieces

Brown sausage in kettle, stirring until crumbly. Add celery. Cook for 10 minutes, stirring occasionally. Add next 9 ingredients. Simmer, covered, for 20 minutes. Add green peppers. Simmer for 1 hour. Yield: 12 servings.

Nancy Fisher, Xi Chi
Butler, Pennsylvania

62 / Soups

♥ CAPTAIN'S SOUP

1 medium onion, chopped
1 teaspoon vegetable oil
1 (10-ounce) can cream of mushroom soup
1 (10-ounce) can cream of celery soup
1 (32-ounce) can V-8 juice
1 (16-ounce) package frozen vegetables
Salt and pepper to taste

Sauté onion in oil in saucepan until transparent. Add soups and juice. Bring to a boil. Add frozen vegetables. Simmer until vegetables are tender. Add salt and pepper. May add sautéed ground beef, chicken or turkey if desired. Yield: 12 servings.

June Snyder, Xi Delta Omega
Smyrna, Georgia

♥ LOW-CALORIE INSPIRATION SOUP

1 (20-ounce) can Chinese mixed vegetables
1 (20-ounce) can asparagus pieces
2 (4-ounce) cans mushrooms with liquid
1 (14-ounce) can French green beans with liquid
3 stalks celery, cut into bite-sized pieces
2 cups water
1 1/4 cups tomato juice
2 envelopes beef broth seasoning
2 envelopes plain gelatin
Onion flakes to taste
Salt and pepper to taste

Combine vegetables, water, tomato juice, seasoning, gelatin, onion flakes, salt and pepper in large kettle. Simmer for 20 minutes. Yield: 12 servings.

Helen T. Forrest
Luverne, Minnesota

♥ SUMMER GARDEN SOUP

1 cup chopped onion
2 cups baby carrots
1 cup chopped celery
2 cups frozen green beans
1 (15-ounce) can garbanzo beans
8 cups vegetable broth
1/2 teaspoon basil
1/2 teaspoon rosemary
1/4 teaspoon thyme
1/2 teaspoon salt
1 (12-ounce) package frozen egg noodles
2 cups chopped fresh tomatoes

Combine first 10 ingredients in large kettle. Bring to a boil. Stir in noodles. Cook for 30 minutes. Add tomatoes. Heat for 5 minutes. Yield: 10 servings.

Mary Aubry, Gamma Theta
Cedar Rapids, Iowa

TORTILLA SOUP

6 corn tortillas
1/2 cup vegetable oil
2 (10-ounce) cans condensed onion soup
1 (10-ounce) can Snap E Tom cocktail drink
1 1/2 cups water
1 (7-ounce) can green chili salsa
1/2 teaspoon coriander
2 cups grated Monterey Jack cheese

Cut tortillas into 1/2-inch strips. Heat oil in skillet. Fry strips until crisp and golden; drain. Combine onion soup, Snap E Tom cocktail drink, water, salsa and coriander in saucepan. Cook until bubbly. Place tortilla strips in 6 large soup bowls, dividing equally. Ladle soup over strips. Sprinkle cheese over top. Serve at once. Yield: 6 servings.

Lori Boyce, Xi Alpha
Polson, Montana

WILD RICE SOUP

1 cup wild rice
8 ounces crisp-fried bacon, crumbled
1 cup chopped onion
1/2 cup chopped carrots
1/2 cup chopped celery
1/2 teaspoon ground pepper
3 (10-ounce) cans cream of mushroom soup
2 (10-ounce) cans chicken soup with rice
5 soup cans milk

Cook rice according to package directions. Combine rice, bacon, onion, carrots, celery, pepper, soups and milk in 5-quart saucepan; mix well. Simmer for 1 hour. Serve hot. Yield: 12 servings.

Mary Ellen Carver, Preceptor Tau
Littleton, Colorado

♥ APPLE SALAD

1 large can apple pie filling
1 cup raisins, softened
1 cup chopped celery (optional)
1 cup vanilla yogurt
Cinnamon to taste
Sugar to taste

Place pie filling in large bowl. Add raisins, celery and yogurt; mix well. Add cinnamon and sugar. Chill until serving time. Yield: 6 servings.

Kay Thornton, Preceptor Mu Tau
Round Rock, Texas

APPLE-PEANUT SALAD

1 small can crushed pineapple
1/2 cup sugar
2 tablespoons cider vinegar
1 egg, beaten
1 tablespoon all-purpose flour
1 (8-ounce) container whipped topping
4 cups chopped, peeled Delicious apples
1 1/2 cups salted dry roasted peanuts

Drain pineapple, reserving juice. Combine reserved pineapple juice, sugar, vinegar, egg and flour in saucepan; mix well. Cook until thickened. Let cool. Add whipped topping. Fold in pineapple, apples and peanuts. Chill until serving time. Yield: 6 to 8 servings.

Helen Janz, Laureate Gamma
Wausau, Wisconsin

♥ APPLE SALAD DELUXE

4 red Delicious apples, chopped
4 bananas, sliced
1 (21-ounce) can peach pie filling
1 (16-ounce) can pineapple
1 cup miniature marshmallows
1/2 cup chopped nuts

Combine ingredients in order listed in bowl. Chill for 1 hour or serve immediately. Yield: 12 servings.

Betty Matschullat, Xi Alpha Chi
Lincoln, Nebraska

TAFFY APPLE SALAD

1 (20-ounce) can pineapple chunks
2 cups miniature marshmallows
1/2 cup sugar
1 tablespoon all-purpose flour
2 tablespoons vinegar
1 egg, beaten
6 to 7 cups cubed cored red and/or green apples
1 (8-ounce) container frozen whipped topping, thawed
1 (10-ounce) jar maraschino cherries, drained, cut into halves
1 cup peanuts

Drain pineapple, reserving juice. Mix pineapple chunks and marshmallows in large bowl. Chill, covered, for 24 hours. Combine sugar and flour in saucepan. Add reserved pineapple juice, vinegar and egg; mix well. Cook over medium heat just until mixture bubbles, stirring constantly. Reduce heat. Cook for 2 minutes longer, stirring constantly. Transfer mixture to small bowl. Cover surface of mixture with plastic wrap. Chill. To serve, add chilled dressing, apples, whipped topping, cherries and peanuts to marshmallow mixture; mix well. Yield: 20 servings.

Gloria Elsbernd, Beta Delta
Calmar, Iowa

CRANBERRY SALAD

1 (6-ounce) package strawberry gelatin
1 cup boiling water
1 can whole cranberry sauce
1/4 cup chopped nuts
1/2 cup chopped celery
1/4 cup chopped apple
1 (6-ounce) package lemon gelatin
1 1/4 cups boiling water
3 ounces cream cheese, softened
1/4 cup mayonnaise
1 1/4 cups whipped topping

Dissolve strawberry gelatin in 1 cup boiling water in bowl. Chill until consistency of egg whites. Fold in cranberry sauce, nuts, celery and apple. Pour into 9-by-10-inch glass dish. Let set until partially thickened. Dissolve lemon gelatin in 1 1/4 cups boiling water in mixer bowl. Chill until consistency of egg whites. Beat in cream cheese and mayonnaise until smooth. Fold in whipped topping. Pour over layer in glass dish. Chill for several hours. Yield: 16 servings.

Arleen Dubbé, Preceptor Alpha Beta
Morgantown, West Virginia

ORANGE SALAD BOWL

1/3 cup sugar
1 teaspoon salt
1 teaspoon dry mustard
1/3 cup vinegar
1 small onion, chopped
1 cup vegetable oil
1 tablespoon celery seeds
1 purple onion, sliced
8 cups torn salad greens
2 cups orange sections or 2 cans mandarin oranges, drained
1 cup sunflower seeds, chopped pecans or peanuts

Combine first 7 ingredients in bowl; mix well. Chill. Separate onion slices into rings. Combine onion and remaining ingredients in salad bowl. Pour dressing over salad mixture. Toss gently. Yield: 12 servings.

Evelyn D. Hill, Nu
Amarillo, Texas

PINEAPPLE-RASPBERRY-BEET SALAD

1 can crushed pineapple
2 cans shoestring beets
3 tablespoons lemon juice
1/4 cup white vinegar
1/4 cup sugar
1 (6-ounce) package raspberry gelatin
8 ounces cream cheese, softened

Drain pineapple and beets, reserving juices. Combine 3 cups reserved juices, lemon juice, vinegar and sugar in saucepan. Bring to a boil. Add gelatin, stirring to dissolve. Add pineapple and beets. Pour into 9-by-12-inch glass serving dish. Chill until set. Garnish with cream cheese. Yield: 20 servings.

Winona Parsons, Xi Lambda Iota
Steinhatchee, Florida

FROSTED FRUIT SALAD

1 large can juice-packed crushed pineapple
1 (6-ounce) package lemon gelatin
2 cups boiling water
2 cups 7-Up
2 or 3 large bananas, chopped
2 cups miniature marshmallows
2 tablespoons all-purpose flour
1/2 cup sugar
1 egg, beaten
2 tablespoons butter or margarine
1 cup whipping cream, whipped
1 cup grated sharp Cheddar cheese

Drain pineapple, reserving juice. Dissolve gelatin in boiling water in bowl. Add 7-Up. Pour into 9-by-12-inch dish. Chill until syrupy. Stir in pineapple, bananas and marshmallows. Chill until firm. Combine flour and sugar in saucepan. Beat in egg. Add reserved pineapple juice. Cook, stirring, over low heat until thickened. Remove from heat. Add butter, stirring until melted. Pour into bowl; chill. Whip cream until stiff. Blend into cooked mixture. Spread over congealed layer. Sprinkle cheese over top. Chill for several hours. Cut into squares. Yield: 12 servings.

Elsie Sheedy, Laureate Xi
Northport, Washington

FRUIT SALAD

1 (20-ounce) can chunk pineapple
1 (11-ounce) can mandarin oranges
1 (3-ounce) package vanilla pudding mix
1 (3-ounce) package tapioca pudding mix
12 maraschino cherries, cut into halves
2 bananas, sliced

Drain pineapple and oranges, reserving juices. Add enough water to juices to equal 3 cups liquid. Combine pudding mixes and liquid in saucepan. Cook according to package directions. Let cool. Add fruit. Pour into 1 1/2-quart glass dish. Chill. Yield: 8 to 10 servings.

Patty Dewalt, Xi Alpha Mu
Terre Haute, Indiana

♥ PARFAIT FRUIT PLATE

2 envelopes plain gelatin
1/4 cup cold water
1 cup boiling water
2/3 cup sugar
24 ounces no-fat cottage cheese
8 ounces no-fat lemon yogurt
1 (9-ounce) container low-fat frozen whipped topping, slightly thawed
Spinach leaves
Bibb lettuce leaves
Fresh fruits

Mix gelatin and cold water in large mixer bowl. Add boiling water. Stir to dissolve gelatin. Add sugar; mix well. Add cottage cheese and yogurt, mixing well with wire whisk. Whip topping into cottage cheese mixture. Pour into large gelatin mold or individual molds. Chill until set. Arrange spinach and lettuce leaves on plate. Unmold gelatin gently onto center of plate. Garnish with fresh fruits. Yield: 10 servings.

Joyce A. Lane, Preceptor Alpha Gamma
Ionia, Michigan

♥ LAYERED FRUIT SALAD WITH YOGURT DRESSING

1 cup seedless grapes, cut into halves
3 bananas, sliced
3 unpeeled apples, cored, chopped
1 (15-ounce) can pineapple tidbits with juice
1/2 cup raisins
1/2 cup chopped dried apricots
1 orange, peeled, sliced, seeded
1/2 cup plain yogurt
1/4 cup undiluted frozen orange juice concentrate, thawed
1/4 cup sugar

Layer grapes, bananas, apples, pineapple, raisins, apricots and orange attractively in glass bowl. Combine yogurt, orange juice concentrate and sugar in bowl; mix well. Pour over fruit. Do not stir. Yield: 8 to 10 servings.

Marilyn R. Buchele, Preceptor Gamma Chi
Emporia, Kansas

ORIENTAL FRUIT SALAD AND DRESSING

1 (8-ounce) can sliced pineapple
1 (8-ounce) can apricot halves
1 (11-ounce) can mandarin oranges
1 banana, sliced
Shredded lettuce
1/4 cup peanut butter
1/4 cup mayonnaise
4 to 6 maraschino cherries

Drain canned fruit, reserving juices in bowl. Let banana slices float in juices; drain. Arrange lettuce, pineapple, apricots, oranges and banana slices on salad plates. Combine peanut butter, mayonnaise and reserved fruit juices to make thick salad dressing. Spoon dressing over salad. Top with cherry. Serve with oriental foods. Yield: 4 to 6 servings.

Esther Westfall, Preceptor Omega
Grand Island, New York

ELEGANT WARM SIRLOIN SALAD

2 1/4 cups water
1 package long grain and wild rice pilaf mix
1/2 cup fresh lemon juice
1/3 cup extra light olive oil
4 cloves of garlic, crushed
Salt and pepper to taste
1/2 cup pecan halves
1 pound beef top sirloin steak, cut into 4-ounce pieces
1 (6-ounce) jar marinated artichoke hearts
8 cups mixed salad greens, broken into bite-sized pieces

Preheat grill. Combine water and rice mix in medium saucepan. Bring to a boil over high heat; cover. Reduce heat to simmer. Cook for 25 minutes or until water is absorbed. Remove from heat. Let stand at room temperature. Preheat oven to broil. Combine lemon juice, olive oil and garlic in small bowl. Season with salt and pepper. Reserve 1/4 cup dressing for basting steaks. Toast pecans under broiler; set aside. Season steaks with salt and pepper. Grill steaks to desired doneness, basting once with reserved dressing. Combine remaining dressing with cooked rice, toasted pecans and artichoke hearts in large bowl. Toss lightly to mix. Arrange mixed greens on 4 dinner-sized plates, dividing equally. Top greens with bed of rice mixture. Carve grilled steak into thin slices. Fan steak slices on top of rice mixture. Serve immediately. Yield: 4 servings.

Lucille Bredy, Laureate Rho
Homedale, Idaho

Winnie Davies, Preceptor Beta Eta, Monmouth, Oregon, makes Honey-Mustard Dressing by combining 1 cup vegetable oil, 1/2 cup vinegar, 3/4 cup Dijon mustard, 3/4 cup honey, 1 teaspoon chopped garlic and dash of pepper in bowl; mix well. Store, covered, in refrigerator. Makes 3 1/2 cups.

♥ FRUIT AND CHICKEN SALAD

16 ounces chicken breast strips
1/2 cup plain low-fat yogurt
1/4 cup reduced-fat mayonnaise
1/4 teaspoon ground cinnamon
3/4 cup unsweetened apple juice
3/4 cup water
2 cups long grain and wild rice
3/4 cup chopped MacIntosh apple
1/2 cup sliced celery
1/2 cup chopped pecans
25 to 30 small seedless red grapes
Spinach leaves or fresh fruit

Rinse chicken pieces; pat dry. Combine yogurt, mayonnaise and cinnamon in small bowl. Cover and chill. Combine chicken, apple juice and water in saucepan. Simmer, covered, over medium heat for 15 to 20 minutes or until chicken tests done. Remove chicken from pan; reserve pan juices. Cut chicken into 1/2-inch cubes. Place in bowl; cover and chill. Cook rice according to package directions, adding enough water to pan juices to equal amount of liquid needed. Toss rice, apple, celery, pecans and grapes together gently in bowl. Stir in chicken and yogurt mixture. Chill until serving time. Garnish with spinach leaves or fresh fruit slices. Yield: 6 servings.

Brenda Mack, Theta Sigma
Hays, Kansas

CHICKEN-PINEAPPLE SALAD

1 (8-ounce) can crushed pineapple with juice
2 teaspoons cornstarch
1/4 teaspoon ground ginger
1/4 teaspoon salt
1/3 cup mayonnaise
1 cup chopped cooked white chicken
1/4 cup chopped green bell pepper
1/4 cup sliced almonds, toasted

Combine pineapple, cornstarch, ginger and salt in small saucepan. Cook for 2 minutes or until thickened. Let cool. Add mayonnaise. Combine chicken, green pepper and almonds in bowl. Add mayonnaise mixture; mix well. Chill. Yield: 2 to 4 servings.

Joanne Melzow, Xi Epsilon
Plano, Texas

CHICKEN SOUP SALAD

2 (10-ounce) cans chicken-rice soup
2 packages sugar-free lemon gelatin
1 cup mayonnaise-type salad dressing
1 cup nondairy whipped topping
2 tablespoons chopped onion
2 cups chopped celery
1 cup chopped walnuts
2 cups chopped cooked chicken or turkey
Lettuce leaves

Bring soup to a boil in saucepan. Pour over gelatin in bowl, stirring until gelatin is dissolved. Let cool until partially set. Whip gelatin mixture until frothy. Add salad dressing, whipped topping, onion, celery, walnuts and chicken; mix well. Pour into 9-by-13-inch pan; chill until set. Cut into squares. Serve on lettuce leaves. Yield: 15 servings.

Florence Helle, Preceptor Phi
Luverne, Minnesota

TROPICANA SALAD

2 cups cubed cooked chicken
1 cup chopped celery
1 cup mayonnaise-type salad dressing
1/2 to 1 teaspoon curry powder
1 (20-ounce) can pineapple chunks, drained
2 large firm bananas, sliced
1 (11-ounce) can mandarin oranges, drained
1/2 cup flaked coconut
3/4 cup cashew halves
Spinach leaves or salad greens

Place chicken and celery in large bowl. Combine salad dressing and curry powder in small bowl. Add to chicken mixture; mix well. Chill, covered, for 30 minutes. Add pineapple, bananas, oranges, coconut and cashews just before serving; toss gently. Serve on spinach leaves. Yield: 4 servings.

Rita Sovanski, Xi Epsilon Delta
Topeka, Kansas

✣ ♥ GRILLED CHICKEN CAESAR SALAD

1 boneless skinless chicken breast
1 clove of garlic, cut in half
Worcestershire sauce
2 cups shredded lettuce
1/2 red bell pepper, sliced into strips
1/2 green bell pepper, sliced into strips
1 carrot, thinly sliced
2 medium mushrooms, thinly sliced
2 tablespoons grated Parmesan or Romano cheese
2 tablespoons crumbled bleu cheese
2 to 4 tablespoons croutons
2 tablespoons olive oil
1 1/2 tablespoons white or cider vinegar
1 teaspoon Dijon mustard
1/4 teaspoon white pepper
1/4 teaspoon salt
1 1/2 tablespoons water

Preheat oven to broil. Pound chicken to flatten. Rub sides with garlic; discard garlic. Brush sides lightly with Worcestershire sauce. Place on rack in broiler pan. Broil until done, turning once and basting again with sauce. Cut chicken into long thin strips. Divide lettuce into 2 bowls. Arrange peppers, carrot and mushrooms over lettuce. Add chicken. Sprinkle Parmesan and bleu cheese over chicken. Top bowls with croutons. Combine remaining ingredients in small bowl. Mix briskly with whisk. Drizzle lightly over salad using small spoon. Yield: 2 servings.

Betsy Fisher, Laureate Omicron
Nashville, Tennessee

FAJITA CHICKEN SALAD

2 boneless skinless chicken breasts	1 1/2 cups shredded Colby or Monterey Jack cheese
1/4 cup chopped onion	
1 envelope fajita marinade	1 medium tomato, chopped
Tortilla chips	Sour cream
4 to 5 cups shredded lettuce	Picante sauce
	Guacamole (optional)

Cut chicken into bite-sized pieces. Place chicken and onion in shallow dish. Prepare fajita marinade according to package directions. Pour 1/2 the marinade over chicken. Let marinate for 15 minutes. Refrigerate remaining marinade for later use. Arrange chips on 2 large plates. Top with lettuce, cheese and tomato. Sauté chicken and onion in hot skillet. Arrange chicken over salad. Serve with sour cream, picante sauce and guacamole. Yield: 2 servings.

Karen Starks, Xi Zeta
Anthony, Kansas

TORTELINI-CHICKEN SALAD

1 (16-ounce) package American mixtures San Francisco-style frozen broccoli, carrots, water chestnuts and red peppers	3 cups cubed cooked chicken
	1 (8-ounce) bottle prepared Italian dressing
	2 tablespoons freshly grated Parmesan cheese
1 (9-ounce) package refrigerated uncooked cheese tortelini	

Cook vegetables according to package directions until crisp-tender; drain. Cook tortelini according to package directions. Rinse in cold water. Combine vegetables, tortelini, chicken and dressing in large bowl. Toss gently to coat. Refrigerate, covered, until well chilled. Sprinkle with cheese just before serving. Yield: 6 servings.

Tammy Smith, Xi Mu Gamma
Lincoln, Illinois

♥ HONEY MUSTARD-TURKEY SALAD

1/2 cup fat-free mayonnaise	1/2 cup chopped celery
2 tablespoons honey	2 small or 1 large apple, cored, cubed
1 1/2 tablespoons Dijon mustard	1/4 green bell pepper, chopped
3/4 teaspoon lite soy sauce	1/4 cup toasted almonds or cashews
3/4 teaspoon lemon juice	1/2 cup raisins or 1 cup red seedless grapes
2 cups chopped cooked turkey	Lettuce leaves
1/4 cup chopped green onions	Chopped nuts or chow mein noodles

Mix mayonnaise, honey, mustard, soy sauce and lemon juice in small bowl. Combine next 7 ingredients in large bowl. Add honey-mustard sauce; mix well. Chill for 2 hours. Serve on lettuce leaves. Garnish with nuts. Yield: 4 to 6 servings.

Karen Witzel, Xi Beta Lambda
Randolph, New Jersey

CLUB SALAD

1 package cherry tomatoes, cut into halves	2 cups seasoned croutons
	4 ounces ham, cubed
2 to 3 cups shredded lettuce	4 ounces Monterey Jack cheese, cubed
1 cup ranch dressing	4 ounces turkey, cubed
1 large tomato, seeded, chopped	1 cup ranch dressing with bacon

Place cherry tomato halves up against side of 3-quart clear glass salad bowl. Layer lettuce, 1 cup ranch dressing, chopped tomato, croutons, ham, cheese and turkey in bowl, making distinct layers. Pour remaining dressing over top. Yield: 4 to 6 servings.

Mrs. Donna Hoendorf, Preceptor Gamma Upsilon
Gladstone, Missouri

ORIENTAL SEAFOOD SALAD

1/2 head lettuce, chopped	2 tablespoons sesame seed
1/2 head cabbage, chopped	1/4 cup vinegar
6 to 8 green onions, chopped	1/4 cup vegetable oil
	2 tablespoons water
1 package top ramen noodles	1/4 cup sugar
1/2 cup sliced almonds	1 envelope top ramen seasoning
3/4 to 1 pound crab meat	

Combine lettuce, cabbage, green onions, ramen, almonds, crab meat and sesame seed in large salad bowl. Blend remaining ingredients in small bowl; mix well. Pour over salad mixture; toss. Chill for 30 minutes to 1 hour. Yield: 10 to 12 servings.

Debbie Doran, Gamma Upsilon
Moses Lake, Washington

SEAFOOD-WILD RICE SALAD

1/2 cup mayonnaise	12 ounces crab meat, chopped
1 tablespoon lemon juice	
1 teaspoon curry powder	2 (4-ounce) cans tiny shrimp
2 cups cold cooked wild rice	Salad greens
1/2 cup frozen peas	Cherry tomatoes

Combine mayonnaise, lemon juice and curry powder in bowl; mix well. Add rice, peas, crab meat and shrimp; mix well. Chill for 1 hour. Spoon on salad greens. Garnish with tomatoes. Yield: 4 servings.

VaLynn Mednansky, Lambda
Belle Fourche, South Dakota

SHELLFISH-PASTA SALAD

1/4 cup chopped parsley
2 cloves of garlic, crushed
1/2 teaspoon salt
1/4 teaspoon pepper
1 cup plain yogurt
1 (7-ounce) package small seashell macaroni
1 onion, finely chopped
1 cup cubed Edam or Gouda cheese
1/2 cup bread and butter pickles, chopped
Paprika to taste
Dill to taste
Beau Monde seasoning to taste
Lemon juice to taste
Mayonnaise to taste
12 ounces imitation crab meat

Combine parsley, garlic, salt, pepper and yogurt in small bowl; mix well. Cook macaroni according to package directions; drain. Combine macaroni, onion, cheese and pickles in salad bowl. Add yogurt mixture, seasonings, lemon juice and mayonnaise; mix well. Fold in crab meat. Chill for 2 hours or overnight. Yield: 8 servings.

Jo Ann Hansler, Laureate Beta Omega
Port Orchard, Washington

SHRIMP AND RICE SALAD

2 (5-ounce) packages sesame chicken rice
4 green onions with tops, chopped
1/2 green bell pepper, chopped
2 (6-ounce) jars marinated artichoke hearts
1 pound shrimp, boiled, peeled
1/2 teaspoon curry powder
1/2 cup lite mayonnaise

Cook rice according to package directions. Let cool. Combine rice, onions and green pepper in bowl. Drain artichoke hearts, reserving juice. Add artichokes and shrimp to rice mixture. Combine reserved juice, curry powder and mayonnaise in bowl; mix well. Pour over rice mixture. Chill for 24 hours. Yield: 8 servings.

Loraine Saylor, Xi Gamma Nu
Dallas, Texas

WARM SALMON AND ASPARAGUS SALAD

1 pound fresh asparagus or broccoli flowerets
1 (15-ounce) can salmon
1 head iceberg lettuce, shredded
1 carrot, julienned (optional)
4 cherry tomatoes (optional)
1/3 cup vegetable oil
1/4 cup apple cider vinegar
1/4 cup finely chopped onion
2 tablespoons chopped fresh parsley
2 tablespoons lemon juice
1 teaspoon grated lemon rind
1 teaspoon sugar
1/2 teaspoon salt
1/2 teaspoon dried basil
1/4 teaspoon pepper

Cook asparagus in small amount of water until tender-crisp. Drain salmon, reserving 1/4 cup liquid. Place lettuce and salmon on 4 serving plates. Arrange asparagus on top. Garnish with carrot and tomatoes. Combine reserved salmon liquid and remaining ingredients in saucepan. Bring to a boil over medium-high heat, stirring occasionally. Pour hot dressing over individual salads. Serve immediately. Yield: 4 servings.

Terry Flesher, Laureate
Kingston, Ontario, Canada

TUNA "JELLY" SALAD

1 cup chopped celery
1 cup shredded carrot
3/4 cup chopped green bell pepper
6 hard-cooked eggs, chopped
6 tablespoons chopped green pimento
3 (6-ounce) cans tuna in water, drained
3/4 cup cold water
3 envelopes plain gelatin
2 cups mayonnaise
1 1/2 teaspoons salt
1 1/2 teaspoons paprika
3 tablespoons white vinegar

Combine celery, carrot, green pepper, eggs, pimento and tuna in bowl. Place cold water in top of double boiler. Sprinkle gelatin in water. Place over boiling water. Stir until gelatin is dissolved. Let cool slightly. Add to tuna mixture; mix well. Pour into 9-by-13-inch serving dish. Chill until set. Yield: 10 to 12 servings.

Dorothy Sumner, Delta Master
Ogden, Utah

LAYERED GARDEN PASTA SALAD

1 (8-ounce) package macaroni shells
1/2 cup sliced green onions
4 tablespoons bacon bits
1/4 cup lemon juice concentrate
1 cup mayonnaise
1 (2-ounce) envelope dry ranch dressing mix
3 tablespoons grated Parmesan cheese
1 teaspoon sugar
1/2 teaspoon garlic powder
3 cups shredded lettuce
1 cucumber, sliced
1 green bell pepper, chopped
2 medium tomatoes, cut into wedges

Cook macaroni according to package directions. Rinse with cold water; drain. Combine macaroni, green onions and 2 tablespoons bacon bits in bowl. Combine lemon juice concentrate, mayonnaise, dressing mix, cheese, sugar and garlic powder in separate bowl; mix well. Layer lettuce, macaroni mixture, cucumber and green pepper in large clear salad bowl. Pour dressing evenly over top. Garnish with tomato wedges and remaining bacon bits. Yield: 10 servings.

Brenda Raven, Pi Nu
Hays, Kansas

RUSH PARTY PASTA SALAD

1 (12-ounce) package corkscrew pasta
1 (20-ounce) can pineapple chunks
1 cup vegetable oil
1/2 cup white vinegar
1 tablespoon Dijon mustard
1 clove of garlic, mashed
1 tablespoon Worcestershire sauce
Salt and pepper to taste
3 cups cauliflowerets
3 cups broccoli flowerets
1 red bell pepper, chopped
1 cup toasted almonds

Cook pasta according to package directions. Drain pineapple, reserving 3 tablespoons juice. Combine reserved juice, oil, vinegar, mustard, garlic, Worcestershire sauce, salt and pepper in screw-top jar; shake well. Combine pasta and cauliflower in large bowl. Add dressing; toss. Marinate, covered, in refrigerator overnight. Add broccoli, red pepper and almonds; toss and serve. Yield: 12 to 15 servings.

Nancie J. Williams, Preceptor Beta Omega
Emporia, Kansas

♥ LASAGNA SALAD

4 lasagna noodles, cooked, drained
1 teaspoon olive oil
16 fresh spinach leaves
2 cups low-fat cottage cheese
1 cup shredded low-fat mozzarella cheese
4 cloves of garlic, finely chopped
12 fresh basil leaves
Fresh ground black pepper to taste
Fresh Tomato Dressing

Place noodles on damp cloth towel. Brush each noodle gently with oil. Rinse spinach; pat dry. Chop spinach coarsely. Combine spinach, cottage cheeese, mozzarella cheese and garlic in bowl; blend well. Spread spinach mixture gently over noodles. Place basil over spinach mixture. Season with pepper. Fold 1 end of each gently over filling. Roll noodle into neat round package, enclosing filling. Serve lasagna rolls with Fresh Tomato Dressing. Yield: 4 servings.

FRESH TOMATO DRESSING

2 ripe tomatoes, chopped
1 stalk celery, chopped
1 carrot, grated
1/2 sweet red pepper, seeded, chopped
1/2 sweet green pepper, seeded, chopped
1/4 cup sliced green onions
2 cloves of garlic, finely chopped
1/4 cup balsamic or red wine vinegar
2 tablespoons olive oil

Combine tomatoes, celery, carrot, red and green peppers, green onions, garlic, balsamic vinegar and oil in medium bowl. Stir dressing thoroughly just before using. May store in refrigerator for up to 3 days. Yield: 2 1/2 cups.

Nina L. Slaton, Laureate Gamma Tau
Lubbock, Texas

TORTELINI SALAD

1 (7-ounce) package cheese tortelini
1 cup fresh broccoli flowerets
1/2 cup chopped parsley
1 tablespoon chopped pimento or red pepper
1 (6-ounce) jar marinated artichokes
2 green onions, chopped
2 1/2 teaspoons chopped fresh basil
1/2 teaspoon garlic powder
1/2 cup Italian salad dressing
Parmesan cheese
Cherry tomatoes

Cook tortelini according to package directions; rinse. Combine tortelini and next 8 ingredients in large bowl. Refrigerate, covered, for 4 to 6 hours. Sprinkle with Parmesan cheese just before serving. Garnish with cherry tomatoes. Yield: 6 servings.

Marjorie Dykstra, Xi Mu
Londonderry, New Hampshire

♥ BLACK BEAN, CORN AND PEPPER SALAD

2 cans black beans, drained, rinsed
1 1/2 cups cooked fresh corn or 1 (10-ounce) package frozen corn, thawed
1 large red bell pepper, finely chopped
2 small fresh jalapeño peppers, seeded, finely chopped
1/2 cup firmly packed chopped cilantro
1/4 cup lime juice
2 tablespoons vegetable oil
Salt and pepper to taste
Lettuce leaves, rinsed, crisped
Lime wedges
Cilantro sprigs (optional)

Combine beans, corn, red bell pepper, jalapeño peppers, cilantro, lime juice and oil in large bowl; mix lightly. Season with salt and pepper. Chill, covered, for 1 to 24 hours. Line serving bowl with lettuce leaves. Spoon mixture into bowl. Garnish with lime wedges and cilantro sprigs. Yield: 6 servings.

Tanya Gunnels, Xi Eta Nu
College Station, Texas

FRESH BROCCOLI SALAD

1 (1-ounce) envelope dry Italian dressing mix
1 medium bunch broccoli, chopped
1 (15-ounce) can dark red kidney beans
1 small red onion, finely chopped
1 cup grated sharp Cheddar cheese

Prepare dressing according to package directions. Combine broccoli, beans, onion and cheese in large bowl. Pour dressing over salad; mix gently. Cover tightly. Refrigerate for 4 hours or overnight. Yield: 8 servings.

Sharon Popp, Xi Theta Zeta
Gilbert, Iowa

♥ CHICK-PEA-FRESH BASIL AND SWEET PEPPER SALAD

1 sweet red pepper
1 (19-ounce) can chick-peas, drained
1 cup chopped cucumbers
1/4 cup packed chopped fresh parsley
1/4 cup minced red onion
1/4 cup packed chopped fresh basil
1/4 cup lemon juice
1 tablespoon olive oil
1 clove of garlic, minced
Salt and pepper to taste

Roast red pepper over grill, turning often, for 15 minutes or until blackened and soft. Peel and seed; chop coarsely. Combine red pepper and next 5 ingredients in salad bowl. Whisk lemon juice, oil, garlic, salt and pepper in bowl. Pour over salad; toss lightly. Chill, covered, for 1 to 24 hours. Yield: 8 servings.

Alison M. Lawlor, Beta Master
Saskatoon, Saskatchewan, Canada

CORN MEDLEY SALAD

3 cups fresh corn
1 cup chopped onion
2 cups cubed zucchini
1 bunch spring onions, sliced
1 1/2 cups chopped red, yellow or green peppers
1 cup chopped broccoli
2/3 cup vegetable oil
1/3 cup white vinegar
1/2 teaspoon salt
1/2 teaspoon pepper
1 tablespoon sugar
1 clove of garlic, minced
1/2 teaspoon Worcestershire sauce
1 teaspoon hot sauce
1 teaspoon mustard

Place corn in saucepan. Add water to cover. Cook, covered, for 10 minutes. Drain; let cool. Combine corn and remaining vegetables in salad bowl. Combine remaining ingredients in small bowl. Pour over vegetables; toss. Serve cold. Yield: 12 servings.

Joyce A. Herian, Preceptor Gamma
Annandale, Virginia

♥ CORN SALAD MOLD

2 cups water
1/4 cup cider vinegar
2 tablespoons Dijon mustard
2 (3-ounce) packages lemon gelatin
1/2 cup chopped red bell pepper
1/2 cup chopped green bell pepper
1 (15-ounce) can whole-kernel corn, drained
1/2 cup chopped green onions
Lettuce leaves

Mix water, vinegar and mustard in saucepan. Sprinkle gelatin over vinegar mixture. Cook over low heat, stirring until gelatin is dissolved. Pour mixture into bowl. Chill, covered, for 1 1/2 hours or until partially congealed. Fold in peppers, corn and green onions. Spoon into 8-inch square dish, coated with vegetable cooking spray. Chill, covered, until firm. Serve on lettuce-lined plates. Yield: 9 servings.

Lenore C. Longnecker, Xi Sigma Mu
Sierra Blanca, Texas

♥ CUCUMBER-YOGURT SALAD

1 sweet white onion
1 cup water
2 tablespoons sugar
2 tablespoons vinegar
3 to 6 drops of hot pepper sauce
1 1/2 teaspoons salt
2 English cucumbers, thinly sliced
1 cup low-fat yogurt
2 tablespoons chopped fresh dillweed

Slice onion into thin slices. Separate into rings. Combine water, 1 tablespoon sugar, vinegar, pepper sauce and 1 teaspoon salt in large glass bowl. Stir until sugar is dissolved. Add cucumber and onion. Place small plate on top mixture; weigh down with heavy can. Chill for 4 hours or overnight. Drain well. Mix yogurt, dillweed, remaining sugar and salt in salad bowl. Add cucumber mixture; toss. Yield: 6 servings.

Gerrie Wise, Laureate Beta Gamma
Langley, British Columbia, Canada

♥ ORIENTAL MUSHROOM SALAD

2 teaspoons honey
2 teaspoons reduced-sodium soy sauce
1/4 teaspoon ground ginger
2 teaspoons red wine vinegar
2 teaspoons oriental sesame or peanut oil
1 clove of garlic, bruised
8 ounces mushrooms, thinly sliced
1 small sweet red pepper, chopped
2 teaspoons minced fresh coriander or parsley
1 teaspoon toasted sesame seed

Whisk honey, soy sauce, ginger, vinegar and sesame oil in bowl. Add garlic, mushrooms and red pepper; toss well. Chill, covered, for 2 hours. Remove garlic; discard. Transfer to serving plate. Sprinkle with coriander and sesame seed. Yield: 2 servings.

Connie Steward, Beta Pi
Lakeview, Oregon

♥ CALICO POTATO SALAD

1/2 cup olive oil
1/4 cup vinegar
1 tablespoon sugar
1 1/2 teaspoons chili powder
1 teaspoon salt
Dash of hot pepper sauce
4 large peeled red potatoes, cooked, cubed
1 1/2 cups cooked whole-kernel corn
1 cup shredded carrot
1/2 cup chopped red onion
1/2 cup chopped green bell pepper
1/2 cup chopped red sweet pepper
1/2 cup sliced pitted black olives

Combine oil, vinegar, sugar, chili powder, salt and pepper sauce in bowl. Cover; chill. Combine remaining ingredients in salad bowl. Pour dressing over mixture; toss lightly. Cover; chill. Yield: 14 servings.

Tara Smith, Alpha Rho Theta
Friendswood, Texas

♥ LOW-FAT SOUR CREAM-POTATO SALAD

7 medium potatoes, cooked in jackets
1/3 cup low-fat Italian dressing
3/4 cup chopped celery
1/3 cup sliced green onions with tops
4 hard-cooked eggs
3/4 cup nonfat mayonnaise
3/4 cup fat-free sour cream
1 1/2 teaspoons horseradish mustard
Salt and pepper to taste

Peel and cube potatoes. Place in salad bowl. Pour dressing over warm potatoes. Chill for 2 hours. Chop egg whites. Add celery, green onions and egg whites to potatoes. Sieve 2 egg yolks into small bowl. Reserve 2 egg yolks for another use. Combine egg yolks, mayonnaise, sour cream and mustard in small bowl; mix well. Fold into salad. Add salt and pepper to taste. Chill for 6 hours. Yield: 12 servings.

Martha J. Gwinn, Xi Eta Pi
Davie, Florida

HONEY-SPINACH SALAD

1/2 teaspoon salt
1 clove of garlic
1 cup honey
1/3 cup olive oil
1 tablespoon lemon juice
12 ounces fresh spinach
1 (11-ounce) can mandarin oranges, drained
3/4 cup toasted walnuts, coarsely chopped

Sprinkle salt in large bowl. Add garlic. Mash garlic to paste consistency, using back of spoon. Combine honey, olive oil and lemon juice in jar with tight-fitting lid; shake vigorously. Add honey mixture to garlic mixture; stir well. Chill, covered, for at least 2 hours. Remove stems from spinach. Wash leaves; cut into bite-sized pieces. Combine spinach, oranges and walnuts in large bowl; toss well. Pour honey mixture over salad, tossing to coat. Yield: 4 servings.

France McIntyre, Kappa Alpha
Pembroke, Ontario, Canada

KOREAN SPINACH SALAD

1 1/2 pounds fresh spinach
8 ounces fresh bean sprouts
1 (8-ounce) can water chestnuts, drained, sliced
5 slices bacon
2/3 cup vegetable oil
1/4 cup sugar
1/3 cup catsup
1/3 cup white wine vinegar
1/3 cup chopped green onions
2 teaspoons Worcestershire sauce
Salt and pepper to taste
2 hard-cooked eggs, sliced

Trim spinach; discard tough stems. Rinse leaves; pat dry. Tear into bite-sized pieces. Combine spinach, bean sprouts and water chestnuts in large bowl. Fry bacon until crisp; drain. Crumble bacon into spinach mixture. Cover and chill. Combine next 6 ingredients in jar with lid; shake well. Chill. Pour dressing over salad just before serving; toss. Sprinkle with salt and pepper. Garnish with egg slices. Yield: 6 servings.

Michelle Bullington, Alpha Alpha Gamma
Redding, California

WARM ALMOND-SPINACH SALAD

10 ounces fresh spinach, rinsed, drained
8 ounces bacon, chopped
1/2 cup slivered almonds
8 ounces mushrooms, sliced
1/4 cup balsamic vinegar
2 tablespoons Dijon mustard
1/2 cup grated Swiss cheese
Pinch of salt
Ground black pepper to taste

Tear spinach into bite-sized pieces. Place in heat-proof salad bowl. Fry bacon in skillet; drain. Reserve pan drippings in skillet. Add almonds. Cook for 5 minutes or until golden; remove from skillet. Add mushrooms to drippings. Sauté for 4 minutes; remove from skillet. Add mushrooms to spinach. Add vinegar to skillet. Cook, stirring, for 1 minute or until vinegar is reduced by half. Stir in mustard. Remove from heat. Drizzle over spinach and mushroom mixture; toss. Add bacon and almonds. Cover salad bowl with warm skillet for 1 minute or until leaves begin to wilt. Add cheese, salt and pepper. Serve immediately. Yield: 6 servings.

Cathy Cole, Xi Alpha Alpha
Dawson Creek, British Columbia, Canada

CALICO SALAD

1 cup small shell macaroni
1 (15-ounce) can green beans, drained
1 (15-ounce) can kidney beans, drained
1 (15-ounce) can wax beans, drained
1 small can mushroom pieces, drained
Salt to taste
1 green bell pepper, chopped
1 small jar pimentos, drained, chopped
1 small onion, chopped
2 cups sugar
1/2 cup vegetable oil
1 cup vinegar

Cook macaroni according to package directions; drain. Combine beans and mushroom pieces in large bowl. Add salt. Add macaroni, green pepper, pimentos and onion; toss lightly. Place in flat container. Combine sugar, oil and vinegar in saucepan. Bring to a boil. Remove from heat; let cool. Pour over vegetable mixture. Let marinate in refrigerator overnight or for several days. Yield: 6 to 8 servings.

Moonyenne Harshman, Preceptor Epsilon Theta
St. Petersburg, Florida

♥ CREAMY CAESAR SALAD

1/2 (300-gram) package soft tofu
1 clove of garlic, minced
1 teaspoon Worcestershire sauce
1 teaspoon Dijon mustard
2 tablespoons anchovy paste
2 tablespoons lemon juice
3 tablespoons plus 1 teaspoon olive oil
2 tablespoons Parmesan cheese
Dash of salt and pepper
1 head romaine lettuce
1 cup croutons
2 tablespoons Parmesan cheese

Place tofu, garlic, Worcestershire sauce, mustard, anchovy paste, lemon juice, olive oil and 2 tablespoons Parmesan cheese in blender container. Add salt and pepper. Blend until smooth and creamy. Tear lettuce into bite-sized pieces. Place in salad bowl. Add dressing and croutons; toss. Sprinkle 2 tablespoons Parmesan cheese over salad. Yield: 6 servings.

Angie Wood, Zeta Gamma
Port Hardy, British Columbia, Canada

♥ LOW-FAT CAESAR SALAD

1/2 cup low-fat cottage cheese
1 clove of garlic, chopped
1 tablespoon lemon juice
2 tablespoons water
2 tablespoons skim milk
3 tablespoons olive oil
2 tablespoons Parmesan cheese
Salt and pepper to taste
1 head romaine lettuce

Combine cottage cheese, garlic, lemon juice, water, skim milk and olive oil in food processor container. Process until smooth. Add Parmesan cheese, salt and pepper. Tear lettuce into bite-sized pieces. Place in salad bowl. Add dressing; toss. Yield: 6 servings.

Betty Smith, Xi Epsilon Iota
Mississauga, Ontario, Canada

♣ GREEK SALAD WITH OREGANO DRESSING

1 tablespoon red wine vinegar
2 teaspoons fresh lemon juice
1 clove of garlic, pressed
1/2 teaspoon salt
1/2 teaspoon dried oregano
Pinch of cinnamon
1/4 teaspoon ground pepper
1/4 cup olive oil
1 large head romaine lettuce
1 pound feta cheese
1 medium cucumber, sliced
2 1/2 cups whole cherry tomatoes
4 ounces black Greek olives
4 ounces green Greek olives
1 small green pepper, chopped
1 avocado, sliced
1 red onion, sliced
Salt and pepper to taste

Combine vinegar, lemon juice, garlic, salt, oregano, cinnamon, pepper and olive oil in jar with tight-fitting lid; shake to mix thoroughly. Tear lettuce into bite-sized pieces. Place in salad bowl. Season with small amount of dressing. Break feta cheese into small pieces; mound in center of lettuce. Arrange cucumber slices, tomatoes, olives, green pepper, avocado slices and onion slices attractively around edge of bowl. Season with salt and pepper. Pour remaining dressing over salad just before serving. Yield: 8 servings.

Maureen Attridge, Preceptor Gamma Rho
Kemptville, Ontario, Canada

TOMORROW'S LAYERED SALAD

1 1/2 cups sour cream
1 1/2 cups mayonnaise
10 ounces spinach, rinsed, torn into bite-sized pieces
4 ounces alfalfa sprouts
4 hard-cooked eggs, chopped
1 bunch scallions with tops, chopped
1 pound bacon, crisp-fried, crumbled
1 (10-ounce) package frozen tiny peas, cooked
2 teaspoons sugar
Salt and pepper to taste
1 cup grated Swiss cheese

Combine sour cream and mayonnaise in small bowl; mix well. Layer half the spinach, alfalfa sprouts, eggs, scallions, bacon and peas in 10-by-13-inch glass dish. Sprinkle with 1 teaspoon sugar, salt and pepper. Frost with half the sour cream mixture. Repeat layers. Garnish with Swiss cheese. Cover with plastic wrap. Chill overnight. Yield: 12 to 15 servings.

Sharon R. Wry, Laureate Beta
Moncton, New Brunswick, Canada

MARINATED MIXED VEGETABLES

3 cloves of garlic, crushed
1 cup canola oil
1 3/4 cups white vinegar
1/3 cup sugar
2 teaspoons dry mustard
Salt and pepper to taste
1 head cauliflower, cut into flowerets
3 carrots, sliced
1 large green bell pepper, cut into strips
1 medium sweet onion, chopped
2 cups fresh green and/or yellow beans, cut up
1 large zucchini, cut into strips
2 yellow summer squash, sliced
2 cups sugar snap peas, cut into pieces

Combine garlic, oil, vinegar, sugar, mustard, salt and pepper in jar with tight-fitting lid; shake well. Place vegetables in container with tight-fitting lid. Pour marinade over vegetables; cover. Let marinate in refrigerator for 48 hours. Stir before serving. Yield: 8 servings.

Arleta Witzki, Preceptor Laureate Alpha Zeta
East Leroy, Michigan

72 / Salads

♥ MIXED GREENS SALAD

1/2 small head iceberg lettuce
1/2 small head romaine lettuce
1/2 small bunch escarole or endive
1 small tomato, cut into chunks
1/2 small cucumber sliced
1/4 cup olive oil
1/4 cup red wine vinegar
1/4 teaspoon salt
1/4 teaspoon pepper

Tear lettuce and escarole into bite-sized pieces. Place in large salad bowl. Add tomato and cucumber slices; toss together. Combine remaining ingredients in jar with tight-fitting lid; shake well. Pour over salad; toss to coat. Serve immediately. Yield: 6 to 8 servings.

Patricia A. Lewis, Theta Chi
Grand Rapids, Michigan

♥ HEALTHY NO-FAT SALAD

1/4 cup apple cider vinegar
1/4 cup apple juice
1/4 cup lemon juice
1 clove of garlic
1/4 teaspoon oregano
1/8 teaspoon thyme
1/8 teaspoon rosemary
1 head Boston lettuce
1 head radicchio
1/2 Spanish onion, chopped
2 plum tomatoes, chopped
1/2 cucumber, sliced

Combine vinegar, juices, garlic, oregano, thyme and rosemary in small bowl; mix well. Chill, covered, for 1 hour. Wash lettuce; pat dry. Tear into bite-sized pieces. Place in salad bowl. Add onion, tomatoes and cucumber. Pour dressing over salad. Toss to coat. Yield: 8 servings.

Lisa Grigg, Beta Mu
North York, Ontario, Canada

SKINNY SALAD

1 (6-ounce) can water chestnuts, sliced
1 (16-ounce) can French-cut green beans
1 can bean sprouts
1 can Chinese mixed vegetables
2 (8-ounce) cans mushrooms
1 (8-ounce) can white corn
1 onion, chopped
1 green bell pepper, chopped
1 cup sliced celery
1 small head cauliflower, broken into pieces
3 carrots, shredded
2 1/2 cups vinegar
1 cup vegetable oil
2 cups sugar
1 teaspoon salt
1 teaspoon pepper

Drain canned vegetables. Place in salad bowl. Add onion, green pepper, celery, cauliflower and carrots; mix well. Combine remaining ingredients in jar with tight-fitting lid; shake well. Pour over vegetables; toss to coat. Yield: 12 servings.

Frances Appelt, Preceptor Phi
Luverne, Minnesota

RENDEZ-VOUS SALAD

10 ounces spinach
2 cups sprouts
2 cups cooked rice
1 cup chopped celery
1/2 cup raisins
1 cup mushrooms
1/2 cup cashews
Parsley to taste
1 to 2 cloves of garlic, minced
1/4 cup soya sauce
1/2 cup vegetable oil

Tear spinach into bite-sized pieces. Place in salad bowl. Add sprouts, rice, celery, raisins, mushrooms, cashews and parsley; mix gently. Combine garlic, soya sauce and oil in jar with tight-fitting lid; shake well. Pour over salad; toss to coat. Yield: 12 to 15 servings.

Elizabeth Newman, Laureate Beta Tau
Delhi, Ontario, Canada

♥ BROWN RICE SALAD

1 cup brown rice
3 green scallions, finely chopped
1 red bell pepper, chopped
1/4 cup raisins
1/4 cup roasted cashews, chopped
2 tablespoons chopped parsley
6 tablespoons Soy Sauce Dressing

Cook rice in boiling water to cover in saucepan for 40 to 45 minutes or until tender. Rinse; drain well. Let cool. Combine rice, scallions, red pepper, raisins, cashews and parsley in salad bowl. Add dressing; toss to coat. Yield: 6 servings.

SOY SAUCE DRESSING

3/4 cup olive oil
1/4 cup lite soy sauce
2 tablespoons lemon juice
1 clove of garlic, crushed
1 (1/2-inch) ginger root, finely chopped

Combine all ingredients in jar with tight-fitting lid. Shake well. Yield: 1 1/8 cups.

Elizabeth McCracken, Beta
Pincourt, Quebec, Canada

♥ ORANGE DRESSING

2 tablespoons plus 2 teaspoons vegetable oil
2 tablespoons plus 2 teaspoons olive oil
1 tablespoon wine vinegar
1 teaspoon sugar
2 teaspoons grated orange peel
1/4 cup frozen orange juice concentrate
1/4 cup orange liqueur

Combine oils, vinegar, sugar, orange peel, orange juice concentrate and liqueur in jar with tight-fitting lid; shake well. Serve over mixed greens such as lettuce and radicchio. Garnish with mandarin oranges and avocado slices. Can be stored in airtight container in refrigerator for several days. Yield: 1 cup.

Jane J. Gelhaus, Laureate Delta Omicron
Sacramento, California

The Main Event

That old saying, "Meat makes the meal" is as true today as it was in grandmother's time. Guests may have seconds and thirds of the potato casserole, or rave about the fruit salad, but it's the main course everyone remembers long after the dinner is over. If you're stuck in a "meat-and-potatoes" rut, or just can't think of a new way to fix the pork chops, here's your answer. You'll find lots of delectable recipes that turn the most ordinary cuts into memorable main courses that your family and guests will devour. Many of the recipes are quick, easy, and can be assembled ahead of time. Then, after a busy day at work or volunteering, dinner is ready for the oven. Whether for a simple family Sunday supper, a casual buffet for friends, or a lavish sit-down dinner for business associates, each of these taste-tempting entrees will impress all who share your table.

✦ FILET OF BEEF WITH FETA AND HERB MEDALLIONS

1/2 cup crumbled feta cheese	Freshly ground lemon pepper to taste
2 tablespoons softened butter or margarine	4 beef tenderloin steaks, cut 1 1/2 to 2 inches thick
1 tablespoon fresh marjoram	1 tablespoon olive oil
1 tablespoon fresh thyme	Salt to taste
1/2 teaspoon Dijon mustard	Fresh marjoram sprigs
1/2 teaspoon lemon juice	Fresh thyme sprigs
	Lemon slices

Combine feta cheese, butter, marjoram, thyme, mustard, lemon juice and lemon pepper in bowl; mix well. Shape into 3-by-3-inch log. Wrap in plastic wrap. Refrigerate for 2 to 3 hours or overnight. Preheat broiler. Brush each steak with olive oil. Sprinkle with salt and lemon pepper. Broil steaks 5 inches from heat source for 6 to 8 minutes per side or until medium-rare. Cut feta cheese mixture into 4 slices. Place 1 slice on top each steak. Return steaks to broiler until feta cheese mixture is warm and softened. Garnish with marjoram sprigs, thyme sprigs and lemon slices. Yield: 4 servings.

Phoebe Richards, Laureate Mu
Montclair, California

♥ RED WINE ONION SAUCE OVER TENDERLOINS

1 teaspoon butter or margarine	1 1/4 cups lite beef consommé, heated
2 onions, sliced	1 teaspoon cornstarch
1/4 teaspoon basil	2 tablespoons cold water
1 tablespoon chopped fresh parsley	4 tenderloin steaks
1/2 cup dry red wine	1 tablespoon vegetable oil
	Salt and pepper to taste

Melt butter in saucepan over medium heat. Add onions, basil and parsley. Cook for 15 minutes over low heat, stirring constantly. Pour in wine; turn heat to high. Cook for 2 to 3 minutes. Add consommé. Bring to a boil. Mix cornstarch with water in small bowl. Stir into sauce, mixing well. Simmer for 6 to 7 minutes. Brush oil over each steak. Season with salt and pepper. Broil or grill as desired. Serve sauce over steaks. Yield: 4 servings.

Doreen MacLean, Zeta
Grand Falls, Newfoundland, Canada

SIRLOIN STEAK SUPREME

2 pounds sirloin steak, cubed	1 package wild rice
1/4 cup vegetable oil	1 (8-ounce) can water chestnuts, sliced
1 medium onion, chopped	2 (10-ounce) cans beef consommé
1 clove of garlic, minced	1/2 cup slivered almonds
1 cup chopped celery	2 tablespoons soy sauce
8 ounces mushrooms, sliced	

Preheat oven to 350 degrees. Brown steak in oil in skillet. Sauté onion and garlic in skillet. Add celery and mushrooms. Discard wild rice seasonings. Add wild rice and remaining ingredients; mix well. Place in 9-by-13-inch baking pan. Cover with cooking foil. Bake for 1 hour. Yield: 6 servings.

Mary Jane Stoltenberg, Laureate Psi
Grand Island, Nebraska

RIB-EYE ROAST

2 cloves of garlic, crushed	1 1/2 teaspoons dry mustard
1 teaspoon salt	1 teaspoon water
1 teaspoon cracked black pepper	1 (12-ounce) jar brown beef gravy
1 teaspoon thyme	1/4 cup currant jelly
1 (4-pound) beef rib-eye roast	

Preheat oven to 350 degrees. Combine garlic, salt, pepper and thyme in small bowl. Press evenly onto surface of roast. Place roast in shallow roasting pan. Insert meat thermometer into thickest part of roast. Do not add water or cover. Roast for 18 to 22 minutes per pound or to desired doneness. Remove roast from oven. Let stand for 15 minutes. Dissolve mustard in water in saucepan. Add remaining ingredients. Cook over medium heat until bubbly. Serve with roast. Yield: 8 to 10 servings.

Lorraine Harrington, Beta Master
Daytona Beach Shores, Florida

"MY SISTER'S" BRISKET MARINADE

My sister ran truck stops in Texas for years. She developed this recipe, a favorite with all the truckers!

3/4 cup soy sauce	1 tablespoon garlic powder
1/4 cup vegetable oil	1/2 teaspoon oregano
1/4 cup lemon juice	1/4 cup Worcestershire sauce
2 tablespoons grated onion	1/4 cup liquid smoke
1 tablespoon pepper	1 (4- to 5-pound) brisket
1/2 teaspoon sage	

Combine first 10 ingredients in bowl; mix well. Pour into baking pan. Place brisket in pan. Refrigerate overnight, turning once. Preheat oven to 250 to 300 degrees. Wrap roast with marinade in cooking foil. Bake for 6 to 8 hours or to desired doneness. Let cool before slicing. Yield: 8 to 12 servings.

Johnnye Clement, Preceptor Mu
Neosho, Missouri

Shannon Buettner, Beta Delta, Harve, Montana, makes a Meat Marinade for all types of meat by combining 1/2 cup vegetable oil, 1/3 cup soy sauce, 1/4 cup lemon juice, 2 tablespoons prepared mustard, 2 tablespoons Worcestershire sauce, 1 clove of garlic, minced and 1 teaspoon pepper in bowl; mix well. Pour over meat. Refrigerate, turning occasionally, for several hours to overnight. The longer, the better!

DRIP BEEF

1 (3- to 5-pound) beef roast
1 bay leaf
1 tablespoon salt
1 tablespoon rosemary
1 tablespoon oregano
1 tablespoon cracked pepper
1 tablespoon savory salt
1 tablespoon garlic powder
1 beef bouillon cube

Place roast in Crock•Pot. Add water to cover roast. Add remaining ingredients. Cook on High for 1 to 2 hours. Reduce temperature to Low. Cook for several hours or until beef is very tender. Shred meat with fork. Serve on buns or hard rolls. Yield: 8 to 12 servings.

Lucille Bingham, Kansas Preceptor Xi
Baxter Springs, Kansas

BRAISED BEEF ROLLS (OXRULADER)

2 pounds round steak, cut 1/4 inch thick
Dijon mustard
Salt and pepper to taste
8 slices bacon, cut into halves
8 hot dogs, cut into halves
All-purpose flour
3 tablespoons butter
1 beef bouillon cube
1 cup boiling water
2 cups cream

Pound steak until thin. Cut into 16 strips. Spread Dijon mustard on 1 side of each strip. Sprinkle with salt and pepper. Place 1 bacon slice half and 1 hot dog half over mustard on each strip. Roll up; secure with toothpicks. Coat with flour. Heat butter in heavy skillet. Add beef rolls. Brown on all sides. Dissolve bouillon cube in boiling water in bowl. Pour into skillet. Simmer, covered, for 1 hour or until tender. Lift beef rolls from pan. Keep warm. Skim fat from drippings. Add cream to skillet, stirring constantly. Bring to a boil. Pour over beef rolls. Yield: 16 rolls.

Judith Putman, Preceptor Gamma Beta
Ada, Michigan

MUSTARD BEEF ROLLS

6 slices bacon, chopped
1/2 bunch green onions, chopped
3 tablespoons bread crumbs
1 1/2 pounds flank steak
2 tablespoons mustard
2 1/2 tablespoons all-purpose flour
1 1/2 tablespoons bacon drippings
1/2 cup water or wine

Preheat oven to 350 degrees. Crisp-fry bacon in skillet. Remove bacon, reserving drippings. Combine bacon, onions and bread crumbs in bowl. Trim fat from steak. Cut into 4-inch strips. Pound steak well to tenderize. Spread each strip with mustard and bacon mixture. Roll up. Secure with toothpicks. Dust each roll with flour. Brown in bacon drippings. Place in baking dish. Pour water in dish; cover tightly. Bake for 1 1/2 hours. Yield: 4 servings.

Susan M. Farkos, Xi Alpha Xi
Las Cruces, New Mexico

♥ INDONESIAN BAMIE

1/8 teaspoon crushed red pepper
3 large cloves of garlic, minced
Butter or margarine
1 (1 1/2-pound) flank steak, cut into thin strips
Salt and pepper to taste
1 large onion, sliced
4 large stalks celery, chopped
2 tablespoons vegetable oil
1 small head cabbage, chopped
12 ounces spaghetti, cooked
1/2 cup soy sauce

Sauté red pepper and garlic in small amount of butter in large electric skillet. Season steak with salt and pepper. Sauté in skillet until pink. Remove from skillet. Sauté onion and celery in oil in skillet. Add cabbage; cook until bright green. Add steak, spaghetti and soy sauce; mix well. Cook until heated through. Serve immediately. Yield: 4 to 6 servings.

Patricia Pryhuber, Preceptor Gamma Zeta
Ballwin, Missouri

MEXICAN STEAK

1 (1 1/4-pound) boneless round steak
2 tablespoons butter or margarine
1 (8-ounce) jar taco sauce
1 (4-ounce) can chopped green chilies, drained
1/2 cup shredded Monterey Jack cheese

Preheat oven to 350 degrees. Trim excess fat from steak. Cut steak into 4 pieces. Pound to 1/4-inch thickness. Brown steak in butter in skillet. Place in lightly greased shallow 2-quart casserole. Top with taco sauce and chilies. Bake, covered, for 40 minutes. Sprinkle with cheese. Bake, uncovered, for 5 minutes. Yield: 3 to 4 servings.

Jean Zeller, Laureate Theta
New Albany, Indiana

SPICY ORANGE BEEF

1 (1-pound) flank or round steak
2 tablespoons vegetable oil
1/4 cup slivered orange peel
1 clove of garlic, minced
1/2 teaspoon ginger
2 tablespoons cornstarch
1 cup beef broth
1/4 cup soy sauce
1/4 cup dry Sherry
1/4 cup orange marmalade
1/2 teaspoon crushed dried pepper
Cooked rice

Slice steak on the diagonal into thin slices. Heat oil in large skillet or wok over medium-high heat. Add steak, 1/3 at a time. Stir-fry for 3 minutes or until browned. Return steak to skillet. Add orange peel, garlic and ginger. Stir-fry for 1 minute. Combine cornstarch, beef broth, soy sauce, Sherry, marmalade and red pepper in bowl. Add to steak, stirring constantly. Bring to a boil over medium heat. Boil for 1 minute. Serve over rice. Yield: 4 servings.

Sharon Boscarelli, Xi Beta Rho
Norman, Oklahoma

BEEF STEW AND DUMPLINGS

1 pound beef, cut into 1-inch cubes
2 tablespoons margarine
3 cups water
2 1/2 tablespoons all-purpose flour
1/4 cup water
2 (10-ounce) cans vegetable soup
2 cups all-purpose flour
1 tablespoon baking powder
1/2 teaspoon salt
3/4 cup milk

Brown beef in margarine in skillet. Add water. Simmer for 1 1/2 hours. Mix 2 1/2 tablespoons flour and 1/4 cup water in bowl. Add to beef, stirring constantly. Cook until thickened. Add soup. Heat to boiling point. Combine 2 cups flour, baking powder and salt in bowl. Add milk, stirring until soft dough consistency. Drop by spoonfuls into stew. Steam, covered, for 15 minutes; do not lift lid. Serve immediately. Yield: 4 to 6 servings.

Phyllis Malm, Epsilon Master
Waukegan, Illinois

BEEF SANDWICHES

3 cups shredded cabbage
1 (3-pound) chuck roast
1 (10-ounce) can tomato soup
1 cup chopped onion
1/2 cup hot-style catsup
2 tablespoons sugar
2 tablespoons Worcestershire sauce
2 tablespoons vinegar
1 bay leaf
1 clove of garlic, minced
1 teaspoon chili powder
1 teaspoon dried oregano
1/2 teaspoon salt
1/4 cup cold water
2 tablespoons all-purpose flour

Place cabbage in Crock•Pot. Trim excess fat from roast. Cut roast in half. Place over cabbage. Combine next 11 ingredients in bowl. Pour over roast; cover. Cook on Low for 10 to 12 hours. Remove roast. Shred. Combine water and flour in bowl. Stir into sauce. Cook on High until thickened. Return beef to sauce. Cook, covered, for 10 minutes longer. Serve on buns. Yield: 12 servings.

Paula A. Disterhaupt, Laureate Beta Beta
Glenwood, Iowa

WESTERN STEW

2 pounds stew beef, cut into 1/2-inch cubes
1 (8-ounce) bottle Catalina dressing
2 cups water
4 small potatoes, cubed
1 1/2 cups sliced carrots
2 small onions, chopped
1/4 cup water
1/4 cup all-purpose flour

Marinate beef in dressing overnight. Drain, reserving marinade. Brown beef in saucepan. Add 2 cups water and marinade. Simmer, covered, for 2 hours. Add vegetables. Simmer until tender. Mix 1/4 cup water and flour in bowl. Add gradually to stew, stirring constantly. Bring to a boil. Cook until thickened. Yield: 8 servings.

Doreen Parker, Xi Epsilon
Hoquiam, Washington

PEANUT BUTTER STEW (DOMADA)

This dish is West African. My brother brought it back from The Gambia where peanuts are the principal crop. It should be hot, with lots of cayenne pepper.

1/2 cup peanut butter
1 pound beef cubes
2 medium onions, chopped
2 tomatoes, quartered
1/4 cup tomato paste
1/2 teaspoon salt
1/4 teaspoon pepper
Cayenne pepper to taste
Mushrooms (optional)
Hot cooked rice

Combine peanut butter with enough water to make smooth paste in large saucepan. Add beef, onions, tomatoes, tomato paste, salt, pepper and cayenne pepper; mix well. Add water to achieve desired consistency. Cook over medium heat for 1 hour. Add mushrooms. Cook for 1 hour or to desired degree of doneness. Serve over rice. Yield: 4 servings.

C. J. Cochrane, Laureate Beta
Winnipeg, Manitoba, Canada

♥ CROCK•POT CORNED BEEF AND CABBAGE

2 medium onions, sliced
1 (3-pound) corned beef brisket
1 cup apple juice
1/4 cup packed dark brown sugar
2 teaspoons finely shredded orange peel
2 teaspoons mustard
6 whole cloves
6 cabbage wedges

Place onions in Crock•Pot. Place brisket over onions. Combine apple juice, sugar, orange peel, mustard and cloves in bowl. Pour over brisket. Add cabbage. Cook, covered, on Low for 10 to 12 hours or on High for 5 to 6 hours. Yield: 6 servings.

Carolyn Cline, Xi Sigma
Jamestown, New York

♥ AMAZING MICROWAVE MEAT LOAF

I put the glass in the dish to form the meat loaf and magical things happened!

2 pounds ground beef
Salt and pepper to taste
1 egg, slightly beaten
1 (8-ounce) can tomato sauce
Crushed cracker crumbs

Combine ground beef, salt, pepper, egg and 1/2 can tomato sauce in large bowl. Add enough cracker crumbs to make meat loaf consistency; mix well. Place drinking glass upside down in microwave-safe glass pie plate. Shape beef mixture around drinking glass, rounding top. Spread remaining tomato sauce over top. Microwave on High for 18 minutes. Let stand for 15 to 20 minutes. Grease will be pulled into drinking glass. Do not remove glass to serve or grease will release. Yield: 8 servings.

Cynthia L. Newton, Gamma Xi
Fulton, Missouri

CALIFORNIA MEAT LOAF

1 pound ground beef
1/2 pound bulk sausage
1 egg, slightly beaten
1 (11-ounce) can mandarin oranges, drained, chopped
3/4 cup mushroom stems and pieces, chopped
1 (2-ounce) jar pimento, chopped
2 or 3 cups cornflakes, crushed

Preheat oven to 350 degrees. Combine ground beef and sausage in large bowl; mix well. Add egg, oranges, mushrooms and pimentos with enough cornflakes for meat loaf consistency; mix well. Shape into meat loaf in 2-quart casserole. Bake for 1 hour. Yield: 10 servings.

Patricia E. Duncan, Laureate Gamma Eta
National City, California

GRILLED MEAT LOAF

2 pounds ground beef
1 1/3 cups catsup
1 cup dried bread crumbs
1/3 cup sour cream
3 tablespoons Parmesan cheese
1 tablespoon instant minced onion
1 1/2 teaspoons salt
2 eggs, slightly beaten

Preheat coals in outdoor grill for 2 hours. Combine ground beef, 1/3 cup catsup and remaining ingredients in large bowl. Shape mixture into 8-inch loaf. Place on sheet of double thickness heavy duty cooking foil. Top with remaining catsup. Wrap loaf, folding several times to seal in juices. Place packet on grill over medium coals. Cook for 1 1/2 hours, turning with tongs every 10 to 15 minutes; do not puncture foil. Yield: 8 servings.

Judith A. Shipman, Laureate Gamma Mu
Jacksonville, Florida

♥ YUMMY LOW-FAT MEAT LOAF

I make this meat loaf in April and freeze 1 or 2 slices per freezer bag. When temperature is 90 to 105 degrees, I just pop a slice in the microwave and beat the heat!

2 pounds ground lean sirloin, 7 to 12% fat
1 pound bulk turkey sausage
2 carrots, grated
1 small potato, grated
1 onion, chopped
1/4 cup egg beaters
2 cups oatmeal
1 tablespoon herb seasonings
Salt and pepper to taste
2 to 4 cloves of garlic
1 (8-ounce) can tomato sauce

Preheat oven to 350 degrees. Combine sirloin, sausage, carrots, potato, onion, egg beaters, oatmeal, seasonings and garlic in large bowl; mix well. Shape into loaf. Place in large nonstick bread pan. Spread tomato sauce over top. Bake for 2 to 3 hours or until internal temperature reaches 180 degrees and sauce is brown and crusty. Yield: 8 to 10 servings.

Robbie Bryan, Preceptor Zeta Beta
Stockton, California

♥ MICROWAVE HEALTH LOAF

3/4 pound lean ground round
1 cup shredded carrots
1/2 cup chopped fresh mushrooms
1/3 cup chopped onion
1/3 cup finely chopped green pepper
3 tablespoons wheat germ
1/4 cup finely chopped celery
1/4 cup unsalted sunflower seeds
1/4 teaspoon salt (optional)
1/4 teaspoon pepper
1 egg, slightly beaten
2 tablespoons skim milk

Combine all ingredients in medium bowl; mix well. Spread into 4-by-8-inch microwave-safe loaf dish. Microwave on Medium-High for 16 to 24 minutes or until internal temperature in center reaches 150 degrees. Rotate dish once or twice. Let stand for 5 minutes before serving. Yield: 4 servings.

Loruss Grasmick, Preceptor Alpha Lambda
Carroll, Iowa

DODIE'S MEAT LOAF

This recipe has been in my family for years. I tried to duplicate it but finally got the recipe from my 90-year-old Aunt Dodie.

2 pounds ground beef
1 egg, slightly beaten
1/4 cup chopped onion
1 1/2 teaspoons salt
1/4 teaspoon pepper
1 (10-ounce) can vegetable soup
2 cups Rice Krispies
1/2 cup water
All-purpose flour

Preheat oven to 425 degrees. Combine beef, egg, onion, salt, pepper, soup and Rice Krispies in bowl; mix well. Shape into loaf in 9-inch square pan. Sprinkle loaf with flour. Sear in hot oven until browned. Pour 1/2 cup water around loaf; cover. Bake for 1 hour. Uncover; brown slightly. Add additional 1/2 cup water if liquid evaporates. Yield: 8 servings.

Shirley Sink, Beta Alpha
Fort Worth, Texas

BURRITO PIE

Vegetable oil
4 (8-inch) flour tortillas
1 pound ground beef
1/2 cup chopped onion
1 (20-ounce) can refried beans
1 (4-ounce) can chopped green chilies
1/3 cup hot taco sauce
3 cups shredded Cheddar cheese

Preheat oven to 350 degrees. Heat small amount of oil in skillet. Fry tortillas, 1 at a time, for 30 seconds on each side or until lightly browned and blistered; let drain. Brown ground beef and onion in skillet, stirring until crumbly; drain off fat. Remove from heat. Stir in beans, chilies and taco sauce. Layer 1 tortilla, 1/3 meat mixture and 1/3 cheese in pie pan. Repeat layers, ending with tortilla. Bake for 25 minutes. Yield: 6 servings.

Tammy Bevel, Lambda
Boise, Idaho

♥ SHEPHERD'S PIE

6 medium potatoes, peeled
3/4 pound low-fat ground beef
1 tablespoon pepper
2 teaspoons unsalted tenderizer
4 teaspoons salt-free Mrs. Dash Original Blend
1 (15-ounce) can no-salt creamed corn

Preheat oven to 350 degrees. Boil potatoes in saucepan in water to cover for 50 minutes or until softened; mash. Brown ground beef in skillet, stirring until crumbly. Season with pepper, tenderizer and Mrs. Dash during browning process. Heat corn in saucepan. Spray casserole with fat-free nonstick vegetable cooking spray. Combine meat and corn in casserole. Top with mashed potatoes. Cover with cooking foil. Bake for 30 minutes. Remove foil. Bake for 15 minutes longer or until potatoes are browned. Yield: 6 servings.

Kathleen Murphy, Xi Eta Nu
College Station, Texas

BUBBLE PIZZA

1 pound ground beef or ground turkey
1/4 cup chopped onion
2 (10-count) packages refrigerator biscuits
1 (14-ounce) jar pizza store
2 cups grated mozzarella cheese
1 cup grated Cheddar cheese

Preheat oven to 400 degrees. Brown ground beef with onion in skillet, stirring until crumbly; drain. Cut individual biscuits into fourths. Combine biscuits and ground beef with pizza sauce in large bowl. Place in 9-by-13-inch baking pan. Bake for 20 minutes. Remove from oven. Top with cheeses. Bake for 10 minutes or until cheese is melted. Yield: 8 servings.

Lisa Rea, Beta
Des Moines, Iowa

ALMOST PIZZA

I made this at a restaurant where I worked. Strangers call me for the recipe.

7 cups thinly sliced potatoes
2 pounds ground beef
1 small onion, chopped
Salt to taste
1 (6-ounce) can sliced mushrooms, drained
1 (10-ounce) can nacho cheese soup
1 cup milk
1 (10-ounce) can tomato soup
1 (3-ounce) package pepperoni, sliced
1 1/2 pounds bulk sausage
3 cups grated mozzarella cheese

Preheat oven to 375 degrees. Parboil potatoes in 1 cup water in saucepan; drain. Place potatoes in ungreased 10-by-15-inch baking dish. Brown ground beef with onion and salt in skillet, stirring until crumbly; drain. Spread mixture over potatoes. Add mushrooms. Combine nacho cheese soup and milk in small microwave-safe dish. Microwave for 1 1/2 minutes; mix well. Pour over mushrooms. Spread tomato soup over mushrooms. Cover with pepperoni slices. Brown sausage in skillet, stirring until crumbly; drain. Spread over pepperoni. Bake, covered, for 45 minutes. Turn oven off. Remove cover. Sprinkle cheese over top. Return to oven, uncovered, for 10 minutes or until cheese is melted. Yield: 12 to 15 servings.

Wanda Laughman, Iota Eta
Russia, Ohio

♥ GA'S HEALTHY LASAGNA

This recipe came from a heart cooking class. The noodles do not have to be cooked beforehand.

1/2 pound ground chuck
1 pound fresh mushrooms, sliced
1 medium onion, chopped
1 to 3 cloves of garlic, minced
1/4 cup low-sodium chicken broth
1 (32-ounce) jar spaghetti sauce
1 cup water
2 carrots, shredded
1 tablespoon sugar (optional)
1 (10-ounce) package frozen chopped spinach, thawed
1 (15-ounce) low-fat ricotta cheese
1/2 cup Parmesan cheese
8 ounces low-fat mozzarella cheese, shredded
2 egg whites
12 uncooked lasagna noodles

Preheat oven to 350 degrees. Brown ground chuck in skillet, stirring until crumbly; drain and rinse. Spray 9-by-13-inch baking pan with nonstick vegetable cooking spray. Sauté mushrooms, onion and garlic in chicken broth in large skillet until mushrooms are tender and onion is limp. Add spaghetti sauce, water, carrots, sugar and ground chuck; mix well. Squeeze spinach dry. Combine spinach, ricotta cheese, Parmesan cheese, mozzarella cheese and egg whites in medium bowl; mix well. Place thin layer of sauce mixture in bottom of prepared pan. Place layer of uncooked noodles over sauce. Spread half cheese mixture over noodles. Cover cheese mixture with half remaining sauce. Repeat layers of noodles and remaining cheese mixture. Add third layer of noodles. Top with remaining sauce. Cover with cooking foil. Bake for 45 minutes. Remove foil. Bake for 15 minutes longer. Remove from oven. Let set for 10 minutes before serving. May be refrigerated for up to 24 hours or frozen if desired. Yield: 6 to 8 servings.

Karen Menard, Laureate Beta Xi
Cape Girardeau, Missouri

♥ PASTA CON BROCCOLI WITH MEAT SAUCE

2 pounds ground beef
2 large jars chunky garden-style spaghetti sauce
2 1/2 teaspoons minced garlic
1 teaspoon Italian seasoning
1 (16-ounce) package seashell noodles
1 (16-ounce) package chopped broccoli
1 pound Velvetta lite cheese
1/2 cup margarine
1 tablespoon Italian seasoning
1 can Milnot milk
Salt and pepper to taste

Brown ground beef in skillet, stirring until crumbly; drain off fat. Add sauce, 1 teaspoon garlic and Italian seasoning; mix well. Let simmer over low heat. Cook noodles and broccoli according to package directions. Combine cheese, 1 1/2 teaspoons garlic and remaining ingredients in microwave-safe dish. Microwave until cheese is melted. Combine cheese mixture, noodles and broccoli in serving dish. Serve topped with meat sauce. Yield: 15 to 20 servings.

Debby Holt, Xi Kappa
Poplar Bluff, Missouri

CROCK•POT SPAGHETTI SAUCE

1/2 pound sweet or hot Italian link sausage
1 pound ground beef
2 onions, chopped
1 large green pepper, chopped
2 cloves of garlic, minced
2 tablespoons sugar
1 tablespoon salt
2 teaspoons leaf basil
1 teaspoon crushed red pepper
2 (16-ounce) cans tomatoes
1 (15-ounce) can tomato sauce
1 (12-ounce) can tomato paste

Remove sausage from casings. Brown sausage with ground beef in skillet, stirring until crumbly; drain well. Place in Crock•Pot with remaining ingredients; mix well. Cook, covered, on Low all day. Sauce may be made 1 to 2 days ahead. Freezes well. Yield: 3 1/2 quarts.

Rose Sadzewicz, Rho Eta
Coshocton, Ohio

WHITE SPAGHETTI WITH MEATBALLS

1 pound ground beef
1/2 cup soda cracker crumbs
1 egg, slightly beaten
1/2 teaspoon salt
1/4 teaspoon pepper
2 tablespoons chili sauce
1 medium onion, finely chopped
2 tablespoons vegetable oil
1 to 2 (5-ounce) cans evaporated milk
Cooked spaghetti

Combine first 7 ingredients in bowl; mix well. Shape into meatballs. Brown meatballs in vegetable oil in skillet; remove from skillet. Pour off drippings, leaving 2 tablespoons in skillet. Add milk. Cook, stirring constantly, until slightly thickened. Return meatballs to sauce. Serve over spaghetti. Yield: 4 servings.

Judy Curtis, Preceptor Alpha Sigma
Kitchener, Ontario, Canada

MACHO MEXICAN SUPPER

1 1/2 pounds ground chuck
2 large onions, julienned
1 green and/or red bell pepper, julienned
2 cloves of garlic, chopped
1 tablespoon taco seasoning
1 (10-count) package soft flour tortillas
1 (29-ounce) can chopped tomatoes
1 (10-ounce) can Ro-Tel tomatoes with green chilies
1 tablespoon sugar
Salt and pepper to taste
4 ounces Cheddar or taco cheese, shredded

Preheat oven to 350 degrees. Sauté ground chuck, onions, peppers, garlic and taco seasoning in skillet, stirring until crumbly; drain. Place 1 tablespoon meat mixture in center of each tortilla. Fold envelope-style to enclose filling. Place in large glass casserole, fold-side down. Combine chopped tomatoes, Ro-Tel tomatoes, sugar, salt and pepper in bowl. Heat tomato mixture in same skillet. Cook for 5 minutes. Pour over casserole. Sprinkle with cheese. Bake for 25 to 30 minutes or until cheese is melted. Yield: 4 to 6 servings.

Jean Crawford, Xi Delta Nu
Mt. Vernon, Ohio

♥ TACO GARDEN RICE

1 pound ground beef or ground turkey
1/2 cup chopped onion
1 (1-ounce) package taco seasoning
1 1/2 cups water
1 1/2 cups thinly sliced zucchini
1 cup frozen niblet corn
1 (14-ounce) can stewed tomatoes
1 1/2 cups uncooked minute rice
1 cup shredded Cheddar cheese
Cilantro (optional)

Brown ground beef and onion in large skillet, stirring until crumbly; drain. Stir in taco seasoning, water, zucchini, corn and tomatoes. Bring to a boil. Stir in rice. Reduce heat to low. Simmer, covered, for 5 to 7 minutes or until liquid is absorbed, stirring occasionally. Remove from heat. Fluff mixture with fork. Sprinkle with cheese. Let cheese melt. Garnish with cilantro. Yield: 6 servings.

Mishelle A. Ringe, Xi Delta Omicron
Stanfield, Oregon

Sharon LaRue, Omicron Eta, Elsmore, Kansas, makes Dump Lasagna by browning 1 pound ground beef, stirring until crumbly; drain. Combine beef, 10 ounces dumpling egg noodles, 24 ounces cottage cheese and 36 ounces spaghetti sauce in large baking dish. Top with 1 pound grated mozzarella cheese. Seal with cooking foil. Bake in preheated 375-degree oven for 45 minutes. Remove foil; serve.

TACOS IN FLOUR TORTILLAS

1 1/4 pounds lean ground beef
1 (3-ounce) package cream cheese with chives, cubed
1 teaspoon chili powder
1/4 teaspoon salt
6 (12-inch) flour tortillas
1 cup taco sauce or picante sauce
1 cup shredded Cheddar cheese
1 cup shredded Monterey Jack cheese
1 1/2 cups crushed tortilla chips
Chopped green onions

Preheat oven to 350 degrees. Brown ground beef in skillet, stirring until crumbly; drain. Stir in cream cheese, chili powder and salt. Simmer for 5 minutes. Spoon 1/6 of mixture onto each tortilla. Fold in sides; roll up. Arrange in greased 9-by-13-inch baking pan. Spoon taco sauce over tortillas. Bake, covered, for 15 minutes. Uncover. Top with cheeses and tortilla chips. Bake for 15 minutes longer. Sprinkle with green onions before serving. Yield: 6 servings.

Jane Bebermeyer, Theta Delta
Reserve, Kansas

❖ LAYERED TORTILLA SANDWICH

3/4 pound lean ground beef
1 cup shredded lettuce
1 (4-ounce) can diced green chili peppers, drained
2 tablespoons snipped fresh parsley
8 (10-inch) flour tortillas
1 (6-ounce) carton frozen avocado dip, thawed
1 (16-ounce) can refried beans
1 cup sour cream
1 1/2 cups shredded Cheddar cheese
1/4 cup chopped tomatoes
2 tablespoons sliced pitted ripe olives
2 tablespoons snipped parsley
Salsa (optional)

Preheat oven to 350 degrees. Brown ground beef in skillet, stirring until crumbly; drain. Combine ground beef, lettuce, chili peppers and parsley in bowl. Place 1 tortilla on large oven-proof platter. Spread with half the avocado dip. Top with second tortilla. Spread with half the refried beans. Cover with third tortilla. Sprinkle with half the ground beef mixture. Add fourth tortilla. Spread with half the sour cream. Sprinkle with half the cheese. Repeat the layers, ending with sour cream and cheese. Bake for 15 to 20 minutes or until cheese is melted. Garnish with tomatoes, olives and parsley. Serve with salsa. Yield: 8 servings.

Juanita McGann, Laureate Iota
Colorado Springs, Colorado

♥ WHOLE WHEAT CABBAGE ROLLS

4 loaves whole wheat bread dough
1 pound ground beef
1 cup chopped onion
1 clove of garlic, minced
1 small head cabbage, shredded
3 cups shredded medium Cheddar cheese
1 cup chives
Butter

Preheat oven to 350 degrees. Prepare bread dough according to package directions. Brown ground beef and onion in 2-quart saucepan, stirring until crumbly. Add garlic and cabbage. Cook until cabbage is tender. Separate dough into 3-inch balls. Roll out each ball to 1/4-inch thickness. Place small portion of beef mixture, cheese and chives in center of dough. Pinch edges to enclose filling. Place on cookie sheet, edge side down. Repeat until all ingredients are used. Bake for 12 minutes. Remove rolls from oven. Brush tops with butter. Bake for 3 minutes longer. Rolls freeze well in plastic container or ziplock bag. Yield: 50 rolls.

Trudy Schlader, Phi
Moscow, Idaho

SPICY BEEF CRÊPES

1/4 cup chopped onion
1 teaspoon minced garlic
2 tablespoons vegetable oil
1 to 1 1/2 pounds ground beef
1 (15-ounce) jar spaghetti sauce
1 tablespoon chili powder
1 can whole kernel corn
1/3 cup sliced mushrooms
1/3 cup raisins
1 (4-ounce) can chopped green chilies
1/3 cup all-purpose flour
2/3 cup yellow cornmeal
1 1/2 cups skim milk
2 eggs, beaten

Preheat oven to 350 degrees. Sauté onion and garlic in oil in large skillet until lightly browned. Add ground beef. Brown, stirring until crumbly; drain. Add spaghetti sauce, chili powder, corn, mushrooms, raisins and chilies; mix well. Heat through. Combine remaining ingredients in bowl; beat until smooth. Batter will be fairly thin. Heat lightly greased 6-inch skillet or omelet pan. Remove from heat. Spoon 2 tablespoons batter into skillet. Lift and tilt skillet to spread batter evenly. Return to heat. Brown on 1 side only. Invert pan over paper towel to remove crêpe. Repeat until all batter is used. Wrap beef mixture in crêpes. Place side by side in 9-by-13-inch casserole. Spread any remaining sauce over crêpes. Cover with cooking foil. Bake for 20 minutes. Yield: 8 servings.

Evelyn Lehmann, Preceptor Alpha Alpha
Foley, Alabama

Mari Vandersloot, Beta Delta, Havre, Montana, makes Barbecue Kabobs by combining 1/2 cup vegetable oil, 1/3 cup soy sauce, 1/4 cup lemon juice, 2 tablespoons prepared mustard, 2 tablespoons Worcestershire sauce, 1 clove of garlic, minced and 1 teaspoon pepper in bowl; mix well. Marinate beef cubes, chicken cubes or shrimp, green pepper, onion, mushrooms and small potatoes for several hours or overnight. Separate meat and vegetables. Thread on skewers in attractive pattern. Place on preheated grill. Grill until done.

GARDEN HARVEST CASSEROLE

1 pound ground beef
1 (10-ounce) package scalloped potatoes
2 cups thinly sliced zucchini
1 cup 1-inch pieces fresh green beans
1 (14-ounce) can diced tomatoes
2 cups chopped fresh carrots
1 medium onion, sliced
2 cups bite-sized fresh broccoli pieces
2 cups water
2/3 cup milk
1 tablespoon dried basil leaves
2 teaspoons dry parsley
1 teaspoon salt
1/4 teaspoon pepper

Preheat oven to 400 degrees. Brown ground beef in skillet, stirring until crumbly; drain. Add remaining ingredients; mix well. Place in ungreased 9-by-13-inch baking pan. Bake, covered, for 45 minutes or until vegetables are tender. Yield: 6 servings.

Bonnie L. Fisher, Preceptor Omega
Niagara Falls, New York

GROUND BEEF AND YORKSHIRE PUDDING

1 cup sifted all-purpose flour
1 teaspoon salt
1 cup milk
2 eggs
1 1/2 pounds ground beef
1/4 cup chopped onion
1/2 teaspoon pepper
1 clove of garlic, minced
1 tablespoon minced parsley
3 tablespoons vegetable oil

Preheat oven to 425 degrees. Sift flour and salt together in bowl. Beat in milk gradually. Add eggs, 1 at a time; mix well. Chill for 30 minutes. Beat until large bubbles form. Combine beef, onion, pepper, garlic and parsley in bowl; mix gently. Oil 8-by-12-inch baking pan. Place pan in oven until oil sizzles. Pour half the batter in pan. Spread meat mixture quickly over batter. Pour in remaining batter. Bake for 15 minutes. Reduce heat to 350 degrees. Bake for 20 minutes longer or until batter is puffy and browned. Serve immediately.
Yield: 6 to 8 servings.

Janice Howe, Xi Gamma
Winnipeg, Manitoba, Canada

MATAMBRE ROLL

2 pounds lean ground beef
1 teaspoon seasoned salt
1/2 teaspoon seasoned pepper
1/4 cup catsup
1/4 cup smoky barbecue sauce
2 cups shredded peeled carrots
1 cup soft bread crumbs
1/2 cup chopped parsley
1 teaspoon salt
2 eggs, beaten
1 cup hot water
1/4 cup all-purpose flour
1 cup milk
Salt to taste

Preheat oven to 350 degrees. Place ground beef, salt and pepper in large bowl; mix well. Pat into 12-by-14-inch thin rectangle on waxed paper slightly larger than meat. Combine catsup and barbecue sauce in bowl. Brush half the mixture on meat. Combine carrots, bread crumbs, parsley, salt and eggs in bowl; spread over meat. Roll up, jelly-roll fashion, using paper as guide. Place on greased shallow baking pan; remove paper. Brush roll with part of remaining sauce. Bake, brushing several times with sauce, for 1 hour or until tests done and glazed. Remove from pan. Stir water into drippings in pan, scraping browned bits. Mix flour and milk in small bowl. Add to drippings, stirring constantly, until thickened. Season with salt. Serve over rolls.
Yield: 8 servings.

Sharon L. Upleger, Laureate Omega
Warren, Michigan

HAM ROLLS

2 pounds ground ham
1 1/2 pounds lean ground pork
2 pounds ground beef
3 eggs, beaten
3 cups graham cracker crumbs
2 cups milk
1 small onion, minced
2 cups tomato soup
1/2 cup vinegar
2 1/4 cups packed dark brown sugar
2 teaspoons dry mustard

Preheat oven to 350 degrees. Combine ham, pork, ground beef, eggs, cracker crumbs, milk and onion in bowl; mix well. Shape into 30 rolls. Place in two 9-by-13-inch baking pans. Combine soup, vinegar, brown sugar and mustard in bowl. Pour over rolls. Bake for 1 hour, basting 2 or 3 times. May be made a day ahead or frozen. Yield: 15 servings.

Karen Ann Crook, Alpha Eta
Moses Lake, Washington

LAMB AND GREEN BEANS

1 pound lamb, cubed
1 large onion, chopped
3 cloves of garlic, minced
1 tablespoon coriander
1 (28-ounce) can tomatoes, crushed
1 cup tomato juice
1/2 can tomato paste
Salt and pepper to taste
2 (16-ounce) cans green beans
Hot cooked rice

Brown lamb with onion and garlic in skillet. Sprinkle with coriander; stir well. Add tomatoes, tomato juice, tomato paste, salt and pepper. Simmer over low heat until lamb is tender. Add green beans; heat through. Serve over rice. Yield: 4 to 6 servings.

Glory Case, Kappa Master
Gabriola, British Columbia, Canada

Judith A. Stramel, Preceptor Tau, Elko, Nevada, makes a Ham Sauce by mixing 1/2 cup sugar, 1/4 teaspoon salt, 3/4 cup vinegar, 1 envelope unflavored gelatin dissolved in water, 4 eggs, 3 to 4 teaspoons dry mustard and 3/4 cup water in blender container; blend until smooth. Cook in top of double boiler until thickened. Fold in 1 small carton whipped topping. Spoon into serving dish. Chill. Serve with ham dinner.

❖ GRILLED BUTTERFLIED PORK CHOPS

2 tablespoons butter or margarine
4 green onions, chopped
1/2 cup sliced fresh mushrooms
2 cloves of garlic, crushed
1/2 teaspoon ginger powder
2 tablespoons white cooking wine
1 1/2 cups imitation crab meat
1/2 cup shredded Swiss cheese
1/2 cup shredded sharp Cheddar cheese
1/4 cup whole cashews
4 (1-inch thick) butterflied pork chops

Preheat grill. Melt butter in large skillet. Add green onions, mushrooms, garlic, ginger and wine. Cook until onions are tender. Add crab meat; mix well. Add cheeses. Cook, stirring, over low heat until cheese is melted. Remove from heat. Add cashews, stirring gently. Stuff chops with filling. Place on grill. Grill until done. Yield: 4 servings.

Kimberly F. Jahde, Lambda
Lincoln, Nebraska

PEACH-GLAZED PORK CHOPS

1 (16-ounce) can sliced peaches
2/3 cup hot water
1/4 cup margarine
1 (18-ounce) package stove-top stuffing mix
10 thick deboned pork chops
1/2 cup peach preserves
1 1/2 tablespoons Dijon mustard

Preheat oven to 350 degrees. Drain peaches, reserving syrup. Chop peaches. Mix water and margarine in bowl. Stir in stuffing mix, peaches and reserved syrup. Trim fat from chops. Place chops in 9-by-13-inch baking pan. Combine preserves and mustard in bowl. Brush over chops. Cover with stuffing mixture. Bake for 45 minutes or until done. Yield: 5 to 10 servings.

Marcia J. Cram, Preceptor Gamma Kappa
Lewiston, Michigan

PORK AND SAUERKRAUT A LA NORMANDE

When newly married to my French chef husband, I was absolutely terrified to cook for him. He patiently taught me some of his professional cooking secrets, and I am still using them after almost 40 years.

4 (1-inch thick) pork chops
1 (16-ounce) jar sauerkraut
2 slices bacon, chopped
3 or 4 peeled Granny Smith apples, sliced
1 medium onion, chopped
2 cloves of garlic, crushed
Dry white wine
Salt and pepper to taste

Preheat oven to 350 degrees. Wash and dry pork chops. Rinse sauerkraut in colander several times under running water. Heat 2-quart heavy ovenproof saucepan over high heat. Add pork chops. Brown on both sides for a few minutes. Remove to platter. Add bacon; reduce heat to medium. Brown bacon; drain. Add apples; brown. Add onion and garlic at same time, stirring often to prevent sticking. Add sauerkraut all at once, stirring to mix well. Add white wine to cover. Bring to a boil over high heat. Reduce heat. Add pork chops. Cover; transfer to oven. Bake for 1 hour, adding water if necessary. Season to taste. To prevent apples from turning brown, cover with water and a few drops lemon juice. Strain; pat dry before adding to pork chops.
Yield: 4 servings.

Annemarie Michel Foulard, Nu
Houston, Texas

TACO PORK CHOPS

6 (1/2-inch thick) lean pork chops
2 tablespoons vegetable oil
Salt and pepper to taste
3/4 cup uncooked rice
1 1/2 cups water
1 (8-ounce) can tomato sauce
2 tablespoons taco seasoning
2 tablespoons chopped green onions
1/2 green pepper, chopped
1/2 cup shredded Cheddar cheese

Preheat oven to 350 degrees. Brown pork chops in oil in large skillet. Sprinkle with salt and pepper. Combine rice, water, tomato sauce and taco seasoning in greased 9-by-13-inch baking dish; mix well. Arrange chops over rice. Top with chopped onions and green pepper. Cover with cooking foil. Bake for 1 1/2 hours. Uncover; sprinkle with cheese. Return to oven until cheese is melted. Yield: 6 servings.

Marlene J. Baucum, Preceptor Omega
Phoenix, Arizona

PORK "EXTRAORDINAIRE"

2 pounds pork tenderloin
Salt and pepper to taste
1 clove of garlic, crushed
Vegetable oil
1/4 cup vinegar
1/4 cup water
1/4 cup sugar
1/2 cup fruit juice
1 1/2 tablespoons soy sauce
1/4 cup chopped dill pickle
1 cup pineapple chunks
1/2 cup mandarin oranges
Cooked wild rice
Sweet carrots and peas

Preheat oven to 350 degrees. Cut tenderloin into bite-sized pieces. Season with salt and pepper. Brown garlic in hot oil in skillet. Add pork; brown lightly. Combine vinegar, water, sugar, fruit juice and soy sauce in saucepan. Simmer for 5 to 10 minutes. Place pork in casserole. Pour sauce over top. Add dill pickle and fruit. Bake, covered, for approximately 1 hour. Serve with wild rice and sweet carrots and peas. Yield: 6 to 8 servings.

Anne C. Perry
Richmond, British Columbia, Canada

"MAMA'S" PORK TENDERLOINS

1 or 2 pork tenderloins, sliced
Salt and pepper to taste
Olive oil
Green onions
Mushrooms
1 tablespoon butter or margarine
Paprika to taste
Salt and pepper to taste
2 shots cognac
1/4 cup white wine
1 cup (about) water
2 chicken bouillon cubes
1/4 cup heavy cream

Cover tenderloin slices with waxed paper. Pound with flat side of tenderizer. Sprinkle with salt and pepper. Fry in olive oil in skillet for 1 1/2 minutes on each side. Sauté green onions and mushrooms in butter in saucepan. Add paprika, salt and pepper. Add shots of cognac and wine. Bring to a boil. Add water and chicken bouillon cubes, stirring to dissolve bouillon. Add cream. Return meat to sauce. Sauce can be thickened with flour or cornstarch. Yield: 4 to 6 servings.

Gisela Goucher, Exemplar
Windham, New Hampshire

TOURTIERE

Britain has its pasties, Italy has its pizzas and Mexico has its tortillas . . . French Canada has always had Tourtiere! Like all traditional recipes, each housewife has her own interpretation, adjusted to mood and available ingredients!

2 cups all-purpose flour
Pinch of salt
1/2 cup butter or margarine
3 tablespoons lard
1 egg, beaten
Cold milk
2 pounds ground pork
1 large onion, chopped
3 cloves of garlic, minced
1/2 teaspoon nutmeg
2 tablespoons chopped parsley
1/4 cup chopped celery
1 tablespoon Worcestershire sauce
1/4 cup sweet fruit sauce
1 can peaches and pears
Salt and pepper to taste
1/4 to 1/2 cup boiling water
1/2 cup bread crumbs

Preheat oven to 400 degrees. Combine flour and pinch of salt in bowl. Cut in butter and lard. Blend in egg and enough cold milk to form stiff dough. Chill for 1 hour. Brown pork, onion and 1 clove of garlic in skillet, stirring until crumbly. Add remaining garlic, nutmeg, parsley, celery, Worcestershire sauce, fruit sauce, peaches and pears, salt and pepper; mix well. Simmer for 25 minutes, adding boiling water as needed. Add bread crumbs. Let stand for 10 minutes; drain. Let cool. Roll out pastry on lightly floured surface. Fit into 10-inch pie plate. Pour cooled filling into shell. Bake, covered, for 25 minutes or until browned. May serve with sweet pickles and sweet fruit sauce if desired. Yield: 8 servings.

D' Herringshaw, Preceptor Laureate Beta Eta
North Delta, British Columbia, Canada

MAPLE BARBECUED SPARERIBS

3 pounds spareribs
1 cup maple syrup
1 tablespoon chili sauce
1 tablespoon vinegar
1 tablespoon Worcestershire sauce
1 small onion, finely chopped
1/2 teaspoon salt
1/4 teaspoon dry mustard
1/8 teaspoon pepper

Preheat oven to 425 degrees. Cut ribs into serving-sized pieces. Place on rack in roasting pan. Roast for 35 minutes. Transfer ribs to 9-by-13-inch baking dish. Combine remaining ingredients in saucepan. Bring to a boil. Boil for 5 minutes. Pour over ribs. Reduce oven temperature to 375 degrees. Bake, uncovered, for 1 hour, basting and turning occasionally. Yield: 6 to 8 servings.

Vivian MacDonald, Theta Alpha
Cache Creek, British Columbia, Canada

SAUSAGE-POTATO QUICHE

3 tablespoons vegetable oil
3 cups coarsely shredded potatoes
1 cup grated Cheddar cheese
3/4 cup chopped browned sausage
1/4 cup chopped onion
1 cup evaporated milk
2 eggs
1/2 teaspoon salt
1/8 teaspoon pepper
1 tablespoon parsley flakes

Preheat oven to 425 degrees. Combine vegetable oil and potatoes in 9-inch pie pan. Press evenly in pan, forming crust. Bake for 15 minutes. Remove from oven. Layer cheese, sausage and onion in crust. Combine remaining ingredients in bowl; beat well. Pour over layered ingredients. Bake for 30 minutes or until knife inserted in center comes out clean. Let cool for 5 minutes. Cut into wedges. Yield: 4 to 6 servings.

Sara Plett, Preceptor Alpha Chi
Wichita, Kansas

SWEET 'N' SOUR SAUSAGE

1 green pepper, sliced
1 medium onion, sliced
1 pound smoked sausage, cut up
1 tablespoon butter or margarine
1/2 teaspoon ground ginger
1 tablespoon cornstarch
1 tablespoon vinegar
1 tablespoon soy sauce
1/2 cup apricot preserves
1 cup pineapple chunks, drained
Hot cooked rice

Sauté green pepper, onion and sausage in butter in large skillet for 5 minutes. Combine ginger and cornstarch in bowl. Stir in vinegar. Add soy sauce and preserves. Stir into sausage mixture. Cook over low heat until sauce is thickened. Stir in pineapple. Heat until hot. Serve over rice. Yield: 4 to 6 servings.

Teri Farney, Zeta Eta
Derby, Kansas

THREE-SAUSAGE CASSEROLE

I created this for my catering company "Magic Spoon" because I had many elderly clients who liked to entertain inexpensively. It was a real hit!

5 spicy beef sausages
4 pork sausages
4 beef sausages
1/2 cup chopped cauliflower
1/2 cup chopped broccoli
1/2 cup sliced carrots
1/2 cup sliced mushrooms
1/2 cup sliced onion
1/2 cup peas
1/2 cup chopped tomatoes
4 cups semi-cooked rice
1 (10-ounce) can cream of mushroom soup
Garlic to taste
Pepper to taste

Preheat oven to 325 degrees. Cook sausages in skillet until done; let cool. Slice sausages diagonally. Cook vegetables in small amount of water in saucepan until tender-crisp. Combine sausage, vegetables and rice in large casserole. Mix soup with water in bowl according to can directions. Add garlic and pepper; mix well. Pour evenly over mixture. Bake for 40 minutes. May substitute cream of celery, broccoli or tomato soup for mushroom soup if desired. Yield: 6 to 8 servings.

L. Paula David-Pigeau
Winnipeg, Manitoba, Canada

ITALIAN VEAL SPECIAL

1 1/2 pounds veal
All-purpose flour
2 tablespoons margarine
2 tablespoons olive oil
1 clove of garlic, crushed
1 bunch green onions, chopped
8 ounces fresh mushrooms, sliced
2 cups chicken broth
3/4 cup dry white wine
3/4 cup tomato juice
1 teaspoon chopped fresh parsley
Dash of nutmeg
Linguine

Pound veal as for scallopini. Dredge in flour. Melt margarine and oil in large skillet. Add garlic and veal. Cook until browned. Remove from skillet. Add onions and mushrooms. Sauté for 5 minutes. Return veal to skillet. Add broth, wine, tomato juice, parsley and nutmeg. Bring to a boil. Reduce heat to simmer. Simmer, covered, for 40 minutes. Serve with linguine.
Yield: 6 to 8 servings.

Betty Carmichael, Laureate Phi
Sun City West, Arizona

Janith Farnham, Preceptor Theta, Pierre, South Dakota, says wild goose is part of growing up in South Dakota, but some people do not care for it so she makes Wild Goose and Roast Beef so we can have our goose and they can eat their meat. Place 2 or 3 carrots in bottom of roasting bag. Sprinkle goose breasts and legs and 1 small beef roast with 1 teaspoon onion salt or sliced onions. Place in roasting bag. Pour 1 cup beef bouillon over all. Close roasting bag according to directions. Place in baking pan. Bake in preheated 300-degree oven for 3 hours.

VEAL MARSALA

4 (6-ounce) veal cutlets
All-purpose flour
1/2 cup butter or margarine
1 clove of garlic, minced
2 shallots, finely chopped
1 cup Marsala
1 cup heavy cream

Dredge cutlets in flour. Sauté cutlets in melted butter in large skillet for 30 seconds. Turn over in skillet. Add garlic and shallots. Tilt up front of skillet. Pour wine around edges. Ignite wine. Let flame reduce by half. Cook for 30 seconds. Add cream. Let mix with wine. Let reduce until sauce is desired thickness. Yield: 6 servings.

Renée Anderson, Mu Epsilon
Holts Summit, Missouri

VENISON MEATBALLS

1 pound ground venison
1/2 cup chopped onion
1 egg, slightly beaten
1/3 cup dry bread crumbs
1/4 cup milk
1/4 teaspoon salt
1/8 teaspoon pepper
1/2 teaspoon cumin
1 (12-ounce) jar salsa

Preheat oven to 400 degrees. Combine venison, onion, egg, bread crumbs, milk, salt, pepper and cumin in large bowl; mix well. Shape into thirty 1-inch balls. Place in ungreased rectangular baking pan. Bake, uncovered, for 15 minutes or until no longer pink in center. Place salsa and meatballs in 2-quart saucepan. Bring to a boil, stirring occasionally; reduce heat. Simmer, covered, for 15 minutes. Serve in chafing dish with wooden picks. Yield: 8 to 12 servings.

Patty Jean Hawkins, Alpha Pi Psi
Mineola, Texas

♥ RICE PIZZA

3 cups cooked brown rice
1 cup shredded mozzarella cheese
1/2 cup sesame seeds
1 (8-ounce) can tomato sauce
1 (6-ounce) can tomato paste
Toppings: cooked bacon, cooked ham, lightly cooked ground beef, pepperoni, anchovies, pineapple tidbits, sliced olives, chopped onion, tomato slices and green or red peppers
Grated mozzarella cheese

Preheat oven to 400 degrees. Combine cooked rice, 1 cup mozzarella cheese and sesame seeds in bowl. Spread in pizza pan to form crust. Bake for 15 minutes. Combine tomato sauce and tomato paste in bowl; mix well. Spread over entire top of crust. Add favorite toppings. Top with mozzarella cheese. Bake for 20 minutes or until golden and cheese is bubbly. Let cool for 10 minutes before serving. Yield: 8 servings.

Ann Walker, Delta Kappa
Mississauga, Ontario, Canada

Delectable Dishes

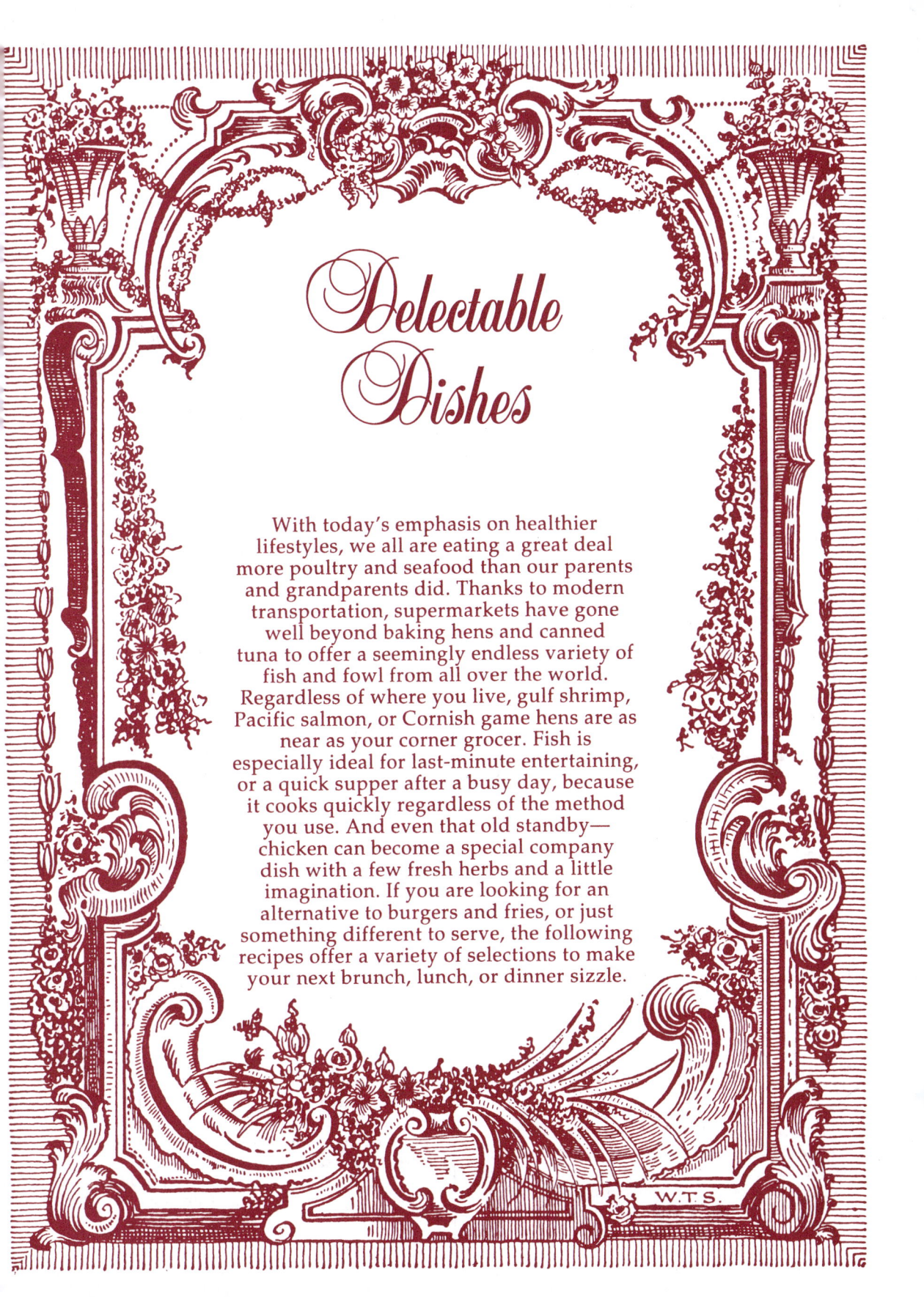

With today's emphasis on healthier lifestyles, we all are eating a great deal more poultry and seafood than our parents and grandparents did. Thanks to modern transportation, supermarkets have gone well beyond baking hens and canned tuna to offer a seemingly endless variety of fish and fowl from all over the world. Regardless of where you live, gulf shrimp, Pacific salmon, or Cornish game hens are as near as your corner grocer. Fish is especially ideal for last-minute entertaining, or a quick supper after a busy day, because it cooks quickly regardless of the method you use. And even that old standby—chicken can become a special company dish with a few fresh herbs and a little imagination. If you are looking for an alternative to burgers and fries, or just something different to serve, the following recipes offer a variety of selections to make your next brunch, lunch, or dinner sizzle.

86 / Poultry

BAKED CHICKEN-PRUNE DELIGHT

1/3 cup Italian salad dressing
1/4 teaspoon pepper
2 tablespoons red wine vinegar
4 boneless skinless chicken breasts
1 cup whole pitted prunes
2 medium apples, cut into 1/2-inch wedges
1 medium onion, sliced
1/3 cup apple juice
1/4 cup packed dark brown sugar
3 tablespoons chopped parsley
3 cups cooked rice

Preheat oven to 350 degrees. Combine first 3 ingredients in 9-inch square glass baking dish. Add chicken breasts. Marinate for 30 minutes, turning several times. Add prunes, apples and onion, mixing with chicken breasts to coat. Add apple juice. Sprinkle brown sugar over all. Bake, covered, for 30 minutes. Turn chicken breasts over; baste. Sprinkle with parsley. Serve over rice. Yield: 4 servings.

Letty L. Clark, Alpha Master
Longview, Washington

BEST-CHOICE-EVER BAKED CHICKEN SUPREME

1 cup fat-free sour cream
4 1/2 tablespoons lemon juice
1 1/2 teaspoons celery salt
1/4 teaspoon paprika
2 teaspoons Worcestershire sauce
Salt and pepper to taste
8 whole boneless skinless chicken breasts
3 cups Italian bread crumbs
1/2 cup margarine, melted

Preheat oven to 350 degrees. Combine sour cream, lemon juice, celery salt, paprika, Worcestershire sauce, salt and pepper in large bowl; mix well. Place chicken breasts in mixture, turning to coat. Cover; refrigerate overnight. Roll each chicken breast in bread crumbs. Place in 9-by-13-inch baking dish. Spoon margarine over each breast. Bake for 1 hour and 15 minutes. Yield: 8 servings.

Jean Ann Robby, Preceptor Zeta
Springdale, Arkansas

CASHEW CHICKEN

4 to 6 boneless skinless chicken breasts
Milk
1 cup all-purpose flour
1 cup cornstarch
Peanut oil
1 (10-ounce) can chicken broth
3 tablespoons oyster sauce
1 tablespoon sugar
1 teaspoon pepper
Cooked rice
3 green onions, chopped
1 cup cashews

Preheat oven to 200 degrees. Cut chicken breasts into bite-sized pieces. Place in bowl. Add milk to cover. Soak for 15 minutes. Coat chicken with flour, then cornstarch. Deep-fry in hot oil. Keep warm in oven. Bring chicken broth to a boil in saucepan. Add water if needed. Add oyster sauce, sugar and pepper. Remove from heat. Combine small amount of cornstarch with water in small bowl. Add to broth, stirring constantly with wire whisk until desired consistency. Serve rice with chicken. Pour sauce over top. Garnish with green onions and cashews. Yield: 4 servings.

Gretchen Thurman, Zeta Eta
Derby, Kansas

♥ CHICKEN BREASTS DIANE

4 chicken boneless skinless breasts
1/2 teaspoon salt
1/4 to 1/2 teaspoon pepper
2 tablespoons vegetable oil
2 tablespoons margarine
3 tablespoons chopped green onions
Juice of 1/2 lemon
3 tablespoons chopped parsley
2 teaspoons Dijon mustard
1/4 cup chicken broth

Pound chicken breasts between waxed paper until flattened. Sprinkle with salt and pepper. Heat 1 tablespoon each of oil and butter in skillet. Cook chicken breasts over high heat for 4 minutes on each side. Do not overcook. Transfer to platter. Add green onions, lemon juice, parsley and mustard to skillet. Cook for 15 seconds. Add broth. Cook, stirring, until smooth. Add remaining butter and oil; mix well. Pour over chicken. Yield: 4 servings.

Shirley Edgar, Beta Master
Courtenay, British Columbia, Canada

CHICKEN BREASTS IN MAPLE SYRUP

1/2 cup all-purpose flour
Salt and pepper to taste
4 boneless skinless chicken breasts
4 large mushrooms, finely chopped
1/2 cup finely chopped cooked ham
1/2 teaspoon dried chives
3 tablespoons butter or margarine
1 onion, thinly sliced
Pinch of savory
1/4 cup maple syrup
1/2 cup water

Preheat oven to 350 degrees. Combine flour, salt and pepper in bowl. Roll each chicken breast in seasoned flour. Sauté mushrooms, ham and chives in 1 tablespoon butter in skillet. Slit thick portion of each chicken breast to form pocket. Insert spoonful of ham mixture. Secure with skewers. Add remaining butter in skillet. Brown chicken breasts over medium heat. Arrange in shallow casserole. Sauté onion with savory in remaining drippings. Spoon over chicken. Pour 1 tablespoon maple syrup over each breast. Add water to skillet, scraping browned bits from skillet. Pour into casserole. Bake, uncovered, for 30 to 40 minutes. Remove skewers to serve. Yield: 4 servings.

Jo Mayes, Xi Zeta
Calgary, Alberta, Canada

♣ CHICKEN BREASTS WELLINGTON

2 large chicken breasts
1 can refrigerated
  crescent dinner rolls
4 slices pepper cheese
Grey Poupon mustard
1 egg, beaten
1 tablespoon dark brown
  sugar
2 tablespoons red wine
  vinegar
1/8 cup corn oil
1/2 teaspoon dry mustard

Preheat oven to 350 degrees. Cover chicken breasts with water in heavy skillet. Simmer for 30 minutes. Let cool; remove skin and bones. Cut chicken breasts in half. Spread crescent rolls on pastry board. Make 4 squares by pinching perforations together. Place 1/2 chicken breast on each square. Top with pepper cheese and Grey Poupon mustard. Wrap pastry to enclose filling. Brush with egg. Place on cookie sheet. Bake for 20 to 25 minutes or until lightly browned. Combine brown sugar, vinegar, oil and dry mustard in saucepan. Simmer, stirring vigorously, for 5 minutes. Serve over chicken. Yield: 4 servings.

Mary Dille, Xi Theta Gamma
Poplar Bluff, Missouri

CHICKEN MARBELLA

10 pounds boneless
  skinless chicken
  breasts, quartered
1 clove of garlic, puréed
1/4 cup dried oregano
Coarse salt to taste
Freshly ground pepper
  to taste
1/2 cup red wine
  vinegar
1/2 cup olive oil
1/2 cup capers with small
  amount of juice
6 bay leaves
1 cup packed dark brown
  sugar
1 cup white wine
1 cup pitted prunes
1/2 cup pitted Spanish
  green olives
1/4 cup finely chopped
  parsley or cilantro

Preheat oven to 350 degrees. Place chicken in large bowl. Combine next 9 ingredients in bowl; mix well. Pour over chicken. Let marinate in refrigerate overnight. Preheat oven to 350 degrees. Arrange chicken breasts in single layer in one or two 10-by-13-inch baking pans. Spoon marinade over breasts. Sprinkle with brown sugar. Pour white wine around breasts. Bake, basting frequently, for 45 minutes to 1 hour or until fork-tender. Remove with slotted spoon to serving platter. Remove bay leaves from drippings. Pour over chicken. Add prunes and olives. Sprinkle with parsley. Yield: 10 to 12 servings.

Dorothy Sayre, Preceptor Beta Beta
Racine, Ohio

♥ CHICKEN WITH PEACHES

Nonstick vegetable
  cooking spray
4 boneless skinless
  chicken breasts
1 (8-ounce) can lite
  sliced peaches
1/2 teaspoon ginger
1 teaspoon cornstarch
1/4 teaspoon salt
1/2 cup water chestnuts,
  drained
2 cups cooked rice
8 ounces fresh or frozen
  pea pods, cooked

Coat large skillet with nonstick spray. Heat skillet over medium heat. Add chicken breasts. Cook for 8 to 10 minutes or until browned on 1 side. Turn; brown on other side. Remove from skillet; keep warm. Drain peaches, reserving juice in bowl. Add water to juice to make 1/2 cup liquid. Mix liquid, ginger, cornstarch and salt in bowl. Pour into saucepan, stirring until thickened and bubbly. Stir in peaches and water chestnuts; heat through. Arrange rice, pea pods and chicken breasts on platter. Pour sauce over chicken. Yield: 4 servings.

Louise W. Paulshock, Preceptor Laureate
Pottsville, Pennsylvania

PEACHY CHICKEN

3 chicken breasts, cut
  into halves
1/2 cup all-purpose flour
Salt and pepper to taste
2 tablespoons butter
  or margarine
2 tablespoons vegetable
  oil
1 1/2 cups orange juice
2 tablespoons cider
  vinegar
2 tablespoons dark
  brown sugar
1 teaspoon basil
1/2 teaspoon nutmeg
1 (16-ounce) can peach
  or apricot halves,
  drained

Preheat oven to 375 degrees. Shake chicken breasts in bag with flour, salt and pepper to coat well. Brown in butter and oil in skillet. Place chicken breasts in 3-quart casserole. Combine orange juice, vinegar, brown sugar, basil and nutmeg in bowl. Pour over chicken breasts. Bake, covered, for 1 hour and 15 minutes. Place peach halves between chicken breasts. Baste well. Bake, uncovered, for 15 to 20 minutes longer. Yield: 6 servings.

Mari Nowak, Xi Zeta Epsilon
Portage, Michigan

CHICKEN PICCATA

1 large lemon
2 whole boneless
  skinless chicken
  breasts
1 1/2 cups fresh bread
  crumbs
1/2 teaspoon salt
1 egg
1 tablespoon milk
1/4 cup butter or
  margarine
1/2 cup water
1/4 cup dry white wine
1 chicken bouillon cube

Cut 6 thin slices from lemon. Squeeze 1 tablespoon juice from remaining lemon. Cut chicken breasts into halves. Pound each half with meat mallet into 1/4 inch-thick cutlet. Mix bread crumbs and salt on waxed paper. Beat egg and milk with fork in pie plate until blended. Dip cutlets into egg mixture, then into bread crumb mixture to coat both sides. Heat butter in skillet over medium heat. Cook cutlets for 5 minutes. Keep warm. Add water, wine, bouillon cube and reserved lemon juice to drippings in skillet. Bring to a boil over high heat, stirring constantly. Simmer for 5 minutes. Spoon sauce over chicken. Garnish with lemon slices. Yield: 4 servings.

Becky McCary, Phi Alpha Epsilon
Great Bend, Kansas

CHICKEN BREASTS IN WINE

15 boneless skinless
  chicken breasts, cut
  into halves
Butter or margarine
1/2 cup warm Cognac
2 1/2 pounds fresh small
  mushrooms
5 1/2 pounds small white
  onions
1 1/2 teaspoons salt
3/4 teaspoon pepper
2 bay leaves
1/8 teaspoon thyme
2 1/3 cups Sauterne
3 (12-ounce) cans
  chicken broth
1/2 cup cornstarch
2 1/2 cups heavy cream

Fry chicken, a few breasts at a time, in butter in 2 skillets until golden. Remove from skillets; let drain. Return to skillets. Pour 1/4 cup Cognac over chicken breasts in each skillet; ignite. Heat 1/4 cup butter in each of 2 large heavy saucepans. Sauté half the mushrooms and onions in each saucepan for about 10 minutes. Add chicken breasts. Add 3/4 teaspoon salt, 3/8 teaspoon pepper, 1 bay leaf, 1/16 teaspoon thyme, 1 cup Sauterne and 1 1/2 cans chicken broth to each saucepan. Cover. Simmer over low heat for 20 minutes or until chicken breasts are fork-tender. Mix cornstarch and 1/3 cup Sauterne in bowl to make a smooth paste. Add gradually to chicken breasts. Stir in cream. Simmer, covered, for 10 minutes. Remove bay leaves. Serve. Yield: 30 servings.

Lynn Turner, Preceptor Laureate Beta Eta
North Delta, British Columbia, Canada

♥ GINGER CHICKEN WITH SPRING ONIONS

1 lemon
4 teaspoons olive oil
4 boneless skinless
  chicken breasts
1 tablespoon cornstarch
1/2 cup low-sodium
  chicken broth
4 slices unpeeled ginger
3 cloves of garlic,
  chopped
1 cup 1- to 2-inch pieces
  spring onions
1/2 teaspoon sugar
1/4 teaspoon red pepper
  flakes
1/4 teaspoon pepper

Grate zest from 1/2 lemon. Cut remaining lemon into thin slices. Heat 2 teaspoons olive oil in large nonstick skillet over medium-high heat. Add chicken breasts. Sauté on each side for 3 minutes or until golden. Remove chicken to plate; keep warm. Dissolve cornstarch in chicken broth in small bowl. Add remaining 2 teaspoons oil to skillet. Add lemon zest, ginger, garlic and onions. Cook, stirring, for 1 minute. Add cornstarch mixture. Bring to a boil, stirring constantly. Return chicken breasts to skillet. Add lemon slices, sugar, red pepper flakes and pepper. Bring to a boil over medium high heat. Cover; reduce heat to low. Simmer for 5 minutes or until chicken breasts are cooked through. Serve hot with additional onions and sauce. Yield: 4 servings.

Marlene Johnston, Preceptor Iota
Fredericton, New Brunswick, Canada

♥ HERBED CHICKEN BREASTS BELLEFONTAINE

2 cups bread crumbs
1 teaspoon freshly
  ground pepper
2 tablespoons dried
  chopped parsley
1 teaspoon dried
  marjoram
1 teaspoon dried thyme
1 teaspoon dried oregano
1 teaspoon garlic powder
4 boneless skinless
  chicken breasts, cut
  into halves
1/2 cup egg substitute,
  lightly beaten
1 tablespoon virgin
  olive oil
1 cup white wine
1 orange, sliced
Sprigs of fresh parsley

Combine bread crumbs, pepper, parsley, marjoram, thyme, oregano and garlic powder in large bowl. Place crumb mixture in large plastic bag. Dip chicken breasts in egg substitute. Place in bag, 1 at a time, shaking gently until coated. Heat olive oil in large skillet over medium-high heat. Brown chicken breasts on both sides. Reduce heat. Add wine; cover. Simmer for 20 to 30 minutes or until chicken breasts are tender. Garnish with orange slices and parsley. Yield: 4 servings.

Louise Norris, Beta Zeta
Bellefontaine, Ohio

♥ CHICKEN IN RASPBERRY-WALNUT SAUCE

1 tablespoon margarine
1 tablespoon sugar
1/3 cup orange juice
2 tablespoons blackberry
  Brandy
1/4 cup chicken broth
1 cup fresh raspberries
1/2 cup seedless raspberry
  preserves
1/8 teaspoon ground
  allspice
1/4 teaspoon ground
  ginger
6 (3-ounce) boneless
  skinless chicken
  breasts
2 tablespoons canola oil
3 tablespoons
  all-purpose flour
Salt to taste
1/4 cup chopped walnuts

Melt margarine in saucepan. Add sugar. Cook until golden. Stir in orange juice, Brandy and broth. Bring to a boil. Boil for 5 minutes or until reduced to approximately 1/3 cup. Add 1/4 cup fresh raspberries, raspberry preserves, allspice and ginger. Simmer for 10 minutes. Pound chicken pieces to 1/2-inch thickness. Heat oil in heavy skillet. Dredge chicken in flour; salt lightly. Brown in hot oil. Reduce heat; cover. Simmer for 5 minutes. Add remaining raspberries and walnuts to raspberry sauce. Serve over chicken. Yield: 6 servings.

Esther Hess, Xi Iota Sigma
Harrisonville, Missouri

LuAnn Sanders, Preceptor Gamma Gamma, Mannford, Oklahoma, makes Picante Chicken by placing 4 skinless chicken breasts in 9-by-13-inch baking pan. Pour a medium jar picante sauce over chicken. Bake at 350 degrees for 1 hour or until done.

♥ HONEY DIJON CHICKEN

6 to 8 boneless chicken breasts
1 jar Honey Dijon low-fat salad dressing
Assorted vegetables: potatoes, onions, parsnips, turnips, etc.
1 teaspoon parsley flakes or chopped fresh parsley
Fresh chives
Salt and pepper to taste
Honey
1 lemon, sliced

Marinate chicken breasts in salad dressing for 6 hours or overnight. Preheat oven to 400 degrees. Place chicken breasts in roasting pan with desired vegetables. Pour remaining salad dressing over all. Add parsley, chives, salt and pepper. Criss-cross honey over top. Arrange lemon slices on top. Squeeze lemon ends over honey. Bake for 1 hour. Yield: 6 to 8 servings.

Donna Knabl, Preceptor Gamma Zeta
Sterling Heights, Michigan

HONEY-PECAN CHICKEN

4 boneless skinless chicken breasts
1/2 cup buttermilk
2 cups all-purpose flour
Dash of cayenne pepper
1/2 teaspoon salt
1/4 teaspoon pepper
1/4 teaspoon garlic powder
Vegetable oil
1/4 cup butter or margarine
1/4 cup honey
1/4 cup roasted pecans

Pound chicken breasts until flattened; cut in half. Soak in buttermilk in bowl for 2 hours. Combine flour and seasonings in bowl. Coat chicken with flour mixture. Let stand for 20 minutes; coat again. Pour oil to 1-inch depth in skillet. Fry chicken until golden brown, turning half way through cooking. Melt butter and honey in saucepan. Stir in pecans. Place chicken in serving dish. Pour honey-pecan sauce over top. Serve. Yield: 4 servings.

Heather Herbert, Phi Iota
Fort Frances, Ontario, Canada

JERK CHICKEN

1 envelope Italian salad dressing mix
1/2 cup vegetable oil
1/4 cup red wine vinegar
2 tablespoons dark brown sugar
2 tablespoons soy sauce
1 teaspoon thyme
1/2 teaspoon allspice
1/2 teaspoon cloves
1/2 teaspoon nutmeg
1/2 teaspoon red pepper
1/4 teaspoon cinnamon
1/4 teaspoon pepper
2 pounds boneless skinless chicken breasts

Combine first 12 ingredients with whisk in large bowl with cover. Add chicken breasts; cover. Shake well to coat all sides of chicken breasts. Refrigerate for 4 to 24 hours. Preheat oven to broil. Spray broiler pan with nonstick vegetable cooking spray. Broil 3 inches from heat for 16 minutes or until cooked, turning and basting often. Discard unused marinade. Yield: 2 to 4 servings.

Carol Clark, Preceptor Alpha Gamma
Madison, Wisconsin

LEMON CHICKEN

2 boneless skinless chicken breasts
Juice of 2 lemons
1/2 cup all-purpose flour
1/2 cup cornstarch
Vegetable oil for frying
2 tablespoons sesame oil
2 tablespoons catsup
2 tablespoons soy sauce
2 tablespoons sugar
2 tablespoons vinegar

Cut chicken breasts into 2-inch pieces. Marinate in lemon juice in bowl for 1 hour. Mix flour and cornstarch in bowl. Dredge chicken in mixture. Deep-fry in hot oil; drain. Heat sesame oil in saucepan. Add remaining ingredients. Heat; pour over chicken. Yield: 2 servings.

Kathy Jenkins, Lambda Eta
Lamar, Missouri

LEMON BAKED CHICKEN

2 boneless skinless chicken breasts
1/4 cup vegetable oil
1/4 cup lemon juice
2 teaspoons oregano or tarragon (optional)
1/8 teaspoon garlic powder
2 tablespoons chopped parsley
1/4 teaspoon paprika

Preheat oven to 350 degrees. Place chicken in casserole. Combine next 4 ingredients in bowl. Brush mixture on chicken. Bake, covered, for 35 minutes. Brush with oil-lemon mixture. Bake, uncovered, for 20 minutes. Sprinkle with parsley and paprika. Yield: 4 servings.

Susan Burns, Preceptor Alpha Rho
Webster, New York

MUSTARD CHICKEN AND PASTA

1/3 cup Dijon mustard
1/3 cup vegetable oil
2 tablespoons red wine vinegar
3 tablespoons balsamic vinegar
1/2 teaspoon ground oregano
1/4 teaspoon salt
1/4 teaspoon pepper
6 boneless skinless chicken breasts
1/2 cup milk
1 (10-ounce) can cream of chicken soup
2 cups rotini, cooked, drained
1 cup 1-inch cubes yellow squash
1 cup 1-inch cubes zucchini
2 (2-ounce) can French-fried onion rings
1 large tomato, cut into wedges

Preheat oven to 375 degrees. Mix first 7 ingredients in large bowl. Toss chicken in mustard mixture until well coated; reserve mixture. Place chicken in 9-by-13-inch baking dish. Bake, uncovered, for 30 minutes. Mix milk, soup, hot pasta, squash, zucchini and 1/2 onion rings with mustard mixture. Spoon into dish around and under chicken. Bake, uncovered, for 20 minutes. Top pasta with tomato wedges. Top chicken breasts with remaining onion rings. Bake for 20 minutes. Yield: 6 servings.

Pat Hildebrant, Alpha Alpha Epsilon
Jacksonville, Florida

TROPICAL CHICKEN

1 (8-ounce) can crushed pineapple with juice	1/3 cup all-purpose flour
1/3 cup lime juice	1 teaspoon salt
1/4 teaspoon ground cloves	2 to 4 tablespoons vegetable oil
4 boneless skinless chicken breasts, cut into halves	1/3 cup slivered almonds
	1/3 cup flaked coconut

Preheat oven to 400 degrees. Combine pineapple, lime juice and cloves in bowl. Pound chicken breasts to 1/4-inch thickness. Place in pineapple mixture. Let marinate for 45 minutes. Drain, reserving marinade. Mix flour and salt in bowl. Dredge chicken breasts in flour mixture. Heat oil in skillet. Brown chicken breasts in oil on both sides. Place in baking dish. Add marinade to skillet. Heat until hot and bubbly. Pour over chicken breasts. Sprinkle almonds and coconut over top. Bake, covered, for 20 to 25 minutes. Yield: 4 servings.

Barbara I. Jacobson, Xi Master
Coos Bay, Oregon

VANILLA AND TARRAGON BAKED CHICKEN

2 chicken breasts with skins	2 tablespoons chicken broth
3 to 6 fresh tarragon sprigs	1 tablespoon pure vanilla extract
Salt and pepper to taste	

Preheat oven to 350 degrees. Line small baking pan with cooking foil. Rinse chicken breasts; pat dry. Place in baking pan. Loosen skin gently with fingers. Place tarragon sprig under skin of each chicken breast. Sprinkle remaining tarragon over top. Season with salt and pepper. Mix broth and vanilla in small bowl. Pour over chicken breasts. Seal chicken breasts securely in foil. Bake for 45 minutes, basting twice during baking. Drizzle basting liquid over chicken breasts; let stand for 5 to 10 minutes. Serve. Yield: 2 servings

Carole Van Hoven, Preceptor Beta
Grand Rapids, Michigan

CHICKEN WITH SPANISH RICE

2 pounds boneless skinless breasts	1 cup canned whole tomatoes with liquid
1 tablespoon plus 1 teaspoon vegetable oil	2 tablespoons chopped parsley
1/2 teaspoon paprika	1/8 teaspoon turmeric
1/2 cup sliced scallions	2 tablespoons dried chopped pimento
8 ounces uncooked rice	1/8 teaspoon freshly ground pepper
1 1/2 cups low-sodium chicken broth	1 1/2 cups green beans

Brown chicken breasts in hot oil in skillet. Sprinkle on both sides with paprika. Remove chicken breasts from skillet. Add scallions and rice to skillet, stirring until rice is golden brown and translucent. Stir in broth, tomatoes, parsley, turmeric, pimento and pepper. Bring to a boil. Return chicken to skillet; cover. Reduce heat to low. Cook for 15 minutes, stirring occasionally. Add green beans. Cook until tender. Yield: 8 servings.

Marjorie Brandon, Laureate Eta Omicron
Madera, California

APPLE CHICKEN

1 (3- to 3 1/2-pound) chicken, cut up	8 ounces mushrooms, sliced
Salt and pepper to taste	1 green apple, cored, chopped
2 tablespoons butter or margarine	1/4 cup cream or milk
1 medium onion, chopped	1 tablespoon cornstarch
1 (6-ounce) can frozen apple juice concentrate	3 tablespoons Brandy
	Chopped parsley

Season chicken pieces with salt and pepper. Melt butter in large skillet with lid. Add chicken; brown well. Add onion and apple juice concentrate. Cover; simmer for 30 minutes. Add mushrooms and apples. Cook, covered, for 15 minutes longer or until chicken is fork-tender. Remove chicken, vegetables and apples to serving platter; keep warm. Mix cream and cornstarch in bowl. Stir into pan drippings with Brandy. Cook, stirring constantly, until thickened. Pour sauce over chicken. Sprinkle with parsley. Yield: 4 to 6 servings.

Kathryn M. Hosman, Preceptor Lambda Pi
Visalia, California

CHICKEN AND ARTICHOKE BUFFET

3 whole chicken breasts, cooked	1/2 cup heavy cream
	1/2 cup Sherry
2 cups 1-inch carrot strips	1 teaspoon salt
4 tablespoons butter or margarine	2 (14-ounce) cans artichoke hearts, drained, quartered
4 cups cooked wild rice	
10 medium mushrooms, sliced	3 cups grated mozzarella cheese
10 small green onions, chopped	Freshly grated Parmesan cheese
2 (10-ounce) cans cream of chicken soup	

Preheat oven to 350 degrees. Cut chicken into bite-sized pieces. Blanch carrots for 5 minutes in saucepan. Rinse well with cold water; drain. Grease 9-by-13-inch casserole with 2 tablespoons butter. Spread cooked rice evenly in casserole. Sauté mushrooms and onions in remaining butter in skillet. Add soup, cream, Sherry and salt; mix well. Combine mushroom mixture, chicken, artichokes, blanched carrots and mozzarella cheese in large bowl; mix well. Spread over rice. Sprinkle with Parmesan cheese. Yield: 8 to 10 servings.

Rowena Caraway, Laureate Delta Alpha
Silsbee, Texas

AJI DE GALLINA

2 cups milk
1 loaf of bread
2 chickens, cut up
Salt to taste
1/2 cup vegetable oil
2 tablespoons garlic
2 green peppers, coarsely chopped
2 medium onions, sliced
4 ounces Parmesan cheese, grated
1/2 cup chopped nuts
Salt and pepper to taste
1 head leaf lettuce
12 potatoes, cooked
10 hard-cooked eggs
1 small can olives, pitted
2 tablespoons chopped parsley

Pour milk over bread in bowl. Let soak for 2 hours. Boil chicken in salted water in saucepan until tender; reserve broth. Debone chicken; cut into 1-inch pieces. Heat oil in electric skillet. Fry bread, garlic, green peppers, onions, cheese and nuts. Add reserved chicken broth if mixture becomes too dry. Add chicken. Cook until heated through. Season with salt and pepper. Arrange lettuce leaves and potatoes on serving platter. Pour chicken mixture over lettuce and potatoes. Garnish with eggs, olives and parsley. Yield: 12 servings.

Oguilvia Skelton, Alpha Delta
Eugene, Oregon

♥ HONEY-CRUNCH CHICKEN

1 1/4 pounds boneless skinless chicken pieces
2 tablespoons plus 2 teaspoons reduced-calorie mayonnaise
1 1/2 ounces Grape Nuts, crushed
1 tablespoon plus 1 teaspoon honey

Preheat oven to 375 degrees. Rinse chicken; pat dry. Spread mayonnaise over both sides of chicken, using pastry brush. Place in shallow baking pan. Sprinkle cereal evenly over chicken. Drizzle honey evenly over cereal. Let stand at room temperature for 10 minutes. Bake, uncovered, for 45 minutes. Yield: 4 servings.

Peggie Helms, Laureate Gamma Mu
Jacksonville, Florida

BAKED CHICKEN PARMESAN

2 eggs or 1/2 cup egg beaters
2 tablespoons milk
1 cup instant potato flakes
1 teaspoon garlic powder
1/4 cup grated Parmesan cheese
3 pounds chicken, cut up
1/4 cup margarine

Preheat oven to 400 degrees. Beat eggs and milk in shallow bowl. Mix potato flakes, garlic powder and Parmesan cheese in medium bowl. Roll chicken in egg mixture, then in potato flake mixture. Melt margarine in 9-by-13-inch baking pan. Roll coated chicken in margarine. Arrange, skin side up, in baking pan. Bake for 45 to 50 minutes or until tender. Yield: 6 servings.

Karla Woodard, Xi Delta
Gillette, Wyoming

CHICKEN PAELLA

4 ounces pork link sausage
1 (2 1/2-pound) chicken, cut up
Salt and pepper to taste
2 cups uncooked quick-cooking brown rice
1/2 onion, chopped
2 cloves of garlic, minced
1 3/4 cups water
1 (6-ounce) can tomato juice
1 (47-ounce) can minced clams

Preheat oven to 350 degrees. Cut sausage into 1-inch lengths. Brown in skillet; remove sausage. Season chicken with salt and pepper. Brown slowly in sausage drippings. Layer 1/2 browned chicken pieces and 1 cup rice in Dutch oven; repeat layers. Combine sausage and remaining ingredients in bowl. Pour over rice, stirring gently to mix. Bake for 1 1/2 hours. Yield: 6 servings.

Susie McKinney, Xi Epsilon Beta
Prosser, Washington

CHICKEN PAPRIKAS AND DUMPLINGS

1 large onion, chopped
1/4 cup butter or margarine
5 pounds chicken, cut up
3 tablespoons paprika
1 1/2 cups water
4 eggs
1/2 cup milk
2 cups sifted all-purpose flour
2 teaspoons salt
Butter or margarine to taste
1 1/2 cups sour cream

Brown onion in butter in skillet. Add chicken. Brown on each side for 10 minutes. Sprinkle chicken with paprika after turning. Add water; cover. Simmer slowly until tender. Remove chicken from skillet. Combine eggs, milk, flour and salt in bowl. Drop small bits of flour mixture into boiling mixture in skillet. Cook for 15 minutes. Remove from skillet. Rinse with cold water; drain. Top with butter. Place sour cream in mixer bowl. Add drippings slowly to sour cream, a little at a time. Add dumplings. Add chicken; mix well. Yield: 8 servings.

Barbara Imber, Laureate Gamma Epsilon
Toledo, Ohio

♥ TANDOORI CHICKEN

1 cup plain nonfat yogurt
1 tablespoon minced gingerroot
2 large cloves of garlic, minced
1 tablespoon paprika
1 1/2 teaspoon coriander
1 1/2 teaspoons cumin
1 teaspoon salt (optional)
1 teaspoon pepper
3/4 teaspoon cayenne
6 pounds skinless chicken pieces, wings removed
Vegetable oil

Mix first 9 ingredients in bowl. Make 1-inch deep slits in chicken at intervals. Coat chicken with marinade, rubbing into slits. Refrigerate, covered, for 6 to 24 hours. Preheat oven to broil. Place chicken on oiled rack in broiler pan. Broil 6 inches from heat for 20 minutes. Turn over. Broil for 15 minutes. Yield: 8 servings.

Vanessa L. Gilmore, Iota Chi
St. Louis, Missouri

92 / Poultry

♥ CHICKEN GARDENER'S-STYLE

Nonstick vegetable cooking spray
1 (3-pound) chicken, skinned, cut into pieces
8 small new potatoes, scrubbed
8 small white onions, peeled
4 medium carrots, peeled, cut into 3-inch pieces
1 1/2 cups low-sodium chicken broth
1/2 cup dry white wine
1 tablespoon lemon juice
3 cloves of garlic, minced
1 teaspoon dried oregano
1/2 teaspoon dried thyme
1/4 teaspoon pepper

Preheat oven to 500 degrees. Coat 9-by-13-inch baking pan with cooking spray. Arrange chicken pieces, potatoes, onions and carrots in pan. Combine chicken broth, wine and lemon juice in bowl. Pour over chicken and vegetables. Sprinkle with garlic, oregano, thyme and pepper. Bake, uncovered, for 40 to 45 minutes or until juices run clear. Turn chicken and vegetables occasionally, basting with pan juices. Add more chicken broth if needed. Yield: 4 servings.

Rosemarie Centola, Laureate Gamma Upsilon
Lady Lake, Florida

♥ CHICKEN AND VEGETABLES IN ROSÉ SAUCE

1 teaspoon vegetable oil
1 teaspoon margarine
1 1/2 pounds skinless chicken pieces
1/4 teaspoon salt
Dash of pepper
2 tablespoons chopped onion
1 cup quartered mushrooms
1/4 cup Rosé
1/4 cup canned chicken broth
3/4 cup frozen artichoke hearts
1/2 cup broccoli flowerets, blanched

Combine oil and margarine in 9-inch skillet. Heat over medium heat until bubbly and hot. Add chicken. Cook, turning frequently, until lightly browned on all sides. Sprinkle with salt and pepper. Remove chicken from skillet. Sauté onion in same skillet until softened. Add mushrooms. Sauté for 2 minutes longer. Stir in Rosé and broth. Bring to a boil. Reduce heat to low. Return chicken to pan. Simmer, covered, for 40 minutes or until chicken is almost tender. Add artichoke hearts. Simmer for 5 minutes. Stir in broccoli. Simmer for 3 minutes. Yield: 2 servings.

Connie Windmiller, Theta Omega
Salisbury, Missouri

Sandy Young, Preceptor Gamma Lambda, Castle Rock, Colorado, makes Curry Marmalade Chicken by mixing 1/2 cup orange marmalade, 2 tablespoons lemon juice and 1/2 teaspoon curry powder in saucepan. Heat until melted. Pour over 4 boneless skinless chicken breasts in baking dish. Bake in preheated 350-degree oven for 1 hour, basting as necessary.

♥ CHICKEN-LINGUINE STIR-FRY

1 (16-ounce) package fresh linguine
Olive oil
2 cloves of garlic, finely minced
Ginger to taste
1 pound chicken breast strips
2 carrots, peeled, thinly sliced
2 cups broccoli flowerets
2 cups cauliflowerets
1 small red bell pepper, julienned
4 cups fresh spinach
1/2 cup chopped green onions
1 cup red wine vinegar
1/4 cup soy sauce

Cook linguine according to package directions; drain. Heat 2 tablespoons olive oil in large skillet or wok over medium-high heat. Add garlic and ginger. Sauté for 1 minute. Add chicken. Sauté for 5 minutes. Add carrots, broccoli, cauliflower and red pepper. Sauté for 5 minutes. Add 1 tablespoon oil at a time as necessary. Add spinach and green onions. Sauté for 2 minutes. Transfer to large bowl. Add linguine; mix well. Mix vinegar, soy sauce and 2 to 4 tablespoons olive oil in same skillet. Simmer for 1 minute. Toss sauce and linguine mixture together. Yield: 8 servings.

Christine McCurry, Pi Zeta
Olathe, Kansas

CHICKEN-VEGETABLE LASAGNA

We served this dish at a Beta Sigma Phi Christmas party. It was enjoyed by all.

1 tablespoon vegetable oil
1 teaspoon butter or margarine
1/2 pound lean ground chicken
1/2 cup chopped onion
2 cloves of garlic, minced
1 (28-ounce) can tomatoes
1 (5-ounce) can tomato paste
3/4 cup water
1 1/2 teaspoons salt
Pinch of pepper
4 medium carrots, chopped
1 bunch broccoli, chopped
8 ounces mushrooms, sliced
12 ounces lasagna noodles
Mozzarella cheese to taste
Parmesan cheese to taste

Preheat oven to 350 degrees. Combine oil and butter in skillet. Add chicken, onion and garlic. Cook until chicken is done, stirring until crumbly. Add tomatoes, tomato paste, water, salt and pepper. Cook, uncovered, for 15 minutes. Add carrots, broccoli and mushrooms. Cook over low heat for 30 minutes. Cook lasagna according to package directions. Spoon 1/4 of the sauce into 9-by-13-inch baking dish. Layer lasagna noodles over sauce. Repeat layers twice, ending with sauce. Top with mozzarella cheese. Sprinkle with Parmesan cheese. Bake for 30 to 45 minutes. Let stand for 10 minutes. Serve. Yield: 8 servings.

Cathy Martindale, Kappa
Beresford, New Brunswick, Canada

♥ PASTA WITH LOVE

This is low fat and heart smart. Serve with bread and a good red wine.

1 pound boneless skinless chicken breasts, cubed	2 teaspoons capers
2 tablespoons water	2 tablespoons chopped cilantro
1 cup chopped scallions	2 cups low-fat ricotta cheese
1 cup chopped red bell pepper	4 cups Penne pasta, cooked
1 cup chopped tomato	

Sauté chicken in water in saucepan until tender. Add scallions, red pepper, tomato, capers and cilantro. Cook until vegetables are tender. Stir in cheese, blending thoroughly. Serve over pasta. Yield: 4 servings.

Ann M. Lang, Xi Tau
Boise, Idaho

CHICKEN SPAGHETTI

I make this recipe for any of my sorority sisters who are in need of help. It makes enough for two meals.

1 cup chopped onion	1 (4-ounce) jar pimentos (optional)
1 green pepper, chopped	5 cups chopped cooked chicken
1/2 cup butter or margarine	1/2 cup black olives, chopped
1 (16-ounce) package spaghetti	8 ounces grated Cheddar cheese
2 (10-ounce) cans cream of mushroom soup	

Preheat oven to 350 degrees. Sauté onion and pepper in butter in medium saucepan. Cook spaghetti according to package directions. Add soup and pimento to sautéed mixture. Remove from heat. Stir in chicken, olives and half the cheese. Add spaghetti; mix. Place in 9-by-13-inch baking pan. Top with remaining cheese. Bake for 45 minutes or until hot and bubbly. Yield: 10 to 12 servings.

Jeanette Geibel, Xi Eta Phi
Pittsburgh, Pennsylvania

CHICKEN POTPIE WITH PHYLLO DOUGH

I have taken this potpie to several covered dish luncheons and received raves.

1 (3- to 3 1/2-pound) chicken	2 stalks celery, chopped
Margarine	6 small red potatoes, cubed
2 cups half and half	1 bunch broccoli, chopped
1 tablespoon all-purpose flour	1 onion, chopped
2 cups chicken broth	1 (10-ounce) package frozen peas
3 carrots, peeled, cubed	1 package phyllo

Preheat oven to 350 degrees. Boil chicken until tender in covered saucepan. Remove bones and skin. Cut into bite-sized pieces. Combine 1/4 cup margarine, half and half, flour and broth in saucepan. Cook until blended and smooth. Remove from heat. Add chicken, carrots, celery, potatoes, broccoli, onion and peas; mix well. Place 3 layers phyllo in 11-by-15-inch baking pan, brushing each layer with melted margarine. Spread half the chicken mixture over top layer. Place 3 more layers phyllo over mixture, brushing each layer with melted margarine. Repeat layers ending with phyllo. Bake for 1 hour. Yield: 12 servings.

Elizabeth F. Curts, Theta Gamma
Ruston, Louisiana

MINIATURE CHICKEN PIES

1 cup frozen green peas	3 tablespoons mayonnaise
1 (10-count) can buttermilk biscuits	1/2 cup sliced water chestnuts
1 (11-ounce) Mexicorn, drained	1/4 cup finely chopped onion
2 (5-ounce) cans chunk white chicken in water, drained	1 cup grated Cheddar cheese
4 ounces cream cheese, softened	Salt and pepper to taste
	Dash of garlic powder

Preheat oven to 325 degrees. Cook peas in small amount of water in saucepan for 3 minutes; drain. Separate each biscuit into 2 halves. Place bottom half of biscuit in greased muffin cup, shaping to form cup. Repeat for each biscuit. Combine peas and remaining ingredients in large bowl; mix well. Spoon mixture into muffin cups, dividing equally. Cover with top portions of biscuits. Press edges to seal. Bake for 25 to 30 minutes or until golden brown and bubbling hot inside. Yield: 10 servings.

Judy Y. Rich, Preceptor Alpha Pi
McMinnville, Tennessee

EASY CROCK•POT CHICKEN ENCHILADAS

4 boneless skinless chicken breasts	8 to 10 corn tortillas
1 (4-ounce) can chopped green chilies	1 cup shredded Cheddar cheese
2 (14-ounce) cans cream of mushroom soup	Sour cream
	Salsa
	Olives

Combine chicken breasts, chilies and soup in Crock•Pot. Cook on Low for 4 1/2 hours, stirring each hour. Preheat oven to 350 degrees. Remove chicken breasts. Cut into bite-sized pieces. Place chicken on tortillas, dividing equally. Roll up tortillas, enclosing chicken. Place in baking dish. Spoon mushroom sauce in Crock•Pot over tortillas to cover. Top with cheese. Bake for 15 to 20 minutes. Garnish with sour cream, salsa and olives. Yield: 8 servings.

Tricia Macrab, Alpha Eta
Nathrop, Colorado

♥ CHICKEN FAJITAS

1 teaspoon vegetable oil	1 teaspoon ground
2 cloves of garlic, minced	cumin
1 large onion, cut into	1 teaspoon dried
bite-sized pieces	oregano
1 large green pepper,	Pepper to taste
cut into strips	1/2 cup lime juice
1 large red pepper,	4 flour tortillas
cut into strips	Salsa
4 chicken breasts, cut	Nonfat sour cream
into bite-sized pieces	

Heat oil in skillet. Add garlic, onion, green pepper, red pepper and chicken. Sauté for 2 minutes. Add seasonings and lime juice. Simmer for 7 minutes or until chicken is done. Warm tortillas in nonstick pan or microwave just until softened. Place on serving dish. Place chicken mixture on each tortilla, dividing equally. Top with salsa and sour cream. Fold tortillas. Yield: 4 servings.

Debbie Windmiller, Theta Omega
Salisbury, Missouri

♥ SOUTH TEXAS-STYLE ROAST CHICKEN

1 (3- to 3 1/2-pound)	Hot green pepper to taste
chicken	1/2 onion, cut in half
Salt to taste	Olive oil
Freshly ground black	Crushed rosemary
pepper to taste	to taste
1 clove of garlic	Thyme to taste
2 or 3 sprigs parsley	Dry white wine

Preheat oven to 350 degrees. Rinse chicken; pat dry. Rub inside and out with salt and pepper. Place garlic, parsley and hot pepper inside chicken. Place chicken in roasting pan, breast-side up. Place onion on each side. Sprinkle oil over all. Sprinkle with rosemary and thyme. Bake for 2 hours, turning and basting occasionally to brown evenly. Pour wine over chicken during last 30 minutes of baking. Baste again. Yield: 6 servings.

Carol Sassin, Xi Psi Beta
Beeville, Texas

♥ PITA PIZZAS

1/2 pound boneless	1/2 teaspoon dried
skinless chicken breasts,	oregano leaves
cut into 1/2-inch cubes	1 cup torn fresh spinach
1/2 cup thinly sliced red	leaves
bell pepper	6 mini whole wheat pita
1/2 cup thinly sliced	bread rounds
mushrooms	1/2 cup shredded
1/2 cup thinly sliced red	mozzarella cheese
onion	1 teaspoon grated
2 cloves of garlic, minced	Parmesan cheese
1 teaspoon dried basil	
leaves	

Preheat oven to 375 degrees. Coat skillet with nonstick vegetable cooking spray. Heat skillet over medium heat. Add chicken. Sauté for 6 minutes or until browned. Remove from skillet. Coat same skillet again with cooking spray. Add red peppers, mushrooms, onion, garlic, basil and oregano. Sauté for 5 to 7 minutes. Add chicken; stir well. Place spinach leaves on each pita bread round. Spoon chicken mixture evenly on spinach, dividing equally. Sprinkle with cheeses. Bake for 7 to 10 minutes or until cheeses are melted. Yield: 6 servings.

Rosanne Richey, Alpha Delta Lambda
Cameron, Missouri

BRUNSWICK STEW WITH POLENTA DUMPLINGS

2 cups cooked chicken	1 (16-ounce) can whole
4 cups defatted chicken	kernel corn
stock	1 (16-ounce) can lima
1 onion, thinly sliced	beans
3 potatoes, thinly sliced	1 cup cornmeal
1 tablespoon sugar	3 cups water
Salt and pepper to taste	Salt to taste (optional)

Combine chicken, chicken stock, onion, potatoes, sugar, salt and pepper in stockpot. Cook until potatoes are tender. Add corn and beans. Cook for 5 minutes. Combine cornmeal and water in saucepan. Add salt. Cook, stirring constantly, until polenta is solid. Ladle stew into bowls. Top with spoonfuls of polenta. Yield: 6 to 8 servings.

Kathy Anderson, Xi Beta Rho
Norman, Oklahoma

♥ GRILLED MARINATED CHICKEN

1 (12-ounce) bottle chili	1 teaspoon salt
sauce	3 pounds boneless
1/2 cup red wine vinegar	skinless chicken
1 tablespoon horseradish	breasts, cubed
1 clove of garlic,	3 large green peppers, cut
quartered	into bite-sized pieces

Combine first 5 ingredients in 9-by-13-inch baking dish; mix well. Place chicken in marinade. Refrigerate, covered, for 2 hours. Preheat grill. Thread chicken pieces and green peppers alternately on skewers. Grill over hot coals until chicken is tender. Yield: 4 servings.

Deanna Beiermann, Rho Sigma
Jerseyville, Illinois

Michelle Austin, Delta Mu, Monticello, Arkansas, makes Oven-Fried Chicken Strips by cutting 4 boneless skinless chicken breasts into strips. Dip chicken strips in 2 slightly beaten egg whites. Coat in 1 1/4 cups Italian bread crumbs. Place in baking pan coated lightly with nonstick vegetable cooking spray. Bake in preheated 400-degree oven for 15 minutes, turning once. Serve with Honey Mustard made by combining 3/4 cup mayonnaise, 1 tablespoon mustard and 2 tablespoons honey in small bowl. Mix well and refrigerate. Yield: 4 servings.

♥ GRILLED CIOPPINO "PACKETS"

12 littleneck clams, scrubbed	4 fresh ears of corn, shucked
4 lobster tails	Salt to taste
4 boneless skinless chicken breasts, cut into halves	Freshly ground black pepper to taste
	Pinch of cayenne pepper
4 whole baking potatoes, scrubbed	1 1/3 cups dry white wine or water
4 large whole carrots, peeled	Peasant bread
4 stalks celery, trimmed	Sweet butter or margarine

Preheat grill to medium heat. Place one 24-inch square piece cooking foil on flat surface. Place one 24-inch square piece of cheesecloth directly over foil. Place 3 clams, 1 lobster tail, 1 chicken breast, 1 potato, 1 carrot, 1 stalk celery and 1 ear of corn in center of cheesecloth. Season with salt, pepper and cayenne pepper. Fold sides of cheesecloth over mixture to enclose completely. Begin to fold sides of foil over mixture. Pour 1/3 cup wine into each packet. Fold edges of foil, sealing tightly. Repeat for remaining 3 packets. Place packets directly on hot grill. Cover. Grill for 30 to 35 minutes or until potatoes are tender. Transfer each packet to large individual serving plate. Let set for 5 minutes. Serve hot with bread and butter. Packets may be baked in preheated 350-degree oven for 40 to 45 minutes or until done. Yield: 4 servings.

Janice DiBeneditto, Laureate Iota
Waterbury, Connecticut

♣ ♥ SUMMER LIME CHICKEN BREASTS

This recipe was prepared by my son and is a favorite at Lewis 'n' Clark Restaurant in St. Charles.

4 boneless skinless chicken breasts	3 tablespoons chopped fresh cilantro
1/3 cup olive oil	1/2 teaspoon salt
Juice of 3 limes	1/2 teaspoon pepper
4 cloves of garlic, minced	

Place chicken in 9-by-13-inch dish. Combine oil, lime juice, garlic, cilantro, salt and pepper in bowl; mix well. Pour over chicken breasts. Refrigerate, covered, for 1 hour. Preheat grill. Grill chicken breasts for 10 minutes on each side. Yield: 4 servings.

Maxine Birdsong, Zeta Phi
St. Charles, Missouri

CAJUN TURKEY

1 (12- to 14-pound) frozen turkey	6 to 8 fresh whole jalapeño peppers
4 to 6 stalks celery, sliced	2 fresh whole green chili peppers
3 medium white onions, quartered	Vegetable oil
	Cajun seasoning to taste

Preheat oven to 250 degrees. Thaw and clean turkey according to label directions. Stuff turkey with half the celery, onions and jalapeño peppers and all the chili peppers. Baste turkey with oil. Coat with cajun seasoning. Place turkey in cooking bag with remaining celery, onions and jalapeño peppers. Cut vent in bag. Bake for 8 hours or until tests done. Adjust baking time according to turkey weight. Serve with cajun recipes. Yield: 12 to 16 servings.

Chele Raasch, Beta
Ankeny, Iowa

KRAUT BURGERS

1 loaf frozen bread dough, thawed	1/2 teaspoon pepper
1 pound ground turkey	1 (16-ounce) can sauerkraut, drained
1 small onion, chopped	1/2 cup catsup
2 teaspoons salt	

Preheat oven to 350 degrees. Let bread dough rise until doubled in bulk. Brown turkey in skillet, stirring until crumbly. Add onion, salt and pepper; mix well. Add sauerkraut and catsup; mix well. Cut bread dough into approximately 8 to 10 equal portions. Roll out each portion. Place 1 large spoonful turkey mixture in center of each portion. Roll up corners of dough; seal. Place on cookie sheet. Bake for 30 to 40 minutes or until browned. Yield: 4 servings.

Julie K. Boettcher, Xi Alpha Iota
Custer, South Dakota

♥ SPINACH-FILLED TURKEY LOAF

1 1/2 pounds ground turkey	2 cups frozen cut leaf spinach, thawed
2 eggs, slightly beaten	1/2 cup shredded part-skim mozzarella cheese
1/2 cup finely chopped onion	
2 cloves of garlic, minced	1/2 cup part-skim ricotta cheese
1/2 teaspoon salt	1/3 cup apple jelly (optional)
Bread crumbs	

Preheat oven to 375 degrees. Combine turkey, eggs, onion, garlic and salt with enough bread crumbs to make firm mixture; mix well. Pat mixture into 8-by-12-inch rectangle on sheet of cooking foil. Combine spinach and cheeses in bowl; blend well. Spread evenly over turkey mixture. Roll up, starting with 8-inch side, using foil to help rolling process. Place loaf, seam-side down, in 5-by-9-inch loaf pan. Heat apple jelly in small saucepan until melted, stirring occasionally. Brush half the melted jelly over loaf. Bake for 55 minutes to 1 hour or until tests done. Brush with remaining jelly mixture half way through baking. Yield: 8 servings.

Elsie M. Green, Preceptor Alpha
Glendale, California

♥ TURKEY LOAF

3/4 cup rolled oats
1/4 to 1/2 cup herbed croutons
3/4 cup skim milk
2 egg whites
1/4 cup chopped onion
1/4 cup chopped green bell pepper
1/2 teaspoon ground sage
1/8 teaspoon pepper
1 teaspoon parsley flakes
1/4 cup honey
1 pound ground turkey
2 tablespoons dark brown sugar
1/4 cup catsup
1 teaspoon dry mustard
1/4 teaspoon ground nutmeg
1/8 teaspoon ground ginger
1 tablespoon honey

Preheat oven to 375 degrees. Combine oats, croutons, milk, egg whites, onion, green pepper, sage, pepper, parsley and 1/4 cup honey in large bowl; mix well. Add ground turkey; blend thoroughly. Mixture should be firm enough to shape; if not, add more croutons. Shape into loaf. Press into 5-by-9-inch loaf pan. Combine brown sugar, catsup, mustard, nutmeg, ginger and 1 tablespoon honey in small bowl; mix well. Pour over loaf. Bake, uncovered, for 1 hour. Yield: 6 servings.

Alicia Proffitt, Xi Eta Kappa
Sterling, Kansas

SHEPHERD'S PIE

2 cups cubed cooked turkey
2 cups frozen mixed vegetables, thawed
1 (10-ounce) can cream of mushroom soup
Skim milk
2 tablespoons finely chopped onion
1/2 teaspoon dried Italian seasoning
1 (22-ounce) package frozen mashed potatoes
1 1/2 cups shredded Cheddar cheese

Preheat oven to 350 degrees. Mix turkey, vegetables, soup, 3/4 cup skim milk, onion and Italian seasoning in large bowl. Place mixture in 9-by-11-inch baking pan. Prepare potatoes according to package directions, using 1 2/3 cups skim milk. Spoon mashed potatoes over turkey mixture. Sprinkle cheese over potatoes. Bake for 25 minutes. Serve immediately. Yield: 6 servings.

Pat Franklin, Epsilon Rho
Alabaster, Alabama

PROUD-TO-SERVE GAME HENS

1/4 cup vegetable shortening
2 teaspoons Kitchen Bouquet
4 game hens, split into halves
1/4 cup butter or margarine
1/4 cup minced onion
1 (6-ounce) can sliced mushrooms
1 (5-ounce) can water chestnuts
1/2 cup white wine
3 tablespoons cornstarch
1/4 cup water
1 bouillon cube
8 ounces margarine
1/2 cup sliced celery
1 cup drained mandarin oranges
2 cups cooked rice

Preheat oven to broil. Combine shortening and Kitchen Bouquet in bowl. Brush over hens. Place hens on broiler rack. Broil for 10 minutes on each side. Melt butter in saucepan. Add onion; simmer for 3 minutes or until tender. Drain mushrooms and chestnuts, reserving liquid. Slice chestnuts. Add wine and enough water to reserved liquid to make 1 pint liquid. Pour into saucepan. Bring to a boil. Blend cornstarch with water. Stir in bouillon cube; blend well. Stir into wine mixture. Cook, stirring, until sauce is transparent. Add chestnuts and mushrooms. Place hens in large electric skillet. Pour sauce over hens. Simmer for 30 minutes or until heated through. Melt margarine in saucepan. Add celery. Sauté until limp. Add mandarin oranges. Add rice; mix gently. Serve rice with hens. Yield: 4 to 8 servings.

Shirley Jones, Laureate Beta Mu
Shingletown, California

BALLOTINE OF CAPON

1 cup pitted prunes
Port or apricot Brandy
4 tablespoons butter
1 Spanish onion, chopped
1 pound freshly ground pork
1 cup fresh bread crumbs
1 tablespoon sage
1 tablespoon chopped parsley
Salt and pepper to taste
1 egg, slightly beaten
1 (6-pound) capon or roasting chicken, boned
1 tablespoon all-purpose flour
2 cups chicken stock
1 teaspoon tomato paste
Bouquet garni (1 parsley sprig, 1 sprig thyme, 1 bay leaf)
Watercress or parsley

Soak prunes in port in saucepan for 2 hours. Simmer for 15 minutes; drain. Preheat oven to 375 degrees. Melt 2 tablespoons butter in skillet. Add onion. Sauté until onion is soft but not brown. Let cool. Combine onion, pork, bread crumbs, sage, chopped parsley, salt and pepper in bowl. Add egg; mix well. Place capon, skin side down, in baking pan. Place 1/3 the pork mixture down center of capon. Place 1/2 the prunes in row over mixture. Repeat, ending with pork mixture. Bring up sides of capon; tuck in ends. Sew up loosely; tie tightly in 3 places. Roast for 1 1/2 hours or until juices run clear. Melt 2 tablespoons butter in saucepan. Add flour, stirring constantly, until deep brown. Remove from heat. Add stock, tomato paste and bouquet garni; mix well. Slice ballotine on serving dish. Pour some sauce over slices. Serve remaining sauce in gravy boat. Garnish with watercress. Yield: 10 servings.

Patricia Crucefix, Preceptor Gamma Lambda
Castle Rock, Colorado

Brenda Boudreaux, Xi Beta Omega, New Iberia, Louisiana, makes Cajun Season-All by mixing 1 (26-ounce) box salt, 1 1/2 ounces ground black pepper, 2 ounces red cayenne pepper, 1 1/2 ounces garlic powder, 1 1/2 ounces onion powder and 1/4 cup dried parsley in bowl. Store in air-tight container.

OVEN-BAKED PHEASANT

2 pheasants	1 teaspoon salt
2 cups milk	1/2 teaspoon pepper
1 medium white onion, sliced	Cayenne pepper (optional)
2 stalks celery, sliced	4 slices bacon
1 small green bell pepper, sliced	1/4 cup melted butter or margarine
1/2 teaspoon garlic	1/2 cup water

Preheat oven to 325 degrees. Rinse pheasants; pat dry. Place in large bowl. Pour milk over pheasants. Refrigerate, covered, overnight. Drain; blot dry. Stuff pheasants with sliced vegetables. Season with garlic, salt, pepper and cayenne pepper. Wrap each pheasant with 2 bacon slices. Secure with toothpicks. Place in large casserole. Pour butter and water over pheasants. Bake, covered, for 2 hours. Yield: 2 servings.

Melissa Newby, Xi Delta Iota
Jay, Florida

PHEASANT CASSEROLE

12 ounces bulk mild pork sausage	1/4 cup butter or margarine
Onions to taste	1/4 cup all-purpose flour
8 ounces fresh mushrooms, sliced	1/2 cup milk
	1 3/4 cups chicken broth
1 (8-ounce) can water chestnuts, chopped	1 teaspoon salt
	1/8 teaspoon pepper
Juice of 1/2 lemon	2 cups chopped cooked pheasant
1 (6-ounce) package minute wild rice mix	1/2 cup toasted slivered almonds

Preheat oven to 350 degrees. Sauté sausage in skillet, stirring until crumbly. Remove from skillet; drain. Sauté onions and mushrooms in sausage drippings. Add water chestnuts. Squeeze lemon juice over mixture. Cook rice according to package directions. Melt butter in saucepan. Add flour, stirring to make a roux. Stir in milk, chicken broth, salt and pepper. Cook, stirring, until thickened. Combine pheasant, sausage, rice and mushroom mixture in bowl; toss lightly. Pour sauce over mixture; toss again. Place in 9-by-13-inch baking pan. Bake for 1 hour. Turn off oven. Let set in warm oven until serving time. Sprinkle with almonds. Yield: 6 servings.

LaVonne Ruse, Preceptor Gamma Gamma
Tulsa, Oklahoma

♥ HERB-BAKED FISH FILETS

2 tablespoons chopped green onions	2 tablespoons chopped parsley
1 clove of garlic, crushed	1/2 teaspoon salt
1/4 teaspoon thyme	Dash of tarragon
1/3 cup dry white wine	3/4 teaspoon basil
3 cups shredded Chinese cabbage	1 pound fish filets

Preheat oven to 450 degrees. Combine first 9 ingredients in bowl; mix well. Spread half the mixture in bottom of large shallow baking dish. Arrange filets over mixture. Cover with remaining mixture. Bake, covered, for 25 minutes or until fish flakes easily. Yield: 4 servings.

Cindy Vierboom, Xi Omicron
Calgary, Alberta, Canada

FISH FILETS WITH HERB-LEMON TOPPING

1 tablespoon butter or margarine	1 tablespoon grated lemon peel
2 tablespoons lemon juice	2 teaspoons chopped chives
1 (16-ounce) package frozen cod, Greenland turbot, flounder or sole filets, thawed	1/4 teaspoon salt
	Dash of pepper
	Cooked potatoes
1/2 cup chopped parsley	Cooked carrots

Preheat oven to broil. Melt butter in 1-quart saucepan over low heat. Stir in lemon juice. Place fish filets in 1 layer on rack in broiler pan. Baste with lemon-butter mixture. Broil for 5 to 8 minutes or until fish flakes easily, basting once. Combine parsley, lemon peel, chives, salt and pepper in small bowl; mix well. Sprinkle over fish and remaining ingredients 10 minutes before serving time. Yield: 4 servings.

Marlene Flowers, Xi Epsilon Delta
Topeka, Kansas

BAKED AMBER JACK FISH

10 (3-by-4-inch) Amber Jack steaks	Parsley flakes to taste
	Salt and pepper to taste
2 quarts milk	Tartar sauce to taste
1/2 cup margarine	Italian salad dressing to taste
1/2 cup lemon juice	
1 large onion, chopped	Cheddar cheese slices to taste
1 large green bell pepper, chopped	
	Monterey Jack cheese slices to taste
4 stalks celery, chopped	
Garlic powder or salt to taste	

Soak steaks in milk in bowl in refrigerator for 4 to 24 hours; drain. Place steaks in individual cooking foil pouches. Combine margarine and lemon juice in saucepan. Add onion, green pepper and celery, garlic powder, parsley flakes, salt and pepper. Sauté until vegetables are slightly softened. Spread thin layer tartar sauce over each steak. Top with sautéed mixture, dividing equally. Drizzle Italian dressing over mixture. Close pouch; seal tightly. Place on cookie sheet. Bake for 45 minutes. Remove from oven. Top with cheese slices. Bake for 15 minutes longer or until cheeses are melted. Yield: 8 to 10 servings.

Bette Hurst, Xi Lambda Iota
Steinhatchee, Florida

♥ CAJUN-STYLE ORANGE ROUGHY

1 (14- to 16-ounce) can stewed tomatoes
1 stalk celery, chopped
1 small onion, chopped
1 clove of garlic, minced
1/2 green pepper, chopped
1 bay leaf
1/4 teaspoon ground thyme
1/4 teaspoon pepper
Dash of salt
1/2 teaspoon Louisiana hot sauce
6 (6- to 8-ounce) orange roughy filets
2 tablespoons melted margarine
2 tablespoons chopped parsley
Cooked thin spaghetti

Preheat oven to 425 degrees. Mix first 10 ingredients in heavy saucepan over medium heat. Bring to a boil; reduce heat. Simmer for 20 minutes or until reduced. Place filets in shallow baking pan. Brush with margarine. Bake for 8 to 12 minutes or until opaque and flakes. Remove bay leaf from sauce. Spoon over fish. Sprinkle with parsley. Serve over spaghetti. Yield: 6 servings.

Beverly Binder, Laureate Gamma Epsilon
Toledo, Ohio

OREGON FLOUNDER AND SALMON ROULADE

1 (1-pound) boneless skinless salmon steak
1 pound flounder filets
1 teaspoon lemon juice
1/4 teaspoon pepper
1/2 cup water
1/2 cup dry white wine
2 shallots, thinly sliced
3/4 teaspoon salt
1 teaspoon leaf tarragon
1 1/2 cups heavy cream
1/8 teaspoon paprika
1 (16-ounce) can lobster or crab meat, drained, shredded
Fresh dill

Halve salmon crosswise; cut each half into 4 strips. Cut each filet in half lengthwise. Sprinkle with lemon juice and pepper. Place 1 salmon strip on each filet. Roll up; secure with toothpicks. Combine water, wine, shallots and 1/2 teaspoon salt in large skillet. Tie tarragon in cheesecloth; drop into skillet. Stand fish rolls in skillet. Bring to a boil; lower heat. Simmer, covered, for 5 minutes or just until fish loses its transparency, becomes white and feels firm. Remove rolls to warm platter; keep warm. Cook pan liquid rapidly until reduced to 1/2 cup; reserve. Cook cream rapidly in saucepan until reduced to 1 cup. Add reserved fish liquid, 1/4 teaspoon salt, paprika and lobster. Heat, stirring, until bubbly. Spoon sauce over fish. Garnish with dill. Yield: 8 servings.

Betty Czulo, Xi Zeta Omicron
Brighton, Ontario, Canada

Kathe Ingham, Laureate Epsilon Kappa, Easton, Pennsylvania, makes Baked Lemon Haddock by placing 2 pounds haddock filets in baking dish. Sprinkle with mixture of 1 cup dry bread crumbs, 1/4 cup melted butter, 2 tablespoons dried parsley, 2 teaspoons grated lemon peel and 1/2 teaspoon garlic powder. Bake at 350 degrees for 25 minutes or until fish flakes easily.

SALMON ALFREDO

8 ounces cream cheese, softened
3/4 cup Parmesan cheese
1/2 cup margarine
1/2 cup milk
1 (16-ounce) can salmon
1 (10-ounce) package frozen snow peas
8 ounces fettucini, cooked

Combine cream cheese, Parmesan cheese, margarine and milk in large saucepan. Cook, stirring, over low heat until smooth. Add salmon and snow peas, mixing gently. Heat through. Serve over fettucini. Yield: 4 servings.

Darlene Monteith, Xi Epsilon Beta
Fort Wayne, Indiana

SUCCULENT STUFFED SALMON

1/2 cup chopped celery
1/2 cup sliced onion
1/2 cup chopped green pepper
1 can sliced mushrooms, drained
1/4 teaspoon lemon pepper
1/4 teaspoon salt
2 tablespoons margarine
1 package stove-top stuffing mix
1 can shrimp
1 (2- to 3-pound) salmon
1 medium onion, sliced into rings
1 lemon, sliced

Preheat oven to 375 degrees. Stir-fry first 6 ingredients in margarine in skillet. Cook stove-top stuffing according to package directions. Combine stir-fried vegetables, stuffing and shrimp in bowl. Rinse salmon; pat dry. Stuff mixture inside salmon. Fold over. Cover with onion rings and lemon slices. Wrap in foil. Place on cookie sheet. Bake for 30 minutes. Yield: 6 to 8 servings.

Julie Anne MacDonell, Laureate Beta Gamma
Sudbury, Ontario, Canada

♥ SALMON-ROSEMARY WITH TOMATO SALSA

4 (1-inch thick) salmon steaks
1 tablespoon olive oil
2 tablespoons lime juice
1 teaspoon fresh rosemary
Salt to taste
Freshly ground pepper to taste
1/2 cup chopped tomatoes
1/4 cup chopped fresh basil or parsley
2 tablespoons finely chopped green onions
1 tablespoon red wine vinegar
1 tablespoon olive oil
1/2 teaspoon grated lime zest
4 tablespoons tomato salsa

Place salmon in large flat dish. Combine 1 tablespoon olive oil with next 4 ingredients in bowl. Pour over salmon; turn salmon. Refrigerate, covered, for 30 minutes to 4 hours. Combine remaining ingredients in small bowl; mix well. Preheat grill. Grill salmon on oiled grill for 4 to 6 minutes on each side, turning once. Serve immediately with 1 tablespoon tomato salsa per person. Yield: 4 servings.

Kelso Reed, Gamma Master
Victoria, British Columbia, Canada

SALMON PATTIES

1 (6-ounce) can salmon, boned, drained
1 teaspoon minced onion
1/2 teaspoon parsley flakes
1 teaspoon lemon juice
Dash of pepper
2 tablespoons sour cream
1 egg, slightly beaten
2 tablespoons dry bread crumbs
2 tablespoons vegetable oil

Combine salmon, onion, parsley, lemon juice and pepper in small bowl. Add sour cream, egg and bread crumbs; mix well. Shape into patties. Heat oil in skillet over medium heat. Cook patties for 4 minutes on each side or until lightly browned. Yield: 2 servings.

Juanita Hill, Laureate Alpha Psi
Lancaster, Ohio

SALMON QUICHE

1 cup whole wheat flour
2/3 cup grated Cheddar cheese
1/4 cup chopped toasted almonds
1/4 teaspoon paprika
6 tablespoons vegetable oil
1 (6-ounce) can salmon
3 eggs, beaten
1/2 cup sour cream
1/2 cup yogurt
1/4 cup mayonnaise
1/2 cup grated Cheddar cheese
1/4 teaspoon dillweed
3 drops of hot pepper sauce

Preheat oven to 350 degrees. Combine flour, 2/3 cup Cheddar cheese, almonds, paprika and vegetable oil in bowl; mix well. Press into 9-inch pie plate. Bake for 10 minutes. Reduce temperature to 325 degrees. Drain and flake salmon, reserving liquid. Blend eggs, sour cream, yogurt, mayonnaise and reserved liquid in bowl. Fold in salmon, 1/2 cup Cheddar cheese, dillweed and pepper sauce. Spoon into shell. Bake for 40 minutes. Yield: 6 servings.

June Bingham, Beta Master
Comox, British Columbia, Canada

SURPRISE SOLE ROLLS

1 (10-ounce) package frozen chopped spinach
3/4 cup plain low-fat yogurt
1 tablespoon cornstarch
1/2 cup chopped green onions
1 1/2 teaspoons lemon juice
1/2 teaspoon garlic powder
6 (4-ounce) sole filets
Paprika to taste

Place spinach in microwave-safe bowl. Microwave on High for 7 minutes; drain well, pressing out water. Combine spinach, yogurt, cornstarch, green onions, lemon juice and garlic powder in medium microwave-safe bowl. Microwave on High for 1 1/2 to 2 minutes. Spread mixture down middle of each filet to 1/4 inch of edges. Roll up jelly-roll fashion. Secure with toothpicks. Arrange in 7-by-11-inch microwave-safe dish. Sprinkle with paprika. Microwave on High for 3 minutes. Rearrange, moving outside rolls to center of dish. Microwave on High for 2 to 3 minutes longer or until fish turns opaque and just begins to flake. Yield: 6 servings.

Frances S. Fogg, Preceptor Lambda
Gorham, Maine

GRILLED BERMUDA WAHOO WITH BANANA SAUCE

2 pounds firm white fish filets
All-purpose flour
Vegetable oil
1 tablespoon butter or margarine
1 cup white rum
1/2 teaspoon salt
1/2 teaspoon freshly ground pepper
2 firm Bermuda bananas, sliced
1 tablespoon sugar
Juice of 1/2 lemon or lime
1 tablespoon curry powder
Rice
Grilled tomatoes
Buttered green peas

Coat filets with flour in bowl. Pan-fry in small amount of oil until tender. Melt 1 tablespoon butter in medium saucepan. Add 1 tablespoon flour; mix well. Add rum gradually, mixing with fork. Add next 6 ingredients. Cook over low heat until slightly thickened. Serve over fish filets. Serve with rice, grilled tomatoes and buttered green peas. Yield: 4 servings.

Margaret Holland, Laureate Phi
Nepean, Ontario, Canada

MIDWEST TUNA CAKES WITH LEMON-DILL SAUCE

1 (12-ounce) can water-packed tuna
3/4 cup seasoned bread crumbs
1/4 cup minced green onions
2 tablespoons chopped pimentos
1/4 cup egg substitute
1/2 cup skim milk
2 tablespoons margarine
1/4 cup chicken broth
1 tablespoon lemon juice
1/4 teaspoon dried dillweed
Lemon slices
Fresh parsley sprigs

Drain and finely flake tuna. Combine tuna, bread crumbs, onions and pimentos in large bowl. Beat egg substitute and milk together in small bowl. Stir into tuna mixture; mix until moistened. Shape into eight 4-inch patties with lightly floured hands. Melt margarine in large nonstick skillet. Fry patties, a few at a time, for 3 minutes on each side or until golden brown. Keep warm in preheated 300-degree oven until ready to serve. Combine chicken broth, lemon juice and dillweed in small saucepan. Cook until heated through. Spoon over tuna cakes. Garnish with lemon slices and parsley. Yield: 4 servings.

Lauren Iannaci, Delta Rho
Lakeville, Minnesota

BROCCOLI-TUNA ROLL-UPS

1 (10-ounce) can cream of mushroom soup
1 cup milk
1 (10-ounce) can tuna drained
1 (10-ounce) package frozen broccoli spears, drained, cut into 1-inch pieces
1 cup shredded Cheddar cheese
1 can French-fried onion rings
6 small flour tortillas
1 tomato, chopped

Preheat oven to 350 degrees. Mix soup and milk in bowl. Combine tuna, broccoli, 1/2 cup cheese and 1/2 can onion rings in bowl. Stir in 3/4 cup soup mixture. Spoon tuna mixture on tortillas, dividing equally; roll up to enclose mixture. Place, seam side down, in 9-by-13-inch greased baking dish. Stir tomato into remaining soup mixture. Pour over tortillas. Bake, covered, for 35 minutes. Top tortillas with remaining cheese and onion rings. Bake, uncovered, for 5 minutes longer. Yield: 6 servings.

Debbie Schultz, Epsilon Beta
Truman, Minnesota

HEARTY TUNA CASSEROLE

2 (6-ounce) cans chunky tuna
3 cups uncooked egg noodles
1/2 cup chopped celery
1/3 cup sliced green onions
1/2 cup sour cream
2 teaspoons mustard
1/2 cup mayonnaise
1/2 teaspoon dried thyme leaves
1/4 teaspoon salt
1 small zucchini, sliced
1 cup shredded Monterey Jack cheese
1 tomato, chopped

Preheat oven to 350 degrees. Drain and flake tuna. Cook noodles according to package directions; drain. Rinse in hot water. Combine noodles with tuna, celery and green onions. Blend next 5 ingredients in bowl. Spoon 1/2 the mixture into 2-quart buttered casserole. Top with half the zucchini. Repeat layers. Top with cheese. Sprinkle with tomato. Bake for 30 minutes. Yield: 4 to 6 servings.

Shirley Hornstein, Beta Master
Courtenay, British Columbia, Canada

SEAFOOD PASTA MELTS

1 to 1 1/2 cups pasta, cooked
3 tablespoons reduced-fat margarine
1 (4- to 6-ounce) can imitation crab meat, chopped
2 ounces grated American cheese
2 ounces grated Cheddar cheese
2 ounces grated mozzarella cheese

Layer pasta, margarine and crab meat in microwave-safe dish. Spread cheeses evenly over top. Microwave on High for 3 minutes. Stir. Microwave for 2 to 2 1/2 minutes or until cheeses are melted. Yield: 1 serving.

Julia Anne Dutton, Xi Delta Psi
Erie, Pennsylvania

VERMICELLI IN WHITE CLAM SAUCE

1 can minced or chopped clams
1 (8-ounce) package vermicelli
1/4 cup finely chopped onion
1 clove of garlic, chopped
1/4 cup margarine
1 cup canned mushrooms
2 tablespoons all-purpose flour
1/2 cup half and half
1/2 cup milk
1/4 cup grated Parmesan cheese

Drain clams, reserving liquid. Prepare vermicelli according to package directions. Cook onion and garlic in margarine in saucepan until soft. Add mushrooms. Stir in flour. Stir in clam liquid, half and half and milk gradually. Cook, stirring constantly, until thickened. Add clams; mix well. Add cheese; mix well. Heat through; do not boil. Serve over hot vermicelli. Yield: 6 servings.

Stacy Matherly, Xi Kappa Pi
Cabool, Missouri

CREAMY BAKED SCALLOPS

2 cups sliced zucchini
3/4 cup thinly sliced carrot strips
2 tablespoons margarine
1/4 cup all-purpose flour
2/3 cup whipping cream
1 pound scallops
Parmesan cheese
1/4 teaspoons salt
1/4 teaspoon pepper
2 tablespoons white wine
1 (4-ounce) can crescent rolls

Preheat oven to 375 degrees. Sauté zucchini and carrots in margarine for 3 to 4 minutes or until crisp-tender. Add flour. Cook for 1 minute. Add cream. Cook for 1 minute longer. Add scallops, 2 tablespoons cheese, salt and pepper. Bring to a boil. Remove from heat. Add wine. Place mixture in greased pie pan. Remove dough from can; do not unroll. Cut roll into 6 slices. Cut each slice in half. Arrange around edge of pan. Sprinkle with additional Parmesan cheese. Bake for 20 to 30 minutes or until browned. Yield: 6 servings.

Pamela Hilliard, Phi
Troy, Idaho

PINEAPPLE-SCALLOP KABOBS

2 tablespoons soy sauce
1 tablespoon lemon juice
1/2 cup pineapple juice
White pepper
10 ounces fresh scallops
2 canned pineapple rings
1 cup 1-inch squares red and green bell pepper
8 cherry tomatoes
Rice

Preheat oven to broil. Combine soy sauce, lemon juice, pineapple juice and white pepper in bowl; mix well. Add scallops and pineapple rings. Marinate for 1 hour. Cut each pineapple ring into 4 equal quarters. Thread 2 skewers with peppers, tomato, pineapple and scallops, alternating colors. Broil for 8 minutes. Serve over rice. Yield: 2 servings.

Sonia Monson, Preceptor Gamma Eta
Lawrenceburg, Indiana

SCALLOPS IN APRICOT BRANDY

1/4 cup butter or
  margarine
1 to 1 1/2 pounds fresh
  scallops
8 scallions, chopped
1/2 cup apricot Brandy
Parsley

Melt butter in skillet over low heat. Add scallops. Cook for 2 minutes. Add scallions and Brandy. Bring to a boil. Cook for 1 1/2 to 2 minutes. Place on serving platter. Pour liquid over scallops. Add parsley. Yield: 4 servings.

Betts Johnson, Preceptor Nu
Kodiak, Alaska

MEDITERRANEAN SCALLOP SAUTÉ

1 tablespoon olive oil
2 cloves of garlic, minced
1/4 cup chopped onion
2 tomatoes, chopped
Juice and grated rind
  of 1/2 lemon
Dash of hot pepper sauce
1 pound scallops
1 teaspoon dried basil
1 teaspoon dried oregano
Pasta
Crumbled feta cheese

Heat oil over medium heat in large skillet. Add garlic and onion. Sauté over medium heat for 5 minutes or until soft. Add tomatoes, lemon juice, lemon rind and hot pepper sauce. Sauté for 1 1/2 minutes or until cooked down. Stir in scallops, basil and oregano. Sauté for 4 minutes or until cooked through. Serve over pasta. Sprinkle with feta cheese. Yield: 4 servings.

Carol Pestor, Laureate Delta Nu
Anaheim Hills, California

❖ ROASTED RED PEPPER AND SCALLOP FETTUCINI

2 whole red peppers
1 (16-ounce) package
  fettucini
1/4 cup margarine
2 teaspoons finely
  chopped garlic
1/2 cup sliced green onions
1 1/2 pounds large scallops
2 cups sour cream
Salt to taste
Ground pepper to taste

Preheat oven to 400 degrees. Place whole red peppers on cookie sheet. Bake, turning occasionally, for 25 minutes or until skins are blackened. Let cool. Remove skins and seeds. Purée peppers in blender on High until smooth. Prepare fettucini according to package directions; drain. Melt butter in 10-inch skillet. Add garlic. Cook over medium heat, stirring occasionally, for 1 minute. Add green onions and scallops. Continue cooking, stirring occasionally, for 5 to 7 minutes or until scallops are tender. Stir in sour cream and red pepper purée; mix well. Continue cooking for 4 to 6 minutes or until heated through. Combine scallop mixture and cooked fettucini in large bowl; toss to mix. Season to taste.
Yield: 6 servings.

Maureen English, Laureate Delta
Nelson-Miramichi, New Brunswick, Canada

STIR-FRIED SCALLOPS AND VEGETABLES

1 pound fresh scallops
1/4 cup lemon juice
1 cup thinly sliced carrots
3 cloves of garlic,
  crushed, chopped
1/3 cup butter or
  margarine
2 cups sliced fresh
  mushrooms
3/4 teaspoon dried thyme
  leaves
2 teaspoons cornstarch
1/2 teaspoon salt
1/4 cup diagonally sliced
  green onions
4 ounces fresh sugar peas
2 tablespoons dry Sherry
Hot cooked rice

Marinate scallops in lemon juice in dish for 30 minutes, stirring occasionally. Cook carrots and garlic in butter in large skillet over high heat for 3 minutes or until tender-crisp. Add mushrooms and thyme. Cook, stirring constantly, for 5 minutes. Stir in cornstarch and salt. Add scallops. Cook until scallops are opaque. Stir in onions, peas and Sherry. Remove from heat. Serve with rice. Yield: 4 servings.

Shirley A. Michaud, Laureate Eta
Prince George, British Columbia, Canada

SCAMPI WITH FETTUCINI

1/2 pound fresh shrimp
1/2 pound fresh scallops
2 tablespoons chopped
  garlic
1/4 cup clarified butter
2 ounces Bianco wine
4 teaspoons lemon juice
1 teaspoon basil
Pepper to taste
2 tablespoons butter
1 pound fettucini,
  cooked al dente

Sauté shrimp and scallops with garlic in clarified butter in skillet over medium heat for 2 minutes. Add wine, lemon juice, basil and pepper. Simmer for 3 to 5 minutes or until seafood is cooked. Remove seafood. Cook until sauce is reduced by half. Whisk in 2 tablespoons butter. Return seafood to sauce. Heat through. Serve over fettucini. Yield: 4 servings.

Julie Cross, Xi Eta Xi
Edinboro, Pennsylvania

BAKED STUFFED SHRIMP

24 large shrimp, with
  tails unpeeled
1 (8-ounce) can lump
  crab meat
1/4 cup butter or
  margarine
1/2 cup grated Cheddar
  cheese
1 (8-ounce) can cream
  of mushroom soup
1/2 cup cream
Fine bread crumbs
Garlic powder to taste
Salt and white pepper
  to taste
Paprika to taste

Preheat oven to 350 degrees. Butterfly shrimp. Sauté crab meat lightly in butter in skillet. Add cheese, soup, cream and enough bread crumbs to hold mixture together. Add garlic powder, salt and white pepper. Mold stuffing into shrimp. Sprinkle with paprika. Place in baking pan. Bake for 10 minutes. Yield: 4 servings.

Eunice French, Preceptor Beta Omicron
Rolla, Missouri

102 / Seafood

DELICIOUS CURRY

1 brown onion, finely chopped
2 large green apples, finely chopped
2 tablespoons vegetable oil
2 tablespoons all-purpose flour
1 (10-ounce) can consommé
2 to 3 heaping teaspoons curry powder
1 1/2 pounds cooked shrimp
Steamed rice
Condiments to taste: crisp-fried crumbled bacon, shredded coconut, chopped green onions, Major Grey's chutney, snipped parsley, currant jelly, crushed or chunky pineapple, pickles, avocado slices, grated orange or lemon rind, thinly sliced cucumbers, watercress, tomato wedges and/or nasturtium blossoms

Stir-fry onion and apples in oil in skillet until tender and lightly browned. Add flour. Remove from heat. Add consommé and enough water to make slightly thick sauce. Add curry; mix well. Add shrimp; mix well. Serve over steamed rice with desired condiments. Yield: 6 to 8 servings.

Billie Porter, Preceptor Iota Beta
Camarillo, California

LINGUINE AND SHRIMP

1 (8-ounce) package linguine
1/2 cup Italian dressing
1/2 pound shrimp, peeled, deveined
1 yellow squash, julienned
1 zucchini, julienned
1 carrot, julienned
3 green onions, cut into strips
1 clove of garlic, minced
2 teaspoons grated lemon peel
1 teaspoon salt
Dash of cayenne pepper

Cook linguine according to package directions; drain. Heat Italian dressing in large skillet. Add remaining ingredients. Cook, stirring constantly, for 8 to 10 minutes. Add linguine; toss to mix. Garnish as desired. Yield: 4 servings.

Jackie Hepler, Xi Alpha Pi
McFarland, Wisconsin

♥ SHRIMP JAMBALAYA

Canola cooking spray
1 tablespoon vegetable oil
1 tablespoon all-purpose flour
1 cup chopped onion
1 cup chopped celery
1 cup chopped green bell pepper
4 ounces low-salt lean ham, chopped
2 cloves of garlic, minced
2 1/2 cups low-salt no-fat chicken broth
1/2 cup chopped fresh parsley
1 teaspoon dried thyme
1/2 teaspoon salt
1/2 teaspoon dried basil
1/4 teaspoon pepper
1/8 teaspoon ground red pepper
1 (14-ounce) can no-salt whole tomatoes, undrained, chopped
1 cup brown rice
8 ounces medium shrimp, peeled, deveined

Coat large nonstick skillet with cooking spray. Add oil; stir in flour. Cook over medium-high heat for 1 1/2 minutes or until brown, stirring constantly. Add next 5 ingredients. Sauté for 7 minutes or until tender. Add chicken broth and next 7 ingredients; stir well. Bring to a boil. Add rice; stir well. Cover. Reduce heat. Simmer for 20 minutes or until rice is tender. Stir in shrimp. Cook, covered, for 5 minutes or until shrimp is pink. Yield: 4 servings.

Anita M. Wilson, Laureate Alpha Mu
Mansfield, Ohio

SHRIMP MARINARA

1 1/2 to 2 pounds fresh medium shrimp
1/4 cup olive oil
2 tablespoons minced garlic
1/8 teaspoon dried red hot pepper flakes
1 (28-ounce) can crushed tomatoes
1 tablespoon dried parsley
1 teaspoon salt
1 teaspoon sugar
1 teaspoon dried oregano
1 teaspoon dried basil
Cooked linguine

Peel and devein shrimp; rinse. Pour oil in hot saucepan to cover bottom. Add garlic and pepper flakes. Sauté just until garlic turns golden. Add tomatoes, parsley and next 4 ingredients; mix well. Simmer for 20 minutes. Add shrimp; cover. Cook for 2 to 4 minutes or until shrimp are pink. Serve over linguine. Yield: 4 servings.

Cheryl Crain
Bethel Park, Pennsylvania

EASY SEAFOOD CHIMICHANGAS

1 cup canola or vegetable oil
Pepper to taste
1 (6-ounce) can scallops
1 (6-ounce) can shrimp
1 (10-ounce) package real or imitation flaked crab meat
1/4 cup shredded Monterey Jack cheese
1/4 cup shredded Swiss cheese
1/4 cup shredded Colby cheese
8 large flour tortillas
Salsa
Sour cream
Guacamole
Cocktail sauce

Heat oil in large skillet. Combine pepper, scallops, shrimp and crab meat in bowl. Add cheeses; mix gently. Place tortillas on flat surface. Place 1/8 mixture directly in center of each tortilla. Fold up edges from top to bottom, then from side to side, making square to completely enclose filling. Secure with toothpicks. Place, folded side down, in skillet. Fry for 5 minutes or until golden. Turn over; fry until golden brown. Remove from skillet to serving dish, placing folded side down. Absorb oil with paper towel. Remove toothpicks. Garnish with salsa, sour cream, guacamole and/or cocktail sauce. Yield: 8 servings.

Dawn Pierce, Theta Rho
Royalton, Illinois

From the Garden

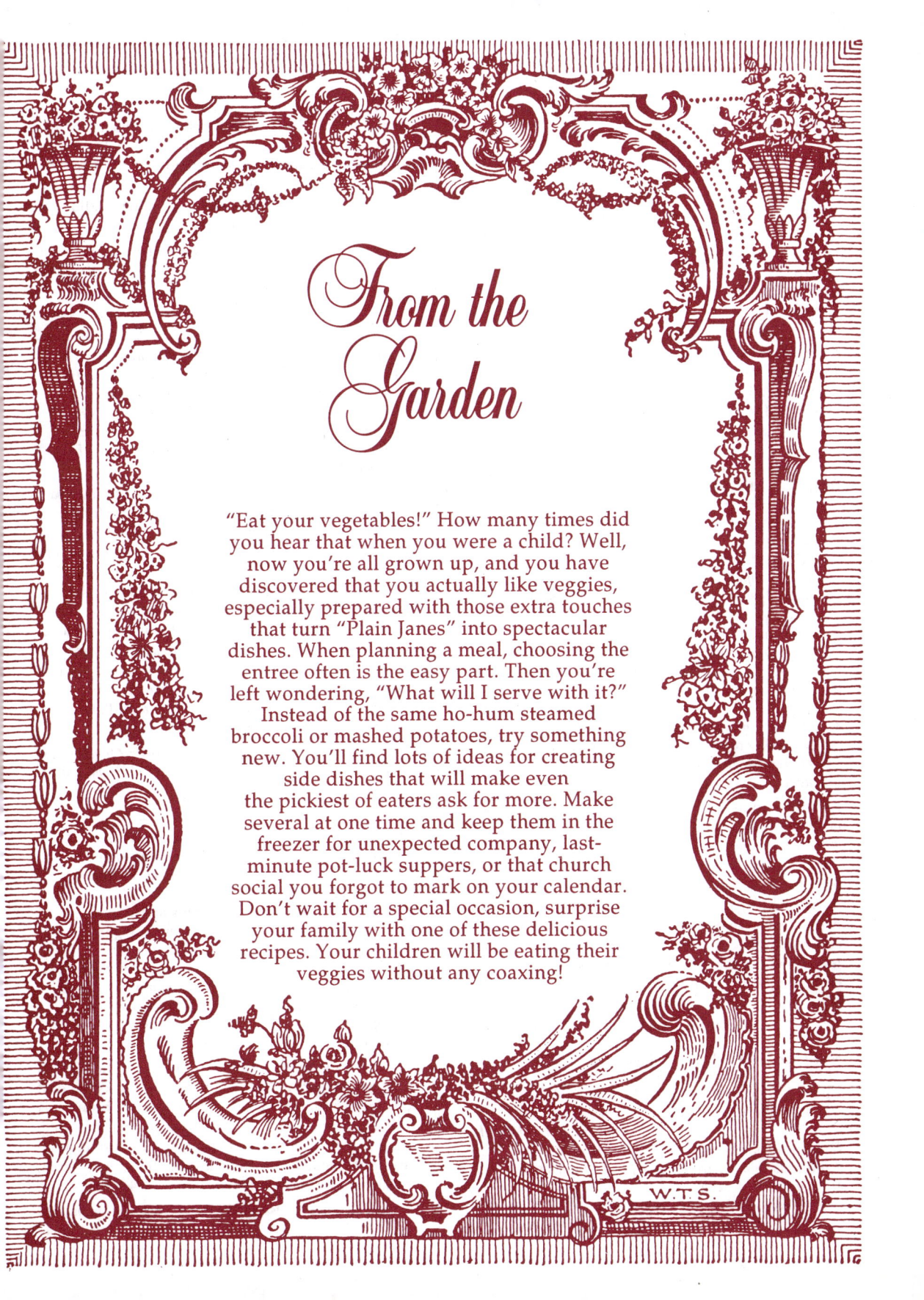

"Eat your vegetables!" How many times did you hear that when you were a child? Well, now you're all grown up, and you have discovered that you actually like veggies, especially prepared with those extra touches that turn "Plain Janes" into spectacular dishes. When planning a meal, choosing the entree often is the easy part. Then you're left wondering, "What will I serve with it?" Instead of the same ho-hum steamed broccoli or mashed potatoes, try something new. You'll find lots of ideas for creating side dishes that will make even the pickiest of eaters ask for more. Make several at one time and keep them in the freezer for unexpected company, last-minute pot-luck suppers, or that church social you forgot to mark on your calendar. Don't wait for a special occasion, surprise your family with one of these delicious recipes. Your children will be eating their veggies without any coaxing!

BARLEY CASSEROLE

1 medium onion, chopped
1 (4-ounce) can mushrooms, drained
1/2 cup butter or margarine
1 cup quick-cooking barley
1 envelope dry onion soup mix
1 (14-ounce) can chicken broth
1 package slivered almonds
1 (8-ounce) can water chestnuts, drained, chopped

Preheat oven to 350 degrees. Sauté onion and mushrooms in butter in skillet. Add barley. Cook until golden. Add onion soup mix, chicken broth, almonds and water chestnuts; mix well. Place in covered 1 1/2-quart casserole. Bake for 30 to 45 minutes. Yield: 6 servings.

Verna L. Carlisle, Preceptor Alpha Rho
St. Simons Island, Georgia

BAKED BEANS ON DARK BREAD

2 tablespoons peanut or corn oil
2 medium yellow onions, finely chopped
4 cloves of garlic, minced
1 small sweet red or green pepper, finely chopped
2 medium carrots, finely chopped
1 tablespoon minced fresh ginger or 1/4 teaspoon ground ginger
1/2 teaspoon red pepper flakes
2 cups pinto beans, cooked, drained
1/4 cup molasses
2 teaspoons dry mustard
1 tablespoon red wine vinegar
2 teaspoons low-sodium tomato paste
3/4 teaspoon dried thyme, crumbled
2 (2-by-1/2-inch) strips orange peel
4 slices pumpernickel

Preheat oven to 325 degrees. Heat peanut oil over moderately low heat in 4-quart Dutch oven for 1 minute. Add onions, garlic, red pepper, carrots, ginger and red pepper flakes; mix well. Cook, covered, for 30 minutes or until vegetables are soft. Stir pinto beans, molasses, mustard, vinegar, tomato paste and thyme into vegetables with orange peel. Add enough water to cover. Bake, covered, for 1 1/2 hours. Add more water if needed. Bake for 1 hour longer. Remove orange peel. Spoon beans over pumpernickel. Yield: 4 servings.

Celia Mortson, Laureate Eta
Prince George, British Columbia, Canada

♥ HERBED GREEN BEANS

1 pound fresh green beans
1/2 cup chopped green onions
1/2 clove of garlic, minced
1 tablespoon margarine
1/2 cup chopped fresh parsley
1 teaspoon dried whole rosemary
1/4 teaspoon dried whole basil
3/4 teaspoon salt

Rinse and trim beans. Place beans in 2 inches boiling water in covered saucepan. Cook for 15 to 20 minutes. Drain; keep warm. Sauté onions and garlic in margarine in skillet. Add remaining ingredients. Simmer, covered, for 20 minutes. Combine beans and butter mixture just before serving. Yield: 4 servings.

Deanna Siemsen, Alpha Rho
Liberal, Kansas

BRUSSELS SPROUTS WITH BACON SAUCE

2 1/2 pounds fresh Brussels sprouts
12 slices bacon, chopped
1/2 cup finely chopped onion
3 tablespoons all-purpose flour
1 1/2 cups milk
1/3 cup dry white wine
1/2 teaspoon salt
1/8 teaspoon pepper
1/2 teaspoon oregano
3/4 teaspoon crumbled dillweed

Rinse Brussels sprouts; trim stem ends. Cut X into each stem end. Cook, uncovered, in boiling water for 7 to 10 minutes or until tender; drain well. Arrange in 2-quart casserole. Fry bacon until crisp. Drain, reserving 4 tablespoons drippings. Add onion to 2 tablespoons in skillet. Cook until limp. Stir in flour. Cook until bubbly. Remove from heat. Stir in milk gradually. Return to heat. Cook, stirring, until thickened. Reserve 2 tablespoons bacon. Add remaining bacon, wine, salt, pepper, oregano and dillweed; mix well. Pour sauce over Brussels sprouts. Sprinkle bacon over top. Refrigerate, covered, until serving time. Preheat oven to 325 degrees. Bake for 35 minutes or until hot. Yield: 8 to 10 servings.

Mary Cooley, Laureate Alpha Epsilon
Langley, British Columbia, Canada

NAVY BEANS AND RICE

1 (8-ounce) package navy beans
1 medium onion, chopped
2 or 3 cloves of garlic, finely chopped
1 green bell pepper, chopped
1 red bell pepper, chopped
3 or 4 stalks celery, chopped
1/3 cup olive oil
1 (14-ounce) can tomatoes, chopped
1 (6-ounce) can tomato paste
3 cups water
1 teaspoon sugar
3/4 teaspoon salt
3/8 teaspoon black pepper
3/8 teaspoon red pepper
1 (8-ounce) can mushrooms, sliced
Hot cooked rice

Soak beans overnight; drain. Sauté onion, garlic, red and green peppers and celery in olive oil in saucepan. Add tomatoes and tomato paste. Add water and beans; mix well. Add sugar, salt, black and red pepper; mix well. Bring to a boil. Simmer, covered, for 2 hours or until beans are cooked. Add mushrooms. Simmer, covered, for 30 minutes. Serve over hot rice. Yield: 4 to 6 servings.

Isobel Hubbard, Laureate Gamma Rho
Winter Haven, Florida

♥ GINGERED BROCCOLI

1 1/2 pounds fresh broccoli
1 tablespoon olive oil
6 (1/8-inch) slices peeled gingerroot
4 large cloves of garlic, halved
2 tablespoons white wine vinegar
1/4 teaspoon salt
1/8 teaspoon pepper

Trim broccoli, discarding large leaves and tough ends of stalks. Rinse thoroughly. Separate into flowerets. Slice stalks into 1/2-inch pieces. Coat large skillet with non-stick vegetable cooking spray. Add oil. Place over medium-high heat until hot. Add gingerroot. Sauté for 2 minutes. Add garlic. Sauté for 1 minute. Discard gingerroot and garlic, reserving oil. Add sliced broccoli. Stir-fry for 2 minutes. Add broccoli flowerets and vinegar. Stir-fry for 3 minutes. Sprinkle with salt and pepper. Toss well. Yield: 12 servings.

JoAnn Mason, Gamma Gamma
Duluth, Minnesota

BROCCOLI CASSEROLE

1 (20-ounce) package frozen broccoli
1 (10-ounce) package frozen baby lima beans
1 (10-ounce) can mushroom soup
2 cups sour cream
1 envelope onion soup mix
1 (8-ounce) can sliced water chestnuts
2 tablespoons margarine, melted
2 cups Rice Krispies

Preheat oven to 325 degrees. Cook broccoli and lima beans according to package directions; drain. Combine soup, sour cream, onion soup mix and water chestnuts in bowl. Add broccoli and lima beans; mix well. Pour into 1 1/2-quart casserole. Combine margarine and Rice Krispies in bowl. Sprinkle over top. Bake for 30 minutes. Yield: 8 servings.

Mary Ann Wasser, Pi Tau
California, Missouri

♥ CONFETTI CABBAGE

1 onion, sliced
2 cloves of garlic, minced
2 tablespoons olive oil
6 cups thinly sliced cabbage
2 carrots, shredded
1 medium zucchini, chopped
1/2 teaspoon salt
1/2 teaspoon caraway seeds

Sauté onion and garlic in oil in wok or large saucepan over high heat until onion is tender. Stir in remaining ingredients. Cook, stirring quickly and frequently, for 10 minutes or until cabbage is tender-crisp. Yield: 8 servings.

Rachel Kirkbride, Preceptor Theta Iota
Tampa, Florida

HOT CABBAGE-MUSHROOM DISH

2 tablespoons bacon drippings
2 tablespoons butter or margarine
1 pound sliced mushrooms
1/2 cup chopped onion
1/4 cup water
4 cups shredded cabbage
8 cooked slices bacon, crumbled
2 tablespoons vinegar
1 tablespoon sugar
1 teaspoon salt
1 teaspoon dillweed
1/4 teaspoon pepper

Heat bacon drippings in skillet over medium heat. Add butter. Heat until melted. Add mushrooms and onion. Sauté for 5 minutes. Add remaining ingredients. Bring to a boil; reduce heat. Simmer, covered, for 8 minutes. Yield: 6 to 8 servings.

Anna Sue Watts, Laureate Gamma Delta
Cinti, Ohio

♥ CARIBBEAN CARROTS

2 cups 1/2-inch carrot slices
2 cups cubed peeled sweet potatoes
1 (20-ounce) can unsweetened pineapple chunks
1/4 cup water
2 tablespoons dark brown sugar
1 tablespoon cornstarch
2 teaspoons low-sodium soy sauce
1 teaspoon vinegar
1/2 teaspoon grated orange rind
1/8 teaspoon salt
1/4 cup golden raisins

Place carrots in vegetable steamer. Steam, covered, over boiling water for 2 minutes. Add sweet potatoes. Steam, covered, for 8 minutes or until tender-crisp. Drain pineapple, reserving 1/2 cup juice. Combine juice, water, brown sugar, cornstarch, soy sauce, vinegar, orange rind and salt in saucepan. Place over medium heat. Bring to a boil, stirring constantly. Add pineapple and raisins. Cook for 2 minutes. Combine vegetables and pineapple mixture in large bowl; mix gently. Yield: 4 to 6 servings.

Barbara R. Quivey, Alpha Iota Preceptor Laureate
Plymouth, Indiana

♥ APPLE AND CARROT CASSEROLE

5 apples, sliced
2 cups cooked sliced carrots
Salt to taste
2 tablespoons all-purpose flour
6 tablespoons sugar
3/4 cup orange juice

Preheat oven to 350 degrees. Place apples and carrots in 9-by-13-inch baking pan. Combine salt, flour and sugar in small bowl. Sprinkle mixture over apples and carrots. Pour orange juice over mixture. Bake for 20 to 30 minutes. Yield: 4 to 6 servings.

Nancy Hutton, Xi Epsilon Beta
Woodstock, Virginia

CARROT CASSEROLE

2 cups mashed carrots
1 cup soda cracker crumbs
1 cup milk
3/4 cup grated
  Cheddar cheese
1/3 cup melted margarine
1/4 cup grated onion
Salt and pepper to taste
3 eggs or 6 egg whites

Preheat oven to 350 degrees. Combine carrots, cracker crumbs, milk, cheese, margarine, onion, salt and pepper in bowl; mix well. Beat eggs until frothy. Fold into carrot mixture. Pour into greased casserole. Bake for 50 minutes to 1 hour. Yield: 6 servings.

Kimberley Myers-Stuart, Theta
Dartmouth, Nova Scotia, Canada

CARROTS L'ORANGE

10 medium carrots, cut
  into 1-inch diagonal
  slices
2 tablespoons dark
  brown sugar
1 tablespoon cornstarch
1/2 teaspoon ground
  ginger
1/4 teaspoon salt
1 cup orange juice
1/4 cup butter or
  margarine

Cook carrots in boiling salted water in saucepan until tender-crisp; drain. Combine brown sugar, cornstarch, ginger and salt in small saucepan. Add orange juice. Bring to a boil. Cook, stirring constantly, for 1 minute or until thickened. Stir in butter. Remove from heat. Pour over hot carrots, tossing gently to coat. Yield: 8 servings.

Patricia Crucefix, Preceptor Gamma Lambda
Castle Rock, Colorado

CLASSY CAULIFLOWER
AND CARROT CASSEROLE

4 cups sliced carrots
Flowerets of 1 head
  cauliflower
2 tablespoons butter or
  margarine
1 teaspoon mustard
2 tablespoons
  all-purpose flour
1 cup chicken broth
1/2 cup milk
1 1/4 cups shredded Swiss
  cheese
1 (16-ounce) can
  French-fried onions

Preheat oven to 350 degrees. Cook carrots and cauliflower in lightly salted water in large saucepan until just tender. Heat butter in small saucepan over medium heat. Stir in mustard and flour. Cook until bubbly. Remove from heat. Stir in chicken broth and milk gradually. Cook, stirring, until thickened. Add 1 cup cheese gradually. Stir until melted. Combine with vegetables and half of French-fried onions. Pour into 1 1/2-quart casserole. Sprinkle with remaining cheese. Bake, uncovered, for 15 minutes. Top with remaining French-fried onions. Bake for 3 minutes longer. Yield: 6 to 8 servings.

Ann P. Horrell, Preceptor Alpha Omicron
Marshall, North Carolina

ZESTY HORSERADISH
CORN ON THE COB

1/2 cup softened
  margarine
1/2 teaspoon salt
1/4 teaspoon pepper
1 tablespoon chopped
  fresh parsley
2 tablespoons
  country-style Dijon
  mustard
2 teaspoons horseradish
8 fresh ears of corn,
  shucked

Preheat oven to 375 degrees. Combine first 6 ingredients in small bowl. Spread 1 tablespoon mixture evenly over each ear of corn. Wrap tightly in heavy-duty cooking foil. Place in jelly-roll pan. Bake for 40 to 45 minutes or until heated through. Yield: 8 servings.

Lynda J. Klasel, Xi Omega Nu
Rosenberg, Texas

♥ HEARTY CORN CASSEROLE

1 (16-ounce) can
  cream-style corn
1/2 cup egg substitute,
  thawed
1/2 cup chopped green
  onions
1/2 cup chopped green
  bell pepper
2 tablespoons
  all-purpose flour
1/4 cup cornmeal
1/4 teaspoon salt
1 (16-ounce) can
  whole-kernel corn,
  drained
1 (8-ounce) carton plain
  nonfat yogurt
1 (2-ounce) can chopped
  ripe olives, drained
Vegetable cooking spray

Preheat oven to 350 degrees. Combine cream-style corn and egg substitute in mixer bowl. Beat until smooth. Add onions and green pepper. Add remaining ingredients; mix well. Pour into 2-quart casserole coated with vegetable cooking spray. Bake, uncovered, for 45 minutes. Remove from oven; stir well. Return to oven. Bake for 25 minutes or until set. Yield: 6 to 8 servings.

Gloria Scherrer, Xi Gamma Iota
Yuma, Arizona

MACQUE CHOUX (MOCK SHOE)

6 to 8 slices bacon
1 large onion, thinly
  sliced
1 green bell pepper,
  chopped
2 large tomatoes, peeled
1/2 teaspoon minced garlic
1/2 teaspoon sugar
2 (17-ounce) cans
  cream-style corn
1/4 teaspoon Tabasco
  sauce
1/4 teaspoon ground
  thyme
Salt and pepper to taste
Steamed rice

Sauté bacon in large skillet until crisp. Remove from skillet; drain and crumble. Sauté onion and green pepper in bacon drippings until transparent. Chop and seed tomatoes. Add tomatoes and garlic to skillet mixture. Simmer for 10 minutes. Add sugar, corn, Tabasco sauce, thyme, salt and pepper. Simmer for 45 minutes or until thickened. Add bacon. Serve over rice. Yield: 6 servings.

Deborah Touchet, Beta Zeta Mu
Malakoff, Texas

♥ MU-JA-DA-RA (GREEK)

This delicious vegetarian dish was an onion contest winner. May be served as an entrée or side dish.

1 cup lentils
7 cups water
1 tablespoon salt
3/4 cup long grain rice
7 small onions
1/2 cup olive oil

Place lentils, water and salt in large saucepan. Cook over medium heat for 15 minutes. Add rice. Cook for 10 minutes longer. Peel onions. Slice from stem down into 1/2-inch slivers. Pour olive oil into skillet. Add onions. Cook until browned. Add sizzling onions and olive oil to lentils and rice. Cook, covered, over low heat, stirring occasionally, for 15 minutes. Remove cover; cook for few minutes longer to reduce liquid if necessary. Yield: 8 servings.

Vickie Thomas, Preceptor Tau
Weiser, Idaho

♥ ZESTY EGGPLANT PARMIGIANA

1 medium eggplant
Salt to taste
Olive oil cooking spray
3 cloves of garlic, minced
2 sweet medium onion, chopped
2 medium green bell pepper, chopped
1/2 cup fresh mushrooms, sliced
2 or 3 (2-inch) jalapeño peppers, chopped
1/2 cup chopped zucchini
4 to 5 medium fresh tomatoes, chopped or 1 (16-ounce) can whole or chopped tomatoes
3 tablespoons tomato paste
1 tablespoon sugar
1/2 cup chopped fresh cilantro
1 tablespoon chopped fresh sweet basil
1/2 tablespoon chopped oregano
Salt and pepper to taste
Garlic powder to taste
8 ounces low-fat mozzarella cheese, grated
2 tablespoons Parmesan cheese

Preheat oven to broil. Peel and slice eggplant into 1/2-inch slices. Sprinkle lightly with salt. Let stand for 10 minutes. Spray large skillet with cooking spray. Sauté garlic, onion, green pepper, mushrooms, jalapeño peppers and zucchini until tender. Add tomatoes, tomato paste, sugar, cilantro, basil and oregano; mix well. Season to taste. Simmer, uncovered, for several minutes. Pat eggplant dry. Arrange on large cookie sheet in single layer. Spray lightly with olive oil spray. Sprinkle with garlic powder. Broil until edges of each slice are browned. Turn slices over; repeat. Preheat oven to 350 degrees. Layer sauce, eggplant and mozzarella cheese in 9-by-12-inch baking pan. Repeat layers, ending with mozzarella cheese. Sprinkle Parmesan cheese over top. Bake until bubbly and cheese is melted and lightly browned. Let stand for 10 minutes. Cut into rectangles to serve. Yield: 6 to 8 servings.

Betsy Messer, Preceptor Beta Eta
Dallas, Oregon

EGGPLANT PARMESAN

1/2 cup whole wheat flour
1 teaspoon salt
2 eggs, slightly beaten
1/4 cup milk
2 1/2 cups whole wheat crackers
Dash of pepper
1/4 teaspoon oregano
1 medium eggplant, cut into 1/4-inch slices
1 1/2 cups tomato sauce
1/2 cup grated Parmesan cheese
1 cup grated mozzarella cheese

Preheat oven to 350 degrees. Combine 1/2 cup whole wheat flour and 1/2 teaspoon salt in bowl. Combine 2 eggs and milk in separate bowl. Combine cracker crumbs, 1/2 teaspoon salt, pepper and oregano in separate bowl. Dip eggplant slices into each mixture, coating completely. Layer, overlapping slightly, in 9-by-13-inch glass dish. Sprinkle each layer with tomato sauce and Parmesan cheese, covering lightly. Bake for 30 to 45 minutes or until fork-tender. Top with mozzarella cheese and remaining Parmesan cheese. Bake until cheese is melted. Yield: 10 servings.

Maureen Stitt, Delta
Brandon, MB, Canada

MUSHROOMS FLORENTINE

2 (10-ounce) packages frozen chopped spinach
1/4 cup chopped onion
1/4 cup melted butter or margarine
1 teaspoon salt
1 cup grated Cheddar cheese
1 pound fresh mushrooms, sliced
2 tablespoons butter or margarine
Garlic powder to taste

Preheat oven to 350 degrees. Cook spinach according to package directions. Drain well; squeeze out water. Place in bottom of 8-by-11-inch casserole. Sprinkle with onion, melted butter and salt. Layer 1/2 cup cheese over spinach. Sauté mushrooms in 2 tablespoons butter. Layer mushrooms over spinach. Sprinkle with garlic powder and remaining cheese. Bake for 20 minutes. Yield: 8 servings.

Patricia M. Pickler, Mu Sigma
Mt. Pleasant, Michigan

BAKED ONIONS

12 medium onions, thinly sliced
1 (3-ounce) package potato chips, crushed
8 ounces Wisconsin mild cheese, grated
2 (10-ounce) cans cream of mushroom soup
1/2 cup milk
1/8 teaspoon cayenne pepper

Preheat oven to 350 degrees. Layer onions, potato chips and cheese in 9-by-13-inch buttered casserole. Pour soup and milk over onion mixture. Sprinkle cayenne pepper over top. Bake for 1 hour. Yield: 8 to 10 servings.

Mary Jane Vaughn, Xi Beta Rho
Purcell, Oklahoma

ONIONS CELESTE

- 2 tablespoons butter or margarine
- 2 large Bermuda or Vidalia onions
- 8 ounces grated Swiss cheese
- 1/4 teaspoon pepper
- 1 (10-ounce) can cream of chicken soup
- 1 cup milk
- 8 slices slightly dry buttered French bread

Preheat oven to 350 degrees. Melt butter in large saucepan. Add onions; cover. Cook slowly over low heat for 20 to 30 minutes or until onions are soft. Spoon into 2-quart baking dish. Sprinkle cheese evenly over top. Sprinkle with pepper. Heat soup and milk in saucepan. Pour over mixture, using knife tip to allow mixture to flow to bottom. Arrange bread slices overlapping in ring on top. Bake for 30 minutes or until toasted and bubbly. Yield: 12 to 18 servings.

Johanna Thomas, Gamma Rho
Lakeside, Arizona

♥ ROASTED MUSTARD POTATOES

- Lite vegetable cooking spray
- 1/4 cup Dijon mustard
- 2 teaspoons paprika
- 1 teaspoon ground cumin
- 1 teaspoon chili powder
- 1/8 teaspoon cayenne pepper
- 16 red new potatoes

Preheat oven to 400 degrees. Spray roasting pan to coat with cooking spray. Combine mustard, paprika, cumin, chili powder and cayenne pepper in large bowl until well blended. Prick potatoes several times with fork. Add to mustard mixture. Toss to coat evenly. Pour potatoes into prepared roasting pan, leaving a little space between potatoes. Bake for 45 minutes to 1 hour or until fork-tender. Yield: 4 servings.

Jean Jarrett, Eta Tau
Falls Mills, Virginia

NEW POTATO CASSEROLE

- 1 1/2 cups shredded Cheddar cheese
- 1/2 cup sour cream
- 1/2 cup ranch-style dressing
- 1/4 cup bacon bits
- 2 tablespoons parsley flakes
- 6 to 8 medium new potatoes, cooked
- 2 cups lightly crushed cornflakes
- 1/4 cup melted butter or margarine

Preheat oven to 350 degrees. Combine 1 cup cheese and next 4 ingredients in bowl; mix well. Place potatoes in greased 9-by-13-inch baking dish. Pour sour cream mixture over potatoes; mix gently. Combine 1/4 cup cheese with remaining ingredients in bowl. Sprinkle over potato mixture. Bake for 40 minutes. Yield: 8 servings.

Katheine Bowles, Laureate Alpha
Storm Lake, Iowa

POTATO CASSEROLE

- 1 (24-ounce) package hashed brown potatoes, thawed
- 1 cup sour cream
- 1 cup bleu cheese salad dressing
- 2 cups grated Cheddar cheese
- 1/4 cup margarine, melted
- 1/2 teaspoon salt
- 1/2 teaspoon pepper
- 1 (10-ounce) can cream of chicken soup
- 1/2 cup chopped onion
- 2 teaspoons chopped parsley

Preheat oven to 350 degrees. Separate potatoes in bowl. Add remaining ingredients; mix well. Spread in 9-by-13-inch casserole. Bake for 45 to 55 minutes. Yield: 6 to 8 servings.

Vicki S. Thacker, Preceptor Rho
Suffolk, Virginia

♥ POTATO CHIPS

- Vegetable cooking spray
- 1 (6-ounce) baking potato, scrubbed
- 1 tablespoon grated Parmesan cheese
- 1/2 teaspoon dried basil
- 1/4 teaspoon salt

Preheat oven to 350 degrees. Spray nonstick baking pan with spray. Slice potato into 1/16-inch thick slices. Place in pan. Sprinkle with cheese, basil and salt. Bake for 18 to 20 minutes. Let cool on wire rack. Yield: 2 servings.

Peggy Camp, Delta Phi
Leesville, South Carolina

SCALLOPED POTATOES

- 1 (10-ounce) can cream of onion soup
- 1/2 cup milk
- Salt to taste
- 1/8 teaspoon pepper
- 4 cups thinly sliced potatoes
- 1 tablespoon margarine

Preheat oven to 350 degrees. Mix soup, milk, salt and pepper in bowl. Layer potatoes and sauce alternately in large casserole. Dot with margarine. Bake, covered, for 1 hour. Uncover; bake for 15 minutes. Yield: 6 servings.

Sharon Ehrsam, Preceptor Beta Xi
Wichita, Kansas

RUTABAGA WITH MASHED POTATOES

- 1 peeled rutabaga, chopped
- 2 quarts water
- 6 peeled potatoes, chopped
- 1/4 cup margarine
- 1/2 cup mayonnaise
- 1/4 cup milk

Cook rutabaga in water in 4-quart saucepan for 1 hour. Add potatoes. Cook for 30 minutes or until tender. Drain; keep hot. Add margarine. Mash into potatoes and rutabagas with potato masher. Add mayonnaise; mash. Add milk; mash. Serve hot. Yield: 6 servings.

Patricia Debow, Preceptor Theta
Daytona Beach, Florida

YAM AND CRANBERRY CASSEROLE

1 (12-ounce) package
 fresh whole cranberries
1 1/2 cups sugar
1 small orange, sliced
1/2 cup pecan halves
1/4 cup orange juice
3/4 teaspoon cinnamon
1/4 teaspoon nutmeg
1/8 teaspoon mace
1 (40-ounce) can yams,
 drained

Preheat oven to 375 degrees. Combine first 8 ingredients in 2-quart casserole. Bake, uncovered, for 30 minutes. Stir yams into cranberry mixture. Bake for 15 minutes longer or until hot. Yield: 8 servings.

Dawn McCuan, Xi Mu Alpha
Harrisburg, Illinois

♥ BAKED SQUASH THE AMERICAN WAY

6 medium yellow
 squash, chopped
2/3 cup skim milk
1/2 cup low-fat
 mayonnaise
1 cup grated low-fat
 Cheddar cheese
1 small onion, chopped
Salt and pepper to taste

Preheat oven to 350 degrees. Cook squash in small amount of water until tender and slightly firm; drain. Add milk slowly to mayonnaise in bowl, stirring constantly. Add cheese, onion, salt and pepper. Layer squash and sauce into 3-quart casserole. Bake for 25 to 30 minutes or until brown on top and firm in center. Yield: 4 to 6 servings.

Kathy Verchick, Omega Lambda
Lake City, Florida

TURNIP CASSEROLE

1 turnip, peeled, cubed
1 large onion, sliced
1/4 cup butter or
 margarine
1/4 cup all-purpose flour
1 1/4 teaspoons salt
1/2 teaspoon dry mustard
1 teaspoon
 Worcestershire sauce
2 cups milk
4 ounces grated
 medium-sharp
 Cheddar cheese

Preheat oven to 350 degrees. Cook turnip with onion in small amount of water until almost tender; drain. Place in greased casserole. Melt butter in saucepan. Blend in flour, salt, mustard and Worcestershire sauce. Stir in milk. Cook until thickened, stirring frequently. Add cheese. Pour over casserole. Bake, covered, for 15 minutes. Uncover; bake for 15 minutes longer. Yield: 4 servings.

Gloria Rayner, Preceptor Laureate Beta Eta
Delta, British Columbia, Canada

OVEN-FRIED ZUCCHINI

6 tablespoons butter
 or margarine
1 egg
2 tablespoons milk
1 cup cracker crumbs
1/2 cup Parmesan cheese
Zucchini

Preheat oven to 400 degrees. Melt butter in 9-by-13-inch baking pan. Mix egg and milk in bowl. Combine cracker crumbs and Parmesan cheese in bowl. Slice zucchini lengthwise into 1/8-inch slices. Dip zucchini in egg mixture. Roll in cracker crumb mixture. Place in buttered pan in single layer. Bake for 10 minutes. Turn over. Bake for 10 minutes longer. Yield: 4 servings.

Pam Gooch, Xi Zeta Iota
Richmond, Missouri

ZUCCHINI AND GREEN CHILI QUICHE

3 cups grated unpeeled
 zucchini
Salt to taste
1 (4-ounce) can whole
 green chilies
3/4 cup sliced green
 onions with tops
2 to 3 tablespoons
 margarine
1 1/2 tablespoons
 all-purpose flour
1 (10-inch) unbaked
 pie crust
1 cup grated Cheddar
 cheese
1/2 cup shredded
 Monterey Jack cheese
3 eggs, beaten
1 1/2 cups undiluted
 evaporated milk
Fresh ground black pepper

Preheat oven to 400 degrees. Place zucchini on cooking foil. Sprinkle with salt. Let stand for 30 minutes. Squeeze out moisture; blot dry. Rinse and seed chilies; blot dry. Cut into 1/2-inch pieces. Cook green onions slowly in melted margarine in saucepan for 1 minute. Stir in zucchini. Cook for a few minutes or until glazed. Blend in flour. Spread in pie crust. Sprinkle with half the chilies and half the cheeses. Combine eggs and milk in bowl. Pour over mixture in pie crust. Sprinkle with remaining cheeses. Sprinkle with pepper. Bake for 15 minutes. Reduce oven temperature to 350 degrees. Bake for 20 to 25 minutes or until tests done. Yield: 10 servings.

Linda Holmes, Xi Alpha Iota
Custer, South Dakota

FANCY VEGETABLE CASSEROLE

1 (10-ounce) package
 frozen corn
1 (16-ounce) package
 frozen French-cut
 green beans
1/2 cup melted margarine
1 roll buttery crackers,
 crushed
1/2 cup slivered almonds
1 (10-ounce) can cream
 of celery soup
1 cup grated sharp
 Cheddar cheese
1 small onion, chopped
1 (4-ounce) jar chopped
 pimentos, drained

Preheat oven to 350 degrees. Cook corn and beans according to package directions until just tender; drain. Combine margarine, cracker crumbs and almonds in bowl. Combine corn and beans with remaining ingredients in 2-quart casserole. Top with cracker mixture. Bake for 45 minutes. Yield: 8 servings.

Jennifer Hodges, Psi Upsilon
Orlando, Florida

♥ GARDEN RATATOUILLE

1/4 cup olive oil
1 large onion, thinly sliced
2 green peppers, julienned
2 cups sliced zucchini
2 large tomatoes, peeled, chopped
1 cup sliced mushrooms
1 cup water
1 cup wide egg noodles
1 teaspoon Italian seasonings
1 tablespoon sugar
Salt and pepper to taste

Heat oil in large skillet. Add onion and peppers. Sauté until tender-crisp. Add zucchini, tomatoes and mushrooms. Simmer for 5 minutes. Add remaining ingredients. Simmer until noodles are tender, stirring frequently. Add more water if needed. Yield: 8 servings.

Kristin Dye, Sigma Eta
Chesterfield, Missouri

VEGETABLE SUPREME

1 (10-ounce) package frozen cauliflower
1 (10-ounce) package sliced carrots
1 (10-ounce) frozen Brussels sprouts
1 (10-ounce) package frozen broccoli
1 (10-ounce) jar button mushrooms, drained
1 (10-ounce) can cream of celery soup
1 (10-ounce) cream of Cheddar soup
1/3 cup milk
1/2 teaspoon seasoning salt
1/2 teaspoon seasoned pepper

Preheat oven to 400 degrees. Parboil cauliflower, carrots and Brussels sprouts in saucepan for 5 minutes. Add broccoli. Cook until vegetables are tender-crisp; drain. Place in casserole. Add mushrooms. Mix remaining ingredients in bowl. Pour over vegetables; stir gently. Bake, uncovered, for 35 minutes. Yield: 10 servings.

Eulora A. Bagley, Iota Xi
Zwolle, Louisiana

♥ VEGETABLE STIR-FRY

1/2 rutabaga, peeled
2 large carrots
2 large parsnips
1 tablespoon butter or margarine
1 tablespoon sesame oil
1 clove of garlic, minced
1/2 cup apple juice
2 tablespoons honey
2 tablespoons soy sauce
1 tablespoon lemon juice
Salt and pepper to taste
1 green onion, chopped
1 tablespoon sesame seeds

Cut rutabaga, carrots and parsnips into 2 1/2-by-1/4-inch strips. Heat butter and sesame oil in large skillet over medium-high heat. Add rutabaga, carrots, parsnips and garlic. Sauté for 5 minutes. Stir in apple juice, honey, soy sauce and lemon juice. Cook, covered, for 2 minutes. Uncover. Sauté for 2 minutes. Add salt and pepper. Transfer to serving platter. Sprinkle green onion and sesame seeds on top. Yield: 4 to 6 servings.

H. Doreen Sanders, Laureate Tau
Penticton, British Columbia, Canada

♥ FETTUCINI WITH ROASTED RED PEPPER SAUCE

2 red bell peppers
2 teaspoons olive oil
2 cloves of garlic
2 (14-ounce) cans Italian stewed tomatoes
1/2 teaspoon oregano
1/2 teaspoon pepper
4 cups hot cooked fettucini
Grated Parmesan cheese

Preheat oven to broil. Cut peppers into halves; remove seeds and membrane. Place peppers, skin-side up, on baking sheet lined with cooking foil. Broil 2 to 3 inches from heat source until charred. Remove; let cool. Peel and chop peppers. Heat oil in nonstick skillet over medium heat. Add garlic. Sauté until browned. Drain and chop tomatoes, reserving liquid. Add tomatoes and reserved liquid to skillet. Cook until heated through. Add roasted peppers, oregano and pepper. Simmer until heated through. Serve over hot fettucini. Sprinkle with Parmesan cheese. Yield: 4 to 6 servings.

Teresa J. Long, Xi Epsilon Theta
Columbia, Missouri

✤ FETTUCINI SPINACH TOSS

2 cups fettucini
1 clove of garlic
1 cup sliced mushrooms
1 medium onion, sliced
2 tablespoons margarine
1 teaspoon basil
1/2 teaspoon salt
1/2 teaspoon pepper
2 tablespoons all-purpose flour
1 cup milk
1 (10-ounce) package chopped spinach, thawed, drained
1/2 cup Parmesan cheese
2 cups cottage cheese

Cook fettucini according to package directions. Sauté garlic, mushrooms and onion in margarine in large skillet. Stir in basil, salt, pepper and flour. Add milk, stirring until thickened. Add remaining ingredients. Cook for 5 minutes or until heated through and thickened. Toss with noodles in serving dish. Yield: 4 servings.

Delinda Tjoelker, Epsilon Rho
La Crescenta, California

FRESH VEGETABLES AND FETTUCINI

8 ounces fettucini
1/4 cup margarine
1 cup chopped broccoli
1 cup 1/4-inch carrot slices
1 cup sliced fresh mushrooms
1/2 teaspoon minced fresh garlic
1/2 cup chopped onion
1 teaspoon dried basil leaves
1/2 teaspoon salt
1/4 teaspoon cracked pepper
1 1/2 cups shredded mozzarella cheese

Cook fettucini according to package directions; drain. Melt margarine in skillet. Add next 5 ingredients. Cook over medium heat for 4 to 5 minutes. Stir in basil, salt and pepper. Add fettucini. Cook for 3 to 5 minutes. Place on serving dish. Sprinkle with cheese. Yield: 6 servings.

Lila Ludwig, Tau
Knoxville, Tennessee

LINGUINE WITH ARTICHOKES

1 (7-ounce) package uncooked dried linguine
3 tablespoons butter or margarine
1/2 cup chopped onion
1 teaspoon finely chopped fresh garlic
1 (16-ounce) can artichoke hearts packed in water
1 (4-ounce) jar olives
1/2 cup freshly grated Parmesan cheese
1/4 cup chopped fresh parsley

Cook linguine according to package directions. Rinse with hot water. Drain; keep warm. Melt butter in 10-inch skillet. Stir in onion and garlic. Cook over medium-high heat, stirring constantly, for 2 to 3 minutes or until onion is softened. Drain artichoke hearts; cut into halves. Add artichoke hearts and olives to skillet. Cook, stirring occasionally, for 4 to 5 minutes or until heated through. Spoon linguine into serving bowl. Toss with artichoke mixture, Parmesan cheese and parsley. Yield: 6 servings.

Audrey Baggett, Beta Pi
Lakeview, Oregon

♥ SPINACH LASAGNA

1 large onion, chopped
2 cloves of garlic, minced
2 tablespoons olive oil
1 pound spinach, rinsed, drained
1 teaspoon oregano
1 tablespoon basil
3 cups tomato sauce
1 (8-ounce) package whole wheat lasagna noodles, cooked
1 cup cottage cheese
1/4 cup grated Parmesan cheese
1/2 cup shredded mozzarella cheese

Preheat oven to 375 degrees. Spray 8-inch square baking dish with nonstick vegetable cooking spray. Sauté onion and garlic in oil in large saucepan. Add spinach, 1/3 at a time; cover. Add oregano, basil and tomato sauce with last 1/3 of spinach; blend. Cook until tender. Remove from heat. Layer noodles, cottage cheese and sauce in prepared baking dish. Top with Parmesan and mozzarella cheeses. Bake for 40 minutes. Yield: 6 to 8 servings.

Jackie Kennedy, Preceptor Gamma Beta
Grand Rapids, Michigan

GARDEN RANCH NOODLES

1 (8-ounce) package egg noodles
1 (4-ounce) can mushrooms, drained
1 green bell pepper, chopped
1 small onion, chopped
2 tablespoons butter or margarine
1 tomato, chopped
Salt and pepper to taste
3/4 cup ranch dressing

Cook noodles according to package directions; drain. Sauté mushrooms, green pepper and onion in butter in skillet. Add tomato. Combine noodles and vegetables in large bowl. Add salt and pepper. Stir in ranch dressing. Serve hot or cold. Yield: 4 to 6 servings.

Jean Harbolt, Preceptor Alpha Alpha
Ironton, Ohio

♣ PASTA WITH PICANTE BLACK BEAN SAUCE

1 medium onion, coarsely chopped
1 clove of garlic, minced
1 tablespoon vegetable oil
1 (15-ounce) can black beans, rinsed, drained
1 (16-ounce) can stewed tomatoes
1 (8-ounce) can stewed tomatoes
1/2 cup picante sauce
1 teaspoon chili powder
1 teaspoon ground cumin
1/4 teaspoon crushed oregano
4 cups hot cooked pasta
Shredded Monterey Jack or Cheddar cheese
Chopped cilantro

Sauté onion and garlic in oil in large skillet until onion is tender. Stir in next 7 ingredients. Bring to a boil; reduce heat. Simmer, covered, for 15 minutes, stirring occasionally. Uncover. Cook over high heat until desired consistency. Serve over pasta. Sprinkle with cheese and cilantro. Serve with additional picante sauce. Yield: 4 servings.

Janet Hosier, Xi Alpha Upsilon
Rudy, Arkansas

♥ PASTA PRIMAVERA

2 cloves of garlic, minced
1/2 cup frozen green beans
1/2 cup frozen broccoli
1/2 cup thinly sliced zucchini
1 cup chopped plum tomatoes
2 teaspoons olive oil
1/2 teaspoon thyme
1/2 teaspoon salt
1/4 teaspoon ground pepper
1 cup cooked pasta
2 teaspoons grated Parmesan cheese
1 ounce salami
3/4 ounce mozzarella cheese, grated

Sauté garlic, green beans, broccoli, zucchini and tomatoes in oil in nonstick skillet. Add remaining ingredients. Cook, covered, for 10 minutes. Yield: 1 serving.

Thelma Woolley, Alpha Iota
Plymouth, Indiana

SOUTHWESTERN TOMATO PASTA

3 small ripe tomatoes
2 tablespoons extra virgin olive oil
3 cloves of garlic, minced
1 tablespoon fresh lime juice
1/2 teaspoon chili powder
1/4 teaspoon salt
1/4 teaspoon ground white pepper
4 ounces angel hair pasta
Grated goat cheese
2 tablespoons pine nuts, toasted

Peel tomatoes. Chop coarsely over bowl, reserving juice. Combine tomatoes, reserved juice, olive oil, garlic, lime juice, chili powder, salt and pepper; mix well. Cover; let stand for 1 hour at room temperature. Cook pasta according to package directions; drain. Serve tomato mixture over pasta. Top with goat cheese and pine nuts. Yield: 2 servings.

Brenda Gobble, Iota Chi
Concord, North Carolina

BROCCOLI-YAMS-MUSHROOMS WITH NOODLES

2 cups uncooked egg noodles
2 cloves of garlic, sliced
1 unpeeled yam, quartered, sliced into 1/4-inch slices
1 cup quartered mushrooms
1 cup chopped broccoli
1 cup shredded mozzarella cheese
2 tablespoons lite soy sauce
1/4 teaspoon dried thyme leaves
1/4 teaspoon pepper

Place noodles and garlic in large saucepan of boiling water. Cook for 4 minutes. Add yam; cook for 4 minutes. Add mushrooms and broccoli. Cook for 2 minutes or until vegetables are tender. Drain well. Place in bowl. Toss with cheese, soy sauce, thyme and pepper until cheese is melted. Serve immediately. Yield: 4 servings.

Jean Sudaby-Stuart, Laureate Tau
Penticton, British Columbia, Canada

BAKED BROCCOLI AND BROWN RICE

1 medium onion, chopped
3 cups chopped broccoli
1 cup minced celery
1 teaspoon dillweed
1 teaspoon dried marjoram
3 tablespoons vegetable oil
1/2 cup fresh minced parsley
3 cups cooked brown rice
4 eggs, slightly beaten
2 cups shredded Swiss cheese
Salt and pepper to taste

Preheat oven to 350 degrees. Sauté onion, broccoli and celery with dillweed and marjoram in oil in skillet until vegetables are tender. Add parsley. Combine rice with eggs and cheese in large bowl. Stir into vegetable mixture. Add salt and pepper. Spoon into buttered 6-by-10-inch shallow baking dish. Bake, uncovered, for 30 to 35 minutes or until golden. Yield: 6 servings.

Marcie Altman, Zeta Eta
Derby, Kansas

HERBED SPINACH AND RICE

1 (10-ounce) package frozen chopped spinach
1 1/2 cups rice, cooked
1 cup shredded sharp American cheese
2 eggs, slightly beaten
2 tablespoons softened butter or margarine
1/3 cup milk
2 tablespoons chopped onion
1/2 teaspoon Worcestershire sauce
1 teaspoon salt
1/4 teaspoon crushed rosemary or thyme

Preheat oven to 350 degrees. Cook spinach according to package directions; drain. Combine spinach and remaining ingredients in bowl; mix well. Pour into baking dish. Bake until knife inserted in center comes out clean. Yield: 4 servings.

Cinstal Weaver, Alpha Eta
Tucson, Arizona

RED HOT BEANS AND RICE

4 teaspoons olive or vegetable oil
1 cup chopped onion
1 cup chopped green bell pepper
2 cloves of garlic, crushed
1 cup chopped fresh tomatoes
8 ounces red kidney beans, cooked, rinsed, drained
1 cup sliced mushrooms
1 cup thawed frozen corn kernels
1 cup tomato sauce
1/4 teaspoon salt
1/4 teaspoon ground red pepper
1/4 teaspoon ground cumin
1/2 cup water
2 cups cooked instant brown rice
1/4 cup sour cream

Heat oil in large nonstick skillet. Add onion, green pepper and garlic. Cook, stirring occasionally, for 5 minutes or until vegetables are tender-crisp. Add tomatoes, beans, mushrooms, corn, tomato sauce, salt, red pepper, cumin and water; stir to combine. Simmer, uncovered, for 10 minutes. Spread rice on serving platter, mounding edges slightly. Spoon bean mixture into center of rice. Top with sour cream. Yield: 4 servings.

Gerrie Heusinger, Preceptor Epsilon Theta
St. Petersburg, Florida

INDIAN PILAF

1/4 cup butter
1 medium onion, chopped
1 1/2 cups uncooked rice
1/2 teaspoon salt
1/2 teaspoon allspice
1/2 teaspoon turmeric
1/4 teaspoon curry powder
1/8 teaspoon pepper
3 1/2 cups chicken broth
1/2 cup raisins
1/4 cup blanched slivered almonds

Preheat oven to 350 degrees. Melt butter in skillet. Add onion and rice. Cook, stirring constantly, until rice is yellow and onion is tender. Stir in seasonings. Pour into ungreased 2-quart casserole. Heat chicken broth in saucepan to boiling. Stir into rice mixture. Bake for 30 to 40 minutes or until liquid is absorbed and rice is tender. Stir in raisins and almonds. Yield: 8 servings.

Marie Melnicheck, Xi Epsilon Gamma
Collinswood, Ontario, Canada

RISOTTO CON FUNGHI (ITALIAN)

2 tablespoons olive oil
2 tablespoons butter or margarine
1/2 cup tomato sauce
1 teaspoon basil
2 cloves of garlic
2 sprigs parsley, minced
2 cups Italian arborio rice
8 cups vegetable or chicken broth
1 pound mushrooms
1/2 cup Parmesan cheese

Heat oil and butter in large skillet. Add tomato sauce, basil, garlic and parsley; mix well. Stir in rice. Add broth, a small amount at a time, until rice is cooked. Sauté mushrooms in small skillet. Add to rice mixture. Add cheese. Serve immediately. Yield: 4 to 6 servings.

Danna Brennink, Gamma Mu
Kelowna, British Columbia, Canada

WILD RICE

1 cup cubed Velveeta cheese
1 cup cubed Cheddar cheese
1 cup chopped black olives
2 (14-ounce) cans tomatoes
1/2 cup chopped onion
1 (4-ounce) can mushrooms, drained
1/2 cup olive oil
1 1/2 teaspoons salt
1 1/2 teaspoons pepper
1/2 cup washed wild rice
1/2 cup uncooked white rice
1 1/2 cups boiling water

Preheat oven to 325 degrees. Combine all ingredients in 2-quart casserole. Bake, covered, for 2 hours, stirring once. Yield: 8 servings.

Rita Opie, Xi Zeta
Billings, Montana

♥ LENTIL SPAGHETTI

1 medium onion, chopped
2 cloves of garlic, chopped
Vegetable oil
2 cups tomato sauce
1 (16-ounce) can whole peeled tomatoes, chopped
1/2 teaspoon oregano
1/2 teaspoon thyme
1/2 teaspoon sweet basil
1/2 teaspoon salt
Pepper to taste
1/2 cup dried lentils, rinsed
Cooked spaghetti or pasta

Sauté onion and garlic in oil in large saucepan until tender. Add tomato sauce, tomatoes, oregano, thyme, basil, salt, pepper and lentils; mix well. Simmer for 45 minutes. Serve over spaghetti. Yield: 4 to 6 servings.

Barbara J. Roberts, Zeta Nu
Princeton, Missouri

♥ TOFU QUICHE

1 1/2 cups whole wheat flour
1/2 cup wheat germ
1 1/2 teaspoons salt
12 tablespoons margarine
4 to 6 tablespoons cold water
3 eggs, beaten
2 cups warm milk
1/4 teaspoon pepper
8 ounces tofu
8 ounces grated Swiss cheese
1/4 teaspoon nutmeg

Preheat oven to 400 degrees. Combine flour, wheat germ and 1 teaspoon salt in bowl. Cut in 10 tablespoons margarine until consistency of rolled oats. Sprinkle with cold water, using just enough to hold together. Shape into ball. Press into 10-inch pie pan. Bake for 7 minutes. Combine eggs, milk, 1/2 teaspoon salt and pepper in bowl; mix well. Crumble tofu over bottom of pie shell. Spread cheese evenly over tofu. Pour milk mixture over cheese. Sprinkle with nutmeg. Dot with 2 tablespoons margarine. Bake for 30 minutes or until set. Let stand for 10 minutes before serving. Yield: 6 to 8 servings.

Thelma Yragui, Laureate Lambda
Walla Walla, Washington

♣ ♥ VEGETARIAN ENCHILADAS

Nonstick vegetable cooking spray
1 clove of garlic, crushed
1 teaspoon vegetable oil
2 1/2 cups shredded zucchini
1/4 cup canned chopped green chilies
1 (9-ounce) package frozen corn kernels
1 (16-ounce) can black beans, drained
2 cups salsa
1/4 teaspoon ground cumin
Salt to taste
10 (5-inch) corn tortillas
1 1/4 cups shredded Cheddar or Monterey Jack cheese

Preheat oven to 350 degrees. Spray 9-inch pie pan with cooking spray. Sauté garlic in oil in large skillet. Add zucchini. Cook for 4 minutes or until limp. Add chilies, corn, beans, salsa, cumin and salt. Simmer for 5 to 6 minutes or until hot and thickened. Place 4 corn tortillas in pie pan to cover bottom. Spoon in 1/3 hot mixture. Sprinkle lightly with 1/3 cheese. Repeat layers with remaining tortillas ending with cheese. Bake for 35 to 40 minutes or until browned. Let stand for 10 minutes. Slice into wedges. Yield: 6 servings.

Kathleen Landreth, Xi Alpha
Albuquerque, New Mexico

TORTILLA-BLACK BEAN CASSEROLE

2 cups chopped onions
1 1/2 cups chopped green bell pepper
1 (14-ounce) can tomatoes, chopped
3/4 cup picante sauce
2 cloves of garlic, minced
2 teaspoons ground cumin
2 (15-ounce) cans black beans, drained
12 (6-inch) corn tortillas, cut up
2 cups shredded Monterey Jack cheese
2 medium tomatoes, sliced
2 cups shredded lettuce
Sliced green onions
Sliced ripe olives
1/2 cup sour cream

Preheat oven to 350 degrees. Combine onions, green pepper, undrained tomatoes, picante sauce, garlic and cumin in large skillet. Bring to a boil; reduce heat. Simmer, uncovered, for 10 minutes. Stir in beans. Spread 1/3 bean mixture in bottom of 9-by-13-inch baking dish. Top with 6 tortillas and 1/2 the cheese. Add 1/3 bean mixture, remaining tortillas and remaining bean mixture. Bake, covered, for 30 to 35 minutes. Sprinkle with remaining cheese. Let stand for 10 minutes. Top with remaining ingredients. Yield: 8 servings.

Jan Temple, Xi Epsilon
Rowlett, Texas

Betty Prusaczyk, Lambda Master, Harrisburg, Illinois, makes Green Tomato Pickles by placing 2 quarts green tomatoes, quartered, 2 cups chopped onions and 3/4 cup hot pepper if desired in saucepan. Mix 2 cups sugar, 3 tablespoons salt, 2 cups vinegar and 1 tablespoon celery seeds in bowl. Pour over tomatoes. Bring to a boil. Remove from heat immediately. Place in sterile pint jars; seal. Serve with fish and hushpuppies.

114 / Side Dishes

♥ VEGETABLE LO MEIN DELIGHT

1 (8-ounce) package angel hair or thin spaghetti
3/4 cup chicken broth
1/4 cup soy sauce
2 teaspoons cornstarch
2 tablespoons vegetable or canola oil
1 3/4 cups sliced celery
1 3/4 cups sliced mushrooms
1 1/2 cups sliced red or green peppers
1/2 cup sliced onion
2 cups bean sprouts
1 1/4 cups sliced cabbage or 1 1/4 cups snow peas
Chow mein noodles

Cook angel hair according to package directions; drain. Combine chicken broth, soy sauce and cornstarch in cup; mix until smooth. Heat oil in wok or large saucepan until hot. Add celery, mushrooms, peppers and onion. Cook, stirring constantly, for 3 minutes or until celery is tender-crisp. Stir in bean sprouts, cabbage and cornstarch mixture until thickened and starts to boil. Stir for 1 minute. Toss vegetables and angel hair together in bowl. Garnish with chow mein noodles. Yield: 4 servings.

Jane E. Fleming, Laureate Gamma Beta
Tampa, Florida

CORN BREAD DRESSING

2 teaspoons salt
1 1/2 teaspoons white pepper
1 teaspoon ground red pepper
1 teaspoon pepper
1 teaspoon dried oregano leaves
1/2 teaspoon onion powder
1/2 teaspoon dried thyme leaves
1/2 cup unsalted butter or margarine
1/4 cup margarine
3/4 cup finely chopped onion
3/4 cup finely chopped green peppers
1/2 cup finely chopped celery
1 tablespoon minced garlic
2 bay leaves
3/4 pound chicken giblets, cooked, finely chopped
1 cup chicken stock
1 tablespoon Tabasco sauce
5 cups crumbled corn bread
1 (13-ounce) can evaporated milk
3 eggs

Preheat oven to 350 degrees. Combine salt, white pepper, ground red pepper, pepper, oregano, onion powder and thyme in small bowl; mix well. Melt butter and margarine in large skillet. Add onion, green peppers, celery, garlic and bay leaves. Sauté over high heat for 2 minutes. Add seasoning mixture. Cook for 5 minutes or until vegetables are barely wilted. Stir in giblets, stock and Tabasco sauce. Cook for 5 minutes, stirring frequently. Turn off heat. Add corn bread, milk and eggs, stirring well. Spoon dressing into greased 9-by-13-inch baking pan. Bake for 35 to 40 minutes or until browned on top. Yield: 6 to 8 servings.

Betty Quinn, Nu
Hampton, New Brunswick, Canada

♥ LOW-FAT SAGE DRESSING

1 tablespoon margarine
7 cups dry bread crumbs
1 cup chopped onion
1 cup chopped celery
3 cups chopped unpeeled apple
1 teaspoon salt
1/4 cup minced fresh parsley
1/4 teaspoon paprika
1/2 teaspoon rubbed sage
1/2 teaspoon dried thyme
1 to 1 1/2 cups turkey stock or broth

Rub walls of Crock•Pot with margarine. Combine remaining ingredients in bowl; mix well. Pour into Crock•Pot. Cook, covered, on High for 1 hour. Stir well. Cook on Low for 2 to 3 hours. Yield: 8 to 10 servings.

Sharon Franklin, Laureate Beta Upsilon
Warrensburg, Missouri

♥ FIRE AND ICE

3/4 cup vinegar
1/4 cup water
1 1/2 teaspoons celery salt
1 1/2 teaspoons mustard seeds
1 teaspoon salt
1 teaspoon garlic salt
1/8 teaspoon red pepper
1/8 teaspoon pepper
1/2 cup sugar
6 large tomatoes, chopped
1 large green bell pepper, chopped
1 large red onion, sliced
4 stalks celery, chopped
2 large cucumbers, sliced

Combine first 9 ingredients in saucepan. Bring to a boil. Boil for 1 minute. Combine tomatoes, green pepper, onion, celery and cucumbers in bowl. Pour vinegar mixture over vegetables; mix well. Chill. Yield: 8 servings.

Phyllis Raymos, Preceptor Beta Xi
Wichita, Kansas

♥ SWEET ONION MARMALADE

2 pounds onions
1/4 cup olive oil
2 tablespoons sugar
1 teaspoon ground white pepper
1 teaspoon ground pepper
1/8 teaspoon ground allspice
1/8 teaspoon ground cloves
1/4 cup red wine vinegar
1/4 cup chicken broth
Salt to taste

Cut onions into halves lengthwise; cut into 1/2-inch wedges. Heat oil in large heavy skillet over medium heat. Add onions. Cook for 15 minutes or until softened, stirring frequently. Add sugar, peppers, allspice and cloves. Cook for 10 minutes, stirring often. Add vinegar. Cook for 5 minutes; stir well. Add broth. Season with salt; stir well. Serve at room temperature. Yield: 2 cups.

Kathleen Blay, Xi Mu
Londonderry, New Hampshire

Judy Selheim, Preceptor Gamma Lambda, Castle Rock, Colorado, makes Mexican Rice by mixing 3 1/2 cups cooked long grain rice, 2 cups sour cream, 1 cup chopped chilies, 8 ounces Monterey Jack cheese, salt and pepper in bowl. Pour into buttered casserole. Bake at 350 degrees for 30 minutes.

Just Loafing Around

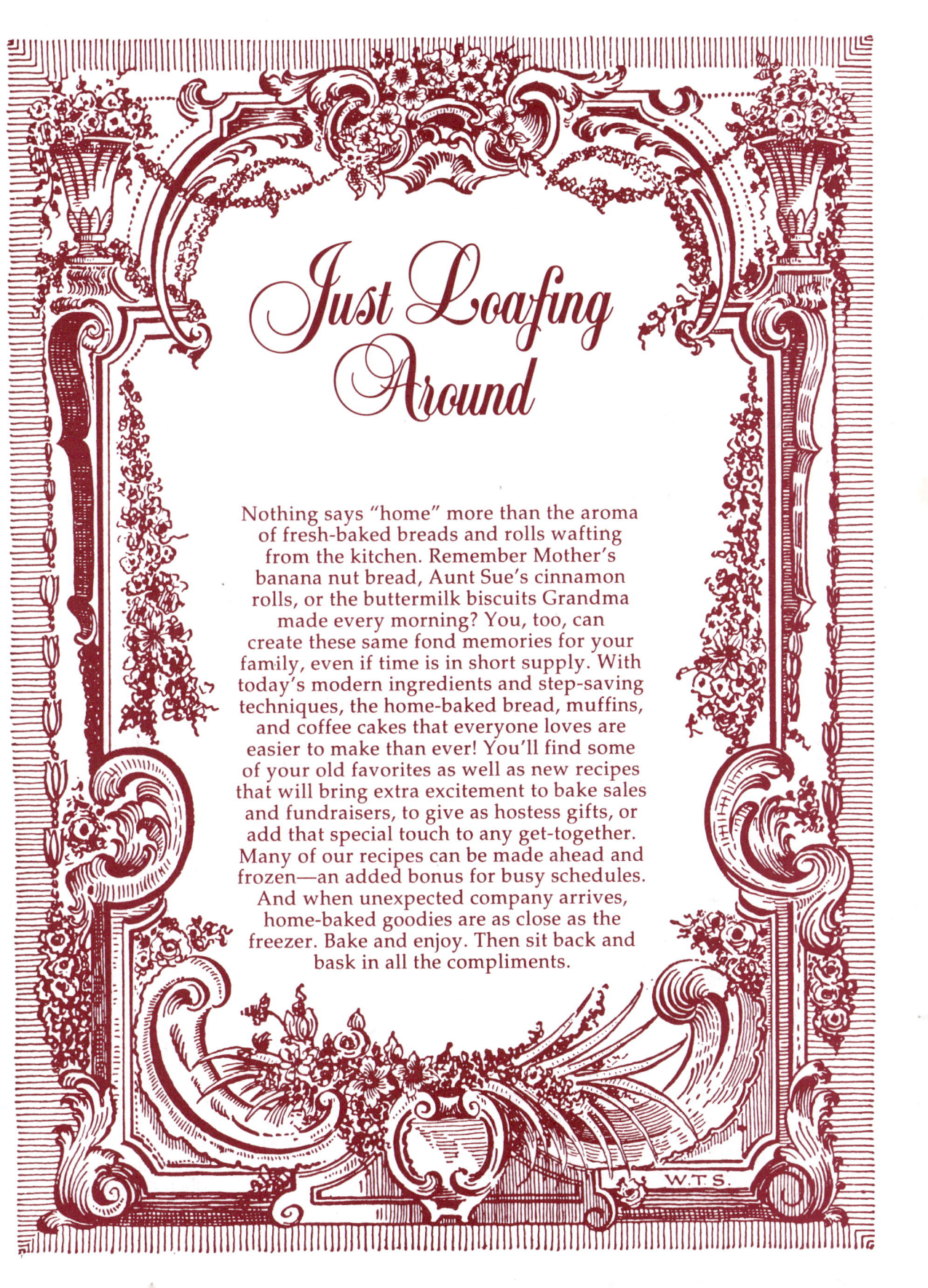

Nothing says "home" more than the aroma of fresh-baked breads and rolls wafting from the kitchen. Remember Mother's banana nut bread, Aunt Sue's cinnamon rolls, or the buttermilk biscuits Grandma made every morning? You, too, can create these same fond memories for your family, even if time is in short supply. With today's modern ingredients and step-saving techniques, the home-baked bread, muffins, and coffee cakes that everyone loves are easier to make than ever! You'll find some of your old favorites as well as new recipes that will bring extra excitement to bake sales and fundraisers, to give as hostess gifts, or add that special touch to any get-together. Many of our recipes can be made ahead and frozen—an added bonus for busy schedules. And when unexpected company arrives, home-baked goodies are as close as the freezer. Bake and enjoy. Then sit back and bask in all the compliments.

APPLE BUTTER-SPICE BREAD

1/2 cup butter or margarine, at room temperature	1 teaspoon salt
	1/2 teaspoon baking soda
3/4 cup sugar	3/4 teaspoon allspice
2 eggs	1 1/4 cups apple butter
2 cups all-purpose flour	1/2 cup chopped nuts
	Cream cheese
2 1/2 teaspoons baking powder	

Preheat oven to 350 degrees. Cream butter and sugar in bowl; mix well. Add eggs, 1 at a time, beating well after each addition. Sift flour, baking powder, salt, baking soda and allspice together. Add to creamed mixture, alternately with apple butter, stirring well after each addition. Add nuts. Pour into greased 5-by-9-inch loaf pan. Bake for 1 hour to 1 hour and 10 minutes or until wooden toothpick inserted in center comes out clean. Remove bread from pan to wire rack. Let cool thoroughly before slicing. Top with cream cheese and additional apple butter. Yield: 12 servings.

Faye Williams, Zeta Xi
Kennett, Missouri

APPLESAUCE-GINGERBREAD LOAF

1 1/2 cups sugar	1 teaspoon baking soda
1/4 cup butter or margarine at room temperature	1/2 teaspoon ground cloves
3 egg whites	1/4 teaspoon salt
2 1/2 cups all-purpose flour	1 cup applesauce
2 teaspoons ground ginger	1/4 cup unsulphured molasses
1 teaspoon ground cinnamon	1/2 cup boiling water

Preheat oven to 350 degrees. Beat sugar and butter in medium mixer bowl at high speed for 2 minutes or until well blended. Beat in egg whites; mix well. Sift flour, ginger, cinnamon, baking soda, cloves and salt together in bowl. Add to egg mixture with applesauce and molasses; beat at low speed until smooth. Beat in boiling water. Pour batter into lightly greased and floured 5-by-9-inch loaf pan. Bake for 55 minutes or until toothpick inserted in center comes out clean. Let cool in pan on wire rack. Yield: 12 servings.

Joanne Pontius, Xi Chi
Butler, Pennsylvania

Clara McCord, Preceptor Theta Sigma, Brackettville, Texas, makes Rise and Shine Biscuits by mixing 1/3 cup sour cream, 1/3 cup club soda and 2 cups biscuit mix in bowl. Shape into biscuits. Place in greased baking pan. Bake in preheated 450-degree oven for 18 minutes. This is a New Mexico guest ranch favorite. Yield: 8 to 10 servings.

♥ CARROT-APRICOT BREAD

1 1/2 cups sifted all-purpose flour	3/4 cup applesauce
	2 eggs
1 teaspoon baking soda	1/2 cup shredded carrots
	1/2 cup chopped dried apricots
1/2 teaspoon cinnamon	1/2 cup coconut
1/4 teaspoon nutmeg	1/2 cup raisins
1/4 teaspoon salt	1/2 cup chopped nuts
1 cup sugar	

Preheat oven to 350 degrees. Sift together flour, baking soda, cinnamon, nutmeg and salt in bowl. Beat sugar, applesauce and eggs in mixer bowl for 2 minutes. Add dry ingredients; stir just until moistened. Stir in remaining ingredients; mix well. Pour into greased 5-by-9-inch loaf pan. Bake for 55 minutes or until toothpick inserted in center comes out clean. Let cool in pan for 10 minutes. Remove to wire rack to cool completely. Yield: 10 servings.

Lillian Cook, Laureate Alpha Zeta
Matheny, West Virginia

BANANA-APPLESAUCE BREAD

1/2 cup unsweetened applesauce	1 cup chopped nuts
	2 cups all-purpose flour
3/4 cup sugar	1 teaspoon baking soda
2 eggs	1/4 teaspoon salt
2 or 3 bananas, mashed	1 teaspoon vanilla extract

Preheat oven to 350 degrees. Combine all ingredients in bowl; mix well with spoon. Grease and flour two 4-by-8-inch bread pans. Pour batter into pans. Bake for 50 minutes to 1 hour or until toothpick inserted in center comes out clean. Yield: 10 to 12 servings.

Judy Newlan, Laureate Iota
Sun City West, Arizona

♥ LOW-FAT BANANA BREAD

1/2 cup unsweetened applesauce	1 cup mashed bananas
	1 1/2 cups all-purpose flour
3/4 cup sugar	1 teaspoon vanilla extract
1 egg plus 1 egg white	
1 teaspoon baking soda	1/4 teaspoon salt
1/4 cup fat-free sour cream	Raisins and nuts to taste

Preheat oven to 350 degrees. Cream applesauce and sugar in mixer bowl. Add eggs. Beat until light and fluffy. Dissolve baking soda in sour cream in bowl. Add to applesauce mixture. Add remaining ingredients; mix well. Pour into greased 5-by-9-inch loaf pan. Bake for 40 to 45 minutes or until toothpick inserted in center comes out clean. Let cool on wire rack. Yield: 10 to 12 servings.

Michelle McNicoll, Iota Epsilon
Baton Rouge, Louisiana

♥ CHOLESTEROL-FREE BANANA BREAD

2 1/4 cups all-purpose flour
2/3 cup honey-crunch wheat germ
1/2 cup oats, uncooked
1/4 cup packed dark brown sugar
1 tablespoon baking powder
1/2 teaspoon salt
1/4 teaspoon baking soda
10 tablespoons light corn-oil spread
1 1/2 cups mashed bananas
1 (6-ounce) can frozen apple juice concentrate, thawed
1/2 cup frozen egg substitute, thawed
1/2 cup chopped walnuts
1 teaspoon vanilla extract

Preheat oven to 350 degrees. Combine flour, wheat germ, oats, brown sugar, baking powder, salt and baking soda in large mixer bowl. Cut in corn-oil spread with pastry blender until mixture resembles coarse crumbs. Stir in bananas, apple juice concentrate, egg substitute, walnuts and vanilla just until flour is moistened. Spoon into greased 5-by-9-inch loaf pan. Bake for 1 hour or until toothpick inserted in center comes out clean. Let cool in pan on wire rack for 10 minutes. Remove from pan. Let cool slightly. Serve warm or let cool completely. Yield: 18 servings.

Joy Murphy, Laureate Beta Eta
Urbandale, Iowa

♣ BANANA-PEANUT BUTTER BREAD

1/2 cup butter
1 cup sugar
2 eggs
1/2 cup peanut butter
2 or 3 bananas, mashed
2 cups all-purpose flour
1 teaspoon baking soda
1/2 cup chopped nuts (optional)

Preheat oven to 325 degrees. Cream butter and sugar in mixer bowl. Add eggs; beat well. Add peanut butter, bananas, flour and baking soda; mix well. Add nuts. Pour into greased 5-by-9-inch loaf pan. Bake for 1 hour and 10 minutes. Remove to wire rack to cool. Yield: 10 to 12 servings.

Jennifer M. Kelly, Zeta Rho
Collins, Colorado

OVEN-BAKED BROWN BREAD

1 1/2 cups all-purpose flour
1 1/2 cups rye flour
1 cup yellow cornmeal
1 teaspoon baking soda
2 cups buttermilk
1/2 cup dark molasses

Preheat oven to 375 degrees. Combine flour, cornmeal and baking soda in mixer bowl. Add buttermilk alternately with molasses, beating at low speed after each addition until well blended. Pour into greased 5-by-9-inch loaf pan. Bake for 50 minutes. Let cool on wire rack. Yield: 10 to 15 servings.

Peggy Woehl, Xi Phi
Hot Springs, South Dakota

GRANDMOTHER'S FAMOUS CRANBERRY BREAD

2 cups sifted all-purpose flour
1 cup sugar
1 1/2 teaspoons baking powder
1 teaspoon salt
1/2 teaspoon baking soda
1/4 cup butter or margarine
1 egg, beaten
1 teaspoon grated orange peel
3/4 cup orange juice
1 1/2 cups light raisins
1 1/2 cups chopped fresh or frozen cranberries

Preheat oven to 350 degrees. Sift flour, sugar, baking powder, salt and baking soda together in large bowl. Cut in butter until mixture is crumbly. Add egg, orange peel and orange juice all at once. Stir just until mixture is moistened. Fold in raisins and cranberries. Pour into greased 5-by-9-inch loaf pan. Bake for 1 hour and 10 minutes. Let cool on wire rack. Yield: 10 servings.

Sharon A. Fahlman, Xi Gamma
Winnipeg, Manitoba, Canada

♥ HEALTHY FRUIT BREAD

2 cups all-purpose flour
12 packets artificial sweetener
1 teaspoon baking soda
4 large bananas, sliced
1/2 cup sugar-free crushed pineapple, well drained
1/2 cup raisins
1/2 cup sugar-free applesauce
1/2 cup dried apricots, chopped

Preheat oven to 325 degrees. Combine all ingredients in order listed in large mixer bowl. Beat at low speed until well blended. Pour into 6-by-9-inch loaf pan coated with cooking spray. Bake for 1 hour or until toothpick inserted in center comes out clean. Let cool on wire rack. Yield: 10 servings.

Archalyn Kibler, Xi Delta Omega
Altamont, Kansas

ORANGE SLICE BREAD

3/4 cup melted butter
1 egg
2 cups sugar
4 cups all-purpose flour
1 teaspoon baking soda
1 teaspoon salt
1 cup chopped nuts
1 cup apple juice
1 cup orange juice
1 pound orange slice candy, cut up

Preheat oven to 325 degrees. Combine butter, egg and sugar in mixer bowl. Sift flour, baking soda and salt into mixture; mix well. Add remaining ingredients; mix well. Pour into greased 5-by-9-inch loaf pan. Bake for 1 hour and 20 minutes. Let cool in pan on wire rack. Yield: 10 to 12 servings.

Laura Baumgart, Zeta Alpha
Quincy, Washington

GARDEN BREAD

3 eggs	1 teaspoon baking
2 cups sugar	soda
1 cup vegetable oil	1/2 teaspoon salt
1 teaspoon vanilla	2 teaspoons cinnamon
extract	1 cup unpeeled shredded
1 cup all-purpose	zucchini
flour	1 cup chopped apple
2 cups whole wheat	1 cup chopped nuts
flour	
1 teaspoon baking	
powder	

Preheat oven to 325 degrees. Cream eggs, sugar, oil and vanilla in large bowl; mix well. Add next 6 ingredients; mix well. Fold in zucchini, apple, carrot and nuts. Pour into well-greased tube pan or 2 greased 5-by-9-inch loaf pans. Bake for 50 minutes to 1 hour or until bread tests done. Let cool on wire rack. Yield: 24 servings.

Mary Ann Christian, Laureate Rho
Richmond, Virginia

POPPY SEED-EGGNOG BREAD

2 1/2 cups all-purpose	3 tablespoons vegetable
flour	oil
1 cup sugar	3 1/2 teaspoons baking
1/4 cup poppy seeds	powder
1 1/4 cups eggnog	1 teaspoon salt
1 tablespoon plus	1 teaspoon ground
1 teaspoon grated	nutmeg
orange peel	1 egg

Preheat oven to 350 degrees. Grease bottom only of 5-by-9-inch loaf pan. Combine all ingredients in large mixer bowl; beat for 30 seconds. Pour into prepared pan. Bake for 55 minutes to 1 hour and 5 minutes or until toothpick inserted in center comes out clean. Let cool slightly on wire rack. Loosen sides from pan; remove to wire rack to cool completely. Wrap; refrigerate for up to 1 week. Yield: 24 servings.

Margaret Lawrence, Laureate Phi
Montgomery, New York

RASPBERRY-NUT BREAD

2 cups all-purpose	1/4 cup shortening
flour	3/4 cup orange juice
1 cup sugar	1 tablespoon orange
1 1/2 teaspoons baking	rind
powder	1 egg, well beaten
1/2 teaspoon baking	1/2 cup chopped nuts
soda	2 cups fresh or frozen
1 teaspoon salt	whole raspberries

Preheat oven to 350 degrees. Sift first 5 ingredients in large bowl. Cut in shortening until mixture resembles coarse cornmeal. Combine orange juice and rind with egg in bowl. Pour all at once into dry ingredients, mixing just enough to moisten. Fold in nuts and raspberries. Pour into greased 5-by-9-inch loaf pan, spreading corners and sides slightly higher than center. Bake for 1 hour or until toothpick inserted in center comes out clean. Let cool for 10 minutes before removing from pan. Yield: 10 to 12 servings.

Betty Fagan, Preceptor Alpha
Cumberland, Maryland

RHUBARB BREAD

2 cups packed dark	1 teaspoon salt
brown sugar	1 teaspoon baking soda
2/3 cup melted vegetable	1 1/2 cups finely chopped
shortening	rhubarb
1 egg	1/2 cup chopped nuts
1 cup sour milk	1/2 teaspoon cinnamon
1 teaspoon vanilla	1 tablespoon melted
extract	margarine
2 1/2 cups all-purpose	
flour	

Preheat oven to 325 degrees. Combine 1 1/2 cups brown sugar and shortening in mixer bowl. Beat in egg, sour milk and vanilla. Sift flour, salt and baking soda together in bowl. Add to mixture, mixing well. Fold in rhubarb and nuts; mix well. Pour into greased 5-by-9-inch loaf pan. Combine remaining 1/2 cup brown sugar and remaining ingredients in bowl. Sprinkle over loaf. Bake for 40 minutes. Let cool in pan for 10 minutes. Remove from pan to wire rack; let cool completely. Yield: 10 to 12 servings.

Doris Claypole, Psi Eta
Orrick, Missouri

SWEDISH PEPPARKAKU BREAD

2 cups plus	1 teaspoon baking
2 tablespoons	soda
all-purpose flour	1 teaspoon cinnamon
2 cups sugar	2 eggs
1 1/4 teaspoons ground	1 cup buttermilk
cloves	1/2 cup melted butter

Preheat oven to 350 degrees. Blend flour, sugar, cloves, baking soda and cinnamon in 8-by-11-inch plastic bag; mix well. Combine eggs and buttermilk in mixer bowl. Blend in butter and dry ingredients; mix well. Pour into 5-by-9-inch loaf pan. Bake for 1 hour. Let cool on wire rack. Yield: 10 to 12 servings.

Charlotte Clements-Freeman, Xi Omicron Gamma
Sacramento, California

Margie Bontz, Alpha Delta Lambda, Cameron, Missouri, makes Cakelike Corn Bread by mixing 2 boxes corn bread mix and 2 boxes single layer yellow cake mix in bowl. Mix 2/3 cup milk, 4 eggs, 1 cup water and 1/2 cup vegetable oil in large bowl. Add corn bread-cake mixture; mix well. Spread in 9-by-13-inch greased pan. Bake in preheated 350-degree oven for 35 minutes.

MICROWAVE BEER BREAD

I wanted a hot bread that could be made in 12 minutes or less so I made up this recipe.

Cornflakes, crushed	12 ounces beer, at room
2 cups self-rising flour	temperature
1 cup all-purpose flour	1 to 2 tablespoons butter
3 tablespoons sugar	or margarine

Grease and flour 4-by-8-inch microwave-safe glass loaf dish. Coat with cornflake crumbs. Combine flour, sugar and beer in bowl; mix well. Pour into prepared pan. Sprinkle additional cornflake crumbs on top. Dot with butter. Microwave on Medium for 9 minutes or on High for 2 minutes. Remove to wire rack to cool. Yield: 8 to 10 servings.

Delone J. Bond, Xi Upsilon
Salt Lake City, Utah

APPLE-PECAN MUFFINS

1 1/2 cups all-purpose flour	2 eggs
1/4 cup oatmeal	1 cup sugar
1 1/2 teaspoons baking soda	1/3 cup vegetable oil
Dash of salt	2 cups chopped peeled apples
1/2 teaspoon cinnamon	1 cup chopped pecans
	1/2 cup coconut

Preheat oven to 350 degrees. Combine flour, oatmeal, baking soda, salt and cinnamon in large bowl; mix well. Combine eggs, sugar and oil in small bowl; mix well. Stir in apples, pecans and coconut. Combine with dry ingredients; mix well. Fill greased muffin cups 3/4 full. Bake for 25 to 30 minutes or until tests done. Let cool on wire rack. Yield: 18 servings.

Paula Boland, Alpha Epsilon
Thunder Bay, Ontario, Canada

CHOCOLATE CHIP-BANANA MUFFINS

2 cups all-purpose flour	2/3 cup packed dark brown sugar
2 teaspoons baking powder	2 eggs
1/2 teaspoon baking soda	1/4 cup vegetable oil
1/2 teaspoon salt	1 teaspoon vanilla extract
1 1/2 cups mashed ripe bananas	1/2 cup mini-chocolate chips

Preheat oven to 400 degrees. Combine flour, baking powder, baking soda and salt in large bowl. Combine bananas, brown sugar, eggs, oil and vanilla in medium bowl. Stir into dry ingredients just until combined. Stir in chocolate chips. Spoon into 12 greased 2 1/2-inch muffin cups. Bake for 25 minutes. Yield: 12 servings.

Rebecca Seeman, Xi Eta Delta
Salina, Kansas

♥ BANANA-ORANGE MUFFINS

These muffins contain no sugar and no salt.

1 banana, sliced	1 1/2 cups rolled oats
1 egg	2 teaspoons baking
3 tablespoons safflower oil	powder
1 cup whole wheat flour	1/2 teaspoon orange rind
	3/4 cup orange juice

Preheat oven to 425 degrees. Blend banana, egg and oil in mixer bowl until smooth. Combine flour, oats, baking powder and orange rind in bowl. Stir into banana mixture; mix well. Add orange juice; mix well. Pour into muffin cups coated with cooking spray. Bake for 15 minutes. Yield: 12 servings.

Sandra Malone
Houston, Texas

♥ FAT-FREE BANANA CRUNCH MUFFINS

1 cup all-purpose flour	1/4 teaspoon salt
1/2 cup wheat and barley nuggets	1 large ripe banana, mashed
1/2 cup sugar	1/2 cup plain yogurt
1/2 teaspoon baking powder	1/4 cup frozen egg substitute, thawed
1/2 teaspoon baking soda	1/2 teaspoon vanilla extract

Preheat oven to 350 degrees. Combine first 6 ingredients in large bowl; mix well. Combine banana, yogurt, egg substitute and vanilla in bowl with whisk. Add banana mixture to flour mixture, stirring just until moistened. Spoon into muffin cups coated with nonfat cooking spray. Bake for 20 minutes. Yield: 12 servings.

Bonnie Jo Nay, Xi Alpha Delta
Pleasant Hill, Oregon

♥ LOW-FAT BANANA MUFFINS

1/2 cup nonfat buttermilk	1/4 cup rolled oats
3 tablespoons applesauce	1/4 cup packed light brown sugar
1/2 cup mashed bananas	1/4 cup sugar
1/4 cup egg substitute	1/4 teaspoon salt
1/4 cup white corn syrup	2 teaspoons baking powder
1 1/4 cups all-purpose flour	1/2 teaspoon cinnamon
1/2 cup whole wheat flour	

Preheat oven to 400 degrees. Spray muffin cups with cooking spray. Combine buttermilk, applesauce, bananas, egg substitute and corn syrup in large bowl. Combine remaining ingredients in large bowl; mix well. Blend dry ingredients into first mixture until just moistened. Fill muffin cups 1/2 full. Bake for 15 to 18 minutes or until golden brown. Yield: 18 servings.

Cathy Brady, Beta Sigma
Kennewick, Washington

♥ NO-SUGAR BANANA-BRAN MUFFINS

8 large overripe bananas, mashed	2 eggs
3 cups all-bran extra fiber cereal	1/4 cup olive oil
	1 cup raisins
	3 cups self-rising flour
2 cups skim milk	1 cup chopped pecans

Preheat oven to 425 degrees. Line two 12-cup muffin pans and one 6-cup muffin pan with paper liners. Spray lightly with cooking spray. Combine bananas, fiber cereal, milk, eggs, oil and raisins in 8-cup mixer bowl. Add flour, 1 cup at a time, mixing well after each addition. Add pecans. Spoon into liners in muffin cups. Bake for 25 minutes. Yield: 30 servings.

Alice C. Yandle, Xi Delta Delta
Mooresville, North Carolina

♥ SIX-WEEK BRAN MUFFINS

2 1/2 cups all-purpose flour	2 teaspoons cinnamon
2 1/2 cups whole wheat flour	1 (8-ounce) package egg substitute
5 teaspoons baking soda	1 quart buttermilk
	1 1/2 cups honey
15 ounces bran cereal with raisins	1/2 cup vegetable oil
	1/2 cup nonfat yogurt

Preheat oven to 400 degrees. Sift flour and baking soda into large bowl. Add cereal and cinnamon; mix well. Add egg substitute, buttermilk, honey, oil and yogurt; mix well. Fill mini-muffin cups 2/3 full. Bake for 15 minutes. May be stored in refrigerator for up to 6 weeks. Yield: 144 mini muffins.

Margaret Jacobs, Laureate Rho
Hutchinson, Kansas

♥ EASY MUFFINS

1 1/2 cups all-purpose flour	1 tablespoon baking powder
1/4 cup packed dark brown sugar	2 cups bran cereal
1 cup chocolate drink mix	1 3/4 cups skim milk
	1 cup raisins
1/4 teaspoon salt	2 eggs
1/2 teaspoon allspice	1/4 cup vegetable oil

Preheat oven to 400 degrees. Combine flour, brown sugar, chocolate drink mix, salt, allspice and baking powder in bowl. Combine cereal, milk and raisins in large bowl. Let stand for 5 minutes or until cereal is softened. Add eggs and oil; mix well. Add flour mixture, stirring until well combined. Pour batter evenly into 12 lightly greased 2 1/2-inch muffin cups, filling 3/4 full. Bake for 20 minutes or until golden brown. Serve warm. Yield: 12 to 18 servings.

Helen E. Smith, Omega Upsilon
Alford, Florida

♣ PEACHES 'N CREAM MUFFINS

1 (14-ounce) can sliced peaches, drained	1 1/2 cups bran cereal
4 ounces cream cheese	2 cups all-purpose flour
2 eggs	1 tablespoon baking powder
1 1/4 cups milk	1 teaspoon cinnamon
1/3 cup honey	1/2 teaspoon salt
1/4 cup melted butter	
1 teaspoon grated lemon rind	

Preheat oven to 400 degrees. Grease 12 large muffin cups or line with paper cupcake liners. Chop peaches and cream cheese into cubes. Beat eggs lightly with fork in bowl. Stir in milk, honey, butter and lemon rind; mix well. Add cereal; mix well. Combine remaining ingredients in large bowl; mix well. Stir peaches and cream cheese into cereal mixture. Stir cereal mixture into liquid mixture, mixing just until moist. Spoon into muffin cups, filling to top. Bake for 20 to 25 minutes or until test done. Let cool on rack. Store in airtight container. Yield: 24 servings.

Irja Hansen, Gamma Zeta
Ramore, Ontario, Canada

PINEAPPLE-CARROT-RAISIN MUFFINS

2 cups all-purpose flour	1/2 cup raisins
1 cup sugar	1/2 cup chopped pecans
2 teaspoons baking powder	1 (8-ounce) can crushed pineapple
1/2 teaspoon ground cinnamon	2 eggs
	1/2 cup melted margarine
1/4 teaspoon ground ginger	1 teaspoon vanilla extract
1/2 cup shredded carrot	Dark brown sugar to taste

Preheat oven to 375 degrees. Combine flour, sugar, baking powder, cinnamon and ginger in large bowl; mix well. Stir in carrot, raisins and pecans; mix well. Combine undrained pineapple, eggs, margarine and vanilla in small bowl. Stir into dry ingredients until just blended. Spoon into 12 greased 2 1/2-inch muffin cups. Bake for 20 to 25 minutes or until golden brown. Remove from pan. Let cool on wire rack. Sprinkle with brown sugar. Yield: 12 servings.

Heather Pihulak, Tau
Keewatin, Ontario, Canada

Judi Tippin, Preceptor Zeta, Anchorage, Alaska, makes Garlic French Bread by combining 1 cup mayonnaise, 2 cups grated cheese, 2 to 3 teaspoons garlic powder and chopped tops of 6 to 8 green onions in bowl; mix well. Refrigerate, covered, overnight. Cut 1 French bread loaf in half lengthwise. Spread each half with mixture. Place in baking pan. Cover with cooking foil. Bake in preheated 350-degree oven for 30 minutes. Fold back foil. Sprinkle with parsley. Broil until brown.

♥ THREE-GRAIN MUFFINS

1/3 cup stoneground cornmeal
1/3 cup raw sugar
1/3 cup soy flour
1 cup whole wheat flour
3/4 teaspoon sea salt
1 teaspoon baking soda
1 egg, lightly beaten
1 cup yogurt
1/3 cup melted butter

Preheat oven to 350 degrees. Combine dry ingredients in bowl. Mix egg and yogurt in small bowl. Add to dry ingredients. Stir in butter. Fill 12 greased muffin cups 2/3 full. Bake for 25 minutes or until golden brown. Yield: 12 servings.

Patty Snyder, Phi
Moscow, Idaho

SOUTHWEST MUFFINS

2 (10-ounce) cans refrigerator biscuits
8 ounces cream cheese, softened
8 ounces shredded Cheddar cheese
7 ounces green chilies, chopped
2 cups chopped ham or chicken
1 (4-ounce) can chopped black olives
Salsa
Sour cream

Preheat oven to 350 degrees. Cut each biscuit in half. Place 1 half in each muffin cup; press to line cups. Combine cream cheese, cheese, chilies, ham and olives in bowl; mix well. Spoon into biscuit-lined muffin cups. Bake for 15 to 20 minutes or until lightly browned. Serve with salsa and sour cream. Yield: 32 servings.

Beth Nelson, Zeta Eta
Derby, Kansas

♥ SCOTTISH SCONES

3 cups sifted all-purpose flour
4 teaspoons baking powder
1/4 cup sugar
1/2 teaspoon salt
1/2 cup softened low-cholesterol margarine
1 cup raisins
1 egg, well beaten
Two-percent milk
1 egg yolk, beaten
2 tablespoons water

Preheat oven to 450 degrees. Sift flour, baking powder, sugar and salt into large bowl. Cut margarine into flour mixture. Add raisins; mix well. Pour beaten egg into measuring cup. Add enough milk to make 1 cup liquid. Stir egg-milk mixture into flour mixture. Turn dough out onto lightly floured board. Knead lightly for 15 to 20 turns or for 30 seconds. Roll out 3/4-inch thick. Cut into triangles with floured knife. Place 1/2-inch apart on cookie sheet. Combine egg yolk and water in cup. Brush tops with mixture. Bake for 10 to 12 minutes or until brown. Yield: 24 servings.

Diane M. Boyd, Preceptor Rho
Balcarres, Saskatchewan, Canada

Just Loafing Around / 121

PARMESAN-WINE MUFFINS

These are very easy and very flavorful.

2 cups buttermilk baking mix
1 tablespoon sugar
1 tablespoon minced green onions
1 teaspoon fresh oregano or 1/2 teaspoon dried oregano
1 teaspoon fresh dillweed or 1/2 teaspoon dried dillweed
1 teaspoon fresh basil or 1/2 teaspoon dried basil
1/4 cup melted margarine
1/4 cup white wine
1 egg
1/2 cup milk
1/4 cup Parmesan cheese

Preheat oven to 400 degrees. Combine first 6 ingredients in large bowl; mix well. Add margarine, wine, egg and milk; mix well. Fill paper-lined muffin cups 2/3 full. Sprinkle with Parmesan cheese. Bake for 10 minutes. Yield: 12 servings.

Connie Myers, Mu Eta
San Antonio, Texas

♥ OLD-FASHIONED SOUTHERN CORN BREAD

1/4 cup vegetable oil
1 cup cornmeal
1 cup whole wheat flour
1 cup milk
Dash of salt
4 teaspoons baking powder
Dash of salt
1/4 to 1/2 cup honey or molasses
2 eggs

Preheat oven to 350 degrees. Pour small amount of oil into cast-iron skillet. Heat skillet in oven. Combine remaining ingredients in bowl; mix well. Pour into heated skillet. Bake for 20 to 30 minutes or until tests done. Yield: 10 servings.

Lynette Baugh, Preceptor Zeta Alpha
Waco, Texas

♥ SHORTCUT CORN LITE BREAD

1/2 cup all-purpose flour
1 cup (scant) sugar
1 teaspoon salt
2 cups cornmeal
1 teaspoon baking soda
2 cups buttermilk

Preheat oven to 350 degrees. Sift flour, sugar and salt together in bowl. Sift cornmeal into small bowl. Dissolve baking soda in buttermilk in small bowl. Combine all ingredients in large bowl; mix well. Heat 5-by-9-inch loaf pan until warm. Grease and flour pan well. Pour cornmeal mixture into pan. Bake for 10 minutes. Increase temperature to 400 degrees. Bake for 15 to 20 minutes longer or until golden brown. Yield: 8 to 10 servings.

Mona Casteel, Xi Epsilon Beta
Maurertown, Virginia

FRENCH CHEESE BREAD

1 loaf French bread
2 ounces Swiss cheese slices
1/2 cup margarine
3 (2-ounce) cans mushrooms
2 tablespoons onion flakes
2 tablespoons poppy seeds
1 1/2 teaspoons season salt
1 tablespoon dry mustard
1/2 teaspoon lemon juice

Preheat oven to 350 degrees. Cut bread lengthwise into slices; do not cut through crust. Place cheese between slices. Melt margarine in skillet. Add mushrooms, onion flakes, poppy seeds, season salt, dry mustard and lemon juice; mix well. Pour between bread slices. Bake for 30 minutes. Yield: 18 servings.

Jucie Philpott, Pi Master
Longview, Washington

GOUGERE

Our daughter has made this bread for the past two Christmas holidays. It became her favorite after taking cooking classes in Washington, D.C.

1/2 cup water
1/4 to 1/2 teaspoon salt
1/4 cup butter
1/2 cup all-purpose flour
Pepper and nutmeg to taste
2 eggs
1 cup grated Swiss cheese
1 egg, beaten

Preheat oven to 425 degrees. Heat water with salt in saucepan. Add butter; bring to a boil. Remove from heat. Add flour; mix well with wooden spoon. Return to medium heat, stirring constantly for 2 minutes to dry out dough or until dough comes away from side of pan while stirring. Remove from heat. Let cool for a few minutes while adding pepper and nutmeg; mix well. Add 2 eggs, 1 at a time, mixing well after each addition. Add 1/2 cup cheese; mix well. Spoon into large pastry bag; pipe into large circle or individual puffs on lightly greased baking sheet. May use spoon instead of pastry bag if desired. Brush top or tops with beaten egg. Sprinkle with remaining cheese. Bake circle for 35 to 45 minutes and puffs for 25 minutes or until golden brown. Serve immediately or let cool and reheat briefly before serving. Yield: 12 servings.

Joyce T. Koster, Alpha Lambda
Carroll, Iowa

IRISH SODA BREAD

2 cups all-purpose flour
1 cup whole wheat flour
1/2 cup sugar
2 teaspoons baking soda
1 teaspoon salt
1/4 cup cold unsalted butter, cut into bits
1 cup raisins
2 teaspoons caraway seeds
1 1/2 cups buttermilk or plain yogurt
Milk

Preheat oven to 350 degrees. Grease 1 1/2-quart round baking dish. Whisk together flours, sugar, baking soda and salt in large bowl. Add butter; toss to coat with flour. Rub in butter with fingertips until mixture resembles coarse meal. Add raisins and caraway seeds; toss until coated. Add buttermilk. Stir until dough is moistened evenly; do not overwork dough. Knead dough for 1 minute on floured surface, sprinkling lightly with additional flour to prevent sticking. Shape dough into ball. Place in baking dish. Cut a shallow X in top of loaf with sharp knife. Brush loaf with milk. Bake in middle of oven for 55 minutes to 1 hour or until golden brown. Turn bread onto wire rack. Let cool completely before slicing. Yield: 12 servings.

Billy Jane Gabel, Xi Mu Eta
Houston, Texas

❖ TOMATO-CHEESE BRAIDS

I sent this recipe in to "Better Homes and Gardens" about 35 years ago and received honorable mention.

2 cups biscuit mix
3/4 cup shredded sharp American cheese
2/3 cup tomato juice
Butter or margarine, melted
Celery seed

Preheat oven to 450 degrees. Combine biscuit mix and cheese in bowl. Add tomato juice, all at once, mixing and kneading dough according to package directions. Roll in 6-by-13-inch rectangle, about 1/2 inch thick. Cut into 3-inch strips, 1/2 inch wide. Shape strips into braid; pinch ends. Place on ungreased baking sheet. Brush with butter. Sprinkle with celery seed. Bake for 10 to 15 minutes or until brown. Yield: 18 servings.

Dorothy Bellis, Xi Lambda Pi
Quincy, Illinois

OLIVE-NUT BREAD

This bread is delicious served with cream cheese or cheese spread.

5 cups all-purpose flour
2 1/2 tablespoons baking powder
2/3 cup sugar
1/2 teaspoon dried thyme
1/2 teaspoon salt
2 eggs
2 cups milk
2 cups sliced stuffed green olives
1/4 cup chopped pimento
2 cups chopped walnuts

Preheat oven to 350 degrees. Grease two 5-by-9-inch loaf pans. Sift together flour, baking powder, sugar, thyme and salt in large bowl. Beat eggs lightly in bowl. Add milk; beat until well blended. Stir mixture into dry ingredients until well blended. Fold in olives, pimento and walnuts. Bake for 55 minutes to 1 hour or until test done. Let cool in pans for 5 minutes. Turn on wire rack to cool completely. Yield: 24 servings.

Marion Hansen, Xi Epsilon Nu
Chicago, Illinois

GRANDMA'S PERFECT BREAD

2 packages yeast	3/4 cup sugar
1/3 cup sugar	4 teaspoons salt
1 cup lukewarm water	7 to 8 cups all-purpose
5 cups all-purpose	flour
flour	Melted butter or
1/2 cup butter	margarine

Dissolve yeast and 1/3 cup sugar in lukewarm water in large mixer bowl. Let stand for 5 minutes or until bubbly. Add 4 cups warm water and 5 cups flour. Beat until smooth. Add butter, 3/4 cup sugar and 4 teaspoons salt. Beat until smooth. Add 7 to 8 cups flour gradually to make stiff dough. Knead dough on floured surface until smooth, adding additional flour to surface as needed. Place dough in greased bowl. Grease top of dough lightly; cover. Let rise for 1 1/2 to 2 hours or until almost doubled in bulk. Shape into 4 loaves. Place in greased 5-by-9-inch loaf pans; cover. Let rise in warm place for 45 minutes or until almost doubled in bulk. Preheat oven to 350 degrees. Brush loaves with melted butter. Bake for 50 minutes. Turn out on wire racks to cool. Brush with melted butter. Yield: 48 servings.

Linda Martin, Xi Epsilon Beta
Woodstock, Virginia

♥ DEUTSCHES BAUERN BROT

This is hardy dark bread called German farmers' bread. It is an old recipe from my German grandmother.

1 large baking potato,	2 packages yeast
peeled, chopped	2 teaspoons sugar
4 teaspoons salt	9 cups all-purpose flour
5 cups water	4 cups rye flour
6 tablespoons margarine	

Boil potato with salt in water in saucepan until done. Let cool slightly. Mash potato. Add margarine. Combine yeast with small amount of warm water and sugar in bowl; let rise. Pour flour into large bowl, making hole in center. Add yeast mixture; mix well. Add mashed potato and water gradually to flour, mixing well after each addition. Turn dough onto floured surface. Knead with hands until smooth, adding additional flour if needed. Place in greased bowl; cover. Let rise until doubled in bulk. Punch down. Shape into 3 loaves. Place in 3 round 9-inch baking pans. Let rise again. Preheat oven to 375 degrees. Bake for 1 hour and 15 minutes. Let cool on wire racks. Yield: 24 servings.

Margot Stryker, Xi Alpha Psi
Prescott, Arizona

♥ ITALIAN FOCACCIA

1 package active dry	3 tablespoons olive oil
yeast	2 teaspoons salt
1 cup warm water	2 1/2 to 3 cups all-purpose
2 to 3 tablespoons	flour
snipped fresh rosemary	Coarsely ground pepper

Dissolve yeast in warm water in large bowl. Stir in rosemary, 3 tablespoons olive oil, salt and enough flour to make dough easy to handle. Turn dough onto lightly floured surface. Knead for 5 to 10 minutes or until smooth and elastic. Place in greased bowl; turn greased side up. Cover. Let rise in warm place for 1 hour or until doubled in bulk. Preheat oven to 400 degrees. Punch dough down. Press into oiled 12-inch pizza pan. Make depressions with fingers about 2 inches apart on top of dough. Brush with additional olive oil. Sprinkle with pepper. Let rise, uncovered, for 30 minutes. Bake for 20 to 25 minutes or until golden brown. Brush with additional olive oil. Serve warm. Yield: 16 servings.

Christine A. Stevenson
Independence, Iowa

♥ JAM AND CHEESE LOAF

1 package active dry	8 ounces low-fat cream
yeast	cheese, softened
1/2 cup warm water	1/2 cup sugar
2 1/2 cups biscuit mix	1 tablespoon lemon juice
1 egg, beaten	1/4 to 3/4 cup cherry
1 tablespoon sugar	preserves

Dissolve yeast in warm water in large bowl. Stir in biscuit mix, egg and 1 tablespoon sugar; mix well. Turn onto floured surface. Knead gently for 20 strokes. Place dough in center of greased baking sheet. Roll to 9-by-14-inch rectangle. Combine cream cheese, 1/2 cup sugar and lemon juice in bowl. Spread mixture down center third of rectangle. Make 3-inch long cuts at 1-inch intervals on both long sides. Fold strips at an angle over filling. Cover. Chill overnight. Preheat oven to 350 degrees. Bake for 20 minutes. Spoon preserves down center of loaf. Bake for 5 minutes longer. Let cool for 10 minutes. Yield: 18 servings.

Scottie Michelle, Preceptor Rho
Asheboro, North Carolina

♥ MIX BREAD

This recipe was brought to Lexington, South Carolina, many years ago.

1 cup quick-cooking	1/2 cup vegetable
grits	shortening, melted
1 package yeast	3 cups all-purpose flour
1 tablespoon salt	1 cup warm water
1 tablespoon sugar	

Prepare grits according to package directions. Dissolve yeast in 1 cup warm water. Combine 1 cup cooked grits, yeast mixture and remaining ingredients in large bowl; mix well. Add water if needed to stir. Let rise until doubled in bulk. Stir down. Pour into 2 greased 5-by-9-inch loaf pans. Let rise again. Preheat oven to 400 degrees. Bake for 35 minutes. Yield: 20 servings.

Inez L. Hyatt, Laureate Mu
Blythewood, South Carolina

♥ ENGLISH MALT BREAD

4 cups whole wheat flour
2 to 2 1/2 cups all-purpose flour
1/4 teaspoon salt
1 cup sultana raisins
1 tablespoon sugar
1/4 cup warm water
1 package active dry yeast
2 1/2 cups warm water
1/4 cup black treacle or molasses
1/4 cup plain light pure malt extract
1/4 cup butter or vegetable shortening, melted
2 tablespoons milk
2 tablespoons sugar

Combine flours, salt and raisins in large bowl. Dissolve sugar in warm water in small bowl. Stir in yeast. Let stand for 10 minutes. Stir again. Combine warm water, molasses, malt and butter in bowl; mix well. Add molasses mixture to flour mixture; mix well. Turn onto floured board; knead well. Place in greased bowl. Cover. Let rise in warm place for 1 to 1 1/2 hours or until doubled in bulk. Punch down. Shape into 2 loaves. Place in 2 greased 5-by-9-inch loaf pans. Let rise for 45 minutes longer or until doubled in bulk. Preheat oven to 375 degrees. Bake for 45 minutes or until brown. Remove from oven. Combine milk with sugar in small bowl. Brush on top of loaves. Remove loaves from pans; let cool. Yield: 24 servings.

Kay Houghton, Xi Chi
Port Alberni, British Columbia, Canada

QUAKER OATS BREAD

2 cups boiling water
2 cups oats
1 cake yeast
1/2 cup lukewarm water
1/2 cup molasses
1/2 teaspoon salt
1 tablespoon butter
5 cups all-purpose flour

Add boiling water to oats in large bowl. Let stand for 1 hour. Dissolve yeast in lukewarm water. Add molasses, salt, butter, yeast and flour to oats; mix well. Let rise until doubled in bulk. Punch down. Turn into 2 buttered 5-by-9-inch loaf pans. Let rise again. Preheat oven to 350 degrees. Bake for 45 minutes. Let cool on wire rack. Yield: 20 servings.

Cheryl Dryer, Preceptor Delta
Klamath Falls, Oregano

♥ OLD MILWAUKEE SOUR RYE BREAD

Starter
1 package active dry yeast
1 cup 105-degree water
1/4 cup dark molasses
1 egg
1 tablespoon salt
1 tablespoon caraway seeds
1 cup rye flour
5 to 5 1/2 cups all-purpose flour
3 tablespoons vegetable oil

Place Starter in large bowl. Dissolve yeast in 1 cup warm water. Add molasses, egg, salt, caraway seeds, rye flour and yeast to Starter; mix well. Add half the all-purpose flour and oil; mix well. Stir in remaining all-purpose flour gradually until dough is too stiff to stir. Cover. Let rise for 30 minutes. Turn dough onto floured surface. Knead for about 10 minutes or until smooth. Place dough in large greased bowl. Coat dough in greased bowl. Cover. Let rise in warm place for 1 hour. Shape dough into 2 round loaves. Place on greased baking sheet. Cover. Let rise until doubled in bulk. Preheat oven to 375 degrees. Cut large X in top of each loaf. Bake for 40 minutes or until loaves sound hollow when tapped. Yield: 20 servings.

STARTER

1 1/2 cups warm water
1 package dry yeast
2 cups rye flour
1 tablespoon caraway seeds

Combine warm water with yeast, flour and caraway seeds in large bowl. Mix for 2 minutes. Cover tightly. Allow to ferment for 12 to 48 hours.

Jeannette Noble, Preceptor Theta Iota
Tampa, Florida

♥ COLORFUL VEGETABLE BREADS

This bread is best served fresh. It is colorful and low in sugar, fat and salt.

1/4 cup warm water
1 package active dry yeast
2 tablespoons sugar
1/2 cup milk at room temperature
1/4 cup butter or margarine at room temperature
1 egg
1 teaspoon nutmeg
1 teaspoon salt
1 1/2 cups Vegetable Purée (beet, carrot, potato, spinach or tomato)
5 1/2 cups (about) all-purpose flour

Combine warm water, yeast and sugar in large bowl. Let stand for 5 minutes or until foamy. Add milk, butter, egg, nutmeg, salt, Vegetable Purée and flour; mix well. Knead on floured surface until smooth and elastic. Let rise until doubled in bulk. Punch down; knead well. Divide dough in half. Shape into 2 round balls. Place each in center of 10-by-15-inch baking pan. Shape into loaves. Dust lightly with additional flour. Cover. Let rise until almost doubled in bulk. Preheat oven to 350 degrees. Make 1/2 inch deep slashes in tops with sharp knife. Bake for 30 to 40 minutes or until golden brown. Yield: 20 servings.

VEGETABLE PURÉES

Beet: Cook and purée 1 1/2 pounds beets.
Carrot: Cook and purée 1 1/2 pounds carrots.
Potato: Mix 1 1/4 cups mashed potatoes with 1/4 cup milk.
Spinach: Purée 1 1/2 cups spinach; mix with 1 1/2 teaspoons oregano leaves.
Tomato: 1 (12-ounce) can tomato paste plus 1 1/2 teaspoons Italian herb seasoning.

Bettie Carson, Preceptor Beta Phi
Huntington, Oregon

♥ TOMATO-HERB BREAD

1 large onion, finely chopped
3 cloves of garlic, crushed
2 tablespoons olive oil
2 teaspoons basil
1 teaspoon whole oregano
2 tablespoons active dry yeast
2 tablespoons sugar
1 cup warm water
2 cups undrained canned tomatoes
3 tablespoons Parmesan cheese
2 teaspoons salt
5 to 6 cups all-purpose flour

Sauté onion and garlic in olive oil in small saucepan until onion is transparent. Add basil and oregano. Let cool to room temperature. Add yeast and sugar to water in small bowl. Let stand until foamy. Add onion mixture, tomatoes, Parmesan cheese, salt and 5 cups flour; mix well. Knead on floured surface, adding flour as needed to make firm smooth dough. Place dough in oiled bowl. Cover. Let rise until doubled in bulk. Turn dough onto lightly floured board. Roll into 2 or 3 loaves. Place in oiled 5-by-9-inch loaf pans. Let rise until doubled in bulk. Preheat oven to 375 degrees. Slit top off loaves with very sharp knife. Sprinkle with additional Parmesan cheese. Bake for 20 to 25 minutes or until tests done. Yield: 20 to 30 servings.

Marlene Gariepy, Preceptor Alpha Upsilon
Parksville, British Columbia, Canada

♥ WAR BREAD

During World War II white flour was scarce and this blend of oats, cornmeal and whole wheat flour was added to the white flour to make it go farther.

1 package dry yeast
1/4 cup warm water
1 cup cornmeal
3 cups boiling water
1 cup oats
1 cup whole wheat flour
2 tablespoons olive oil
1/3 cup molasses
1 tablespoon salt
5 to 6 cups all-purpose flour

Dissolve yeast in 1/4 cup warm water in small bowl. Let cool. Add cornmeal to boiling water in large bowl, stirring until smooth. Add oats, whole wheat flour, olive oil, molasses and salt; mix well. Add yeast mixture; mix well. Add all-purpose flour, 1/2 cup at a time, mixing well after each addition. Turn dough onto lightly floured surface. Knead until smooth and elastic. Place dough in greased bowl. Cover. Let rise until doubled in bulk. Shape dough into 2 loaves. Place in 2 greased 5-by-9-inch loaf pans. Cover. Let rise until doubled in bulk. Preheat oven to 375 degrees. Bake for 35 minutes. Remove from pans to wire rack to cool. Yield: 20 servings.

Emily Larsen, Preceptor Beta Epsilon
Bay Village, Ohio

♥ EGG BAGELS

3 cups all-purpose flour
1 1/2 teaspoons salt
4 tablespoons sugar
1 package dry yeast
3/4 cup lukewarm water
2 tablespoons vegetable oil
1 egg, beaten
4 quarts water
1 egg yolk
1 tablespoon water

Sift flour, salt and 2 tablespoons sugar into bowl. Dissolve yeast in 1/4 cup lukewarm water in large bowl. Stir in oil and remaining lukewarm water. Stir 1/2 the yeast mixture into flour. Add egg; mix well. Add remaining yeast; mix well. Knead on lightly floured surface for 5 minutes. Return to bowl. Cover. Let rise for 40 minutes. Punch down. Knead on floured surface for 10 minutes. Divide into 12 equal pieces. Roll each piece with palms of hands into 5 to 6-inch long roll. Join ends of each roll to form ring. Cover. Let rise for 15 minutes. Preheat oven to broil. Place on cookie sheet. Place under broiler for 4 minutes. Reduce oven temperature to 425 degrees. Boil 4 quarts water with 2 tablespoons sugar in large saucepan. Drop bagels into boiling water. Let surface; turn and boil for 2 minutes longer. Place on greased cookie sheet. Combine egg yolk with 1 tablespoon water in cup. Brush with yolk mixture. Bake for 20 to 25 minutes or until brown. Yield: 12 servings.

Rettie B. Isett, Mu Tau
James Creek, Pennsylvania

♥ WHOLE WHEAT BAGUETTES

2 1/2 to 3 cups all-purpose flour
2 packages active dry yeast
1 tablespoon sugar
1 1/2 teaspoons salt
2 cups warm water
2 cups whole wheat flour
1 egg white, slightly beaten
1 tablespoon water

Combine 2 cups all-purpose flour, yeast, sugar and salt in large mixer bowl. Add warm water. Beat at low speed for 30 seconds, scraping sides of bowl constantly. Beat for 3 minutes at high speed. Stir in whole wheat flour and enough remaining all-purpose flour to make stiff dough. Turn onto lightly floured surface. Knead for 8 to 10 minutes or until smooth and elastic. Shape into ball. Place in lightly greased bowl; turn once to grease surface. Cover. Let rise in warm place for 1 hour and 15 minutes or until doubled in bulk. Punch down. Turn onto lightly floured surface. Divide into thirds. Cover. Let rest for 10 minutes. Roll each third into 10-inch square. Roll up tightly; seal well. Taper ends. Place, seam-side down, in greased baking pan. Combine egg white with 1 tablespoon water in cup. Brush each loaf with mixture. Cover. Let rise for 30 to 45 minutes or until doubled in bulk. Preheat oven to 450 degrees. Make 3 diagonal 1/4-inch deep cuts across top of each loaf. Bake for 15 to 20 minutes or until brown. Yield: 24 servings.

Mary Ford, Psi Iota
Theodosia, Missouri

BRAN BUNS

1/2 cup sugar
3 teaspoons salt
1/2 cup margarine
6 tablespoons molasses
4 cups warm boiled
   water
2 cups bran
1/2 cup wheat germ
4 eggs, beaten
2 packages yeast
2 teaspoons sugar
1/2 cup warm water

Dissolve 1/2 cup sugar, salt, margarine and molasses in 4 cups warm water in large bowl. Let cool. Add bran and wheat germ; mix well. Add eggs to mixture. Dissolve yeast and 2 teaspoons sugar in 1/2 cup warm water in small bowl. Add to molasses-bran mixture. Add flour, a few cups at a time, stirring well after each addition. Knead on floured surface for 10 minutes. Shape into ball. Rub with small amount vegetable oil. Let rise for 2 hours or until doubled in bulk. Knead down. Let rise again. Preheat oven to 375 degrees. Shape into buns. Let rise for 1 1/2 hours. Bake for 20 minutes. Yield: 12 servings.

Joyce Hayes, Epsilon
Saskatoon, Saskatchewan, Canada

OLD-FASHIONED HOT CROSS BUNS

After trying for 10 years to find a good recipe for hot cross buns, I found this one and revised it. I think the oats make these buns extra special.

2 teaspoons sugar
1/2 cup lukewarm water
2 packages active dry
   yeast
1 cup boiling water
1 cup oats
3/4 cup hot water
1/2 cup margarine
5 cups all-purpose
   flour
2 teaspoons cinnamon
1/2 teaspoon cloves
1 1/2 teaspoons salt
1 cup packed dark
   brown sugar
2 eggs
1 cup raisins
Vegetable oil

Dissolve sugar in lukewarm water in bowl. Sprinkle yeast over sugar water. Pour boiling water over oats in large bowl. Let stand for 20 minutes. Pour hot water over margarine in bowl; let melt. Place flour, cinnamon, cloves, salt and brown sugar in large bread bowl. Add lukewarm oats mixture. Beat eggs with wire whisk in small bowl. Add to water and melted margarine. Add to flour mixture. Add in yeast. Knead dough on floured surface until smooth and elastic. Knead raisins into dough. Shape dough into ball. Brush top with oil. Cover with waxed paper, then soft dishcloth. Let rise in warm place for 1 1/2 to 2 hours. Punch dough down. Let rise for 1 hour longer. Punch down. Shape dough into 2 1/2-inch balls. Place 1/2 inch apart on greased 15-by-18-inch cookie sheet, in rows of 4 across. Let rise for 1 hour. Preheat oven to 350 degrees. Bake for 35 to 40 minutes or until brown. Brush tops with butter while hot. Yield: 20 servings.

Florence Brendon, Laureate Nu
London, Ontario, Canada

SOFT PRETZELS

1 package active dry
   yeast
1 1/2 cups warm water
1 tablespoon sugar
4 1/2 cups all-purpose
   flour
1 1/2 teaspoons salt
1 egg, slightly beaten
1 1/2 teaspoons coarsely
   ground salt or
   sea salt

Preheat oven to 425 degrees. Combine yeast, warm water and sugar in bowl. Let stand for 5 minutes or until yeast is dissolved and begins to foam. Sift flour and salt together into yeast mixture; mix well. Turn onto lightly floured surface. Knead for 8 to 10 minutes or until smooth and elastic. Separate into 16 equal pieces. Roll each into 20-inch rope. Shape into pretzel shape. Cover. Let rise for 20 minutes. Brush with egg. Sprinkle with coarse salt. Bake for 15 minutes. Yield: 16 servings.

Colleen Gauthier, Xi Gamma Omega
Quesnel, British Columbia, Canada

CRESCENT ROLLS

1 1/2 cups boiling water
1/3 cup sugar
3 tablespoons butter
1 2/3 cups shredded
   wheat, crushed
2 packages yeast
1/4 cup warm water
1 egg, beaten
3 1/4 to 3 1/2 cups
   all-purpose flour

Combine first 4 ingredients in bowl. Let cool to lukewarm. Dissolve yeast in warm water. Add to shredded wheat mixture; mix well. Add egg and 2 cups flour; mix well. Stir in remaining flour; mix well. Cover tightly. Refrigerate for 3 hours or up to 2 days. Punch dough down; divide in half. Roll each half on floured surface into 13-inch circle. Cut into wedges. Roll each from wide end to small end to form crescent. Place on greased cookie sheets. Cover. Let rise for 1 hour or until doubled in bulk. Preheat oven to 375 degrees. Bake for 18 to 20 minutes or until brown. Yield: 24 to 36 servings.

Betty Stonecipher, Laureate Beta Eta
Urbandale, Iowa

♥ EASY HOT ROLLS

1 package yeast
2 1/4 cups warm water
1/2 cup plus
   1 tablespoon sugar
1/4 cup shortening
1 tablespoon salt
6 cups all-purpose
   flour

Combine yeast and 1/4 cup warm water in bowl. Combine 2 cups warm water, sugar, shortening and salt in large bowl; mix well. Add yeast mixture. Let stand for 5 minutes. Add 3 cups flour; mix well. Add remaining flour, stirring just until well mixed. Cover. Let rise in warm place for 2 hours. Shape into 18 rolls. Place in greased 9-by-13-inch baking pans. Let rise for 2 hours. Preheat oven to 350 degrees. Bake for 30 minutes. Yield: 18 servings.

Carol Stinebaugh, Eta Omicron
Rogers, Arkansas

Rise and Shine

In today's fast-paced world, breakfast often means a hastily-gulped cup of coffee, or something from the drive-through window on the way to work. For a change this weekend, invite some friends over to help you ease into your day with some good conversation and festive food. A breakfast or brunch can be as casual or as formal as you like, and it's a great way to entertain a large group without breaking the budget! Whether for a get-together before the big game, a brunch after church, or that special wedding breakfast, you'll find lots of ideas and scrumptious recipes for any size crowd. If a family sit-down breakfast has become a thing of the past in your household, why not plan a special Sunday breakfast just for family? When the aroma from those special dishes reaches your sleepy heads, they'll be up and in the kitchen before you have the juice poured!

BAGEL CASSEROLE

4 bagels, cut into halves horizontally	1/4 teaspoon freshly ground paprika
1/4 cup plus 1 tablespoon butter or margarine	6 ounces grated Monterey Jack cheese
7 eggs	6 ounces grated Cheddar cheese
1/2 teaspoon salt	Salsa
2 cups milk	
Chopped cooked ham or bacon (optional)	

Grease 9-by-13-inch casserole with 2 tablespoons butter. Butter each bagel half with 1 teaspoon margarine. Cut into small bite-sized pieces. Beat eggs, salt, milk, ham and paprika with wire whisk in medium bowl. Place half the bagel cubes in baking dish. Combine cheeses in bowl. Sprinkle half the cheese mixture over bagels. Repeat layers. Spoon egg mixture into casserole, covering bagels completely. Refrigerate, covered, overnight. Preheat oven to 350 degrees. Bake, uncovered, for 1 hour. Serve with salsa. Yield: 8 servings.

Anita Peschka, Gamma Mu
Tulsa, Oklahoma

ASPARAGUS BREAKFAST CASSEROLE

3 tablespoons butter	6 eggs
1 loaf white bread slices, crusts removed	3 cups milk
1 cup shredded Cheddar cheese	1 tablespoon dry minced onion
2 cups cubed cooked ham	1/2 teaspoon salt
2 (8-ounce) cans asparagus, chopped, drained	1/2 teaspoon dry mustard

Spread butter on 1 side of half the bread slices. Place slices, buttered side down, in 9-by-13-inch baking dish. Sprinkle with 1/2 cup cheese. Layer ham and asparagus over cheese. Place remaining buttered bread slices on top. Beat eggs lightly in bowl. Add milk, onion, salt and mustard; mix well. Pour over bread. Refrigerate, covered, overnight. Preheat oven to 325 degrees. Bake for 50 minutes. Sprinkle with remaining cheese. Bake for 10 minutes longer or until knife inserted in center comes out clean. Yield: 10 servings.

Joy R. Griffin, Laureate Gamma Mu
Jacksonville, Florida

BREAKFAST CASSEROLE

8 slices bread, crusts removed	1 cup milk
16 ounces cream cheese	1/2 cup maple syrup
6 eggs	1 teaspoon cinnamon
	1/2 teaspoon ginger
	1 teaspoon nutmeg

Cut bread into cubes. Spread in greased 9-by-13-inch baking dish. Cut cream cheese into cubes. Layer over bread cubes. Beat eggs, milk, syrup, cinnamon, ginger and nutmeg in bowl. Pour over bread and cheese. Cover with cooking foil. Refrigerate overnight. Preheat oven to 350 degrees. Bake for 30 to 45 minutes or until knife inserted in center comes out clean. Yield: 9 servings.

Julie Holt, Beta Delta
Havre, Montana

BEST BREAKFAST CASSEROLE

2 tablespoons butter or margarine	3 tablespoons butter or margarine
2 1/2 tablespoons all-purpose flour	12 eggs, beaten
2 cups milk	1 (4-ounce) can sliced mushrooms, drained
1 cup grated sharp Cheddar cheese	1/4 teaspoon salt
1/4 teaspoon salt	1/8 teaspoon pepper
1/8 teaspoon pepper	1 pound bacon, crisp-fried, crumbled
1/4 cup chopped green onions	

Melt butter in saucepan over medium heat. Add flour; mix well. Cook for 1 to 2 minutes or until bubbly. Remove from heat. Stir in milk. Return to heat. Cook, stirring constantly, until thickened. Add cheese, salt and pepper, stirring until cheese is melted. Sauté onions in butter in skillet until transparent. Add eggs. Scramble until soft. Do not overcook. Add mushrooms, salt and pepper. Fold in cheese sauce and bacon. Spoon into lightly greased 9-by-13-inch baking dish. Cover with plastic wrap. Chill until ready to bake. May be refrigerated up to 2 days. Preheat oven to 350 degrees. Bake for 30 minutes. Yield: 8 servings.

Doris H. Olesen, Beta Gamma
Severna Park, Maryland

BREAKFAST CORN BREAD

1 pound sausage	1 teaspoon salt
6 large eggs	1/2 cup vegetable oil
1 (15-ounce) can creamed corn	1 cup milk
2 eggs, beaten	8 ounces grated Cheddar cheese
1 cup yellow cornmeal	1 large onion, chopped
1/2 teaspoon baking soda	3 large baked potatoes, chopped

Preheat oven to 350 degrees. Brown sausage in skillet, stirring until crumbly. Remove from skillet; let drain. Scramble 6 eggs in same skillet. Combine next 7 ingredients in large bowl; mix well. Grease cast-iron skillet. Heat in oven. Pour half the corn mixture into heated skillet. Layer cheese, onion, scrambled eggs, potatoes and sausage in skillet. Top with remaining corn mixture. Bake for 45 minutes or until lightly browned and mixture pulls from side of skillet. Yield: 6 servings.

Rebecca Fillmore, Theta Sigma
Hays, Kansas

BREAKFAST-IN-A-LOAF

1 tablespoon butter
 or margarine
6 eggs, lightly beaten
1/2 teaspoon salt
1/4 teaspoon pepper
1 (8- to 9-inch) round
 loaf bread
4 ounces sliced ham
1/2 red bell pepper,
 thinly sliced
 crosswise
1/2 cup shredded
 Monterey Jack cheese
1/2 cup shredded Cheddar
 cheese
1/2 cup sliced ripe olives
1 medium tomato,
 thinly sliced
8 ounces mushrooms,
 sliced, cooked

Preheat oven to 350 degrees. Melt butter in skillet over medium heat. Season eggs with salt and pepper. Add eggs to skillet. Cook, stirring gently, and lifting to allow uncooked eggs to flow under cooked portion. Do not overcook. Cut 2-inch slice from top of loaf. Hollow out bread, leaving 1-inch thick wall and bottom. Place ham in bottom of loaf. Top with bell pepper rings. Sprinkle with half the cheeses. Layer scrambled eggs, olives and tomato over cheeses. Top with remaining cheeses and mushrooms. Place top on bread. Wrap in cooking foil. Bake for 30 minutes or until thoroughly heated. Cut into 8 wedges. Yield: 8 servings.

Christy Grossheim, Zeta Gamma
Farmington, New Mexico

MAKE-AHEAD BRUNCH BAKE

1 pound bulk pork
 sausage
6 eggs, beaten
2 cups cream
1/2 teaspoon salt
1 teaspoon mustard
1 cup shredded Cheddar
 cheese
1 can French-fried
 onions

Brown sausage in large skillet over medium-high heat, stirring until crumbly; drain off fat. Stir in eggs, cream, salt, mustard, 1/2 cup cheese and 1/2 can fried onions; mix well. Pour into greased 8-by-12-inch baking dish. Refrigerate for 8 hours or overnight. Preheat oven to 350 degrees. Bake, uncovered, for 45 minutes or until knife inserted in center comes out clean. Top with remaining cheese and fried onions. Bake, uncovered, for 5 minutes longer. Let stand for 15 minutes before serving. Yield: 6 servings.

Mildred E. Mitchke, Preceptor Epsilon
Bigfork, Montana

❖ CHILI RELLENOS CASSEROLE

9 eggs, beaten
4 1/2 cups cream-style
 cottage cheese
27 butter-flavor
 crackers, finely
 crushed
1 1/2 (4-ounce) cans diced
 chilies
1 1/4 cups shredded mild
 Cheddar cheese
1 1/4 cups shredded
 Monterey Jack cheese

Preheat oven to 350 degrees. Combine eggs, cottage cheese, cracker crumbs, chilies and 1/2 the cheeses in bowl; mix well. Pour into 9-by-13-inch baking dish. Bake for 45 minutes or until knife inserted in center comes out clean. Sprinkle with remaining cheeses. Bake for 2 to 3 minutes longer or until cheese is melted. Yield: 12 to 15 servings.

Carolyn English, Xi Theta Lambda
Patterson, California

EGGS FANTASTIC

1 (12-ounce) package
 bulk sausage
1 medium onion,
 chopped
Salt and pepper
 to taste
6 eggs
3 tablespoons sour
 cream
1/3 cup plus 2
 tablespoons salsa
8 ounces Cheddar
 cheese
8 ounces mozzarella
 cheese
8 ounces Velveeta
 cheese

Preheat oven to 400 degrees. Sauté sausage, onion, salt and pepper in skillet. Combine eggs and sour cream in blender container. Process for 1 minute. Pour into greased 7-by-11-inch baking dish. Bake for 8 to 10 minutes. Reduce oven temperature to 300 degrees. Spoon salsa over eggs. Add sausage. Layer Cheddar cheese, mozzarella cheese and Velveeta cheese over sausage. Bake, uncovered, for 45 minutes. Let stand for 5 to 10 minutes before serving. Yield: 9 servings.

Virginia Bergemann, Epsilon Beta
Truman, Minnesota

GOLD RUSH BRUNCH

1 (2-pound) package
 frozen hashed brown
 potatoes
1/2 cup chopped onion
2 tablespoons chopped
 parsley
1 (4-ounce) can chopped
 green chilies
1/4 cup melted margarine
1/2 cup all-purpose flour
1 teaspoon salt
1/4 teaspoon pepper
1 1/2 cups milk
1/2 cup sour cream
12 slices Canadian bacon
12 eggs

Preheat oven to 350 degrees. Cook potatoes according to package directions. Add onion, parsley, green chilies; mix well. Combine margarine, flour, salt, pepper and milk in saucepan. Cook, stirring constantly, until thick. Add sour cream. Place potatoes in 9-by-13-inch baking pan. Top with sauce; mix lightly. Place bacon on top. Bake for 45 minutes. Press down on each bacon round to form cups. Break an egg into each cup. Bake for 15 to 20 minutes longer or until eggs are set. Yield: 12 servings.

Billie Freiberger, Delta Master
Roswell, New Mexico

130 / Breakfast and Brunch

♥ HAM AND CHEESE POWER SQUARES

1 pound frozen hashed brown potatoes, thawed
6 ounces cooked turkey ham, cubed
1 cup shredded Cheddar or Swiss cheese
6 eggs, beaten
1 cup plain nonfat yogurt
1/2 teaspoon salt
1/4 teaspoon pepper
Apple slices

Preheat oven to 350 degrees. Combine potatoes, turkey ham, cheese, eggs, yogurt, salt and pepper in bowl; mix well. Spread evenly in greased 9-by-13-inch baking pan. Bake for 40 to 45 minutes or until golden brown and center is firm. Let stand for 5 minutes. Cut into squares. Garnish with apple slices. Serve immediately. Yield: 12 servings.

Carol Hinson, Xi Alpha Tau
Monroe, North Carolina

SWISS HAM RING-AROUND

1 cup fresh or frozen chopped broccoli
1/4 cup chopped parsley
2 tablespoons finely chopped onion
1 tablespoon mustard
1 tablespoon butter or margarine, softened
1 teaspoon lemon juice
3/4 cup shredded Swiss or mozzarella cheese
1 can chunk ham, drained
1 (8-count) can crescent dinner rolls
Grated Parmesan cheese

Preheat oven to 350 degrees. Cook broccoli according to package directions; drain. Combine parsley, onion, mustard, butter and lemon juice in bowl; mix well. Add cheese, broccoli and ham; mix lightly. Separate rolls into triangles. Place on cookie sheet in circle with points toward outside and bases overlapping. Center opening should be 3 inches in diameter. Spoon ham filling in ring evenly over bases of triangles. Fold points of triangle over filling; tuck under bases of triangles at center of circle. Sprinkle with Parmesan cheese. Bake for 25 to 30 minutes or until golden brown. Serve hot. To make ahead, refrigerate, covered, for up to 3 hours and bake for 30 to 35 minutes. Yield: 6 to 8 servings.

Meryl White, Xi Omicron Sigma
Lakehead, California

TACO-CHEESE BREAKFAST CASSEROLE

1 pound pork sausage
4 ounces fresh mushrooms, chopped
1 medium onion, chopped
1/4 teaspoon salt
1/4 teaspoon pepper
5 eggs
3 tablespoons sour cream
3 tablespoons Mexican taco sauce
8 ounces cream cheese, grated
8 ounces grated mozzarella cheese
8 ounces Velveeta cheese, cubed

Preheat oven to 400 degrees. Brown sausage, mushrooms, onion, salt and pepper in skillet, stirring until sausage is crumbly; drain. Beat eggs and sour cream in bowl. Pour into greased 9-by-13-inch baking pan. Bake for 5 to 7 minutes. Remove from oven. Spoon taco sauce over top. Add sausage mixture. Top with cheeses in order listed. Bake for 30 minutes longer or until cheeses are melted. Yield: 12 servings.

Judy Behnke, Xi Gamma Alpha
Norfolk, Nebraska

♥ LOW-CHOLESTEROL SAUSAGE AND EGG BAKE

1 pound turkey-pork sausage
6 slices sour dough or Italian bread, cubed
1 cup grated low-cholesterol low-sodium sharp Cheddar cheese
Egg substitute equivalent to 6 eggs
2 cups skim or 1% milk
1 teaspoon dry mustard
Salt and pepper to taste
2 tablespoons chives
Paprika to taste

Brown sausage in skillet, stirring until crumbly; drain. Place bread cubes in 9-inch square glass baking dish. Top with cooked sausage and half the grated cheese. Combine egg substitute and milk in bowl; mix well. Add mustard, salt, pepper and chives; mix well. Pour over layered ingredients. Top with remaining cheese. Sprinkle with paprika. Refrigerate overnight. Preheat oven to 325 degrees. Bake for 30 to 45 minutes or until firm. Yield: 6 servings.

Mildred M. Reiberg, Zeta Master
Lakeland, Florida

SPINACH SOUFFLÉ

2 (10-ounce) packages frozen chopped spinach
1 tablespoon finely chopped onion
1 tablespoon butter or margarine
1 1/2 tablespoons all-purpose flour
1 cup milk
3/4 teaspoon salt
1/2 teaspoon pepper
4 egg yolks
1 1/2 cups shredded sharp cheese
4 egg whites, at room temperature

Preheat oven to 350 degrees. Cook spinach according to package directions. Drain; press dry. Sauté onion in butter in saucepan over low heat until transparent. Blend in flour gradually. Stir in milk. Cook over medium heat until thickened. Add salt and pepper. Beat egg yolks in bowl. Stir in 1/4 the hot white sauce, mixing well. Return yolk mixture to white sauce. Add spinach and cheese; mix well. Beat egg whites in mixer bowl until stiff but not dry. Fold into spinach mixture. Spoon into well-greased 2-quart casserole. Bake for 45 minutes or until golden brown. Yield: 6 to 8 servings.

Mary P. Tartaglino, Xi Alpha Phi
Millersville, Maryland

SPINACH-SAUSAGE CASSEROLE

1 1/2 pounds pork breakfast sausage
1 cup chopped onions
1 red pepper, chopped
1 (10-ounce) package chopped frozen spinach, thawed, drained
1 cup flour
1/2 teaspoon salt
1/4 cup grated Parmesan cheese
1 tablespoon basil
8 eggs
2 cups milk
1 cup shredded provolone cheese
Cantaloupe slices
Melon slices
Kiwifruit slices

Preheat oven to 425 degrees. Brown sausage in skillet, stirring until crumbly. Remove from skillet; drain. Sauté onions in same skillet until lightly browned. Layer sausage and onions in bottom of 9-by-13-inch casserole. Sprinkle 1/2 the red pepper over top. Top with spinach. Combine flour, salt, Parmesan cheese and basil in bowl. Beat eggs in large bowl. Add milk; mix well. Beat dry ingredients into egg mixture. Pour over casserole. Bake for 30 to 45 minutes or until firm. Sprinkle remaining red pepper and provolone cheese on top. Bake for 2 minutes longer or until cheese is melted. Let stand for 5 minutes before serving. Serve with cantaloupe, melon and kiwifruit slices. Yield: 10 to 12 servings.

Yvonne Nelson, Laureate Eta
Prince George, British Columbia, Canada

JACK CHEESE OMELET

8 slices bacon, coarsely chopped
4 green onions, thinly sliced
1/2 green bell pepper, chopped
1/2 red bell pepper, chopped
2 stalks celery, chopped
8 eggs
1 cup milk
1/2 teaspoon seasoning salt
4 ounces cream cheese
6 teaspoons water
1 tomato, chopped
2 1/2 cups shredded Monterey Jack cheese

Preheat oven to 350 degrees. Fry bacon in skillet until crisp; drain and crumble. Reserve 2 teaspoons drippings in skillet. Sauté onions, green pepper, red pepper and celery in drippings until soft. Beat eggs in bowl. Add milk, salt, cream cheese and water; mix well. Add bacon, sautéed mixture, tomato and 2 cups cheese. Pour into 7-by-11-inch greased baking pan. Bake for 35 to 40 minutes. Remove from oven. Top with remaining cheese. Bake until cheese is melted. Yield: 8 to 10 servings.

Margaret Chadek
Walla Walla, Washington

TORTILLA ESPAÑOLA

3 tablespoons olive oil
5 or 6 medium potatoes, peeled, cubed
Salt and pepper to taste
1 medium onion, chopped
1 medium green or red bell pepper, chopped
4 eggs

Heat olive oil in skillet. Add potatoes. Cook over medium heat for 6 minutes, stirring occasionally. Season with salt and pepper. Add onion and green pepper. Cook for 6 minutes or until tender. Beat eggs in bowl. Add to potato mixture in skillet; mix well. Reduce temperature to simmer. Cook, covered, for 2 to 3 minutes or until firm. Loosen tortilla from skillet around edges with spatula. Place flat dish over skillet. Invert tortilla onto flat dish. Slide carefully back into skillet, trying not to break tortilla. Cook for 2 minutes or until brown. Cut into wedges. Serve hot or cold. Yield: 6 to 8 servings.

Rita T. Prado, Xi Theta Psi
Placentia, California

SPANISH-POTATO OMELET

6 potatoes, peeled, thinly sliced
1 tablespoon salt
1 cup olive oil
2 onions, thinly sliced
6 eggs
1 1/4 teaspoons salt
2 tablespoons cold water

Preheat oven to 425 degrees. Place potatoes in bowl. Add cold water to cover and 1 tablespoon salt. Soak for 5 minutes. Preheat oil in 10-inch nonstick skillet. Drain potatoes. Cook potatoes and onions in oil over medium heat until tender, stirring frequently. Do not brown. Drain onion-potato mixture in colander, reserving drippings. Combine eggs and 1 1/4 teaspoons salt and cold water in blender container. Process until blended. Mix eggs with onion-potato mixture in bowl. Heat 2 tablespoons reserved oil in skillet. Pour egg mixture into skillet, spreading to smooth top. Cook, covered, over low to medium heat for 20 minutes or until eggs are set. Place, uncovered, in oven. Bake until top is lightly browned. Turn onto platter. Garnish with pimento strips. May serve warm or at room temperature, cut into 1 to 2-inch cubes. Flavor improves if allowed to remain at room temperature for 1 hour. Yield: 8 servings.

Georgina Staggs, Xi Alpha Omega
Story, Wyoming

PIZZA EGGS

1 pound ground sausage
2 tablespoons curry powder
10 eggs, beaten
1 (8-ounce) can Italian tomato sauce
2 1/2 cups shredded Cheddar cheese
1/2 cup grated Parmesan cheese

Preheat electric skillet to 300 degrees. Brown sausage in skillet, stirring until crumbly; drain off fat. Add curry powder. Pour eggs evenly over sausage; cover. Let set for 10 minutes or until eggs are firm. Spread tomato sauce evenly over eggs. Top with cheeses. Cook, covered, for 10 minutes or until cheeses are melted. Let set for 5 minutes. Cut into squares. Yield: 8 servings.

Marsha Rudy, Upsilon Theta
Flora, Illinois

132 / Breakfast and Brunch

QUICHE

1 1/4 cups all-purpose flour
1/2 teaspoon salt
1/3 cup vegetable shortening
3 to 4 tablespoons cold water
12 ounces bulk sausage
4 eggs, beaten
1 cup heavy cream
1 tablespoon all-purpose flour
1/4 cup chopped green pepper
1/2 cup chopped onion
1/2 teaspoon minced garlic
3/4 teaspoon Tabasco sauce
1/2 cup shredded mozzarella cheese
1/4 cup grated fresh Parmesan cheese
1/4 cup grated Swiss cheese
1/4 cup grated Cheddar cheese
Nutmeg to taste

Preheat oven to 350 degrees. Combine 1 1/4 cups flour and salt in bowl; mix well. Cut in 1/3 cup shortening until crumbly. Add water, 1 tablespoon at a time, mixing with fork until mixture forms a ball. Flatten dough with hands on floured surface. Roll to fit 9-inch pie plate. Brown sausage in skillet, stirring until crumbly; drain. Combine sausage, eggs, cream, 1 tablespoon flour, green pepper, onion, garlic, Tabasco sauce and cheeses in bowl; mix well. Pour into unbaked pie shell. Sprinkle with nutmeg. Bake for 45 to 50 minutes or until knife inserted in center comes out clean. Let set for 10 minutes before serving. Yield: 6 servings.

Theresa Miller, Theta
Peculiar, Missouri

SUNDAY MORNING STEAK AND EGGS

1/2 onion, finely minced
1 tablespoon vegetable oil
1 cup leftover barbecued steak, cut up
Salt and pepper to taste
10 eggs, beaten
1 cup shredded cheese
1 tomato, chopped (optional)
Fried mushrooms

Preheat oven to broil. Sauté onion in oil in cast-iron skillet over medium heat until softened. Add steak, salt and pepper. Add eggs. Cook, stirring constantly, until almost set. Sprinkle cheese over top. Place under broiler for 5 to 7 minutes or until cheese is melted. Top with tomato. Serve with fried mushrooms. Yield: 4 servings.

Deborah Henderson, Psi
Alouette, Quebec, Canada

♥ SOUTH-OF-THE-BORDER SKILLET-SCRAMBLE

2 teaspoons vegetable oil
4 corn tortillas, cut into strips
1/3 cup chopped onion
2 cups egg substitute
1 tablespoon chopped jalapeño pepper
1/2 teaspoon ground cumin
1/4 teaspoon salt
Picante sauce
Fat-free sour cream
Chopped green onions

Heat oil in nonstick 10-inch skillet over medium-high heat. Cook tortilla strips and onion in oil for 5 to 7 minutes or until crisp, stirring often. Combine egg substitute, jalapeño pepper, cumin and salt in bowl. Reduce temperature to medium-low. Pour egg mixture over tortilla mixture, lifting edges to allow uncooked liquid to flow underneath. Cook for 5 minutes or until cooked through. Serve each portion with picante sauce, sour cream and green onions. Yield: 4 servings.

Dianne L. Waldo, Lambda Lambda
Emporia, Kansas

BRUNCH PIE

3 tablespoons margarine
2 (15-ounce) cans beef hash
1 egg, beaten
1/2 cup chopped onion
1 cup grated Cheddar cheese
1 (16-ounce) can mixed vegetables, drained
1/2 cup evaporated milk
2 eggs
1 tablespoon all-purpose flour
1/2 teaspoon dry mustard
Dash of garlic powder
Dash of pepper

Preheat oven to 350 degrees. Coat 9-inch pie plate with small amount of margarine. Combine hash and beaten egg in bowl. Press into pie plate to form crust. Bake for 10 minutes. Sauté onion in 3 tablespoons margarine in skillet. Layer cheese, sautéed onion and vegetables in crust. Combine remaining ingredients in bowl; mix well. Pour over mixture in crust. Bake for 20 to 30 minutes longer. Let stand for 10 minutes before serving. Yield: 6 servings.

Berlita Anderson
Beatrice, Nebraska

"THOSE DARN THINGS"

2 (8-count) cans crescent rolls
12 hard-cooked eggs, mashed
1/4 cup chopped celery
1/4 cup chopped onion
1/2 cup cubed Cheddar cheese
1/2 to 3/4 cup crumbled crisp-fried bacon or cubed ham
2 tablespoons sour cream
1/2 cup butter or mayonnaise-type salad dressing
Chopped green pepper to taste
Canned mushrooms to taste

Preheat oven to 350 degrees. Unroll crescent rolls. Place 1 triangle in each greased muffin cup, leaving tip of triangle over edge of cup. Combine remaining ingredients in bowl; mix well. Fill each muffin cup 2/3 full. Bring hanging tips over tops of filling. Bake for 15 minutes. May substitute salmon or tuna for bacon if desired. Yield: 16 servings.

Shirley Wasson, Laureate Sigma
Belleville, Ontario, Canada

LATTICE HAM AND CHEESE PIE

2 (8-count) cans crescent rolls
1 cup chopped leftover ham
1 cup chopped Monterey Jack cheese
1 egg, well beaten
Pepper to taste

Preheat oven to 325 degrees. Unroll 1 can rolls; do not separate. Line 9-inch pie plate with dough, pressing perforations to seal. Mix ham, cheese, egg and pepper in bowl. Pour into pie shell. Unroll remaining rolls; do not separate. Press perforations to seal. Cut into strips. Place on top of pie in crisscross fashion. Place pie on baking sheet. Bake for 35 to 45 minutes or until browned. Let stand for 10 minutes. Yield: 4 to 6 servings.

Robin Anne Breslauer, Iota Epsilon
Suffolk, Virginia

♥ BLACKBERRY TEA BARS

3/4 cup reduced-calorie margarine
1 1/2 cups confectioners' sugar
2 egg whites
3/4 teaspoon almond extract
2 1/4 cups sifted all-purpose flour
1/8 teaspoon salt
1/2 teaspoon baking soda
1/2 cup blackberry jam

Preheat oven to 350 degrees. Combine margarine, confectioners' sugar and egg whites in mixer bowl at medium speed. Blend in almond extract, flour, salt and baking soda at low speed. Do not overbeat. Spread dough in 9-by-13-inch baking pan coated with cooking spray. Smooth top of dough with rubber spatula. Run spatula lightly over top of dough to make 7 to 8 crisscross diagonal grooves. Fill grooves with jam. Bake for 20 to 25 minutes or until top is firm and edges are brown. Let cool. Refill grooves with jam. Cut into bars. Yield: 28 servings.

Carole Yost, Zeta Eta
Salisbury, North Carolina

❖ EASY CARAMEL-CHOCOLATE STICKY BUNS

1 (15-ounce) can coconut-pecan frosting
1 cup pecan halves
2 (10-count) cans refrigerator biscuits
20 chocolate kisses, unwrapped

Preheat oven to 375 degrees. Spread frosting in bottom of lightly greased 9-inch square baking pan. Arrange pecan halves over frosting. Separate biscuits; flatten each to 1/4-inch thickness. Place chocolate kiss to 1 side of center on each biscuit. Fold biscuit in half over chocolate kiss, forming a semi-circle. Press edges together to seal. Arrange over pecans. Bake for 28 to 30 minutes or until lightly browned. Let cool for 5 minutes. Invert onto serving tray. Yield: 20 servings.

Janette Haynes, Nu Kappa
Guthrie, Oklahoma

Rise and Shine / 133

MAPLE-CREAM COFFEE TREATS

1 cup packed dark brown sugar
1/2 to 3/4 cup chopped pecans
1/3 cup maple-flavored or corn syrup
1/4 cup margarine, melted
8 ounces cream cheese
2 tablespoons margarine, softened
1/4 cup confectioners' sugar
1/2 cup coconut
2 (10-count) cans refrigerator biscuits

Preheat oven to 350 degrees. Combine brown sugar, pecans, syrup and melted margarine in 9-by-13-inch baking pan. Spread evenly to cover bottom. Blend cream cheese, 2 tablespoons margarine and confectioners' sugar in mixer bowl until smooth. Add coconut; mix well. Separate biscuits. Press out each biscuit with fingers to form 4-inch circle. Spoon cream cheese mixture into circle. Roll into finger-shaped roll. Place, seam-side down, over brown sugar mixture. Bake for 25 to 30 minutes or until brown. Yield: 20 servings.

Mary Lynn Lethcoe, Eta Alpha
Powell, Tennessee

ROLL-UPS

1 king-size sliced loaf white bread
16 ounces cream cheese, softened
1 1/2 cups sugar
2 egg yolks
1 tablespoon sour cream
2 1/2 cups margarine
1 tablespoon cinnamon

Remove crusts from bread slices. Roll, 3 slices at a time, with rolling pin to flatten. Mix cream cheese, 1/2-cup sugar, egg yolks and sour cream in mixer bowl. Spread mixture on each bread slice; roll up. Melt margarine in small saucepan. Combine 1 cup sugar and cinnamon in bowl. Roll bread rolls in margarine, then in sugar mixture. Place on large cookie sheet. Freeze for 30 minutes. Store in freezer bags. To serve, bake frozen rolls in preheated 350-degree oven for 30 minutes. Serve warm or let cool. Yield: 60 servings.

Grace E. Black, Preceptor Psi
Aurora, Colorado

DOUGHNUTS

1 cup warm water
3 tablespoons sugar
1 package dry yeast
1 egg, beaten
1 teaspoon salt
3 tablespoons melted vegetable shortening
3 cups all-purpose flour
Vegetable oil for frying
Confectioners' sugar

Combine water, 3 tablespoons sugar and yeast in bowl. Let stand until foamy. Add egg, salt, shortening and flour; mix well. Roll out dough on floured board. Cut into doughnuts. Let rise on slightly greased waxed paper for 30 minutes. Fry in deep hot oil until golden brown; drain. Roll in sugar. Yield: 12 to 16 servings.

Karla Edwards, Xi Eta
Omaha, Nebraska

BLUEBERRY-SAUSAGE BREAKFAST CAKE

1 pound bulk pork sausage
2 cups all-purpose flour
1 teaspoon baking powder
1/2 teaspoon baking soda
1/2 cup margarine or butter
3/4 cup sugar
1/4 cup packed dark brown sugar
2 eggs
1 (8-ounce) container sour cream or low-fat sour cream
1 cup blueberries
1/2 cup chopped pecans
Blueberry Sauce

Brown sausage in skillet, stirring until crumbly; drain well. Sift flour, baking powder and baking soda in medium bowl. Beat margarine in large mixer bowl at medium to high speed until fluffy. Add sugar and brown sugar; beat until combined. Add eggs, 1 at a time, beating for 1 minute after each addition. Add flour mixture and sour cream to egg mixture alternately, beating after each addition just until combined. Fold in sausage and blueberries. Pour batter into ungreased 9-by-13-inch baking pan. Spread batter evenly in pan. Sprinkle pecans on top. Chill, covered, overnight. Preheat oven to 350 degrees. Bake for 35 to 40 minutes or until toothpick inserted in center comes out clean. Let cool on wire rack. Serve warm with Blueberry Sauce. Chill leftover cake and Blueberry Sauce. Yield: 15 servings.

BLUEBERRY SAUCE

1/2 cup sugar
2 tablespoons cornstarch
1/2 cup water
2 cups fresh or frozen blueberries
1/2 teaspoon lemon juice

Combine sugar, cornstarch, water and blueberries in medium saucepan. Cook over medium heat, stirring constantly, until thick and bubbly. Cook, stirring constantly, for 2 minutes longer. Stir in lemon juice. Let cool slightly. Yield: 2 cups.

Beverly Rippey, Preceptor Beta Phi
Bryan, Texas

ANY-FRUIT COFFEE CAKE

We served this coffee cake with breakfast burritos and fruit at a Western Round-up Rush Party.

4 cups chopped apples, apricots, peaches, pineapple, blueberries or raspberries
1 cup water
2 tablespoons lemon juice
2 3/4 cups sugar
1/3 cup cornstarch
3 1/2 cups all-purpose flour
1 tablespoon baking powder
1 teaspoon cinnamon
1 teaspoon salt
1 1/3 cups butter or margarine
2 eggs, slightly beaten
1 cup milk
1 teaspoon vanilla extract
1/2 cup chopped walnuts

Preheat oven to 350 degrees. Combine fruit and water in saucepan. Simmer, covered, for 5 minutes or until fruit is tender. Stir in lemon juice. Combine 1 1/4 cups sugar and cornstarch in bowl. Stir into fruit mixture. Cook, stirring constantly, until thickened. Let cool. Combine 3 cups flour, 1 cup sugar, baking powder, cinnamon and salt in large bowl. Cut in 1 cup butter until mixture resembles fine crumbs. Combine eggs, milk and vanilla in bowl. Add to flour mixture, mixing until blended. Spread half the batter in greased 9-by-13-inch baking pan. Spread cooled fruit mixture over batter. Spoon remaining batter in small mounds over fruit mixture, spreading to cover fruit. Combine 1/2 cup sugar and 1/2 cup flour in bowl. Cut in 1/3 cup butter until mixture resembles coarse crumbs. Stir in walnuts. Sprinkle over batter. Bake for 45 to 50 minutes or until cake tests done. Yield: 12 servings.

Susan Mercer, Xi Beta Gamma
Overland Park, Kansas

OVERNIGHT CRUNCH COFFEE CAKE

2/3 cup margarine, softened
1 cup sugar
1 cup packed dark brown sugar
2 eggs
2 cups all-purpose flour
1 teaspoon baking soda
1/2 teaspoon salt
1 teaspoon baking powder
1 1/2 teaspoons cinnamon
1 cup buttermilk or sour milk
1/2 cup chopped pecans
1/2 teaspoon nutmeg

Cream margarine, 1 cup sugar and 1/2 cup brown sugar in mixer bowl until light and fluffy. Add eggs, 1 at a time, beating well after each addition. Combine flour, baking soda, salt, baking powder and 1 teaspoon cinnamon in bowl. Add to creamed mixture alternately with buttermilk. Spread into greased and floured 9-by-13-inch baking pan. Combine 1/2 cup brown sugar, 1/2 teaspoon cinnamon, pecans and nutmeg in bowl. Sprinkle over cake batter. Must refrigerate, covered, for 8 hours or overnight. Preheat oven to 350 degrees. Bake, uncovered, for 30 minutes or until toothpick inserted in center comes out clean. Cut into squares. Serve warm. Yield: 10 to 15 servings.

Janie Kuddes, Preceptor Zeta Phi
St. Peters, Missouri

Diane Crane, Laureate Alpha Eta, Plantation, Florida, makes Cheese Spread for Breads by combining 1 pound grated sharp Cheddar cheese, 4 ounces grated Romano cheese and 1 pound softened butter or margarine in bowl. Add 2 tablespoons Worcestershire sauce and 1/4 teaspoon minced garlic; mix well. Spread on slices of sourdough, Italian or French bread. Place bread on cookie sheet. Broil on middle rack in oven until brown and bubbly. May be frozen in small containers for later use.

ORANGE-OATMEAL COFFEE CAKE

1 1/2 cups all-purpose flour
2 teaspoons baking powder
1/2 teaspoon cinnamon
1/4 teaspoon salt
1 cup quick-cooking oats
1/2 cup butter
1 cup sugar
2 eggs
1 cup milk
1/4 cup butter, softened
1/2 cup packed dark brown sugar
1/2 cup chopped nuts
3 tablespoons orange juice

Preheat oven to 350 degrees. Sift first 4 ingredients together into bowl. Add oats; mix well. Cream 1/2 cup butter in large mixer bowl. Add sugar gradually, beating until light and fluffy. Add eggs, 1 at a time, beating well after each addition. Add flour mixture alternately with milk, beating well after each addition. Pour into greased 8-inch square baking pan. Bake for 35 to 45 minutes or until tests done. Combine remaining ingredients in bowl. Spread over warm cake. Place under broiler for 2 minutes or until bubbly. Yield: 8 servings.

Alma Bucklin, Xi Mu
Londonderry, New Hampshire

♥ SCONES

3/4 cup all-purpose flour
1/2 cup oats
1/2 cup whole wheat flour
1/4 cup packed dark brown sugar
1 teaspoon baking powder
1/2 teaspoon baking soda
1/2 teaspoon salt
1 teaspoon cinnamon
1/4 cup butter or margarine
1/2 cup lemon-flavored nonfat or low-fat yogurt
1/2 cup light or nonfat sour cream
3/4 cup blueberries
1/4 cup chopped nuts

Preheat oven to 350 degrees. Combine first 8 ingredients in food processor container. Process until smooth. Cut in butter until mixture becomes fine crumbs. Add remaining ingredients, stirring until evenly moistened. Mound dough in lightly oiled 12-by-15-inch baking pan. Pat mound with lightly floured hands into smooth 7-inch round. Cut into 8 wedges with sharp floured knife. Separate wedges. Sprinkle tops with additional brown sugar if desired. Bake for 25 minutes. Yield: 8 servings.

Eileen Sanders, Preceptor Iota
Eugene, Oregon

BREAKFAST LASAGNA

1 cup sour cream
1/3 cup packed dark brown sugar
2 (9-ounce) packages frozen French toast or 12 slices homemade French toast
8 ounces sliced boiled ham
2 cups shredded Cheddar cheese
1 cup apple pie filling
1 cup granola with raisins

Preheat oven to 350 degrees. Blend sour cream and brown sugar in bowl; chill. Prepare French toast according to package directions. Place 6 slices toast in bottom of 9-by-13-inch baking pan coated with cooking spray. Layer ham, 2 cups cheese and remaining toast over toast. Spread pie filling over top. Sprinkle granola over filling. Bake for 25 to 35 minutes or until tests done. Top with remaining cheese while hot. Let cheese melt. Serve with sour cream mixture. Yield: 6 to 8 servings.

"Al" Smit Briggs, Xi Kappa Upsilon
Cameron, Missouri

OVERNIGHT FRENCH TOAST

1 cup butter, softened
1/3 cup orange juice
1/2 cup confectioners' sugar
12 (1-inch thick) slices French bread
6 eggs
4 cups milk
1/2 teaspoon salt
1/2 teaspoon nutmeg
1/2 teaspoon vanilla extract
2 tablespoons butter or margarine

Cream 1 cup butter in mixer bowl until light and fluffy. Add orange juice and confectioners' sugar. Beat until well blended. Place bread in 9-by-13-inch baking pan. Combine eggs, milk, salt, nutmeg and vanilla in bowl; mix well. Pour over bread. Refrigerate, covered, overnight. Preheat electric skillet to 300 degrees. Melt 2 tablespoons butter in skillet. Fry bread for 10 to 12 minutes or until golden. Place in warm oven. Serve hot with orange butter. Yield: 4 servings.

Diana O'Conor, Alpha Iota
Wallkill, New York

OVERNIGHT EGGNOG FRENCH TOAST

9 eggs
3 cups half and half
1/3 cup sugar
1/2 teaspoon nutmeg
2 teaspoons vanilla extract
1 1/2 teaspoons rum extract
24 (3/4-inch thick) slices French bread or Texas-cut bread
Confectioners' sugar

Grease two 10-by-15-inch baking pans. Combine eggs, half and half, sugar, nutmeg, vanilla and rum extract in large mixer bowl. Beat until well blended. Arrange bread slices in greased pans. Pour egg mixture over bread, lifting and moving bread until all egg mixture is absorbed. Cover with cooking foil. Refrigerate overnight or freeze for up to 1 week. Preheat oven to 500 degrees. Remove from refrigerator or freezer; do not thaw. Remove foil. Bake 1 pan for 15 minutes or until golden brown. Sprinkle with confectioners' sugar. Repeat for second pan. Cut into squares. Serve hot. Yield: 6 to 8 servings.

Lorraine Bates, Laureate Tau
Summerland, British Columbia, Canada

APPLE-OATMEAL-CRANBERRY MUFFINS

3/4 cup quick oats
1/4 cup oat bran
1/2 cup all-purpose flour
3 tablespoons packed dark brown sugar
2 1/2 teaspoons baking powder
1/8 teaspoon salt
1 teaspoon cinnamon
1/2 cup unsweetened apple-cranberry juice
1/4 cup low-fat milk
1 egg
2 tablespoons vegetable oil
1 medium apple, grated
2 tablespoons raisins

Preheat oven to 400 degrees. Coat 12 muffin cups with nonstick cooking spray. Combine oats, oat bran, flour, brown sugar, baking powder, salt and cinnamon in bowl; mix well. Combine apple-cranberry juice, milk, egg and oil in large bowl; mix well. Add dry ingredients; mix well. Stir in grated apple and raisins. Do not overmix. Fill greased muffin cups. Bake for 20 minutes or until golden brown. Yield: 12 servings.

Patricia M. Spencer
Langlois, Oregon

♥ HEALTHY SESAME-BANANA CRUNCH MUFFINS

2 ripe bananas
1 cup low-fat milk
2 egg whites
2 tablespoons vegetable oil
1 teaspoon vanilla extract
1 1/2 cups quick-cooking rolled oats
1/2 cup all-purpose flour
1/2 cup whole wheat flour
1 tablespoon baking powder
2 tablespoons sugar
1/2 teaspoon salt
Sesame Crunch Topping

Preheat oven to 400 degrees. Purée bananas in blender container. Combine bananas, milk, egg whites, oil and vanilla in large bowl; mix well. Combine oats, flour, whole wheat flour, baking powder, sugar and salt in bowl; mix well. Stir in banana mixture until just moistened; batter will be lumpy. Fill muffin cups coated with cooking spray 3/4 full. Sprinkle 2 teaspoons Sesame Crunch Topping over batter in each cup. Bake for 20 to 25 minutes or until golden brown. Let cool slightly in pan before turning onto wire rack. Serve warm. Yield: 17 servings.

SESAME CRUNCH TOPPING

2 tablespoons whole wheat flour
2 tablespoons chopped walnuts
1/4 cup packed dark brown sugar
1 tablespoon margarine
1/4 teaspoon cinnamon
1/4 teaspoon nutmeg
1 tablespoon sesame seeds

Combine wheat flour and remaining ingredients in bowl; mix well. Yield: 1/2 cup.

Maryanne Denisi
Mishawaka, Indiana

CHEDDAR CHEESE MUFFINS WITH APPLE BUTTER

2 cups all-purpose flour
1/2 cup sugar
1 tablespoon baking powder
1/2 teaspoon salt
1/2 teaspoon baking soda
2 cups grated Cheddar cheese
1 cup plain yogurt
1/4 cup melted margarine
2 eggs, beaten
Apple Butter

Preheat oven to 400 degrees. Line large muffin cups with paper liners or grease well. Combine flour, sugar, baking powder, salt and baking soda in large bowl. Stir with fork until blended. Stir in cheese gradually until evenly mixed. Make well in center of mixture. Whisk yogurt, melted butter and eggs together in small bowl. Add to dry ingredients all at once. Stir until evenly moistened. Batter will be very thick. Spoon into muffin cups. Bake in center of oven for 18 to 20 minutes or until tests done. Serve with Apple Butter. Muffins can be stored in refrigerator for several days and freeze well. Yield: 12 servings.

APPLE BUTTER

1/2 cup butter, softened
1/2 cup apple jelly
1/4 teaspoon cinnamon

Beat butter in mixer bowl until creamy. Beat in jelly and cinnamon until evenly blended. Serve with warm muffins. Yield: 1 cup.

Berny Suchan, Theta
Moose Jaw, Saskatchewan, Canada

PUMPKIN-BUTTERSCOTCH MUFFINS

1 3/4 cups sifted all-purpose flour
1/2 cup sugar
1/2 cup packed dark brown sugar
1/2 teaspoon ground ginger
1/2 teaspoon nutmeg
1 teaspoon cinnamon
1/4 teaspoon ground cloves
1 teaspoon baking soda
1/4 teaspoon baking powder
1/4 teaspoon salt
2 eggs
1/2 cup melted butter
1 cup canned pumpkin
1/2 cup chopped pecans
1 cup butterscotch chips

Preheat oven to 350 degrees. Combine flour, sugar, brown sugar, ginger, nutmeg, cinnamon, cloves, baking soda, baking powder and salt in large bowl; mix well. Make well in center of mixture. Combine eggs, butter and pumpkin in bowl; mix well. Stir in pecans and butterscotch chips. Pour into center of dry mixture. Fold until ingredients are moistened; do not overmix. Pour into greased muffin cups. Bake for 25 minutes. Let cool on wire rack. Yield: 18 servings.

Christina Maring
Columbia, Missouri

♥ BANANA-APPLESAUCE PANCAKES

2 eggs, lightly beaten
1 1/2 cups all-purpose flour
1/2 cup whole wheat flour
2 tablespoons applesauce or yogurt
2 tablespoons sugar
2 tablespoons baking powder
1/2 teaspoon salt
1/4 teaspoon nutmeg
2 bananas, cut into 1/4-inch pieces

Preheat nonstick griddle on medium heat. Beat eggs in large bowl until fluffy. Add all-purpose flour, whole wheat flour, applesauce, sugar, baking powder, salt and nutmeg; mix well. Add bananas; mix well. Pour batter onto hot griddle. Cook until puffed and dry around edges. Yield: 4 to 6 servings.

Lorraine M. Watry, Eta Omega
Colorado Springs, Colorado

BLUEBERRY-SOUR CREAM PANCAKES

1 1/3 cups all-purpose flour
1/2 teaspoon baking soda
1 teaspoon salt
1 tablespoon sugar
1/4 teaspoon ground nutmeg or cinnamon
1 egg, beaten
1 cup nonfat sour cream
1 cup skim milk
1 cup fresh blueberries

Preheat griddle. Combine flour, baking soda, salt, sugar and nutmeg in bowl; mix well. Combine egg, sour cream and milk in bowl; mix well. Add to dry ingredients, stirring just enough to moisten. Fold in blueberries. Drop batter by spoonfuls onto hot greased griddle. Cook until surface is covered with bubbles. Turn pancakes; cook until brown. Serve with syrup. Yield: 12 servings.

Juanita W. Gray, Xi Omicron
Bluefield, West Virginia

♥ COTTAGE CHEESE PANCAKES

2 cups low-fat cottage cheese
4 egg whites
6 teaspoons all-purpose flour
Nonstick vegetable cooking spray
Fruit spread or syrup

Preheat nonstick skillet. Combine cottage cheese, egg whites and flour in blender container. Process until smooth. Coat skillet with cooking spray. Pour 1/8 portion batter into hot skillet. Cook over medium heat until bubbly. Turn pancake; cook until brown. Repeat until batter is used. Serve with fruit spread or syrup. Yield: 8 servings.

Cheryl Miller, Preceptor Epsilon Upsilon
East Sparta, Ohio

♥ LIGHT AND FLUFFY PANCAKES

1 cup plus 2 tablespoons all-purpose flour
1 tablespoon sugar
1 teaspoon baking powder
1/2 teaspoon baking soda
2 tablespoons plus 2 teaspoons soft whipped margarine, melted
1 cup vanilla yogurt
2 eggs
2 teaspoons vanilla extract
1/4 cup water
1 cup fresh or frozen blueberries
Nonstick vegetable cooking spray

Preheat griddle. Combine first 4 ingredients in bowl; mix well. Combine margarine, yogurt, eggs, vanilla and water in bowl; mix well. Add dry ingredients; mix until blended, adding additional water if needed. Fold in blueberries. Spray griddle with cooking spray. Drop batter by spoonfuls onto hot griddle. Cook until bubbles form on top. Turn and cook until brown. Yield: 12 pancakes.

Rose Wojnar, Delta Sigma
Lafayette, Colorado

♥ OAT-BUTTERMILK PANCAKE MIX

3 cups old-fashioned oats
2 1/4 cups all-purpose flour
1 1/2 cups whole wheat flour
1 1/2 cups oat bran
1/2 cup buttermilk mix
5 teaspoons baking powder
2 teaspoons baking soda
1 teaspoon salt
1/3 cup packed dark brown sugar (optional)

Combine all ingredients in bowl; mix well. Store, covered, in large container. To prepare batter, combine desired amount of mix with water, egg and vegetable oil; mix well. Cook over medium heat on griddle sprayed with nonstick cooking spray. Serve with applesauce or pancake syrup. Yield: variable.

Joy Patty, Xi Beta Kappa
Prattville, Arizona

♥ OATMEAL PANCAKES

2 1/2 cups milk
2 cups oats
1 cup all-purpose flour
1 tablespoon sugar
1/4 teaspoon salt
1 tablespoon baking powder
1 egg
2 tablespoons vegetable oil

Preheat griddle. Pour milk over oats in bowl. Let stand for 5 minutes. Add remaining ingredients; mix well. Spoon batter onto hot griddle. Cook until brown, turning once. Yield: 12 pancakes.

Noreen Tetz, Xi Gamma
Winnipeg, Manitoba, Canada

138 / Breakfast and Brunch

PANCAKES, WAFFLES AND BISCUITS

10 cups all-purpose flour
10 cups whole wheat flour
1 cup baking powder
4 cups instant milk powder
2 tablespoons salt
1/2 cup sugar
4 cups shortening

Combine first 6 ingredients in large container; mix well. Cut in shortening until cornmeal consistency. Store, covered, in refrigerator for up to 2 months or in freezer for up to 6 months.

PANCAKES OR WAFFLES

1 cup milk
1 egg
1 1/2 cups dry mix
1/2 teaspoon cinnamon
1/4 teaspoon cloves
Fruit to taste

Combine milk and egg in bowl; mix well. Add dry mix, cinnamon and cloves; mix well. Fold in fruit. Ladle batter onto lightly greased hot griddle. Cook until bubbles form. Turn; cook until brown.
Yield: 8 to 12 servings.

BISCUITS

2 cups dry mix
1/2 cup milk

Combine dry mix and milk in bowl. Knead lightly on floured surface until blended. Roll out to 1/2-inch thickness. Cut with biscuit cutter. Place in ungreased baking pan. Bake for 8 to 10 minutes or until browned.
Yield: 8 to 12 servings.

Janet Bodner, Kappa Alpha
Petawawa, Ontario, Canada

❖ GINGERBREAD WAFFLES

2 cups all-purpose flour
1 teaspoon salt
1 1/4 teaspoons baking soda
2 1/2 teaspoons ginger
1 1/4 teaspoons cinnamon
1/4 teaspoon cloves
1 cup dark molasses
1/2 cup sour milk
1 egg, slightly beaten
1/3 cup vegetable oil
1 egg white, stiffly beaten
French vanilla ice cream

Preheat waffle iron on medium heat. Sift first 6 ingredients together into bowl. Combine molasses, sour milk and egg in bowl; mix well. Add dry ingredients; mix well. Add oil; mix well. Fold in egg white. Pour into hot waffle iron. Bake for 3 minutes or until lightly browned. Serve with ice cream. Yield: 6 servings.

Malinda Hamilton, Gamma Rho
Pinetop, Arizona

Betty Glavas, Preceptor Gamma Gamma, Tulsa, Oklahoma, makes Sunrise-In-A-Glass by combining 6 ounces pineapple juice, 8 ounces strawberry yogurt, 1 tablespoon wheat germ and 1 large banana in blender container. Purée until smooth. Pour into glass. Yield: 1 serving.

APPLE BUTTER

5 pounds Granny Smith apples, peeled, chopped
3 cups water
3 cups sugar
3 cups packed dark brown sugar
1 (1 3/4-ounce) package powdered pectin
1 tablespoon ground cinnamon
1 teaspoon ground allspice
1/4 teaspoon ground cloves
1/4 teaspoon ground nutmeg

Combine apples and water in large saucepan. Bring to a boil. Reduce heat. Simmer for 20 to 25 minutes or until tender. Mash apples. Stir in remaining ingredients. Bring to a boil. Cook for 2 minutes, stirring constantly. Pour mixture quickly into 6 hot sterilized jars, leaving 1/4-inch headspace. Seal with 2-piece lids. Process in boiling water bath for 5 minutes. Yield: 6 pints.

Phyllis T. Ohm, Epsilon Alpha
Salisbury, North Carolina

BLUEBERRY BREAKFAST PUDDING

1 large egg
1/3 cup packed light or dark brown sugar
1 cup skim milk
1 teaspoon ground cinnamon
1 teaspoon grated lemon rind
Pinch of ground nutmeg
1 teaspoon vanilla extract
6 slices whole wheat bread, cubed
Nonstick vegetable cooking spray
2 cups fresh or frozen dry-pack blueberries
1 1/2 cups plain low-fat yogurt (optional)

Beat egg and brown sugar together in large bowl with fork until well blended. Stir in milk, cinnamon, lemon rind, nutmeg and vanilla; mix well. Stir bread cubes into mixture. Refrigerate, covered, for 1 hour or overnight. Preheat oven to 375 degrees. Coat 8-inch square baking pan lightly with cooking spray. Stir blueberries into bread mixture. Spoon into pan, spreading evenly. Bake for 40 minutes or until firm. Serve warm. Top each portion with 2 tablespoons yogurt. Yield: 6 servings.

Peg McVitty, Laureate Beta Mu
Forest, Ohio

Marti Paulin, Preceptor Gamma Beta, Grand Rapids, Michigan, makes Rosy Jelly by combining 2 cups Rosé wine and 3 cups sugar in saucepan. Bring to a boil over medium heat, stirring frequently. Add 1 (3-ounce) package liquid pectin. Return to a boil, stirring for 1 minute. Pour into 3 sterilized wine glasses. Seal with thin layer of melted paraffin. Each wine glass can be wrapped with colored cellophane, a decorative bow added to the stem of wine glass and given as a great gift. Cheers!

GLAZED FRUIT IN ORANGE CUPS

This was quick and easy to make for our chapter Thanksgiving dinner. It can be made ahead of time and refrigerated.

1 (20-ounce) can pineapple chunks, drained
1 (29-ounce) can fruit cocktail, drained
2 (11-ounce) cans mandarin oranges, drained
8 bananas, sliced
2 tablespoons lemon juice
1 (22-ounce) can apricot or pineapple pie filling
6 oranges

Combine pineapple, fruit cocktail, mandarin oranges, bananas, lemon juice and pie filling in large bowl. Chill, covered, overnight. Cut each orange in half. Scoop out pulp. Serve fruit mixture in orange shells. Yield: 12 servings.

Diana Kratchman, Preceptor Beta Phi
College Station, Texas

PINEAPPLE CASSEROLE

1 (20-ounce) can crushed pineapple
1/4 cup sugar
3 tablespoons all-purpose flour
1 cup grated sharp Cheddar cheese
1/2 cup butter-flavor cracker crumbs
1/4 cup margarine, melted

Preheat oven to 350 degrees. Drain pineapple, reserving juice. Combine pineapple juice, sugar and flour in bowl; mix well. Add pineapple and cheese. Pour into buttered 9-inch pie plate. Sprinkle crumbs on top. Pour melted margarine over all. Bake for 25 to 30 minutes. Yield: 6 servings.

Ruth Ann Connell, Preceptor Laureate
Chadron, Nebraska

♥ MUSICAL FRUIT MELODIES

2 cups chunk fresh pineapple
1 firm large banana, sliced
1 cup seedless grapes
1 orange, peeled, sliced, seeded
1 red apple, cored, sliced
1 cup pitted prunes
1 cup pitted dates
1 (8-ounce) carton low-fat yogurt
1 cup chopped strawberries

Arrange pineapple chunks, banana slices, grapes, orange slices, apple slices, prunes and dates on serving platter. Combine yogurt with strawberries in small bowl. Place bowl in center of platter for dipping. Yield: 8 servings.

Jean Hoehn, Preceptor Eta Theta
Lynn Haven, Florida

♥ SPARKLING FRUIT COMPOTE

1 cup seedless grapes
1 (11-ounce) can mandarin oranges, drained
1 (8-ounce) can pineapple chunks with juice
1 pear, cored, cubed
1/4 cup frozen orange juice or lemonade concentrate, thawed
1/4 teaspoon ground ginger
1 banana, sliced
1/2 cup ginger ale or sparkling wine

Combine grapes, orange segments, pineapple chunks with juice, pear cubes, orange juice concentrate and ground ginger in large bowl; blend well. Refrigerate, covered, for 1 hour to blend ingredients. Add banana slices and ginger ale just before serving; mix well. Yield: 8 servings.

Nancy Robeson, Preceptor Alpha
Frostburg, Maryland

MY FAVORITE CHEESE GRITS

4 1/2 cups water
1 1/2 cups grits
1/2 teaspoon salt (optional)
1/4 cup butter or margarine
3 eggs, beaten
1 pound grated Velveeta cheese
Dash of Tabasco sauce
Dash of paprika
Dash of garlic powder
1/3 cup grated Velveeta cheese

Preheat oven to 250 degrees. Bring water to a rolling boil in saucepan. Add grits and salt to boiling water. Cover; reduce heat. Cook until grits are thick, stirring occasionally. Add butter, eggs, 1 pound cheese, Tabasco sauce, paprika and garlic powder, cooking slowly. Pour into greased baking dish. Sprinkle with 1/3 cup grated cheese. Bake for 1 hour. Yield: 4 to 6 servings.

Stephanie Wood, Delta
Okinawa, Japan

GREAT SAUSAGE AND GRITS

1 1/2 to 2 pounds bulk sausage
Few drops of Tabasco sauce
1/3 clove of garlic
1/4 teaspoon salt
1 cup instant grits
2 cups boiling water
1 cup grated Colby or Cheddar cheese
1/4 cup butter, melted
2 eggs, beaten

Preheat oven to 350 degrees. Brown sausage in skillet, stirring until crumbly; drain. Add Tabasco sauce, garlic and salt. Cook grits in boiling water according to package directions. Combine all ingredients in large bowl; mix well. Pour into buttered 9-by-13-inch baking dish. Bake for 1 hour. Yield: 4 to 6 servings.

Kathi Brewer, Rho Xi
Spickard, Missouri

SPICY GRITS

1 cup grits
8 ounces Velveeta mild Mexican cheese, cubed
1 teaspoon Worcestershire sauce
2 to 4 drops of Tabasco sauce
2 eggs, beaten
1 cup cornflakes, crushed
2 tablespoons margarine, melted

Preheat oven to 350 degrees. Cook grits according to package directions. Remove from heat. Add cheese; stir until cheese is melted. Add Worcestershire sauce, Tabasco sauce and eggs; mix well. Pour into greased 9-by-11-inch casserole. Combine cornflakes with margarine in bowl. Sprinkle over casserole. Bake for 45 minutes. May be chilled for several hours before baking. Yield: 6 to 8 servings.

Charlotte Wilson, Preceptor Beta Alpha
Santa Fe, New Mexico

BAKED OATMEAL

This tastes like an oatmeal cookie. It is also a nice ice cream topping.

3 cups quick-cooking oats
1 cup packed dark brown sugar
2 teaspoons baking powder
1 teaspoon ground cinnamon
1 teaspoon salt
1 cup milk
1/2 cup margarine, melted
2 eggs, beaten

Preheat oven to 350 degrees. Combine all ingredients in large bowl. Spoon into greased 9-inch square pan. Bake for 40 to 45 minutes. Serve warm with milk. Yield: 9 servings.

Michelle L. Gerke, Theta Chi
Jenison, Michigan

GRANOLA

3/4 cup vegetable oil
1/4 cup honey
1 cup packed dark brown sugar
1 teaspoon vanilla extract
1/2 teaspoon salt
8 cups rolled oats
3/4 cup toasted slivered almonds
1/2 cup toasted sunflower seeds (optional)
1/2 cup dry coconut (optional)

Preheat oven to 325 degrees. Combine oil, honey, brown sugar, vanilla and salt in medium saucepan. Cook until brown sugar is melted and oil and sugar remain separated. Combine remaining ingredients in large bowl. Pour honey mixture over oat mixture, stirring well. Mix with hands. Knead mixture thinly on foil-lined jelly roll pans. Bake for 10 to 15 minutes, stirring frequently, until cereal is golden brown. Repeat process several times to cook all mixture. Let cool completely. Store in airtight covered container. Yield: 16 servings.

Ginny Shoaf, Xi Epsilon Delta
Topeka, Kansas

♥ LOW-FAT GRANOLA

2 cups old-fashioned or quick-cooking oats
2 to 4 tablespoons packed dark brown sugar
1 tablespoon vegetable oil
1/4 cup wheat germ
1 teaspoon cinnamon
1/4 cup slivered almonds
1/4 cup sunflower seeds
1/4 to 1/2 cup dried fruits (optional)

Combine all ingredients in microwave-safe bowl. Microwave on High for 2 minutes. Stir well. Microwave for 1 1/2 to 2 minutes longer. Let cool. Store in covered airtight container. Yield: 6 to 8 servings.

Kathy L. Frieling, Xi Zeta Mu
Smith Center, Kansas

♥ MUESLI

1 cup skim milk
2 cups uncooked oats
1 large apple, chopped
1/4 cup slivered almonds
1/2 cup raisins
2 packets artificial sweetener or 1/4 cup sugar
1 tablespoon fresh lemon juice
1 (8-ounce) container nonfat no-sugar vanilla yogurt
2 tablespoons wheat germ
Dash of cinnamon
Fresh fruit, chopped

Combine milk and oats in bowl. Let stand for 30 minutes or overnight in refrigerator. Combine all ingredients in large bowl; mix well. Store in covered container in refrigerator for 2 to 3 days. Yield: 6 cups.

Phyllis Kerr, Laureate Sigma
Brookings, Oregon

SUNNY RAISIN-PEANUT BARS

3/4 cup chopped peanuts
2 1/2 cups toasted rice cereal
2 cups quick-cooking oats
1 cup raisins
1/2 cup peanut butter
1/2 cup packed dark brown sugar
1/2 cup light corn syrup
1 teaspoon vanilla extract

Combine peanuts, rice cereal, oats and raisins in large bowl. Place peanut butter, brown sugar and corn syrup in large microwave-safe glass bowl. Microwave on High for 2 minutes. Add vanilla; stir until smooth. Stir in cereal mixture; mix well. Press mixture in greased 9-inch square pan. Let cool. Cut into 10 bars. Wrap each bar in plastic wrap. Store in airtight container.
Yield: 10 servings.

Adele Kaufman, Epsilon Beta
Truman, Minnesota

Rave Reviews

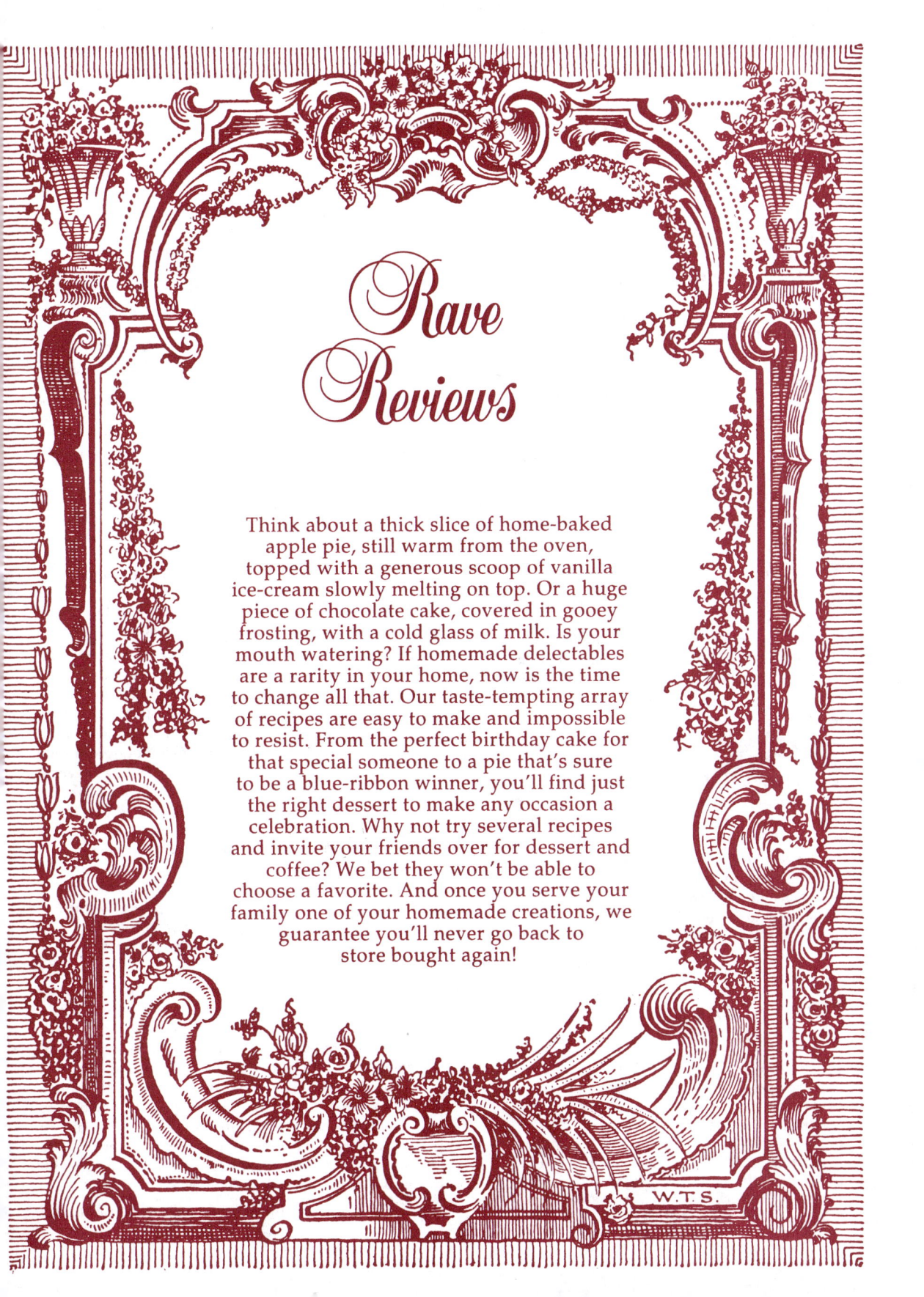

Think about a thick slice of home-baked apple pie, still warm from the oven, topped with a generous scoop of vanilla ice-cream slowly melting on top. Or a huge piece of chocolate cake, covered in gooey frosting, with a cold glass of milk. Is your mouth watering? If homemade delectables are a rarity in your home, now is the time to change all that. Our taste-tempting array of recipes are easy to make and impossible to resist. From the perfect birthday cake for that special someone to a pie that's sure to be a blue-ribbon winner, you'll find just the right dessert to make any occasion a celebration. Why not try several recipes and invite your friends over for dessert and coffee? We bet they won't be able to choose a favorite. And once you serve your family one of your homemade creations, we guarantee you'll never go back to store bought again!

AMARETTO DI SARONNO CAKE

4 eggs
1 (2-layer) package orange cake mix
1 (3-ounce) package lemon instant pudding mix
2 tablespoons Amaretto Di Saronno
1/2 cup plus 2 tablespoons water
1/2 cup butter-flavored vegetable oil
1 (10-ounce) jar orange marmalade
1/2 (5-ounce) jar apricot preserves
1/2 cup Amaretto
1 cup chopped toasted almonds

Preheat oven to 350 degrees. Beat eggs in mixer bowl until light. Add cake mix, pudding mix, 2 tablespoons Amaretto, water and oil. Beat for 5 minutes. Pour into greased bundt pan. Bake for 40 to 45 minutes or until cake tests done. Let cool. Place marmalade, apricot preserves and 1/2 cup Amaretto in saucepan. Cook until ingredients are heated. Drizzle over cooled cake. Top with almonds. Yield: 16 servings.

Norma Harris, Preceptor Alpha Mu
Knoxville, Tennessee

♥ LITE WALDORF ANGEL CAKE

1 (2-layer) package angel food cake mix
1 1/2 cups confectioners' sugar
3/4 cup baking cocoa
1/4 teaspoon salt
2/3 cup toasted slivered almonds
2 (12-ounce) containers lite whipped topping

Prepare and bake cake according to package directions. Invert cake on funnel to cool completely. Place cooled cake upside down on plate. Cut 1-inch layer off top of cake. Cut cake 1 inch from outer and inner edges of cake, leaving 1 inch on bottom. Remove cake within well. Place cake on serving plate. Combine confectioners' sugar, cocoa, salt and 1/3 cup almonds with whipped topping in bowl; mix well. Spoon 1/2 the mixture into cake well. Press mixture firmly to avoid air bubbles. Replace top cake layer. Press down gently. Frost cake with remaining whipped topping mixture. Sprinkle remaining almonds on top of cake. Chill for at least 4 hours. Yield: 14 to 16 servings.

Shirley Gratto, Xi Beta Alpha
Menasha, Wisconsin

BROWN SUGAR ANGEL FOOD CAKE WITH FROSTING

1 1/2 cups egg whites, at room temperature
2 teaspoons vanilla extract
1 1/2 teaspoons cream of tartar
1 teaspoon salt
2 cups packed dark brown sugar
1 1/4 cups sifted cake flour
1 cup sugar
1/4 cup milk
1/2 cup margarine
1 teaspoon vanilla extract
Sliced strawberries

Preheat oven to 350 degrees. Beat egg whites with 2 teaspoons vanilla, cream of tartar and salt until soft peaks form. Sift 1 cup brown sugar gradually over egg whites. Beat until soft peaks form. Sift remaining brown sugar with flour in bowl. Fold into egg whites. Turn into ungreased 10-inch tube pan. Cut through batter 1 inch from center of pan with knife. Bake for 45 to 50 minutes or until top is brown and dry. Invert cake on funnel to cool completely. Loosen cake from side of pan. Invert onto cake plate. Serve with sliced strawberries. Yield: 12 to 16 servings.

Peggy L. Fox, Delta Pi
Norfolk, Nebraska

CHOCOLATY ANGEL FOOD CAKE WITH PLUM SAUCE

There is no cholesterol and only a trace of saturated fat in this luscious dessert.

1/2 cup plus 2 tablespoons cake flour
1/2 cup baking cocoa
1 1/2 cups sugar
12 egg whites, at room temperature
1 teaspoon cream of tartar
1 teaspoon vanilla extract
1/2 teaspoon almond extract
Fresh spearmint leaves
Plum Sauce

Preheat oven to 350 degrees. Sift flour, cocoa and 1/2 cup sugar into medium bowl; stir until well blended. Place egg whites in large mixer bowl. Beat whites until foamy. Add cream of tartar. Beat at high speed until stiff but not dry. Fold in remaining sugar, 1/4 cup at a time. Fold in vanilla and almond extract. Sprinkle flour-cocoa mixture over egg whites, a little at a time, folding in gently. Spoon batter into ungreased 10-inch tube pan. Bake for 40 to 45 minutes or until top is brown and dry. Invert cake on funnel to cool completely. Loosen cake from side of pan. Invert onto cake plate. Yield: 12 servings.

PLUM SAUCE

1 (16-ounce) can purple plums in heavy syrup
1 tablespoon cornstarch
Juice of 1/2 lemon
3/4 cup plum preserves

Drain plums, reserving syrup. Pit plums. Reserve 1/4 cup plum syrup. Combine plums and remaining syrup in food processor container. Process until puréed. Blend cornstarch with reserved 1/4 cup plum syrup in small bowl. Pour puréed plums into medium saucepan. Add lemon juice. Bring to a boil. Add cornstarch mixture. Reduce heat. Cook, stirring constantly, until thickened. Remove from heat. Stir in plum preserves. Return to food processor container. Process until smooth. Chill. To serve, spread 2 tablespoons plum sauce on plate. Place chocolaty angel food cake slice on sauce. Garnish with spearmint sprig. Yield: 12 servings.

Helen Chambers, Preceptor Gamma Nu
Bethel Park, Pennsylvania

APPLE CAKE

2 1/2 cups sugar
1 teaspoon baking powder
1 teaspoon cinnamon
2 eggs
1 cup vegetable oil
3 cups all-purpose flour
1 teaspoon baking soda
1 teaspoon salt
1 teaspoon vanilla extract
1/2 cup cold water
5 or 6 apples, peeled, sliced
Cinnamon-sugar mixture to taste

Preheat oven to 350 degrees. Combine sugar, baking powder, cinnamon, eggs, oil, flour, baking soda, salt, vanilla and water in large bowl; mix well. Fold in apples. Pour into greased 9-by-13-inch baking pan. Bake for 55 minutes. Sprinkle cinnamon-sugar mixture over top of hot cake. Yield: 12 servings.

Kate R. Fortunato, Preceptor Kappa
Merrimack, New Hampshire

APPLE CHEESECAKE

1 1/4 cups graham cracker crumbs
1/4 cup finely chopped walnuts
2 tablespoons dark brown sugar
1/4 cup butter, melted
2 Granny Smith apples, peeled, thinly sliced
3 tablespoons butter
1/2 teaspoon cinnamon
1/2 teaspoon nutmeg
32 ounces cream cheeese, softened
1 cup sugar
5 eggs, at room temperature
1/2 cup sour cream
3/4 cup chopped toasted walnuts
1 bottle cream caramel sauce

Preheat oven to 350 degrees. Combine graham cracker crumbs, 1/4 cup chopped walnuts, brown sugar and 1/4 cup butter in bowl; mix well. Press on bottom and side of 10-inch springform baking pan. Bake for 5 minutes. Sauté apples in 3 tablespoons butter in saucepan until tender. Combine cinnamon, nutmeg, cream cheese and sugar in mixer bowl; beat until creamy. Add eggs; beat. Fold in sour cream and walnuts. Fold in apples. Pour into prepared springform pan. Bake for 1 hour. Serve with warmed caramel sauce. Yield: 10 servings.

Deborah Crawford, Zeta Theta
Olathe, Kansas

APPLE-NUT CAKE

1 cup packed dark brown sugar
1 cup sugar
1 1/4 cups vegetable oil
2 eggs
2 cups all-purpose flour, sifted
3/4 teaspoon baking soda
1/4 teaspoon baking powder
1 teaspoon cinnamon
2 teaspoons vanilla extract
3 cups chopped apples
1/2 cup chopped nuts

Preheat oven to 350 degrees. Beat brown sugar, sugar and oil in large mixer bowl until creamy. Add eggs; mix well. Add flour, baking soda, baking powder and cinnamon. Add vanilla. Add apples and nuts. Dough will be very stiff. Pour into greased 9-by-13-inch baking pan. Bake for 45 minutes. Yield: 8 to 10 servings.

Millie Hill, Eta Alpha
Powell, Tenneseee

CRAZY APPLE CAKE

4 cups finely chopped apples
2 cups sugar
1/2 cup vegetable oil
2 eggs, beaten
2 cups sifted all-purpose flour
2 teaspoons cinnamon
2 teaspoons baking soda
1/2 teaspoon salt
2 teaspoons vanilla extract
1 cup chopped walnuts

Preheat oven to 350 degrees. Place apples in large bowl. Add sugar; stir to mix well. Let stand for 30 minutes. Add oil and eggs; mix well. Sift flour, cinnamon, baking soda and salt together in bowl. Stir into apple mixture. Add vanilla and walnuts. Pour into well-greased and floured 9-by-13-inch pan. Bake for 40 to 50 minutes or until cake tests done. Let cool in pan.
Yield: 15 to 18 servings.

Denise Evans, Iota Delta
Oskaloosa, Iowa

DOUBLE APPLE CAKE

1/2 cup raisins
Wine
2 cups sugar
1 1/4 cups applesauce
2 eggs or 4 egg whites
1 teaspoon vanilla extract
3 cups all-purpose flour
1 teaspoon salt
1 teaspoon baking soda
1 teaspoon cinnamon
1/4 teaspoon ginger
1/4 teaspoon nutmeg
1/4 teaspoon cloves
3 cups finely chopped apples
1/4 cup chopped nuts (optional)
Confectioners' sugar or whipped topping

Preheat oven to 350 degrees. Soak raisins in wine to cover in bowl; drain. Beat sugar, applesauce, eggs and vanilla in large mixer bowl. Add flour, salt, baking soda, cinnamon, ginger, nutmeg and cloves; mix well. Add apples, raisins and nuts; mix well. Batter will be stiff. Pour into greased 9-by-13-inch baking pan. Bake for 45 to 50 minutes or until cake tests done. Sprinkle with confectioners' sugar or serve with whipped topping. Yield: 12 servings.

Shirley E. Baker, Laureate Beta Psi
Springfield, Ohio

144 / Cakes

FAMOUS APPLE CAKE

My Aunt Cindy gave me this recipe which has made her famous in her hometown of Port Orange, Florida.

4 cups sliced apples	2 teaspoons nutmeg
2 cups sugar	1 teaspoon salt
2 cups all-purpose flour	2 eggs
1 1/2 teaspoons baking soda	3/4 cup vegetable oil
2 teaspoons cinnamon	2 teaspoons vanilla extract
	1 cup chopped nuts

Preheat oven to 350 degrees. Combine apples and sugar in large bowl; stir with spoon. Add flour, baking soda, cinnamon, nutmeg and salt; stir with spoon. Combine eggs, oil and vanilla in bowl; mix well. Pour over dry ingredients. Add nuts; mix thoroughly. Pour into greased and floured 9-by-13-inch baking pan. Bake for 50 minutes. Yield: 12 servings.

Diane Frame, Xi Delta Gamma
Manassas, Virginia

FAVORITE APPLE CAKE

6 apples, peeled, cored	2 teaspoons cinnamon
2 cups sugar	1/2 teaspoon salt
1/2 cup vegetable oil	2 cups all-purpose flour
2 teaspoons vanilla extract	2 eggs
2 teaspoons nutmeg	1 teaspoon baking soda

Chop apples into nickle-sized pieces into bowl. Add sugar and oil; mix with spoon. Let stand for 30 minutes. Preheat oven to 350 degrees. Add vanilla, nutmeg, cinnamon, salt, flour, eggs and baking soda; mix well. Pour into greased and floured 9-by-13-inch baking pan. Bake for 25 minutes or until golden brown. Yield: 24 servings.

Elaine Wendel, Mu Kappa
Ellinwood, Kansas

FRESH APPLE CAKE

2 cups chopped peeled apples	1 egg, beaten
1 cup sugar	1 cup all-purpose flour
1/2 cup chopped nuts	1 teaspoon baking soda
	1 teaspoon cinnamon

Preheat oven to 325 degrees. Combine apples and sugar in large bowl. Let stand for 15 minutes. Add remaining ingredients; mix well. Pour into 9-inch square or round baking dish coated with nonstick vegetable cooking spray. Bake for 25 minutes. Yield: 6 to 8 servings.

Phyllis M. Bailey, Beta Chi
Ocala, Florida

MOM'S FRESH APPLE CAKE

2 cups sugar	1 teaspoon salt
3 cups all-purpose flour	1 teaspoon cinnamon
1 1/4 cups vegetable oil	2 teaspoons vanilla extract
2 eggs	1 cup or less chopped nuts (optional)
3 cups chopped unpeeled red apples	Whipped topping
1 teaspoon baking soda	

Preheat oven to 325 degrees. Do not use mixer. Mix sugar, flour, oil and eggs in large bowl. Stir in apples. Add baking soda, salt and cinnamon; mix well. Add vanilla and nuts; mix well. Batter will be very stiff. Pour into greased and floured 9-by-13-inch baking pan. Bake for 40 to 45 minutes or until tests done. Serve with whipped topping. Yield: 24 servings.

Jo Ann Schlup, Pi Tau
California, Missouri

APPLE HARVEST CAKE

This cake can be baked in an 11-by-15-inch baking pan and served without icing as coffee cake.

2 eggs, beaten	1/2 teaspoon salt
2 cups sugar	1 teaspoon cinnamon
1 1/2 cups vegetable oil	3 cups finely chopped peeled apples
3 cups all-purpose flour	1 cup chopped nuts
1 teaspoon baking soda	Cream Cheese-Cinnamon Icing
	Whole or chopped nuts

Preheat oven to 350 degrees. Combine eggs, sugar and oil in mixer bowl; beat well. Add flour, baking soda, salt and cinnamon. Mix by hand until dry ingredients are moistened. Stir in apples and nuts. Mixture will be stiff. Pour into well-greased and floured 9-by-13-inch baking pan. Bake for 1 hour or until wooden pick inserted in center comes out clean. Let cool in pan for 10 minutes. Turn out onto wire rack. Let cool. Ice with Cream Cheese-Cinnamon Icing. Yield: 15 servings.

CREAM CHEESE-CINNAMON ICING

2 (3-ounce) packages cream cheese, softened	2 teaspoons vanilla extract
3 tablespoons milk or cream	1 teaspoon cinnamon
4 1/2 cups sifted confectioners' sugar	Halved or chopped nuts (optional)

Beat cream cheese with milk in mixer bowl. Beat in confectioners' sugar gradually. Stir in vanilla and cinnamon. Top with nuts. Yield: 3 cups.

Judy Bolton, Preceptor Nu
Atlantic, Iowa

LOW-FAT APPLE CAKE

2 cups sugar
3 eggs or 6 egg whites
2 teaspoons vanilla extract
1 1/2 cups applesauce
3 cups all-purpose flour
1 teaspoon salt
1 teaspoon baking soda
1 1/4 teaspoons cinnamon
3 cups chopped apples

Preheat oven to 350 degrees. Combine sugar, eggs, vanilla and applesauce in bowl; mix well. Sift flour, salt, baking soda and cinnamon together into bowl. Add to sugar mixture; mix well. Fold in apples. Pour into greased and floured 9-by-13-inch baking pan. Bake for 55 minutes to 1 hour and 5 minutes or until cake tests done. Yield: 12 to 15 servings.

Carol R. Roth
Metairie, Louisiana

MIX-DUMP-AND-EAT APPLE CAKE

This is wonderful served warm when you want a fairly simple dessert for a sorority meeting in fall weather.

2 eggs, well beaten
1 cup vegetable oil
2 cups sugar
2 cups all-purpose flour
1 cup raisins
1 cup chopped nuts
2 teaspoons baking soda
1 teaspoon cinnamon
1 teaspoon salt
1 teaspoon vanilla extract
1 (16-ounce) can apple pie filling
Nonstick vegetable cooking spray

Preheat oven to 350 degrees. Mix eggs, oil, sugar, flour, raisins, nuts, baking soda, cinnamon, salt and vanilla in large bowl. Chop apples in pie filling into bite-sized pieces. Fold into mixture. Pour into 9-by-13-inch baking pan coated with nonstick cooking spray. Bake for 1 hour. Serve warm or cold. Yield: 12 servings.

Roberta L. Chargin, Preceptor Chi
Tacoma, Washington

APPLE-RUM DUM CAKE

1 cup sugar
1/2 cup butter
1 egg
2 cups chopped apples
1 cup all-purpose flour
1 teaspoon baking soda
1 teaspoon cinnamon
1/4 teaspoon salt
1/2 cup chopped nuts
1/2 cup sugar
1/2 cup packed dark brown sugar
1/2 cup butter
1/2 cup whipping cream
Whipped cream

Preheat oven to 350 degrees. Mix 1 cup sugar, 1/2 cup butter and egg in large bowl. Add apples; mix well. Add flour, baking soda, cinnamon and salt; mix well. Fold in nuts. Pour into greased and floured 9-inch square baking pan. Bake for 35 to 40 minutes or until tests done. Combine 1/2 cup sugar, brown sugar, 1/2 cup butter and whipping cream in saucepan; mix well. Bring to a boil over medium heat. Boil for 2 minutes. Serve over cake. Top with whipped cream. Yield: 9 servings.

Nancy Anderson, Preceptor Zeta
Moorhead, Minnesota

SPICED APPLE-CARROT CAKE

3 cups all-purpose flour
2 teaspoons ground cinnamon
1 teaspoon baking powder
1 teaspoon baking soda
3/4 teaspoon salt
1/4 teaspoon ground nutmeg
1/4 teaspoon ground cloves
1 1/2 cups vegetable oil
1 cup packed light brown sugar
3/4 cup sugar
3 eggs
2 teaspoons vanilla extract
2 cups coarsely grated, peeled apples, excess juice squeezed out
1 cup coarsely grated carrots
1 cup chopped pecans
Cream Cheese-Orange Frosting

Preheat oven to 350 degrees. Sift together flour, cinnamon, baking powder, baking soda, salt, nutmeg and cloves into medium bowl. Combine oil, brown sugar, sugar, eggs and vanilla in large bowl. Beat with wooden spoon until thoroughly combined and smooth. Stir in flour mixture; beat until smooth. Stir in apples, carrots and pecans. Spoon into greased 9-by-13-inch baking pan, smoothing top evenly. Bake for 40 to 50 minutes or until toothpick inserted in center comes out clean. Let cool in pan on wire rack. Spread Cream Cheese-Orange Frosting over top of cooled cake. Yield: 12 servings.

CREAM CHEESE-ORANGE FROSTING

8 ounces cream cheese, softened
1/2 cup butter, softened
1 cup confectioners' sugar
Grated rind of 1 orange
1 teaspoon vanilla extract

Combine cream cheese and butter in small mixer bowl; beat until smooth and creamy. Beat in confectioners' sugar, orange rind and vanilla until smooth and of spreading consistency. Yield: 2 cups.

Paulette Hedden, Laureate Lambda
Bonner Springs, Kansas

Betty J. Loring, Laureate Beta Omega, Kankakee, Illinois, makes a German Apple Cake by combining 2 cups sugar, 2 cups all-purpose flour, 1 tablespoon baking soda, 1 cup vegetable oil, 1/2 tablespoon salt, 1 cup chopped nuts, 2 eggs, 2 tablespoons cinnamon, 1 teaspoon vanilla extract and 4 cups sliced apples in large bowl; mix with spoon. Batter will be thick. Pour into greased and floured 9-by-13-inch baking pan. Bake in preheated 350-degree oven for 45 minutes to 1 hour or until cake tests done. Serve with whipped cream. Yield: 12 servings.

APPLE AND MINCEMEAT CAKE

5 ounces butter
5 ounces dark brown sugar
3 eggs
2 cups self-rising flour
1 teaspoon mixed spice
1 (14-ounce) can mincemeat
2 small apples, peeled, cored, sliced
2 ounces sultanas
2 tablespoons Demerara sugar
2 tablespoons clear honey, warmed

Preheat oven to 325 degrees. Cream butter and brown sugar in mixer bowl until fluffy. Beat in eggs gradually. Fold in flour and spice. Add mincemeat. Spoon mixture into 8-inch round baking pan. Arrange apple slices over top. Cover with sultanas and Demerara sugar. Place in center of oven. Bake for 1 hour and 45 minutes to 2 hours or until toothpick inserted in center comes out clean. Brush top of warm cake with honey. Yield: 8 servings.

Doreen Whyte, Beta Master
Comox, British Columbia, Canada

APPLESAUCE FRUITCAKE

2 cups all-purpose flour
1 1/2 cups sugar
1 1/2 teaspoons baking soda
1 teaspoon salt
2 tablespoons baking cocoa
1/2 teaspoon cinnamon
1/2 teaspoon cloves
1/2 teaspoon nutmeg
1/2 teaspoon allspice
1/2 cup vegetable oil
1 1/2 cups applesauce
2 eggs
3/4 cup raisins
3/4 cup chopped nuts
1 cup candied fruit
2 tablespoons sugar
1/2 cup chopped nuts

Preheat oven to 350 degrees. Sift flour, 1 1/2 cups sugar, baking soda, salt, cocoa, cinnamon, cloves, nutmeg and allspice together into large bowl. Add oil. Add 1 cup applesauce; mix well. Scrape bowl and spoon frequently. Add eggs; mix well. Add remaining applesauce; beat 50 strokes. Add raisins, nuts and candied fruit; mix well. Pour into greased 10-inch tube pan. Mix 2 tablespoons sugar and 1/2 cup nuts in bowl. Sprinkle over top of cake. Bake for 55 minutes to 1 hour and 5 minutes or until cake tests done. Yield: 15 servings.

Dorothy L. Brown, Preceptor Beta Xi
Wichita, Kansas

RASPBERRY-FILLED APRICOT CAKE

1 (2-layer) package yellow cake mix
1 1/3 cups plus 2 tablespoons apricot nectar
2 eggs
1 cup raspberry Simply Fruit
1 (3-ounce) package sugar-free vanilla instant pudding mix
1/2 cup skim or low-fat milk
1 (8-ounce) carton frozen lite whipped topping, thawed

Preheat oven to 350 degrees. Prepare cake mix using 1 1/3 cups apricot nectar and eggs in mixer bowl. Pour into 2 greased and floured 9-inch round cake pans. Bake for 25 to 35 minutes or until cake tests done. Let cool completely. Split layers in half. Spread layers with Simply Fruit. Combine pudding mix, milk and 2 tablespoons apricot nectar in bowl; mix until thickened. Fold in whipped topping. Frost top and side of cake.
Yield: 12 servings.

Linda Perry, Preceptor Theta
Virginia Beach, Virginia

BANANA CAKE

3/4 cup vegetable shortening
3/4 teaspoon salt
2 eggs
1 1/2 cups sugar
1/4 cup buttermilk
1 teaspoon vanilla extract
2 cups all-purpose flour
1/2 teaspoon baking powder
3/4 teaspoon baking soda
2 large bananas, cut into chunks

Preheat oven to 350 degrees. Combine shortening, salt, eggs and sugar in large bowl; mix well. Add buttermilk and vanilla; mix well. Add flour, baking powder and baking soda; mix well. Fold in bananas. Pour into 8-by-11-inch baking pan. Bake for 30 to 35 minutes or until tests done. Yield: 12 to 15 servings.

Marcia L. Freeman, Nu Gamma
Salina, Kansas

♥ BANANA-NUT SNACKING CAKE

2 1/4 cups all-purpose flour
2 teaspoons baking powder
1 teaspoon baking soda
1/3 cup margarine, softened
1 1/4 cups sugar
3/4 cup egg substitute
1 1/4 cups mashed bananas
2/3 cup plain nonfat yogurt
1/2 cup chopped walnuts
Confectioners' sugar

Preheat oven to 350 degrees. Combine flour, baking powder and baking soda in small bowl. Cream margarine and sugar in mixer bowl at medium speed until well combined. Blend in egg substitute and bananas at low speed. Add flour mixture alternately with yogurt, mixing until smooth after each addition. Stir in walnuts. Spoon batter into greased and floured 9-by-13-inch baking pan. Bake for 45 minutes or until toothpick inserted in center comes out clean. Let cool in pan on wire rack. Dust with confectioners' sugar before serving.
Yield: 16 to 20 servings.

Katherine I. Kamradt, Xi Eta Pi
Davie, Florida

BANANA SPLIT CAKE

1/2 cup margarine, melted	1 (16-ounce) package confectioners' sugar
2 cups graham cracker crumbs	1 (16-ounce) can crushed pineapple, drained
1 teaspoon sugar	3 or 4 bananas, sliced
1 cup margarine, softened	1 (20-ounce) carton whipped toppng
1 teaspoon vanilla extract	1 (4-ounce) jar maraschino cherries
2 eggs	1/2 cup chopped pecans

Combine 1/2 cup melted margarine, cracker crumbs and sugar in bowl; mix well. Press into 9-by-13-inch baking pan. Combine 1 cup margarine, vanilla, eggs and confectioners' sugar in mixer bowl; beat for 15 minutes. Pour over cracker crumb crust. Layer pineapple and bananas over mixture. Top with whipped topping, maraschino cherries and pecans. Yield: 6 to 8 servings.

Glenda C. Bell, Xi Delta Iota
Woodstock, Georgia

SUMMERTIME BANANA SPLIT CAKE

1 1/2 cups graham cracker crumbs	4 or 5 bananas, cut in half lengthwise
4 ounces butter, softened	1 quart frozen presweetened strawberries
2 cups confectioners' sugar	
2 egg whites	3 teaspoons cornstarch
4 ounces butter, softened	2 cups heavy cream, whipped

Preheat oven to 325 degrees. Combine cracker crumbs and 4 ounces butter in bowl; mix well. Press on bottom of 3-quart shallow baking dish. Bake for 10 minutes. Let cool. Combine confectioners' sugar, egg whites and 4 ounces butter in mixer bowl. Beat until creamy. Spread over cooled crumb crust. Arrange bananas over mixture. Place strawberries in medium saucepan. Add cornstarch; mix well. Bring to a boil over low heat. Boil until thickened. Chill. Spread over bananas. Spread whipped cream over top. Refrigerate until serving time. Yield: 8 to 10 servings.

Lavon Ace, Xi Alpha Pi
Oregon, Wisconsin

ALMOST BETTER-THAN-SEX CAKE

This cake can be cut for appeal or laughs. It is good for congratulations for making a diet goal. Cut a half circle out of each side of cake in middle to create waist. Place half circles at top, lining up edges to form breasts.

1 (2-layer) package yellow cake mix	2 packages vanilla instant pudding mix
1 (15-ounce) can crushed pineapple	3/4 cup coconut
3/4 cup sugar	Whipped topping

Mix and bake cake mix according to package directions for 9-by-13-inch baking pan. Combine pineapple and sugar in saucepan. Bring to a boil over medium-low heat. Boil for 20 minutes. Poke holes in top of hot cake with fork. Pour pineapple mixture slowly over cake. Prepare pudding mix according to package directions. Spread over cake. Sprinkle coconut over pudding. Top with whipped topping. Yield: 16 servings.

Kim Ehrensbeck, Xi Gamma Iota
Old Forge, New York

BETTER-THAN-SEX CAKE

1 (2-layer) package yellow cake mix	3 medium bananas, chopped
1 cup sugar	1 (8-ounce) carton frozen whipped topping, thawed
1 (15-ounce) can crushed pineapple	
8 ounces cream cheese, softened	1 cup chopped pecans
	1 cup coconut
1 (3-ounce) package vanilla instant pudding mix	Cherries to taste

Mix and bake cake according to package directions for 9-by-13-inch baking pan. Combine sugar and pineapple in saucepan. Bring to a boil over medium-low heat. Boil for 6 minutes; let cool. Pour over cooled cake. Combine cream cheese and pudding; mix well. Spread over pineapple mixture. Layer bananas over pudding. Top with whipped topping. Sprinkle with pecans and coconut. Decorate with cherries. Refrigerate for 1 hour. Yield: 16 to 20 servings.

Donna Tarpley, Epsilon Omicron
Hope, Arkansas

BLACKBERRY WINE CAKE

1 (2-layer) package white cake mix	1/2 cup chopped pecans
	1 cup confectioners' sugar
1 (3-ounce) package blackberry gelatin	1/2 cup butter or margarine
4 eggs	1/2 cup blackberry wine
1/2 cup vegetable oil	
1 cup blackberry wine	

Preheat oven to 325 degrees. Combine cake mix and gelatin in mixer bowl; mix well. Add eggs, oil and 1 cup wine. Beat at low speed until moistened. Beat at medium speed for 2 minutes, scraping bowl frequently. Grease and flour bundt cake pan. Sprinkle pecans in bottom of pan. Pour in batter. Bake for 45 to 50 minutes or until cake tests done. Remove from oven. Combine remaining ingredients in saucepan. Bring to a rolling boil. Pour half the glaze over warm cake while still in pan. Let cool for 30 minutes. Turn cake out of pan; let cool. Add additional confectioners' sugar to glaze to thicken. Pour glaze over cooled cake. Yield: 12 servings.

Paula Lyens, Preceptor Epsilon Theta
Treasure Island, Florida

GOOEY BUTTER CAKE

1 (2-layer) package
   yellow cake mix
1/2 cup butter
1 egg
1 cup chopped pecans
2 eggs
8 ounces cream cheese,
   softened
1 (16-ounce) package
   confectioners' sugar
1 (8-ounce) container
   whipped topping

Preheat oven to 350 degrees. Blend cake mix and butter in bowl with pastry blender. Add 1 egg and pecans; mix well. Press on bottom of 9-by-13-inch baking pan. Combine 2 eggs, cream cheese and confectioners' sugar in mixer bowl; mix well. Spread over mixture in baking dish. Bake for 35 to 40 minutes or until tests done. Do not overbake. Top with whipped topping.
Yield: 12 to 15 servings.

Jeanne Ritter, Preceptor Tau
Denver, Colorado

BUTTERSCOTCH CAKE

1 (3-ounce) package
   butterscotch
   pudding mix
2 cups milk
1 (2-layer) package
   white cake mix
1/4 cup vegetable oil
6 ounces butterscotch
   chips
Whipped topping

Preheat oven to 350 degrees. Cook butterscotch pudding mix according to package directions using milk. Let cool slightly. Combine cake mix and oil in mixer bowl. Add pudding to cake mix. Pour into greased 9-by-13-inch cake pan. Sprinkle with butterscotch chips. Bake for 30 to 35 minutes or until cake tests done. Serve with dollop of whipped topping on each serving.
Yield: 15 servings.

Kathy Pitcher, Upsilon Omicron
Jewett, Illinois

CARROT CAKE

4 eggs
1 1/2 cups vegetable oil
1 1/2 cups sugar
2 cups all-purpose
   flour
2 teaspoons baking
   soda
1/2 teaspoon salt
2 teaspoons cinnamon
2 1/2 cups shredded
   carrots
8 ounces cream cheese,
   softened
3 cups confectioners'
   sugar
1/2 cup butter
2 teaspoons vanilla
   extract

Preheat oven to 350 degrees. Combine eggs, oil and sugar in large bowl; mix well. Add flour, baking soda, salt and cinnamon. Mix just until moist. Fold in carrots. Spread in greased 9-by-13-inch baking pan. Bake for 40 to 45 minutes or until cake tests done. Let cool completely. Combine cream cheese, confectioners' sugar, butter and vanilla in mixer bowl. Beat until creamy. Spread on cooled cake. Yield: 12 servings.

Kathleen White, Mu
Tonopah, Nevada

♥ FAT-FREE CARROT CAKE

1/2 cup sugar
1 cup applesauce
3 eggs or equivalent
   egg substitute
2 teaspoons vanilla
   extract
2 cups sifted
   all-purpose flour
1 teaspoon salt
2 teaspoons baking
   soda
2 teaspoons cinnamon
2 teaspoons nutmeg
1/4 teaspoon cardamom
1 cup chopped walnuts
1/2 cup crushed
   pineapple, drained
1/2 cup raisins
2 cups packed shredded
   carrots
Cream Cheese-Pineapple
   Icing

Preheat oven to 350 degrees. Combine sugar and applesauce in bowl; mix well. Add eggs; mix well. Add vanilla. Combine flour and next 5 ingredients in bowl; mix well. Add walnuts, pineapple, raisins and carrots to egg mixture. Add flour mixture; mix well. Pour into greased and floured 9-by-13-inch baking pan. Bake for 45 minutes to 1 hour or until cake tests done. Top with Cream Cheese-Pineapple Icing. Yield: 12 servings.

CREAM CHEESE-PINEAPPLE ICING

3 ounces nonfat cream
   cheese, softened
1/2 cup nonfat margarine
1 1/4 cups confectioners'
   sugar
3 tablespoons
   well-drained crushed
   pineapple
1/4 cup chopped walnuts
1/8 teaspoon cardamom

Combine cream cheese, margarine and confectioners' sugar in mixer bowl; mix well. Add pineapple, walnuts and cardamom; mix well. Yield: 1 to 1 1/2 cups.

Arlene Kerscher, Preceptor Alpha Mu
San Jose, California

CARROT-CHOCOLATE CAKE

1 1/2 cups vegetable
   oil
2 cups sugar
4 cups eggs, beaten
1 1/2 cups all-purpose
   flour
1/2 cup baking cocoa
2 teaspoons baking
   powder
2 teaspoons cinnamon
3 cups grated carrots
1 1/2 cups chopped
   walnuts or raisins
1/4 cup butter
8 ounces cream cheese,
   softened
1 (1-pound) package
   confectioners' sugar
2 teaspoons vanilla
   extract
1 tablespoon baking
   cocoa

Preheat oven to 325 degrees. Blend oil, sugar and eggs in mixer bowl. Sift flour and next 3 ingredients together into bowl. Add to egg mixture alternately with carrots, beating well after each addition. Pour into greased 9-by-12-inch baking pan. Bake for 1 hour and 15 minutes. Cream butter and cream cheese in mixer bowl. Add confectioners' sugar, vanilla and 1 tablespoon cocoa; mix well. Spread on cooled cake. Dust top with additional confectioners' sugar. Yield: 15 servings.

Sheila Kalvn, Zeta Rho
Orangeville, Ontario, Canada

FAVORITE CARROT CAKE

2 cups all-purpose flour	2 cups sugar
2 teaspoons baking powder	1 teaspoon vinegar
2 teaspoons baking soda	4 eggs, beaten
2 tablespoons cinnamon	1 1/2 cups vegetable oil
1 teaspoon salt	3 cups grated carrots
	Cream Cheese Icing
	Whole nuts

Preheat oven to 375 degrees. Combine flour and next 4 ingredients in large bowl; mix well. Add sugar, vinegar, eggs and oil; mix well. Fold in carrots. Pour into 3 greased and floured 8-inch cake pans. Bake for 30 minutes. Let cool on wire racks. Frost with Cream Cheese Icing. Arrange whole nuts on top. Yield: 16 servings.

CREAM CHEESE ICING

1/2 cup margarine, softened	1 (16-ounce) package confectioners' sugar
8 ounces cream cheese, softened	1 cup chopped pecans

Combine margarine and cream cheese in mixer bowl; mix until creamy. Add confectioners sugar; beat until of spreading consistency. Add pecans. Yield: 2 to 3 cups.

Mary Ann Valley, Xi Gamma Lambda
Goodrich, Michigan

CHERRY CHOCOLATE CAKE

3 eggs	1 cup sugar
1 (2-layer) package chocolate cake mix with pudding	5 tablespoons margarine
	1/3 cup milk
1 (21-ounce) can cherry pie filling	1 (6-ounce) package chocolate chips
1 teaspoon almond extract	

Preheat oven to 350 degrees. Beat eggs in large mixer bowl. Add cake mix; mix well. Fold in cherry pie filling and almond extract. Pour into greased and floured 9-by-13-inch baking pan. Bake for 35 to 40 minutes or until tests done. Combine sugar, margarine and milk in saucepan. Bring to a boil over medium-low heat. Boil for 1 minute; remove from heat. Add chocolate chips. Beat until creamy and smooth. Punch holes in top of hot cake. Spread frosting over cake. Yield: 15 servings.

Margie Shanafect, Nu Master
Centralia, Illinois

GREAT CHERRY-CHOCOLATE CAKE

2 1/4 cups all-purpose flour	1 egg, slightly beaten
2 teaspoons baking powder	2 ounces baking chocolate, melted
3/4 teaspoon baking soda	6 ounces maraschino cherries
1 1/4 teaspoons salt	
1 1/4 cups sugar	1 1/4 cups sour cream
10 tablespoons butter	3/4 cup chopped pecans

Preheat oven to 350 degrees. Sift flour, baking powder, baking soda and salt together into bowl. Cream sugar and butter in large mixer bowl. Add egg; mix well. Stir in chocolate; mix well. Drain cherries, reserving 1/4 cup juice. Cut cherries into small pieces. Combine sour cream and reserved cherry juice in small bowl; mix well. Add flour mixture alternately with sour cream mixture to chocolate mixture. Beat until smooth. Stir in pecans and cherries. Spoon into greased and floured bundt pan. Bake for 50 minutes to 1 hour or until cake tests done. Let cool in pan for 10 minutes. Remove to wire rack to cool completely. Frost as desired. Yield: 16 servings.

Linda Collobert, Laureate Lambda
Kansas City, Missouri

CHOCOLATE-CHERRY UPSIDE DOWN CAKE

1 (21-ounce) can cherry pie filling	1 1/2 cups sugar
1 1/2 cups water	1 1/2 tablespoons baking soda
1/2 cup vegetable oil	3/4 teaspoon salt
1/4 cup vinegar	3/4 cup baking cocoa
1 1/2 teaspoons vanilla extract	Slivered almonds (optional)
2 1/4 cups all-purpose flour	

Preheat oven to 350 degrees. Spread cherry pie filling in 9-by-13-inch baking pan. Combine water, oil, vinegar and vanilla in bowl. Combine flour, sugar, baking soda, salt and cocoa in bowl. Add liquid mixture to flour mixture all at once. Stir just until moistened. Pour into greased 9-by-13-inch baking pan. Bake for 30 to 35 minutes or until cake tests done. Let cool for 10 minutes in pan. Invert on rack; let cool. Sprinkle with almonds. Yield: 10 to 12 servings.

Sherrie Bennett, Preceptor Gamma Zeta
North Delta, British Columbia, Canada

LUSCIOUS CHERRY CAKE

1 (2-layer) package white cake mix	1 (21-ounce) can cherry pie filling
1 small package vanilla instant pudding mix	1 (9-ounce) container whipped toppng
	Coconut (optional)
8 ounces cream cheese, softened	Ground nuts (optional)

Preheat oven to 350 degrees. Prepare cake mix according to package directions. Pour into greased 9-by-13-inch baking pan. Bake for 30 to 35 minutes or until tests done. Let cool. Prepare pudding mix according to package directions. Add cream cheese; mix well. Spread over cooled cake. Spread cherry pie filling over pudding mixture. Top with whipped topping. Sprinkle with coconut. Top with nuts. Refrigerate. Yield: 15 servings.

Margarette Karakas, Laureate Gamma Theta
Alta Loma, California

150 / Cakes

EASY BLACK FOREST CAKE

1 (2-layer) package chocolate cake mix
1 package chocolate instant pudding mix
1 cup milk
8 ounces cream cheese, softened
1 (19-ounce) can cherry pie filling
1 large carton whipped topping

Preheat oven to 350 degrees. Mix and bake cake mix according to package directions for 9-by-13-inch cake. Let cool. Combine pudding mix, milk and cream cheese in mixer bowl. Whip until smooth. Spread on top of cake. Layer cherry pie filling and whipped topping over pudding. Yield: 6 to 8 servings.

Jean Parri, Laureate Beta Gamma
Sudbury, Ontario, Canada

BLACK FOREST TORTE

1 1/2 cups grated toasted filberts
1/4 cup all-purpose flour
4 ounces semisweet baking chocolate
1/2 cup butter
1 cup sugar
6 egg yolks
2 tablespoons Kirsch
6 egg whites
Cherry Filling
Whipped Cream Filling
Chocolate curls

Preheat oven to 375 degrees. Blend filberts and flour in bowl. Melt chocolate in saucepan; let cool. Cream butter in mixer bowl until softened. Beat in sugar gradually until mixture is light and fluffy. Add egg yolks, 1 at a time, beating well after each addition. Blend in chocolate and Kirsch. Stir in filberts-flour mixture until blended. Beat egg whites in mixer bowl until stiff, not dry. Fold into batter. Pour into 3 greased and lightly floured 8-inch cake pans. Bake for 15 minutes or until test done. Let cool for 10 minutes in pans on wire rack. Remove from pans; let cool. Place 1 layer on cake plate. Spread with half the Cherry Filling. Top with 1 cup Whipped Cream Filling, spreading evenly. Cover with second layer. Top with remaining Cherry Filling. Spread 1 cup Whipped Cream Filling over Cherry Filling. Top with third layer. Frost top and side of torte with remaining Whipped Cream Filling. Garnish with reserved cherries and chocolate curls. Yield: 12 servings.

CHERRY FILLING

1 (16-ounce) jar maraschino cherries
1/4 cup Kirsch
1 1/2 tablespoons cornstarch
1 tablespoon lemon juice

Drain cherries, reserving 1/2 cup syrup. Reserve 13 cherries for garnish. Slice remaining cherries. Combine reserved syrup and Kirsch in saucepan. Blend cornstarch gradually into syrup mixture. Add lemon juice. Bring to a boil over medium heat. Boil mixture for 30 seconds. Add sliced cherries. Let cool. Yield: 1 1/2 cups.

WHIPPED CREAM FILLING

3 cups chilled heavy cream
1/3 cup confectioners' sugar
2 tablespoons Kirsch

Whip cream, 1 1/2 cups at a time, in mixer bowl until soft peaks form. Add 1/2 the confectioners' sugar and 1 tablespoon Kirsch to each portion. Yield: 6 cups.

Diane Burling, Iota Nu
Iroquois Falls, Ontario, Canada

CHOCOLATE BETTER-THAN-SEX CAKE

1 (2-layer) package German chocolate cake mix
1 cup semisweet chocolate chips
1 (14-ounce) can sweetened condensed milk
1/2 cup caramel ice cream topping
1 (12-ounce) carton frozen whipped topping, thawed
3 Heath candy bars, crushed

Preheat oven to 350 degrees. Mix cake mix according to package directions. Pour into greased and floured 9-by-13-inch baking pan. Bake for 10 minutes. Sprinkle with chocolate chips. Bake for 25 to 35 minutes longer or until cake tests done. Poke holes in hot cake with handle of wooden spoon. Pour condensed milk over cake. Let cool. Top with caramel topping. Spread with whipped topping. Sprinkle with crushed candy bars. Refrigerate. Yield: 20 servings.

Rosa Michel Vornkahl, Beta Omega
Kankakee, Illinois

CHOCOLATE BIRTHDAY CAKE

1 cup butter
2 cups sugar
3 eggs
1/2 cup buttermilk
1 cup water
2 cups all-purpose flour
1 teaspoon baking soda
3/8 teaspoon vanilla extract
1 teaspoon cinnamon
1/2 cup butter
6 tablespoons buttermilk
3 tablespoons baking cocoa
1 (16-ounce) package confectioners' sugar

Preheat oven to 325 degrees. Combine 1 cup butter and sugar in mixer bowl. Mix for 10 to 15 minutes or until creamy. Add eggs, 1 at a time, beating after each addition. Add 1/2 cup buttermilk, water, flour, baking soda, vanilla and cinnamon. Mix at high speed until creamy. Pour into 2 greased and floured 9-inch cake pans. Bake for 20 to 30 minutes or until cakes test done. Let cool in pan for 10 minutes. Remove to wire rack to cool completely. Combine 1/2 cup butter and 6 tablespoons buttermilk in mixer bowl; beat until smooth. Add cocoa and confectioners' sugar gradually, beating until creamy. Frost cake. Yield: 12 servings.

Louise Rustad
Rose Valley, Saskatchewan, Canada

CHOCOLATE CAKE

1/2 cup butter
2 cups packed dark brown sugar
1 egg
1/2 cup baking cocoa
1/2 cup milk
2 cups all-purpose flour
1 teaspoon baking soda
2 teaspoons baking powder
1 cup boiling water

Preheat oven to 350 degrees. Grease and flour 9-by-13-inch baking pan. Cream butter in bowl. Add brown sugar and egg; mix with spatula. Add cocoa and milk; mix well. Blend in flour, baking soda and baking powder. Add boiling water; mix well. Pour batter into 9-by-13-inch baking pan. Bake for 35 to 40 minutes or until cake tests done. Yield: 15 servings.

Sarron Murphy, Laureate Alpha Alpha
Kingston, Ontario, Canada

CHOCOLATE CAKE WITH CREAMY CHOCOLATE ICING

2 cups unbleached flour
2 cups sugar
1 1/4 teaspoons baking soda
1 teaspoon salt
1/4 teaspoon baking powder
1 cup water
1 teaspoon vanilla extract
2 eggs
3/4 cup sour cream
1/4 cup butter
4 ounces unsweetened baking chocolate, melted
Creamy Chocolate Icing

Preheat oven to 350 degrees. Combine flour, sugar, baking soda, salt, baking powder, water, vanilla, eggs, sour cream, butter and chocolate in mixer bowl. Mix for 1 minute at low speed. Beat for 3 minutes at high speed. Pour into 2 greased and floured 9-inch cake pans. Bake for 40 to 45 minutes or until cakes test done. Let cool in pans for 10 minutes. Invert onto wire rack to cool completely. Frost cake with Creamy Chocolate Icing. Store in refrigerator. Yield: 12 servings.

CREAMY CHOCOLATE ICING

1/3 cup butter, slightly softened
3 ounces unsweetened baking chocolate, melted
3 cups confectioners' sugar
1/2 cup sour cream
2 teaspoons vanilla extract

Mix butter and chocolate in mixer bowl. Blend in confectioners' sugar. Stir in sour cream and vanilla. Beat at high speed until smooth. Yield: 3 to 4 cups.

Jodi Kowalski, Alpha Iota
Carson City, Nevada

COCA-COLA CHOCOLATE CAKE

1 cup butter, softened
1 3/4 cups sugar
1/2 cup buttermilk
2 eggs
2 cups all-purpose flour
3 tablespoons baking cocoa
1 teaspoon baking soda
1 teaspoon cinnamon
1 teaspoon vanilla extract
1 cup Coca-Cola
1 1/2 cups marshmallows
Coca-Cola Icing

Preheat oven to 350 degrees. Combine butter, sugar, buttermilk and eggs in large mixer bowl. Add flour and next 4 ingredients; mix well. Beat at medium speed for 1 minute. Add Coca-Cola; blend well. Stir in marshmallows. Pour into greased 9-by-13-inch baking pan. Bake for 40 to 45 minutes or until cake tests done. Spread Coca-Cola Icing over warm cake. Yield: 12 servings.

COCA-COLA ICING

4 cups confectioners' sugar
3 tablespoons baking cocoa
1/2 cup butter
1/3 cup Coca-Cola
1/2 cup toasted chopped pecans

Sift confectioners' sugar and cocoa together into bowl. Cream butter in mixer bowl. Add sugar-cocoa mixture gradually; beat until creamy. Add Coca-Cola. Beat until smooth. Stir in pecans. Yield: 3 to 4 cups.

Cindy Free, Beta Gamma
Siloam Springs, Arkansas

QUICK CHOCOLATE-COLA CAKE

1 (2-layer) package Devil's Food cake mix
1 (4-ounce) package chocolate instant pudding mix
1/2 cup vegetable oil
4 eggs
1 1/4 cups carbonated cola
2 cups miniature marshmallows
Cola Frosting

Preheat oven to 350 degrees. Combine cake mix, pudding mix, oil and eggs in large mixer bowl. Beat at low speed until well blended. Bring cola to a boil in saucepan. Pour hot cola over cake batter beating at low speed. Beat for 2 minutes at medium speed. Pour into 9-by-13-inch greased baking pan. Bake for 30 minutes. Frost hot cake with Cola Frosting. Yield: 12 servings.

COLA FROSTING

1/2 cup butter
6 tablespoons carbonated cola
3 tablespoons baking cocoa
1 (16-ounce) package confectioners' sugar
1 teaspoon vanilla extract
1 cup chopped pecans

Combine butter, cola and cocoa in saucepan. Cook over medium heat, stirring, until butter is melted. Do not boil. Remove from heat. Add confectioners' sugar and vanilla; stir until smooth. Stir in pecans. Yield: 3 cups.

Shelly Allison, Nu Kappa
Guthrie, Oklahoma

DIRT CAKE

This cake requires no cooking and makes a great centerpiece. Just add flowers to the pot and serve with garden trowel. It is lots of fun to watch your guests when you start serving them the "dirt" from the pot!

2 (20-ounce) packages Oreo cookies
1/4 cup butter, softened
8 ounces cream cheese, softened
1 cup confectioners' sugar
3 1/2 cups milk
2 (3-ounce) packages chocolate instant pudding mix
1 (12-ounce) carton frozen whipped topping, thawed

Crush cookies until texture resembles potting soil. Cream butter, cream cheese and confectioners' sugar in mixer bowl until fluffy. Combine milk and pudding mix in large bowl; mix until well blended. Fold in whipped topping. Fold in cream cheese mixture; mix well. Place 1/3 crushed cookies in bottom of foil-lined clay pot or plastic pail. Add 1/2 pudding mixture. Top with 1/3 crushed cookies, then remaining pudding. Top with remaining crumbs. Chill overnight. Yield: 10 to 12 servings.

*Sue Conning, Preceptor Delta Omega
London, Ontario, Canada*

♥ HOT FUDGE PUDDING CAKE

1 cup self-rising flour
1/2 cup sugar
2 tablespoons baking cocoa
1/2 cup skim milk
2 tablespoons liquid Butter Buds
1 cup Grape Nuts
1 cup packed dark brown sugar
1/4 cup baking cocoa
1 3/4 cups hot water

Preheat oven to 350 degrees. Combine flour, sugar and 2 tablespoons cocoa in bowl. Blend in milk and Butter Buds. Stir in Grape Nuts. Pour into 8-inch square baking pan coated with nonstick vegetable cooking spray. Combine brown sugar and 1/4 cup cocoa; mix well. Sprinkle over batter. Pour hot water over batter. Bake for 45 minutes. Cut into squares. Serve hot. Yield: 16 servings.

*Juanita Fleming, Preceptor Beta Mu
Prineville, Oregon*

CHOCOLATE FUDGE CAKE

2 cups sugar
2 cups all-purpose flour
1 cup margarine
1/4 cup baking cocoa
1 cup water
1/2 cup buttermilk
2 eggs, slightly beaten
1 teaspoon baking soda
1 teaspoon vanilla extract
1/2 cup margarine
1/4 cup baking cocoa
6 tablespoons milk
1 (16-ounce) package confectioners' sugar
1 teaspoon vanilla extract
1 cup chopped nuts

Preheat oven to 400 degrees. Sift sugar and flour together into large bowl. Combine 1 cup margarine, 1/4 cup cocoa and water in saucepan; mix well. Bring to a rapid boil over medium-low heat. Pour over flour-sugar mixture. Stir until well mixed. Add buttermilk, eggs, baking soda and 1 teaspoon vanilla; mix well. Pour into greased and floured 11-by-16-inch baking pan. Bake for 20 minutes or until cake tests done. Combine 1/2 cup margarine, 1/4 cup cocoa and milk in saucepan. Bring to a boil over medium-low heat. Remove from heat. Add confectioners' sugar, vanilla and nuts. Beat well with spoon. Spread on hot cake. Yield: 12 servings.

*Lela Patteson, Exemplar
Ardmore, Oklahoma*

CHOCOLATE CAKE WITH PEANUT BUTTER-FUDGE FROSTING

This cake was served at the installation and in honor of the beginning of our chapter and Marilyn Ross' birthday. It is now the official dessert of our chapter — a group of chocolate lovers!

1/4 cup vegetable shortening
2 cups sugar
2 eggs
3/4 cup baking cocoa
2 cups all-purpose flour
1 teaspoon baking powder
1/4 teaspoon salt
1 cup milk
1 teaspoon vanilla extract
2 teaspoons baking soda
1 cup boiling water
Peanut Butter-Fudge Frosting

Preheat oven to 350 degrees. Cream shortening, sugar and eggs in mixer bowl. Fold in cocoa. Sift flour, baking powder and salt together. Add flour mixture alternately with milk and vanilla to creamed mixture. Add baking soda to boiling water in medium bowl. Add to batter. Batter will be very thin. Pour into two 7-inch round cake pans. Bake for 35 minutes or until cake tests done. Let cool. Frost with Peanut Butter-Fudge Frosting. Yield: 12 servings.

PEANUT BUTTER-FUDGE FROSTING

3 cups confectioners' sugar
3/4 cup baking cocoa
1/8 teaspoon salt
6 tablespoons milk
2 teaspoons vanilla extract
1/3 cup butter or margarine, softened
1 to 2 tablespoons peanut butter

Combine confectioners' sugar, cocoa and salt in large mixer bowl. Add milk and vanilla. Blend until smooth. Add butter. Beat until of spreading consistency. Add peanut butter; mix well. Yield: 3 to 4 cups.

*Phyllis Kulp, Preceptor Delta Delta
Shawnee, Kansas*

GERMAN CHOCOLATE UPSIDE DOWN CAKE

1 (2-layer) package German chocolate cake mix
1 1/2 cups chopped pecans
1 cup coconut
1/2 cup margarine
8 ounces cream cheese, softened
1 (16-ounce) package confectioners' sugar

Preheat oven to 350 degrees. Mix cake mix according to package directions. Spread pecans evenly in bottom of greased and floured 9-by-13-inch baking pan. Spread coconut over pecans. Pour cake mix evenly over pecans and coconut. Cream margarine, cream cheese and confectioners' sugar in mixer bowl. Spoon evenly over cake. Bake for 1 hour. Let cool in pan. Invert onto serving plate. Yield: 12 servings.

Susan Hinkhouse, Theta Delta
Burlington, Colorado

♥ CHOCOLATE ICE CREAM CAKE

My mother-in-law is on a low-fat, low-cholesterol diet so I made this for her 66th birthday so she could celebrate "legally."

Nonstick vegetable cooking spray
1 (2-layer) package chocolate cake mix
1 1/3 cups water
1/2 cup plain nonfat yogurt
4 egg whites
1 quart cherry-nut ice milk, softened
1 pint chocolate ice milk, softened
1 (1-ounce) envelope whipped dessert topping mix
1 tablespoon baking cocoa
1/2 cup skim milk
1 teaspoon vanilla extract

Preheat oven to 350 degrees. Spray two 8-inch round cake pans with cooking spray. Prepare cake mix according to package directions with 1 1/3 cups water, yogurt and egg whites. Divide batter equally between prepared pans. Bake for 35 to 40 minutes or until toothpick inserted in center comes out clean. Let cool in pans on wire racks for 10 minutes. Remove from pans; let cool completely on racks. Slice each cake layer in half horizontally to make 4 layers. Place bottom half of cake layer on serving plate. Spread with half the cherry-nut ice milk. Top with second layer. Spread with chocolate ice milk. Top with third layer. Spread with remaining cherry-nut ice milk. Top with fourth layer. Cover. Freeze for at least 1 hour. Combine dessert topping mix, cocoa, milk and vanilla in medium mixer bowl. Beat at high speed until thickened and of spreading consistency. Spread side and top of cake with mixture. Cover. Freeze until firm. Remove cake from freezer 10 minutes before serving. Cut into wedges using wet knife.
Yield: 12 servings.

Julie E. Jones, Xi Delta Chi
Broken Arrow, Oklahoma

MICROWAVED MISSISSIPPI MUD CAKE

1 cup butter or margarine
1/2 cup baking cocoa
4 eggs
2 cups sugar
1 1/2 cups all-purpose flour
Miniature marshmallows
Chocolate-Pecan Fudge Frosting

Place butter and cocoa in microwave-safe glass bowl. Microwave on high until butter is melted. Beat eggs in large mixer bowl at medium speed until lightly beaten. Add sugar, flour and cocoa mixture. Beat at medium speed until well blended. Pour into 9-by-13-inch glass baking dish. Microwave on high for approximately 8 minutes, rotating dish 1/2 turn after 4 minutes. Time may vary with different microwaves. Top of cake will look moist. Do not overcook. Place marshmallows in single layer over top of cake. Microwave on high for 1 1/2 to 3 minutes longer. Let cake cool for 30 minutes. Frost with Chocolate-Pecan Fudge Frosting. Yield: 15 servings.

CHOCOLATE-PECAN FUDGE FROSTING

1/2 cup butter or margarine
3 tablespoons baking cocoa
2 tablespoons corn syrup
2 cups confectioners' sugar
3 tablespoons milk
1/2 to 1 cup chopped pecans

Place butter and cocoa in glass bowl. Microwave on high for 1 to 1 1/2 minutes or until melted. Combine corn syrup and confectioners' sugar with cocoa mixture in mixer bowl; blend well. Add milk slowly until frosting is of smooth consistency. Add pecans. Yield: 2 to 3 cups.

Donna M. Coleman, Gamma
Jeffersonville, Indiana

CHOCOLATE MOIST CAKE

2 cups all-purpose flour
2 cups sugar
1/2 cup baking cocoa
2 1/2 teaspoons baking soda
1/2 teaspoon salt
1 cup vegetable oil
1 cup hot water
1 cup buttermilk
2 eggs
1 teaspoon vanilla extract
1 cup sugar
1/2 cup milk
6 tablespoons margarine
1/4 cup baking cocoa

Preheat oven to 350 degrees. Combine flour, 2 cups sugar, 1/2 cup cocoa, baking soda and salt in large bowl. Combine oil, water, buttermilk, eggs and vanilla in large mixer bowl; mix well. Add flour mixture slowly; blend until smooth. Pour into greased and floured 9-by-13-inch baking pan. Bake for 20 to 30 minutes or until cake tests done. Combine 1 cup sugar, milk, margarine and 1/4 cup cocoa in saucepan. Bring to a boil over medium-low heat. Boil for 1 minute. Remove from heat. Spread over hot cake. Yield: 12 servings.

Jana Burdge, Xi Epsilon Omega
Laverne, Oklahoma

CHOCOLATE-OATMEAL CAKE

1 1/2 cups boiling water
1 cup oats
1 1/2 cups sugar
1 cup all-purpose flour
1/2 cup margarine
1/2 cup baking cocoa
2 eggs
1 teaspoon vanilla extract
1 teaspoon baking soda
1/2 teaspoon salt

Preheat oven to 350 degrees. Pour boiling water over oats in bowl; let stand for 5 to 10 minutes. Combine remaining ingredients in large bowl; mix well. Add oats mixture; mix well. Pour into greased 9-by-13-inch baking pan. Bake for 25 minutes. Yield: 15 servings.

Dana McDaniel, Lambda Nu
Pattonsburg, Missouri

♥ OIL-FREE COCOA FUDGE CAKE

1 2/3 cups all-purpose flour
1 1/2 cups sugar
2/3 cup baking cocoa
1 1/2 teaspoons baking soda
1 teaspoon salt
1 1/2 cups buttermilk or sour milk
1/2 cup applesauce
2 eggs
1 teaspoon vanilla extract

Preheat oven to 350 degrees. Combine all ingredients in mixer bowl. Beat for 30 seconds at low speed. Beat for 3 minutes longer at high speed. Pour into greased 9-by-13-inch baking pan. Bake for 35 to 40 minutes or until cake tests done. Yield: 15 servings.

Lynne McCaughey, Delta
Brandon, Manitoba, Canada

♥ LOW-FAT CHOCOLATE-POTATO CAKE

This is a unique sweet recipe using potato flakes.

1 (2-layer) package chocolate fudge cake mix
1 1/2 cups water
2 small jars baby food prunes
3 egg whites
1/3 cup sugar
1 cup Irish potato flakes

Preheat oven to 350 degrees. Combine cake mix, water, prunes, egg whites and sugar in bowl; mix well. Beat for 2 minutes. Add potato flakes; mix well. Beat for 1 minute longer. Adjust water or potato flakes accordingly if batter is too dry or too moist. Pour into greased 9-by-13-inch baking pan. Bake for 27 to 35 minutes or until cake tests done. Let cool. Frost as desired or top with sifted confectioners' sugar. Yield: 16 to 20 servings.

Pam Dalke, Xi Alpha Upsilon
Roland, Oklahoma

CHOCOLATE-PISTACHIO CAKE

1 (2-layer) package white cake mix
1 package pistachio instant pudding mix
1/2 cup orange juice
1/2 cup cold water
4 eggs
1/2 cup vegetable oil
3/4 cup chocolate syrup
Smooth Chocolate Icing

Preheat oven to 350 degrees. Combine cake mix, pudding mix, orange juice, cold water, eggs and oil in large mixer bowl. Beat for 5 minutes. Pour 3/4 batter into well-greased and floured tube pan. Add chocolate syrup to remaining batter; mix well. Pour over batter in pan. Run knife through batter. Bake for 55 minutes or until wooden pick inserted in center comes out clean. Let cool in pan on wire rack for several hours. Remove from pan. Frost with Smooth Chocolate Icing. Yield: 16 servings.

SMOOTH CHOCOLATE ICING

2 squares unsweetened chocolate
2 tablespoons butter
1/4 cup cold water
2 cups confectioners' sugar
1 teaspoon vanilla extract

Combine chocolate, butter and water in saucepan. Heat until melted. Remove from heat. Add confectioners' sugar and vanilla; mix well. Yield: 2 cups.

Joyce Upton, Preceptor Eta
Morna Saint John, New Brunswick, Canada

BEST EVER RED DEVIL'S FOOD CAKE

1 tablespoon vinegar
1 cup milk
2 cups sugar
2 eggs
2 1/2 cups all-purpose flour
2 teaspoons baking soda
1/2 teaspoon salt
1 cup margarine, softened
1 teaspoon vanilla extract
1/2 cup baking cocoa
1 to 2 ounces red food coloring
1 cup boiling water
6 tablespoons margarine
6 tablespoons milk
1 1/2 cups sugar
1/2 cup chocolate chips

Preheat oven to 350 degrees. Stir vinegar into 1 cup milk in small bowl; set aside. Combine 2 cups sugar, eggs, flour, baking soda, salt, 1 cup margarine, vanilla, cocoa and food coloring in large mixer bowl; mix well. Add soured milk; mix well. Add water; mix well. Pour into greased 9-by-13-inch baking pan. Bake for 40 to 45 minutes or until toothpick inserted in cake comes out clean. Combine 6 tablespoons margarine, 6 tablespoons milk and 1 1/2 cups sugar in saucepan; mix well. Bring to a boil, stirring constantly. Boil, stirring, for 2 minutes. Remove from heat. Add chocolate chips. Stir for 2 minutes. Spread on cake. Continue spreading with knife until frosting starts to set up. Yield: 12 to 15 servings.

Jeanette A. Tims, Xi Gamma Alpha
Norfolk, Nebraska

MAMA'S RED CAKE

1/2 cup vegetable shortening
1 1/2 cups sugar
2 eggs
2 ounces red food coloring
2 teaspoons baking cocoa
2 1/4 cups cake flour
1 teaspoon salt
1 cup buttermilk
1 teaspoon baking soda
1 teaspoon vinegar
1 teaspoon vanilla extract

Preheat oven to 350 degrees. Cream shortening and sugar in mixer bowl. Add eggs; beat thoroughly. Mix food coloring and cocoa in small bowl. Add to creamed mixture. Beat for several minutes. Sift together flour and salt in large bowl. Stir in buttermilk alternately with creamed mixture. Mix baking soda and vinegar in small bowl. Fold carefully into batter. Pour into greased 9-by-13-inch baking pan or 2 greased 9-inch cake pans. Bake for 35 to 40 minutes or until cake tests done. Let cool. Frost with your favorite frosting. Yield: 12 servings.

Daphna June Cummings, Xi Iota Tau
Pattonsburg, Missouri

RED VELVET CAKE

2 ounces red food coloring
3 tablespoons instant cocoa drink powder
1 1/2 cups sugar
1/2 cup vegetable shortening
2 eggs
2 1/4 cups all-purpose flour
1/2 teaspoon salt
1 cup buttermilk
1 teaspoon baking soda
1 tablespoon vanilla extract
1 tablespoon vinegar
Creamy White Icing

Preheat oven to 350 degrees. Mix food coloring and cocoa drink powder in small bowl; set aside. Do not use mixer to mix cake. Cream sugar, shortening and eggs in large bowl. Stir in cocoa mixture; beat well. Mix buttermilk and baking soda together in medium bowl. Add flour and salt; mix. Add to creamed mixture. Fold in vanilla and vinegar. Pour into 2 greased and floured 8-inch cake pans. Bake for 35 minutes. Let cool. Slice each layer in half to make 4 layers. Frost cake with Creamy White Icing. Yield: 12 to 16 servings.

CREAMY WHITE ICING

1 cup milk
5 tablespoons all-purpose flour
1 1/2 cups sugar
3/4 cup margarine
4 1/2 tablespoons vegetable shortening
3 teaspoons vanilla extract

Combine milk and flour in saucepan. Cook over low heat until of paste consistency. Remove from heat. Chill overnight. Cream sugar, margarine, shortening, sugar and vanilla in mixer bowl. Add flour mixture. Beat until consistency of whipped cream. Yield: 2 to 3 cups.

Stephanie Small, Chi Psi
Marseilles, Illinois

GRANDMA'S RED VELVET CAKE

1 1/2 cups sugar
1/2 cup vegetable shortening
1 ounce red food coloring
1 ounce water
2 eggs
2 cups cake flour
1 tablespoon baking cocoa
1/2 teaspoon salt
1 cup buttermilk
1 tablespoon vinegar
1 teaspoon baking soda
Fluffy White Icing
Coconut to taste

Preheat oven to 350 degrees. Cream sugar and shortening in bowl. Add food coloring and water. Add eggs, 1 at a time; mix well. Sift flour, cocoa and salt together into bowl. Add to creamed mixture alternately with buttermilk. Mix vinegar and baking soda in small bowl. Fold into batter. Pour into 2 greased and floured 9-inch cake pans. Bake for 25 minutes. Let cool. Frost with Fluffy White Icing. Sprinkle with coconut. Yield: 12 servings.

FLUFFY WHITE ICING

1/4 cup all-purpose flour
1 cup milk
Dash of salt
1 cup sugar
1 cup vegetable shortening

Combine flour, milk and salt in saucepan. Cook until fluffy. Let cool. Combine flour mixture, sugar and shortening in mixer bowl. Beat until fluffy. Yield: 2 to 3 cups.

Teresa Sickels
St. Peters, Missouri

THE WALDORF ASTORIA RED CAKE

1/2 cup margarine
1 1/2 cups sugar
2 eggs
1 1/2 ounces red food coloring
1/4 cup baking cocoa
2 1/2 cups cake flour
1 teaspoon salt
1 1/2 teaspoons baking soda
1 cup buttermilk
1 teaspoon vanilla extract
Fluffy Butter Icing

Preheat oven to 350 degrees. Cream margarine and sugar in mixer bowl. Add eggs; mix well. Mix food coloring and cocoa in bowl. Add to creamed mixture. Sift flour, salt and baking soda together into bowl. Add to creamed mixture alternately with buttermilk; do not beat. Fold in vanilla. Pour into 2 greased and floured 9-inch cake pans. Bake for 30 to 35 minutes. Let cool. Frost with Fluffy Butter Icing. Yield: 12 servings.

FLUFFY BUTTER ICING

3 tablespoons (heaping) all-purpose flour
1 cup milk
1 cup sugar
1 cup butter
1 teaspoon vanilla extract

Mix flour and milk in saucepan. Cook over low heat until slightly clear. Let cool. Cream sugar and butter in mixer bowl. Add vanilla. Add flour mixture. Beat until fluffy. Yield: 3 cups.

Sharon Mashek, Beta Delta
Spillville, Iowa

DOUBLE CHOCOLATE-RUM CAKE

1 (2-layer) package chocolate cake mix
1 package chocolate instant pudding mix
4 eggs
1 cup Bacardi dark rum
3/4 cup water
1/2 cup vegetable oil
1 (12-ounce) package semisweet chocolate morsels
1 cup raspberry preserves
2 tablespoons vegetable shortening
1 (1-ounce) baking white chocolate bar
1 teaspoon water

Preheat oven to 350 degrees. Combine cake mix, pudding mix, eggs, 1/2 cup rum, 3/4 cup water and oil in large mixer bowl. Beat at low speed until moistened. Beat at medium speed for 2 minutes. Stir in 1 cup chocolate morsels. Pour batter into greased 12-cup bundt pan. Bake for 50 minutes to 1 hour or until cake tests done. Let cool in pan for 15 minutes. Remove from pan. Let cool on wire rack. Heat raspberry preserves and 1/2 cup rum in small saucepan. Strain through sieve to remove seeds. Place cake on serving plate. Prick surface of cake with fork. Brush raspberry glaze evenly over cake, allowing cake to absorb glaze. Repeat until all glaze has been absorbed. Combine 1 cup chocolate pieces and shortening in microwave-safe bowl. Microwave on High for 1 minute or until melted. Stir until smooth. Spoon chocolate icing over cake. Let stand for 10 minutes. Combine white chocolate and 1 teaspoon water in small microwave-safe bowl. Microwave on High for 30 seconds or until melted. Drizzle over icing. Yield: 16 servings.

Darlene Morris, Laureate Alpha Delta
Columbus, Kansas

GRANDMOTHER'S CHOCOLATE SHEET CAKE

2 cups sugar
2 cups all-purpose flour
1 teaspoon baking soda
1 cup margarine
1/4 cup baking cocoa
1 cup water
1/2 cup buttermilk
2 eggs
1 teaspoon vanilla extract
Creamy Chocolate-Pecan Icing

Preheat oven to 350 degrees. Sift sugar, flour and baking soda together into bowl. Combine 1 cup margarine, 1/4 cup baking cocoa and 1 cup water in saucepan. Bring to a boil. Pour over dry ingredients; mix well. Add buttermilk, eggs and vanilla, mixing well after each addition. Pour into 10-by-15-inch baking pan. Bake for 15 to 20 minutes or until cake tests done. Spread Creamy Chocolate-Pecan Icing over warm cake. Yield: 12 servings.

CREAMY CHOCOLATE-PECAN ICING

1/2 cup margarine
1/4 cup baking cocoa
1/3 cup buttermilk
1 (16-ounce) package confectioners' sugar
1 teaspoon vanilla extract
1 cup chopped nuts

Combine margarine, cocoa and buttermilk in saucepan. Bring to a boil. Remove from heat. Add confectioners' sugar; beat well. Add vanilla and nuts; mix well. Yield: 2 to 3 cups.

Alison Sperry, Lambda Nu
Pattonsburg, Missouri

CHOCOLATE SHEATH CAKE

2 cups sugar
2 cups self-rising flour
1/4 teaspoon salt
1/2 cup margarine or butter
1/2 cup vegetable shortening
1/4 cup baking cocoa
1 cup water
1/2 cup buttermilk
2 eggs, slightly beaten
1 teaspoon baking soda
1 teaspoon cinnamon
1 teaspoon vanilla extract
Chocolate-Pecan Frosting

Preheat oven to 350 degrees. Sift together sugar, flour and salt into large bowl. Place margarine, shortening, cocoa and water in saucepan. Bring to a rapid boil. Pour over flour mixture; mix well. Add buttermilk, eggs, baking soda, cinnamon and vanilla, mixing well after each addition by hand. Batter will be thin. Pour into greased 11-by-16-inch baking pan. Bake for 40 minutes to 1 hour or until center springs back after touch of finger. Do not remove from pan. Spread Chocolate-Pecan Frosting over hot cake. Let cool. Yield: 12 servings.

CHOCOLATE-PECAN FROSTING

1/2 cup butter
1/4 cup cocoa
6 tablespoons milk
1 (16-ounce) package confectioners' sugar
1 teaspoon vanilla extract
1 cup chopped pecans

Combine butter, cocoa and milk in saucepan. Bring to a rapid boil. Remove from heat. Add confectioners' sugar, vanilla and pecans; beat well. Yield: 2 to 3 cups.

Sheryl A. Porter, Preceptor Zeta
Jacksonville, Alabama

SNICKER BAR CAKE

1 (2-layer) package German chocolate cake mix
30 caramels
1/2 cup margarine
1 tablespoon milk
3/4 cup chocolate chips
1 cup chopped nuts
Ice cream or whipped cream

Preheat oven to 350 degrees. Mix cake mix according to package directions. Pour half the batter into greased 9-by-13-inch baking pan. Bake for 20 minutes. Melt caramels with margarine and milk in saucepan over low heat; mix well. Pour over cake. Spread chocolate chips over caramel. Sprinkle with nuts. Spread remaining batter over mixture. Bake for 10 to 20 minutes longer. Test with finger for doneness. Serve with ice cream or whipped cream. Yield: 15 servings.

Mylo Unruh, Preceptor Theta Sigma
Brackettville, Texas

TURTLE CAKE

1 (2-layer) German
  chocolate cake mix
1 (14-ounce) package
  caramels
3/4 cup butter
1 cup semisweet
  chocolate chips
1/2 cup evaporated
  milk
1/2 cup chopped nuts

Preheat oven to 350 degrees. Mix cake mix according to package directions. Pour half the batter into ungreased 9-by-13-inch baking pan. Bake for 15 minutes. Melt caramels and butter in saucepan over low heat. Add evaporated milk; blend well. Pour over partially baked cake. Sprinkle with chocolate chips. Pour remaining batter over top. Sprinkle with nuts. Bake for 20 minutes longer. Yield: 12 servings.

Shirley Morrison, Alpha Delta Lambda
Cameron, Missouri

TURTLE CAKE
WITH CHOCOLATE FUDGE FROSTING

1 (2-layer) package
  German or Swiss
  chocolate cake mix
1 (14-ounce) package
  caramels
1/2 cup butter
1 cup chocolate chips
1 cup chopped pecans
  or walnuts
Chocolate Fudge Icing

Preheat oven to 375 degrees. Mix cake mix according to package directions. Pour half the batter into lightly greased and floured 9-by-13-inch baking pan. Bake for 15 minutes. Melt caramels and butter in saucepan over low heat; mix well. Pour caramel mixture over partially baked cake. Sprinkle with chocolate chips and pecans. Pour remaining batter over top. Bake for 20 minutes longer. Pour Chocolate Fudge Icing over warm cake in pan. Let cool thoroughly. Yield: 10 servings.

CHOCOLATE FUDGE ICING

2 tablespoons (heaping)
  cornstarch
1/4 cup cold water
1/2 cup butter
3/4 cup sugar
2 tablespoons baking
  cocoa
3/4 cup boiling water
1/2 teaspoon vanilla
  extract

Dissolve cornstarch in cold water in small saucepan. Add butter, sugar, cocoa, boiling water and vanilla; mix well. Cook, stirring, over medium-low heat until thickened. Yield: 1 to 2 cups.

Audrey Casey, Gamma Pi
Paris, Ontario, Canada

Cindi Burgess, Zeta Gamma, Farmington, New Mexico, makes a Heath Bar Cake by mixing and baking 1 (2-layer) chocolate cake mix according to package directions for 9-by-13-inch cake. Make holes in cake using fork. Let cool partially. Pour 1 (14-ounce) can sweetened condensed milk over cake. Let cool completely. Spread with whipped topping. Sprinkle crushed Heath candy bars over topping. Refrigerate. Serve cold.

WACKY CAKE

This is a very moist chocolaty tasting cake.

1 1/2 cups all-purpose
  flour
1 cup sugar
3 tablespoons baking
  cocoa
1 teaspoon baking
  soda
1/2 teaspoon salt
6 tablespoons
  vegetable oil
1 tablespoon (scant)
  vinegar
1 teaspoon vanilla
  extract
1 cup water
Confectioners' sugar

Preheat oven to 350 degrees. Mix flour, sugar, baking cocoa, baking soda and salt together in ungreased 8-inch baking pan. Punch 1 small hole, 1 medium hole and 1 large hole in dry ingredients. Pour oil in largest hole, vinegar in medium hole and vanilla in smallest hole. Cover with water. Mix with fork. Bake for 25 minutes. Frost or sprinkle with confectioners' sugar. Yield: 9 servings.

Patricia Premo, Laureate Alpha Delta
Saginaw, Michigan

WONDERFUL CHOCOLATE CAKE

1/2 cup buttermilk
1 teaspoon baking
  soda
2 cups all-purpose
  flour
2 cups sugar
1 cup water
1/4 cup vegetable
  shortening
1/2 cup margarine
1/4 cup baking cocoa
2 eggs
1 teaspoon vanilla
  extract
1 teaspoon cinnamon
Wonderful Chocolate
  Icing
1 cup chopped nuts

Preheat oven to 400 degrees. Mix buttermilk and baking soda in cup. Mix flour and sugar in mixer bowl. Combine water, shortening, margarine and cocoa in saucepan. Bring to a boil over medium-low heat. Add hot mixture to flour mixture in bowl. Add 1 egg at a time, beating after each addition. Add buttermilk mixture; mix well. Add vanilla and cinnamon; beat well. Pour into greased and floured 11-by-15-inch baking pan. Batter will be thin. Bake for 20 minutes or until cake tests done. Spread Wonderful Chocolate Icing over hot cake. Sprinkle with nuts. Yield: 12 to 15 servings.

WONDERFUL CHOCOLATE ICING

1/2 cup margarine
1/4 cup baking cocoa
1 (16-ounce) package
  confectioners' sugar
4 to 6 tablespoons milk
1 teaspoon vanilla
  extract

Melt margarine with cocoa in saucepan over low heat. Remove from heat. Add confectioners' sugar, milk and vanilla. Beat until smooth. Yield: 2 cups.

Claudine R. Carson, Xi Sigma Mu
Sierra Blanca, Texas

158 / Cakes

CHRISTMAS WELCOME CAKE

1 package chopped dates
1 teaspoon baking soda
1 cup hot water
1 cup margarine
1 cup sugar
2 eggs, beaten
1 3/4 cups all-purpose flour
Pinch of salt
2 tablespoons baking cocoa
1 teaspoon vanilla extract
1 (12-ounce) package chocolate chips
1 cup chopped pecans
Whipped topping (optional)

Preheat oven to 350 degrees. Combine dates, baking soda and hot water in saucepan. Heat to boiling point; remove from heat. Cream margarine and sugar in mixer bowl. Add eggs; blend well. Mix flour, salt and cocoa in bowl. Combine date mixture, sugar mixture and flour mixture in large mixer bowl; blend well. Stir in vanilla. Pour into greased and floured 9-by-13-inch baking pan. Sprinkle 1/2 the chocolate chips over batter. Bake for 5 minutes. Sprinkle with remaining chocolate chips and pecans. Bake for 25 to 30 minutes or until tests done. Cut into squares. Serve plain or with whipped topping. Yield: 20 servings.

Laura Leigh Wilkinson, Laureate Pi
Double Oak, Texas

COCONUT CAKE

1 (2-layer) package yellow cake mix
1 package vanilla instant pudding mix
1 1/2 cups water
4 eggs
1/4 cup vegetable oil
2 1/4 cups coconut
1 cup chopped walnuts or pecans
Coconut Cream Cheese Frosting

Preheat oven to 350 degrees. Combine cake mix, pudding mix, water, eggs and oil in large mixer bowl. Beat at medium speed for 4 minutes. Stir in 2 cups coconut and walnuts. Pour into 3 greased and floured 9-inch cake pans. Bake for 35 minutes or until cakes test done. Let cool for 15 minutes. Remove from pans. Let cool on wire rack. Frost with Coconut Cream Cheese Icing. Sprinkle remaining coconut on top. Yield: 12 servings.

COCONUT-CREAM CHEESE ICING

4 tablespoons margarine
1 3/4 cups coconut
8 ounces cream cheese, softened
2 teaspoons milk
3 1/2 cups confectioners' sugar
1/2 teaspoon vanilla extract

Melt 2 tablespoons margarine in skillet. Add coconut. Cook, stirring constantly, over low heat until golden brown. Spread coconut on absorbent paper to cool. Cream 2 tablespoons margarine with cream cheese in mixer bowl. Add milk. Beat in sugar gradually. Blend in vanilla. Stir in coconut. Yield: 3 to 4 cups.

Marilyn Shrader, Xi Lambda Pi
Quincy, Illinois

COCONUT SHEET CAKE

1 (2-layer) package yellow cake mix
1 teaspoon coconut flavoring
2/3 cup evaporated milk
1/2 cup sugar
1 (12-ounce) carton whipped topping
1 (8-ounce) package frozen coconut

Mix and bake cake according to package directions for 9-by-13-inch cake, adding coconut flavoring. Let cool. Combine evaporated milk and sugar in saucepan. Bring to a boil over medium-low heat. Remove from heat. Punch holes in cake. Pour hot mixture over cake. Let cool. Spread whipped topping over cake. Sprinkle with coconut. Refrigerate overnight. Yield: 12 servings.

Ann Southerland, Preceptor Beta Zeta
Greensboro, North Carolina

FLUFFY COCONUT CAKE

1 (2-layer) package white cake mix
1 1/4 cups water
1/4 cup vegetable oil
2 eggs
1 can cream of coconut
1 (16-ounce) carton whipped topping
1 (7-ounce) package flake coconut

Preheat oven to 350 degrees. Mix cake according to package directions, using water, oil and eggs. Pour into greased and floured 9-by-13-inch baking pan. Bake for 35 minutes or until cake tests done. Do not remove from pan. Punch several holes in top of cake with fork. Pour cream of coconut over hot cake. Let cool. Spread with whipped topping. Sprinkle with coconut. Refrigerate. Yield: 20 servings.

Kitty Waddell, Gamma Masters
Vero Beach, Florida

EXQUISITE COCONUT CREAM CAKE

1 (2-layer) package white cake mix
4 egg whites
1/2 cup vegetable oil
1 cup sour cream
1 (14-ounce) can sweetened condensed milk
2 cups sugar
2 cups sour cream
1 (12-ounce) package coconut
1 (16-ounce) carton frozen whipped topping, thawed

Preheat oven to 350 degrees. Combine cake mix, egg whites, oil, 1 cup sour cream and condensed milk in mixer bowl. Beat at medium speed for 2 to 3 minutes. Pour into 3 greased and floured cake pans, dividing equally. Bake for 20 minutes or until cakes test done. Let cool on wire rack. Combine sugar and 2 cups sour cream in bowl. Stir until sugar is dissolved. Add coconut and whipped topping; mix well. Frost cake, spreading generous amount between layers. Refrigerate overnight. Store in refrigerator. Yield: 12 servings.

Martie Nickerson, Preceptor Sigma
Victor, Montana

CRANBERRY SAUCE CAKE

This very moist cake comes from Indiana and is beautiful when sliced.

3 cups all-purpose flour	1 teaspoon salt
1 1/2 cups sugar	1 teaspoon orange extract
1 cup mayonnaise	1 cup chopped walnuts
1 (16-ounce) can whole cranberry sauce	Nonstick vegetable cooking spray
1/3 cup orange juice	1 cup confectioners' sugar
1 tablespoon grated orange rind	1 to 2 tablespoons orange juice
1 teaspoon baking soda	

Preheat oven to 350 degrees. Combine flour, sugar, mayonnaise, cranberry sauce, 1/3 cup orange juice, orange rind, baking soda, salt and orange extract in mixer bowl; mix well. Fold in walnuts. Line bottom of 10-inch tube pan with waxed paper. Coat tube pan and waxed paper with cooking spray. Pour batter into prepared pan. Bake for 1 hour to 1 hour and 10 minutes or until cake tests done. Let cool in pan for 10 minutes. Combine confectioners' sugar and 1 to 2 tablespoons orange juice in mixer bowl; mix well. Drizzle icing over warm cake. Yield: 12 to 16 servings.

Betty J. Miller, Laureate Alpha Epsilon
Tucson, Arizona

CRATER CAKE

1 cup margarine	2 teaspoons baking powder
2 cups sugar	2 teaspoons baking soda
2 eggs, beaten	1 teaspoon cinnamon
1 teaspoon vanilla extract	1/2 cup packed dark brown sugar
3 ripe bananas, cut up	1 1/2 cups chocolate chips
1 cup sour cream	
3 cups all-purpose flour	

Preheat oven to 350 degrees. Combine margarine, sugar, eggs and vanilla in mixer bowl; mix well. Add bananas and sour cream; mix well. Add flour, baking powder and baking soda; mix well. Combine cinnamon, brown sugar and chocolate chips in bowl. Pour half the batter into greased and floured 8-by-12-inch baking pan. Sprinkle with half the chocolate chips mixture. Pour remaining batter over mixture. Sprinkle with remaining chocolate chips mixture. Bake for 45 minutes. Yield: 12 servings.

Shauna Mackay, Gamma Omega
Courtenay, British Columbia, Canada

CRUNCH CAKE

1 (21-ounce) can cherry pie filling	1 cup melted butter
1 small can crushed pineapple	1 cup coconut
	3/4 cup chopped nuts
1 (2-layer) package yellow cake mix	Whipped topping or ice cream

Preheat oven to 350 degrees. Spread pie filling evenly over bottom of buttered 9-by-13-inch glass baking dish. Spoon pineapple with juice evenly over pie filing. Sprinkle dry cake mix evenly over pineapple. Drizzle melted butter over cake mix. Sprinkle coconut and nuts on top. Bake for 45 minutes or until golden brown. Serve plain or with whipped topping. Yield: 10 servings.

Carol Jean Moyer, Delta Sigma Preceptor
Waverly, Missouri

EARTHQUAKE CAKE

The cream cheese mixture on top of this cake forms "craters" much like those caused by an earthquake.

1 cup coconut	1/2 cup margarine
1 cup chopped pecans	8 ounces cream cheese, softened
1 (2-layer) package German chocolate cake mix	1 (16-ounce) package confectioners' sugar

Preheat oven to 350 degrees. Spread coconut and pecans on bottom of greased 9-by-13-inch baking pan. Prepare cake mix according to package directions. Pour over coconut and pecans. Melt margarine and cream cheese in saucepan over very low heat. Add confectiners' sugar; mix well. Drop mixture by spoonfuls on top of cake. Bake for 45 minutes. Yield: 24 servings.

Valerie Dahlke, Xi Upsilon
Wichita, Kansas

♥ CAKE WITH FRUIT

3/4 can frozen concentrated apple juice	2 small unpeeled apples, cored, chopped
2 cups all-purpose flour	1 teaspoon vanilla extract
2 eggs, slightly beaten	No-fat ice cream (optional)
2 teaspoons baking soda	
1 (20-ounce) can unsweetened pineapple with juice	

Preheat oven to 350 degrees. Combine apple juice, flour, eggs, baking soda, pineapple, apples and vanilla in large bowl. Stir with spoon until well mixed. Do not use mixer. Pour into 9-by-13-inch baking pan coated with nonstick vegetable cooking spray. Bake for 35 minutes. Serve with ice cream. Yield: 10 to 12 servings.

Marlynne Snare, Xi Iota Sigma
Garden City, Missouri

160 / Cakes

♥ ALL-SEASON FRUIT CAKE

We have a Western Sizzler and I fix this cake for special occasions for customers, using sparklers instead of candles. I use strawberries in May, peaches in July, lemons and oranges in the winter months and cherries for Christmas. It is a wonderful secret sister cake.

1 (2-layer) package butter golden cake mix	1 package vanilla instant pudding mix
1 cup sugar	1/4 cup confectioners' sugar
3 tablespoons cornstarch	1 cup milk
1 cup water	1 (8-ounce) container whipped topping
3 tablespoons favorite gelatin	Fresh fruit in season

Prepare and bake cake according to package directions for 9-inch layer cake. Let cool. Place sugar, cornstarch and water in saucepan. Cook over medium heat, stirring constantly, until thickened. Let cool. Add gelatin; mix well. Spread layer of filling and fresh fruit between layers. Combine pudding mix, confectioners' sugar and milk in bowl; mix well. Fold in whipped topping. Spread on top and side of cake. Top with fresh fruit. Yield: 12 servings.

Loma Sexton, Xi Gamma Omicron
Clarksville, Arkansas

FRUIT COCKTAIL CAKE

2 cups all-purpose flour	1/2 cup margarine
1 1/2 cups sugar	1 cup sugar
1/4 teaspoon salt	1 cup evaporated milk
2 teaspoons baking soda	1 teaspoon vanilla extract
2 eggs, slightly beaten	1 cup coconut
1 (14-ounce) can fruit cocktail	1 cup chopped nuts
1/2 cup packed dark brown sugar	

Preheat oven to 350 degrees. Mix flour, 1 1/2 cups sugar, salt and baking soda in bowl. Stir in eggs and fruit cocktail; mix well. Pour into greased and floured 9-by-13-inch baking pan. Sprinkle brown sugar over top. Bake for 45 minutes or until cake tests done. Combine margarine, 1 cup sugar and evaporated milk in saucepan. Bring to a boil over medium-low heat. Boil for 5 minutes. Remove from heat. Beat until slightly thickened. Add vanilla, coconut and nuts; mix well. Spread over warm cake. Yield: 12 servings.

Penny Pangborn, Beta Sigma Phi
Tuscola, Illinois

♥ FAST FIXIN' FRUITCAKE

This is great served with coffee after chapter meetings.

1/4 cup vegetable oil	1/2 cup water
1 (2-layer) package lite white cake mix	1 (21-ounce) can lite cherry pie filling
2 eggs	

Preheat oven to 350 degrees. Pour oil into 9-by-13-inch baking pan. Tilt to cover bottom of pan. Place cake mix, eggs and water into baking pan. Stir with fork until blended. Spoon pie filling over mixture. Create marbled effect using fork. Bake for 40 to 50 minutes or until toothpick inserted in center comes out clean.
Yield: 12 to 15 servings.

Rose N. Czap, Delta Beta
South Williamsport, Pennsylvania

BRAZIL NUT FRUITCAKE

This cake is made with nuts and cherries instead of candied fruits. Nuts are easier to shell if they are put in freezer overnight.

3/4 cup all-purpose flour	2 (8-ounce) packages whole dates
3/4 cup sugar	1 cup maraschino cherries
1/2 teaspoon baking powder	3 eggs
1/2 teaspoon salt	1 teaspoon vanilla extract
3 cups whole Brazil nuts	

Preheat oven to 300 degrees. Sift flour, sugar, baking powder and salt together in bowl. Place Brazil nuts, dates and cherries in large bowl. Sift flour mixture over fruit; mix well with hands. Beat eggs well in bowl. Add vanilla. Add to fruit mixture; mix well. Grease and line two 5-by-9-inch baking pans with waxed paper. Pour batter into prepared pans. Bake for 1 hour and 45 minutes. Let cool for 15 minutes in pans. Let cool completely on wire rack. Yield: 12 to 16 servings.

Marilynn J. Jossy, Laureate Epsilon Tau
Thousand Oaks, California

MEXICAN FRUITCAKE

1 (20-ounce) can crushed pineapple with juice	1 cup chopped pecans
2 cups sugar	8 ounces cream cheese, softened
2 teaspoons baking soda	1/2 cup butter
2 cups all-purpose flour	2 cups confectioners' sugar
2 eggs, slightly beaten	1 teaspoon vanilla extract

Preheat oven to 350 degrees. Place pineapple in large bowl. Add sugar, baking soda, flour and eggs; mix well. Fold in pecans. Pour into greased and floured 9-by-13-inch baking pan. Bake for 45 minutes. Blend cream cheese and butter in mixer bowl. Add confectioners' sugar and vanilla. Beat until creamy and of spreading consistency. Spread over hot cake. Yield: 12 servings.

Peggy C. Sawyer, Xi Alpha Tau
Morristown, Tennessee

PEACH FRUITCAKE

1 cup butter
1 1/2 cups sugar
3 eggs, well beaten
1 (20-ounce) can peaches, drained, crushed
3 cups sultana raisins
1 1/2 cups chopped maraschino cherries
1 cup coconut
3 cups all-purpose flour
1 teaspoon baking powder
1/2 teaspoon salt
2 teaspoons vanilla extract

Preheat oven to 275 degrees. Cream butter and sugar in mixer bowl. Add eggs. Blend in peaches, raisins, cherries and coconut; mix well. Sift dry ingredients into bowl. Add to fruit mixture; mix well. Add vanilla. Add small amount of peach juice if batter is dry. Pour into greased and waxed paper lined 9-inch square baking pan. Bake for 3 hours. Let cool on wire rack. Yield: 8 servings.

Marie Newville, Tau
Happy Valley, Labrador

APPLE GINGERBREAD

This is a special Nova Scotia recipe that has been in my family for over 100 years. It is great on a cold winter night.

1/2 cup water
1/2 cup packed dark brown sugar
3 large apples, peeled, thinly sliced
2 eggs, beaten
1/2 cup sour milk
1/2 cup molasses
1/4 cup packed dark brown sugar
1 1/2 cups all-purpose flour
1 teaspoon baking soda
1 teaspoon ginger
1/4 teaspoon salt
1/2 cup melted butter or margarine
1/2 cup packed dark brown sugar
2 tablespoons cornstarch
2 cups boiling water
2 teaspoons vanilla extract
2 tablespoons butter

Preheat oven to 350 degrees. Combine 1/2 cup water and 1/2 cup brown sugar in 9-inch square baking pan. Add apples. Cook for 10 minutes. Beat eggs in large bowl. Add sour milk, molasses and 1/4 cup brown sugar; mix well. Combine flour, baking soda, ginger and salt in bowl. Add to egg mixture; mix well. Add melted butter; mix well. Pour mixture over apples. Bake for 30 to 35 minutes or until cake tests done. Let cool. Combine 1/2 cup brown sugar and cornstarch in saucepan. Add boiling water. Boil, stirring constantly, until mixture is clear. Add vanilla and 2 tablespoons butter; mix well. Cut gingerbread into 9 servings. Serve with brown sugar sauce. Yield: 9 servings.

Sandra Amon, Preceptor Zeta
Truro, Nova Scotia, Canada

GUMDROP CAKE

This cake is a great substitute for holiday fruitcake.

2 cups butter
2 cups sugar
4 eggs
2 teaspoons vanilla extract
8 cups all-purpose flour
1/2 teaspoon ground cloves
1/2 teaspoon nutmeg
1 teaspoon salt
2 teaspoons cinnamon
2 tablespoons baking soda
2 tablespoons hot water
3 cups applesauce
2 pounds gumdrops with black and white gumdrops discarded
2 pounds raisins
2 cups chopped pecans

Preheat oven to 300 degrees. Cream butter and sugar in mixer bowl. Add eggs and vanilla; beat until smooth. Combine flour, cloves, nutmeg, salt and cinnamon in bowl. Add gradually to creamed mixture; beat until smooth. Dissolve baking soda in hot water in bowl. Add baking soda mixture and applesauce to batter. Fold in gumdrops, raisins and pecans. Divide batter evenly among 4 greased and floured loaf pans. Bake for 3 hours. Let cool on wire rack. Yield: 20 servings.

Kimberly Barnes, Iota Theta
Duncan, Oklahoma

ALL-OCCASION GUMDROP CAKE

8 ounces white or golden raisins
16 ounces cooking gumdrops, cut in half
8 ounces slivered almonds or chopped pecans (optional)
8 ounces glazed red cherries, cut in half
8 ounces glazed green cherries, cut in half
8 ounces glazed mixed fruit and peel, cut into small pieces
1 cup all-purpose flour
1 cup butter
1 cup sugar
4 eggs
1 teaspoon baking powder
1/2 teaspoon salt
1/2 teaspoon cinnamon or nutmeg
1 cup milk
1 teaspoon vanilla or almond extract
2 cups all-purpose flour

Place raisins in bowl. Cover with hot water. Let stand for 1 hour; pat dry. Combine raisins, gumdrops, almonds, cherries and mixed fruit in large bowl. Add 1 cup flour, mixing to coat. Let stand overnight. Preheat oven to 300 degrees. Cream butter and sugar in mixer bowl. Add eggs, 1 at a time, mixing after each addition. Add baking powder, salt and cinnamon; mix well. Add milk and vanilla; mix well. Add flour; mix well. Fold in flour-coated raisins, gumdrops, almonds, cherries and mixed fruit with flour. Stir until mixed. Pour into 2 loaf pans lined with waxed paper. Bake for 1 hour and 45 minutes to 2 hours. Yield: 20 servings.

Bernice Manuel, Laureate Beta Gamma
Sudbury, Ontario, Canada

HAWAIIAN CAKE

This is a good cake to use when serving large groups.

1 (2-layer) package white cake mix	1 (15-ounce) can crushed pineapple, well drained
8 ounces cream cheese, softened	1 large container whipped topping
2½ cups milk	Shredded coconut
1 large package vanilla instant pudding mix	

Preheat oven to 350 degrees. Prepare cake mix according to package directions. Pour into greased and floured 9-by-13-inch baking pan. Bake for 20 minutes or until cake tests done. Combine cream cheese with small amount of milk in mixer bowl; mix well. Add remaining milk and pudding mix; mix well. Spread on cooled cake. Spoon pineapple evenly over mixture. Top with whipped topping. Sprinkle with coconut. Yield: 24 servings.

Peggy Moore, Laureate Xi
Belle Fourche, South Dakota

ITALIAN LOVE CAKE

Chapter members are always requesting this scrumptious cake for dessert. Even the husbands enjoy it at our parties!

2 pounds ricotta cheese	1 (2-layer) package marble cake mix
4 eggs	1 (12-ounce) carton whipped topping
¼ cup sugar	1 package chocolate instant pudding mix
2 teaspoons vanilla extract	

Preheat oven to 350 degrees. Beat cheese, eggs, sugar and vanilla in mixer bowl until smooth. Prepare cake mix according to package directions. Pour into greased 9-by-15-inch baking pan. Drizzle ricotta mixture over batter. Bake for 45 to 55 minutes or until cake tests done. Let cool. Combine whipped topping and pudding mix in bowl; mix well. Spread over cake. Refrigerate. Yield: 15 servings.

Barbara Kennedy, Preceptor Eta Omega
Fort Pierce, Florida

Kristi Hirzel, Nu Kappa, Guthrie, Oklahoma, makes a Dump Cake by dumping 1 (21-ounce) can cherry pie filling into greased 9-by-13-inch baking pan; spread evenly. Dump 1 (15-ounce) can crushed pineapple, drained, over pie filling; spread evenly. Shake 1 (2-layer) package yellow cake mix evenly over pineapple. Drizzle ¼ cup melted butter over cake mix. Bake in preheated 350-degree oven for 30 minutes. Sprinkle 1½ cups coconut evenly over top of cake. Bake for 10 minutes longer. Let cool. Serve with whipped topping. Yield: 12 to 15 servings.

ITALIAN CREAM CAKE

This cake is very moist and rich and will stay fresh for several days. I was served this cake on my sixteenth birthday. The taste was such a memorable one for such a memorable day.

½ cup margarine	1 teaspoon vanilla extract
½ cup vegetable shortening	1 cup coconut
2 cups sugar	1 cup chopped pecans
5 egg yolks	5 egg whites, stiffly beaten
1 teaspoon baking soda	Cream Cheese Icing WithNuts
1 cup buttermilk	
2 cups cake flour	

Preheat oven to 325 to 350 degrees. Cream margarine and shortening in mixer bowl. Add sugar gradually, cream well. Add egg yolks; beat well. Mix soda and buttermilk in small bowl. Add buttermilk mixture and flour alternately to creamed mixture, beating slowly. Add vanilla. Add coconut and pecans. Fold in beaten egg whites. Pour into 3 greased and floured 9-inch cake pans. Bake for 40 minutes or until test done. Let cool on wire racks. Frost with Cream Cheese Icing With Nuts. Yield: 12 to 16 servings.

CREAM CHEESE ICING WITH NUTS

8 ounces cream cheese, softened	1 teaspoon vanilla extract
¼ cup margarine	1 cup chopped nuts
1 (16-ounce) package confectioners' sugar	

Combine cream cheese, margarine, confectioners' sugar and vanilla in mixer bowl. Beat until creamy. Add nuts; mix well. Yield: 2 to 3 cups.

Peggy Tillery, Xi Epsilon Omega
Laverne, Oklahoma

SIMPLY DELICIOUS LEMON ANGEL FOOD CAKE

1 large baked angel food cake	½ cup lemon juice
1 (14-ounce) can sweetened condensed milk	1 cup whipping cream

Slice angel food cake in half horizontally. Pinch out tunnel in bottom half. Mix condensed milk and lemon juice in bowl. Let stand for 30 minutes. Whip cream in mixer bowl until stiff. Add lemon juice mixture; mix well. Pour some of mixture into tunnel of cake. Replace top half of cake. Frost cake with remaining mixture. Chill until ready to serve. Yield: 12 servings.

Eddie McCullin, Laureate Beta Phi
Longview, Texas

LEMON REFRIGERATOR CAKE

2 tablespoons gelatin	2 tablespoons grated
1/2 cup cold water	lemon rind
8 egg yolks	8 egg whites
1 cup fresh lemon	2 packages ladyfinger
juice	cookies
1 teaspoon salt	1 cup whipping cream
2 cups sugar	1/4 cup sugar

Soften gelatin in 1/2 cup cold water. Combine egg yolks, lemon juice, salt and 1 cup sugar in double boiler. Cook for 5 to 10 minutes or until mixture coats back of spoon. Remove from heat. Add gelatin and grated rind, stirring until gelatin is dissolved. Let cool. Beat egg whites in mixer bowl until stiff. Beat in 1 cup sugar gradually. Fold lemon mixture into egg white mixture. Beat whipping cream in mixer bowl at high speed until thick. Add 1/4 cup sugar; mix well. Fold into egg white mixture. Split ladyfingers. Line bottom and sides of buttered 9-by-13-inch pan with ladyfingers. Pour mixture into lined pan. Chill for 4 hours. Yield: 12 servings.

Merry Phillips, Alpha Chi Chi
Pleasanton, Texas

LUCKY LEMON CAKE

2 (3-ounce) packages	14 to 15 tablespoons
ladyfingers	lemon juice
2 (14-ounce) cans	8 egg whites
sweetened	1/4 teaspoon cream
condensed milk	of tartar
8 egg yolks	

Preheat oven to 375 degrees. Cover bottom of lightly greased 9-inch springform pan with ladyfingers. Cut ladyfingers so when placed around edge of pan they are even with top of side of pan. Combine condensed milk, egg yolks and lemon juice in large mixer bowl; mix well. Beat egg whites with cream of tartar in medium mixer bowl until stiff. Fold into lemon mixture. Pour into prepared pan. Bake for 25 minutes or until top is lightly browned. Let cool thoroughly. Cover with foil; freeze up to 3 months. Yield: 12 servings.

Corinne Trefz, Omega Upsilon
Alford, Florida

SPECIAL BIRTHDAY CAKE

1 baked angel food	2 tablespoons lemon
cake	juice
2 (6-ounce) packages	2 cups frozen whipped
sugar-free lemon	topping
gelatin	1 (8-ounce) container
3 1/2 cups boiling water	frozen whipped
1 (8-ounce) can crushed	topping, thawed
pineapple	Maraschino cherries

Tear angel food cake into bite-sized pieces. Place in tube cake pan without removable middle. Mix gelatin and water in bowl, stirring until gelatin is dissolved. Add pineapple and lemon juice. Let stand for 1 hour. Add 2 cups whipped topping; mix until melted. Pour over cake pieces. Chill overnight. Remove from pan. Frost with thawed whipped topping. Garnish with cherries. Yield: 12 servings.

Peggy Wallis, Laureate Delta
Pueblo, Colorado

ST. PATRICK'S DAY KEY LIME CAKE

3/4 cup vegetable oil	6 tablespoons
3/4 cup orange juice	confectioners' sugar
5 eggs	8 ounces cream cheese,
1 (3-ounce) package	softened
lime gelatin	1/4 cup butter
1 (2-layer) package	1 teaspoon vanilla
lemon cake mix	extract
1/4 cup Key lime or	1 (16-ounce) package
lemon juice	confectioners' sugar

Preheat oven to 350 degrees. Combine oil, orange juice, eggs, gelatin and cake mix in mixer bowl. Beat until smooth. Pour into greased 9-by-13-inch baking pan. Bake for 30 to 40 minutes or until cake tests done. Let cool slightly. Remove cake from pan. Pierce top of cake all over with toothpick. Combine lime juice and 6 tablespoons confectioners' sugar in mixer bowl. Drizzle over cake. Let cool completely. Combine remaining ingredients in mixer bowl; mix well. Frost cake. Yield: 12 to 15 servings.

Robyn Courtright, Preceptor Epsilon Phi
Homestead, Florida

♥ KEY LIME CAKE

1 (2-layer) package	1/2 cup water
lemon cake mix	1/2 cup vegetable oil
1 (3-ounce) package	1/2 cup Key lime juice
lemon instant	1 cup confectioners'
pudding mix	sugar
1 cup egg substitute	2 tablespoons Key lime
or 4 eggs	juice

Preheat oven to 350 degrees. Combine cake mix, pudding mix, egg substitute, water, oil and 1/2 cup Key lime juice in mixer bowl. Beat for 2 minutes at medium speed. Pour batter into greased and floured 9-by-13-inch baking pan. Bake for 35 minutes or until wooden pick inserted in center comes out clean. Let cake cool in pan on wire rack. Combine remaining ingredients in mixer bowl, adding additional juice if needed. Drizzle over cake. Cut into squares. Yield: 15 to 18 servings.

Trevetta Wunderlin, Preceptor Iota
Lutz, Florida

MOIST 'N NUTTY CAKE

1 (20-ounce) can crushed pineapple with juice
2 cups all-purpose flour
2 teaspoons baking soda
2 cups sugar
2 eggs
1 1/2 cups chopped pecans
8 ounces cream cheese, softened
2 cups confectioners' sugar
1 teaspoon vanilla extract
1/2 cup melted margarine

Preheat oven to 350 degrees. Combine pineapple, flour, baking soda, sugar and eggs in large bowl; mix well by hand. Fold in 1 cup pecans. Pour into greased 9-by-13-inch baking pan. Bake for 45 minutes. Place cream cheese in mixer bowl; mix until smooth. Add confectioners' sugar and vanilla; mix well. Add melted margarine gradually; mix until creamy. Spread over cake. Sprinkle 1/2 cup pecans over top. Yield: 12 servings.

Carol Brinkman, Theta Nu
Batesville, Indiana

MOON CAKE

The surface of this cake looks like the moon's surface.

1 cup water
1/2 cup margarine
1 cup all-purpose flour
4 eggs
2 small packages vanilla instant pudding mix
8 ounces cream cheese, softened
1 (8-ounce) container whipped topping
Chocolate sauce to taste
1 cup chopped nuts

Preheat oven to 400 degrees. Mix water and margarine in saucepan. Bring to a boil. Add flour all at once, stirring rapidly until mixture forms a ball. Remove from heat. Let cool. Place in mixer bowl. Beat in eggs, 1 at a time. Spread mixture in ungreased 11-by-15-inch baking pan. Bake for 30 minutes. Let cool. Do not prick surface of cake. Mix pudding mix according to package directions. Beat in cream cheese; blend well. Spread on crust. Refrigerate for 20 minutes. Top with whipped topping. Drizzle with chocolate sauce. Sprinkle with nuts. Refrigerate. Yield: 12 to 15 servings.

Beth Egel, Alpha Chi
Algona, Iowa

OATMEAL CAKE

1/2 cup butter
1 cup quick oats
1 1/4 cups boiling water
1 1/3 cups all-purpose flour
1 cup sugar
2 cups packed dark brown sugar
2 eggs
1 teaspoon cinnamon
1 teaspoon vanilla extract
1 teaspoon baking soda
1 teaspoon salt
1 cup coconut
1/4 cup melted margarine
1/4 cup milk
1/4 cup chopped nuts

Preheat oven to 325 degrees. Combine butter, oats and water in large bowl; mix well. Let stand until cool. Add flour, sugar, 1 cup brown sugar, eggs, cinnamon, vanilla, baking soda and salt; mix well. Pour into greased and floured 9-by-13-inch baking pan. Bake for 40 minutes. Let cool for 5 minutes. Combine 1 cup brown sugar, coconut, margarine, milk and nuts in bowl; mix well. Sprinkle over cake. Broil until bubbly. Yield: 12 servings.

Marilyn Glenn, Preceptor Mu Kappa
Sanger, California

TRIPLE ORANGE JELLY ROLL

I make this at special times and always at Christmas. It is easy to double and freeze without the icing.

4 eggs
2/3 cup sugar
2 teaspoons vanilla extract
3 teaspoons grated orange rind
1/4 teaspoon salt
1 cup sifted all-purpose flour
3/4 cup confectioners' sugar
1/2 cup sugar
1/4 cup cornstarch
1 1/2 cups fresh orange juice
2 egg yolks
1 tablespoon butter
1 cup heavy cream
1/3 cup confectioners' sugar
2 tablespoons fresh orange juice
Thin orange slices
Lemon leaves

Preheat oven to 375 degrees. Grease 10-by-15-inch cookie sheet. Line with waxed paper; grease paper. Combine eggs, 2/3 cup sugar, vanilla, 1 teaspoon grated orange rind and salt in large mixer bowl. Beat at high speed for 3 minutes or until thick and lemon-colored. Sift flour over egg mixture. Fold in gently. Pour batter into prepared pan, spreading gently but evenly. Bake for 8 minutes or until cake springs back when lightly touched in center. Sprinkle 3/4 cup confectioners' sugar evenly over kitchen towel. Invert hot cake onto towel. Remove waxed paper gently. Roll up warm cake with towel, jelly roll fashion, beginning at long side. Place on wire rack to cool. Combine 1/2 cup sugar and cornstarch in medium saucepan. Stir in 1 1/2 cups orange juice until smooth. Bring to a boil over low heat, stirring constantly. Remove from heat. Add in egg yolks, 1 at a time, beating well after each addition. Stir in butter and 1 teaspoon orange rind. Let cool at room temperature, stirring occasionally. Unroll cooled cake gently. Spread evenly with filling. Reroll carefully. Place on serving plate. Refrigerate. Beat cream in mixer bowl at medium speed until soft peaks form. Beat 1/3 cup confectioners' sugar, 1 tablespoon at a time, until stiff. Fold in 2 tablespoons orange juice and 1 teaspoon grated orange rind. Swirl frosting over jelly roll. Garnish with orange slices and lemon leaves. Yield: 16 servings.

Cathy Burgess, Gamma Omega
Fanny Bay, British Columbia, Canada

FLUFFY ORANGE CAKE

1 (2-layer) package yellow cake mix
1 cup orange juice
3/4 cup mayonnaise-type salad dressing
3 eggs
1/4 cup poppy seeds (optional)
Confectioners' sugar

Preheat oven to 350 degrees. Combine cake mix, orange juice, salad dressing, eggs and poppy seeds in large mixer bowl; mix well. Beat at medium speed for 2 minutes. Pour into greased and floured 10-inch tube pan. Bake for 35 to 40 minutes. Let cool for 10 minutes. Remove from pan. Sprinkle with confectioners' sugar. Yield: 12 servings.

Barbara Ann Verble, Theta Phi
Cairo, Illinois

♥ LOW-FAT MANDARIN ORANGE CAKE

1 cup all-purpose flour
3/4 cup sugar
Dash of salt
1 teaspoon baking soda
1/4 cup chopped walnuts
1 egg
1 (11-ounce) can mandarin oranges with juice
12 ounces low-fat cream cheese, softened
2 tablespoons butter
2 to 4 tablespoons sugar

Preheat oven to 350 degrees. Combine flour, 3/4 cup sugar, salt, baking soda and walnuts in bowl. Add egg and oranges with juice. Beat well. Pour into greased 8-inch square baking pan. Bake for 35 to 40 minutes or until toothpick inserted in cake comes out clean. Let cool. Beat cream cheese and butter in mixer bowl until smooth. Beat in sugar to taste. Frost cake. Yield: 8 servings.

Elsie Dereniwski, Chi
Strathclair, Manitoba, Canada

ORANGE-LEMON CAKE

1 (2-layer) package lemon cake mix
1 (3-ounce) package lemon instant pudding mix
4 eggs
1/2 cup vegetable oil
1 3/4 cups water
2 cups sifted confectioners' sugar
2 tablespoons vegetable oil
1/3 cup orange juice concentrate
2 tablespoons warm water

Preheat oven to 325 degrees. Combine cake mix, pudding mix, eggs, oil and 1 3/4 cups water in mixer bowl; mix well. Pour into foil-lined 9-by-13-inch baking pan. Bake for 45 minutes or until cake tests done. Pierce top of warm cake all over with toothpick. Combine remaining ingredients in mixer bowl; mix well. Pour over cake. Yield: 15 servings.

Barbara Korn, Preceptor Alpha Gamma
Nampa, Idaho

♥ FLUFFY PEACH CAKE

1 (2-layer) package super moist yellow cake mix
1 (16-ounce) can sliced peaches in juice
1 (8-ounce) container frozen lite whipped topping, thawed
1 small package sugar-free vanilla instant pudding mix

Preheat oven to 350 degrees. Prepare cake mix according to package directions, using no-cholesterol recipe. Spoon batter evenly into three 8-inch cake pans coated with nonstick cooking spray. Bake for 25 minutes or until toothpick inserted in center of cake comes out clean. Let cakes cool in pans on wire racks for 10 minutes. Remove cakes from pans to wire racks; let cool completely. Drain peach juice into large bowl. Chop peaches coarsely. Add whipped topping, pudding mix and chopped peaches to juice, stirring gently to combine. Refrigerate, covered, until ready to assemble cake. Place 1 cake layer on cake plate. Spread with 3/4 cup peach mixture. Top with second layer; spread with 3/4 cup peach mixture. Place third layer on top. Frost top and side of cake with remaining peach mixture. Refrigerate until serving time. Yield: 16 servings.

Florence Barron, Preceptor Gamma Beta
Lexington, Missouri

♥ APRICOT-FILLED PEAR CAKE

1 (16-ounce) can pear halves in extra lite syrup
1 (2-layer) package low-fat white cake mix
3 eggs
1 (10-ounce) jar apricot spreadable jam
1 3/4 cups lite whipped topping

Preheat oven to 350 degrees. Grease lightly 9-by-13-inch baking pan. Line bottom with waxed paper. Grease and flour entire pan. Drain pears, reserving 1/2 cup liquid. Blend pears in mixer bowl until smooth. Combine cake mix, puréed pears, reserved juice and eggs in large mixer bowl until moist. Beat at high speed for 2 minutes. Pour into prepared pan. Bake for 25 to 30 minutes or until top is golden brown and springs back when touched in center. Let cool in pan for 10 minutes. Remove from pan; remove waxed paper. Let cool completely. Slice cake in half horizontally to make 2 layers. Spread 1 layer, cut-side up, with 3/4 cup jam. Place remaining layer, cut-side down, on top. Spread whipped topping over top. Cut cake into squares or diamonds. Spoon 1/2 teaspoon jam on top of each piece. Store in refrigerator. Yield: 24 servings.

Kelly Young, Xi Zeta
Kincardine, Ontario, Canada

PEANUT BUTTER CAKE

2 1/4 cups all-purpose flour
2 cups packed dark brown sugar
1 cup peanut butter
1/2 cup butter or margarine
1 teaspoon baking powder
1/2 teaspoon baking soda
1 teaspoon vanilla extract
3 eggs
1 cup milk
1 (12-ounce) package semisweet chocolate morsels

Preheat oven to 350 degrees. Combine flour, sugar, peanut butter and butter in mixer bowl; mix well. Reserve 1 cup mixture. Add baking powder, baking soda, vanilla, eggs and milk to remaining mixture; mix until smooth. Pour into greased and floured 9-by-13-inch baking pan. Sprinkle with reserved peanut butter mixture. Sprinkle with chocolate morsels. Bake for 30 to 35 minutes or until knife inserted in center comes out clean. Yield: 15 servings.

Paula L. Nelson, Beta Eta
Hamlin, West Virginia

PEPSI COLA CAKE

This is a good cake for meeting night. It is better if made the day before.

2 cups sifted all-purpose flour
3 tablespoons baking cocoa
2 cups sugar
1 cup butter, melted
1 cup Pepsi Cola
1/2 cup buttermilk
2 eggs
1 teaspoon baking soda
1 teaspoon vanilla extract
1 1/2 cups miniature marshmallows
1/2 cup butter
3 1/2 cups confectioners' sugar
2 tablespoons baking cocoa
1/3 cup Pepsi cola

Preheat oven to 350 degrees. Combine flour, 3 tablespoons cocoa and sugar in large mixer bowl; mix well. Beat in 1 cup melted butter, 1 cup Pepsi Cola, buttermilk, eggs, baking soda and vanilla. Fold in marshmallows. Pour into greased and floured 9-by-13-inch baking pan. Bake for 40 minutes. Combine 1/2 cup butter and confectioners' sugar in mixer bowl; beat until creamy. Beat in 2 tablespoons cocoa. Add 1/3 cup Pepsi Cola. Beat until smooth. Spread on warm cake. Yield: 12 to 16 servings.

Elaine Wilson, Preceptor Beta
Warwick, Rhode Island

PIG PICKIN' CAKE

1 (2-layer) package white or yellow cake mix
1 (11-ounce) can mandarin oranges with juice
1/2 cup vegetable oil
3 eggs
1 (20-ounce) can crushed pineapple
1 (12-ounce) container frozen whipped topping, thawed

Preheat oven to 350 degrees. Combine cake mix, oranges, oil and eggs in mixer bowl; blend well. Pour into greased and floured 9-by-13-inch baking pan. Bake for 30 minutes or until cake tests done. Drain pineapple, reserving juice. Pour pineapple juice over hot cake. Let cool. Spoon pineapple over cake. Top with whipped topping. Refrigerate overnight. Yield: 12 servings.

Joan Huebener, Preceptor Gamma
Charlotte, North Carolina

♥ ORANGE-PINEAPPLE CAKE

This is a great cake for healthy eating and for diabetics. It freezes well.

1 (2-layer) lite white cake mix
4 eggs
1 1/2 cups vegetable oil or applesauce
1 (11-ounce) can mandarin oranges
1 teaspoon vanilla extract
1 (9-ounce) carton lite whipped topping
1 package sugar-free vanilla instant pudding mix
1 (20-ounce) can crushed pineapple in juice
1 teaspoon vanilla extract

Preheat oven to 350 degrees. Combine cake mix, eggs, oil, mandarin oranges with liquid and 1 teaspoon vanilla in mixer bowl; mix well. Pour into greased 9-by-13-inch baking pan. Bake for 30 to 40 minutes or until cake tests done. Let cool. Combine remaining ingredients in mixer bowl; mix well. Spread over top of cake. May also be baked in three 9-inch cake pans. Yield: 12 servings.

Willie Sloan, Preceptor Omega
La Mesa, New Mexico

THIRTY-MINUTE PINEAPPLE CAKE

1 3/4 cups all-purpose flour
1 3/4 cups sugar
1 teaspoon baking soda
2 eggs
1 (20-ounce) can crushed pineapple with juice
2 teaspoons vanilla extract
1/4 cup margarine, melted
3 ounces cream cheese, softened
2 cups confectioners' sugar

Preheat oven to 350 degrees. Combine flour, sugar, baking soda, eggs, pineapple with juice and 1 teaspoon vanilla in large bowl; mix well. Pour into greased and floured 9-by-13-inch baking pan. Bake for 30 minutes or until tests done. Combine margarine and cream cheese in mixer bowl. Beat until creamy. Add confectioners' sugar and 1 teaspoon vanilla. Beat until fluffy. Frost hot cake. Yield: 12 servings.

Gail O'Connor, Lambda
Boulder City, Nevada

THE BEST PINEAPPLE CAKE

1/2 cup egg substitute
2 cups sugar
2 cups all-purpose flour
2 teaspoons baking soda
1 (20-ounce) can crushed pineapple with juice
1 teaspoon vanilla extract
1 cup chopped nuts (optional)
8 ounces fat-free cream cheese, softened
1 1/2 cups confectioners' sugar
1/4 teaspoon vanilla extract

Preheat oven to 350 degrees. Combine egg substitute and sugar in mixer bowl; beat well. Mix flour and baking soda in bowl. Beat into egg mixture. Add pineapple with juice; blend well. Stir in 1 teaspoon vanilla and nuts. Pour into 9-by-13-inch baking pan coated with nonstick cooking spray. Bake for 40 minutes or until cake tests done. Place cream cheese in bowl; stir with wire whisk. Do not use mixer. Beat in confectioners' sugar gradually. Stir in 1/4 teaspoon vanilla. Let cake cool for 10 minutes. Frost cake with cream cheese mixture. Sprinkle with additional nuts if desired.
Yield: 12 to 15 servings.

Irene E. Urbanek, Gamma Tau
Ellsworth, Kansas

PUMPKIN-PINEAPPLE CAKE

2 cups all-purpose flour
2 teaspoons baking powder
1/2 teaspoon baking soda
1/2 teaspoon salt
1 teaspoon ground cinnamon
1/2 teaspoon ground nutmeg
1/8 teaspoon ground ginger
1 cup sugar
1/2 cup packed dark brown sugar
1 cup vegetable oil
3 eggs
1 cup canned pumpkin
1 (8-ounce) can crushed pineapple in unsweetened juice
1 1/2 cups bite-sized crispy wheat cereal squares, crushed
Chopped walnuts

Preheat oven to 350 degrees. Grease 9-by-13-inch baking pan. Sift flour, baking powder, baking soda, salt, cinnamon, nutmeg and ginger together into bowl. Combine sugar and brown sugar in large mixer bowl; mix well. Add oil; mix well. Beat in eggs. Add pumpkin, pineapple with juice and cereal; mix thoroughly. Add flour mixture; mix until just combined. Pour into prepared pan. Bake for 30 to 35 minutes or until cake tests done. Let cool in pan. Frost with desired frosting. Garnish with chopped walnuts. Yield: 12 servings.

Patricia A. Butler, Alpha Iota Preceptor Laureate
Culver, Indiana

PINEAPPLE-ZUCCHINI CAKE

Nonstick vegetable cooking spray
2 cups all-purpose flour
1 1/2 cups sugar
2 teaspoons baking soda
2 teaspoons cinnamon
3/4 teaspoon salt
1/2 teaspoon allspice
3 eggs
3/4 cup vegetable oil
1/3 cup frozen pineapple juice concentrate, thawed
1 teaspoon vanilla extract
2 cups shredded zucchini
1 (8-ounce) can crushed pineapple
3/4 cup chopped walnuts
1/2 cup golden raisins
4 ounces cream cheese, softened
2 cups confectioners' sugar
1 1/2 teaspoons pineapple juice concentrate

Preheat oven to 350 degrees. Coat 10-inch tube pan with nonstick cooking spray. Combine flour, sugar, baking soda, cinnamon, salt and allspice in large bowl. Combine eggs, oil, pineapple juice concentrate and vanilla in mixer bowl; mix well. Add dry ingredients; mix well. Press zucchini to remove excess liquid. Add zucchini, pineapple, walnuts and raisins; mix with wooden spoon. Pour into prepared tube pan. Bake for 50 to 55 minutes or until cake tests done. Let cool on wire rack. Combine remaining ingredients in mixer bowl; beat until light and fluffy. Frost cake. Yield: 16 servings.

Linda Cope, Pi Xi
Suisun City, California

OLD-FASHIONED PORK "BANG-BELLY" CAKE

This cake was a favorite of Newfoundland fishermen who spent long hours fishing. It was called "Bang-Belly" because it was so filling and would keep them from getting hungry during the working day.

1 cup finely ground salt pork
1 cup hot strong coffee
1 cup sugar
1 teaspoon allspice
1 teaspoon nutmeg
1 teaspoon cinnamon
1 teaspoon baking soda
2 eggs, well beaten
2/3 cup molasses
3 cups all-purpose flour
2 cups raisins

Preheat oven to 300 to 325 degrees. Place pork in large bowl. Pour coffee over pork. Let stand until cold. Stir in sugar, spices and baking soda. Add eggs and molasses. Sprinkle flour over raisins. Add flour and raisins to mixture. Stir until well blended. Pour into round iron baking pan. Bake for 2 hours and 15 minutes.
Yield: 6 to 8 sevings.

Marie Noble, Preceptor Eta
Lewisporte, Newfoundland, Canada

♥ NO-CHOLESTEROL MILLION-DOLLAR POUND CAKE

2 1/2 cups sugar
2 cups margarine
1 teaspoon almond extract
1 teaspoon lemon extract
1 teaspoon vanilla extract
1 teaspoon butter flavoring
1/4 cup skim milk
3 3/4 cups all-purpose flour
1/2 teaspoon salt
1 teaspoon baking powder
Egg substitute equivalent to 6 eggs
1 1/2 cups confectioners' sugar
1/4 cup lemon juice

Preheat oven to 325 degrees. Cream sugar and margarine in mixer bowl for 7 minutes. Add almond, lemon and vanilla extracts, butter flavoring, skim milk, flour, salt and baking powder; mix well. Add egg substitute, a small amount at a time, beating well after each addition. Pour into greased and floured tube pan. Bake for 1 1/2 hours or until cake tests done. Let cool in pan for 10 minutes. Combine confectioners' sugar and lemon juice in mixer bowl. Pour over cake immediately after removing from oven. Yield: 16 servings.

Ola M. Chapman, Laureate Kappa Beta
Salem, Illinois

PUMPKIN CAKE

1 (2-layer) package yellow cake mix
1/2 cup butter, melted
1 egg, slighty beaten
1 (28-ounce) can seasoned pumpkin
2 eggs
2/3 cup milk
1/4 cup sugar
1/4 cup butter
1 teaspoon cinnamon
Whipped topping

Preheat oven to 350 degrees. Reserve 1 cup cake mix. Combine remaining cake mix, melted butter and slightly beaten egg in large mixer bowl; mix well. Press in bottom of greased 9-by-13-inch baking pan. Combine pumpkin, 2 eggs and milk in mixer bowl; mix until smooth. Pour over crust mixture. Place reserved cake mix, sugar and butter in bowl; mix with fork. Sprinkle over pumpkin mixture. Bake for 45 to 50 minutes or until knife inserted in center comes out clean. Let cool. Top servings with dollops of whipped topping. Yield: 15 servings.

Nancy Ross, Xi Nu
Las Vegas, Nevada

PUMPKIN BUNDT CAKE

1 (2-layer) package spice cake mix
1 cup canned pumpkin
1/2 cup vegetable oil
1 small package vanilla instant pudding mix
3 eggs
1 teaspoon cinnamon
1/2 cup sugar
Whipped cream

Preheat oven to 350 degrees. Combine cake mix, pumpkin, oil, pudding mix, eggs, cinnamon and water in large mixer bowl. Beat at medium speed for 5 minutes. Pour into greased and floured bundt pan. Bake for 40 to 45 minutes. Let cool for 5 to 10 minutes in pan. Invert on serving tray. Serve with whipped cream. Yield: 12 to 15 servings.

Diana Osika, Xi Eta Chi
Niles, Ohio

RHUBARB CAKE

1 cup margarine
1 1/2 cups packed dark brown sugar
1 egg
2 cups all-purpose flour
1 teaspoon baking soda
1 cup sour cream
1 teaspoon vanilla extract
2 cups finely chopped rhubarb
1/4 cup packed dark brown sugar
1 teaspoon cinnamon
1/2 cup chopped nuts

Preheat oven to 350 degrees. Cream margarine and 1 1/2 cups brown sugar in mixer bowl. Add egg; mix well. Sift flour and baking soda in bowl. Add to creamed mixture alternately with sour cream, beating well after each addition. Add vanilla and rhubarb; mix well. Pour into greased 9-by-13-inch baking pan. Combine remaining ingredients in bowl; mix well. Sprinkle over batter. Bake for 50 minutes. Yield: 15 servings.

Susan Townsend-Kaus, Phi
Moscow, Idaho

BACARDI RUM CAKE

1 cup chopped pecans or walnuts
1 (2-layer) package yellow cake mix
1 package vanilla instant pudding mix
4 eggs
1/2 cup cold water
1/2 cup vegetable oil
1/3 cup Bacardi Amber Rum
Bacardi Rum Glaze

Preheat oven to 325 degrees. Sprinkle nuts over bottom of greased and floured 10-inch tube pan. Combine cake mix, pudding mix, eggs, water, oil and rum in large mixer bowl. Beat at medium speed until well mixed. Pour batter over nuts. Bake for 1 hour. Let cool. Invert onto serving plate. Prick top. Drizzle and smooth Glaze over top and side of cake. Repeat until all Glaze is used. Yield: 12 servings.

BACARDI RUM GLAZE

1/2 cup butter
1/4 cup water
1/2 cup sugar
1/3 cup Bacardi Amber rum

Melt butter in suacepan. Stir in water and sugar. Boil for 5 minutes, stirring constantly. Remove from heat. Stir in rum. Yield: 1 cup.

Pauline Ash, Beta Sigma Phi
Corner Brook, Newfoundland, Canada

GLAZED RUM CAKE

1 package pistachio instant pudding mix
1 (2-layer) package yellow cake mix without pudding
1/2 cup rum
1/2 cup vegetable oil
4 eggs
1 cup sugar
1/2 cup margarine
1/2 cup rum
1/4 cup water

Preheat oven to 350 degrees. Mix pudding mix and cake mix in large mixer bowl. Add 1/2 cup rum, oil and eggs. Mix according to package directions for bundt cake. Pour into greased and floured bundt pan. Bake for 1 hour. Combine sugar, margarine, 1/2 cup rum and water in saucepan. Bring to a boil over medium-low heat. Cook, stirring, for 2 minutes or until sugar is dissolved. Remove cake from pan. Poke holes on surface of cake with fork. Pour warm glaze slowly over entire cake. Yield: 12 servings.

Norma Mahagan, Preceptor Gamma Lambda
Castle Rock, Colorado

GRANDMOTHER'S RUM CAKE

1 1/2 cups butter, softened
10 ounces sugar
8 egg yolks
10 ounces sifted all-purpose flour
1 (12-ounce) package chocolate chips
1 (8-ounce) package finely chopped walnuts
3 tablespoons white rum
8 egg whites, beaten
1 cup sugar
1/4 cup butter, softened
1 teaspoon water
3 tablespoons white rum

Preheat oven to 350 degrees. Combine butter, sugar and egg yolks in mixer bowl; mix well. Add flour, chocolate chips, walnuts and 3 tablespoons rum; mix well. Beat egg whites until stiff peaks form. Fold into mixture. Pour into ungreased 10-by-16-inch jelly roll pan. Bake for 20 to 25 minutes or until cake tests done. Let cool for 15 minutes. Combine remaining ingredients in bowl; mix well. Frost cake. Let stand for 3 hours or until cold. Cut into 1-inch squares to serve. Yield: 144 squares.

Andrea M. Swartzman, Preceptor Alpha Upsilon
Bemus Point, New York

RUM CAKE

1/2 cup chopped nuts
1 (2-layer) package yellow cake mix with pudding
4 eggs
1/2 cup vegetable oil
1/2 cup cold water
1/2 cup rum
Rum Sauce

Preheat oven to 325 degrees. Sprinkle nuts on bottom of generously greased large bundt pan. Combine cake mix, eggs, oil, water and rum in large mixer bowl. Beat at medium speed for 6 minutes. Pour over nuts in pan. Bake for 55 minutes to 1 hour or until toothpick inserted in cake comes out clean. Pour Rum Sauce over cake in pan. Let stand for 20 to 30 minutes or until sauce is well absorbed. Invert onto plate. Yield: 12 to 16 servings.

RUM SAUCE

1/2 cup margarine
1 cup sugar
1/4 cup rum
1/4 cup water

Combine margarine, sugar, rum and water in saucepan. Bring to a boil, stirring constantly. Boil slowly, stirring, for 2 minutes. Yield: 1 cup.

Sybil Shell, Xi Alpha Lambda
Whitesburg, Kentucky

CREAM SHERRY CAKE

1 (2-layer) package yellow cake mix
1 package vanilla instant pudding mix
2 teaspoons nutmeg
4 eggs
1 cup cream Sherry
3/4 cup vegetable oil
1/2 cup cream Sherry
1/2 cup sugar
1/2 cup water

Preheat oven to 350 degrees. Combine cake mix, pudding mix, nutmeg, eggs, 1 cup cream Sherry and oil in large mixer bowl. Beat until well mixed. Pour batter into greased tube pan. Bake for 50 minutes or until tests done. Let cool in pan for 10 minutes. Combine 1/2 cup cream Sherry, sugar and water in saucepan. Bring to a boil over medium-low heat. Boil, stirring, until sugar is dissolved. Pour over warm cake.
Yield: 12 to 16 servings.

Mary Nell Watson, Laureate Delta Delta
Fort Worth, Texas

♥ LIGHT-AS-A-FEATHER SPONGE CAKE

6 egg yolks
1/2 cup cold water
1 1/2 cups sugar
1/2 teaspoon vanilla extract
1/2 teaspoon lemon juice
1/2 teaspoon grated lemon rind
1/4 teaspoon almond extract
1 1/2 cups cake flour
1/4 teaspoon salt
6 egg whites
3/4 teaspoon cream of tartar
Butter icing or whipped cream topping

Preheat oven to 325 degrees. Beat egg yolks in mixer bowl until thick and lemon-colored. Add water; continue beating until thick. Add sugar gradually; mix well. Add vanilla, lemon juice, lemon rind and almond extract; mix well. Fold in flour, sifted with salt, a little at a time. Beat egg whites until foamy. Add cream of tartar. Beat until stiff peaks form. Fold into egg mixture. Pour into ungreased tube pan. Bake for 1 hour. Invert on rack to cool. Frost with butter icing or whipped topping. Yield: 12 servings.

Alice Schmelz, Laureate Gamma Theta
Whittier, California

STRAWBERRY ANGEL FOOD CAKE

1 angel food cake mix
1 cup hot water
1 (3-ounce) package strawberry gelatin
1 small package frozen strawberries
1 (16-ounce) container whipped topping
1 small package vanilla instant pudding mix
Fresh strawberries

Bake angel food cake according to package directions. Invert on funnel to cool completely. Loosen cake from side of pan. Invert onto cake plate. Slice 2-inch layer off top of cake; set aside. Dig 1 to 2-inch tunnel into cake. Break removed cake into bite-sized pieces. Mix water and gelatin in bowl; stir until gelatin is dissolved. Add partially frozen strawberries; stir until well mixed. Let stand until soft-set. Add cake pieces; stir. Spoon into cake tunnel. Place top on cake. Combine whipped topping and pudding mix in bowl; mix well. Frost cake. Garnish with fresh strawberries. Chill for several hours. Yield: 8 to 12 servings.

Tina Kerian, Kappa
Sioux City, Iowa

STRAWBERRY CAKE

1 (2-layer) package white cake mix
1 (3-ounce) package strawberry gelatin
4 eggs
1 cup vegetable oil
8 ounces frozen strawberries with juice
1/2 cup margarine, melted
1/2 cup frozen strawberries with juice
3 cups confectioners' sugar

Preheat oven to 350 degrees. Mix cake mix and gelatin together in large mixer bowl. Add eggs, oil and 8 ounces strawberries with juice. Beat until well blended. Pour into greased and floured 9-by-13-inch baking pan. Bake for 25 to 30 minutes or until tests done. Let cool. Blend margarine, 1/2 cup strawberries with juice and confectioners' sugar in mixer bowl. Blend until of frosting consistency. Frost cooled cake. Yield: 12 to 15 servings.

Karen Legleiter, Laureate Beta Epsilon
Arkansas City, Kansas

Barbara Miller, Xi Omega, Bowling Green, Kentucky, makes a Strawberry Cake by combining 1 (2-layer) package white cake mix, 1 cup vegetable oil, 1 cup thawed frozen strawberries, 4 eggs and 1 (3 ounce) package strawberry gelatin in large mixer bowl. Beat for 2 to 3 minutes. Pour into 2 greased and floured 9-inch cake pans. Bake in preheated 350-degree oven for 30 minutes or until toothpick inserted in center of cakes comes out clean. Let cool on wire racks. Frost with your favorite white butter or cream cheese frosting tinted with red food coloring. Yield: 12 to 16 servings.

TREASURE TOFFEE CAKE

1/4 cup sugar
1 teaspoon cinnamon
2 cups all-purpose flour
1 cup sugar
1 1/2 teaspoons baking powder
1 teaspoon baking soda
1/4 teaspoon salt
1 teaspoon vanilla extract
1 cup sour cream
1/2 cup butter, softened
2 eggs
1 cup chopped nuts
3 (1-ounce) chocolate toffee candy bars, crushed
1/4 cup butter, melted

Preheat oven to 325 degrees. Combine 1/4 cup sugar and cinnamon in small bowl. Combine flour, sugar, baking powder, baking soda, salt, vanilla, sour cream, 1/2 cup butter and eggs in large mixer bowl. Blend at low speed until moistened. Beat at medium speed for 3 minutes. Spoon half the batter into greased and floured 10-inch bundt pan. Sprinkle with 2 tablespoons sugar-cinnamon mixture. Pour remaining batter into pan. Top with remaining cinnamon-sugar mixture, nuts and crushed candy. Pour melted butter over top. Bake for 45 minutes or until cake tests done. Yield: 16 servings.

Marilyn Borras, Xi Epsilon Xi
Stafford, Virginia

GREEN TOMATO CAKE

2 or 3 green tomatoes, quartered
2/3 cup butter
1 3/4 cups sugar
2 eggs
4 ounces unsweetened chocolate
1 teaspoon vanilla extract
2 1/2 cups all-purpose flour
1/2 cup baking cocoa
2 teaspoons baking powder
2 teaspoons baking soda
1/4 teaspoon salt
1 cup beer
Cream cheese frosting

Preheat oven to 350 degrees. Purée tomatoes in blender. Reserve 1 cup puréed tomatoes. Cream butter and sugar in mixer bowl until light and fluffy. Add eggs; mix well. Melt chocolate in top of double boiler over boiling water. Let cool. Add chocolate, vanilla and reserved puréed mixture to creamed mixture; mix well. Sift flour, cocoa, baking powder, baking soda and salt together in bowl. Add half the dry ingredients to creamed mixture; mix well. Add beer and remaining dry ingredients; mix well. Spoon batter into 2 greased and floured 9-inch cake pans, spreading top of batter until smooth. Bake for 35 minutes. Let cool. Frost with cream cheese frosting. Yield: 12 servings.

Mary Ann Shealy, Laureate Delta Beta
Cocoa, Florida

TOMATO SOUP CAKE

1/2 cup butter
  or margarine
1 cup sugar
1 egg
1 teaspoon baking
  soda
2 (10-ounce) cans
  tomato soup
2 cups all-purpose
  flour
2 teaspoons baking
  powder
1 cup raisins
1 cup chopped nuts
1 teaspoon cinnamon
1 teaspoon nutmeg
1 teaspoon cloves
Cream Cheese-Lemon
  Frosting

Preheat oven to 350 degrees. Cream butter and sugar in mixer bowl. Add egg; beat well. Combine baking soda and tomato soup in small bowl. Sift flour and baking powder in bowl. Add to creamed mixture; mix well. Add tomato mixture; mix well. Add raisins, nuts, cinnamon, nutmeg and cloves. Pour into 9-by-13-inch baking pan. Bake for 40 minutes. Let cool completely. Ice with Cream Cheese-Lemon Frosting.

CREAM CHEESE-LEMON FROSTING

1/2 cup butter
  or margarine
3 ounces cream cheese,
  softened
4 cups confectioners'
  sugar
1 teaspoon vanilla
  extract
3 tablespoons lemon
  juice
2 teaspoons grated
  lemon rind

Cream butter and cream cheese in mixer bowl. Add confectioners' sugar, vanilla, lemon juice and lemon rind. Beat until fluffy and of spreading consistency. Add more lemon juice if necessary. Yield: 3 to 4 cups.

Sheryl Lynn Hartranft, Epsilon Omega
Tucson, Arizona

SPICY ZUCCHINI CAKE

2 cups finely chopped
  zucchini
1/3 cup boiling water
2 cups all-purpose
  flour
1 1/4 cups sugar
1 1/4 teaspoons baking
  powder
1 teaspoon salt
1 teaspoon cinnamon
1 teaspoon nutmeg
1 teaspoon cloves
1/2 cup vegetable oil
3 eggs
1 teaspoon vanilla
  extract

Preheat oven to 350 degrees. Mix zucchini and boiling water in large mixer bowl. Add flour, sugar, baking powder, salt, cinnamon, nutmeg and cloves. Add oil, eggs and vanilla. Beat at low speed for 1 minute, scraping bowl constantly. Beat at medium speed for 2 minutes, scraping bowl occasionally. Spoon into greased and floured 9-by-13-inch baking pan. Bake for 45 to 50 minutes or until toothpick inserted in center comes out clean. Let cool in pan on wire rack. Yield: 12 servings.

Beverly Wilczek, Alpha Rho Theta
Friendswood, Texas

APPLE-APRICOT PIE

1/3 cup sugar
1/3 cup packed dark
  brown sugar
3 tablespoons
  all-purpose flour
1/4 teaspoon salt
1/4 teaspoon cinnamon
1 (20-ounce) can
  pie-sliced apples,
  undrained
1 tablespoon lemon juice
1 (30-ounce) can apricot
  halves, well drained
Pastry for 9-inch
  2-crust pie
1 tablespoon butter
  or margarine
1 tablespoon sugar

Preheat oven to 400 degrees. Combine sugar, brown sugar, flour, salt and cinnamon in bowl. Place apples in large bowl. Stir sugar mixture into apples. Add lemon juice; mix well. Cut apricot halves in half; fold into apple mixture. Line 9-inch pie plate with pastry. Pour fruit mixture into pastry-lined pie plate. Dot with butter. Place top crust on pie. Cut slits in crust. Seal; flute edge. Sprinkle with 1 tablespoon sugar. Bake for 40 minutes or until crust is golden brown. Yield: 6 servings.

Norma Rowland, Xi Kappa Phi
Glendora, California

APPLE-CRANBERRY PIE

3 cups chopped apples
1 cup cranberries
1 1/2 cups sugar
3 tablespoons minute
  tapioca
1/4 teaspoon salt
1 (15-ounce) package
  refrigerated pie crust
1 tablespoon margarine

Preheat oven to 400 degrees. Combine apples, cranberries, sugar, tapioca and salt in bowl. Let stand for 15 minutes. Prepare pie crust according to package directions for 2-crust pie. Line 9-inch pie pan with 1 crust. Fill with fruit mixture. Dot with margarine. Cut second pie crust into 1/2-inch strips. Arrange lattice-fashion on top. Bake for 1 hour or until bubbly. Yield: 6 servings.

Barbara Wiscarson, Preceptor Beta Lambda
Cottage Grove, Oregon

♥ SUGARLESS APPLE PIE

1 (12-ounce) can frozen
  unsweetened
  apple juice
3 tablespoons
  cornstarch
1/3 cup brown Sugartwin
1 teaspoon cinnamon
1/8 teaspoon salt
5 or 6 apples, peeled,
  sliced
Pastry for 9-inch
  2-crust pie

Preheat oven to 350 degrees. Place apple juice in heavy saucepan over medium heat. Mix cornstarch with small amount of apple juice in cup. Add Sugartwin, cinnamon and salt. Stir into apple juice. Cook, stirring, until thickened. Add apples. Cook for 1 minute. Pour into pie crust. Cover with top crust. Bake for 45 minutes to 1 hour or until lightly browned. Yield: 6 to 8 servings.

Mary C. Distefano, Beta Mu
Macomb, Illinois

SOUR CREAM-APPLE PIE

3/4 cup sugar
2 tablespoons all-purpose flour
1 cup sour cream
1 egg
1/2 teaspoon vanilla extract
1/8 teaspoon salt
2 cups chopped apples
1 (9-inch) unbaked pie shell
1/3 cup sugar
1/3 cup all-purpose flour
1 teaspoon cinnamon
1/4 cup margarine

Preheat oven to 450 degrees. Combine 3/4 cup sugar and 2 tablespoons flour in mixer bowl. Add sour cream, egg, vanilla and salt. Beat until smooth. Add apples to mixture. Pour into unbaked pie shell. Bake for 15 minutes. Reduce oven temperature to 325 degrees. Combine 1/3 cup sugar, 1/3 cup flour and cinnamon in bowl; mix well. Cut in margarine until crumbly. Sprinkle over pie. Bake for 20 minutes longer. Yield: 6 to 8 servings.

Marilyn Lefholz, Preceptor Gamma Beta
Lexington, Missouri

APPLE CANDY PIE

6 cups thinly sliced tart apples
3/4 cup sugar
1/4 cup all-purpose flour
1/2 teaspoon ground cinnamon
1/8 teaspoon nutmeg
1/4 teaspoon salt
Pastry for 9-inch 2-crust pie
2 tablespoons butter or margarine
2 tablespoons lemon juice
1/4 cup butter
1/2 cup packed dark brown sugar
2 tablespoons cream
1/2 cup chopped pecans

Preheat oven to 400 degrees. Combine apples, sugar, flour, cinnamon, nutmeg and salt in large bowl; toss to mix. Pour mixture into pastry-lined pie plate. Dot with 2 tablespoons butter; sprinkle with lemon juice. Top with remaining pastry, fluting edge and cutting vents in top. Bake for 50 minutes. Melt 1/4 cup butter in saucepan. Stir in brown sugar and cream. Bring slowly to a boil. Remove from heat. Stir in pecans. Pour onto baked pie. Bake for 5 minutes longer. Let cool for 1 hour. Yield: 8 to 12 servings.

Barbara Brond, Alpha Rho
Liberal, Kansas

APPLE-CHEESE PIE

1 1/2 cups all-purpose flour
1 teaspoon salt
1/2 cup vegetable shortening
1/2 cup grated Cheddar cheese
1/4 cup sugar
1/2 teaspoon cinnamon
4 tart apples, peeled, cored
1 teaspoon butter
1 teaspoon lemon juice
3/4 cup sugar
3 tablespoons butter
3/4 cup packed dark brown sugar
1 cup water

Preheat oven to 375 degrees. Sift flour and salt together in bowl. Cut in shortening and cheese. Add enough cold water to make firm dough. Roll out on floured surface. Cut into 4 squares. Combine 1/4 cup sugar and cinnamon in cup. Pour 1 tablespoon mixture into each apple. Dot with 1/4 teaspoon butter and 1/4 teaspoon lemon juice. Place 1 apple on each dough square. Fold dough to enclose each apple; seal. Place in 4-by-6-inch baking pan. Place 3/4 cup sugar, 3 tablespoons butter, brown sugar and 1 cup water in saucepan. Cook, stirring constantly, until hot. Pour over dumplings. Bake for 45 minutes, basting 2 times during baking. Yield: 4 servings.

Joyce Kirk
Corpus Christi, Texas

APPLE-RASPBERRY PIE

2 cups all-purpose flour
7 ounces lard
1 tablespoon apple cider vinegar
1/2 teaspoon salt
6 tablespoons cold water
8 large Granny Smith apples
1 1/2 tablespoons lemon juice
1/2 cup sugar
2 tablespoons all-purpose flour
1 teaspoon cinnamon
2 cups nutmeg
2 cups cloves
2 cups raspberries
1 tablespoon sugar

Freeze 2 cups flour in medium bowl for 1 hour. Refrigerate lard for 1 hour. Cut chilled lard into cubes. Combine vinegar, salt and water in cup. Place 1 cup flour onto flat surface. Place lard cubes on top. Cover with 1 cup flour. Roll rolling pin over mixture until all pieces have been flattened and slightly incorporated. Scrape into bowl. Add vinegar mixture; mix. Turn dough out onto lightly floured surface. Roll out to 8-by-12-inch rectangle with lightly floured rolling pin. Fold to center and roll out slightly to form 8-inch square. Roll and fold once more. Wrap in parchment or waxed paper. Refrigerate until needed. Preheat oven to 425 degrees. Peel, core and cut apples into eighths. Cut crosswise into 1 1/2-inch chunks. Toss apples with lemon juice in bowl. Combine 1/2 cup sugar, 2 tablespoons flour, cinnamon, nutmeg and cloves in large bowl; mix well. Add apples; toss until evenly coated. Add raspberries; toss lightly. Reserve 1/3 of dough. Roll remaining dough into circle 5 inches larger than pie dish. Fit into dish; trim overhang to 1 inch. Spoon in apples; dome evenly. Roll out remaining dough. Place over apples; crimp. Cut 5 slits in center. Sprinkle remaining sugar over crust. Bake for 10 minutes. Reduce oven temperature to 400 degrees. Bake for 40 minutes or until golden brown. Let cool. Yield: 8 servings.

Karen Lea Walsh, Preceptor Eta
Saint John, New Brunswick, Canada

BITTER SWEET PIE

1 cup milk
2 cups miniature marshmallows
1/4 teaspoon salt
1/2 teaspoon almond extract
1 cup heavy cream, whipped or 8 ounces whipped topping
1/2 cup shaved German's chocolate
1 (8-inch) baked pie shell

Heat milk and marshmallows in saucepan, stirring until marshmallows are melted. Add salt and almond extract. Chill thoroughly. Fold in whipped cream. Fold in shaved chocolate, reserving enough for garnish. Pour into pie shell. Chill for several hours. Garnish with reserved chocolate shavings. Yield: 6 servings.

Carol A. Scheele, Beta Sigma Chi
Odell, Nebraska

BUTTERMILK PIE

For those who do not keep buttermilk on hand, powdered buttermilk works just as well as fresh. This is a favorite pie for bake sales. Being from Texas and living in Alaska, southern dishes like this are new to a lot of people.

2 cups sugar
1/2 cup butter or margarine
3 tablespoons (heaping) all-purpose flour
3 eggs, beaten
1 cup buttermilk
1 teaspoon vanilla extract
2 (9-inch) unbaked pie shells

Preheat oven to 350 degrees. Cream sugar and butter in mixer bowl. Add flour and eggs; beat well. Add buttermilk and vanilla. Pour into pie shells, dividing equally. Bake for 45 to 50 minutes or until lightly browned. Yield: 12 servings.

S. Zann Reid, Xi Xi
Eielson Air Force Base, Alaska

FRESH CHERRY PIE

3 cups ripe red cherries, pitted
1/4 cup all-purpose flour
1 1/2 cups sugar
Dash of salt
Pastry for 9-inch 2-crust pie
1 tablespoon butter or margarine

Preheat oven to 400 degrees. Combine cherries, flour, sugar and salt in large bowl. Pour into pastry shell. Dot with butter. Cut second crust into 1/2-inch strips. Arrange in lattice design over cherry mixture. Bake for 50 minutes. Yield: 6 servings.

Vickie Dillard, Eta Sigma
Mineral Bluff, Georgia

CANDY BAR PIE

1 (9-inch) unbaked pie shell
5 Snicker or Milky Way candy bars
1/2 cup sugar
12 ounces cream cheese, softened
2 eggs, beaten
1/3 cup sour cream
1/3 cup peanut butter
2/3 cup semisweet chocolate chips
2 tablespoons whipping cream

Preheat oven to 450 degrees. Bake pie shell for 5 minutes. Reduce oven temperature to 325 degrees. Cut candy bars into 1/4-inch pieces. Line pie shell with candy. Beat sugar and cream cheese in mixer bowl until smooth. Add eggs; mix well. Add sour cream and peanut butter. Blend until smooth. Pour into pie shell. Bake for 30 to 40 minutes or until set. Melt chocolate chips and whipping cream in saucepan. Pour over top. Refrigerate for several hours. Yield: 8 to 10 servings.

Judy Woltz, Laureate Epsilon Tau
Simi Valley, California

CHOCOLATE ANGEL PIE

4 egg whites
1/4 teaspoon cream of tartar
1/4 teaspoon vanilla extract
1 1/2 cups sugar
1/4 cup cocoa
1/8 teaspoon salt
1/2 teaspoon vanilla extract
1 1/2 cups heavy cream

Preheat oven to 275 degrees. Beat egg whites in mixer bowl until frothy. Add cream of tartar. Beat until stiff peaks form. Add 1/4 teaspoon vanilla and 1 cup sugar. Place mixture in buttered and floured 9-inch pie plate, pushing mixture up around edge. Bake for 1 hour. Let pie crust stand overnight. Combine 1/2 cup sugar, cocoa, salt, vanilla and heavy cream in mixer bowl; mix well. Chill for 1 hour. Beat until stiff. Spoon into pie crust. Yield: 8 servings.

Sharon Kelly, Xi Delta Phi
Lowville, New York

CHOCOLATE-BUTTERFINGER PIE

1 large package chocolate instant pudding mix
2 3/4 cups low-fat milk
1 (9-inch) baked pie shell
Lite whipped topping
1 Butterfinger candy bar

Combine pudding mix and milk in mixer bowl; mix well. Pour into cooled pie shell. Chill for 15 minutes. Top with whipped topping. Crush Butterfinger candy bar in bowl. Sprinkle on top. Chill for 2 hours. Yield: 6 servings.

Melinda Dudeck, Xi Iota Iota
Oregon, Missouri

174 / Pies

FUDGE PIE

2/3 cup margarine	1 cup sugar
6 tablespoons baking cocoa	2 eggs
	1 cup chopped pecans
1/4 cup all-purpose flour	Whipped cream (optional)

Preheat oven to 350 degrees. Melt margarine and cocoa in small saucepan over low heat. Remove from heat. Combine flour and sugar in bowl. Add flour-sugar mixture and eggs to chocolate mixture; mix well. Add pecans. Pour into lightly greased 8-inch cake pan. Bake for 30 minutes. Cut into 6 wedges. Top with whipped cream. Yield: 6 servings.

Hazel I. Ivey, Beta Sigma Phi
Brackettville, Texas

GERMAN CHOCOLATE PIE

3 tablespoons (heaping) all-purpose flour	1 cup chopped pecans
1 cup sugar	Nonstick vegetable cooking spray
3 eggs	
2/3 German's sweet chocolate bar	All-purpose flour
1/2 cup margarine	Whipped topping
1 teaspoon vanilla extract	

Preheat oven to 325 degrees. Combine 3 tablespoons flour, sugar and eggs in mixer bowl. Beat for 3 minutes at medium speed. Melt chocolate and margarine in saucepan. Fold into sugar mixture. Add vanilla and pecans. Coat 9-inch pie pan with cooking spray. Sprinkle lightly with flour. Pour chocolate mixture into pan. Bake for 35 minutes. Let cool for 3 hours at room temperature before refrigerating. Top with whipped topping. Yield: 6 to 8 servings.

Emma Jo McCormack, Laureate Delta Delta
Fort Worth, Texas

♣ ♥ LOW-FAT MOCHA FUDGE PIE

1/3 cup hot water	1 (3-ounce) package chocolate instant pudding mix
2 teaspoons instant coffee granules	
2 cups light fudge brownie mix	1 1/2 cups frozen reduced-calorie whipped topping, thawed
1 teaspoon vanilla extract	
2 egg whites	1 tablespoon Kahlua
Nonstick vegetable cooking spray	1 teaspoon instant coffee granules
3/4 cup 1% low-fat milk	1 1/2 cups frozen reduced-calorie whipped topping, thawed
2 tablespoons Kahlua	
1 teaspoon instant coffee granules	Chocolate curls
1 teaspoon vanilla extract	

Preheat oven to 325 degrees. Combine hot water and 2 teaspoons coffee granules in medium bowl; mix well. Add brownie mix, 1 teaspoon vanilla and egg whites; stir until well blended. Pour mixture into 9-inch pie plate coated with cooking spray. Bake for 22 minutes. Let crust cool completely. Combine milk, 2 tablespoons Kahlua, 1 teaspoon coffee granules, 1 teaspoon vanilla and pudding mix in mixer bowl. Beat at medium speed for 1 minute. Fold in 1 1/2 cups whipped topping gently. Spread pudding mixture evenly over brownie crust. Combine 1 tablespoon Kahlua and 1 teaspoon coffee granules in bowl; mix well. Fold in 1 1/2 cups whipped topping gently. Spread evenly over pudding mixture. Garnish with chocolate curls. Serve immediately or store loosely covered in refrigerator. Yield: 8 servings.

Lisa Haugen, Beta Delta
Havre, Montana

MALT SHOP PIE

1 quart vanilla ice cream	3 tablespoons marshmallow topping
1 tablespoon milk	
1/2 cup crushed malted milk balls	1 tablespoon milk
1 (9-inch) graham cracker crumb pie crust	1 cup whipping cream, whipped
	1/4 cup crushed malted milk balls
3 tablespoons chocolate malted milk instant powder	

Stir ice cream in bowl until softened. Add 1 tablespoon milk and 1/2 cup crushed malted milk balls. Pour into pie shell; freeze. Combine malted milk powder, marshmallow topping and 1 tablespoon milk in bowl; mix well. Add to whipped cream. Spread over ice cream layer. Sprinkle with remaining crushed malted milk balls. Freeze for 4 hours before serving. Yield: 6 servings.

Shirley Cook, Xi Beta Iota
Marshall, Michigan

MEXICAN CHOCOLATE PIE

I served this at a chapter Mexican progressive dinner.

24 large marshmallows	2 tablespoons Kahlua
6 ounces chocolate chips	1 cup whipping cream, whipped
1/2 cup milk	1 (9-inch) chocolate wafer pie shell
2 tablespoons Crème de Cacao	

Combine marshmallows, chocolate chips and milk in microwave-safe bowl. Microwave on medium for 3 to 4 minutes; let cool. Add Crème de Cacao and Kahlua. Chill for 30 minutes. Fold in whipped cream. Pour into chocolate wafer pie shell. Freeze. Remove from freezer 5 to 10 minutes before serving. Yield: 12 servings.

Nancy Hearn, Xi Lambda Eta
West Chester, Ohio

QUICKIE CHOCOLATE PIE

1 cup sugar
1/4 cup all-purpose flour
2 tablespoons baking cocoa
1/2 cup water
1 (12-ounce) can evaporated milk
3 egg yolks
2 tablespoons margarine
1 teaspoon vanilla extract
1 (10-inch) lightly browned baked deep-dish pie shell
Whipped topping

Combine sugar, flour and cocoa in microwave-safe bowl; mix well. Add water, evaporated milk and egg yolks; mix well. Microwave on high for 3 minutes; mix well. Repeat for 2 more times, totaling 7 to 9 minutes or until mixture becomes thick. Do not scorch. Add margarine and vanilla; stir well. Pour immediately into cooled pie shell. Let cool. Top with whipped topping. Yield: 4 to 6 servings.

Ralfie Flowers, Beta Zeta Phi
Wichita Falls, Texas

CHOCOLATE ALMOND PIE

1 (7-ounce) chocolate almond candy bar
1 (12-ounce) carton frozen whipped topping, thawed
1 tablespoon Bourbon or rum
1 (9-inch) graham cracker crumb pie crust

Chop candy bar into small pieces in top of double boiler. Cook over hot water until melted. Mix with whipped topping in bowl. Add Bourbon; mix well. Pour into pie crust. Freeze. Yield: 6 servings.

June C. Foster, Laureate Omega
Charlottesville, Virginia

COCONUT AND CARAMEL PIE

2 unbaked 10-inch deep-dish pie shells
1 1/4 cups margarine
1 (7-ounce) package coconut
1 1/2 cups chopped pecans
8 ounces cream cheese, softened
1 (14-ounce) can sweetened condensed milk
1 (16-ounce) carton whipped topping
1 (6-ounce) jar caramel topping

Bake pie shells according to package directions. Let cool. Melt margarine in large skillet over medium heat. Add coconut and pecans. Sauté until brown. Spread out on cooking foil; let cool. Combine cream cheese and condensed milk in mixer bowl until smooth. Fold in whipped topping. Pour 1/4 mixture in bottom of each pie shell. Drizzle with caramel topping. Sprinkle with coconut-pecan mixture. Repeat layers until each pie shell is full. Freeze, covered, for 24 hours. Remove from freezer 1 hour before serving. Yield: 12 servings.

Kathy Sturgill, Xi Delta Mu
Johnson City, Tennessee

AMARETTO-COCONUT PIE

1/2 cup butter
7/8 cup graham cracker crumbs
3/4 cup sugar
1 1/4 cups shredded coconut
4 eggs
1 1/4 cups sugar
1 quart heavy cream
1/4 cup favorite flavored gelatin
3 ounces water
4 ounces Amaretto liqueur
Dash of almond extract
Toasted almonds

Melt butter in saucepan. Add cracker crumbs and 3/4 cup sugar; mix well. Press into bottom of 10-inch deep springform pan. Toast coconut in pan until golden brown. Reserve small amount toasted coconut for garnish. Combine remaining coconut, eggs and 1 1/4 cups sugar in mixer bowl. Beat at medium speed until fluffy. Beat cream in mixer bowl until soft peaks form. Dissolve gelatin in water. Blend gelatin, Amaretto and almond extract into egg mixture; mix well. Fold whipped cream into blended ingredients. Pour mixture over crust in mold; chill. Unmold onto serving plate. Sprinkle with reserved coconut and almonds. Yield: 12 servings.

Beth Koenig, Gamma Chi
Houston, Texas

GREAT IMPOSSIBLE COCONUT PIES

These are great for bridge parties and covered dishes.

4 eggs, well beaten
1 3/4 cups sugar
1/4 cup butter
Dash of salt
1/2 cup self-rising flour
1 cup milk
1 teaspoon vanilla extract
1 (7-ounce) can flaked coconut

Preheat oven to 350 degrees. Combine eggs, sugar, butter, salt, flour, milk and vanilla in mixer bowl; mix well. Fold in coconut. Pour into 2 well-greased and floured 8-inch pie pans, dividing equally. Bake for 30 minutes or until lightly browned. Yield: 12 servings.

Minnie K. Stapleton, Xi Alpha Tau
Morristown, Tennessee

IMPOSSIBLE COCONUT PIE

1/2 cup biscuit mix
3/4 cup sugar
4 eggs
2 cups milk
1 teaspoon vanilla extract
3 tablespoons margarine
1 cup coconut

Preheat oven to 400 degrees. Combine biscuit mix, sugar, eggs, milk, vanilla and margarine in mixer bowl; mix well. Fold in coconut; mix well. Pour into 9-inch buttered pie plate. Let stand for 5 minutes. Bake for 30 to 35 minutes or until lightly browned. Yield: 8 servings.

Deanna Oldham, Zeta Gamma
Bloomfield, New Mexico

CRANBERRY-RASPBERRY PIE

1 (10-ounce) package
    frozen raspberries
3 cups fresh
    cranberries
1 1/2 cups sugar
3 tablespoons cornstarch
1/4 teaspoon salt
Pastry for 9-inch
    2-crust pie

Preheat oven to 400 degrees. Drain raspberries, reserving syrup. Add enough water to syrup to make 1 cup. Combine cranberries and syrup mixture in large saucepan. Bring to a boil. Simmer for 5 minutes. Combine sugar, cornstarch and salt in bowl. Add to hot cranberry mixture. Cook quickly, stirring constantly, until thickened. Remove from heat. Stir in raspberries. Pour into 9-inch pastry-lined pie plate. Top with remaining pastry, sealing edge and cutting vents in top. Bake for 35 to 40 minutes. Yield: 6 servings.

Sister in Beta Sigma Phi

CONCORD GRAPE PIE

3 1/2 cups Concord
    grapes
1 cup sugar
1/4 cup all-purpose
    flour
1/4 teaspoon salt
1 tablespoon lemon
    juice
1 1/2 tablespoons butter
    or margarine, melted
1 (9-inch) unbaked
    pie shell
3/4 cup all-purpose
    flour
1/2 cup sugar
1/3 cup butter
    or margarine

Preheat oven to 400 degrees. Remove and reserve skins from grapes. Bring pulp to the boiling point in saucepan. Press through sieve to remove seeds. Add skins. Combine 1 cup sugar, 1/4 cup flour and salt in bowl; mix well. Add lemon juice, 1 1/2 tablespoons butter and grape pulp; mix well. Pour into pie shell. Sift 3/4 cup flour and 1/2 cup sugar in bowl. Cut in 1/3 cup butter until crumbly. Sprinkle over pie. Bake for 40 to 50 minutes or until top is lightly browned. Yield: 6 servings.

Jane O'Rourke, Preceptor Alpha Alpha
LaVale, Maryland

ICE CREAM PIE

1/2 gallon coffee or
    coffee-oreo ice cream,
    softened
2 (9-inch) graham
    cracker crumb
    pie crusts
2 or 3 Skor or Heath
    candy bars, crushed

Spread ice cream in each crust, dividing equally. Sprinkle crushed candy on top of each pie, dividing equally. Freeze solid. Remove from freezer 30 minutes before serving. May also be made in a springform pan as for cheesecake. Yield: 12 servings.

Helen L. Turner, Preceptor Alpha Tau
Lawton, Oklahoma

BLENDER LEMON PIE FILLING

3/4 cup sugar
1/4 cup cornstarch
Dash of salt
1 cup water
1/4 cup lemon juice
Grated rind
    of 1 lemon
3 egg yolks
1 tablespoon butter
    or margarine,
    softened
1 (9-inch) baked
    pie shell
1 (3-egg white) recipe
    meringue

Combine sugar, cornstarch, salt, water, lemon juice, lemon rind, egg yolks and butter in blender container. Process at high speed for 20 seconds. Pour into saucepan. Cook over low heat, stirring constantly, until thickened. Pour into baked pie shell; let cool. Preheat oven to 350 degrees. Top with meringue. Bake for 5 minutes or until brown on top. Yield: 6 servings.

A. Chris Free, Delta Omicron
West Columbia, South Carolina

EASY LEMON OR LIME PIE

1 (6-ounce) can frozen
    lemonade or
    limeade
1 (14-ounce) can
    sweetened
    condensed milk
1 (8-ounce) carton
    whipped topping
6 drops of yellow or
    green food coloring
1 (9-inch) graham
    cracker crumb pie crust

Combine lemonade, condensed milk, whipped topping and food coloring in mixer bowl. Mix thoroughly at slow speed. Pour into pie crust. Freeze. Remove from freezer shortly before serving. Yield: 6 to 8 servings.

Phyllis Blaney, Xi Chi Nu
San Marcos, California

COOL 'N EASY LIME PIE

2/3 cup boiling water
1 (3-ounce) package
    lime gelatin
1/2 cup cold water
Ice cubes
1 (8-ounce) carton
    frozen whipped
    topping, thawed
1 (9-inch) graham
    cracker crumb
    pie crust
Whipped topping
    to taste
Favorite topping
    sprinkles

Stir boiling water into gelatin in bowl, stirring for 2 minutes or until gelatin is dissolved. Mix cold water and ice cubes to make 1 1/4 cups. Stir into gelatin until thickened. Remove any remaining ice. Stir in 8 ounces whipped topping until smooth. Spoon into pie crust. Chill for 4 hours or until firm. Garnish with whipped topping to taste and favorite topping sprinkles. Yield: 8 servings.

Lorie Berndt, Xi Kappa Phi
San Dimas, California

✦ ♥ GUILTLESS KEY LIME PIE

2/3 cup yogurt cheese
1 envelope unflavored gelatin
1/4 cup lime juice
1/4 cup milk
1 egg, separated
2/3 cup 1% cottage cheese
1/4 cup sugar substitute
Grated lime rind
3 tablespoons sugar substitute
1 (9-inch) graham cracker crumb pie shell

Line strainer with cheesecloth or paper filter. Spoon yogurt into strainer. Cover. Refrigerate overnight. Sprinkle gelatin over lime juice in 2-cup glass measure. Microwave on high until gelatin is dissolved. Stir in milk and egg yolk. Microwave on medium for 30 seconds to 1 minute or until hot and slightly thick. Process cottage cheese until smooth in food processor. Stir in yogurt cheese, 1/4 cup sugar substitute and lime rind. Add gelatin mixture. Process until blended. Refrigerate until consistency of egg white. Beat egg white in mixer bowl until soft peaks form. Add 3 tablespoons sugar substitute. Fold into cheese mixture. Pour into pie shell. Refrigerate for several hours. Drizzle small amount of lime juice and rind over pie just before serving. Yield: 6 servings.

Andrea Wood, Xi Alpha
Winnipeg, Manitoba, Canada

FAVORITE KEY LIME PIE

3 eggs
3/4 cup sugar
1/2 cup Key lime juice
1 teaspoon grated lime rind
8 ounces cream cheese, softened
1 (9-inch) baked pie shell
1 cup heavy cream, whipped

Beat eggs and sugar in top of double boiler until thick and fluffy. Continue beating while gradually adding lime juice and rind. Cook over hot water, stirring constantly, until custard is thick. Let cool slightly. Add cream cheese gradually, blending until smooth. Pour into pie shell. Garnish with whipped cream. Yield: 6 to 8 servings.

Pam Edwards, Preceptor Alpha
Columbia, South Carolina

KEY LIME PIE

4 egg yolks
1 (14-ounce) can sweetened condensed milk
1/2 cup fresh lime juice
1 (9-inch) graham cracker crumb pie crust
4 egg whites
1/2 cup sugar

Combine egg yolks and condensed milk in medium bowl. Fold in lime juice using spoon or rubber spatula. Pour into pie crust. Refrigerate for 1 hour. Preheat oven to 400 degrees. Beat egg whites in large mixer bowl until foamy. Add sugar gradually, beating constantly until stiff and glossy. Spread over filling, sealing to edge. Bake for 5 minutes or until meringue is golden. Let cool slightly. Refrigerate overnight. Yield: 6 servings.

Linda Boyle, Xi Alpha Zeta
Columbia, Maryland

GRAND HOTEL MACADAMIA PIE

I served this pie at a luau. It was "almost" like being there!

1/2 cup sugar
1/4 cup sifted cornstarch
1/2 teaspoon salt
2 cups milk
4 egg yolks, lightly beaten
1 tablespoon butter or margarine
2 teaspoons Kahlua
3/4 cup macadamia nuts
1 cup whipped cream
1 (9-inch) baked pie shell
1 cup whipped cream

Combine sugar, cornstarch and salt in top of double boiler. Add milk slowly, stirring constantly. Place over gently boiling water. Cook for 10 to 15 minutes, stirring until mixture is thickened to a custard consistency. Blend 1/2 cup hot sugar mixture into beaten egg yolks, 1 tablespoon at a time. Pour slowly back into remaining sugar mixture, mixing well. Cook for 3 to 5 minutes longer or until custard is thick. Add butter. Let cool to room temperature. Stir in Kahlua. Reserve 1 tablespoon chopped macadamia nuts. Stir remaining nuts into custard. Fold in 1 cup whipped cream. Spoon into pie shell. Garnish with remaining whipped cream and reserved macadamia nuts. Chill. Yield: 6 servings.

Judy P. Newman, Xi Beta Rho
Norman, Oklahoma

MARGARITA PIE

1/2 cup butter or margarine
1 1/4 cups finely crushed pretzels
1/4 cup sugar
1 (14-ounce) can sweetened condensed milk
1/3 cup lime juice from concentrate
2 to 3 tablespoons Tequila
2 tablespoons Triple Sec or other orange-flavored liqueur
1 cup whipping cream, whipped
Pretzel crumbs (optional)
Lime slices (optional)

Melt butter in small saucepan. Stir in 1 1/4 cups pretzel crumbs and sugar. Press mixture on bottom and side of 10-inch pie plate. Chill. Combine sweetened condensed milk, lime juice, Tequila and Triple Sec in medium bowl; blend well. Fold in whipped cream. Spoon into pie crust. Freeze for 4 hours or refrigerate for 2 hours. Garnish with pretzel crumbs or lime slices. Freeze or refrigerate leftovers. Yield: 6 servings.

Cletah M. Garen, Zeta Kappa
Defiance, Ohio

MACAROON-CUSTARD PIE

4 eggs
1 cup sugar
1/2 teaspoon salt (optional)
1/4 teaspoon nutmeg
1 2/3 cups milk
1 teaspoon vanilla extract
1 1/4 cups chopped, shredded or flaked coconut
1 (9-inch) unbaked pie shell

Preheat oven to 425 degrees. Beat eggs in bowl. Add sugar, salt, nutmeg, milk and vanilla; mix well. Stir in coconut. Pour into pie shell. Bake for 15 minutes. Reduce temperature to 350 degrees. Bake for 30 minutes longer or until knife inserted in center comes out clean. Yield: 6 servings.

Kathleen Bennett, Laureate Epsilon Kappa
Easton, Pennsylvania

MILLION DOLLAR PIE

1/4 cup lemon juice
1 (14-ounce) can sweetened condensed milk
1 (8-ounce) carton whipped topping
3/4 cup chopped pecans
3/4 cup coconut
1 (15-ounce) can pineapple, drained
2 (9-inch) graham cracker crumb pie crusts

Combine lemon juice and sweetened condensed milk in mixer bowl; mix well. Fold in whipped topping, pecans, coconut and pineapple. Pour into pie shells, dividing equally. Chill. Yield: 12 to 16 servings.

Cheryl Bennett, Preceptor Tau
Slater, South Carolina

OATMEAL PIE

2 eggs, beaten
1/2 cup sugar
1/3 cup butter
2/3 cup packed dark brown sugar
3/4 cup quick-cooking oats
2/3 cup shredded coconut
1 teaspoon vanilla extract
1 (8-inch) unbaked pie shell

Preheat oven to 350 degrees. Beat eggs. Cream sugar and butter in mixer bowl. Add eggs; mix well. Add brown sugar, oats, coconut and vanilla; mix well. Pour into pie crust. Bake for 35 to 40 minutes or until tests done. Yield: 4 servings.

Mary Bradshaw, Xi Alpha
Omaha, Nebraska

PEACH PEASANT BERRY PIE

Pastry for 9-inch pie shell
2/3 cup sugar
3 tablespoons cornstarch
3 pounds ripe or frozen peaches
1/2 cup blueberries
1/2 cup raspberries
1 tablespoon sugar

Preheat oven to 450 degrees. Roll out pastry dough on lightly floured surface to about 14-inch circle. Place in 9-inch pie pan. Blend 2/3 cup sugar with cornstarch in large bowl. Add peaches, tossing gently to cover with mixture. Let stand for 10 minutes. Combine blueberries and raspberries in bowl. Stir gently into peaches. Pour fruit into pie shell. Fold overhanging edge of dough to cover outer portion of filling. Sprinkle 1 teaspoon sugar over dough. Bake for 20 minutes or until crust begins to brown. Reduce oven temperature to 375 degrees. Bake for 35 to 45 minutes longer or until fruit is bubbling and crust is golden. Yield: 6 to 8 servings.

Claudia M. Long, Kappa Kappa
Meriden, Kansas

APPALACHIAN PEACH PIE

3/4 cup vanilla wafers, finely crushed
1/2 cup chopped almonds
3 tablespoons margarine, melted
1 (9-inch) unbaked pie shell
2 eggs, beaten
1 tablespoon lemon juice
1/4 cup sugar
3 (16-ounce) cans peach slices

Preheat oven to 450 degrees. Combine crushed wafers, almonds and margarine in bowl; mix well. Cover pie shell with double thickness of cooking foil. Bake for 5 minutes. Remove foil. Bake for 5 minutes longer. Reduce oven temperature to 375 degrees. Combine eggs and lemon juice in mixer bowl; beat until well blended. Stir in sugar. Fold in peaches. Spoon mixture into pie shell. Sprinkle with topping. Cover edge of pie shell with cooking foil. Bake for 20 minutes. Remove foil. Bake for 15 to 20 minutes longer. Yield: 8 servings.

Margaret Buckhorn, Beta Pi
Lakeview, Oregon

FAVORITE PEANUT BUTTER PIE

This is a great pie for reunions. You never have to carry any home.

2 tablespoons (heaping) cornstarch
2 eggs, well beaten
1 cup sugar
2 cups milk
1 teaspoon vanilla extract
1/2 cup creamy peanut butter
1 (9-inch) baked pie shell
Whipped topping

Combine cornstarch, eggs, sugar and milk in saucepan; mix well. Bring to a boil over medium heat, stirring constantly, until thickened. Add vanilla and peanut butter; mix well. Pour into pie shell. Chill. Top with whipped topping just before serving. Yield: 6 to 8 servings.

Betty A. King, Laureate Alpha Epsilon
Independence, Missouri

PEANUT BUTTER PIE

1 cup sugar
4 tablespoons (heaping) all-purpose flour
3 egg yolks
2 cups milk
1 tablespoon butter
1 teaspoon vanilla extract
6 tablespoons confectioners' sugar
2 tablespoons peanut butter
1 (9-inch) baked pie shell
3 egg whites
6 tablespoons sugar
1 teaspoon vanilla extract

Preheat oven to 350 degrees. Combine 1 cup sugar and flour in bowl; mix well. Combine egg yolks, milk, butter and 1 teaspoon vanilla in saucepan; mix well. Add sugar-flour mixture. Cook, stirring, over medium heat until thickened. Combine confectioners' sugar and peanut butter in bowl; mix well. Spread in pie crust. Pour filling on top of peanut butter mixture. Beat egg whites in mixer bowl until stiff. Add 6 tablespoons sugar, 1 tablespoon at a time, beating constantly. Add 1 teaspoon vanilla, beating until stiff peaks form. Spoon meringue onto pie, sealing to edge. Bake for 10 minutes or until lightly browned. Yield: 8 servings.

Kathy Williams, Preceptor Beta Pi
Yorktown, Indiana

FLUFFY PEANUT BUTTER PIE

1/3 cup margarine
1 (6-ounce) package chocolate chips
2 1/2 cups Rice Krispies
8 ounces cream cheese, softened
1 (14-ounce) can sweetened condensed milk
3/4 cup chunky peanut butter
3 tablespoons lemon juice
1 teaspoon vanilla extract
1 cup whipped cream
1 to 2 teaspoons chocolate syrup

Combine margarine and chocolate chips in heavy saucepan. Place over low heat, stirring until melted. Remove from heat. Stir in Rice Krispies gently until completely coated. Press into buttered 9-inch pie pan. Chill for 30 minutes. Beat cream cheese in large mixer bowl until fluffy. Add condensed milk and peanut butter; mix well. Stir in lemon juice and vanilla. Fold in whipped cream. Turn into chocolate crust. Drizzle with chocolate syrup. Chill for 4 hours. Store leftovers in refrigerator. Yield: 6 to 8 servings.

Kathleen Radcliffe, Laureate Beta
Lancaster, Pennsylvania

Barbara Paradis, Psi Sigma, Tequesta, Florida, makes an Easy Chocolate Pie by beating 2 packages chocolate instant pudding mix and 1 quart vanilla ice cream together until pudding is dissolved. Pour into 9-inch graham cracker pie crust. Refrigerate until set. Serve with whipped topping. Yield: 8 servings.

REESE'S PEANUT BUTTER PIE

1 quart chocolate ice cream, softened
1/2 cup peanut butter
1 (9-inch) graham cracker crumb pie crust
1/4 cup hot fudge sauce

Combine ice cream and peanut butter in bowl; mix well. Spoon into crust. Freeze until firm. Spoon fudge sauce over top. Return to freezer. Remove from freezer 15 minutes before serving. Yield: 6 to 8 servings.

Vivian Windhorn, Laureate Beta Omega
Bourbonnais, Illinois

FROZEN PEANUT BUTTER PIES

8 ounces cream cheese, softened
2/3 cup peanut butter
2/3 cup milk
2 cups confectioners' sugar
1 (12-ounce) carton frozen whipped topping, thawed
2 (9-inch) baked pie shells

Mix cream cheese, peanut butter and milk in mixer bowl. Add confectioners' sugar and whipped topping; mix well. Pour into pie shells, dividing equally. Freeze until firm. Store in freezer. Yield: 12 servings.

Patricia Mullens, Laureate Alpha Eta
Beckley, West Virginia

❖ FROZEN PEANUT BUTTER BRICKLE PIE

4 ounces fat-free cream cheese, softened
1 cup confectioners' sugar
1 cup chunky peanut butter
1/2 cup milk
1 (8-ounce) carton frozen whipped topping, thawed
1 (6-ounce) package Bits o'Brickle
1/4 cup chocolate chips
Chocolate syrup

Beat cream cheese in mixer bowl for 20 seconds. Add confectioners' sugar; mix well. Add peanut butter; mix until blended. Add milk. Fold in whipped topping and Bits o'Brickle. Sprinkle chocolate chips in crust. Pour cream cheese mixture into crust over chips. Freeze. Drizzle with chocolate syrup just before serving. Yield: 8 to 10 servings.

Dolores Durnwald, Preceptor Alpha Tau
Whitesburg, Georgia

Shirley Emaar, Xi Zeta Epsilon, Kalamazoo, Michigan, makes a Dream Peanut Butter Pie by whipping 8 ounces cream cheese in mixer bowl until soft. Add 1/2 cup crunchy peanut butter, 1 cup confectioners' sugar and 1/2 cup milk; mix well. Fold in 8 ounces whipped topping. Pour into 9-inch graham cracker crumb pie crust. Freeze. Serve frozen as it thaws quickly. Yield: 6 servings.

CRUNCHY PEAR PIE

1/2 cup butter
1/4 cup packed dark brown sugar
1 1/3 cups all-purpose flour
1/2 cup flaked coconut
1/2 cup packed dark brown sugar
1/4 teaspoon salt
3/4 cup pear juice
3/4 cup milk
2 eggs, slightly beaten
2 tablespoons butter
1/2 teaspoon vanilla extract
1 cup whipping cream, whipped
2 tablespoons sugar
1 1/2 teaspoons cinnamon
6 pear halves, well drained

Preheat oven to 400 degrees. Combine 1/2 cup butter, 1/4 cup brown sugar, 1 cup flour and coconut in bowl; mix well. Spread in 9-by-13-inch baking pan. Bake for 15 minutes. Remove from oven; stir. Press 2 cups hot crunch in buttered pan. Combine 1/2 cup brown sugar, 1/3 cup flour and salt in saucepan; mix well. Add pear juice and milk. Cook over low heat, stirring, until mixture comes to a full boil. Remove from heat. Add eggs; mix well. Cook for 1 minute. Add 2 tablespoons butter and vanilla. Pour into crust. Chill. Spread whipped cream over filling. Combine 2 tablespoons sugar and cinnamon in bowl. Dip pear halves into mixture. Place, cut-side down, over whipped cream. Sprinkle remaining hot crunch mixture over pears and whipped cream. Yield: 8 servings.

Arlene P. Burton, Laureate Beta Omega
Manchester, Washington

GRANDPA'S PECAN PIE

3 eggs, beaten
1 cup dark corn syrup
1/2 cup sugar
1/4 cup melted margarine
2 cups cooked squash or pumpkin
1 (9-inch) unbaked pie shell
1 cup pecan halves
Whipped cream or ice cream

Preheat oven to 350 degrees. Combine eggs, corn syrup, sugar, margarine and squash in bowl; mix well. Pour into pie crust. Place pecan halves on top. Bake for 1 hour or until knife inserted 1 inch from edge comes out clean. Serve hot or cold with whipped cream or ice cream. Yield: 6 servings.

Eleanor Parker, Xi Alpha Xi
North Bridgton, Maine

MOCK PECAN PIE

2 cups packed dark brown sugar
1/2 cup melted margarine
1 tablespoon vanilla extract
4 eggs, beaten
1 cup mashed cooked pinto beans
1 (10-inch) unbaked pie shell
Whipped cream or vanilla ice cream

Preheat oven to 350 degrees. Combine brown sugar, margarine, vanilla and eggs in mixer bowl; beat until well blended. Stir in pinto beans. Pour into pie shell. Bake for 45 to 50 minutes or until knife inserted in center comes out clean. Serve warm or chilled with whipped cream. Yield: 6 servings.

Debbie Mistler, Alpha Gamma Theta
Owensville, Missouri

PUMPKIN PIE TROPICAL

2 eggs, slightly beaten
1 1/2 cups solid-pack pumpkin
1 large ripe banana, mashed
1/2 cup packed dark brown sugar
3/4 teaspoon ground ginger
3/4 teaspoon ground cloves
1 1/4 teaspoons nutmeg
1 1/4 teaspoons cinnamon
1/2 teaspoon salt
1 2/3 cups evaporated milk
1 (9-inch) unbaked pie shell
1/2 cup pecan halves (optional)
1 tablespoon honey
1 tablespoon creamed margarine or butter
1/2 cup flaked coconut

Preheat oven to 425 degrees. Combine eggs, pumpkin, banana, brown sugar, ginger, cloves, nutmeg, cinnamon, salt and evaporated milk in mixer bowl; mix well. Cover bottom of pie shell with pecan halves. Pour filling over pecans. Cover fluted edge of crust with 2-inch strip cooking foil to prevent excessive browning. Bake for 15 minutes. Reduce oven temperature to 350 degrees. Bake for 45 minutes longer or until knife inserted in center comes out clean. Let pie cool completely. Increase oven temperature to broil. Combine honey and margarine in bowl. Drizzle over top of cool pie. Spread gently and evenly over pie surface. Sprinkle with flaked coconut. Place under broiler 5 inches from heat for 5 minutes or until toasted. Yield: 8 to 12 servings.

Joyce G. Weckerly, Preceptor Beta
Honolulu, Hawaii

SPICY PUMPKIN PIE

3 cups pumpkin
1 1/2 cups sugar
2 1/4 teaspoons cinnamon
1 1/2 teaspoons ginger
3/4 teaspoon nutmeg
1 teaspoon cloves
5 eggs
2 (13-ounce) cans evaporated milk
1/3 cup Brandy
2 (9-inch) unbaked pie shells
Whipped topping

Preheat oven to 400 degrees. Combine pumpkin, sugar, cinnamon, ginger, nutmeg, cloves, eggs, evaporated milk and Brandy in mixer bowl. Beat at medium speed until well blended. Pour into unbaked pie shells. Bake for 50 minutes to 1 hour or until knife inserted 1/2 way between center and edge comes out clean. Let cool. Serve with whipped topping. Yield: 12 to 16 servings.

Vivian Firlein, Epsilon Xi
Page, Arizona

RHUBARB PIE

4 cups cut-up rhubarb
1 cup sugar
1 (3-ounce) package raspberry gelatin
1 drop of red food coloring
1 teaspoon vanilla extract
1 1/2 cups milk
1 (3-ounce) package vanilla instant pudding mix
8 ounces whipped topping
1 cup marshmallows
2 (9-inch) baked pie shells

Combine rhubarb and sugar in saucepan; mix well. Let stand for 30 minutes. Cook until tender. Add gelatin, food coloring and vanilla; mix well. Let stand until syrupy. Add milk to pudding mix in mixer bowl; mix well. Add whipped topping; mix well. Add pudding mixture to cold rhubarb mixture; mix well. Stir in marshmallows. Spoon into pie shells. Refrigerate. Yield: 12 servings.

Velda M. Kloke, Preceptor Alpha Chi
Harvard, Nebraska

RHUBARB SOUR CREAM CRUNCH PIE

1 egg
1 cup sour cream
1 cup sugar
3 tablespoons cornstarch
1/2 teaspoon cinnamon
1/2 teaspoon nutmeg
3 cups coarsely sliced rhubarb
1 (9-inch) unbaked pie shell
1/2 cup rolled oats
1/3 cup packed dark brown sugar
1/3 cup all-purpose flour
1/3 cup butter, or margarine, softened

Preheat oven to 400 degrees. Whisk egg with sour cream in medium bowl. Combine sugar, cornstarch, cinnamon and nutmeg in bowl; stir into egg mixture. Stir in rhubarb. Spoon into pastry shell. Combine oats, brown sugar and flour in medium bowl. Cut in butter until mixture is crumbly. Sprinkle over rhubarb filling. Bake for 15 minutes. Reduce oven temperature to 375 degrees. Bake for 40 to 50 minutes longer or until top is golden brown and filling is puffed and set. Serve warm. Yield: 6 servings.

Michelle Fox, Zeta Kappa
Harrow, Ontario, Canada

RHUBARB CREAM PIE

This was my grandmother's and daddy's favorite pie.

1 1/2 cups sugar
3 tablespoons all-purpose flour
1/2 teaspoon nutmeg
1 tablespoon butter or margarine
2 eggs, well beaten
3 cups cubed rhubarb
Pastry for 9-inch 2-crust pie
Milk

Preheat oven to 450 degrees. Blend sugar, flour, nutmeg and butter in mixer bowl; mix well. Add eggs; beat until smooth. Place rhubarb in pastry-lined pie plate. Pour mixture over rhubarb. Top with remaining pastry. Brush small amount of milk over pastry. Bake for 10 minutes. Reduce oven temperature to 350 degrees. Bake for 30 minutes longer. Yield: 6 servings.

Jill Coté, Preceptor Theta
Virginia Beach, Virginia

SHERRY PIE

1 (10-ounce) package marshmallows
1/2 cup Sherry
1 cup whipping cream, whipped
1 (9-inch) graham cracker crumb pie crust
Bitter chocolate to taste

Melt marshmallows in saucepan. Stir in Sherry. Fold in whipped cream. Pour into crust. Grate chocolate over top. Chill. Yield: 6 servings.

Emily A. Mullis, Laureate Alpha Sigma
Panama City Beach, Florida

SODA CRACKER PIE

This recipe has been passed down through generations.

12 soda crackers
1/2 teaspoon baking powder
1 cup chopped walnuts or pecans
3 egg whites
1 cup sugar
1 teaspoon vanilla extract
1 (8-ounce) carton whipped topping

Preheat oven to 350 degrees. Crush crackers in bowl. Add baking powder and walnuts; mix well. Beat egg whites in mixer bowl until foamy. Add sugar gradually, beating constantly until stiff and glossy. Add vanilla. Fold into cracker mixture. Spoon into greased pie pan. Bake for 30 minutes. Let cool at room temperature for 2 hours. Refrigerate for 6 to 8 hours. Spread whipped topping on pie just before serving. Yield: 6 servings.

Stacey Stone, Xi Theta
Kearns, Utah

EASY STRAWBERRY PIE

8 ounces cream cheese, softened
1 cup sugar
1 (9-inch) baked pie shell
1 package frozen strawberries
1 (8-ounce) carton whipped topping

Beat cream cheese in mixer bowl. Add sugar, a small amount at a time, while beating. Spread in cooled pie shell. Use only a small amount of juice if strawberries are frozen in juice. Spoon strawberries on top. Cover with whipped topping. Chill. Yield: 6 servings.

Mable Shields, Preceptor Alpha Mu
Knoxville, Tennessee

FAVORITE FRESH STRAWBERRY PIE

1 cup all-purpose flour
1/2 teaspoon salt
1/3 cup vegetable shortening
7 to 8 tablespoons ice water
3/4 cup sugar
2 tablespoons cornstarch
2 tablespoons white corn syrup
1 cup water
3 tablespoons strawberry gelatin
Few drops of red food coloring
1 quart fresh strawberries
1 (8-ounce) carton whipped topping

Preheat oven to 375 degrees. Sift flour into bowl. Add salt; mix well. Cut in shortening until mixture is size of peas. Add 7 to 8 tablespoons ice water. Form into ball. Sift additional flour onto waxed paper. Roll crust 1 1/2-inches larger than pie plate. Press into glass pie plate. Turn under top edge; crimp. Prick with fork. Bake for 15 minutes. Combine sugar, cornstarch, corn syrup and 1 cup water in saucepan. Bring to a boil, stirring constantly, until clear and thickened. Remove from heat. Stir in strawberry gelatin until dissolved. Add red food coloring. Rinse and stem strawberries in bowl. Remove excess water from berries. Cut strawberries lengthwise. Fold into cooled glaze mixture. Pour into pie shell. Top with whipped topping. Place whole strawberry in center of pie. Chill for 1 hour or until firm. Yield: 8 servings.

Sandra K. Hausner, Preceptor Beta Epsilon
Drumright, Oklahoma

FRESH STRAWBERRY PIE

1 1/2 cups all-purpose flour
1 1/2 teaspoons sugar
1 teaspoon salt
1/2 cup vegetable oil
2 tablespoons cold milk
6 cups strawberries
1 cup sugar
3 tablespoons cornstarch
1/2 cup water
Few drops of red food coloring
3 ounces cream cheese, softened

Preheat oven to 425 degrees. Combine flour, 1 1/2 teaspoons sugar and salt in 9-inch pie plate; mix well. Combine oil and milk in bowl; mix thoroughly with fork. Pour over dry ingredients; mix well. Press into pie plate. Prick with fork. Bake for 8 minutes or until lightly browned. Let cool completely. Mash enough strawberries to measure 1 cup. Mix 1 cup sugar and cornstarch in saucepan. Stir in water and crushed berries gradually. Cook over medium heat, stirring constantly, until mixture is thickened and begins to boil. Boil, stirring, for 1 minute. Stir in food coloring; let cool. Beat cream cheese in mixer bowl until smooth. Spread on bottom of cooled baked pie shell. Fill shell with remaining strawberries. Pour cooked mixture over strawberries. Chill for 3 hours or until set. May substitute 6 cups raspberries for strawberries if desired. Yield: 6 to 8 servings.

Gigi Bradshaw, Epsilon Omicron
Hope, Arkansas

QUICK FRESH STRAWBERRY PIE

1 quart fresh strawberries
2 containers strawberry jell
1 (10-inch) baked pie shell
1 (8-ounce) carton whipped topping

Hull and rinse strawberries. Let drain until dry. Fold strawberries into jell in bowl. Pour into pie shell. Dollop whipped topping around rim of pie. Yield: 8 servings.

Mary Ann O'Sullivan, Preceptor Alpha Beta
Terrytown, Louisiana

STRAWBERRY DELIGHT PIE

1 (3-ounce) package strawberry gelatin
2/3 cup boiling water
2 cups ice cubes
1 (8-ounce) carton whipped topping
1 cup fresh strawberries, sliced
1 (9-inch) graham cracker crumb pie crust

Dissolve gelatin in boiling water in bowl, stirring for 3 minutes. Add ice cubes, stirring constantly for 2 to 3 minutes or until gelatin is thickened. Remove any unmelted ice. Blend in whipped topping with wire whisk. Fold in strawberries. Spoon into pie crust. Chill for 3 hours. Garnish as desired. Yield: 6 servings.

Roberta T. White, Eta Master
Las Cruces, New Mexico

SURPRISE PIE

1/4 cup lemon juice
1 can sweetened condensed milk
1 (16-ounce) carton whipped topping
2 cans fruit cocktail, well drained
Coconut to taste (optional)
Chopped nuts to taste (optional)
2 (9-inch) graham cracker crumb pie crusts

Combine lemon juice, condensed milk and whipped topping in mixer bowl; mix well. Fold in fruit cocktail, coconut and nuts by hand. Pour into pie crusts, dividing equally. Chill for 2 hours. Yield: 12 servings.

Henrietta Wright, Beta Kappa
Mayking, Kentucky

BEST PIE CRUST

3 cups all-purpose flour
1 teaspoon salt
1 cup vegetable shortening
1 teaspoon vinegar
5 tablespoons milk
1 egg, beaten

Combine flour and salt in bowl. Cut in shortening until crumbly. Add vinegar, milk and egg; blend well. Divide dough into 4 equal portions. Refrigerate. Yield: 2 (2-crust) pie shells.

Sandra Hollingsworth, Chi Psi
Marseilles, Illinois

Sweets Treats

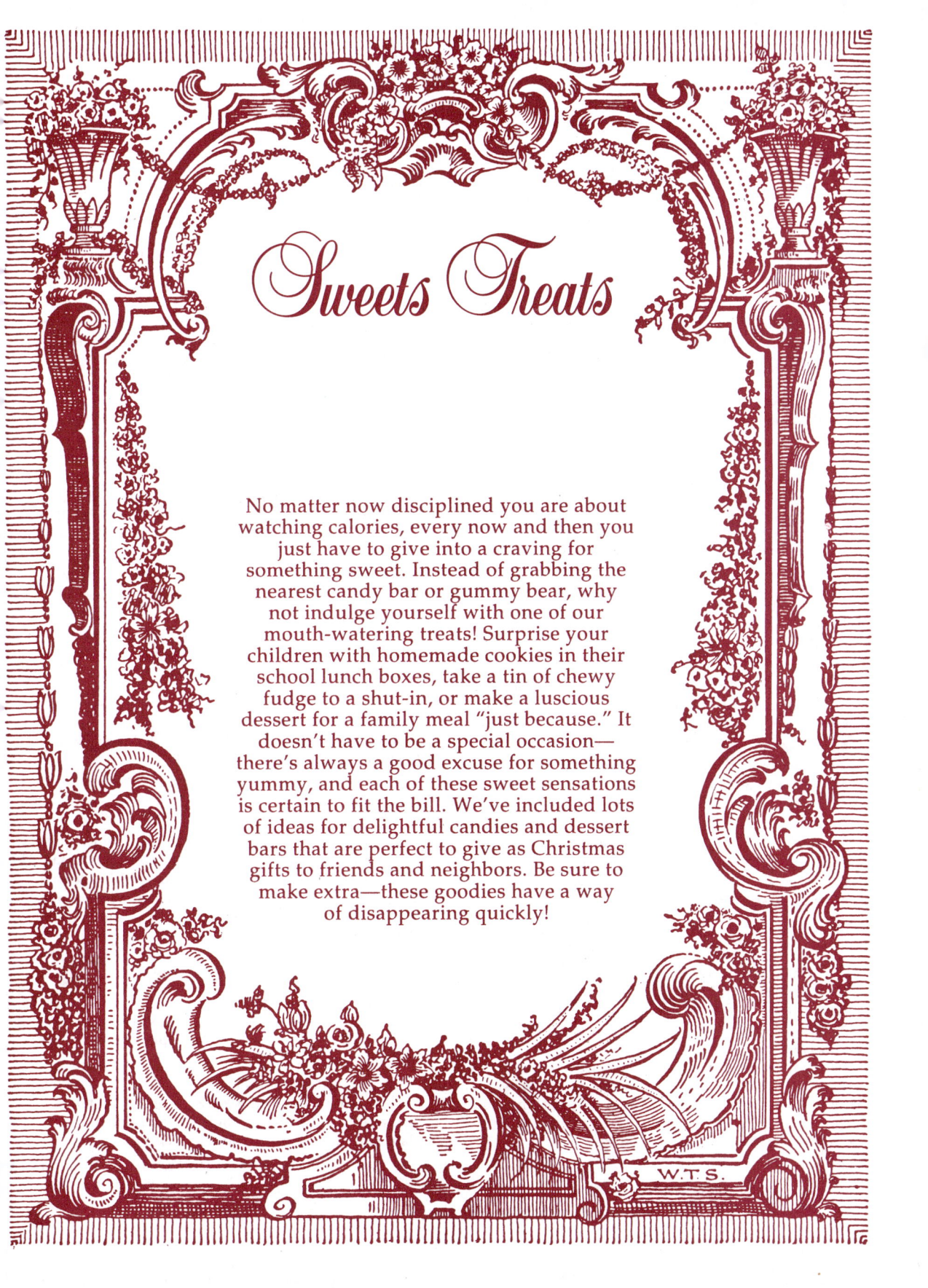

No matter now disciplined you are about watching calories, every now and then you just have to give into a craving for something sweet. Instead of grabbing the nearest candy bar or gummy bear, why not indulge yourself with one of our mouth-watering treats! Surprise your children with homemade cookies in their school lunch boxes, take a tin of chewy fudge to a shut-in, or make a luscious dessert for a family meal "just because." It doesn't have to be a special occasion—there's always a good excuse for something yummy, and each of these sweet sensations is certain to fit the bill. We've included lots of ideas for delightful candies and dessert bars that are perfect to give as Christmas gifts to friends and neighbors. Be sure to make extra—these goodies have a way of disappearing quickly!

ALMOND BARS

8 ounces cream cheese, softened
3/4 cup butter or margarine
3/4 cup sugar
2 cups all-purpose flour
1/2 teaspoon baking powder
1 teaspoon vanilla extract
1 1/2 cups chocolate chips
1/2 cup sliced almonds

Preheat oven to 375 degrees. Combine cream cheese and butter in mixer bowl; beat well. Add sugar gradually, beating until light and fluffy. Add flour and baking powder; mix well. Stir in vanilla. Spread in buttered 9-by-13-inch baking pan. Bake for 15 minutes. Spread chocolate chips over top; let melt. Sprinkle almonds over melted chocolate. Let cool completely. Yield: 12 servings.

June Gentray, Preceptor Laureate Beta Eta
Delta, British Columbia, Canada

BOURBON-SOAKED CHOCOLATE TRUFFLES

7 ounces semisweet baking chocolate
1 ounce unsweetened baking chocolate
1/4 cup Bourbon
2 tablespoons strong coffee
1/2 cup unsalted butter, cut in 1-inch pieces
6 ounces gingersnaps
1/2 cup baking cocoa
1/4 cup instant coffee powder

Break chocolate into small pieces. Combine chocolate pieces, Bourbon and coffee in top of double boiler over boiling water. Turn off heat. Let set over hot water for 5 minutes or until smooth. Pour into mixer bowl. Add butter; mix well. Place gingersnaps in blender container. Process until smooth. Add to chocolate mixture; mix well. Chill for several hours. Combine cocoa and instant coffee powder in bowl. Spread on plate. Spoon small spoonfuls of chocolate mixture onto plate. Shape into balls. Roll in cocoa mixture. Place in paper or foil candy cups. Chill in covered container. May be refrigerated for several weeks or frozen. Yield: 20 to 40 truffles.

Jeanne Carr, Gamma Upsilon
Ephrata, Washington

❖ LOW-FAT CHOCOLATE-WALNUT FUDGE

2 tablespoons butter or margarine
2/3 cup evaporated skim milk
2 1/2 cups sugar
1 (12-ounce) package chocolate chips
1 (2-ounce) jar baby food prunes
1 (7-ounce) jar marshmallow creme
2/3 cup chopped walnuts
1 1/2 teaspoons vanilla extract

Melt butter in large saucepan. Stir in skim milk and sugar. Bring to a boil over medium heat, stirring constantly. Boil for 5 minutes, stirring constantly. Remove from heat. Stir in chocolate chips gradually. Add prunes, marshmallow creme, walnuts and vanilla. Pour into 9-by-13-inch pan lined with waxed paper. Chill until firm. Cut into pieces. Yield: 48 servings.

Carol Ann Blair, Delta Beta
Hazard, Kentucky

CRANBERRY CANDY

1 (16-ounce) can cranberry sauce
1 cup sugar
1 (3-ounce) package orange gelatin
2 (3-ounce) packages pineapple gelatin
1 cup chopped walnuts
Confectioners' sugar

Heat cranberry sauce in saucepan over low heat until melted. Add sugar and gelatins; mix well. Bring to a boil over medium heat. Boil for 2 minutes. Remove from heat. Add walnuts. Pour mixture into buttered 8-inch square pan. Refrigerate overnight. Cut into pieces. Roll in confectioners' sugar. Cover cookie sheet with confectioners' sugar. Place candy pieces on confectioners' sugar. Let stand for 3 days. Store candy in container with tight-fitting lid. This must dry out for 3 days to keep from being sticky. Yield: 12 servings.

Shasta L. Anker, Omicron Master
Los Angeles, California

MICROWAVE SALTED NUT ROLLS

1 (16-ounce) package dry roasted peanuts
1 (12-ounce) package peanut butter chips
3 tablespoons butter or margarine
1 (14-ounce) can sweetened condensed milk
1 (10-ounce) package miniature marshmallows

Place half the peanuts in buttered 9-by-13-inch pan. Place peanut butter chips and butter in microwave-safe dish. Microwave on low until melted. Add condensed milk; do not boil. Fold in marshmallows. Spread mixture over peanuts. Top with remaining peanuts. Chill. Yield: 16 to 20 servings.

Jan Campbell, Gamma Xi
Shakopee, Minnesota

PEANUT BUTTER FUDGE

2 cups sugar
1 cup milk
3 tablespoons peanut butter

Combine sugar and milk in saucepan. Bring to a boil. Cook over medium heat to soft-ball stage. Do not stir. Add peanut butter. Beat until hard. Pour onto buttered plate. Cut into squares. Yield: 12 servings.

Reta Durham, Xi Delta Nu
Fredericktown, Ohio

CREAMY PEANUT BUTTER FUDGE

8 ounces Velveeta cheese
1 cup margarine
1 cup peanut butter
2 teaspoons vanilla extract
2 pounds confectioners' sugar
Chopped nuts (optional)

Melt cheese and margarine in saucepan over low heat. Place peanut butter and vanilla in large bowl. Add cheese mixture; mix well. Add confectioners' sugar and nuts; mix well. Spread in lightly buttered jelly roll pan. Cut into squares. Store in refrigerator. Yield: 18 servings.

Myrna L. Liepins, Laureate Alpha Omega
Birmingham, Michigan

ACADIAN PRALINES

1 cup sugar
1/2 cup heavy cream
3 tablespoons corn syrup
1/16 teaspoon baking soda
1/16 teaspoon salt
1 cup pecan halves
1/2 teaspoon vanilla extract

Combine sugar, cream, corn syrup, baking soda and salt in heavy 2-quart saucepan; mix well. Cook over medium heat, stirring occasionally, until sugar dissolves and mixture comes to a boil. Cook, without stirring, until mixture reaches 234 degrees on candy thermometer or to soft-ball stage. Remove from heat. Add pecans and vanilla, beating until creamy and thick. Drop by heaping teaspoonfuls onto waxed paper-lined dish. Yield: 8 servings.

Sallie G. Caulfield, Preceptor Omega
West Monroe, Louisiana

FROSTED PECANS

1/2 cup sour cream
1 1/2 cups sugar
1 1/2 teaspoons vanilla extract
3 cups pecan halves

Combine sour cream, sugar and vanilla in 2-quart heavy saucepan. Cook to soft-ball stage or 234 degrees on candy thermometer, stirring frequently. Add pecans. Stir to coat. Turn onto buttered baking sheet. Separate with 2 forks into individual pieces. Yield: 12 servings.

Juanita Salazar, Alpha Omicron
Anthony, New Mexico

Margaret Mahoney, Mu Master, LaMarque, Texas, makes a Ritz Cracker Snack by combining 1 (8-ounce) package chopped dates and 1 (14-ounce) can sweetened condensed milk in saucepan; mix well. Cook until a thin consistency; remove from heat. Stir in 1 cup chopped pecans. Spread date mixture on 1 side of Ritz cracker. Cream 8 ounces softened cream cheese and 1/2 cup margarine in small mixer bowl. Add 1 (16-ounce) package confectioners' sugar. Beat until creamy. Spread over date mixture on each cracker. Let stand until firm. Yield: variable.

CINNAMON POPCORN

1 cup margarine
1/2 cup white corn syrup
1 (9-ounce) package cinnamon Emperials
14 cups popped popcorn

Preheat oven to 250 degrees. Combine margarine, corn syrup and Emperials in saucepan. Bring to a boil over medium heat. Boil for 15 minutes. Pour over popcorn. Stir to coat. Place in 9-by-13-inch baking pan. Bake for 1 hour, stirring every 15 minutes. Yield: 24 servings.

Karen L. Sawyer, Xi Lambda Mu
Bartlett, Illinois

BABY FOOD BARS

2 cups sugar
3 eggs
1 1/4 cups vegetable oil
2 cups all-purpose flour
1/4 teaspoon salt
2 teaspoons baking soda
2 teaspoons cinnamon
1 (4-ounce) jar baby food strained carrots
1 (4-ounce) jar baby food strained applesauce
1 (4-ounce) jar baby food strained apricots
2 cups confectioners' sugar
1/2 teaspoon vanilla extract
3 ounces cream cheese, softened
1 cup butter or margarine, softened
1/8 teaspoon Realemon juice

Preheat oven to 350 degrees. Cream sugar and eggs in bowl. Add next 8 ingredients; mix well. Pour into greased and floured 10-by-15-inch jelly roll pan. Bake for 25 minutes or until knife inserted in center comes out clean. Let cool. Combine remaining ingredients in order given in mixer bowl. Beat until creamy. Frost cooled bars. Yield: 24 servings.

Barbara Brown, Beta Omega
Kankakee, Illinois

BETTER-THAN-SEX BROWNIES

1 cup butter or margarine
4 ounces semisweet baking chocolate
4 eggs
2 cups sugar
1 cup all-purpose flour
1 teaspoon vanilla extract
1 cup chopped pecans

Preheat oven to 350 degrees. Place butter and chocolate in microwave-safe dish. Microwave until melted. Let cool. Beat eggs in mixer bowl until foamy. Add sugar slowly, beating until sugar is dissolved. Add flour; mix well. Fold in chocolate mixture. Add vanilla and pecans; mix well. Spread evenly in 11-by-13-inch baking pan. Bake for 30 to 45 minutes or until tests done. Yield: 24 servings.

Barbara Parham, Preceptor Beta Chi
Richmond, Virginia

♥ FAT-FREE BROWNIES

3/4 cup all-purpose flour
6 tablespoons baking cocoa
1 cup sugar
1/4 teaspoon salt (optional)
1/3 cup unsweetened applesauce
3 egg whites
1 teaspoon vanilla extract
1/4 cup chopped nuts (optional)
Nonstick vegetable cooking spray

Preheat oven to 325 degrees. Combine flour, cocoa, sugar and salt in bowl. Stir to mix well. Stir in applesauce, egg whites and vanilla; mix well. Fold in nuts. Coat 8-inch square pan with cooking spray. Spread batter evenly in pan. Bake for 23 to 25 minutes or until tests done. Let cool. Cut into squares. Yield: 16 servings.

Norma Nemec, Alpha Delta
Baker City, Oregon

KAHLUA DREAMS

1/3 cup packed light brown sugar
1/3 cup butter
2/3 cup sifted all-purpose flour
1/2 cup chopped pecans
2 squares unsweetened baking chocolate
1/4 cup vegetable shortening
1/4 cup butter
2 eggs, slightly beaten
1/2 cup sugar
1/2 cup packed light brown sugar
1 teaspoon vanilla extract
1/4 cup Kahlua
1/2 cup sifted all-purpose flour
1/4 teaspoon salt
1/2 cup chopped pecans
2 tablespoons butter
2 cups sifted confectioners' sugar
1 tablespoon Kahlua
1 tablespoon cream
2 squares semisweet baking chocolate
1 square unsweetened baking chocolate
2 teaspoons vegetable shortening

Preheat oven to 350 degrees. Combine 1/3 cup brown sugar, 1/3 cup butter, 2/3 cup flour and 1/2 cup pecans in bowl; mix well. Pat evenly into buttered 9-inch square baking pan. Melt 2 squares unsweetened chocolate, 1/4 cup shortening and 1/4 cup butter in saucepan over low heat. Let cool. Combine eggs with 1/2 cup sugar, 1/2 cup brown sugar and vanilla in bowl; mix well. Stir into cooled chocolate mixture. Add 1/4 cup Kahlua; mix well. Add 1/2 cup flour and salt; mix well. Add 1/2 cup pecans; mix well. Pour into crust. Bake for 25 minutes. Let cool. Combine 2 tablespoons butter, confectioners' sugar, 1 tablespoon Kahlua and cream in bowl; mix until smooth and creamy. Add additional Kahlua if needed for spreading consistency. Spread over top of baked mixture. Refrigerate for 30 minutes. Combine remaining ingredients in saucepan. Cook over low heat until melted, stirring to blend. Let cool. Spread over brownies. Cut into 1 1/2-inch squares. Yield: 36 servings.

Glenda Armstrong, Xi Beta Kappa
Prattville, Alabama

SNICKER BARS

1 (2-layer) package German chocolate cake mix
1/2 cup butter, melted
4 eggs
5 chopped Snicker candy bars, melted
1 (1-pound) package confectioners' sugar
8 ounces cream cheese, softened

Preheat oven to 375 degrees. Combine cake mix, butter and 2 eggs in bowl; mix well. Spread in 9-by-13-inch buttered baking pan. Combine candy bars, 2 eggs, confectioners' sugar and cream cheese in bowl; mix well. Pour over cake mixture. Bake for 30 to 35 minutes or until tests done. Yield: 16 servings.

Debbie Steelman, Pi Upsilon
Odessa, Missouri

SAVANNAH PECAN BARS

1 1/3 cups all-purpose flour
1/2 cup packed light brown sugar
1/3 cup margarine, melted
1 cup chopped pecans
3/4 cup dark corn syrup
1/4 cup packed light brown sugar
1/4 cup all-purpose flour
2 eggs
1 teaspoon vanilla extract
1/2 teaspoon salt

Preheat oven to 350 degrees. Combine 1 1/3 cups flour, 1/2 cup brown sugar and margarine in bowl; mix well. Press into buttered 9-by-13-inch baking pan. Combine pecans, corn syrup, 1/4 cup brown sugar, 1/4 cup flour, eggs, vanilla and salt in bowl; mix well. Pour over crust. Bake for 30 to 35 minutes or until top is set. Let cool. Cut into bars. Yield: 32 servings.

Darlene F. Gudgeon, Xi Alpha Sigma
Thermopolis, Wyoming

ALMOND SLICE

1/2 cup butter
1/2 cup sifted confectioners' sugar
1 cup all-purpose flour
1/4 teaspoon salt
1/4 cup butter
1/3 cup honey
2 teaspoons lemon juice
1 cup sliced almonds
1/2 teaspoon almond extract

Preheat oven to 350 degrees. Cream 1/2 cup butter and confectioners' sugar in mixer bowl. Stir in flour and salt; mix well. Pat into 9-inch square baking pan. Bake for 12 to 15 minutes or until golden brown. Melt 1/4 cup butter in small saucepan. Stir in honey and lemon juice. Bring to a boil over medium heat, stirring constantly. Remove from heat. Add almonds and almond extract. Spread over hot crust. Return to oven. Bake for 15 minutes longer or until golden brown. Cut into squares while hot. Yield: 16 servings.

Cynthia Reynolds, Gamma Phi
Maple Ridge, British Columbia, Canada

SWEDISH WALNUT SQUARES

1/2 cup butter
1 cup all-purpose flour
1 1/2 cups packed dark brown sugar
1/4 teaspoon salt
1/2 teaspoon baking powder
2 tablespoons all-purpose flour
3 eggs, beaten
1 teaspoon vanilla extract
3/4 cup coconut
3/4 cup chopped walnuts
1 1/2 cups confectioners' sugar
2 tablespoons butter or margarine
2 tablespoons orange juice
1 teaspoon lemon juice

Preheat oven to 350 degrees. Blend 1/2 cup butter and 1 cup flour in bowl until crumbly. Press into 9-by-12-inch glass baking dish. Bake for 12 minutes. Combine brown sugar, salt, baking powder, 2 tablespoons flour, eggs, vanilla, coconut and walnuts in bowl; mix well. Pour over baked crust. Bake for 20 or 25 minutes. Let cool. Combine confectioners' sugar, 2 tablespoons butter, orange juice and lemon juice in bowl; mix well. Frost baked mixture. Cut into squares. Yield: 18 servings.

Ann Blair, Preceptor Laureate Alpha Theta
Everett, Washington

♥ APPLE COOKIES

1/2 cup unsweetened applesauce
1 cup packed light brown sugar
4 egg whites
2 cups whole wheat pastry flour
1/2 cup rolled oats
2 teaspoons baking powder
1 teaspoon cinnamon
1 cup chopped walnuts
2 apples, chopped

Preheat oven to 350 degrees. Combine applesauce, brown sugar, egg whites, flour, oats, baking powder, cinnamon and walnuts in mixer bowl; mix until blended. Stir in apples; mix gently until evenly distributed through batter, being careful not to mash apples. Drop by rounded teaspoonfuls onto buttered cookie sheet. Bake for 20 minutes or until lightly browned. Yield: 30 servings.

Susan L. Yergler, Xi Alpha Sigma
Crescent City, Illinois

♥ SUGAR-FREE CARROT-APPLE COOKIES

1/2 cup butter
3/4 cup molasses
1 egg, beaten
2 cups all-purpose flour
1/2 teaspoon cinnamon
1/2 teaspoon nutmeg
1/4 teaspoon cloves
1/2 teaspoon baking soda
1/2 teaspoon baking powder
1 teaspoon salt
1 cup rolled oats
1/2 cup raisins
1/2 cup chopped walnuts
1 apple, peeled, shredded
1 cup grated carrots

Preheat oven to 350 degrees. Combine butter and molasses in mixer bowl; mix well. Add egg; mix well. Sift flour with next 6 ingredients. Add to butter mixture with oats, raisins and walnuts; mix well. Add apple and carrots; mix well. Place by spoonfuls onto buttered cookie sheet. Bake for 10 minutes. Yield: 48 servings.

Kathy Fike, Preceptor Epsilon Gamma
Lordstown, Ohio

BROWN SUGAR COOKIES

My fondest memory of these cookies is sneaking out to my grandmother's freezer to eat the cookie dough.

2 cups vegetable shortening
2 cups margarine or butter
3 cups sugar
3 cups packed dark brown sugar
6 eggs
6 teaspoons vanilla extract
9 3/4 cups all-purpose flour
3 teaspoons baking soda
3 teaspoons salt

Preheat oven to 375 degrees. Cream shortening, margarine, sugar and brown sugar in mixer bowl. Add eggs and vanilla; mix well. Sift flour, baking soda and salt together in bowl. Add to mixture; mix well. Shape dough into 2-by-8-inch rolls. Slice into 1/4-inch slices. Place on buttered cookie sheet. Bake for 11 minutes. This recipe is tripled. May be refrigerated for 1 month or frozen for 3 months. Wrap dough in waxed paper, then in foil to store. Variations: Chocolate Chip Cookies: Add 3 cups chocolate chips and 3 cups chopped nuts. Oatmeal-Coconut Cookies: Reduce flour by 3 cups and add 3 cups oatmeal and 3 cups coconut. Peanut Butter Cookies: Mix 3 cups peanut butter with shortening and margarine. Chocolate-Nut Cookies: Add 3 cups chopped nuts and 1 1/2 cups baking cocoa with flour. Fruit Cookies: Add 3 cups cherries, 1 1/2 cups nuts and 1 1/2 cups chopped candied fruit. Yield: 96 servings.

Fara Cornett Ashcraft, Eta Mu
Van Vleck, Texas

QUICK BROWNIES

3 1/2 cups Brownie Mix
1 teaspoon vanilla extract
2 eggs, beaten
2 tablespoons water
1/2 cup chopped nuts

Preheat oven to 350 degrees. Combine all ingredients in bowl; mix well. Pour into buttered 9-by-13-inch baking pan. Bake for 25 minutes. Yield: 20 servings.

BROWNIE MIX

6 cups all-purpose flour
4 teaspoons baking powder
4 teaspoons salt
8 cups sugar
2 1/2 cups baking cocoa
2 cups vegetable shortening

Sift first 5 ingredients into bowl. Cut in shortening, mixing well. Store in airtight container in refrigerator. Yield: 12 to 14 cups.

Valorie Stone
Pattonsburg, Missouri

♥ "LIGHT" CHOCOLATE CHEWY COOKIES

1 egg
1/2 cup sugar
1/2 cup packed light brown sugar
1/4 cup vegetable oil
1/4 cup plain yogurt
1 teaspoon vanilla extract
1 teaspoon chocolate extract
1 cup quick-cooking oats
1/2 cup baking cocoa
1 1/2 cups all-purpose flour
1/2 teaspoon baking powder
1/2 teaspoon baking soda
1/4 teaspoon salt
Nonstick vegetable cooking spray

Preheat oven to 375 degrees. Combine egg, sugar, brown sugar and oil in mixer bowl; beat until smooth. Add yogurt, vanilla, chocolate extract, oats and cocoa powder; beat well. Add flour, baking powder, baking soda and salt; beat until mixed. Let set for 10 minutes. Coat cookie sheet with cooking spray. Drop by teaspoonfuls 2 inches apart onto cookie sheet. Bake for 7 to 8 minutes or until puffy. Yield: 48 cookies.

Michelle Wendling, Beta Sigma Phi
Fort St. John, British Columbia, Canada

QUICK AND EASY CHOCOLATE SHORTBREAD

1 cup butter or margarine
1 cup packed dark brown sugar
2 cups all-purpose flour
1/4 teaspoon salt
1 teaspoon baking powder
2 teaspoons instant coffee powder
1 (16-ounce) package chocolate chips
1/4 teaspoon almond extract

Preheat oven to 325 degrees. Cream butter in mixer bowl until light and creamy. Add brown sugar; cream thoroughly. Add flour and salt; mix well. Add baking powder, instant coffee, chocolate chips and almond extract; mix well. Spread in buttered 10-by-15-inch baking pan. Bake for 25 minutes. Slice when slightly cool. Yield: 42 servings.

Lynda Wagoner, Xi Alpha Epsilon
Whitecourt, Alberta, Canada

MACAROON KISS COOKIES

A special way to give kisses away on Valentine's Day!

1/3 cup butter or margarine, softened
3 ounces cream cheese, softened
3/4 cup sugar
1 egg yolk
2 teaspoons almond extract
2 teaspoons orange juice
1 1/4 cups all-purpose flour
2 teaspoons baking powder
1/4 teaspoon salt
5 cups flaked coconut
1 (9-ounce) package chocolate kisses, unwrapped

Beat butter, cream cheese and sugar in large mixer bowl until well blended. Add egg yolk, almond extract and orange juice; beat well. Combine flour, baking powder and salt in bowl. Add gradually to butter mixture, mixing well. Stir in 3 cups coconut. Cover tightly. Refrigerate for 1 hour or until firm enough to handle. Preheat oven to 350 degrees. Shape dough into 1-inch balls. Roll balls in 2 cups coconut. Place on ungreased cookie sheet. Bake for 10 to 12 minutes or until lightly browned. Remove from oven. Press chocolate piece immediately on top each cookie. Let cool for 1 minute. Remove carefully from cookie sheet to wire rack. Let cool completely. Yield: 54 cookies.

Jill Huettenmueller, Xi Mu Delta
Excelsior Springs, Missouri

PEANUT BUTTER TREATS

1 egg, beaten
1 cup honey
3/4 cup vegetable oil
1/4 cup water
1 teaspoon salt
1 teaspoon vanilla extract
3 cups quick-cooking rolled oats
1 cup whole wheat flour
3/4 cup wheat germ
1 cup peanut butter-flavored candy pieces
1/2 cup sunflower seeds

Preheat oven to 350 degrees. Combine egg, honey, oil, water, salt and vanilla in bowl; mix well. Combine oats, flour and wheat germ in bowl. Add egg mixture to dry ingredients; mix well. Stir in peanut butter pieces and sunflower seeds. Drop by 1/4-cup measure 2 inches apart onto buttered cookie sheet. Flatten each mound to 3 inches in diameter. Bake for 15 to 20 minutes or until lightly browned. Let cool on wire rack. Yield: 20 cookies.

Gladys Weems, Laureate Eta Iota
Highland, California

♥ LOW-FAT NO-SUGAR PEANUT BUTTER COOKIES

1 cup whole wheat pastry flour
1/2 teaspoon salt
1 1/2 teaspoons baking soda
1 cup creamy peanut butter
1 cup frozen apple juice concentrate, thawed
1 teaspoon vanilla extract

Preheat oven to 350 degrees. Sift first 3 ingredients together into bowl. Blend peanut butter, apple juice and vanilla in bowl. Add peanut butter mixture to dry ingredients; mix well. Drop by spoonfuls onto cookie sheet. Score top with fork. Bake for 15 to 18 minutes. Yield: 24 cookies.

Roxanna E. Cooper, Alpha Sigma
Elkins, West Virginia

CAFÉ AU LAIT CHEESECAKE WITH CHOCOLATE GLAZE

1 3/4 cups chocolate graham cracker crumbs
1/3 cup margarine, melted
2 ounces semisweet chocolate, chopped
2 tablespoons water
1 tablespoon instant coffee powder
2 tablespoons coffee liqueur or water
8 ounces cream cheese, softened
1 cup sugar
2 tablespoons all-purpose flour
1 teaspoon vanilla extract
4 eggs, slightly beaten
1/2 cup whipping cream
9 ounces semisweet baking chocolate

Combine cracker crumbs and margarine in bowl; mix well. Press mixture evenly onto bottom and 2 inches up side of ungreased 8-inch springform pan. Chill. Combine 2 ounces chocolate, water and instant coffee in saucepan. Cook, stirring, over low heat until chocolate begins to melt. Remove from heat. Stir until smooth. Stir in liqueur; mix well. Let cool. Beat cream cheese, sugar, flour and vanilla in large mixer bowl at medium speed until smooth. Add eggs all at once, beating at low speed just until mixed. Do not overbeat. Reserve 2 cups cream cheese mixture; cover. Chill. Preheat oven to 350 degrees. Stir cooled chocolate-coffee mixture into remaining cream cheese mixture, stirring just until combined. Pour chocolate mixture into crust. Bake for 30 minutes or until side is set. Center will be soft. Remove reserved mixture from refrigerator 10 minutes before needed. Pull out oven rack gently just enough to reach inside of pan. Pour reserved mixture carefully into ring over outside edge of chocolate mixture. Spread gently and evenly over entire surface. Bake cheesecake for 20 to 25 minutes longer or until center appears nearly set when gently shaken. Let cool for 10 minutes on wire rack. Loosen side of cheesecake from pan. Chill overnight. Bring cream to a simmer in heavy medium saucepan. Reduce heat to low. Add remaining chocolate. Stir until melted and smooth. Let cool to lukewarm. Release pan side from cheesecake. Place cheesecake on rack set over baking sheet. Pour glaze over cheesecake spreading with spatula to cover top and side, allowing excess to drip onto baking sheet. Refrigerate for 30 minutes or until glaze sets. May be prepared 1 day ahead. Cover; refrigerate. Yield: 12 servings.

Cheril Roberts, Xi Lambda Mu
Sunrise Beach, Missouri

Vivian Sykes, Pi, Killarney, Manitoba, Canada, makes Hot Fudge Topping by microwaving 2 tablespoons butter in microwave-safe dish on medium for 1 minute. Stir in 6 tablespoons dark brown sugar, 3 tablespoons baking cocoa, 3 tablespoons milk and 1 1/2 teaspoons vanilla extract. Microwave, uncovered, on medium for 2 minutes. Serve over ice cream.

CHOCOLATE-GLAZED IRISH CREAM CHEESECAKE

6 whole graham crackers, crushed
1/4 cup unsalted butter, melted
24 ounces cream cheese, softened
7 tablespoons sugar
1 tablespoon all-purpose flour
2 eggs
6 tablespoons sour cream
6 tablespoons Irish cream liqueur
1 teaspoon vanilla extract
1/2 cup whipping cream
8 ounces semisweet chocolate

Preheat oven to 350 degrees. Combine crushed crackers and butter in bowl; mix well. Press in bottom of 9-inch springform pan. Bake for 8 minutes. Combine cream cheese and sugar in mixer bowl. Beat until creamy. Add flour and eggs, 1 at a time, just until combined. Add sour cream, Irish cream and vanilla; mix well. Pour into crust. Bake for 10 minutes. Reduce temperature to 250 degrees. Bake for 40 minutes or until set. Let cool in pan for 10 minutes. Loosen edge with sharp knife. Let cool. Refrigerate overnight. Bring whipping cream to a simmer in saucepan. Reduce heat to low. Add chocolate. Cook until melted. Let cool to lukewarm. Remove side of pan. Place cheesecake on rack over baking sheet. Pour glaze over cheesecake, spreading with spatula to cover top and side. Refrigerate until glaze sets.
Yield: 12 servings.

Kathryn B. Sides, Epsilon Rho
Brierfield, Alabama

FROZEN MOCHA CHEESECAKE

1 1/4 cups chocolate wafer cookie crumbs
1/4 cup sugar
1/4 cup margarine or butter, melted
8 ounces cream cheese, softened
1 (14-ounce) can sweetened condensed milk
2/3 cup chocolate syrup
2 tablespoons instant coffee powder
1 teaspoon hot water
1 cup whipping cream, whipped

Combine crumbs, sugar and margarine in small bowl. Pat crumbs firmly on bottom and up side of buttered 9-inch springform pan. Chill. Beat cream cheese in large mixer bowl until fluffy. Add condensed milk and chocolate syrup; mix well. Dissolve coffee in water in small bowl. Add to milk mixture; mix well. Fold in whipped cream. Pour into prepared pan. Cover. Freeze for 6 hours or until firm. Garnish with additional chocolate crumbs. Yield: 12 to 15 servings.

Sheila Nemeth, Delta Omicron
Campbell River, British Columbia, Canada

FUDGE TRUFFLE CHEESECAKE

2 cups semisweet chocolate chips
24 ounces cream cheese, softened
1 (14-ounce) can sweetened condensed milk
4 eggs
2 teaspoons vanilla extract
1 (9-inch) chocolate crumb pie shell

Preheat oven to 300 degrees. Melt chocolate chips in heavy saucepan over very low heat, stirring constantly. Beat cream cheese in large mixer bowl until fluffy. Add condensed milk; mix until smooth. Add melted chocolate, eggs and vanilla; mix well. Pour into pie crust. Bake for 1 hour or until center is set. Let cool. Yield: 12 servings.

Annette Ahmann, Alpha Lambda
Carroll, Iowa

WHITE CHOCOLATE CHEESECAKE

2 cups graham cracker crumbs
1/4 cup sugar
1 teaspoon cinnamon
1/2 cup melted butter
32 ounces cream cheese, softened
1 cup sugar
4 eggs
6 ounces white chocolate, melted, cooled
2 ounces Cassis liqueur
1 1/2 cups sour cream
1/3 cup sugar
1/2 teaspoon vanilla extract

Preheat oven to 350 degrees. Combine cracker crumbs, 1/4 cup sugar, cinnamon and butter in bowl; mix well. Press into 10-inch pie plate. Bake until lightly browned. Beat cream cheese, 1 cup sugar and eggs in mixer bowl until fluffy. Add cooled chocolate and Cassis; beat until smooth. Pour into crust. Bake for 30 to 40 minutes. Combine sour cream, 1/3 cup sugar and vanilla in bowl; mix well. Pour over cake. Bake for 5 minutes longer. Chill before serving. Yield: 12 servings.

Rhea Hicks
Goodlettsville, Tennessee

RASPBERRY WHITE CHOCOLATE CHEESECAKE

11 vanilla sandwich cookies, crushed
3 tablespoons butter, melted
16 ounces cream cheese, softened
1 (14-ounce) can sweetened condensed milk
2 eggs
8 ounces white chocolate, melted
1/2 cup raspberry syrup
16 ounces cream cheese, softened
16 ounces white chocolate, melted
3/4 cup butter or margarine, softened
2 tablespoons lemon juice
1 cup seedless raspberry jam

Preheat oven to 350 degrees. Stir crushed cookies and 3 tablespoons melted butter together in bowl until well combined. Line 9-inch heart-shaped pan with cooking foil, extending foil above edge of heart. Press crumbs into bottom of buttered pan. Beat 16 ounces cream cheese in bowl until smooth. Add sweetened condensed milk; mix well. Add eggs, 1 at a time, beating well after each addition. Pour in 8 ounces melted chocolate slowly, mixing well. Reserve 1/2 cup filling. Pour remaining filling in pan. Blend reserved filling with raspberry syrup in bowl. Drop raspberry filling gently by tablespoonfuls on top of filling in pan. Use tip of knife to gently swirl fillings to create marbled effect. Bake for 50 minutes to 1 hour or until set. Let cool completely at room temperature. Cover. Refrigerate for 8 hours or overnight. Remove cake from pan. Trim foil carefully from cake. Beat 16 ounces cream cheese in bowl until smooth. Add 16 ounces chocolate, 3/4 cup butter and lemon juice. Beat until smooth and fluffy. Reserve 1 1/2 cups icing. Spread remaining icing over side and top of cake. Refrigerate cake for 1 hour or until icing is firm. Melt jam in small saucepan. Let cool slightly. Spread glaze over top of cake to within 1/4 inch of edge. Pipe a decorative boarder around top edge and base of cake with reserved icing. Refrigerate for 30 minutes or until glaze is set. Bring to room temperature before serving. Yield: 10 servings.

Sandra Acre, Xi Alpha Zeta
Sterling, Colorado

CRANBERRY CHEESECAKE

1 cup graham cracker crumbs
3 tablespoons butter or margarine, melted
24 ounces cream cheese, softened
3/4 cup sugar
2 tablespoons all-purpose flour
4 eggs
3/4 cup sour cream
1/2 teaspoon almond extract
1 teaspoon vanilla extract
1 cup chopped cranberries
1 cup cranberry juice
1 tablespoon cornstarch

Preheat oven to 325 degrees. Combine cracker crumbs and margarine in bowl; mix well. Press into springform pan. Bake for 10 minutes. Remove from oven. Increase oven temperature to 450 degrees. Combine cream cheese, sugar and flour in mixer bowl. Beat at medium speed until smooth. Add eggs, 1 at a time, beating well after each addition. Add sour cream, almond extract and vanilla; mix well. Stir in cranberries. Pour over crust. Bake for 10 minutes. Reduce temperature to 250 degrees. Bake for 40 minutes. Run knife around edge of cake. Let cool in pan. Combine cranberry juice and cornstarch in saucepan. Cook until clear and thick. Spoon half the glaze over cake. Let stand for 10 minutes. Spoon remaining glaze over cake and on side. Refrigerate for 2 to 5 hours. Yield: 12 servings.

Wanda Towns, Lambda Theta
Red Lake, Ontario, Canada

SICILIAN CHEESECAKE

The ricotta cheese will drop to the bottom of cake while baking. It is light and delicious.

1 (2-layer) package chocolate pudding cake mix
3 eggs
1/2 cup sugar
32 ounces ricotta cheese
Confectioners' sugar (optional)

Preheat oven to 350 degrees. Prepare cake mix according to package directions. Pour into greased and floured 9-by-13-inch baking pan. Beat eggs and sugar in mixer bowl. Fold in ricotta cheese. Spoon cheese mixture carefully over cake batter. Bake for 1 hour or until cake tests done. Let cool on wire rack. Cut into serving portions. Sprinkle with confectioners' sugar. Yield: 12 servings.

Frances Gaglio, Laureate Alpha Beta
Fullerton, California

MAPLE MOUSSE

3 cups 2% yogurt
1 teaspoon lemon rind
1/2 cup maple syrup
1/4 cup Brandy
2 egg whites
2 teaspoons sugar

Place yogurt in cheesecloth draped over sieve. Let drain overnight. Add lemon rind. Boil maple syrup in saucepan until reduced to 1/4 cup. Let cool. Add syrup and Brandy to drained yogurt in serving bowl. Combine egg whites and sugar in mixer bowl; beat until stiff peaks form. Fold into yogurt mixture. Yield: 4 to 6 servings.

Murielle Bowman, Preceptor Beta Lambda
Mississauga, Ontario, Canada

COCOA-ALMOND-AMARETTO MOUSSE

2 cups sweetened flaked coconut
6 ounces semisweet chocolate chips
2 tablespoons unsalted butter
1 tablespoon white corn syrup
2 teaspoons unflavored gelatin
1/4 cup Amaretto liqueur
1/2 cup sour cream at room temperature
1 1/2 cups whipping cream
1 cup confectioners' sugar
3/4 cup lightly toasted finely ground almonds
Chocolate Cigars
Toasted almonds, chopped (optional)

Preheat oven to 150 degrees. Grease 9-inch pie plate lightly. Place coconut in medium heat-resistant bowl. Warm in oven. Combine chocolate chips, butter and corn syrup in top of double boiler over very hot water, stirring until smooth. Pour chocolate over warmed coconut; mix with 2 forks until blended. Press evenly into bottom and up side of pie plate. Chill. Combine gelatin and liqueur in small heat-resistant cup; mix until softened. Place cup in simmering water. Heat for 2 to 3 minutes or until gelatin is completely dissolved. Transfer gelatin in large bowl. Add sour cream, blending well. Stir in cream and confectioners' sugar. Whip until stiff. Fold in almonds gently. Spoon into pie plate. Garnish with Chocolate Cigars and chopped toasted almonds. Refrigerate for 2 hours or until set. Yield: 6 servings.

CHOCOLATE CIGARS

6 ounces semisweet chocolate chips

Melt chocolate chips in top of double boiler over hot water, stirring until smooth. Spread chocolate over back of baking sheet into 4-by-6-inch rectangle. Let cool to room temperature. Using cheese-shaver server (wire cheese cutter will not work), start 1 inch from short end of chocolate and pull server toward you in an upward motion so chocolate will curl up and around. Use fingers to aid in curling if necessary. Wrap cigars in plastic and refrigerate. Yield: variable.

Jan D. Moser, Tau Pi
Sterling, Illinois

WIKI WIKI MOUSSE

This was served as a pre-concert picnic dessert at Waikiki Shell. It was prepared in clear plastic short-stem wine glasses with lids, transported in a cooler and topped with a fresh strawberry just before serving. Very elegant!

1 (6-ounce) package semisweet chocolate bits
2 eggs
2 tablespoons Grand Marnier
2 to 3 tablespoons strong coffee
3/4 cup milk, scalded
1/2 cup walnuts

Combine first 5 ingredients in blender container. Process for 1 1/2 minutes. Add walnuts. Blend for 30 seconds longer. Pour into 4 large or 6 small wine glasses or pudding cups. Refrigerate for at least 2 hours before serving. Yield: 4 to 6 servings.

Eleanor Elwyn, Preceptor Beta
Honolulu, Hawaii

STRAWBERRY ANGEL FOOD DESSERT

1 (6-ounce) package strawberry gelatin
2 1/2 cups hot water
1 (20-ounce) package frozen strawberries
1 (19-ounce) angel food cake, cubed
Whipped cream

Dissolve gelatin in hot water in bowl. Add frozen strawberries; stir until strawberries are thawed and mixture begins to set. Add cake cubes. Pour into tube cake pan. Chill until firm. Frost with whipped cream. Yield: 12 to 18 servings.

Kerrie Sonnenberg, Xi Alpha
Belgrade, Montana

MERINGUE TORTE

4 egg whites
1/4 teaspoon cream of tartar
1 cup sugar
1/2 teaspoon vanilla extract
2 cups whipping cream
3 tablespoons confectioners' sugar
3 tablespoons orange liqueur
2 tablespoons butter
8 ounces semisweet chocolate
3 bananas, sliced

Preheat oven to 250 degrees. Beat egg whites in mixer bowl until stiff. Add cream of tartar, sugar and vanilla gradually, beating constantly. Spread mixture in foil-lined pan. Bake for 2 hours or until meringue is dry. Let cool; break into pieces. Whip cream in mixer bowl until soft peaks form. Add confectioners' sugar and liqueur. Melt butter and chocolate in saucepan. Layer whipped cream, pieces of baked meringue and banana slices in glass serving bowl. Drizzle with butter-chocolate mixture. Repeat layers ending with whipped cream. Drizzle remaining chocolate over top. Yield: 6 servings.

Sue Lloyd, Preceptor Beta
Beaconsfield, Quebec, Canada

PUMPKIN TRIFLE

4 packages butterscotch instant pudding mix
2 1/2 cups cold milk
1 teaspoon ground cinnamon
1/4 teaspoon nutmeg
1/4 teaspoon ginger
1/4 teaspoon allspice
1 (16-ounce) can pumpkin
2 cups whipping cream
2 tablespoons confectioners' sugar
1 teaspoon vanilla extract
3 cups crumbled spice or carrot cake
Maraschino cherries

Prepare pudding mix according to package directions using 2 1/2 cups milk. Add cinnamon, nutmeg, ginger and allspice; mix well. Add pumpkin; mix well. Whip cream with confectioners' sugar and vanilla in mixer bowl until soft peaks form. Reserve 1 cup cake crumbs for topping. Layer in glass trifle bowl as follows: 1/2 cup cake crumbs, half of pudding mixture, 1/2 cup cake crumbs and half of whipped cream. Repeat layers. Sprinkle reserved cake crumbs over top. Garnish with cherries. Refrigerate overnight. Yield: 10 to 12 servings.

Denise Elgert, Epsilon Omega
Mission, British Columbia, Canada

♣ STRAWBERRY PAVLOVA WITH LEMON CREAM

3 egg whites
Pinch of cream of tartar
3/4 cup sugar
1 teaspoon vanilla extract
4 cups low-fat yogurt, drained
1/3 cup sugar
2 tablespoons lemon juice
Grated rind of 1 lemon
4 cups strawberries

Preheat oven to 275 degrees. Beat egg whites with cream of tartar in mixer bowl until soft peaks form. Beat in 3/4 cup sugar, 1 tablespoon at a time, until glossy peaks form. Beat in vanilla. Spread meringue into 10-inch circle on foil-lined baking sheet, pushing up edge to form ring. Bake for 1 1/2 hours. Turn off oven. Leave in oven to dry. Combine yogurt, 1/3 cup sugar, lemon juice and rind in bowl; mix well. Spread over meringue. Cover with strawberries. Cut into wedges. Yield: 12 servings.

Wendy Ledwidge
Alton, Ontario, Canada

GERMAN CHRISTMAS TORTE

12 egg yolks
2 cups sugar
4 ounces unblanched almonds, grated
1 teaspoon cinnamon
1/4 teaspoon ground cloves
1 teaspoon baking powder
1/2 teaspoon orange rind
1 teaspoon lemon rind
Juice of 1 lemon
1 cup dry white bread crumbs
1 cup dry rye bread crumbs
12 egg whites, stiffly beaten
2 cups sugar
1 tablespoon butter
2 egg whites, stiffly beaten
Toasted almonds
Red candied cherries

Preheat oven to 325 degrees. Beat egg yolks and 2 cups sugar in large mixer bowl. Add next 7 ingredients; mix well. Add bread crumbs; mix well. Fold in 12 stiffly beaten egg whites. Spoon gently into 11-inch torte pan. Bake for 40 minutes to 1 hour or until lightly browned. Let cool. Cream 2 cups sugar and butter in small mixer bowl. Fold in 2 stiffly beaten egg whites. Spread over cold torte. Decorate top with almonds and cherries. Yield: 12 servings.

Jackolyn Soliday, Alpha Upsilon
Wooster, Ohio

♥ DIETER'S RASPBERRY TORTE

1 (16-ounce) package graham crackers
1 (23-ounce) jar natural applesauce
1 (6-ounce) package sugar-free raspberry gelatin
1 (12-ounce) carton lite frozen whipped topping, thawed
Fresh raspberries

Line 9-by-13-inch pan with whole graham crackers. Combine applesauce and gelatin in medium bowl; mix well. Spread 1/4 the applesauce mixture in very thin layer over crackers. Cover with thin layer of whipped topping. Repeat layers 3 times. Refrigerate for 3 to 4 hours. Garnish with fresh raspberries. Yield: 12 servings.

Gloria Thompson, Preceptor Beta
Wyoming, Michigan

MIDNIGHT VELVET TORTE

1 cup crushed chocolate wafers
1/4 cup melted butter or margarine
2 eggs
1 (12-ounce) package semisweet chocolate baking chips
1 teaspoon vanilla extract
1 1/4 cups milk
2 tablespoons instant coffee powder
1/2 cup coffee-flavored liqueur or Kaluha
Whipped cream

Preheat oven to 350 degrees. Combine wafer crumbs and melted butter in bowl; mix well. Spread evenly over bottom of 8-inch round cake pan. Bake for 10 minutes. Let cool. Combine eggs, chocolate chips and vanilla in blender container. Combine milk and instant coffee in saucepan. Cook over medium heat, stirring occasionally, until scalded. Pour hot mixture into blender container. Process at low speed for 1 minute or until mixture is smooth. Add liqueur. Process until blended. Pour into 9-inch square pan. Freeze for 1 hour or until mixture thickens but is not firm. Stir until smooth and blended. Pour into crust-lined pan. Chill for 6 hours or until firm or up to 5 days. Cut into small slices. Serve topped with whipped cream. Yield: 12 servings.

Lexie Jayne Foster, Preceptor Beta Nu
La Habra, California

♥ SNOWBALL

1 1/2 tablespoons gelatin
1/4 cup cold water
1 cup boiling water
1 cup sugar
Dash of salt
1 cup orange juice
Juice of 1 lemon
1 cup whipping cream, whipped
1 angel food cake
1 cup whipping cream
2 tablespoons sugar
1 teaspoon vanilla extract
Coconut

Dissolve gelatin in cold water in large mixer bowl. Add boiling water, 1 cup sugar, salt, orange juice and lemon juice. Chill until partially set. Whip in mixer bowl. Fold in 1 cup whipped cream. Trim crust from cake; cut into cubes. Line deep bowl with plastic wrap. Cover bottom with cake cubes. Add layers of sauce and cake cubes, ending with sauce. Chill overnight. Unmold on serving dish. Whip 1 cup whipping cream, 2 tablespoons sugar and vanilla in small mixer bowl until small peaks form. Spread over torte. Sprinkle with coconut. Chill. Yield: 12 servings.

Marguerite Duffell
Nanton, Alberta, Canada

Dottie Vonderhaar, Laureate Theta, Benson, Minnesota, makes Creme De Menthe Delight by mixing 1/2 gallon pineapple sherbet that is soft enough to stir, 2 mashed bananas, 1 can crushed pineapple, drained, and 3 tablespoons creme de menthe in large bowl. Pour into 8-inch square pan. Refreeze.

♥ TIRAMISU

1/3 cup Italian cappuccino coffee powder
2 tablespoons hot water
1 (3-ounce) package ladyfingers, split
1/2 cup cold skim milk
8 ounces fat-free cream cheese, softened
1 (6-ounce) package fat-free sugar-free vanilla instant pudding mix
1 cup frozen lite whipped topping, thawed

Dissolve 1 tablespoon coffee powder in hot water in small bowl. Cover bottom and side of 2-quart dessert dish with ladyfingers. Sprinkle with dissolved coffee. Place 1/2 cup milk, cream cheese and remaining coffee powder in blender container. Cover; process until smooth. Add pudding mix and remaining milk. Cover; process until smooth. Pour into prepared dish. Top with whipped topping. Sprinkle with coffee powder. Refrigerate for 3 hours or until set. Yield: 10 servings.

Kay Poling, Xi Eta Nu
College Station, Texas

APPLE FLOATING ISLAND

2 eggs, separated
1/4 cup sugar
1/8 teaspoon salt
2 cups milk, scalded
1 teaspoon vanilla extract
1 (20-ounce) can applesauce, chilled
2 tablespoons sugar
Dash of cinnamon
Nutmeg to taste

Beat egg yolks slightly in bowl. Add 1/4 cup sugar and salt; mix well. Stir in hot milk gradually. Cook in top of double boiler, stirring constantly, until mixture coats a metal spoon. Remove from heat. Add vanilla. Chill. Fold chilled applesauce into custard when ready to serve. Beat egg whites in mixer bowl until stiff peaks form. Add 2 tablespoons sugar; mix well. Drop by spoonfuls on top of custard. Sprinkle with cinnamon and nutmeg. Yield: 6 to 8 servings.

Mary Lee Walzel, Xi Kappa Chi
Refugio, Texas

DELICIOUS BANANA PUDDING

8 ounces cream cheese, softened
1 (14-ounce) can sweetened condensed milk
1 (6-ounce) package vanilla instant pudding mix
3 cups cold milk
1 teaspoon vanilla extract
8 ounces whipped topping
1 (16-ounce) package vanilla wafers
6 large bananas, sliced

Beat cream cheese in bowl. Add condensed milk, pudding mix, milk, vanilla and whipped topping; mix well. Layer vanilla wafers and bananas in 9-by-13-inch dish. Top with 1/2 the pudding mixture. Repeat layers. Refrigerate overnight. Yield: 12 servings.

Karen Doss, Chi Pi
Bay City, Texas

194 / Desserts

FAVORITE BANANA PUDDING

6 ripe bananas, sliced
1 (12-ounce) package
  vanilla wafers
1 teaspoon lemon juice
1/3 cup butter or
  margarine
1/2 cup all-purpose
  flour
1/2 cup sugar
2 cups milk
1 (14-ounce) can
  sweetened
  condensed milk
2 egg yolks
2 teaspoons vanilla
  extract

Combine bananas, wafers and lemon juice in large bowl; cover. Melt butter in saucepan over medium heat. Blend in flour and sugar using wire whisk. Add milk and condensed milk; mix well. Heat until warm. Add 1/2 cup warm mixture to egg yolks; mix well. Add back to milk mixture. Heat until bubbly, stirring constantly. Remove from heat. Add vanilla. Pour over bananas and wafers. Chill. Yield: 12 servings.

Jeanne G. Smith, Epsilon Mu
Mansfield, Louisiana

♥ LOW-FAT BREAD PUDDING

This is a good way to use leftover bread.

6 to 8 slices diet white
  bread
4 ounces egg substitute
1/2 cup sugar
1 1/2 teaspoons cinnamon
3 teaspoons vanilla
  extract
1 1/4 cups evaporated
  skim milk
1/2 cup golden raisins
1 teaspoon butter buds
1/2 cup whole berry
  cranberry sauce
Nonstick vegetable
  cooking spray
1/2 cup Special K cereal

Preheat oven to 350 degrees. Tear bread into bite-sized pieces. Combine egg substitute, sugar, cinnamon, vanilla, evaporated milk, raisins, butter buds and cranberry sauce in large bowl; mix well. Stir in bread; mix well. Pour into 9-inch square baking dish coated with cooking spray. Crumble cereal. Sprinkle on top. Bake for 20 to 30 minutes or until knife inserted in center comes out clean. Do not overbake. Cut into squares to serve. May vary consistency by using more or less bread. Yield: 6 to 8 servings.

Doris Elaine Wilson, Alpha Pi Master
El Campo, Texas

Betty L. Bishop, Xi Gamma Mu, Ontario, Oregon, makes Orange Tapioca by combining 2 (3-ounce) packages vanilla-tapioca pudding mix and 1 (3-ounce) package orange gelatin in bowl; mix well. Pour 3 cups boiling water over pudding mixture, stirring until gelatin is dissolved. Refrigerate for 2 hours, stirring every 15 minutes. Fold in 2 (11-ounce) cans mandarin oranges, drained, and 1 (9-ounce) carton whipped topping; blend well. Pour into 9-by-13-inch dish. Refrigerate for 3 to 4 hours or until firm. Cut into squares to serve. Yield: 12 to 15 servings.

CRÈME BRÛLÉE

4 cups heavy cream
1 vanilla bean
Pinch of salt
3/4 cup sugar
8 egg yolks
1/2 cup packed light
  brown sugar

Preheat oven to 300 degrees. Heat cream with vanilla bean and salt in medium saucepan. Blend sugar and egg yolks in large mixer bowl. Remove vanilla bean. Pour cream into egg yolks; mix well. Pour mixture into 6 custard cups. Place in shallow baking pan with 1 inch hot water. Bake for 40 minutes. Let cool for 30 minutes. Sieve brown sugar over tops. Broil for 15 seconds. Sugar will form hardened glaze. Yield: 6 servings.

Linda Hinnenkamp, Xi Eta Delta
Salina, Kansas

PUDDING-ON-THE-RITZ

65 butter-flavor crackers,
  crushed
1 cup margarine
2 (3-ounce) packages
  favorite pudding
  mix
1 1/2 cups milk
1 quart vanilla ice cream
12 ounces frozen
  whipped topping,
  thawed
1/2 cup chopped nuts
10 butter-flavor
  crackers, crushed

Combine 65 crushed crackers and margarine in bowl; mix well. Spread evenly in bottom of 9-by-13-inch baking pan. Combine pudding mix, milk and ice cream in bowl; mix well. Pour evenly over crust. Combine whipped topping, nuts and 10 crushed crackers in bowl; mix well. Spread gently over filling. Refrigerate until serving time or freeze up to 1 week. Yield: 16 servings.

Kym Fennema, Alpha
Abilene, Kansas

♥ FRUITY BURRITOS

2/3 cup fresh raspberries
1/3 cup fresh blueberries
1/3 cup sliced strawberries
1/4 cup low-fat cottage
  cheese
4 teaspoons skim milk
3/4 teaspoon lemon juice
1/2 teaspoon liquid
  sweetener
8 (6-inch) flour tortillas

Preheat oven to 350 degrees. Combine fruit in shallow dish; stir lightly to mix. Do not crush. Place cottage cheese, skim milk, lemon juice and sweetener in blender container. Process until smooth. Heat tortillas in covered container in oven until warm. Fold in half, then in half again. Lift 1 side to form hollow. Spoon 2 1/2 tablespoons fruit into hollow of each tortilla. Add 1 teaspoon cottage cheese mixture while holding tortilla upright and let run down through fruit. Add more milk if cottage cheese mixture is too thick. Yield: 8 servings.

Donna Ryan, Alpha Kappa
Petawawa, Ontario, Canada

VERY-BERRY CHERRY COBBLER

- 1 (18-ounce) can cherry pie filling
- 1 (10-ounce) package frozen blueberries, thawed
- 1 (10-ounce) package frozen raspberries, thawed
- 2 tablespoons cornstarch
- 2 tablespoons sugar
- 2 cups all-purpose flour
- 1/4 cup sugar
- 1 tablespoon baking powder
- 3/4 teaspoon salt
- 1/2 cup cold butter or margarine
- 1 cup milk

Preheat oven to 375 degrees. Combine pie filling, blueberries, raspberries, cornstarch and 2 tablespoons sugar in ungreased 9-by-13-inch baking pan. Combine flour, 1/4 cup sugar, baking powder and salt in bowl. Cut in butter with pastry blender until mixture is crumbly. Add milk; mix lightly with fork until just combined. Drop by spoonfuls onto fruit mixture. Bake for 35 to 40 minutes or until brown and bubbly. Serve hot or cold. Yield: 8 to 10 servings.

Fern E. Reid
Nanton, Alberta, Canada

HIPPOPOTOMUS

These are funny shaped homemade doughnuts and a real quick comfort food.

- 1 (2-loaf) package frozen bread dough
- 2 cups vegetable oil
- 1/2 cup chocolate chips
- 1/2 cup sugar

Thaw frozen bread dough on greased cookie sheet. Let rise until double in bulk. Heat oil in medium saucepan. Cut bread dough into 1/2 cup-sized chunks with sharp knife. Irregular shapes are fine. Poke hole inside. Fill with 6 to 12 chocolate chips. Pinch sides to seal. Fry until lightly browned, turning once. Drain. Let cool to warm. Coat with sugar. Yield: 12 to 16 servings.

Jackie Cicora, Xi Eta Pi
Plantation, Florida

CHERRY ENCHILADAS

- 1 (21-ounce) can cherry pie filling
- 20 small flour tortillas
- Cinnamon to taste
- 3/4 cup margarine
- 1 cup water
- 1 cup apple juice
- 1 1/2 cups sugar

Preheat oven to 350 degrees. Place 1 1/2 tablespoons pie filling on each tortilla; roll up. Place in 8-by-11-inch casserole. Sprinkle with cinnamon. Combine remaining ingredients in saucepan. Heat to boiling point. Pour 1 cup hot apple juice mixture over tortillas. Bake for 50 minutes, adding apple juice mixture every 10 minutes. Yield: 12 servings.

Ann Harms Baldwin, Laureate Gamma Sigma
Anson, Texas

❖ CHOCOLATE CHIP-CHEESE LOAVES

- 24 ounces cream cheese, softened
- 1 1/2 cups semisweet chocolate chips
- 1 cup sifted confectioners' sugar
- 1 tablespoon ground cinnamon
- 1 (7-ounce) milk chocolate candy bar
- 1 1/4 cups chopped pecans
- Gingersnaps

Combine cream cheese, chocolate chips, confectioners' sugar and cinnamon in bowl, stirring until blended. Divide mixture in half. Spoon each half into 3-by-7-inch loaf pan lined with plastic wrap. Chill, covered, for 5 hours or until ready to serve. Pull vegetable peeler down long edge of candy bar, letting chocolate curl. Invert each loaf onto serving platter. Remove plastic wrap. Press pecans around sides of loaves. Sprinkle chocolate curls on top. Serve with gingersnaps. Yield: 12 to 16 servings.

Wendy Epting, Beta Rho
Batesburg, South Carolina

♥ CREAM CHEESE POPOVERS

- 6 eggs
- 1 1/2 cups all-purpose flour
- 1 teaspoon salt
- 1/2 teaspoon pepper
- 1 teaspoon dried thyme leaves
- Dash of ground nutmeg
- 2 cups 2% milk
- 1/4 cup lite whipping cream
- 4 ounces fat-free cream cheese, cubed

Preheat oven to 400 degrees. Combine eggs, flour, salt, pepper, thyme and nutmeg in blender container. Process for 15 seconds or until well blended. Add milk and cream. Scrape down sides of blender container. Place muffin pan in oven to warm slightly. Remove from oven. Fill each muffin cup 1/2 full with batter. Place 1 cube cream cheese in center of each cup. Pour in remaining batter to fill each cup 2/3 full. Bake for 40 minutes or until puffed and golden brown. Serve immediately. Yield: 12 servings.

Eva R. Jackovich, Zeta Eta
Roosevelt, Arizona

Darlene Brummond, Epsilon Beta, Truman, Minnesota, makes Frozen Snicker Bars by combining 1 (4-serving) package sugar-free chocolate pudding mix, 12 ounces vanilla or chocolate frozen dietary ice cream, softened, 1 cup whipped topping and 1/4 cup chunky peanut butter in large bowl. Stir in 3 ounces Grape Nuts. Pour into 8-inch square pan. Freeze. Cut into 8 or more bars. Wrap each bar in foil; refreeze.

Diana Pella, Alpha Beta, Saskatoon, Saskatchewan, Canada, makes a Fresh Fruit Dessert by mixing 2 quarts large strawberries, sliced, 6 sliced bananas, sugar to taste and 3 cups white wine in large bowl. Chill for 2 hours or overnight.

FAVORITE DESSERT

1 (2-layer) package white cake mix
1 quart vanilla ice cream
1 1/2 cups packed dark brown sugar
1/2 cup sugar
3/4 cup half and half
1/2 cup butter or margarine
Dash of salt
1/2 teaspoon vanilla extract
3/4 cup chopped pecans, lightly toasted

Prepare and bake cake mix according to package directions, baking in two 9-inch round greased and floured cake pans. Let cool. Remove from pans. Split each cake layer in half horizontally. Soften ice cream slightly. Spread ice cream 1/2 inch thick on each bottom layer half. Replace top halves. Freeze. Combine brown sugar, sugar, half and half and butter in saucepan. Heat until smooth over low heat. Add salt and vanilla. Add pecans. Slice cakes into wedges. Spoon warm sauce over cake slice to serve. Yield: 16 servings.

Lois Ostash, Chi
Shoal Lake, Manitoba, Canada

MANDARIN ORANGE SALAD

60 butter-flavor crackers, finely crushed
1/2 cup butter, melted
1/4 cup sugar
1 (6-ounce) can frozen orange juice, thawed
1 can sweetened condensed milk
8 ounces whipped topping
2 (11-ounce) cans mandarin oranges, drained

Combine crushed crackers, melted butter and sugar in bowl; mix well. Reserve enough mixture for garnish. Press remaining mixture firmly into 9-by-13-inch baking dish. Blend orange juice and condensed milk in bowl. Fold in whipped topping and oranges. Do not beat. Pour mixture over crumb crust. Top with reserved crumbs. Freeze until serving time. Yield: 12 servings.

Betty Smith, Laureate Pi
LaGrange, Georgia

FRUIT CONSERVE

8 cups fresh peaches, pears, blueberries or figs
5 1/3 cups sugar
Juice and grated rind of 2 oranges
1 cup chopped pecans
1 package Sure-Jel

Cover fruit with sugar in bowl. Refrigerate overnight. Place in saucepan. Bring to a boil over medium-high heat. Reduce heat. Add orange juice and rind. Cook over low heat for 1 1/2 hours, stirring occasionally. Add pecans and Sure-Jel; mix well. Cook for 5 minutes. Pour into hot sterilized 1/2-pint jelly jars, leaving 1/2-inch headspace. Seal. Yield: 5 or 6 jars.

Marti Holloway, Theta Iota
Marietta, Georgia

♥ TROPICAL FRUIT TART

1 1/4 cups all-purpose flour
1/4 cup confectioners' sugar
1/3 cup margarine
3 tablespoons cold water
Nonstick vegetable cooking spray
1 3/4 cups 2% yogurt
2/3 cup sugar
1/2 cup lite sour cream
3 tablespoons frozen orange juice concentrate, thawed
2 tablespoons all-purpose flour
1 1/2 teaspoons orange rind
3 cups sliced fruit (kiwifruit, mangos, papayas, star fruit)
2 tablespoons apple jelly

Preheat oven to 400 degrees. Combine 1 1/4 cups flour and sugar in bowl; mix well. Cut in margarine with fork until crumbly. Stir in water gradually, adding 1 tablespoon more if necessary to make dough hold together. Press into 9-inch tart pan coated with nonstick cooking spray. Bake for 15 minutes or until browned. Reduce heat to 375 degrees. Combine yogurt, sugar, sour cream, orange juice concentrate, 2 tablespoons flour and orange rind in bowl; mix well. Pour over crust. Bake for 35 to 45 minutes or until filling is set. Let cool. Refrigerate until chilled. Brush fruit with apple jelly. Place on torte. Yield: 12 servings.

Jane Pelletier, Gamma Rho
Kemptville, Ontario, Canada

WONDERFUL FRUIT

1/2 cup Bourbon or apple juice
1/3 cup packed dark brown sugar
1/2 teaspoon cinnamon
1/2 teaspoon nutmeg
1 (8-ounce) package mixed dried fruit
1 (21-ounce) can cherry pie filling
1 (11-ounce) can mandarin oranges, drained

Preheat oven to 350 degrees. Combine Bourbon, brown sugar, cinnamon and nutmeg in baking pan; mix well. Bake for 45 minutes or until crystallized. Combine dried fruit, pie filling and oranges in bowl; mix well. Pour hot mixture over fruit. Yield: 8 to 10 servings.

Jan Cripe, Xi Beta Kappa
Greensboro, North Carolina

Isabella Worthen, Xi Gamma Iota, Old Forge, New York, makes Whipped Ricotta Cream by combining 1/4 cup apple juice, 1/4 cup sugar and 1 envelope unflavored gelatin in saucepan. Cook, stirring, over medium heat for 2 minutes or until gelatin is dissolved. Place mixture in blender container. Add 1 cup nonfat ricotta cheese, 1 cup nonfat buttermilk and 1 teaspoon vanilla extract. Cover; blend for 30 seconds or until smooth. Refrigerate, covered, for 30 minutes or until set. Use as frosting for carrot cake or as dessert topping. Store leftover cream in refrigerator and blend again before using. Yield: 2 1/2 cups.

Spouses' Specials

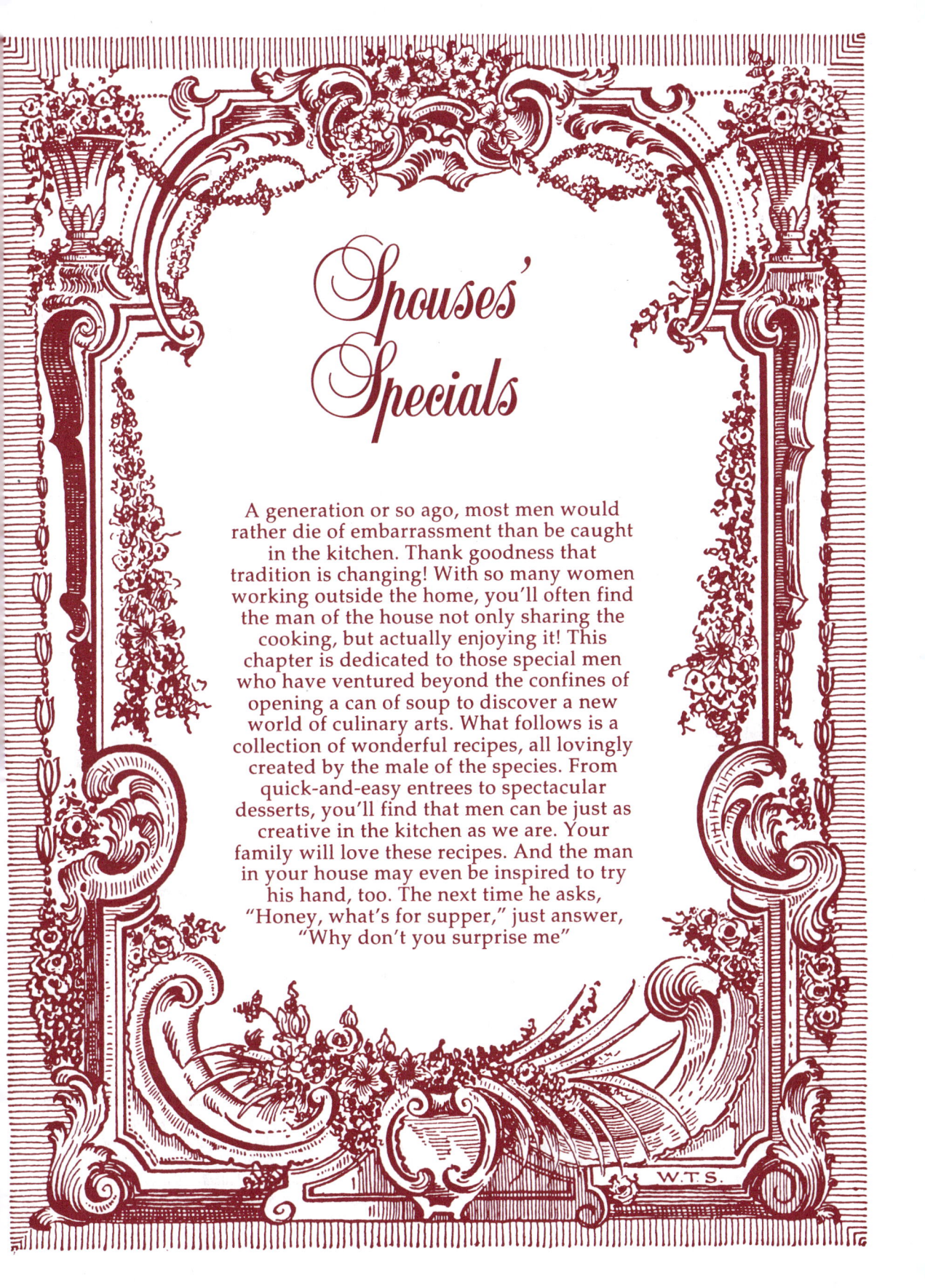

A generation or so ago, most men would rather die of embarrassment than be caught in the kitchen. Thank goodness that tradition is changing! With so many women working outside the home, you'll often find the man of the house not only sharing the cooking, but actually enjoying it! This chapter is dedicated to those special men who have ventured beyond the confines of opening a can of soup to discover a new world of culinary arts. What follows is a collection of wonderful recipes, all lovingly created by the male of the species. From quick-and-easy entrees to spectacular desserts, you'll find that men can be just as creative in the kitchen as we are. Your family will love these recipes. And the man in your house may even be inspired to try his hand, too. The next time he asks, "Honey, what's for supper," just answer, "Why don't you surprise me"

198 / Recipes Submitted By Husbands

APPETIZER MEATBALLS

These can be made ahead of time and frozen until needed.

2 pounds lean ground beef
1 tablespoon catsup
2 eggs, lightly beaten
1 cup shredded mozzarella cheese
1/2 cup dry bread crumbs
1/4 cup finely chopped onion
2 tablespoons grated Parmesan cheese
2 teaspoons Worcestershire sauce
1 teaspoon Italian seasoning
1 teaspoon dried basil
1 teaspoon salt
1/4 teaspoon pepper
1 (14-ounce) bottle catsup
2 tablespoons cornstarch
1 (12-ounce) jar apple jelly
1 (12-ounce) jar currant jelly

Preheat oven to 350 degrees. Combine ground beef, 1 tablespoon catsup, 2 eggs, mozzarella cheese, bread crumbs, onion, Parmesan cheese, Worcestershire sauce, Italian seasoning, basil, salt and pepper in large bowl; mix well. Shape into 1-inch balls. Place on rack in shallow roasting pan. Bake for 15 minutes. Remove meatballs and rack; let drain. Combine 1 bottle catsup and cornstarch in roasting pan. Stir in jellies. Add meatballs; cover. Bake for 30 minutes longer. Yield: 96 meatballs.

Robert (Margaret) Lawrence, Laureate Phi
Montgomery, New York

TEXAS AGGIE-LONGHORN DIP

Being an avid Texas A&M fan and father of 2 Aggie graduates, rival Longhorns are always hoping to top some feat or another. Thus, the name for this dip. It really has a bite to it and is definitely not for those with delicate taste.

2 pounds ground beef
1 onion, chopped
Salt and pepper to taste
Garlic powder to taste
1 (10-ounce) can cream of mushroom soup
1 (10-ounce) can cream of celery soup
1 (10-ounce) can Ro-Tel tomatoes, drained
1 (4-ounce) can green chilies, drained

Brown ground beef with onion in skillet, stirring until crumbly; drain. Season with salt, pepper and garlic powder. Add soups, tomatoes and green chilies. Simmer over low heat until hot. Make a day or 2 ahead for best flavor. Do not freeze. Serve with any chips. Yield: 8 to 10 servings.

Donald (Joan) Menn, Preceptor Eta Phi
Sweetwater, Texas

BREAKFAST TACOS

2 eggs
1 (10-count) package soft shell tacos
1 cup chopped ham
1 cup sliced mushrooms
1/2 cup shredded cheese

Scramble eggs as desired in skillet. Spoon into each taco shell. Add ham, mushrooms and cheese. Place taco shells in microwave-safe dish. Microwave for 30 seconds or until cheese is melted. Yield: 10 servings.

Jim (Kimberly K.) Tjugum, Xi Beta
Madison, Wisconsin

FRENCH CRÊPES

1 1/2 cups milk
1 tablespoon vegetable oil
3 eggs, well beaten
1 1/2 cups sifted all-purpose flour
1/2 teaspoon salt
Butter
Dark brown sugar
Maple syrup or fruit

Beat milk and oil into eggs in bowl. Add sifted flour and salt. Beat with rotary beater or blender until smooth. Batter will be thin. Pour small amount of batter into hot greased griddle. Tilt pan to allow batter to run over griddle thinly. Cook until golden brown. Turn; brown other side, keeping soft enough to roll. Cooked crêpes are thinner than pancakes. Turn out onto dish. Spread each crêpe with butter and brown sugar. Roll up. Top with maple syrup or serve with fruit. Yield: 6 crêpes.

Richard (Ellen M.) Harbour, Preceptor Beta
Coventry, Rhode Island

OATBRAN MUFFINS

2 cups oatbran cereal
1/4 cup packed light brown sugar
2 teaspoons baking powder
1/2 teaspoon salt
2 eggs, beaten
1/2 cup orange juice
2 tablespoons grated orange rind
1/4 cup honey
2 medium bananas, mashed
2 tablespoons vegetable oil
1/2 cup chopped walnuts

Preheat oven to 425 degrees. Combine cereal, brown sugar, baking powder and salt in large bowl; mix well. Beat egg with orange juice, orange rind, honey, bananas, oil and walnuts in bowl. Stir into dry ingredients until just moistened. Fill nonstick muffin cups 2/3 full. Bake for 17 minutes. Yield: 12 servings.

Larry (Donna) Willer, Xi Kappa
Prince Albert, Saskatchewan, Canada

Dave (Shirley J.) Bird, Xi Alpha Nu, Eureka Springs, Arkansas, makes Best Biscuits by mixing 2 cups biscuit mix, 1/2 cup sour cream and 1/2 cup 7-Up in bowl just until blended. Drop onto cookie sheet. Bake in preheated 425-degree oven for 10 to 12 minutes or until golden brown. Yield: 12 biscuits.

BUTTERMILK PANCAKES

2 cups all-purpose flour
1/2 teaspoon salt
1 1/4 teaspoons baking soda
3/4 teaspoon baking powder
1 egg
2 1/4 cups buttermilk
1 tablespoon vegetable oil
2 to 3 tablespoons applesauce

Blend all ingredients with wire whisk in bowl. Preheat nonstick griddle. Spoon batter onto hot griddle. Cook until top side is bubbly. Flip to brown on second side. Yield: 20 pancakes.

John (Lou Ann V.) Knorr, Alpha Lambda
Carroll, Iowa

NO-BEAT POPOVERS

2 eggs
1 cup milk
1 cup sifted all-purpose flour
1/2 teaspoon salt

Butter muffin cups well. Place eggs in bowl. Add milk, flour and salt. Stir with spoon only until mixed but still lumpy. Spoon into muffin cups, dividing equally. Place in cold oven. Set oven at 450 degrees. Bake for 35 minutes. Do not open door during cooking. Serve with prime rib or other casseroles. Yield: 8 servings.

Harvey (Donna J.) Myers, Preceptor Beta Nu
LaHabra, California

OVERNIGHT BUNS

These are a family tradition at all holidays and social events. They can be rolled and cut into crescent shapes.

1 package yeast
1 cup warm water
1 cup sugar
1/3 cup plus 1 tablespoon margarine
1 tablespoon salt
1 cup hot water
2 eggs, beaten
1 cup warm water
10 cups all-purpose flour

Dissolve yeast in 1 cup warm water in bowl. Combine sugar, margarine, salt and 1 cup hot water in mixer bowl, stirring until dissolved. Add eggs, 1 cup warm water, yeast mixture and flour. Beat until thoroughly blended. Let rise. Punch down. Let rise again. Grease 2 cookie sheets. Shape dough with greased hands into 48 buns, 2 to 2 1/2 inches in diameter. Dough will be very sticky. Do not use more flour. Cover with light cloth. Let rise at room temperature overnight. Preheat oven to 350 degrees. Bake for 18 to 20 minutes or until brown. Yield: 48 buns.

Bert (Sharon) Esau, Laureate Beta Zeta
Port Orchard, Washington

DATE-NUT BREAD

My husband has been making this bread for the Christmas holidays for 25 years. It has become a special treat for our family.

1/2 cup boiling water
1/2 cup chopped dates
1 1/2 tablespoons margarine or butter
3/4 teaspoon baking soda
3/4 cup plus 2 tablespoons all-purpose flour
1/2 cup sugar
1/4 teaspoon salt
1 egg
1/2 teaspoon vanilla extract
1/4 cup chopped nuts
Butter or cream cheese

Preheat oven to 350 degrees. Pour boiling water over dates, margarine and baking soda in bowl. Add flour, sugar, salt, egg, vanilla and nuts; beat well. Pour into greased and floured 8-inch loaf pan. Bake for 1 hour to 1 hour and 10 minutes or until bread tests done. Spread with butter or cream cheese. Yield: 10 to 12 servings.

Steve (Linda) Bond, Xi Beta Lambda
Dover, New Jersey

PUMPKIN BREAD

1 1/2 cups pitted prunes
6 tablespoons hot water
1 cup packed dark brown sugar
1 cup sugar
Egg substitute to equal 4 large eggs
1 cup pumpkin purée
2 2/3 cups all-purpose flour
2 teaspoons baking powder
1 teaspoon baking soda
1 teaspoon cinnamon
1/2 teaspoon salt
1/4 teaspoon ground ginger
1/2 teaspoon ground cloves
1/4 teaspoon nutmeg
Nonstick vegetable cooking spray

Preheat oven to 350 degrees. Combine prunes and water in food processor container. Pulse on and off until prunes are finely chopped. Blend prune mixture with brown sugar and sugar in mixer bowl. Beat in egg substitute and pumpkin until just blended. Combine flour, baking powder, baking soda, cinnamon, salt, ginger, cloves and nutmeg in bowl. Add to pumpkin mixture; blend thoroughly. Spray two 4-by-9-inch loaf pans with cooking spray. Spoon batter into pans. Bake for 1 hour or until toothpick inserted into center comes out clean. Yield: 16 servings.

David (Alice) Crouse, Preceptor Beta Pi
Albany, Indiana

SWEET AND SPICY MUSTARD

My husband always makes this mustard to serve with his homemade salami and smoked turkey on special occasions.

4 eggs
1/2 cup firmly
  packed dark
  brown sugar
1/2 cup honey
1/2 cup apple cider
1/2 cup apple cider
  vinegar
1/2 cup dry mustard
1 tablespoon cornstarch
1/2 teaspoon ground
  cardamom
1/8 teaspoon ground
  cloves

Beat eggs in medium heavy saucepan. Add remaining ingredients; mix well. Cook over low heat, stirring constantly, for 10 to 15 minutes or until mixture thickens. Yield: 2 to 3 cups.

Mike (Deborah K.) Wood, Beta Phi
Challis, Idaho

CHILI PETIN JELLY

Chili petins are very small round peppers that grow on bushes around cattle pens in south Texas. They are very hot! Our sorority sold 40 jars of this jelly in our food booth at a craft show. It was the best selling item. We fondly called it "Daryl's Jelly from Hell." It is warm! It is very good served over cream cheese with plain crackers or melba toast rounds.

1 1/2 cups white
  vinegar
3/4 cup chopped green
  or red bell pepper
1/4 cup red or green
  chili petins
6 1/2 cups sugar
1/2 teaspoon butter
  or margarine
6 ounces liquid fruit
  pectin
Red or green food
  coloring
Mint extract to taste

Combine 3/4 cup vinegar and green pepper in blender container. Process until chopped to desired consistency. Pour into large saucepan. Combine whole chili petins and 3/4 cup vinegar in blender container. Process until chopped to desired consistency. Pour into small saucepan. Cook until fully cooked. Strain over saucepan with green peppers, working pulp through strainer with back of spoon. Discard seeds. Add sugar and butter. Bring to a full boil on high heat for 2 minutes. Remove from heat; let cool for 5 minutes. Add fruit pectin, food coloring and 1 drop mint extract. Bring to a full boil for 1 minute on high heat. Do not exceed time or jelly will sugar. Pour into hot sterilized 1/2-pint jars, leaving 1/2-inch headspace. Seal with 2-piece lids. Process in hot waterbath for 10 minutes. Yield: 7 (1/2-pint) jars.

Daryl (Lisa M.) Fowler, Alpha Kappa Rho
Yoakum, Texas

♥ DAD'S PRIZE SOUP

Dad won a prize in the local "Groundhog Day Cook-Off" with this soup.

2 cups chopped celery
1 cup chopped onion
1 (10-ounce) package
  chopped broccoli
2 cups cottage cheese
2 cups milk
1 (10-ounce) can cream
  of chicken soup
1/2 teaspoon seasoned
  salt
1/4 teaspoon pepper

Place celery, onion and broccoli in microwave-safe dish. Microwave on high for 6 minutes, stirring once. Blend cottage cheese in food processor until smooth. Combine broccoli mixture, cottage cheese, milk, cream of chicken soup, salt and pepper in 3-quart saucepan. Heat until hot, but do not boil. Yield: 6 servings.

Arlin (Ninajean) Rohlfs, Preceptor Tau
Unadilla, Nebraska

BEEF-BARLEY SOUP

1 large beef bone
1 1/2 pounds cubed
  stew beef
1/2 cup pot barley
2 large carrots,
  sliced, chopped
1/2 cup white beans
2 stalks celery,
  chopped
1 (28-ounce) can
  stewed tomatoes
1 large onion,
  chopped
Salt to taste
2 handfuls macaroni

Bring beef bone and beef to a boil in large saucepan. Reduce heat; simmer for 2 hours. Remove meat; refrigerate. Discard beef bone. Let liquid stand overnight in refrigerator. Grease will rise to top and harden; remove. Strain remaining liquid into large stockpot. Add barley, carrots, beans, celery, tomatoes, onion, salt and beef. Bring to a boil slowly. Reduce heat; simmer for several hours. Add macaroni after 2 hours. Yield: 12 servings.

William (Pauline) Barber, Preceptor Gamma Rho
Kemptville, Ontario, Canada

BREAD SOUP

1 large onion, finely
  chopped
1 (28-ounce) can diced
  tomatoes
4 cups water
4 cloves of garlic
1/4 teaspoon salt
1/4 teaspoon pepper
1 teaspoon thyme
Dash of Worcestershire
  sauce
1 teaspoon sugar
2 bread slices,
  crumbled

Sauté onion in skillet. Add tomatoes, water, garlic, salt, pepper, thyme, Worcestershire sauce, sugar and bread crumbs. Simmer for 10 minutes. Serve hot or refrigerate for 1 to 2 days. May be frozen for future use. Yield: 4 servings.

Jack (Flora) Cadwallader, Gamma Master
Victoria, British Columbia, Canada

POTATO-CORN CHOWDER

This is an easy dinner to serve on Christmas Eve.

8 slices bacon	2 cups milk
1 onion, chopped	Salt and pepper
4 cups cubed peeled	to taste
potatoes	Dash of dry mustard
1 cup water	1 (17-ounce) can
1 (10-ounce) can	cream-style corn
cream of chicken	Chives or chopped
soup	green onions
1 cup sour cream	(optional)

Fry bacon in skillet until crisp; reserve drippings. Let bacon drain; crumble. Sauté onion in reserved drippings in skillet; drain. Cook potatoes in water in large saucepan until tender. Add chicken soup, sour cream, milk, salt, pepper, mustard and corn. Reserve some bacon for garnish. Add remaining bacon to mixture. Simmer for 1 hour; do not boil. Garnish with reserved bacon and chives. Yield: 8 to 10 servings.

J. D. "Butch" (Jamie) Whitten, Jr., Iota Theta
Duncan, Oklahoma

MINESTRONE

1 (10-ounce) package	2 cloves of garlic,
minestrone soup	minced
beans	8 ounces smoke sausage
3 quarts water	8 ounces browned
1 (15-ounce) can Great	Italian sausage
Northern beans	1 1/2 teaspoons dried
1 (15-ounce) can	basil
Italian-style	1/4 teaspoon dried
stewed tomatoes	oregano
1 (15-ounce) can	1/4 teaspoon pepper
whole-kernel corn	2 ounces elbow or
1 large onion,	shell macaroni
chopped	or spaghetti

Soak minestrone soup beans overnight in water to cover; rinse. Place beans in 8-quart stockpot with 3 quarts water. Add Great Northern beans, tomatoes, corn, onion, garlic, smoke sausage, Italian sausage, basil, oregano and pepper. Cover; bring to a boil. Reduce heat; cook until beans are tender. Add macaroni; cook for 20 minutes. Serve with sourdough breadsticks. May add carrots, red cabbage and/or squash for color. Yield: 24 servings.

Ronald (Louise) Morrison, Xi Kappa Iota
Wilmington, Ohio

Steve (Janice) Willardson, Xi Beta Phi, Lakewood, Colorado, makes Seafood Salad Melt by mixing 8 ounces imitation crabmeat, 1/2 cup mayonnaise, 1/2 cup sliced celery and 1 teaspoon dillweed in bowl. Place 1/2 cup mixture on each of 4 lightly toasted English muffin halves. Top each with 1 cheese slice. Microwave on High for 40 seconds or until cheese is melted.

Spouses' Specials / 201

ARIZONA SUMMER SOUP

Although Charlie has perfected his chili recipe and has won numerous competitions in the United States, Canada and Mexico, he has also developed this easy to prepare soup which is the Southwest's version of the traditional gazpacho soup.

1 (16-ounce) can	1 (10-ounce) can Ro-Tel
stewed tomatoes	hot tomato sauce
1 (16-ounce) can red	1 medium red onion,
kidney beans,	finely chopped
undrained	1/4 teaspoon crushed
1 (8-ounce) can tomato	garlic
sauce	Salt to taste

Combine all ingredients in covered bowl. Refrigerate overnight. Add finely diced jalapeño peppers to make soup hotter or spicier. Yield: 6 servings.

Charlie (Barbara) Ward, Xi Gamma Beta
Lake Havasu City, Arizona

CREAM OF SHRIMP SOUP

1 (4-ounce) can baby	Salt and pepper
shrimp	to taste
2 (10-ounce) cans	1 tablespoon butter
shrimp soup	Salt to taste
1/2 cup milk	Pepper to taste

Rinse shrimp. Combine shrimp, shrimp soup, milk, salt and pepper in saucepan. Bring to a boil. Reduce heat; simmer until flavors are blended. Add butter and salt. Pour into serving bowls. Sprinkle with pepper. Serve with hot rolls or crackers. Yield: 6 servings.

Ray (Valdessa) Stuempfle, Laureate Alpha Epsilon
Bloomsburg, Pennsylvania

QUICK TRICK CLAM CHOWDER

2 (10-ounce) packages	1 teaspoon garlic salt
scalloped potatoes	1 teaspoon pepper
1 1/2 cups milk	1/2 cup butter
5 cups boiling water	3 (6-ounce) cans minced
3 large onions, thinly	or chopped clams
sliced	1 quart half and half
2 jars clam juice	Butter
1 teaspoon seasoned	
salt	

Crush potato flakes. Combine potatoes with seasoning packets, milk, water, onions, clam juice, seasoned salt, garlic salt, pepper and butter in 5-quart stockpot. Bring to a boil. Boil for 30 minutes. Add clams. Add half and half. Heat; do not boil. Serve in mugs with pat of butter in each serving. May let cool, refrigerate prior to adding half and half and serve next day. Yield: 10 servings.

Jimmy (Lerliene) Connolly, Laureate Gamma Mu
Jacksonville, Florida

VEGETARIAN FOUR-BEAN CHILI

- 1 tablespoon vegetable oil
- 2 large onions, chopped
- 1 sweet green pepper, chopped
- 3 cloves of garlic, finely chopped
- 2 carrots, pared, cut into 1/2-inch cubes
- 1 small zucchini, halved, thickly sliced
- 1 summer squash, halved, thickly sliced
- 2 tablespoons chili powder
- 1/2 teaspoon oregano, crumbled
- 1 teaspoon ground cumin
- 2 (28-ounce) cans tomatoes
- 1 (12-ounce) can beer
- 1 teaspoon salt
- 1 (16-ounce) can black beans, drained, rinsed
- 1 (16-ounce) can kidney beans, drained, rinsed
- 1 (16-ounce) can black-eyed peas
- 1 (16-ounce) can chick-peas, drained, rinsed

Heat oil in stockpot over medium heat. Add onions, green pepper and garlic. Sauté for 4 minutes or until onions are softened. Add carrots. Cook, covered, for 2 minutes. Add zucchini, squash, chili powder, oregano and cumin. Sauté for 1 minute. Add tomatoes, carefully breaking with spoon, beer and salt. Bring to a boil. Reduce heat; simmer, partially covered, for 15 minutes. Stir in beans and peas. Simmer, stirring frequently, for 10 minutes to heat through. May serve with rice and grated cheese or as a "bowl of chili." Yield: 8 servings.

Charles (Frances) Lorenz, Laureate Chi
Pottsville, Pennsylvania

OVEN BEEF AND VEGETABLE STEW

- 1 1/2 pounds stew beef, cubed
- 1/4 cup all-purpose flour
- 3 cloves of garlic, minced
- 1 (10-ounce) can beef bouillon
- 1 (7-ounce) can tomato sauce
- 1 teaspoon dried thyme
- 1/2 teaspoon oregano
- 1/4 teaspoon pepper
- 1/2 teaspoon grated orange rind
- 6 small onions
- 6 small potatoes
- 2 carrots
- 2 cups cubed turnip
- 2 parsnips, cubed
- 3 stalks celery, sliced
- 3 cups water
- 1 bay leaf
- 1 (14-ounce) can peas

Preheat oven to 300 degrees. Roll beef cubes in flour. Stir-fry in skillet. Add garlic, beef bouillon, tomato sauce, thyme, oregano, pepper and orange rind. Heat, stirring constantly. Place onions, potatoes, carrots, turnip, parsnips and celery with water in Dutch oven. Add beef mixture and bay leaf; mix well. Bake, covered, for 3 hours, stirring every hour. Add peas the last hour. Remove bay leaf before serving. Yield: 8 to 10 servings.

Terry (Jill) Greenham, Laureate Psi
Ottawa, Ontario, Canada

FESTIVE SALSA MEATBALLS

- 2 pounds lean ground beef
- 1 cup thick mild salsa
- 2 eggs
- 2 teaspoons chili powder
- 1/2 teaspoon salt
- 1/2 teaspoon pepper
- 1/4 teaspoon cayenne pepper
- 1 cup finely chopped corn chips or tortilla chips
- 1 cup fresh coriander
- 4 green onions, thinly sliced
- 1 cup salsa
- 1 cup sour cream

Preheat oven to 400 degrees. Brown ground beef in skillet, stirring until crumbly; drain. Combine salsa, eggs, chili powder, salt, pepper and cayenne pepper in large bowl until blended. Stir in crushed chips. Add ground beef, coriander and onions; mix well. Shape into 1-inch balls. Place in well-greased baking pan. Bake for 15 to 18 minutes or until done. Combine 1 cup salsa sauce and sour cream in bowl; mix well. Serve hot or cold over meatballs. Yield: 8 servings.

Vern (Jan) Aikens, Preceptor Alpha Delta
St. Albert, Alberta, Canada

KILLER STROGANOFF

R. John's day was made when he served this stroganoff to a chef who had cooked at the Air Force Academy for Presidents and the chef raved about the stroganoff.

- 2 pounds round steak
- 1 (10-ounce) can mushroom pieces, drained
- 1 cup finely chopped onion
- 1/4 cup butter
- 3 beef bouillon cubes
- 1 cup boiling water
- 2 tablespoons tomato paste
- 2 teaspoons dry mustard
- 1/2 teaspoon salt
- 2 tablespoons all-purpose flour
- 1/2 cup cold water
- 1 cup sour cream
- Buttered cooked noodles

Cut steak into thin strips 1/8 inch thick and 2 inches long with grain of meat running with 1/8 inch. Sauté mushrooms and onion in 3 tablespoons butter in large skillet until golden brown. Remove from skillet. Add remaining tablespoon of butter. Brown meat on all sides for about 15 minutes. Dissolve bouillon cubes in boiling water in bowl. Pour over meat. Add tomato paste, mustard and salt. Simmer, covered, for 45 minutes or until tender. Combine flour and cold water in small bowl. Stir slowly into meat mixture. Cook, stirring constantly, until mixture boils. Reduce heat. Add mushrooms, onion and sour cream. Heat but do not boil. Serve over hot buttered noodles. Yield: 4 to 6 servings.

R. John (Judy) Kutcher, Preceptor Delta Delta
Eldridge, Iowa

MANICOTTI WITH CRÊPES

Tom prepareed this for many special occasions and several times when we entertained guests. They always asked for the recipe.

1/2 pound ground beef	1/2 teaspoon salt
1 clove of garlic, crushed	1/2 cup mayonnaise
	Crêpes
1 cup small-curd cottage cheese	1 (16-ounce) jar spaghetti sauce
4 ounces shredded mozzarella cheese	1/2 teaspoon oregano
	Parmesan cheese

Preheat oven to 350 degrees. Brown beef with garlic in skillet, stirring until crumbly; drain off fat. Combine cottage cheese, mozzarella cheese, salt and mayonnaise in bowl. Stir into beef; mix well. Fill each crêpe with 1/4 cup meat mixture. Place in 9-by-13-inch baking dish. Cover with spaghetti sauce. Sprinkle with oregano and Parmesan cheese. Cover with cooking foil. Bake for 15 minutes. Remove foil. Bake for 10 minutes longer. Yield: 8 to 10 servings.

CRÊPES

2 eggs	1/4 teaspoon salt
2/3 cup milk	1 tablespoon vegetable shortening
1/2 cup all-purpose flour	

Combine eggs, milk, flour and salt in bowl; mix well. Melt shortening in small skillet. Drop small amount of batter into skillet, tilting skillet to thinly cover bottom. Cook until lightly browned on both sides, turning once. Repeat until all batter is used. Yield: 8 to 10 crêpes.

Tom (Diane) Mallinson, Iota Chi
Ballwin, Missouri

TACOS WITH HOMEMADE SOFT SHELLS

2 pounds ground beef	1 tablespoon salt
1 envelope onion soup mix	1/2 cup yellow cornmeal
2 cups tomato juice	2 tablespoons melted butter
1 cup catsup	
1/4 cup packed dark brown sugar	1 tablespoon vegetable oil
2 tablespoons vinegar	Sour cream
2 teaspoons salt	Grated cheese
3 eggs	Shredded lettuce
1 1/2 cups milk	Chopped tomatoes
1 cup all-purpose flour	Chopped green peppers

Combine ground beef, soup mix, tomato juice, catsup, brown sugar, vinegar and 2 teaspoons salt in large saucepan. Cook slowly for 2 hours. Beat eggs with milk in bowl. Add flour, 1 tablespoon salt, cornmeal and butter; mix well. Heat wok with oil. Spoon 1/2 cup batter into hot wok, circulating around to create large shell. Flip over. Cook until brown. Make 1 at a time; keep warm in tea towel. Top each shell with meat sauce. Fold over jelly-roll fashion. Top with sour cream, cheese, lettuce, tomatoes and green peppers.
Yield: 6 to 8 servings.

Don (Colleen) Middlemiss, Alpha
Regina, Saskatchewan, Canada

VERY BEST EGG FOO YONG

On our first date after World War II we ate at Toy's Restaurant in Milwaukee, Wisconsin and have been improving the recipe ever since!

2 cups hot water	1/2 cup canned or fresh bean sprouts
2 chicken bouillon cubes	1/4 cup yellow onion, thinly sliced
3 tablespoons cornstarch	1/4 cup chopped fresh spinach leaves, stems discarded
2 tablespoons soy sauce	
1/2 teaspoon grated fresh gingerroot	1 teaspoon chopped pimento
1 clove of garlic, crushed	1/4 cup chopped canned mushrooms
1 tablespoon olive oil	4 eggs
	1 tablespoon olive oil
1/2 cup lean pork, julienned	Green onion tops, cut up

Place hot water in blender container. Add bouillon cubes. Let stand for a few minutes. Add cornstarch, soy sauce, gingerroot and garlic. Process at high speed until smooth. Pour into saucepan. Bring to a boil over medium heat, stirring constantly. Boil for 1 minute. Remove from heat. Place 1 tablespoon olive oil in 6-inch cast-iron skillet. Sauté pork. Place in bowl. Add bean sprouts, onion, spinach, pimento and mushrooms; mix well. Break eggs over mixture. Fold in lightly with fork. Add 1 tablespoon olive oil to skillet. Bring to high heat. Add 1/4 cup mixture to pan. Fry until edges lace and are singed slightly. Reduce temperature to medium. Turn patty. Cook to desired doneness. Spoon a small amount of sauce into glass dish. Transfer patty from skillet to dish. Cover with 1 or 2 spoonfuls sauce. Place dish in slightly heated oven to keep warm. Repeat process until all mixture is used. Serve with sauce spooned over patty. Garnish with green onions. Do not add any salt to mixture. Yield: 4 servings.

Jack (Betty) Hanson, Iota Iota
Blue Ridge, Georgia

Michael (Kacy) Boyett, Xi Chi Delta, Corcoran, California, makes California Marinade by combining 1 cup vegetable oil, 3/4 cup soy sauce, 1/2 cup lemon juice, 1/4 cup prepared mustard, 1/4 cup Worcestershire sauce, 1 to 2 teaspoons coarsely cracked pepper and 2 cloves of fresh garlic, minced, in bowl; mix well. Refrigerate marinade for at least 24 to 36 hours.

HUSBAND PLEASING RIBS

3 slabs baby back ribs
1/2 can pickling spice
2 cups barbecue sauce
2 tablespoons Worcestershire sauce

Place ribs in large saucepan in water to cover. Add pickling spice. Bring to a boil. Boil for 45 minutes. Remove ribs; drain. Combine barbecue sauce and Worcestershire sauce in bowl. Grill ribs over medium hot coals for 30 minutes or until tender and meat pulls away from bone, turning and basting frequently with sauce. Yield: 6 servings.

Weldon (Jackie) Meadows, Xi Omicron Nu
Webster, Texas

KRAUT AND RIBS

This is a favorite of those who hate kraut. It is easy and quick to prepare.

1 (27-ounce) can sauerkraut
1 (16-ounce) can chopped tomatoes
1/2 teaspoon salt
1 tablespoon caraway seeds
1 tablespoon dried onion
1 tablespoon dark brown sugar
3 to 5 pounds country-style pork ribs

Place sauerkraut in large saucepan on top of stove. Combine tomatoes, salt, caraway seeds, onion and brown sugar in bowl; mix well. Pour mixture over sauerkraut. Place ribs on top. Simmer, covered, for 2 1/2 to 3 hours or until tender. Yield: 6 servings.

John W. (Gig) Jones, Xi Eta Delta
Salina, Kansas

❖ JAMAICAN PORK TENDERLOIN

This is as close to Jamaican food as we can get without actually being there.

1 pound lean pork tenderloin
3 tablespoons fresh lime juice
1 tablespoon bottled chopped jalapeños
1 teaspoon bottled minced fresh garlic
1 cup bottled minced fresh gingerroot
1/4 teaspoon salt
1/4 teaspoon ground allspice
Nonstick vegetable cooking spray

Trim fat from pork. Combine lime juice, jalapeños, garlic, gingerroot, salt and allspice in large zip-top heavy-duty plastic bag. Add pork. Seal bag. Marinate in refrigerator for 30 minutes. Remove pork from bag, reserving marinade. Coat grill rack with cooking spray. Place over medium coals. Place pork on rack; cover. Grill for 27 minutes or until meat thermometer registers 160 degrees. Cut into 1/4 inch thick slices. Yield: 4 servings.

David (Charlene M.) Reid, Preceptor Gamma Alpha
Okmulgee, Oklahoma

CHICKEN DELIGHT

4 to 6 pounds chicken thighs or drumettes
1 clove of garlic, peeled, puréed
1/4 cup dried oregano
Salt and pepper to taste
1/2 cup red wine vinegar
1/2 cup olive oil
1 cup pitted prunes
Olives to taste
1/2 cup capers and small amount of juice
6 bay leaves
1 cup packed dark brown sugar
1 cup white wine
1/4 cup Italian parsley

Combine chicken, garlic, oregano, salt, pepper, vinegar, olive oil, prunes, olives, capers with juice and bay leaves in large bowl. Cover. Let marinate in refrigerator overnight. Preheat oven to 350 degrees. Arrange chicken in large baking pan. Spoon marinade evenly over chicken. Sprinkle with brown sugar. Pour white wine around chicken. Bake for 50 minutes to 1 hour, basting frequently with pan juices. Remove bay leaves. Transfer chicken, prunes, olives and capers with slotted spoon to serving platter. Moisten with a few spoonfuls of juice. Sprinkle with parsley. Serve remaining pan juices in sauceboat. Yield: 10 to 12 servings.

Arnold (Janet A.) Davis, Omega Xi
Haines City, Florida

♥ CHICKEN LASAGNA

3 tablespoons low-fat margarine
1/2 cup chopped onion
1/2 cup chopped green pepper
1 (8-ounce) can mushroom pieces
1/2 cup low-sodium chicken broth
2 ounces pimento, chopped
1 (10-ounce) can low-fat cream of mushroom soup
1 cup skim milk
Nonstick vegetable cooking spray
8 ounces lasagna noodles
2 cups low-fat cottage cheese
8 ounces low-fat shredded American cheese
2 pounds chopped cooked chicken
1/4 cup low-fat Parmesan cheese

Preheat oven to 350 degrees. Sauté margarine, onion, green pepper and mushrooms in skillet until tender. Combine broth, pimento, soup and milk in bowl; add to skillet. Cook, stirring, until heated. Spray 9-by-13-inch baking pan with cooking spray. Spread dry noodles evenly in bottom of prepared pan. Layer 1/2 milk sauce, 1/2 cottage cheese, 1/2 shredded cheese, 1/2 chopped chicken and 1/2 Parmesan cheese over noodles. Repeat layers. Cover with foil. Bake for 1 hour. Uncover. Bake for 15 minutes longer or until golden brown. Let stand for 20 minutes before serving. Yield: 10 servings.

Danny (Robin Austen-Lovelady) Lovelady, Xi Alpha Phi
Beatrice, Nebraska

CARIBBEAN CHICKEN

6 boneless skinless
  chicken breasts,
  cut into halves
6 thin slices
  lean ham
1 banana
1 egg
1/4 teaspoon coconut
  flavoring (optional)
1 tablespoon
  all-purpose flour
6 tablespoons grated
  coconut
Nonstick vegetable
  cooking spray

Preheat oven to 350 degrees. Flatten chicken breasts. Place ham slice on each breast half. Cut banana into thirds crosswise, then cut each third in half lengthwise. Place 1 piece banana on each ham slice. Roll up chicken egg-roll style. Place in freezer for 15 minutes. Combine egg and coconut flavoring in small bowl; mix well. Roll each chicken piece in flour, then in egg mixture. Roll in grated coconut. Arrange in single layer on baking sheet coated with cooking spray. Bake for 25 minutes. Yield: 6 servings.

Bill (Mary Lou) Gleeson
Punta Gorda, Florida

KUNG PAO CHICKEN

1 pound boneless
  skinless chicken
  breasts
1 tablespoon cornstarch
1 bunch green onions
2 teaspoons peanut oil
2 cloves of garlic,
  minced
1/4 to 1/2 teaspoon red
  pepper flakes
1/4 to 1/2 teaspoon
  ground ginger
2 tablespoons wine
  vinegar
2 tablespoons soy
  sauce
2 teaspoons sugar
1/3 to 1/2 cup dry
  roasted peanuts

Cut chicken into 1-inch pieces. Combine with cornstarch in small bowl; toss to coat. Cut onions, including tops, into small pieces. Heat oil in large skillet or wok on medium-high heat. Add chicken. Fry, stirring constantly, for 5 to 7 minutes or until chicken is no longer pink in the center. Remove chicken from skillet. Add onions, garlic, red pepper and ginger. Stir-fry for 15 seconds. Remove from heat. Combine vinegar, soy sauce and sugar in small bowl; mix well. Add to skillet. Return chicken to skillet. Stir until chicken is well coated. Stir in peanuts. Heat thoroughly, stirring occasionally. Serve over rice. Yield: 2 to 4 servings.

David (Sarah) Baumann, Theta Kappa
Belleville, Illinois

Jim (Deborah) Herwick, Xi Eta Eta, Latrobe, Pennsylvania, makes Secret Chicken Sauce by mixing 9 tablespoons salt, 1 tablespoon white pepper, 1 tablespoon black pepper and 2 to 3 teaspoons meat tenderizer in paper bag; shake well. Rub on both sides of chicken with skin on, then coat with vegeable oil and barbecue. Store remaining mixture for later use.

Spouses' Specials / 205

CASHEW CHICKEN

3 cloves of garlic
1 tablespoon ground
  ginger
1 tablespoon soy
  sauce
12 ounces boneless
  skinless chicken,
  cut into strips
1 1/2 tablespoons
  vegetable oil
3 cups broccoli
  flowerets
1 cup snow pea pods,
  cut into halves
1 1/2 cups water
1/3 cup dry chicken
  noodle soup mix
2 tablespoons
  cornstarch
1 cup sliced radishes
1/2 cup lightly salted
  cashews
4 cups cooked rice

Combine garlic, ginger and soy sauce in bowl; mix well. Add chicken; coat well. Heat oil in wok. Stir-fry broccoli for 1 minute. Add snow peas. Cook for 3 minutes or until crisp-tender. Remove to plate. Add chicken to wok; brown. Add water, soup mix and cornstarch; cover. Simmer for 5 minutes. Return vegetables to wok. Add radishes and cashews. Cook until hot. Serve over cooked rice. Yield: 4 to 6 servings.

Larry (Michelle Leger-Forman) Forman
Petawawa, Ontario, Canada

♥ OVEN-BAKED CHICKEN AND POTATOES

1 1/2 tablespoons olive
  oil
1 (3-pound) chicken,
  cut up
1 cup lemon juice
2 cups seasoned
  bread crumbs
2 tablespoons grated
  Parmesan cheese
4 potatoes, peeled,
  cut into sixths
  lengthwise
1 tablespoon olive oil
1 medium onion, sliced
Garlic powder
  to taste
1 tablespoon lemon
  juice

Preheat oven to 350 degrees. Coat bottom of 9-by-13-inch glass baking dish with 1 1/2 tablespoons olive oil. Rinse chicken; pat dry. Dip in 1 cup lemon juice. Roll in mixture of bread crumbs and Parmesan cheese. Place in baking dish. Rub potatoes with 1 tablespoon olive oil. Roll in remaining bread crumbs mixture. Place potatoes between chicken pieces. Top with onion. Drizzle with 1 tablespoon olive oil. Sprinkle with garlic and 1 tablespoon lemon juice. Bake for 1 hour. Yield: 4 servings.

Ron (Bonnie) Hershey, Beta Lambda
Dayton, Ohio

Tim (Darla) Lowry, Lambda Omega, Weatherford, Oklahoma, makes Barbecue Sauce by mixing 1/2 cup catsup, 1/4 cup mustard, 1/4 cup honey, 1 tablespoon liquid smoke and 2 teaspoons barbecue spice in bowl; mix well. Refrigerate, covered, overnight. Serve on all smoked meats including brisket, turkey and ham. Warm slightly in microwave if desired. Yield: 1 cup.

Recipes Submitted By Husbands

♥ PEPPER CHICKEN FETTUCINI TOSS

3 whole boneless skinless chicken breasts
1 (16-ounce) package fettucini
1/4 cup olive or vegetable oil
2 large red bell peppers, cut into strips
2 large yellow bell peppers, cut into strips
1 medium green bell pepper, cut into strips
1 medium onion, cut into chunks
2 cups sliced fresh mushrooms
1 teaspoon salt-free herb seasoning
2 tablespoons grated Parmesan cheese

Cut chicken breasts into strips. Prepare fettucini according to package directions; drain. Heat oil in large skillet. Add chicken, red, yellow and green peppers, onion, mushrooms and seasonings. Cook, stirring constantly, over medium heat for 8 to 20 minutes or until chicken is cooked through. Add hot cooked fettucini and Parmesan cheese. Toss to coat. Serve immediately. Refrigerate leftovers. Yield: 8 servings.

Ronald (Constance) Tyhurst, Xi Tau
Boise, Idaho

RUM JAMBALAYA

It has been noted that consumption of unused rum may cause alterations in quantities of ingredients and cooking time.

3/4 cup grated onion
2 tablespoons vegetable oil
4 chicken breasts, cut into 1/2-inch cubes
1 teaspoon salt
1 teaspoon red pepper
12 drops of Tabasco sauce
2 cups chopped Polish sausage
1/3 cup rum
2 (16-ounce) cans whole tomatoes
1 (11-ounce) can tomato juice
1 can Ro-Tel tomatoes
2 cups cooked rice
1 1/2 cups chopped celery
12 ounces shrimp

Sauté onion in oil in saucepan until transparent. Add chicken; cook until done. Add salt, red pepper, Tabasco sauce and sausage. Cook for 3 minutes; drain. Add rum. Simmer for 5 minutes. Add tomatoes, tomato juice and Ro-Tel tomatoes. Simmer for 5 minutes. Add rice, celery and shrimp. Simmer for 15 minutes. Yield: 12 servings.

Steve (Carla Sue) Jones, Xi Beta Lambda
Conway, Arkansas

Frank (Terri) Pellegrino, Zeta Eta, Roosevelt, Arizona, makes Grilled Trout by cleaning 1 (3 1/2 to 4-pound) trout, leaving head and tail intact. Sprinkle cavity with lemon-pepper. Place 3 pats butter inside cavity. Stuff with red onion slices. Wrap in cooking foil. Grill on hot coals. This is great for camping.

BACALAO A LA VIZCAINA

This recipe is "Dried Cod in the Style of Vizcaya."

2 pounds dried cod filets
1 onion, sliced
2 cloves of garlic, chopped
1 onion, chopped
1 pound tomatoes, peeled, seeded, chopped
1 (7-ounce) can pimentos
2 tablespoons olive oil
Salt and pepper to taste
1 tablespoon capers
6 medium potatoes, freshly cooked, peeled, cubed
1/2 cup Sherry
Chopped fresh parsley to taste
Stuffed green olives

Soak cod for several hours in cold water or overnight, changing water several times; drain. Cover with fresh cold water. Add sliced onion. Bring to a simmer. Cook gently for about 15 minutes or until fish flakes easily with fork; drain well. Cut into small pieces. Combine garlic, chopped onion and tomatoes in blender container. Chop half the pimentos; add to blender container. Process until puréed. Heat oil in skillet. Add puréed mixture. Cook for 5 minutes, stirring constantly. Season with salt and pepper. Cut remaining pimentos into strips. Add pimento, capers, potatoes and cod to skillet. Add Sherry. Cook for 5 minutes or until fish and potatoes are heated through. Garnish cod with chopped parsley and olives. Serve immediately. Yield: 6 servings.

Tony (Susana) Jauregui, Xi Chi Nu
San Marcos, California

FISH-ON-THE-PIT

Fish will have a unique smoke flavor if pit is covered.

4 large fish filets
Lemon juice to taste
Cajun seasoning to taste
Salt and pepper to taste
1/2 cup butter
1 onion, sliced
1 green bell pepper, cut into strips
Fresh mushrooms
Fresh broccoli flowerets

Rub filets with lemon juice; season to taste. Place filets in melted butter in disposable baking pan. Coat filets on both sides with butter. Arrange side-by-side in pan. Place vegetables in layers over fish. Grill over hot coals, basting frequently. Do not cover pan. Yield: 4 servings.

Tommy (Lou) Myers, Xi Beta Theta
Eunice, Louisiana

Steven (Jean) Roby, Theta Iota, Cordova, Tennessee, makes Barbecue Shrimp by placing 1 pound shrimp with heads on, 1 tablespoon cracked black pepper, 1 chicken bouillon cube, 1 tablespoon chopped garlic, 1 teaspoon cayenne pepper, 1 tablespoon paprika, 1/2 cup beer and 2 tablespoons butter in covered saucepan. Cook over medium flame until shrimp turn pink. Turn off heat. Leave in covered pan for 2 minutes. Serve.

TUNA ROLL-UPS

1 (10-ounce) can cream
   of mushroom soup
1 cup skim milk
1 cup tuna, drained
1/2 cup shredded
   Cheddar cheese
1 (3-ounce) can
   French-fried onions
1 (10-ounce) package
   frozen chopped
   broccoli, thawed
1 teaspoon garlic salt
   with parsley
1 teaspoon white
   pepper
6 small flour tortillas
Nonstick vegetable
   cooking spray
1 large tomato,
   chopped
1/2 cup shredded
   Cheddar cheese

Preheat oven to 350 degrees. Combine soup and milk in small bowl; mix well. Combine tuna, 1/2 cup cheese, 1/2 can onion rings and broccoli in bowl; mix well. Add 3/4 cup soup mixture, garlic salt and pepper; mix well. Divide mixture evenly to fill tortillas. Roll up tortillas. Place, seam-side down, in 9-by-13-inch baking dish lightly coated with cooking spray. Stir tomato pieces into remaining soup mixture. Pour over tortillas. Bake, uncovered, for 35 minutes. Sprinkle 1/2 cup cheese and onions over tortillas. Bake for 5 minutes longer. Yield: 6 servings.

William (Janice G.) Mathews, Jr., Preceptor Beta Delta
Jacksonville, Florida

SKEWERED SCALLOPS

2 tablespoons butter
6 medium mushrooms,
   peeled, quartered
Salt and white
   pepper to taste
Juice of 1/2 lemon
32 small scallops
Sea salt to taste
Freshly ground white
   pepper
2 tablespoons unsalted
   butter
2 tablespoons soy sauce
2 teaspoons red wine
   vinegar
1 tablespoon unsalted
   butter
1 teaspoon fresh
   thyme leaves

Melt 2 tablespoons butter in saucepan over medium heat. Sauté mushrooms, adding salt, white pepper and lemon juice. Cover. Shake pan several times. Cook for 2 to 3 minutes longer; let cool. Thread scallops and mushrooms alternately on 8 wooden skewers, starting with scallops for a total of 4 scallops and 3 mushroom pieces per skewer. Sprinkle lightly with sea salt and pepper just before cooking. Melt 2 tablespoons butter in sauté pan over medium heat until foaming. Place skewers in pan. Cook for 2 minutes; turn over. Add soy sauce, wine vinegar and 1 tablespoon butter. Cook for 2 minutes longer. Turn skewers over again, coating with sauce. Remove from pan; drain. Place 2 skewers on each serving plate immediately after draining. Add a few drops of sauce; sprinkle with thyme. Yield: 4 servings.

Hans (Jeanne) Denee, Laureate Theta
Granville Ferry, Nova Scotia, Canada

SALMON LOAF

2 (14-ounce) cans salmon
1 quart canned
   home-grown
   tomatoes
1/2 teaspoon pepper
1 small onion,
   chopped
2 eggs, beaten
1 cup cracker crumbs

Preheat oven to 350 degrees. Place salmon in bowl. Remove bones; break into small pieces. Add tomatoes, pepper and onion. Add eggs to mixture; mix well. Add cracker crumbs; mix thoroughly. Place in ungreased meat loaf pan. Bake for 1 hour. Yield: 8 servings.

Frank (Ruth) McGill, Preceptor Alpha Sigma
Knoxville, Tennessee

PHEASANT IN SOUR CREAM SAUCE

When we married, my husband, an avid hunter, had to learn to cook his own wild game since I did not like any of it. In the nearly 18 years since then, he has become a great cook and I have learned to like some wild game.

1 pheasant, cut up
3/4 cup all-purpose
   flour
1/8 teaspoon salt
1/8 teaspoon pepper
1/4 teaspoon nutmeg
1/8 teaspoon garlic
   powder
2 tablespoons canola
   oil
2 cups dry white wine
1 cup lite sour cream

Preheat oven to 350 degrees. Rinse pheasant; pat dry. Combine flour, salt, pepper, nutmeg and garlic powder in plastic bag. Shake several pheasant pieces at a time in mixture until well coated. Reserve remaining flour mixture. Brown pheasant in oil in skillet. Place pheasant in casserole. Stir 1 1/2 cups wine into skillet drippings. Blend 1 1/2 tablespoons reserved flour mixture with 1/2 cup wine in small bowl; add to skillet. Cook until thickened, stirring constantly. Blend in 1/2 cup sour cream. Pour over pheasant. Drop remaining sour cream by teaspoonfuls over pheasant. Bake, uncovered, for 1 1/2 hours or until tender. Add additional heated wine if necessary. Yield: 4 servings.

Steve (Annette) Porter, Alpha
West Fargo, North Dakota

Ralph (Patricia A.) Siron, Preceptor Delta Rho, Mexico, Missouri, makes Sugar Bait for Butterflies by combining 1 (12-ounce) can regular beer, 2 pounds dark brown sugar, 2 cups molasses or syrup and 2 pounds well-ripened fruit such as bananas or peaches in large jar or crock. Cover loosely. Place in sun. Let ferment for 1 day. Make sure cover is loose fitting as it expands with fermentation. Store in shady area after fermenting. Dab mixture on posts, rocks or tree trunks. An old paint brush works fine for this. Results will improve as time goes by. Butterflies seem to find it more easily on a large rock in flower bed. This mixture attracts butterflies by day and moths by night.

ROAST DUCKLING

3/4 cup orange marmalade
2 tablespoons butter
1 tablespoon Worcestershire sauce
1/2 teaspoon onion powder
1/4 teaspoon garlic powder
1/2 teaspoon thyme
1/2 teaspoon ginger
1/2 teaspoon salt
1/2 teaspoon pepper
1 frozen duckling, thawed

Preheat oven to 475 degrees. Melt marmalade and butter in saucepan. Add Worcestershire sauce, onion powder and garlic powder; mix well. Cook over low heat, stirring constantly. Combine thyme, ginger, salt and pepper in bowl; mix well. Season inside of duckling. Make 1-inch slits in skin at 4-inch intervals. Place on rack in roasting pan. Baste duckling thoroughly with marmalade sauce. Bake for 45 minutes. Reduce oven temperature to 325 degrees. Bake for 1 hour. Let cool. Yield: 4 servings.

Doug (Karen) Schnell, Xi Epsilon Beta
Fort Wayne, Indiana

CORNED VENISON

1 (2- to 3-pound) brisket, flank or shoulder venison roast, cut 1 inch thick
2 quarts spring or distilled water
1/2 cup canning and pickling salt
1/2 cup Tenderquick
3 tablespoons sugar
2 tablespoons mixed pickling spice
2 bay leaves
8 whole black peppercorns
1 or 2 cloves of garlic, minced

Roll brisket loosely; tie with cooking string. Place in large glass bowl. Combine remaining ingredients in enamel saucepan; bring to a boil. Remove from heat; let cool. Pour cooled brine over meat. Cover bowl with plastic wrap. Refrigerate for 4 to 5 days, turning meat occasionally. Drain. Rinse meat with cold water. Place meat in heavy kettle. Cover with cold water. Bring to a boil; drain. Cover with cold water. Bring to a boil. Reduce heat; cover. Simmer for 3 1/2 to 4 1/2 hours or until tender. Yield: 4 to 6 servings.

Marty (Cyndy) Conlee, Pi Beta
Oswego, Illinois

❖ ♥ FAT-FREE FETTUCINI ALFREDO

1 1/3 cups skim milk
2 cloves of garlic, minced
2 teaspoons all-purpose flour
2 tablespoons fat-free cream cheese
1 cup fat-free Parmesan cheese
2 tablespoons fat-free margarine or butter
4 cups cooked hot fettucini
2 teaspoons fresh parsley, chopped
Pepper to taste

Whisk milk, garlic, flour and cream cheese in medium saucepan. Bring to a boil, whisking constantly. Reduce heat. Simmer for 2 minutes or until thickened. Add Parmesan cheese. Whisk until blended. Remove from heat. Stir in butter. Pour over hot fettucini. Garnish with parsley and pepper. Yield: 4 servings.

Lebro (Claire) Evangelista, Xi Kappa Psi
Westlake, Ohio

RISOTTO

2 tablespoons olive oil
1 onion, chopped
1 teaspoon garlic
1/2 cup white wine
1/2 cup chopped cooked bacon or ham
1 cup long grain rice
8 cups chicken or vegetable stock
1 cup frozen peas
3/4 cup freshly grated Parmesan cheese

Heat olive oil in saucepan over medium heat. Sauté onion and garlic in oil until transparent. Add wine. Cook until liquid is reduced by half. Add bacon and rice. Stir in stock, 1 cup at a time, cooking until absorbed before adding next cup. Rice should be creamy. Add frozen peas and cheese; mix well. Serve immediately. Yield: 4 servings.

Myron (Hope) Dukeshire, Xi Theta Psi
Santa Ana, California

ITALIAN ARTICHOKE PIE

3 eggs, beaten
1 (3-ounce) package cream cheese with chives, softened
3/4 teaspoon garlic powder
1/4 teaspoon pepper
1 cup shredded mozzarella cheese
1 cup ricotta cheese
1/2 cup mayonnaise or mayonnaise-type salad dressing
1 (13-ounce) can artichoke hearts
1 cup cooked garbanzo beans
1/2 cup sliced pitted ripe olives
1 (2-ounce) jar chopped pimento, drained
2 tablespoons snipped parsley
1 (9-inch) unbaked deep-dish pastry shell
1/3 cup grated Parmesan cheese
1/2 cup shredded mozzarella cheese
4 tomato slices, cut into halves

Preheat oven to 350 degrees. Combine eggs, cream cheese, garlic powder and pepper in bowl; mix well. Stir in 1 cup mozzarella cheese, ricotta cheese and mayonnaise. Drain artichokes. Cut 2 hearts into fourths; reserve. Chop remaining artichoke hearts. Fold into cheese mixture with beans, olives, pimento and parsley. Turn into pastry shell. Bake for 30 minutes. Top with remaining cheeses. Bake for 15 minutes or until set. Let stand for 10 minutes. Garnish with reserved artichoke quarters and tomato slices. Yield: 8 servings.

Joe (Ruth) Martinez, Alpha Rho
Durant, Oklahoma

BARBECUE-STYLE BAKED BEANS

2 (16-ounce) cans pork and beans, drained
3/4 cup mesquite barbecue sauce
2 tablespoons golden raisins
1/2 small onion, chopped
1/2 cup packed dark brown sugar
3 bacon slices, cut up
1 tart apple, peeled, chopped
1/2 teaspoon liquid smoke
1/4 teaspoon ginger

Preheat oven to 350 degrees. Combine all ingredients in 2-quart casserole. Bake, uncovered, for 1 hour. Yield: 6 servings.

Courtney (Mariam A.) Goforth, Laureate Alpha Omega
Stanberry, Missouri

BLACK BEAN BURGERS

2 cups black beans
3/4 cup milk
1 cup oats
1/2 cup bread crumbs
1 tablespoon olive oil
1 tablespoon all-purpose flour
1 tablespoon dry vegetable or chicken broth granules

Preheat oven to 350 degrees. Soak black beans in water to cover in bowl overnight; drain. Place beans in small amount of water in pressure cooker. Cook according to manufacturer's instructions until tender. Mash black beans in bowl. Add remaining ingredients; mix well. Shape into patties. Place on greased cookie sheet. Bake for 10 minutes on each side. Serve in buns with fixings. Yield: 6 servings.

Ron (Michelle) Harvey
Boulder, Colorado

BEAN SAUSAGE

2 cups pinto beans
2 eggs, beaten
1 cup bread crumbs
1 tablespoon chopped onion
1/4 teaspoon Italian seasoning
Dash of garlic salt
1/2 teaspoon sage

Cook beans in water in saucepan until tender; drain. Mash beans in bowl. Add remaining ingredients; mix well. Shape into patties. Fry in lightly oiled skillet until browned. Yield: 4 to 6 servings.

Jack (Carole) Stokes, Xi Zeta Epsilon
Portage, Michigan

Nicholas (Karen) Casson, Beta Nu, Encampment, Wyoming, makes Easy Fireman's Meat Loaf by mixing 1 1/2 pounds lean ground beef, 1 (8-ounce) can tomato sauce with mushrooms, 1 beaten egg and 1 (3-ounce) can French-fried onion rings, coarsely crumbled, in large bowl; mix well. Place in 5-by-9-inch loaf pan. Bake in preheated 350-degree oven for 1 hour. Yield: 4 to 6 servings. Nick is a retired fireman and was a cook at many firehouses. This was a good stand-by meal with baked potatoes and salad. Also easy and quick to fix between runs.

RED CABBAGE WITH WINE AND APPLES

This is wonderful with pork chops, grilled sausage and roasted duck.

2 medium heads red cabbage
1/4 cup unsalted butter
1 1/2 tablespoons dark brown sugar
2 medium onions, finely chopped
2 small apples, peeled, coarsely chopped
6 tablespoons red wine vinegar
1 teaspoon coarse salt
6 tablespoons dry red wine
1 to 1 1/2 cups meat stock or water
3 tablespoons red currant jelly

Quarter and core cabbage; shred into 1/4-inch pieces. Melt butter over medium-low heat in large heavy skillet. Stir in brown sugar until melted. Add onions and apples; cover tightly. Cook over low heat for 5 minutes, stirring twice. Add cabbage; toss to coat. Pour vinegar over mixture; mix well. Cover. Cook for 10 minutes. Sprinkle salt over cabbage. Add wine and 1 cup stock. Cover. Simmer over medium-low heat for 1 1/2 hours or until cabbage is very tender. Add additional stock if necessary to keep moist but not soupy. Add jelly; stir until melted. Remove from heat. Serve hot. May be made up to 2 days ahead. Yield: 8 servings.

T. J. (Peggy) Barnes, Preceptor Alpha Kappa
San Antonio, Texas

GRILLED POTATOES AU GRATIN

5 crisp-fried bacon slices, drained, crumbled
1/2 cup shredded Cheddar cheese
1/4 cup chopped onion
7 cups sliced pared potatoes
1/2 teaspoon salt
1/8 teaspoon pepper
1/2 cup butter or margarine, melted

Combine bacon, cheese and onion in bowl. Cover; refrigerate. Arrange potatoes on 24-inch length cooking foil. Sprinkle with salt and pepper. Spread bacon-cheese mixture over potatoes. Drizzle butter over top. Wrap mixture securely into loose packet. Grill 4 inches from medium-hot coals for 1 hour or until tender. Yield: 6 servings.

Gerald (Barbara L.) Godsey, Omega Phi
Ravenwood, Missouri

Ron (Paula) Harmon, Zeta Pi, Burlison, Texas, makes Pickled Eggs by combining 1/2 cup beet juice, 1/2 cup vinegar, 1/4 cup sugar and 1 tablespoon mixed pickling spices in saucepan; mix well. Bring to a boil. Pour over 6 peeled hard-cooked eggs in bowl. Refrigerate, covered, for 12 to 24 hours before serving. These are great served with finger foods and at barbecues. Yield: 6 to 10 servings.

STREUSEL-TOPPED SWEET POTATOES

We have served this dish at Thanksgiving for the past 25 years.

- 3 (16-ounce) cans sweet potatoes, drained, mashed
- 1/2 cup pancake syrup
- 1/3 cup all-purpose flour
- 1/3 cup uncooked oats
- 1/3 cup packed dark brown sugar
- 1/4 teaspoon cinnamon
- 1/4 cup margarine
- 1/4 cup chopped pecans

Preheat oven to 350 degrees. Combine sweet potatoes and syrup in bowl until blended. Spoon into 1 1/2-quart casserole. Combine flour, oats, brown sugar and cinnamon in bowl; mix well. Cut in margarine until mixture resembles coarse meal. Stir in pecans. Sprinkle mixture over sweet potatoes. Bake for 40 minutes. Yield: 8 to 10 servings.

Orion (Leota) Reagan, Preceptor Beta Psi
Fredericktown, Missouri

♥ VEGETARIAN BURRITOS

- 1 pound frozen tofu, thawed
- 1 cup salsa
- 8 flour tortillas, warmed
- 1 cup shredded Colby and Monterey Jack cheese
- 2 cups refried beans
- 1 cup shredded lettuce
- 1/2 cup chopped tomatoes
- 1 cup salsa

Squeeze tofu to remove excess moisture. Place in small bowl; mash with fork. Stir in 1 cup salsa. Let marinate at room temperature for 30 minutes. Place large spoonful tofu on each tortilla. Top with cheese, beans, lettuce and tomatoes. Serve with 1 cup salsa. Yield: 8 servings.

Robert (Dona K.) Spence, Xi Epsilon Epsilon
Evansville, Indiana

HUNTERS' VEGETABLE SPECIAL

- 8 ounces bacon, cut into 2-inch pieces
- 3 cups large chunks zucchini
- 2 cups large chunks yellow squash
- 1 cup large chunks cabbage
- 1 cup large chunks onion
- 1/2 cup large chunk green bell pepper
- 1/2 cup large chunks carrot
- 1/2 cup large chunks celery
- 2 cups large chunks potatoes
- 1 tablespoon oregano
- Salt and pepper to taste

Fry bacon in skillet until almost crisp. Remove from skillet; drain. Reserve drippings in skillet. Combine bacon, zucchini, squash, cabbage, onion, green pepper, carrot and celery in large saucepan. Cook potatoes in reserved bacon drippings until almost tender. Add to saucepan mixture. Add oregano and season to taste. Fill saucepan with water to almost cover vegetables. Bring to a vigorous boil. Reduce heat to simmer. Cover partially. Cook, stirring once or twice, for 8 to 10 minutes or until vegetables are crisp-tender. Yield: 8 servings.

Darrell (Diane) Clarke, Zeta Alpha
Marion, Kentucky

PINEAPPLE-ANGEL FOOD CAKE

- 1 cup cake flour
- 1 1/2 cups confectioners' sugar
- 1 1/2 cups egg whites
- 1/4 teaspoon salt
- 1 1/2 teaspoons cream of tartar
- 1 teaspoon vanilla extract
- 1 teaspoon almond flavoring
- 1 cup sugar
- 1/2 cup butter or margarine
- 3 tablespoons (heaping) all-purpose flour
- 1 (20-ounce) can crushed pineapple
- 1 1/2 cups sugar
- 1/2 carton whipped topping

Preheat oven to 350 degrees. Sift cake flour and confectioners' sugar into bowl. Beat egg whites in mixer bowl at low speed until foamy. Add salt, cream of tartar, vanilla and almond flavoring. Beat at medium speed until soft peaks form. Add 1 cup sugar gradually, 1 tablespoon at a time, beating constantly at high speed until stiff peaks form; do not underbeat. Fold in flour mixture gently, 1/4 cup at a time. Spoon into ungreased tube pan. Cut through batter with knife 1 inch from center of pan. Bake for 35 to 45 minutes or until top is brown and dry. Invert on funnel for 1 hour. Invert onto cake plate. Melt butter in medium saucepan. Add all-purpose flour; mix well. Add pineapple and 1 1/2 cups sugar. Cook until mixture is thick and clear. Let cool. Cut cake into 3 equal layers. Spread 1/4 filling over each layer. Add whipped topping to remaining filling. Frost top of cake. Refrigerate until serving time. Yield: 12 to 16 servings.

Fred (Brenda) Kressig, Theta Omega
Salisbury, Missouri

KAHLUA-GLAZED BANANAS

- 4 small firm ripe bananas, peeled
- 1 cup water
- 1 tablespoon instant coffee granules
- 1/3 cup packed dark brown sugar
- 3 tablespoons low-calorie margarine
- 1/4 cup Kahlua
- 1 1/3 cups vanilla nonfat frozen yogurt

Cut bananas in half lengthwise, then crosswise. Bring water to a boil in large nonstick skillet. Add coffee granules, brown sugar and margarine. Reduce heat to medium. Cook until sugar is dissolved, stirring frequently. Add bananas. Cook for 5 minutes, turning occasionally. Remove from heat. Stir in Kahlua. Spoon over frozen yogurt. Yield: 4 servings.

Dave (Joanne) Pomerleau, Theta
Moose Jaw, Saskatchewan, Canada

CHUNKY PEANUT BUTTER FUDGE

1 cup sugar	2 tablespoons white
1 cup packed light	corn syrup
brown sugar	1/4 cup crunchy
1/2 cup milk	peanut butter
1/4 cup strong liquid	1 teaspoon vanilla
coffee	extract

Combine sugar, brown sugar, milk, coffee and corn syrup in large heavy saucepan; mix well. Bring to a boil, stirring until sugars are dissolved. Reduce heat. Cook, uncovered, over medium heat without stirring until mixture reaches soft-ball stage or 238 degrees on candy thermometer. Remove from heat. Add peanut butter and vanilla. Do not mix. Let stand until mixture is lukewarm. Beat until thick and creamy. Pour quickly into greased 7-inch square pan. Let stand until firm. Cut into squares. Yield: 24 servings.

Joel (Donna S.) Laws, Preceptor Theta Iota
Tampa, Florida

FRENCH APPLE PIE

When we lived in the Middle East, Bob's "apple pie Sunday afternoons" drew Americans and local people for companionship, friendship and a delicious dessert!

1 cup sugar	1 1/2 tablespoons
1 1/4 teaspoons	butter
cinnamon	1/2 cup packed dark
6 cups sliced tart	brown sugar
apples	1 cup all-purpose
1 (10-inch) unbaked	flour
pie shell	1/2 cup butter

Preheat oven to 425 degrees. Combine sugar and cinnamon in bowl. Add apples, stirring until well coated. Place apples in pie shell. Dot with 1 1/2 tablespoons butter. Combine brown sugar, flour and 1/2 cup butter in bowl using pastry blender or 2 knives until crumbly. Sprinkle over apples; pat down lightly. Bake for 50 minutes or until topping is brown. Yield: 6 or 8 servings.

Robert (Muriel M.) Hollenbeck, Preceptor Gamma Lambda
Sedalia, Colorado

Al (Daughn M.) Connarn, Xi Gamma Zeta, Pisgah Forest, North Carolina, makes Better Butter and Garlic Better Butter by placing 1 cup canola oil in blender container. Blend in 1 cup softened butter, a little at time, until smooth. Pour mixture into container. Chill overnight. This simplified version cuts saturated fats in half while actually enhancing the unmatched butter taste. To make Garlic Better Butter, place 1 cup olive oil in blender container. Add 12 to 15 cloves of peeled garlic; blend well. Blend in 1 cup softened butter, a little at time, until smooth. Pour mixture into container. Chill overnight. This is an original spread for garlic bread or an addition to soups, stews or any recipe that needs both garlic and oil. Each recipe makes 1 pound butter.

CHOCOLATE MOUSSE SUPREME

1 1/2 cups all-purpose	4 egg yolks
flour	2 cups whipping
3/4 cup softened	cream
butter	6 tablespoons
1 (12-ounce) package	confectioners' sugar
semisweet chocolate	4 egg whites, at room
pieces	temperature
2 eggs	

Preheat oven to 350 degrees. Combine flour and butter in bowl to form ball. Line bottom and side of 10-inch springform pan with mixture, spreading with hands. Bake for 20 to 30 minutes or until golden. Let cool. Melt chocolate in top of double boiler over simmering water. Remove from heat. Let cool. Add whole eggs; mix well. Add yolks; mix until thoroughly blended. Whip cream with confectioners' sugar in large mixer bowl. Beat egg whites in medium mixer bowl until peaks form. Stir small amount of cream and egg whites into chocolate mixture. Fold in remaining cream and egg whites until completely mixed. Pour into crust-lined pan. Chill for 6 hours. Loosen with sharp knife. Remove from springform pan. Serve with sweetened whipped cream. Yield: 10 servings.

Brad (Diana) Cook, Theta Lambda
Colorado Springs, Colorado

CHERRIES JUBILEE

We had cherries jubilee on our honeymoon and improved upon the recipe, ending up with this.

1 (14-ounce) can	Juice of 1 orange
pitted cherries	Juice of 1/2 lemon
4 ounces Brandy	1 ounce Grand Marnier
2 teaspoons cornstarch	or Kirsch
2 tablespoons	Vanilla ice cream
confectioners' sugar	

Drain cherries, reserving juice. Soak cherries in Brandy for 1 hour. Combine reserved cherry juice, cornstarch and confectioners' sugar in mixer bowl; beat until thick. Add orange and lemon juices, Grand Marnier, cherries and Brandy; mix well. Pour over individual servings of ice cream. Yield: 4 servings.

Graham (Susan) Thomson, Xi Gamma
Winnipeg, Manitoba, Canada

Bruce (Karen) Berning, Xi Iota Beta, Robertsville, Missouri, makes Creamed Eggs on Toast by combining 10 chopped hard-cooked eggs, 1/2 cup butter or margarine and 1/4 cup all-purpose flour in medium saucepan. Stir in 2 cups milk and 1 teaspoon Worcestershire sauce. Cook, stirring, over medium-high heat until thickened. Serve over toasted bread. Yield: 6 servings.

Recipes Submitted By Husbands

FIRST-GENTLEMAN HOMEMADE ICE CREAM

When I was installed as Chapter President, I introduced my husband as the "First Gentleman." He has not baked any cookies, but has made ice cream for our chapter! This ice cream is not as sweet as some homemade recipes; we add fresh fruit, sundae toppings, etc.

12 eggs
4 cups sugar
6 tablespoons vanilla extract
6 cans Milnot
Skim milk

Combine eggs and sugar in mixer bowl; beat well. Add vanilla and Milnot; mix well. Pour into 2-gallon ice cream freezer. Fill to top with skim milk. Freeze according to manufacturer's instructions. Leftover ice cream may be frozen. Yield: 32 servings.

Gary (J. Elaine) Bultemeier, Xi Kappa Omicron
Lampe, Missouri

1-2-3 HOT FUDGE SAUCE

1 (13-ounce) can evaporated milk
2 cups sugar
3 squares unsweetened chocolate
1 to 2 tablespoons peanut butter (optional)
1 teaspoon vanilla extract

Combine evaporated milk, sugar, unsweetened chocolate and peanut butter in saucepan. Bring to a boil over medium heat. Cook for 5 minutes, stirring vigorously. Remove from heat. Add vanilla. Beat with rotary beater for 1 minute. Serve hot or cold on ice cream or cake. Yield: 8 to 10 servings.

Charles (Pat) McCourry, Preceptor Gamma Theta
Canton, Ohio

❖ NEW ZEALAND SHORTBREAD

3/4 cup butter
6 tablespoons confectioners' sugar
1 1/4 cups all-purpose flour
1/2 teaspoon baking powder
1/2 can sweetened condensed milk
2 tablespoons white corn syrup
2 tablespoons butter
1/2 teaspoon vanilla extract

Preheat oven to 350 degrees. Cream 3/4 cup butter with confectioners' sugar in mixer bowl. Add flour and baking powder; mix well. Press 3/4 the mixture into buttered 8-inch square baking pan. Combine condensed milk, corn syrup, 2 tablespoons butter and vanilla in top of double boiler. Cook, stirring, until smooth. Pour over shortbread in pan. Crumble remaining shortbread; sprinkle over condensed milk mixture. Bake for 25 to 30 minutes or until golden. Yield: 12 to 16 servings.

James (Susan M.) Rollo, Preceptor Alpha Sigma
Petersburg, Ontario, Canada

PEARS IN RED WINE

4 large Ajou or Bartlett pears
1 1/2 cups dry red wine
1/3 cup sugar
2 to 3 strips lemon peel
3 tablespoons lemon juice
Few drops of red food coloring

Peel and seed pears, leaving pears whole and stems on. Place pears in saucepan. Add wine, sugar, lemon peel and lemon juice. Bring to a boil. Reduce heat; cover. Simmer for 25 minutes, turning pears frequently. Add food coloring the last few minutes of cooking time. Adjust cooking time according to softness or hardness of pears. Place each pear in a deep serving bowl. Add sauce. Refrigerate. Sauce will thicken as pears chill. Yield: 4 servings.

Fred (Roberta E.) Hanson, Laureate Chi
Munster, Indiana

POPCORN BALLS

3/4 cup white or dark corn syrup
1/2 cup butter
2 tablespoons water
1 pound confectioners' sugar
2/3 (10-ounce) bag miniature marshmallows
5 quarts popped popcorn

Combine corn syrup, butter, water, confectioners' sugar and marshmallows in saucepan. Cook over low heat until just boiling, stirring constantly. Pour over popcorn in bowl. Shape into balls. Yield: 24 to 48 servings.

Dale (Patricia) Pownall, Xi Delta Theta
Rock Creek, British Columbia, Canada

PRETZELS-WITH-A-PUNCH

1 (16-ounce) package pretzel sticks
1/2 cup butter
3 tablespoons whiskey
1 tablespoon dark brown sugar
1 teaspoon garlic powder
1/2 teaspoon cayenne pepper

Preheat oven to 250 degrees. Place pretzels in single layer in 9-by-13-inch baking pan. Melt butter in saucepan. Stir in remaining ingredients. Pour over pretzels, turning to coat evenly. Bake for 20 minutes, turning after 10 minutes. Let cool completely. Store in airtight container. Yield: 4 to 8 servings.

Mike (Jenny) Poole, Preceptor Mu
Lexington, Kentucky

Edward (Judy A.) Finan, Preceptor Gamma Mu, Bingham Farms, Michigan, makes Special Greek-Italian Dressing by mixing 2 cups vegetable oil, 10 tablespoons apple cider vinegar, 1 tablespoon salt, 1 tablespoon garlic salt, 1/2 tablespoon Accent and 1/2 tablespoon oregano in jar. Shake vigorously.

CHOCOLATE-CHERRY VALENTINE TORTE

2 eggs, separated
1/2 cup sugar
1 1/4 cups unsifted all-purpose flour
1 cup sugar
1/2 cup unsweetened baking cocoa
3/4 teaspoon baking soda
1/2 teaspoon salt
1/2 cup vegetable oil
1 cup buttermilk
Cream Filling
Chocolate Whipped Cream
1 (21-ounce) can cherry pie filling

Preheat oven to 350 degrees. Beat egg whites in small mixer bowl until foamy. Beat in 1/2 cup sugar gradually until stiff peaks form. Combine flour, 1 cup sugar, cocoa, baking soda and salt in large mixer bowl. Add oil, buttermilk and egg yolks; beat until smooth. Fold egg whites gently into batter. Grease and flour 2 heart-shaped cake pans. Pour about 1 2/3 cups batter into each pan. Reserve remaining batter in refrigerator while first 2 layers bake. Bake for 18 to 20 minutes or until cake springs back when lightly touched in center. Let cool for 5 minutes. Invert onto wire rack. Bake remaining layer; let cool completely. Prepare Cream Filling. Place 1 cake layer on serving plate. Pipe or spoon Cream Filling 1-inch edge 1/2-inch thick around layer. Spread 1/2 the cherry filling in center. Top with second layer. Spread with 1/2 remaining Cream Filling. Top with third layer. Spoon remaining cherry filling onto top of cake, leaving 1-inch edge. Prepare Chocolate Whipped Cream. Frost sides of cake with Chocolate Whipped Cream. Pipe top edge with remaining Cream Filling. Chill completely; Refrigerate until serving time. Yield: 8 to 10 servings.

CREAM FILLING

1 cup heavy cream
2 tablespoons sugar
1 teaspoon vanilla extract

Whip cream with sugar and vanilla in small mixer bowl until stiff peaks form.

CHOCOLATE WHIPPED CREAM

1/2 cup sugar
1/4 cup unsweetened baking cocoa
1 cup heavy cream
1 teaspoon vanilla extract

Combine sugar and cocoa in small mixer bowl. Add cream and vanilla. Beat on low speed to combine. Beat on medium speed until stiff peaks form.

Photograph for this recipe is on the cover.

CHOCOLATE KISS MOUSSE

1 1/2 cups miniature or 15 regular marshmallows
1/3 cup milk
1/4 teaspoon almond extract or
2 teaspoons Kirsch
6 to 7 drops of red food coloring
36 milk chocolate kisses, unwrapped
1 cup heavy cream
4 milk chocolate kisses (optional)

Combine marshmallows and milk in small saucepan. Cook over low heat, stirring constantly, until marshmallows are melted and mixture is smooth. Remove from heat. Pour 1/3 cup marshmallow mixture into medium bowl; blend in almond extract and food coloring. Set aside. Add 36 milk chocolate kisses to remaining marshmallow mixture. Return to low heat; stir until kisses are melted. Remove from heat. Let cool to room temperature. Whip cream in mixer bowl until stiff. Fold 1 cup into chocolate mixture. Fold remaining whipped cream gradually into almond mixture. Fill parfait glasses about 3/4 full with chocolate mixture. Top with almond cream. Chill for 3 to 4 hours or until set. Garnish with a kiss. Yield: 4 servings.

Photograph for this recipe is on the cover.

PEPPERED HAMBURGERS

1 1/4 pounds ground beef
1 1/2 teaspoons salt
1 teaspoon paprika
1/2 teaspoon pepper
1 egg yolk
6 tablespoons cola beverage
3/4 tablespoon all-purpose flour
1 onion, sliced
1 green pepper, cut into rings
1 red pepper, cut into rings
Butter or margarine

Combine ground beef, salt, paprika, pepper, egg yolk, cola beverage and flour in bowl; mix well. Chill for about 1 hour. Sauté onion and green and red peppers in a small amount of butter in skillet until soft. Remove; set aside. Shape beef mixture into thick patties. Cook in skillet until browned on both sides. Top with onion mixture; serve. Yield: 6 to 8 servings.

Photograph for this recipe on page 1.

PEAR-CHOCOLATE CHIP MUFFINS

1 3/4 cups all-purpose flour
1 cup sugar
2 teaspoons baking powder
1/4 teaspoon salt
2 eggs, slightly beaten
1 cup sour cream
1/4 cup melted butter
1 teaspoon vanilla extract
1 1/2 cups chopped pears
1 cup miniature chocolate chips
1/4 cup chopped walnuts
1/4 cup sugar
2 tablespoons butter, softened

Preheat oven to 400 degrees. Combine flour, 1 cup sugar, baking powder and salt in bowl. Add mixture of eggs, sour cream, 1/4 cup butter, vanilla, pear chunks and chocolate chips; mix just until moistened. Fill 12 greased muffin cups 3/4 full. Mix walnuts, 1/4 cup sugar and 2 tablespoons butter in bowl until crumbly. Sprinkle over muffins. Bake for 18 to 20 minutes or until muffins test done. Yield: 12 servings.

Photograph for this recipe on page 2.

Metric Equivalents

Although the United States has opted to postpone converting to metric measurements, most other countries, including England and Canada, use the metric system. The following chart provides convenient approximate equivalents for allowing use of regular kitchen measures when cooking from foreign recipes.

Volume

These metric measures are approximate benchmarks for purposes of home food preparation.
1 milliliter = 1 cubic centimeter = 1 gram

Liquid
1 teaspoon = 5 milliliters
1 tablespoon = 15 milliliters
1 fluid ounce = 30 milliliters
1 cup = 250 milliliters
1 pint = 500 milliliters

Dry
1 quart = 1 liter
1 ounce = 30 grams
1 pound = 450 grams
2.2 pounds = 1 kilogram

Weight
1 ounce = 28 grams
1 pound = 450 grams

Length
1 inch = 2½ centimeters
1/16 inch = 1 millimeter

Formulas Using Conversion Factors

When approximate conversions are not accurate enough, use these formulas to convert measures from one system to another.

Measurements	Formulas
ounces to grams:	# ounces x 28.3 = # grams
grams to ounces:	# grams x 0.035 = # ounces
pounds to grams:	# pounds x 453.6 = # grams
pounds to kilograms:	# pounds x 0.45 = # kilograms
ounces to milliliters:	# ounces x 30 = # milliliters
cups to liters:	# cups x 0.24 = # liters
inches to centimeters:	# inches x 2.54 = # centimeters
centimeters to inches:	# centimeters x 0.39 = # inches

Approximate Weight to Volume

Some ingredients which we commonly measure by volume are measured by weight in foreign recipes. Here are a few examples for easy reference.

flour, all-purpose, unsifted	1 pound = 450 grams = 3½ cups
flour, all-purpose, sifted	1 pound = 450 grams = 4 cups
sugar, granulated	1 pound = 450 grams = 2 cups
sugar, brown, packed	1 pound = 450 grams = 2¼ cups
sugar, confectioners'	1 pound = 450 grams = 4 cups
sugar, confectioners', sifted	1 pound = 450 grams = 4½ cups
butter	1 pound = 450 grams = 2 cups

Temperature

Remember that foreign recipes frequently express temperatures in Centigrade rather than Fahrenheit.

Temperatures	Fahrenheit	Centigrade
room temperature	68°	20°
water boils	212°	100°
baking temperature	350°	177°
baking temperature	375°	190.5°
baking temperature	400°	204.4°
baking temperature	425°	218.3°
baking temperature	450°	232°

Use the following formulas when temperature conversions are necessary.

Centigrade degrees x 9/5 + 32 = Fahrenheit degrees
Fahrenheit degrees - 32 x 5/9 = Centigrade degrees

American Measurement Equivalents

1 tablespoon = 3 teaspoons	12 tablespoons = ¾ cup
2 tablespoons = 1 ounce	16 tablespoons = 1 cup
4 tablespoons = ¼ cup	1 cup = 8 ounces
5 tablespoons + 1 teaspoon = ⅓ cup	2 cups = 1 pint
	4 cups = 1 quart
8 tablespoons = ½ cup	4 quarts = 1 gallon

Merit Winners

MOUTHWATERING MENUS
First Prize
Collier, Marlene, page 18
Second Prize
Black, Lois C., page 9
Third Prize
Webb, Carol, page 24
JUST FOR STARTERS
First Prize
James, Carol, page 50
Second Prize
Campbell, Robin, page 47
Third Prize
Iberg, Colette, page 42
IT'S A TOSS-UP
First Prize
Attridge, Maureen, page 71
Second Prize
Taylor, Jennifer, page 57
Third Prize
Fisher, Betsy, page 65
THE MAIN EVENT
First Prize
McGann, Juanita, page 80
Second Prize
Richards, Phoebe, page 74
Third Prize
Jahde, Kimberly F., page 82
DELECTABLE DISHES
First Prize
Birdsong, Maxine, page 95
Second Prize
Dille, Mary, page 87
Third Prize
English, Maureen, page 101
FROM THE GARDEN
First Prize
Landreth, Kathleen, page 113
Second Prize
Hosier, Janet, page 111
Third Prize
Tjoelker, Delinda, page 110
JUST LOAFING AROUND
First Prize
Hansen, Irja, page 120
Second Prize
Kelly, Jennifer M., page 117
Third Prize
Bellis, Dorothy, page 122
RISE AND SHINE
First Prize
Hamilton, Malinda, page 138
Second Prize
Haynes, Janette, page 133
Third Prize
English, Carolyn, page 129

RAVE REVIEWS
First Prize
Wood, Andrea, page 177
Second Prize
Durnwald, Dolores, page 179
Third Prize
Haugen, Lisa, page 174
SWEET TREATS
First Prize
Ledwidge, Wendy, page 192
Second Prize
Blair, Carol Ann, page 184
Third Prize
Epting, Wendy, page 195
SPOUSES' SPECIALS
First Prize
Reid, David (Charlene M.), page 204
Second Prize
Evangelista, Lebro (Claire), page 208
Third Prize
Rollo, James (Susan M.), page 212
HONORABLE MENTION
Abraham, Gail, page 57
Ahmann, Annette, page 190
Aho, Anne B., page 57
Amon, Sandra, page 161
Anker, Shasta L., page 184
Armstrong, Glenda, page 186
Ashcraft, Fara Cornett, page 187
Aubry, Mary, page 62
Baggett, Audrey, page 111
Baker, Shirley E., page 143
Barnes, Kimberly, page 161
Barnes, T.J. (Peggy), page 209
Bates, Lorraine, page 135
Baumgart, Laura, page 117
Bay, Shelley, page 46
Beiermann, Deanna, page 94
Bennett, Sherrie, page 149
Bergemann, Virginia, page 129
Binder, Beverly, page 98
Bingham, Lucille, page 75
Bolton, Judy, page 144
Bond, Delone J., page 119
Boyce, Lori, page 62
Bredy, Lucille, page 64
Brendon, Florence, page 126
Briggs, "Al" Smit, page 135
Bryan, Robbie, page 77
Buchele, Marilyn R., page 64
Burgess, Cathy, page 164
Burkhardt, Nancy, page 43
Burling, Diane, page 150
Burnap, Beverly, page 37
Burton, Arlene P., page 180
Busko, Beatrice G. page 10

Butler, Patricia A., page 167
Caraway, Rowena, page 90
Carr, Jeanne, page 184
Carson, Bettie, page 124
Casteel, Mona, page 121
Centola, Rosemarie, page 92
Chambers, Helen, page 142
Chargin, Roberta L., page 145
Christian, Mary Ann, page 118
Clark, Joanie, page 49
Clement, Johnnye, page 74
Cline, Carolyn, page 76
Cole, Cathy, page 70
Coleman, Donna M., page 153
Conlee, Marty (Cyndy), page 208
Connolly, Jimmy (Lerliene), page 201
Cook, Lillian, page 116
Cook, Shirley, page 174
Courtright, Robyn, page 163
Couture, Joan E., page 39
Crook, Karen Ann, page 81
Culen, Sharon, page 60
Curts, Elizabeth F., page 93
Czulo, Betty, page 98
Dacquisto, Joy, page 40
Dalke, Pam, page 154
David, L. Paula, page 84
DeFillipo, Kathryn, page 58
Deniston, Bette, page 61
DiBeneditto, Janice, page 95
Dilworth, Mary, page 56
Disterhaupt, Paula A., page 76
Doherty, Margaret, page 44
Duncan, Patricia E., page 77
Dye, Kristin, page 110
Elgert, Denise, page 192
Elsbernd, Gloria, page 63
Fagan, Betty, page 118
Fillmore, Rebecca, page 128
Fleming, Jane E., page 114
Fleming, Juanita, page 152
Flesher, Terry, page 67
Ford, Mary, page 125
Foreman, Larry (Michelle Leger-Foreman), page 205
Foulard, Annemarie Michel, page 82
Fouts, Wanda, page 61
Fox, Peggy L., page 142
Freiberger, Billie, page 129
French, Eunice, page 101
Gariepy, Marlene, page 125
Geibel, Jeanette, page 93
Gilmore, Vanessa L., page 91
Gleeson, Bill (Mary Lou), page 205
Greason, Doreen, page 48
Green, Elsie M., page 95

Merit Winners / 217

Griffin, Joy R., page 128
Grossheim, Christy, page 129
Gubbrud, Amy, page 40
Gunnels, Tanya, page 68
Gwinn, Martha J., page 70
Hansen, Marion, page 122
Hanson, Jack (Betty), page 203
Harbolt, Jean, page 111
Harris, Norma, page 142
Harshman, Moonyenne, page 70
Hearn, Nancy, page 174
Hedden, Paulette, page 145
Herbert, Heather, page 89
Herczeg, Mae Bele, page 43
Herian, Joyce A., page 69
Hess, Esther, page 88
Hildebrant, Pat, page 89
Hodge, Nancy, page 58
Hoendorf, Mrs. Donna, page 66
Holland, Margaret, page 99
Hollett, Martha, page 58
Holmes, Linda, page 109
Holroyd, Jean G., page 56
Holt, Debby, page 79
Holt, Julie, page 128
Horrell, Ann P., page 106
Hosman, Kathryn M., page 90
Howe, Janice, page 81
Huettenmueller, page 188
Hurst, Bette, page 97
Hutton, Nancy, page 105
Isett, Bettie B., page 125
Jacobson, Barbara I., page 90
Janz, Helen, page 62
Jarrett, Jean, page 108
Johnston, Marlene, page 88
Jones, Julie E., page 153
Jones, Shirley, page 96
Jones, Steve (Carla Sue), page 206
Jossy, Marilynn J., page 160
Kalvn, Sheila, page 148
Kemerling, Carmel-Beth, page 61
Kennedy, Barbara, page 162
Kennedy, Jackie, page 111
Kibler, Archalyn, page 117
Kirkbride, Rachel, page 105
Klasel, Lynda J., page 106
Koster, Joyce T., page 122
Kratchman, Diana, page 139
Kulp, Phyllis, page 152
Kutcher, R. John (Judy), page 202
Lang, Pamela, page 38
Laughman, Wanda, page 78
Lawrence, Margaret, page 118
Legge, Penny, page 44
Lehmann, Evelyn, page 80
Lethcoe, Mary Lynn, page 133
Liepins, Myrna L., page 185
Long, Claudia M., page 178
Long, Teresa J., page 110
Lorenz, Charles (Frances), page 202
Lovelady, Danny (Robin Austen-Lovelady), page 204

Lyens, Paula, page 147
Mack, Brenda, page 65
MacLean, Doreen, page 74
MacLeod, Susan, page 55
Mahagan, Norma, page 169
Mallinson, Tom (Diane), page 203
Martindale, Cathy, page 92
Martinez, Joe (Ruth), page 208
Mason, JoAnn, page 105
Mathews, Jr., William (Janice G.), page 207
Mayes, Jo, page 86
McCary, Becky, page 87
McCauley, Patricia, page 61
McCullin, Eddie, page 162
McVitty, Peg, page 138
Meegan, Debbie, page 18
Mendro, Joan, page 38
Mercer, Susan, page 134
Messer, Betsy, page 107
Michelle, Scottie, page 123
Middlemiss, Don (Colleen), page 203
Miller, Betty J., page 159
Mitchke, Mildred E., page 129
Monson, Sonia, page 100
Monteith, Darlene, page 98
Morris, Darlene, page 156
Morrison, Imogene, page 45
Morrison, Ronald (Louise), page 201
Mortson, Celia, page 104
Moser, Jan D., page 191
Murphy, Sarron, page 151
Myers, Connie, page 121
Myers, Gayle, page 12
Myers, Tommy (Lou), page 206
Nay, Bonnie Jo, page 119
Nelson, Beth, page 121
Nemeth, Sheila, page 189
Newman, Judy P., page 177
Newton, Cynthia L., page 76
Noble, Jeannette, page 124
Noble, Marie, page 167
Nowak, Mari, page 87
Olivas, Viki, page 50
Parakin, Karin, page 59
Parsons, Connie, page 60
Parsons, Tien, page 40
Paulshock, Louise W., page 87
Perry, Anne C., page 82
Perry, Linda, page 146
Peschka, Anita, page 128
Pessano, Jeannie, page 57
Pestor, Carol, page 101
Phares, Martha S., page 14
Pickler, Patricia M., page 107
Pitcher, Kathy, page 148
Poling, Kay, page 193
Pomerleau, Dave (Joanne), page 210
Pontius, Joanne, page 116
Poole, Mike (Jenny), page 212
Porter, Steve (Annette), page 207
Pryhuber, Patricia, page 75
Quivey, Barbara R., page 105

Raasch, Chele, page 95
Raven, Brenda, page 67
Ray, Doris V., page 56
Reed, Kelso, page 98
Reid, Fern E., page 195
Reisen, Becky, page 45
Richey, Rosanne, page 94
Rippey, Beverly, page 134
Robbins, Pam, page 54
Roberts, Cheril, page 189
Rohfs, Arlin (Ninajean), page 200
Rowland, Norma, page 171
Salazar, Juanita, page 185
Schmalfuss, Sue, page 36
Schultz, Debbie, page 100
Sebba, Chris, page 41
Sexton, Loma, page 160
Shrader, Marilyn, page 158
Sides, Kathryn B., page 189
Slaton, Nina L., page 68
Smith, Tammy, page 66
Smith, Tara, page 69
Snare, Marlynne, page 159
Soper, Carla, page 43
Spence, Robert (Dona K.), page 210
Starks, Karen, page 66
Steelman, Debbie, page 186
Stevenson, Christine A., page 123
Steward, Connie, page 69
Stisser, Betty E., page 49
Stone, Valorie, page 187
Suchan, Berny, page 136
Thurman, Gretchen, page 86
Tomson, Kristy, page 47
Touchet, Deborah, page 106
Towns, Wanda, page 190
Tyhurst, Ronald (Constance), page 206
Unruh, Mylo, page 156
Upleger, Sharon L., page 81
Upton, Joyce, page 154
Vandersloot, Mari, page 80
Van Hoven, Carole, page 90
Van Winkle, Sharon, page 60
Vaughn Mary Jane, page 107
Verble, Barbara Ann, page 165
Vierboom, Cindy, page 97
Vogt, Tahnell, page 56
Walker, Ann, page 84
Wallis, Peggy, page 163
Walsh, Karen Lea, page 172
Wells, Pamela, page 55
White, Meryl, page 130
Wilson, Elaine, page 59
Windmiller, Debbie, page 94
Witzel, Karen, page 66
Witzki, Arleta, page 71
Wobito, Liane, page 39
Wood, Mike (Deborah K.), page 200
Wry, Sharon R., page 71
Young, Kelly, page 165
Young, Maxine L., page 55
Zeler, Jean, page 75

Index

ACCOMPANIMENTS
Chili Petin Jelly, 200
Converted Pickles, 13
Dr. Pepper Jelly, 50
Fruit Conserve, 196
Green Tomato Pickles, 113
Pickled Beets, 17
Pickled Carrot Sticks, 46
Sweet and Spicy Mustard, 200
Sweet Onion Marmalade, 114

APPETIZERS. *See also* Cheese Balls; Dips; Spreads; Snacks
Armadillo Eggs, 45
Artichoke Appetizers, 46
Baked Potato Skins, 49
Blue Cheese Pepper Strips, 41
Bruschetta, 40
C.C.C. Dip, 45
Charritos, 42
Cucumber Party Sandwiches, 47
Date-Nut Lettuce Sandwiches, 47
Garden Greek Appetizer, 47
Hilo Hot Dogs, 44
Jalapeño Pastrami Cake, 45
Marinated Peppers, 47
Mexican Snack Squares, 47
Pinwheels, 45
Sausage Balls, 45
Stuffed Jalapeño Peppers, 47
Surimi Salad (Crab Salad), 40
Tortilla Roll-Ups, 48
Won Tons, 23
Zucchini Puffs, 49

APPETIZERS, CHEESE
Cheesy Bread Appetizers, 41
Cream Cheese Tarte, 40
Fried Cheese Squares, 41
Gougères (Goo-Share), 41
Herbed Cheese Bites, 42
Hot Cheese Squares, 41
Mexican Cheesecake, 42
Mini Jarlsberg-Onion Quiches, 49
Mock Cream Cheese, 47
Pizza Cheese Bread, 42
Raspberry-Glazed Cheese Pie, 42

APPETIZERS, CHICKEN
Chicken Cups, 43
Curried Chicken Balls, 43
Finger Chicken Pie, 42
Ginger Chicken-Bacon Bites, 43
Hot Buffalo Wings, 43
Lemonade Chicken Wings, 43
Marinated Chicken Wings, 43
Meat Puffs, 43

APPETIZERS, GROUND BEEF
Appetizer Meatballs, 198
Meatballs to Go, 44
Teriyaki Miniatures with Sweet Sour Sauce, 45

APPETIZERS, HAM
Ham Fingers, 44
Honey Ham Tortilla Rolls with Honey Dip, 44
Party Swirls, 44
Rolled Ham-Crab Tortillas, 44

APPETIZERS, MUSHROOM
Cheesy Mushroom Puffs, 48
Freezer Mushroom Rolls, 48
Hongos (Mushrooms), 48
Mushroom Toasties, 48
Pickled Mushrooms, 48
Stuffed Mushroom Caps, 49
Stuffed Mushrooms, 49

APPETIZERS, SHRIMP
Cold Deviled Shrimp, 46
Golden Shrimp Shells, 46
Shrimp Nachos, 46
Vietnamese Spring Rolls, 46

BEEF. *See also* Ground Beef; Soup, Beef; Veal
Beef Rouladen with Bow Tie Noodles, 8
Beef Sandwiches, 76
Braised Beef Rolls (Oxrulader), 75
California Marinade, 203
Crock• Pot Corned Beef and Cabbage, 76
Drip Beef, 75
Fillet of Beef with Feta and Herb Medallions, 74
Indonesian Bamie, 75
Killer Stroganoff, 202
Mexican Steak, 75
Mustard Beef Rolls, 75
"My Sister's" Brisket Marinade, 74
Red Wine Onion Sauce over Tenderloins, 74
Rib-Eye Roast, 74
Roast Beef au Jus, 10
Sirloin Steak Supreme, 74
Spicy Orange Beef, 75
Steak Teriyaki, 19
Wild Goose and Roast Beef, 84

BEEF, STEWS
Beef Stew and Dumplings, 76
Hearty Beef Stew, 11
Oven Beef and Vegetable Stew, 202
Peanut Butter Stew (Domada), 76
Western Stew, 76

BEVERAGES
Brazilian Float, 51
California Lemonade, 51
Champagne Punch, 51
Cran Tea, 52
Dandelion Tonic, 52
French Iced Coffee, 51
Glögg, 52
Grape Juice Float, 51

Hot Wine Drink, 52
Iced Tea, 52
Killer Coffee, 52
Moose Milk, 52
Passionate Punch, 19
Refreshing Margaritas, 51
Rhubarb Juice, 51
Root Beer, 51
Strawberry Shrub Soda, 51
Strawberry-Watermelon Slush, 51
Sunrise-in-a-Glass, 138

BISCUITS
Best Biscuits, 198
Rise and Shine Biscuits, 116
Scones, 135
Scottish Scones, 121

BREADS. *See also* Biscuits; Coffee Cakes; Corn Bread; Muffins; Pancakes; Rolls
Date-Nut Bread, 199
Doughnuts, 133
Egg Bagels, 125
French Crêpes, 198
No-Beat Popovers, 199
Overnight Buns, 199
Pumpkin Bread, 199
Soft Pretzels, 126
Stacked Breadsticks, 21
Yorkshire Pudding, 10

BREADS, LOAVES
Apple Butter-Spice Bread, 116
Applesauce-Gingerbread Loaf, 116
Banana-Applesauce Bread, 116
Banana-Peanut Butter Bread, 117
Carrot-Apricot Bread, 116
Cholesterol-Free Banana Bread, 117
Colorful Vegetable Breads, 124
Deutsches Bauern Brot, 123
English Malt Bread, 124
French Cheese Bread, 122
Garden Bread, 118
Garlic French Bread, 120
Gougere, 122
Grandma's Perfect Bread, 123
Grandmother's Famous Cranberry Bread, 117
Healthy Fruit Bread, 117
Irish Soda Bread, 122
Italian Focaccia, 123
Jam and Cheese Loaf, 123
Low-Fat Banana Bread, 116
Microwave Beer Bread, 119
Mix Bread, 123
Old Milwaukee Sour Rye Bread, 124
Olive-Nut Bread, 122
Orange Slice Bread, 117
Oven-Baked Brown Bread, 117
Poppy Seed-Eggnog Bread, 118
Quaker Oats Bread, 124
Raspberry-Nut Bread, 118
Rhubarb Bread, 118

Index / 219

Swedish Pepparkaku Bread, 118
Tomato-Cheese Braids, 122
Tomato-Herb Bread, 125
War Bread, 125
Whole Wheat Baguettes, 125

BREADS, SPREADS
Apple Butter, 136, 138
Cheese Spread for Breads, 134
Rosy Jelly, 138

BREAKFAST. *See also* Egg Dishes; French Toast; Pancakes
Baked Oatmeal, 140
Blueberry Breakfast Pudding, 138
Granola, 140
Low-Fat Granola, 140
Muesli, 140
Sunny Raisin-Peanut Bars, 140

BROWNIES
Better-Than-Sex Brownies, 185
Fat-Free Brownies, 186
Quick Brownies, 187

CAKES
Almost Better-Than-Sex Cake, 147
Amaretto Di Saronno Cake, 142
Apricot-Filled Pear Cake, 165
Better-Than-Sex Cake, 147
Blackberry Wine Cake, 147
Butterscotch Cake, 148
Cranberry Sauce Cake, 159
Cream Sherry Cake, 169
Crunch Cake, 159
Fluffy Peach Cake, 165
Gooey Butter Cake, 148
Green Tomato Cake, 170
Italian Cream Cake, 162
Light-as-a-Feather Sponge Cake, 169
Lime Meringue Cake, 14
Luscious Cherry Cake, 149
Moon Cake, 164
No-Cholesterol Million-Dollar Pound Cake, 168
Oatmeal Cake, 164
Old-Fashioned Pork "Bang-Belly" Cake, 167
Peanut Butter Cake, 166
Pineapple-Angel Food Cake, 210
Raspberry-Filled Apricot Cake, 146
Rhubarb Cake, 168
Treasure Toffee Cake, 170

CAKES, ANGEL FOOD
Brown Sugar Angel Food Cake with Frosting, 142
Chocolaty Angel Food Cake with Plum Sauce, 142
Lite Waldorf Angel Cake, 142
Simply Delicious Lemon Angel Food Cake, 162
Strawberry Angel Food Cake, 170

CAKES, APPLE
Apple and Mincemeat Cake, 146
Apple Cake, 143
Apple Gingerbread, 161
Apple Harvest Cake, 144
Apple-Nut Cake, 143
Apple-Rum Dum Cake, 145

Applesauce Fruitcake, 146
Cake with Fruit, 159
Crazy Apple Cake, 143
Double Apple Cake, 143
Famous Apple Cake, 144
Favorite Apple Cake, 144
Fresh Apple Cake, 144
German Apple Cake, 145
Low-Fat Apple Cake, 145
Mix-Dump-and-Eat Apple Cake, 145
Mom's Fresh Apple Cake, 144
Spiced Apple-Carrot Cake, 145

CAKES, BANANA
Banana Cake, 146
Banana-Nut Snacking Cake, 146
Crater Cake, 159

CAKES, CARROT
Carrot Cake, 148
Carrot-Chocolate Cake, 148
Fat-Free Carrot Cake, 148

CAKES, CHOCOLATE
Best Ever Red Devil's Food Cake, 154
Carrot-Chocolate Cake, 148
Chocolate Better-Than-Sex Cake, 150
Chocolate Birthday Cake, 150
Chocolate Cake, 151
Chocolate Cake with Creamy Chocolate Frosting, 151
Chocolate Cake with Peanut Butter-Fudge Frosting, 152
Chocolate-Cherry Valentine Torte, 213
Chocolate Fudge Cake, 152
Chocolate Ice Cream Cake, 153
Chocolate Moist Cake, 153
Chocolate-Oatmeal Cake, 154
Chocolate-Pistachio Cake, 154
Chocolate Sheath Cake, 156
Chocolaty Angel Food Cake with Plum Sauce, 142
Coca-Cola Chocolate Cake, 151
Coconut Cake, 158
Double Chocolate-Rum Cake, 156
Earthquake Cake, 159
Favorite Carrot Cake, 149
German Chocolate Upside Down Cake, 153
Grandmother's Chocolate Sheet Cake, 156
Heath Bar Cake, 157
Hot Fudge Pudding Cake, 152
Italian Love Cake, 162
Low-Fat Chocolate-Potato Cake, 154
Mama's Red Cake, 155
Microwaved Mississippi Mud Cake, 153
Oil-Free Cocoa Fudge Cake, 154
Pepsi Cola Cake, 151
Quick Chocolate Cola Cake, 151
Red Velvet Cake, 155
Texas Sheet Cake, 8
Turtle Cake, 157
Turtle Cake with Chocolate Fudge Frosting, 157
Wacky Cake, 157
Wonderful Chocolate Cake, 17

CAKES, CHOCOLATE, CHERRY
Black Forest Torte, 150
Cherry-Chocolate Cake, 149

Chocolate-Cherry Upside Down Cake, 149
Easy Black Forest Cake, 150
Great Cherry-Chocolate Cake, 149

CAKES, COCONUT
Coconut Sheet Cake, 158
Exquisite Coconut Cream Cake, 158
Fluffy Coconut Cake, 158

CAKES, DATE
Brazil Nut Fruitcake, 160
Christmas Welcome Cake, 158

CAKES, FRUIT
All-Season Fruit Cake, 160
Dump Cake, 162
Fast Fixin' Fruit Cake, 160
Fruit Cocktail Cake, 160

CAKES, FRUITCAKE
Applesauce Fruitcake, 146
Brazil Nut Fruitcake, 160
Peach Fruitcake, 161

CAKES, GUMDROP
All-Occasion Gumdrop Cake, 161
Gumdrop Cake, 161

CAKES, KEY LIME
Key Lime Cake, 163
St. Patrick's Day Key Lime Cake, 163

CAKES, LEMON
Orange-Lemon Cake, 165
Simply Delicious Lemon Angel Food Cake, 162
Special Birthday Cake, 163

CAKES, ORANGE
Fluffy Orange Cake, 165
Low-Fat Mandarin Orange Cake, 165
Orange-Lemon Cake, 165
Orange-Pineapple Cake, 166
Pig Pickin' Cake, 166
Triple Orange Jelly Roll, 164

CAKES, PINEAPPLE
Cake with Fruit, 159
Hawaiian Cake, 162
Mexican Fruit Cake, 160
Moist 'n Nutty Cake, 164
Orange-Pineapple Cake, 166
Pineapple-Zucchini Cake, 167
Pumpkin-Pineapple Cake, 167
The Best Pineapple Cake, 167
Thirty-Minute Pineapple Cake, 166

CAKES, PUMPKIN
Pumpkin Bundt Cake, 168
Pumpkin Cake, 168

CAKES, RUM
Bacardi Rum Cake, 168
Glazed Rum Cake, 169
Grandmother's Rum Cake, 169
Rum Cake, 169
Snicker Bar Cake, 156

CAKES, SPICE
Spicy Zucchini Cake, 171
Tomato Soup Cake, 171

Index / 220

CAKES, STRAWBERRY
Strawberry Angel Food Cake, 170
Strawberry Cake, 170

CAKES, VELVET
Grandma's Red Velvet Cake, 155
Red Velvet Cake, 155

CAKES, WALDORF
Lite Waldorf Angel Cake, 142
The Waldorf Astoria Red Cake, 155

CANDY
Acadian Pralines, 185
Chunky Peanut Butter Fudge, 211
Cranberry Candy, 184
Creamy Peanut Butter Fudge, 185
Frosted Pecans, 185
Low-Fat Chocolate-Walnut Fudge, 184
Microwave Salted Nut Rolls, 184
Peanut Butter Fudge, 184

CHEESE BALLS
"A Diet" Cheese Ball, 36
Beef and Cheese Ball, 36
Carrot-Cheese Balls, 36
Cheese Ball, 36
Fruit Cocktail Ball, 36
Tuna Ball, 37
Yuletide Ham-Cheese Ball, 36

CHEESECAKES
Apple Cheesecake, 143
Café au Lait Cheesecake with Chocolate Glaze, 189
Chocolate-Glazed Irish Cream Cheesecake, 189
Cranberry Cheesecake, 190
Frozen Mocha Cheesecake, 189
Fudge Truffle Cheesecake, 190
Raspberry White Chocolate Cheesecake, 190
Sicilian Cheesecake, 191
White Chocolate Cheesecake, 190

CHICKEN. *See also* Appetizers, Chicken; Salads, Chiccken; Soups, Chicken
Aji de Gallina, 91
Apple Chicken, 90
Baked Chicken Parmesan, 91
Baked Chicken-Prune Delight, 86
Best-Choice-Ever Baked Chicken Supreme, 86
Brunswick Stew with Polenta Dumplings, 94
Caribbean Chicken, 205
Cashew Chicken, 86, 205
Chicken and Artichoke Buffet, 90
Chicken and Vegetables in Rosé Sauce, 92
Chicken Breasts Diane, 86
Chicken Breasts in Maple Syrup, 86
Chicken Breasts in Wine, 88
Chicken Breasts Melvina, 23
Chicken Breasts Wellington, 87
Chicken Delight, 204
Chicken Fajitas, 94
Chicken Gardener's-Style, 92
Chicken in Raspberry-Walnut Sauce, 88
Chicken Lasagna, 204
Chicken-Linguine Stir-Fry, 92
Chicken Marbella, 87

Chicken Paella, 91
Chicken Paprikas and Dumplings, 91
Chicken Piccata, 87
Chicken Pot Pie with Phyllo Dough, 93
Chicken Spaghetti, 93
Chicken-Succotash Stew, 55
Chicken with Peaches, 87
Chicken with Spanish Rice, 90
Cupid's Casserole, 19
Curry Marmalade Chicken, 92
Easy Crock•Pot Chicken Enchiladas, 93
Ginger Chicken with Spring Onions, 88
Grilled Marinated Chicken, 94
Herbed Chicken Breasts Bellefontaine, 88
Honey-Crunch Chicken, 91
Honey-Pecan Chicken, 89
Jerk Chicken, 89
Kung Pao Chicken, 205
Lemon Baked Chicken, 89
Lemon Chicken, 89
Low-Fat Chicken Enchiladas, 12
Miniature Chicken Pies, 93
Mustard Chicken and Pasta, 89
Nutty Chicken Dijon with White Rice, 14
Olympic Honey Dijon Chicken, 89
Oven-Baked Chicken and Potatoes, 205
Oven-Fried Chicken Strips, 94
Pasta with Love, 93
Peachy Chicken, 87
Pepper Chicken Fettucini Toss, 206
Picante Chicken, 88
Pita Pizzas, 94
Rum Jambalaya, 206
South Texas-Style Roast Chicken, 94
Summer Lime Chicken Breasts, 95
Tandoori Chicken, 91
Tropical Chicken, 90
Vanilla and Tarragon Baked Chicken, 90

COFFEE CAKES
Any-Fruit Coffee Cake, 134
Blueberry-Sausage Breakfast Cake, 134
Orange-Oatmeal Coffee Cake, 135
Overnight Crunch Coffee Cake, 134

COOKIES. *See also* Brownies
Almond Bars, 184
Almond Slice, 186
Apple Cookies, 187
Baby Food Bars, 185
Bourbon-Soaked Chocolate Truffles, 184
Brown Sugar Cookies, 187
Kahlúa Dreams, 186
"Light" Chocolate Chewy Cookies, 188
Low-Fat No-Sugar Peanut Butter Cookies, 188
Macaroon Kiss Cookies, 188
New Zealand Shortbread, 212
Peanut Butter Treats, 188
Quick and Easy Chocolate Shortbread, 188
Ritz Cracker Snack, 185
Savannah Pecan Bars, 186
Snicker Bars, 186
Sugar-Free Carrot-Apple Cookies, 187
Swedish Walnut Squares, 187

CORN BREAD
Breakfast Corn Bread, 128
Cakelike Corn Bread, 118
Old-Fashioned Southern Corn Bread, 121
Shortcut Corn Lite Bread, 121

CRAFTS
Clever Candlesticks, 28
Fast and Festive Centerpieces, 32
Fun Frames, 28
Gifts from the Hearth, 27
Gingerbread Man Spiced Mug Mats, 30
Glitter Stars, 33
Leather-Look Bill Holder, 27
Remnant Wrappings, 33
Sequined Sweatshirt, 34
Southwestern Place Setting, 31
Starfish Santa and Snowman, 26
Surprise Gift Bags, 30

DESSERTS. *See also* Cakes; Candy; Cheesecakes; Cookies; Pies
Cherries Jubilee, 211
Cherry Enchiladas, 195
Chocolate Chip-Cheese Loaves, 195
Creme De Menthe Delight, 193
Dieter's Raspberry Torte, 192
Favorite Dessert, 196
First-Gentleman Homemade Ice Cream, 212
Fresh Fruit Dessert, 16, 195
Frozen Snicker Bars, 195
Cream Cheese Popovers, 195
Fruity Burritos, 194
German Christmas Torte, 192
Hippopotomus, 195
Kahlúa-Glazed Bananas, 210
Mandarin Orange Salad, 196
Meringue Torte, 192
Midnight Velvet Torte, 193
Pears in Red Wine, 212
Pudding-on-the-Ritz, 194
Snowball, 193
Strawberry Angel Food Dessert, 191
Strawberry Pavlova with Lemon Cream, 192
Tiramisu, 193
Tropical Fruit Tart, 196
Tropical Pineapple Dreams, 9
Very-Berry Cherry Cobbler, 195
Whipped Ricotta Cream, 196
Wonderful Fruit, 196

DESSERTS, BANANA
Banana Split Cake, 147
Summertime Banana Split Cake, 147
Warm Bananas in Brandy Sauce, 22

DESSERTS, CHOCOLATE
Chocolate Mousse Supreme, 211
Dirt Cake, 152
Hot Fudge Sauce, 11
Hot Fudge Topping, 189
1-2-3 Hot Fudge Sauce, 212

DESSERTS, LEMON
Lemon Refrigerator Cake, 163
Lucky Lemon Cake, 163

DESSERTS, PUDDINGS
Apple Floating Island, 193
Chocolate Kiss Mousse, 213
Cocoa-Almond-Amaretto Mousse, 191
Crème Brûlée, 24, 194
Delicious Banana Pudding, 193
Favorite Banana Pudding, 194
Lime Custard, 14

Index / 221

Low-Fat Bread Pudding, 194
Maple Mousse, 191
Marshmallow Custard, 12
Orange Tapioca, 194
Wiki Wiki Mousse, 191

DESSERTS, TRIFLES
Pumpkin Trifle, 192
Sherry Trifle, 10

DIPS. *See also* Fondues; Salsa
Apple Dip, 52
Bagel Dip, 37
Cheese Dip with Pita Chips, 37
Mexican Bean Dip with Pita Chips, 37
Mexican Fiesta Dip, 37
Northshore Shrimp Dip, 38
Out-of-This-World Dip, 38
Queso Especial, 13
Sensational Crab Dip, 38
Skinny Dip, 38
Spinach and Artichoke Dip, 38
Texas Aggie-Longhorn Dip, 198

EGG DISHES
Asparagus Breakfast Casserole, 128
Bagel Casserole, 128
Baked Lakeside Eggs, 13
Best Breakfast Casserole, 128
Breakfast Casserole, 128
Breakfast Corn Bread, 128
Breakfast-in-a-Loaf, 129
Breakfast Tacos, 198
Brunch Pie, 132
Chili Rellenos Casserole, 129
Creamed Eggs on Toast, 211
Eggs Fantastic, 129
Eggs Mornay, 22
Gold Rush Brunch, 129
Ham and Cheese Power Squares, 130
Italian Artichoke Pie, 208
Jack Cheese Omelet, 131
Lattice Ham and Cheese Pie, 133
Low-Cholesterol Sausage and Egg Bake, 130
Make-Ahead Brunch Bake, 129
Pickled Eggs, 209
Pizza Eggs, 131
Quiche, 132
Scotch Eggs, 15
South-of-the-Border Skillet-Scramble, 132
Spanish-Potato Omelet, 131
Spinach-Sausage Casserole, 131
Spinach Soufflé, 130
Sunday Morning Steak and Eggs, 132
Swiss Ham Ring-Around, 130
Taco-Cheese Breakfast Casserole, 130
"Those Darn Things," 132
Tortilla Española, 131
Very Best Egg Foo Yong, 203

FISH. *See also* Salmon; Tuna
Bacalao a la Vizcaina, 206
Baked Amber Jack, 97
Baked Lemon Haddock, 98
Cajun-Style Orange Roughy, 98
Fish Filets with Herb-Lemon Topping, 97
Fish-on-the-Pit, 206
Grilled Bermuda Wahoo with Banana Sauce, 99
Grilled Trout, 206

Herb-Baked Fish Filets, 97
Surprise Sole Rolls, 99

FONDUES
Beer-Cheese Fondue Dip, 37
Fantasy Fondue, 19

FRENCH TOAST
Breakfast Lasagna, 135
Overnight Eggnog French Toast, 135
Overnight French Toast, 135

FROSTINGS
Bacardi Rum Glaze, 168
Chocolate Fudge Icing, 157
Chocolate-Pecan Fudge Frosting, 153
Coca-Cola Icing, 151
Coconut-Cream Cheese Icing, 158
Cola Frosting, 151
Cream Cheese-Cinnamon Icing, 144
Cream Cheese Icing, 149
Cream Cheese Icing with Nuts, 162
Cream Cheese-Orange Frosting, 145
Cream Cheese-Pineapple Icing, 148
Creamy Chocolate Icing, 151
Creamy White Icing, 155
Fluffy Butter Icing, 155
Fluffy White Icing, 155
Peanut Butter Fudge Frosting, 152
Smooth Chocolate Icing, 154
Wonderful Chocolate Icing, 157

GAME. *See also* Venison
Open-Baked Pheasant, 97
Pheasant Casserole, 97
Pheasant in Sour Cream Sauce, 207

GROUND BEEF. *See also* Appetizers, Ground Beef; Soups, Ground Beef
Almost Pizza, 78
Bubble Pizza, 78
Burrito Pie, 77
Crock• Pot Spaghetti Sauce, 79
Easy Fireman's Meat Loaf, 209
Festive Salsa Meatballs, 202
Filipino Roast, 12
Garden Harvest Casserole, 81
Ground Beef and Yorkshire Pudding, 81
Layered Tortilla Sandwich, 80
Macho Mexican Supper, 79
Manicotti with Crêpes, 203
Matambre Roll, 81
Miniature Meatballs, 21
Pasta con Broccoli with Meat Sauce, 79
Pasticcio, 18
Peppered Hamburgers, 213
Shepherd's Pie, 78
Spicy Beef Crêpes, 80
Taco Garden Rice, 79
Tacos in Flour Tortillas, 80
Tacos with Homemade Soft Shells, 203
White Spaghetti with Meatballs, 79
Whole Wheat Cabbage Rolls, 80

GROUND BEEF, MEAT LOAVES
Amazing Microwave Meat Loaf, 76
California Meat Loaf, 77
Dodie's Meat Loaf, 77
Grilled Meat Loaf, 77
Microwave Health Loaf, 77
Microwave Stuffed Meat Loaves, 22

Yummy Low-Fat Meat Loaf, 77

HAM. *See also* Appetizers, Ham; Soups, Ham
Ham Rolls, 81
Ham Sauce, 81

KABOBS
Barbecue Kabobs, 80
Kabobs, 16
Pineapple-Scallop Kabobs, 100
Vegetable Kabobs, 49

LAMB
Lamb and Green Beans, 81

LASAGNA
Chicken-Vegetable Lasagna, 92
Dump Lasagna, 79
GA's Healthy Lasagna, 78
Lasagna, 8
Spinach Lasagna, 111
Vegetarian Lasagna, 17

MARINADE
Meat Marinade, 74

MEATLESS MAIN DISHES
Tofu Quiche, 113
Tortilla-Black Bean Casserole, 113
Vegetable Lo Mein Delight, 114
Vegetarian Enchiladas, 113

MENUS
A Favorite Dinner, 15
All-Occasion Dinner, 8
An Oriental Dinner, 23
Basic-Is-Best Dinner, 8
Candlelight Gourmet Dinner, 9
Celebration Dinner, 10
Christmas Brunch, 22
Christmas Dinner, 23
Elegant New Year's Day Dinner, 24
Family Favorite Dinner, 11
Foyers Group Dinner, 11
Grandma's Moving Dinner, 12
Home-for-the-Weekend Special Dinner, 12
Labor Day Supper, 19
Lakeside Breakfast, 13
Moving Day Special Dinner, 14
Old-Fashioned Thanksgiving Dinner, 20
Old-Fashioned Wartime Picnic, 15
Outdoor Grilling Party, 16
Potluck Dinner for a Special Friend, 22
Romantic Social, 18
Snow-Day Lite Supper, 20
Soup Get-Together, 21
Surprise Birthday Party, 16
The-Way-to-a-Man's Heart Dinner, 18
Vegetarian Company Dinner, 17

MUFFINS
Apple-Oatmeal-Cranberry Muffins, 136
Apple-Pecan Muffins, 119
Cheddar Cheese Muffins with Apple Butter, 136
Easy Muffins, 120
Healthy Sesame-Banana Crunch Muffins, 136
Oatbran Muffins, 198
Parmesan-Wine Muffins, 121

Index / 222

Pear-Chocolate Chip Muffins, 213
Peaches 'n Cream Muffins, 120
Pineapple-Carrot-Raisin Muffins, 120
Pumpkin-Butterscotch Muffins, 136
Six-Week Bran Muffins, 120
Southwest Muffins, 121
Three-Grain Muffins, 121

MUFFINS, BANANA
Banana-Orange Muffins, 119
Chocolate Chip-Banana Muffins, 119
Fat-Free Banana Crunch Muffins, 119
Low-Fat Banana Muffins, 119
No-Sugar Banana-Bran Muffins, 120

PANCAKES
Banana-Applesauce Pancakes, 137
Blueberry-Sour Cream Pancakes, 137
Buttermilk Pancakes, 199
Cottage Cheese Pancakes, 137
Gingerbread Waffles, 138
Light and Fluffy Pancakes, 137
Oat-Buttermilk Pancake Mix, 137
Oatmeal Pancakes, 137
Pancakes, Waffles and Biscuits, 138

PIES
Best Pie Crust, 182
Buttermilk Pie, 173
Concord Grape Pie, 176
Cranberry-Raspberry Pie, 176
Crunchy Pear Pie, 180
Fresh Cherry Pie, 173
Grand Hotel Macadamia Pie, 177
Ice Cream Pie, 176
Macaroon-Custard Pie, 178
Million Dollar Pie, 178
Oatmeal Pie, 178
Sherry Pie, 181
Soda Cracker Pie, 181
Surprise Pie, 182

PIES, APPLE
Apple-Apricot Pie, 171
Apple Candy Pie, 172
Apple-Cheese Pie, 172
Apple-Cranberry Pie, 171
Apple-Raspberry Pie, 172
French Apple Pie, 211
Sour Cream-Apple Pie, 172
Sugarless Apple Pie, 171

PIES, CHOCOLATE
Bitter Sweet Pie, 173
Candy Bar Pie, 173
Chocolate Almond Pie, 175
Chocolate Angel Pie, 173
Chocolate-Butterfinger Pie, 173
Easy Chocolate Pie, 179
Fudge Pie, 174
German Choolate Pie, 174
Low Fat Mocha Fudge Pie, 174
Malt Shop Pie, 174
Mexican Chocolate Pie, 174
Quickie Chocolate Pie, 175

PIES, COCONUT
Amaretto-Coconut Pie, 175
Coconut and Caramel Pie, 175
Great Impossible Coconut Pies, 175
Impossible Coconut Pie, 175

PIES, KEY LIME
Favorite Key Lime Pie, 177
Guiltless Key Lime Pie, 177
Key Lime Pie, 177

PIES, LEMON
Blender Lemon Pie Filling, 176
Easy Lemon or Lime Pie, 176

PIES, LIME
Cool 'n Easy Lime Pie, 176
Margarita Pie, 177

PIES, PEACH
Appalachian Peach Pie, 178
Peach Peasant Berry Pie, 178

PIES, PEANUT BUTTER
Dream Peanut Butter Pie, 179
Favorite Peanut Butter Pie, 178
Fluffy Peanut Butter Pie, 179
Frozen Peanut Butter Brickle Pie, 179
Frozen Peanut Butter Pies, 179
Peanut Butter Pie, 179
Reese's Peanut Butter Pie, 179

PIES, PECAN
Grandpa's Pecan Pie, 180
Mock Pecan Pie, 180

PIES, PUMPKIN
Pumpkin Pie Tropical, 180
Spicy Pumpkin Pie, 180

PIES, RHUBARB
Rhubarb Cream Pie, 181
Rhubarb Pie, 181
Rhubarb Sour Cream Crunch Pie, 181

PIES, STRAWBERRY
Easy Strawberry Pie, 181
Favorite Fresh Strawberry Pie, 182
Fresh Strawberry Pie, 182
Quick Fresh Strawberry Pie, 182
Strawberry Delight Pie, 182

PORK. See also Ham; Sausage
Chasu, 23
Grilled Butterflied Pork Chops, 82
Husband Pleasing Ribs, 204
Jamaican Pork Tenderloin, 204
Kraut and Ribs, 204
"Mama's" Pork Tenderloins, 83
Maple Barbecued Spareribs, 83
Peach-Glazed Pork Chops, 82
Pork and Sauerkraut a la Normande, 82
Pork "Extraordinaire," 82
Pork Tenders Supreme, 11
Taco Pork Chops, 82
Tourtiere, 83

POULTRY. See also Chicken; Turkey
Ballotine of Capon, 96
Proud-to-Serve Game Hens, 96
Roast Duckling, 208

Rice Pizza, 84

ROLLS
Angel Buns, 13
Bran Buns, 126

Crescent Rolls, 126
Easy Hot Rolls, 126
Old-Fashioned Hot Cross Buns, 126

ROLLS, SWEET
Blackberry Tea Bars, 133
Chocolate-Filled Caramel Buns, 20
Easy Caramel-Chocolate Sticky Buns, 133
Maple-Cream Coffee Treats, 133
Roll-Ups, 133

SALADS
Deviled Egg Salad, 10

SALADS, APPLE
Apple-Peanut Salad, 62
Apple Salad, 62
Apple Salad Deluxe, 63
Taffy Apple Salad, 63

SALADS, CHICKEN
Chicken-Pineapple Salad, 65
Chicken Soup Salad, 65
Fajita Chicken Salad, 66
Fruit and Chicken Salad, 65
Grilled Chicken Caesar Salad, 65
Tortelini-Chicken Salad, 66
Tropicana Salad, 65

SALADS, DRESSINGS
Fresh Tomato Dressing, 68
Honey-Mustard Dressing, 64
Orange Dressing, 72
Soy Sauce Dressing, 72
Special Greek-Italian Dressing, 212

SALADS, FRUIT
Apple-Almond Salad, 17
Cranberry Salad, 63
Frosted Fruit Salad, 63
Fruit Salad, 64
Layered Fruit Salad with Yogurt
   Dressing, 64
Orange Salad Bowl, 63
Oriental Fruit Salad and Dressing, 64
Parfait Fruit Plate, 64
Pineapple-Raspberry-Beet Salad, 63

SALADS, MAIN DISH
Elegant Warm Sirloin Salad, 64

SALADS, PASTA
Frog-Eye Salad, 17
Lasagna Salad, 68
Layered Garden Pasta Salad, 67
Rush Party Pasta Salad, 68
Tortelini Salad, 68

SALADS, POTATO
Calico Potato Salad, 69
Fat-Free Potato Salad, 16
Low-Fat Sour Cream-Potato Salad, 70
Potato Salad, 17

SALADS, RICE
Brown Rice Salad, 72
Rendez-Vous Salad, 72

SALADS, SEAFOOD
Macaroni-Shrimp Salad, 16
Oriental Seafood Salad, 66

Index / 223

Seafood-Wild Rice Salad, 66
Shellfish-Pasta Salad, 67
Shrimp and Rice Salad, 67

SALADS, SPINACH
Honey-Spinach Salad, 70
Korean Spinach Salad, 70
Warm Almond-Spinach Salad, 70

SALADS, TURKEY
Club Salad, 66
Honey Mustard-Turkey Salad, 66

SALADS, VEGETABLE
Almond-Orange Salad, 9
Black Bean, Corn and Pepper Salad, 68
Calico Salad, 70
Chick-Pea-Fresh Basil and Sweet Pepper Salad, 69
Corn Medley Salad, 69
Corn Salad Mold, 69
Creamy Caesar Salad, 71
Cucumber-Yogurt Salad, 69
Fancy Sliced Tomatoes, 19
Fire and Ice, 114
Fresh Broccoli Salad, 68
Greek Salad, 18
Greek Salad with Oregano Dressing, 71
Healthy No-Fat Salad, 72
Low-Fat Caesar Salad, 71
Marinated Mixed Vegetables, 71
Mixed Greens Salad, 72
Oriental Mushroom Salad, 69
Parmesan Salad, 9
Skinny Salad, 72
Summer Salad Bowl, 14
Tomato-Rice Salad, 10
Tomorrow's Layered Salad, 71
Vegetable Salad, 20

SALMON
Oregon Flounder and Salmon Roulade, 98
Salmon Alfredo, 98
Salmon Loaf, 207
Salmon Patties, 99
Salmon Quiche, 99
Salmon-Rosemary with Tomato Salsa, 98
Succulent Stuffed Salmon, 98
Warm Salmon and Asparagus Salad, 67

SALSA
Cabbage Salsa, 50
Cranberry Salsa, 50
Pico de Gallo, 38
Salsa Cruda, 50

SANDWICHES
Black Bean Burgers, 209
Seafood Salad Melt, 201
Vegetarian Burritos, 210

SAUCES. *See also* Salsa
Barbecue Sauce, 205
Plum Sauce, 142
Rum Sauce, 169
Secret Chicken Sauce, 205

SAUSAGE
Sausage-Potato Quiche, 83
Sweet 'n' Sour Sausage, 83
Three-Sausage Casserole, 84

SCALLOPS
Mediterranean Scallop Sauté, 101
Roasted Red Pepper and Scallop Fettucini, 101
Scallops in Apricot Brandy, 101
Skewered Scallops, 207
Stir-Fried Scallops and Vegetables, 101

SEAFOOD. *See also* Fish; Salads, Seafood; Scallops; Shrimp; Soups, Seafood
Creamy Baked Scallops, 100
Easy Seafood Chimichangas, 102
Grilled Cioppino "Packets," 95
Seafood Pasta Melts, 100
Vermicelli in White Clam Sauce, 100

SEASONINGS
Cajun Season-All, 96
Chili Powder, 56

SHRIMP
Baked Stuffed Shrimp, 101
Barbecue Shrimp, 206
Delicious Curry, 102
Gingered Shrimp Roughy, 9
Linguine and Shrimp, 102
Scampi with Fettucini, 101
Shrimp Jambalaya, 102
Shrimp Marinara, 102

SIDE DISHES
Barley Casserole, 104
Fat-Free Fettucini Alfredo, 208
Risotto, 208

SIDE DISHES, DRESSINGS
Corn Bread Dressing, 114
Low-Fat Sage Dressing, 114
Turkey Dressing, 20

SIDE DISHES, FRUIT
Glazed Fruit in Orange Cups, 139
Musical Fruit Melodies, 139
Pineapple Casserole, 139
Sparkling Fruit Compote, 139

SIDE DISHES, GRAVY
Marinade Gravy, 24

SIDE DISHES, GRITS
Great Sausage and Grits, 139
My Favorite Cheese Grits, 139
Spicy Grits, 140

SIDE DISHES, PASTA. *See also* Salads, Pasta
Fettucini Spinach Toss, 110
Fettucini with Roasted Red Pepper Sauce, 110
Fresh Vegetables and Fettucini, 110
Garden Ranch Noodles, 111
Lentil Spaghetti, 113
Linguine with Artichokes, 111
Pasta Primavera, 111
Pasta with Picante Black Bean Sauce, 111
Southwestern Tomato Pasta, 111

SIDE DISHES, RICE. *See also* Salads, Rice
Asparagus-Rice Pilaf, 9
Baked Broccoli and Brown Rice, 112
Dill Rice, 11

Herbed Spinach and Rice, 112
Indian Pilaf, 112
Mexican Rice, 13, 114
Red Hot Beans and Rice, 112
Risotto con Funghi (Italian), 112
Wild Rice, 113

SNACKS
Cinnamon Popcorn, 185
Honey-Fruit Snack, 50
Microwave Bits and Bites, 50
Popcorn Balls, 212
Pretzels-with-a-Punch, 212

SOUPS
Avocado Soup, 60
Black-Eyed Pea Soup, 60
Bread Soup, 200
Cabbage-Tomato Soup, 59
Captain's Soup, 62
Cheesy Chunky Tomato Soup, 61
Corn Chowder, 58
Cream of Asparagus Soup, 24
Creamy Five-Onion Soup, 59
Dad's Prize Soup, 200
French Onion Soup, 60
Green Chili-Cheese Soup, 59
Low-Calorie Inspiration Soup, 62
Low-Fat Sausage Soup, 15
Minestrone, 60, 201
Parsnip Soup, 60
Roasted Carrot and Brie Soup, 59
Summer Garden Soup, 62
Super Soups, 21
Tomato Soup, 61
Tortilla Soup, 62
Watercress Soup, 61
Wild Rice Soup, 62
Zucchini Soup, 61

SOUPS, BEAN
Bean and Rice Soup, 58
Cuban Black Bean Soup, 58
Tomato and Black Bean Soup, 57
Vegetarian Four-Bean Chili, 202

SOUPS, BEEF
Barley Peasant Soup, 54
Beef-Barley Soup, 200
Beef Soup Base, 21
Black Forest Potato Soup, 54
Sauerkraut-Beef Soup, 54

SOUPS, BROCCOLI
Broccoli-Cheese Soup, 58
Broccoli Soup, 59
Cheesy Broccoli and Cauliflower Soup, 59

SOUPS, CHICKEN
Chicken Soup Base, 21

SOUPS, COLD
Arizona Summer Soup, 201
They-Won't-Believe-It Fruit Soup, 57

SOUPS, CRAB
Crab Soup, 56
Cream of Crab-Broccoli Soup, 56

SOUPS, GROUND BEEF
Black Bean Soup, 54

Index / 224

Hamburger Soup, 55
Meatball-Vegetable Soup, 55

SOUPS, HAM
Canadian Soup, 54
Healthy Vegetable and Ham Soup, 55

SOUPS, LENTIL
Lentil and Vegetable Soup, 58
My Favorite Lentil Soup, 58

SOUPS, POTATO
Cheese-Potato Soup, 61
I'm-in-a-Hurry Hearty Potato Soup, 61
Pea Pod-Potato Soup, 60
Potato-Corn Chowder, 201

SOUPS, SEAFOOD
Bay Chowder, 57
Cream of Shrimp Soup, 201
Fish Stew, 56
Italian Clam Chowder, 57
Large Gourmet Chowder, 57
Quick Trick Clam Chowder, 201

SOUPS, TURKEY
Taco Soup, 55
Three-Bean Chili, 56
Turkey Soup, 56

SPREADS. *See also* Cheese Balls
All American Reuben Spread, 38
Better Butter, 211
Better Garlic Butter, 211
Creton (Pork Spread), 39
Five-Alarm Fire, 49
Foie Gras, 39
Good Liver Paste, 40
Salmon Pâté, 40

SPREADS, CHEESE
Layered Cheese Spread, 39
Pimento Cheese, 39
Pimento Spread with Herbed Crostini, 39
Savory Herbed Baked Brie, 40

STEW
Oven Beef and Vegetable Stew, 202

Sugar Bait for Butterflies, 207

TUNA
Broccoli-Tuna Roll-Ups, 100
Hearty Tuna Casserole, 100
Midwest Tuna Cakes with Lemon-Dill Sauce, 99
Tuna "Jelly" Salad, 67
Tuna Roll-Ups, 207

TURKEY. *See also* Salads, Turkey
Cajun Turkey, 95
Kraut Burgers, 95
Shepherd's Pie, 96
Spinach-Filled Turkey Loaf, 95
Turkey Loaf, 96

VEAL
Italian Veal Special, 84
Veal Marsala, 84

VEGETABLES
Baked Beets, 12
Baked Onions, 107
Baked Sauerkraut, 24
Baked Squash the American Way, 109
Broccoli Casserole, 105
Broccoli-Yams-Mushrooms with Noodles, 112
Brussels Sprouts with Bacon Sauce, 104
Confetti Cabbage, 105
Eggplant Parmesan, 107
Fancy Vegetable Casserole, 109
Garden Ratatouille, 110
Gingered Broccoli, 105
Herbed Green Beans, 104
Hot Cabbage-Mushroom Dish, 105
Hunters' Vegetable Special, 210
Mu-Ja-Da-Ra (Greek), 107
Mushrooms Florentine, 107
Onions Celeste, 108
Oven-Fried Zucchini, 109
Red Cabbage with Wine and Apples, 209
Streusel-Topped Sweet Potatoes, 210
Turnip Casserole, 109
Turnip Puff Diane, 23

Vegetable Stir-Fry, 110
Vegetable Supreme, 110
Vegetarian Burritos, 210
Yam and Cranberry Casserole, 109
Zesty Eggplant Parmigiana, 107
Zucchini and Green Chili Quiche, 109

VEGETABLES, BEANS
Baked Beans on Dark Bread, 104
Barbecue-Style Baked Beans, 209
Bean Sausage, 209
Black Bean Burgers, 209
Black Beans, 13
Navy Beans and Rice, 104

VEGETABLES, CARROT
Apple and Carrot Casserole, 105
Baby Carrots, 10
Caribbean Carrots, 105
Carrot Casserole, 106
Carrots l'Orange, 106
Classy Cauliflower and Carrot Casserole, 106

VEGETABLES, CORN
Hearty Corn Casserole, 106
Macque Choux (Mock Shoe), 106
Zesty Horseradish Corn on Cob, 106

VEGETABLES, POTATO. *See also* Salads, Potato; Soups, Potato
Grilled Potatoes au Gratin, 209
Onion-Cream Cheese Whipped Potatoes, 24
New Potato Casserole, 108
Potato Casserole, 108
Potato Chips, 108
Potato Kugel, 13
Roasted Mustard Potatoes, 108
Rutabaga with Mashed Potatoes, 108
Scalloped Potatoes, 108

VENISON
Corned Venison, 208
Venison Meatballs, 84

Beta Sigma Phi Cookbooks

available from *Favorite Recipes® Press* are chock-full of home-tested recipes from Beta Sigma Phi members that earn you the best compliment of all... "More Please!"

Every cookbook includes:

- ☆ color photos or black-and-white photos
- ☆ delicious, family-pleasing recipes
- ☆ lay-flat binding
- ☆ wipe-clean color covers
- ☆ easy-to-read format
- ☆ comprehensive index

To place your order, call our **toll free** number **1-800-251-1520** or clip and mail the convenient form below.

BETA SIGMA PHI COOKBOOKS	Item #	Qty.	U.S. Retail Price	Canadian Retail Price	Total
The Best of Beta Sigma Phi Cookbook	88285		$9.95	$12.95	
Home Sweet Home Cooking: Company's Coming	01260		$9.95	$12.95	
Home Sweet Home Cooking: Family Favorites	01252		$9.95	$12.95	
Food In The Fast Lane	94323		$9.95	$12.95	
Shipping and Handling		1	$1.95	$2.95	
TOTAL AMOUNT					

☐ Payment Enclosed
☐ Please Charge My   ☐ MasterCard   ☐ Visa
☐ Discover
Canadian orders: Visa or checks only
Signature _____
Account Number _____
Name _____
Address _____
City _____ State ____ Zip _____

No COD orders please.
Call our toll free number for faster ordering.
Prices subject to change.
Books offered subject to availability.
Please allow 30 days for delivery.

Mail completed order form to:

Favorite Recipes® Press
P.O. Box 305141
Nashville, TN 37230